COMPARATIVE HUMAN RIGHTS LAW

Comparative Human Rights Law

SANDRA FREDMAN

Great Clarendon Street, Oxford, OX2 6DP,
United Kingdom

Oxford University Press is a department of the University of Oxford. It furthers the University's objective of excellence in research, scholarship, and education by publishing worldwide. Oxford is a registered trade mark of Oxford University Press in the UK and in certain other countries

First Edition published in 2018

Impression: 1

Published in the United States of America by Oxford University Press
198 Madison Avenue, New York, NY 10016, United States of America

British Library Cataloguing in Publication Data
Data available

Library of Congress Control Number: 2018952547

ISBN 978–0–19–968941–5 (pbk.)
ISBN 978–0–19–968940–8 (hbk.)

Printed and bound by
CPI Group (UK) Ltd, Croydon, CR0 4YY

To my children,
Jem, Kim, and Dan

To my husband,
Alan

And to my mother and late father,
Naomi and Mike

Acknowledgements

I have many people to thank for their help and support in writing this book. I was introduced to comparative human rights law when I took the pioneering course taught by Chris McCrudden and Eric Barendt during my BCL year, and this has fundamentally shaped my thinking on the subject ever since. At that time, very few students took the course, and one of them was Edwin Cameron. From the very start, Edwin and I were able to share our early mixture of anxiety and fascination about the course, and this was the beginning of our long and deep friendship. In subsequent years, I have benefited hugely from co-teaching the course with Chris McCrudden and, more recently, Nick Bamforth.

My warm thanks are due to the generations of BCL students from all over the world who have taken the course in Comparative Human Rights law. My own understanding has been immeasurably enriched by the many and varied perspectives they brought, sharing their experience from their own jurisdictions and their fascination with gaining new insights and perceptions.

Particular thanks are due to Chris McConnachie and Meghan Campbell, who helped with the research in the early years, and to Nomfundo Ramalekana and Emilie McDonnell, without whom I would never have got beyond the finishing line. My editors at OUP, Eve Ryle-Hodges and Natasha Fleming, have been infinitely patient and supportive. I am enormously grateful to them and to Arokia Anthuvan Rani who steered the book so efficiently to publication. My very warm thanks go to my doctoral students and post-doctoral fellows and the participants of my research group for all the lively and challenging interactions we have had over the years: Laura Hilly, Chris McConnachie, Meghan Campbell, Anup Surendranath, Shreya Atrey, Helen Taylor, Victoria Miyandazi, Jason Brickhill, Tom Lowenthal, Nomfundo Ramalekana, Ndjodi Ndeunyema, Richard Martin, Max Harris, Rishika Sahgal, Jaakko Kuosmanen, Farrah Raza, Yishai Mishor, Barbara Havelkova and Miles Jackson, and also to our academic visitors Anne Lofaso, Fiona da Londras, and Dhaya Pillay. Many thanks too to Kira Allmann and Claudia Pozo for their help in designing the cover.

I am enormously grateful to Mark Freedland, Paul Davies, and the late Bob Hepple, who have been my academic mentors over all the years, for their warm friendship, and support, their academic leadership and encouragement, and for being role-models of generosity and humanity.

I dedicate this book with boundless love and admiration to my children, Jem, Kim, and Dan, and to my husband, Alan, for all the inspiration they are to me, and for the warmth and light they bring to all around them. I dedicate it too to my mother, Naomi, and my late father, Mike, with deepest love and appreciation.

Acknowledgements

Contents

Table of Cases

INTERNATIONAL AND REGIONAL CASES

African Commission on Human and Peoples' Rights

Committee on Economic, Social and Cultural Rights (UN)

European Court of Human Rights

European Court of Justice

Human Rights Committee (UN)

Permanent Court of International Justice

NATIONAL CASES

Australia

(High Court)

Canada

(Supreme Court unless otherwise indicated)

France

Germany

(Constitutional Court)

India

(Supreme Court unless otherwise indicated)

Ireland

(Supreme Court)

Jamaica

(Privy Council)

South Africa

(Constitutional Court unless otherwise indicated)

Trinidad and Tobago

United Kingdom

United States

(Supreme Court unless otherwise indicated)

Table of Legislation

INTERNATIONAL AND REGIONAL INSTRUMENTS

NATIONAL LEGISLATION

Australia

Canada

Germany

Hungary

India

Ireland

Jamaica

New Zealand

South Africa

List of Abbreviations

ABA/IBI	applied behavioural analysis/intensive behavioural intervention
ANC	African National Congress
CEDAW	Convention on the Elimination of All Forms of Discrimination Against Women
CERD	International Convention on the Elimination of All Forms of Racial Discrimination
CESCR	Committee on Economic, Social and Cultural Rights
CFE	Campaign for Fiscal Equity
CRC	Convention on the Rights of the Child
CRPC	Code of Criminal Procedure 1973
CTOPA	Choice on Termination of Pregnancy Act 1996
ECHR	European Convention on Human Rights
ECtHR	European Court of Human Rights
ERC	Ethics and Religious Culture
ESC	European Social Charter
EU	European Union
EWS/DG	economically weaker section/disadvantaged group
FCC	German Federal Constitutional Court
GDP	gross domestic product
HRA	Human Rights Act 1998
HRC	United Nations Human Rights Committee
ICCPR	International Covenant on Civil and Political Rights
ICESCR	International Covenant on Economic, Social and Cultural Rights
ICJ	International Court of Justice
ICPD	International Conference on Population and Development
ILO	International Labour Organization
IMF	International Monetary Fund
MDG	Millennium Development Goal
NGO	non-governmental organization
NIHRC	Northern Ireland Human Rights Commission
OECD	Organization for Economic Cooperation and Development
OHCHR	Office of the High Commissioner for Human Rights
PEPUDA	The Promotion of Equality and Prevention of Unfair Discrimination Act 2000
PIE Act	Prevention of Illegal Eviction from Unlawful Occupation of Land Act 1998
PIL	public interest litigation
PUCL	People's Union of Civil Liberties
RFRA	Religious Freedom Restoration Act 1993
RTE Act	Right of Children to Free and Compulsory Education Act 2009
SACC	South African Constitutional Court
SCA	Supreme Court of Appeal
SDG	Sustainable Development Goal
SERAC	Social and Economic Rights Action Centre
SGB	school governing body

TBKP	United Communist Party of Turkey
TRAP	Targeted Regulation of Abortion Providers
TRIPS	Agreement on Trade-Related Aspects of Intellectual Property Rights
TWU	Trinity Western University
UDHR	Universal Declaration of Human Rights
UNFPA	United Nations Population Fund
USAID	United States Agency for International Development
WHO	World Health Organization

Note on the Cover

The cover features the aguayo, a multicolour, hand-made rectangular woven blanket that is used by women to carry small children, or all sorts of products, on their backs. It is mostly associated with Aymara and Quechua cultures, along the Andean regions. The colours, stripes, and other geometrical figures, are unique to every ethnic group, and convey a symbolic meaning. The colourful contrasts featured in the aguayo are known to represent diverging entities that are intertwined and come together into a unit.

Introduction

As we celebrate the seventieth anniversary of the United Nations Declaration of Human Rights, the project of creating a global conversation to further human rights is more urgent than ever. On the day of the adoption of the Declaration, one of its drafters, Chilean jurist Hernán Santa Cruz, was moved to state:

> I perceived clearly that I was participating in a truly significant historic event in which a consensus had been reached as to the supreme value of the human person, a value that did not originate in the decision of a worldly power, but rather in the fact of existing—which gave rise to the inalienable right to live free from want and oppression and to fully develop one's personality.

Yet, seven decades on, the space for asserting the supreme value of the human person, and for developing the inalienable right to live free from want and oppression, is narrowing rapidly. In established democracies, populism threatens to engulf political processes, while autocratic governments, having extinguished popular uprisings at home, are increasingly expansionist. Human rights, both at the international and the national level, are more contested than ever. In an era dominated by claims of 'fake news', freedom of speech is ever more dislocated from any attempt to further the quest for truth, and is instead harnessed to the pursuit of personal and political power. Freedom of religion is asserted to defeat rights to equality and tolerance. At the same time, the ascendancy of neo-liberal policies has legitimated the claim that shortage of resources justifies displacing rights to health, housing, and education in favour of ideologies of efficiency and private profit. It is in this climate that the need for a vigorous transnational interaction on the meaning and application of human rights becomes particularly pressing.

This is not to say that we should expect to find a single meaning or truth in all jurisdictions. We need not agree with Cicero that 'there is a true law, a right reason, conformable to nature, universal, unchangeable, eternal ... [a] universal law of justice'.[1] But nor do we need to subscribe to the view that all values are culturally relative, and claims of universality merely a cover for a particular perspective, a hegemonic exercise of the 'West'. Instead, we should continue to participate in a collaborative development and implementation of a set of human rights which is both sensitive to local context and true to universal values rooted in the intrinsic worth of each person and their right to be free of fear and want.

The human rights contestations facing courts in different jurisdictions are remarkably similar. Does the death penalty breach human rights? Does freedom of speech include racist speech? What are the appropriate limits of freedom of religion? Is there

[1] Cicero, *De Re Republica* Book III (translated by Francis Barham).

a right to health? On the one hand, the shared language of human rights suggests that there should be similar solutions to comparable problems. On the other hand, there are important differences. Constitutional texts are worded differently; courts have differing relationships with the legislature; and there are divergences in socio-economic development, politics, and history. This book uses the prism of comparative law to examine the growing transnational conversation between courts and the myriad ways in which these difficult questions are decided.

The first part of the book sets out the cross-cutting themes which shape the ways judges respond to challenging human rights issues. Chapter 1 examines the role of comparative materials. Is US Supreme Court Justice Scalia correct to dismiss comparative legal materials as 'foreign fads or fashions'? The chapter argues that the main role of comparative law is to enhance the reasoning process of judges by requiring them to consider a range of possibilities. Chapter 2 asks whether there can be a universal understanding of human rights and sets out ways in which universality and cultural relativity are balanced in human rights law. How can the liberal ideal of tolerance embrace disagreement, without permitting intolerance to thrive? Chapter 3 challenges the traditional distinction between socio-economic rights and civil and political rights and shifts the focus to duties to respect, protect, and fulfil human rights.

Chapter 4 confronts the difficult question of how to reconcile justiciable human rights with a commitment to participative democracy. It argues that, properly configured, justiciable human rights should contribute to rather than detract from democracy. As well as addressing the question from the perspective of judicial legitimacy, this chapter examines limits on judicial competence and assesses different ways in which such limits can be addressed. Chapter 5 examines the challenging question of how judges interpret open-textured and abstract human rights instruments. Can decisions which inevitably require value judgments be made without bringing into play judges' personal predilections? The chapter assesses different theories of interpretation, including 'original intent', textualism, 'living tree' approaches, and 'transformative constitutionalism'. It shows that, on closer inspection from a comparative perspective, the contrasts between these approaches are less vivid than one would expect.

The second part of the book uses these five cross-cutting themes to assess comparative human rights law across seven substantive topics. Each chapter considers the crucial role of the textual mandate given to courts, as well as the interpretive theory judges use and the values they draw on. Comparative law is used to cast light on both the contrasting ways judges make decisions and the extent to which judges expressly draw on comparative materials. Framing these questions is the judicial consciousness of the limits of their own role, from both a legitimacy and a competence perspective. Since the substance of the chapters spans both civil and political rights and socio-economic rights, it is possible to highlight their interaction, particularly when it comes to positive duties. The book focuses on four jurisdictions: the US, Canada, India, and South Africa. These jurisdictions are chosen because they use English as their legal medium, share a colonial history, and largely use the common law method. They also span the global North and the global South, and have differing social organization and levels of economic development. The book also draws on the European Convention on Human Rights, as well as international human rights instruments.

Chapter Six considers whether capital punishment is compatible with human rights. This is a complex issue, since the text in several of the jurisdictions appears to mandate the death penalty, and other jurisdictions are silent on this issue. Judges' own interpretive theory is therefore put to the test. The chapter explores divergent judicial approaches on three main issues: whether there can be a fair procedure for imposing the death penalty; whether it can be justified by penological goals; and whether there are clear value-based reasons for determining compliance with human rights. It shows how judges' choice of answers to these issues further depends on their background positions on the cross-cutting issues identified earlier, particularly their constitutional interpretation, their view of the proper role of the court, their approach to comparativism, and their background values.

Chapter 7 turns to the highly contested issue of abortion. Given the emotive nature of abortion, there are many trenchant voices that argue that, like capital punishment, this should be an issue left entirely to the legislature. However, a comparative insight demonstrates that in all jurisdictions there has been a complex relationship between legislatures and courts, both complementary and conflictual. The comparative approach also reveals the pivotal role of the characterization of the rights at stake. Is this an issue of the right to life, the right to privacy, or the right to equality and reproductive freedom?

From the chapters on capital punishment and abortion, we turn to two different sorts of challenges, namely health and housing, whose very status as fundamental rights remains controversial. Here the background values of human rights, including dignity and equality, play a central role in determining whether and in what ways these fundamental human needs can be addressed through justiciable human rights, rather than being left to the political process.

Chapter 10 on freedom of speech moves back into the heartland of justiciable human rights. Despite judicial confidence in courts' counter-majoritarian role in this context, the values behind freedom of speech remain highly contested. Freedom of speech is clearly crucial to counter the State's power to intrude on individuals' right to speak. But is it legitimate to limit the speech of powerful individuals and corporations whose speech might silence those who have less power and wealth? These challenges are highlighted by the transnational power of the internet, which has both democratized speech and magnified the voices of the powerful.

Chapter 11 turns to the right to education, which is characterized as a freedom right, an equality right, and a social right. A comparative approach casts important light on the interface between these facets of the right. The final substantive chapter, on freedom of religion, is perhaps the most complex, given the great diversity in the State-religion relationship, the nature of religious demands, and the need to balance freedom of religion with equality concerns.

The coverage of *Comparative Human Rights Law* is not intended to be complete. Instead, it aims to provide a lively account of the study of comparative human rights, asking similar questions across jurisdictions and human rights topics, with the aim of inspiring further comparative examination of other pressing human rights issues. Judges faced with acutely difficult questions must refer to their textual mandate, the fundamental values informing the text, their own interpretive philosophy, and their perception of their role relative to the legislature. But their decision-making is undoubtedly enriched by considering, in a deliberative sense, how judges in other jurisdictions have faced these questions. This is true whether or not they regard other approaches as relevant to their own.

My own journey of discovery of comparative human rights began with the experience of growing up in the totalitarian apartheid state of South Africa with its total denial of human rights and negation of human dignity. The value of human rights can never be forgotten by anyone who has lived with the brutal daily reality of institutionalized racism, the prohibitions on freedom of speech and of assembly, the blatant denial of the right to a fair trial, the uncontrolled use of torture and detention without trial, and the stripping of property rights, citizenship, and the right to vote. At the same time, the Nazi atrocities, which included the extermination of many members of my extended family in Eastern Europe, were a very raw recent memory.

It was, therefore, initially a relief to come to the UK as a graduate student. I was struck then at the ways in which a well-developed welfare state aimed to provide public services to everyone and to ensure that no one was left hungry, homeless or without health care. Equally striking was that freedom of speech and assembly and a well-developed collective bargaining system were respected without a written bill of rights enshrining either social rights or civil and political rights. Instead, this was achieved through reliance on the political process, and indeed a scepticism of the role of judges and courts. However, with the advent of neo-liberal policies originated under the Thatcher Government, easily implemented through executive-dominated Parliaments, it quickly became clear that reliance on the political process only works in fair weather. The enactment of the Human Rights Act 1998 by the subsequent Labour Government was a recognition of the need to constrain executive power. But given its focus on political and civil rights, and its shallow roots in the political and social culture, the Act, too, has provided little by way of a bulwark against the deprivation of basic civil and social rights.

This does not mean that justiciable human rights can substitute for political action. They need to work together. As Eleanor Roosevelt put it in her remarks delivered at the United Nations in New York on 27 March 1958:

> Where, after all, do universal human rights begin? In small places, close to home—so close and so small that they cannot be seen on any maps of the world. Yet they are the world of the individual person; the neighborhood [she] lives in; the school or college [she] attends; the factory, farm or office where [she] works. Such are the places where every man, woman, and child seeks equal justice, equal opportunity, equal dignity without discrimination. Unless these rights have meaning there, they have little meaning anywhere. Without concerned citizen action to uphold them close to home, we shall look in vain for progress in the larger world.

Sandra Fredman
Oxford
August 2018

PART I

1

Foreign Fads or Fashions: The Role of Comparativism in Human Rights Law

> The Court's discussion of these foreign views ... is therefore meaningless dicta. Dangerous dicta, however, since 'this Court ... should not impose foreign moods, fads, or fashions on Americans'.[1]
>
> (Scalia J, Justice of the US Supreme Court)

> The importance of comparative law lies in extending the judge's horizons. Comparative law awakens judges to the potential latent in their own legal systems. It informs judges about the successes and failures that may result from adopting a particular legal solution ... Thus, comparative law acts as an experienced friend.[2]
>
> (Aharon Barak, former President of the Supreme Court of Israel)

I. Introduction

The field of human rights law seems to be particularly ripe for a comparative approach. There is a broadly similar common core of human rights both internationally and domestically, and when analogous issues arise we would expect to see equivalent answers.[3] Yet, as is strikingly demonstrated by these two statements, the role of comparative human rights law remains highly controversial. Scalia J is well known for his implacable opposition to what he regards as an attempt to impose foreign moods and fashions through the citation of foreign law. For him, such citation is no more than a thinly veiled pretext for a judge to impose his or her own subjective values. Foreign law is invoked, in his view, 'when it agrees with one's own thinking', which, he argues, is 'not reasoned decision making, but sophistry'.[4] From the opposite end of the spectrum, Jeremy Waldron sees the citation of foreign law as the manifestation of a nascent system of law in itself, a system of law common to mankind, which we are all partly governed by.[5]

These disagreements reflect the real complexities raised by the use of comparative human rights law. The charge of 'cherry picking', or choosing cases *ex post facto* to support a pre-determined outcome, is easily made and difficult to refute. Which

[1] *Lawrence v Texas* (2003) 123 S Ct 2472 (US Supreme Court) per Scalia J (dissenting) at 598 citing *Foster v Florida* (2002) 537 US 990 (US Supreme Court) (Thomas J, concurring in denial of certiorari).

[2] A Barak, 'Response to the Judge as Comparatist: Comparison in Public Law' (2005–06) 80 Tul L Rev 195 at 195.

[3] This chapter is largely drawn from S Fredman, 'Foreign Fads or Fashions? The Role of Comparativism in Human Rights Law' (2015) 64 ICLQ 631.

[4] *Roper v Simmons* (2005) 543 US 551 (US Supreme Court) per Scalia J at 627.

[5] J Waldron, *Partly Laws Common to All Mankind: Foreign Law in American Courts* (Yale University Press 2012).

jurisdictions form appropriate comparators, and which issues are appropriate for comparison? Given the important social, political, and legal differences between jurisdictions, how can the conclusions reached by judges in other jurisdictions be evaluated and weighed against each other? Where there is no express constitutional mandate to refer to foreign norms, is it illegitimate and undemocratic for courts to do so?[6]

While these difficulties arise in comparative law more generally, human rights law is arguably distinctive. On the one hand, there is a broadly similar common core of human rights both internationally and domestically, and human rights guarantees in different jurisdictions have important central affinities, often through conscious adoption or adaptation. The major international human rights instruments have been widely ratified, forming a shared international frame of reference even where individual jurisdictions do not automatically incorporate international law. Moreover, the human rights questions posed to courts in different jurisdictions are often the same. Is freedom of speech compatible with the prohibition of hate speech? Is capital punishment a breach of human rights? Are housing and health fundamental human rights, or do they belong entirely in the realm of politics? On the other hand, human rights are inevitably formulated in open-textured terms, requiring interpretation and application in specific contexts. The differences in text, culture, history, and institutions might be more important than the similarities. Thus, posing the same questions does not necessarily entail that different jurisdictions should give the same answers. Comparative law is particularly challenging when the issue before the court is whether the State has justifiably limited the right. Balancing public interests against individual human rights might seem to be a paradigmatically domestic exercise.[7] Yet many bills of rights allow States to limit rights only when necessary in a democratic society, suggesting that there are common values in democratic societies.

In practice, the question is no longer *whether* comparative law should be used in a human rights context, but *how* and *why* it should be used.[8] There is a growing tendency for judges to cite cases from other jurisdictions in reaching their own decisions on human rights law. However, while there is now a rich academic literature on comparative constitutional law,[9] judges themselves rarely articulate expressly the role of comparative materials in human rights cases.[10] Kriegler J, in an early case in the South African Constitutional Court (SACC), declared his 'wish to discourage the frequent—and, I suspect, often facile—resort to foreign "authorities"'.[11] While not opposed in

[6] I Cram, 'Resort to Foreign Constitutional Norms in Domestic Human Rights Jurisprudence with Reference to Terrorism Cases' (2009) 68 CLJ 118–41 at 140.

[7] L Hoffman, 'Human Rights and the House of Lords' (1999) 62 MLR 159, 165.

[8] C McCrudden, 'Common Law of Human Rights? Transnational Judicial Conversations on Constitutional Rights' (2000) 20 OJLS 499.

[9] O Kahn-Freund, 'The Uses and Misuses of Comparative Law' [1973] 37 MLR 1; Barak (n 2); D Davis, 'Constitutional Borrowing: The Influence of Legal Culture and History in the Reconstitution of Comparative Influence: The South African Experience' (2003) 1 Int'l J Const L 181; Waldron (n 5); A Slaughter, 'A Typology of Transjudicial Communication' (1994–95) 29 U Rich L Rev 99; R Posner, *How Judges Think* (Harvard University Press 2008) Ch 8; R Hirschl, *Comparative Matters: The Renaissance of Comparative Constitutional Law* (OUP 2014); M Tushnet, *Advanced Introduction to Comparative Constitutional Law* (Edward Elgar 2014).

[10] Cram (n 6); J Allan, G Huscroft, and N Lynch, 'The Citation of Overseas Authority in Rights Litigation in New Zealand: How Much Bark? How Much Bite?' (2007) 11 Otago L Rev 433.

[11] *Bernstein v Bester* (1996) 2 SALR 751 (South African Constitutional Court).

principle to such citation, Kriegler J regarded it as important to articulate its function precisely. Thus where 'courts in exemplary jurisdictions have grappled with universal issues confronting us'; or 'where a provision in our Constitution is manifestly modelled on a particular provision in another country's constitution, it would be folly not to ascertain how the jurists of that country have interpreted their precedential provision'. Considering such materials, however, 'is a far cry from blithe adoption of alien concepts or inapposite precedents'.[12]

It is argued in this book that the main function of the use of comparative law is deliberative. Judges making decisions on complex issues of human rights law need to adopt a reasoning process which is thorough and persuasive. Judicial accountability depends centrally on the quality of the reasons adduced. In contested human rights cases, there can be no single right answer; but the suspicion that judges are imposing their own subjective beliefs can only be dispelled by reasoning which is capable of being persuasive and openly canvasses a range of alternative solutions. Comparative materials constitute an important contribution to the rigour of this process, particularly with respect to canvassing alternative solutions. A deliberative approach does not regard the function of comparativism as tending towards convergence in human rights decision-making world-wide. Even apart from the difficulty in establishing a universal meaning of human rights, there are important and relevant differences in constitutional texts, legal institutions, and social, cultural, historical, and political contexts. But whether the outcomes converge or diverge, there need to be good reasons articulated in the decision explaining why the textual, institutional, legal, social, or cultural context demands convergence or divergence.

Scalia's critique of the use of comparative law in US courts assumes that the aim is to impose binding foreign law. However, in this respect, he is tilting at windmills. Outside of expressly binding meta-legal systems like the European Union (EU), foreign materials are not regarded as having the same binding value or authoritativeness as those which form binding precedents in the domestic jurisdiction. In the end result, it is the judge's decision as to the appropriateness and value of the deliberative resource which is controlling. Rather than imposing 'foreign law', the deliberative approach incorporates insights from other jurisdictions where appropriate and useful.

Once it is recognized that their function is deliberative rather than binding, the force of many of the criticisms falls away. For the very reason that comparative materials are not binding precedent, they need only be chosen for the force of their reasoning, rather than for their legal status in foreign countries. This undercuts the basis of the cherry-picking critique: judgments can be chosen from those countries where there is relevant and valuable material, and dissents could be preferred to majorities. Foreign judgments can even be referred to for the main purpose of demonstrating why they should not be followed. A similar response can be made to the argument that it is illegitimate to refer to foreign judgments where there is no specific mandate in the constitution to do so.[13] By considering how courts in other jurisdictions have answered similar questions, particularly where they reference similar human rights

[12] ibid. [13] Cram (n 6) 140.

norms, judges improve the range and quality of the reasoning. But because foreign judgments are persuasive but not binding, judges in the domestic court remain the final arbiters of the value to be accorded to such materials.

However, viewing comparative law as a deliberative resource itself places certain constraints on its appropriate use. Viewing comparative law as a deliberative resource does not sanction, in Kriegler J's words, 'blithe adoption of alien concepts or inapposite precedents'. To be of deliberative value, judgments must be read and understood in their legal and social context. Judgments based on a legal text with important differences in wording may not be as persuasive as those based on more similar constitutional texts, so the text must be taken into account. Similarly, institutional and doctrinal differences, such as the relationship between the court and the legislature, the separation of powers principle, and the role of precedent, should also be accounted for. For these reasons, we would not necessarily expect to see a convergence of outcomes, although we would hope to see good reasons for divergence. Indeed, as Choudhry argues, comparative constitutional experiences can also entail the avoidance of certain options by highlighting their potentially problematic implications.[14]

This chapter elaborates on these arguments. Section II critically assesses various alternative potential functions of comparative law, section III develops the deliberative model, section IV addresses the main critiques of comparative law, and section V tests the deliberative approach against a selection of cases where courts have confronted broadly similar questions in human rights law.

II. Why Comparative Human Rights Law?

A. Universalism and natural law

The most intuitive but ultimately least persuasive reason for using comparative human rights law is based on the theory that human rights are universal. If we take the view that human rights are based on universal values, then we would expect that judges would seek to articulate those values in interpreting human rights.[15] This argument goes beyond the expectation of consistency in interpretation. It assumes that there is a 'right answer' to fundamental questions of interpretation of human rights. In Posner's more florid words: 'To cite foreign decisions as precedents is indeed to flirt with the idea of universal natural law, or, what amounts to almost the same thing, to suppose fantastically that the world's judges constitute a single, elite community of wisdom and conscience'.[16] It also implies that if judgments contradict each other on core human rights issues, some are correct and others are not.

Put in these terms, the hazards of using comparative law to find the right answer to human rights questions are immediately apparent. As is discussed further in Chapter 2, it is not easy to tell which answer is the correct one: 'There is pervasive disagreement on its actual content, on how to ascertain it, and on how to resolve disagreements

[14] S Choudhry, 'The *Lochner* Era and Comparative Constitutionalism' (2004) 2(1) I.CON 1, 4.

[15] R Posner, 'The Supreme Court 2004 Term—Foreword: A Political Court' (2005–06) 119 Harv L Rev 32 at 85.

[16] ibid, 86–87. McCrudden (n 8); Slaughter (n 9).

over it'.[17] Moreover, as Waldron points out, there is no real need to look to foreign decisions for the 'right' answer: 'Natural law only guarantees that there is a right moral answer; it does not guarantee that any existing consensus embodies it'.[18] Similarly, Slaughter argues that 'the premise of universalism ... does not anoint any one tribunal with universal authority to interpret and apply these rights'.[19] Even if there were universal human rights values, there would be a need to determine how they applied to the local context in different jurisdictions. It is unlikely that we will find universal answers to institutional questions, such as the appropriate separation of power between the judiciary and executive; or to the fair balance between human rights fulfilment and appropriate limitations and indeed between conflicting rights. In any event, courts in practice do not see themselves as using comparative law as a means of discovering the truth behind human rights.[20]

B. Self-understanding

If the use of comparative materials is not part of a quest for universal or absolute values, what is its function? We might start with a relatively minimal approach to the use of comparative human rights law, and simply see it as a mode of self-understanding. As Barak puts it, a key function of comparative law is to 'awaken judges to the potential latent in their own legal systems'. This is true not just for judges, but also for academics and students. Once we are exposed to other legal frameworks, our own assumptions are uncovered. Basic premises which we have regarded as universal and 'normal' may be revealed to be specific to our system; principles which were invisible may become visible. Self-understanding[21] in this sense entails taking a fresh look at our own legal system.

However, the process is not automatic or self-executing. Self-understanding only follows from a pre-existing openness to self-appraisal. Using the metaphor of a mirror to represent the process of comparative law, Michelman asks: 'Can comparative encounter with another country's constitutional–legal choices ... ever help us to see ourselves clearly?'[22] Many jurists simply assume that the specifics of their own legal systems are universals, against which other systems can be judged. One example, which we encounter in Chapter 4, arises in the context of the debate about the ostensible anti-democratic nature of judicially enforceable human rights. Much of the opposition to justiciability on democratic grounds has come from US jurists who have based their critique on the premise that justiciability entails courts having the power to strike down legislation. There is little recognition of the assumption that the US model is universal.[23]

[17] Posner (n 15). [18] Waldron (n 5) 41. [19] Slaughter (n 9) 122.
[20] McCrudden (n 8) 528.
[21] The term is taken from C Mendes, 'A Global Constitution of Rights: The Ethics, the Mechanics and the Geopolitics of Comparative Constitutional Law' in U Baxi, F Viljoen, and O Velhena (eds), *Transformative Constitutionalism: Comparing the Apex Courts of Brazil, India and South Africa* (Pretoria University Press 2014).
[22] F Michelman, 'Reflection' (2003–04) 82 Tex L Rev 1737–62 at 1738.
[23] See eg J Waldron, *Law and Disagreement* (OUP 1999).

C. Learning lessons and mutual co-operation

From self-understanding, we may take a further step and look to comparative human rights law for the lessons we can draw from other jurisdictions' experiences. Thus, Barak suggests that comparative law 'informs judges about the successes and failures that may result from adopting a particular legal solution'.[24] Similarly, Choudhry argues that the use of comparative constitutional materials clarifies the implications of certain institutional, textual, and interpretive options.[25] This can operate both at the drafting stage of human rights instruments, and in relation to their interpretation and application. Mendes argues for a stronger interaction, which he calls mutual co-operation. For Mendes, this entails the 'appreciation that, at least in some aspects, we are part of a single, despite thin, community—which is surely subdivided into thicker ones. Morally meaningful comparisons assume a sense of partnership and reciprocity and lead to a horizontal and respectful conversation. The product of this exercise is not only mutual understanding, but also reciprocal improvement'.[26] Slaughter goes even further. She sees transnational sharing as part of a common enterprise in developing a universal meaning for human rights. Slaughter argues that such sharing 'suggests recognition of a global set of human rights issues to be resolved by courts around the world in colloquy with each other. Such recognition flows from the ideology of universal human rights embedded in the UN Declaration of Human Rights'.[27]

There has indeed been much cross-fertilization in the human rights field. The major international human rights documents are widely ratified. Moreover, the intensity of constitution-making in the post-colonial, post World War II period has witnessed much conscious borrowing, adaption, and interaction in framing human rights. The Irish concept of non-justiciable directive principles directly influenced the incorporation of directive principles of social policy into the Indian Constitution.[28] The Canadian Charter served as the model for the South African constitutional text, with 'liberal borrowings from Germany and the USA'.[29]

It is important, nevertheless, to be cautious about what lessons should be learned, given the differences in legal and constitutional frameworks between jurisdictions. As Kahn-Freund so cogently argued, wholesale transplantation is hazardous, and a legal model which has flourished in one jurisdiction might not take well to transplantation in a very different legal environment.[30] Notably too, the trajectory of development of an initially similar model is influenced by the particular legal and cultural environment, with often radically different results. Thus, the Irish directive principles have remained sternly non-justiciable, while the Indian Supreme Court, impatient at the lack of compliance by the political wing with the constitutional obligations enshrined

[24] Barak (n 2) 195. [25] Choudhry (n 14) 52. [26] Mendes (n 21) 55.

[27] Slaughter (n 9) 121–22.

[28] See further S Fredman, *Human Rights Transformed: Positive Rights and Positive Duties* (OUP 2008) 93.

[29] Davis (n 9) 191. See further D Law and M Versteeg, 'The Declining Influence of the United States Constitution' (2012) 87 NYU L Rev 762.

[30] Kahn-Freund (n 9).

in the Directive Principles, found ways of enforcing them by using them to shape the interpretation of justiciable rights.[31]

Rather than wholesale importation, therefore, the aim is to explore the possible implications of different options, whether positive or negative. Indeed, the perceived failures of specific options might be particularly influential in shaping responses which deliberately aim to avoid such negative outcomes. For example, according to Choudhry,[32] the drafters of the Canadian Charter deliberately set out to avoid the US experience in the *Lochner* era. *Lochner v New York*[33] was the notorious US Supreme Court decision which invalidated New York State's maximum working hours legislation on the grounds that such regulation interfered with the employer's freedom of contract and therefore the right to liberty under the Fourteenth Amendment.[34] The case has come to represent a forty-year period of US jurisprudence (from 1897 to 1937) in which the Court routinely struck down nearly two hundred state and federal laws, many of them aiming to institute social welfare and redistributive policies which had the backing of the elected representatives of the people. To preclude such results, the right to life and liberty in section 7 of the Canadian Charter deliberately omits any reference to a right to property and substitutes the phrase 'principles of fundamental justice' for 'due process of law'. Thus, whereas the Fourteenth Amendment states that 'no State can deprive any person of life, liberty or property without due process of law', section 7 of the Canadian Charter reads: 'Everyone has the right to life, liberty and security of the person and the right not to be deprived thereof except in accordance with the principles of fundamental justice'. Similarly, the *Lochner* experience convinced Canadian drafters that the courts should not have the final say over legislation. Thus, the Canadian Charter includes a 'legislative override', permitting the federal parliament and provincial legislatures to expressly declare that legislation will operate 'notwithstanding' its potential breach of specified Charter rights.[35] This rebalances the relationship between the legislature and courts, so that the court does not have the final say.[36]

Such textual differences mean that citation of comparative law can lead to appropriate divergence in outcomes. A particularly salient example is the right to freedom of speech, where the US First Amendment stands out for including no explicit limitation clause. By contrast, like other freedom-of-speech guarantees, the Canadian Charter permits the right to be subject to 'such reasonable limits prescribed by law as can be demonstrably justified in a free and democratic society'.[37] This difference has been particularly important in addressing the question of whether prohibiting hate speech contravenes freedom of expression. In the Canadian hate speech case of *Keegstra*, Dickson CJ made it clear that: 'It is only common sense to recognize that, just as similarities will justify borrowing from the American experience, differences may require that Canada's constitutional vision depart from that endorsed in the United States'.[38]

[31] See Chapter 3. [32] Choudhry (n 14).

[33] *Lochner v New York* 198 US 45, 25 S Ct 539 (United States Supreme Court).

[34] 'No State shall deprive any person of life, liberty or property without due process of law'.

[35] Canadian Charter, s 33. [36] Choudhry (n 14) 43–45.

[37] Canadian Charter, s 1; see similarly European Convention on Human Rights (ECHR) 213 UNTS 222, entered into force 3 September 1953, Article 10(2).

[38] *R v Keegstra* [1990] 3 SCR 697 (Supreme Court of Canada).

In particular, since the limitation clause in the Canadian Charter 'operates to accentuate a uniquely Canadian vision of a free and democratic society ... we must not hesitate to depart from the path taken in the United States'.[39]

D. *Ius gentium?*

Waldron takes a stronger position. For him, citation of foreign law is a manifestation of a wider *ius gentium* or a set of laws partly common to all humankind.[40] Convergent currents of foreign statutes, constitutional provisions, and precedents can add up to 'a body of law that has its own claim on us, the law of nations, or *ius gentium* which applies to us simply as law, not as the law of any particular jurisdiction'.[41] In this way, governance by law can be recognized, not just as the idiosyncratic traditions of particular countries, but at least in part as a shared or common enterprise in human civilization.[42] Like science, law becomes a 'global enterprise'.[43] Courts in different jurisdictions regularly cite one another because they value one another's assistance; they see each country as 'contributing to a common storehouse of intellectual legal resources', linking to an overarching system: 'laws common to all mankind'.[44]

This raises the question of how we determine which laws constitute *ius gentium*. Waldron accepts that this task cannot be done in a technical, value-neutral way: *ius gentium* is 'a body of principles, discerned interpretively from the commonalities that exist among the positive laws of various countries, by a legal sensibility that is both lawyerly and moralized'.[45] Waldron is careful to distance himself from natural law. He makes it clear that *ius gentium* is not a guarantor of truth: consensus in both law and science can be wrong. However, it is a repository of wisdom to which many have contributed over the years. There is therefore no sensible alternative but to pay attention to it.[46] Moreover, *ius gentium*, although not enacted as such by any sovereign legislature, is nevertheless positive law. It has its source in municipal legal systems of the world, but its legal effect presents itself as 'a body of principles that particular systems may draw down from when seeking to resolve difficult issues in a way that is wise and just and in harmony with the way those issues are resolved elsewhere in the world'.[47] Waldron makes a strong argument that in this way it is binding, as 'a sort of law, the law of the whole world'.[48]

Waldron is able to take this step while remaining a legal positivist by drawing on Hart's understanding that something is called law, not because there is a sovereign authority behind it, but because there is a settled practice among a group of officials, such as judges, of recognizing and acting on it. Therefore, he argues, 'if judges were to develop a settled practice of inferring, citing, manipulating and applying principles from decisions by courts in foreign countries, then that might make the results "law" for their system'.[49] For him, we are at a 'Tinkerbell' moment: this material will exist as a body of law if judges believe in it enough and begin articulating this belief into

[39] ibid. See further Chapter 10 (freedom of speech).
[40] Waldron (n 5) 3. He uses the term 'partly common to all mankind'. [41] ibid.
[42] ibid, 3. [43] ibid, 5. [44] ibid, 20. [45] ibid, 35. [46] ibid, 41. [47] ibid, 51.
[48] ibid, 48. [49] ibid, 54.

practice.[50] This echoes Barak's description of how comparative law becomes widely received. For Barak, 'this vicious circle is coming to its end. Judges will start to rely on comparative law; lawyers will tend to cite it to judges; law schools will start teaching comparative law; scholars will be encouraged to research in comparative law; judges will rely more and more on comparative law'.[51]

Waldron's development of the concept of *ius gentium* is ambitious and challenging. However, it is problematic in two respects. First, his claims for a systematic set of principles in the form of *ius gentium* are too strong. Even within international law, it has become increasingly difficult to find a cohesive set of central principles.[52] How much more so for comparative law? Second, to regard *ius gentium* as 'binding' is to invite many of the criticisms that have been levelled against the use of comparative law, such as that it is undemocratic, not comprehensive, and methodologically unsound. Waldron deals with this criticism by adopting a particular understanding of what is 'binding'. Like precedents, *ius gentium* may only be binding if the reasons against it are not very strong;[53] but the court still has a duty to take it into account and give it appropriate weight.[54] Nevertheless, 'binding' has stronger connotations in law than is necessary to give a true picture of the value of comparative law as a deliberative resource.

III. Comparative Law as a Deliberative Resource

It is not necessary to go so far as to regard comparative law as *ius gentium* to see it as playing a role in the evolution of human rights law. Instead, drawing together much of what has been said above, I would articulate its role as a valuable deliberative resource. While there can be no absolute right answers to human rights questions, judges are required to make their decisions on the basis of the best reasons they can find.[55] Comparative materials, on this approach, constitute an important contribution to the rigour of the deliberative process. If other jurisdictions, faced with similar dilemmas, have discussed and weighed up the arguments in either direction, these should be canvassed as part of the decision-making process. In Waldron's terms, this is equivalent to consulting the laboratory of the world;[56] for Barak, this is the judge's 'experienced friend'.[57] In the context of international law, Koskenniemi refers to 'Kant's cosmopolitan project rightly understood: not an end-state or party programme but a project of critical reason that measures today's state of affairs from the perspective of an ideal of universality that cannot be reformulated into an institution, a technique of rule, without destroying it'.[58] The deliberative approach suggests that comparative law should do more than just confirm a judge's predetermined opinion. It should also be

[50] ibid, 55. [51] Barak (n 2) 195.

[52] M Koskenniemi, 'The Fate of Public International Law: Between Technique and Politics' (2007) 70 MLR 1.

[53] Waldron (n 5) 61.

[54] ibid, 62. For a discussion of comparative law as persuasive authority, see McCrudden (n 8).

[55] On deliberative approaches, see J Cohen, 'Deliberation and Democratic Legitimacy' in A Hamlin and P Pettit (eds), *The Good Polity* (Blackwell 1989); S Fredman, 'From Dialogue to Deliberation: Human Rights Adjudication and Prisoners' Right to Vote' (2013) PL 292; and see further Chapter 4.

[56] Waldron (n 5) 89, 199. [57] Barak (n 2) 195. [58] Koskenniemi (n 52) 30.

persuasive in a deliberative sense. It is neither binding nor a fig leaf, but rather a resource to be considered as part of the judicial decision-making process, a process by judges of 'getting their bearings among a tangle of issues, exploring options, considering various possible models of analysis'.[59] This is not blind deference, but a nuanced discussion of the different possible approaches.

Although a deliberative approach entails regarding comparative law as a valuable and sometimes essential part of judicial decision-making on human rights issues, it does not require judges to regard foreign materials as binding at any level.[60] In the end, it is the judge's decision as to the appropriateness and value of the deliberative resource which is controlling. This is expressly reflected in the South African constitution, which states that when interpreting the Bill of Rights, courts may consider foreign law and must consider international law.[61] Under the UK Human Rights Act 1998 (HRA), courts must 'take into account' the judgments of the European Court of Human Rights (ECtHR).[62] Both require the court to consider comparative law rather than regard it as binding. However, the fact that it is not binding does not mean that recourse to comparative law commits judges to embarking on moral rather than legal decision-making. Dworkin argues that to discern the principles already embedded in the law, a judge must 'grappl[e] with a whole set of shifting, evolving and interacting standards ... about institutional responsibility, statutory interpretation, the persuasive force of various sorts of precedent, the relation of all of these to contemporary moral practices and hosts of other such standards'.[63] Comparative human rights materials should be one of the sources in this exercise;[64] and in fact, this is how many judges regard its role. In her important study, Mak found that the majority of interviewed judges focused more on finding relevant arguments for their decision than the status of the source. In particular, arguments from comparative law were 'valued for the insights which they provide regarding the possible interpretation of the law'.[65]

A deliberative approach permits judges to choose what they regard as the most persuasive authority but requires persuasive deliberative reasons for such choices. We have already rejected the possible role of comparative law in discovering a universal meaning. Nevertheless, there may be good deliberative reasons to expect that similarly worded human rights should be given similar meanings; or at least that judges should consider whether it was appropriate to expect such a convergence. This could be because consistency is valued in itself, especially where a domestic instrument is specifically intended to function as the State's compliance with the mutually shared international human rights provision. But it could also be because judges in different jurisdictions might find the same reasons equally persuasive.

[59] Waldron (n 5) 80.

[60] Except if required by the domestic law of the jurisdiction in question, as is the case for EU law.

[61] Constitution of the Republic of South Africa, 1996, s 39.

[62] Human Rights Act 1998 (UK) s 3. This point is discussed further below at n 77.

[63] R Dworkin, *Taking Rights Seriously* (Duckworth 1977) 40; see also R Alexy, *A Theory of Constitutional Rights* (OUP 2004).

[64] Waldron (n 5) 64.

[65] E Mak, *Judicial Decision-making in a Globalised World* (Hart 2013) 4.

However, viewing comparative law as a deliberative resource itself places important constraints on its appropriate use.[66] Most important is the role of the text itself. Judgments based on a legal text with significant differences in wording may not be as persuasive as those based on more similar constitutional texts. A second set of constraints arises from institutional and doctrinal differences, such as the relationship between the court and the legislature, the separation of powers principle, and the role of precedent. Third, and equally important, are differences in social, economic, historical, and political contexts. It is therefore appropriate, as McCrudden found, that 'it is the judiciaries of liberal democratic regimes that cite each other'.[67] The balance is summed up neatly by Sachs J in the SACC, where he reiterated that 'in developing doctrine we had to take account both of our specific situation and of problems which we shared with all humanity'.[68]

At the same time, simply citing such difference is not sufficient: the deliberative approach requires good reasons for divergence as much as for convergence. For example, in a model deliberative approach, Kriegler J rejected the relevance of US First Amendment jurisprudence in interpreting freedom of speech in the South African Constitution. Thus, he stated: 'The First Amendment declaims an unequivocal and sweeping commandment; ... With us the right to freedom of expression cannot be said automatically to trump the right to human dignity. The right to dignity is at least as worthy of protection as is the right to freedom of expression'.[69] More complex is a situation in which foreign materials point in opposite directions. In the *Keegstra* hate speech case, the Canadian Supreme Court was faced with the decision as to whether the Canadian guarantee of freedom of speech was closer to the US provision or that of international human rights documents, which saw the right to freedom of expression as compatible with a ban on hate speech. In the result, Dickson CJ regarded the existence of a global consensus as good reason to prefer the international understanding to that of the US Supreme Court: 'That the international community has collectively acted to condemn hate propaganda and to oblige State Parties to CERD [International Convention on the Elimination of All Forms of Racial Discrimination] and ICCPR [International Covenant on Civil and Political Rights] to prohibit such expression, thus emphasizes the importance of the objective behind [the Canadian prohibition on hate speech] and the principles of equality and the inherent dignity of all persons that infuse both international human rights and the Charter'.[70] As we have seen, he was fortified in this view by the textual difference between the Canadian and the US guarantees of freedom of speech. McLachlan J, however, came to a different conclusion. For her, 'the experience most relevant to Canada is that of the United States, since its Constitution, like ours, places a high value on freedom of expression, raising starkly the conflict between freedom of speech and the countervailing values of individual dignity and social harmony'.[71]

That judges using the same comparative material reach opposing conclusions does not, however, undermine the deliberative model. Rather, provided both sides make it clear how and why they are using comparative sources, this contributes to the

[66] McCrudden (n 8) 517. [67] ibid.

[68] *Lawrence v State* [1997] ZACC 11 (South African Constitutional Court) citing the earlier case of *Prinsloo v Van der Linde* 1997 (6) BCLR 759 (CC) (South African Constitutional Court).

[69] *S v Mamabolo (CCT 44/00)* [2001] ZACC 17 (South African Constitutional Court) 41–42.

[70] *R v Keegstra* (n 38) 754. [71] ibid.

deliberative legitimacy of the decision. At the same time, judges themselves can be convinced by reasons which diverge from their own. In the 2012 hate speech case of *Whatcott*, McLachlan CJ appeared to have been persuaded that 'the balancing of competing Charter rights should also take into account Canada's international obligations with respect to international law treaty commitments . . . [which] reflect an international recognition that certain types of expression may be limited in furtherance of other fundamental values'.[72]

Less convincing from a deliberative standpoint has been the Indian Court's reference to social and historical differences to justify rejecting the relevance of foreign materials. In *Koushal*,[73] the Supreme Court referred to only two previous decisions to reject the Delhi High Court's use of comparative law in determining whether the criminalization of sodomy was a breach of the rights to life and equality. The first was an early death penalty case where the Court had expressed 'grave doubts about the expediency of transplanting western experience in our country. Social conditions are different and so also the general intellectual level. Arguments which would be valid in respect of one area of the world may not hold good in respect of another area'.[74] The second was a 1974 ruling which rejected the relevance of Halsbury's Laws of England, cited by Counsel on the issue of undue influence in relation to engagement to be married.[75] In that case, the Court explained that the context in which marriage took place in India, and in particular, the continued prevalence of arranged marriages, made Halsbury's Laws irrelevant.

The Court's reasons, however, fall below the deliberative standard required to give cogency to that rejection. The cases cited by the Delhi High Court in support of striking down the provision were not wholly 'western' but also included South Africa, where conditions are arguably comparable. Moreover, the assumption that comparative experience is irrelevant ignores the fact that section 377 of the Indian Penal Code, which criminalizes sodomy as an 'unnatural offence' was never explicitly enacted by the Indian legislature, but instead imported from British law through the colonial code drawn up in the nineteenth century.[76] The result was that in practice a British colonial relic was upheld. It might well be that the specific laws in some areas, such as marriage, might differ in differing contexts. But under the deliberative model much more is needed to support the view that social conditions are sufficiently different to make it plausible that opposing answers should be given to the same fundamental human rights questions in different jurisdictions.

The deliberative approach is particularly helpful in providing a framework for what has become a somewhat fraught relationship between the UK courts and the ECtHR. The HRA was deliberately formulated to require courts to 'take into account'

[72] *Saskatchewan (Human Rights Commission) v Whatcott* 2013 SCC 11 (Supreme Court of Canada).

[73] *Suresh Kumar Koushal v Naz Foundation* (2014) 1 SCC 1 (Indian Supreme Court).

[74] *Jagmohan Singh v State of UP* (1973) 1 SCC 20 (Indian Supreme Court). For the same dictum, see also *Bachan Singh v State of Punjab* 1983 SCR (1) 145 (Indian Supreme Court).

[75] *Surendra Pal v Saraswati Arora* AIR 1974 SC 1999 (Indian Supreme Court).

[76] M Kirby, 'Sodomy Revived: The Supreme Court of India Reverses Naz' (Oxford Human Rights Hub Seminar, Oxford, 22nd April 2014) <http://ohrh.law.ox.ac.uk/the-hon-michael-kirby-sodomy-revived-the-supreme-court-of-india-reverses-naz/140422_001/> (accessed 20 February 2018).

judgments of the ECtHR, rather than regarding them as binding.[77] Nevertheless, for a period, the superior courts in the UK took the view that they should defer to the interpretation given by the ECtHR. In the words of Lord Rodgers, when 'Strasbourg has spoken, the case is closed'.[78] This seems to have been based on a strong sense that there should be convergence in the interpretation of the European Convention on Human Rights (ECHR).[79] This can be contrasted with the deliberative approach of Lord Phillips in the later case of *Horncastle*,[80] which was more in tune with the textual mandate of the HRA and also better reflected the dynamic and evolutionary nature of human rights interpretation:

> The requirement to 'take into account' the Strasbourg jurisprudence will normally result in the domestic court applying principles that are clearly established by the Strasbourg court. There will, however, be rare occasions where the domestic court has concerns as to whether a decision of the Strasbourg court sufficiently appreciates or accommodates particular aspects of our domestic process. In such circumstances it is open to the domestic court to decline to follow the Strasbourg decision, giving reasons for adopting this course. This is likely to give the Strasbourg court the opportunity to reconsider the particular aspect of the decision that is in issue, so that there takes place what may prove to be a valuable dialogue between the domestic court and the Strasbourg court.[81]

Holding that it would not be right to apply the principle laid down by the Strasbourg court in the case before him, he stressed that 'I have taken careful account of the Strasbourg jurisprudence. I hope that in due course the Strasbourg court may also take account of the reasons that have led me not to apply the sole or decisive test in this case'.[82] The Strasbourg court did indeed take into account those views.[83] As Sir Nicolas Bratza, previous President of the ECtHR put it: 'I believe it is right and healthy that national courts should continue to feel free to criticize Strasbourg judgments where those judgments have applied principles which are unclear or inconsistent or where they have misunderstood national law or practices'.[84]

It could be asked how the relevance or persuasiveness of a foreign authority can be assessed, without measuring it against a background moral position. This is, of course, a question which arises for all judicial decision-making, even when solely citing domestic sources. As McCrudden points out, the 'rules of relevance' in determining the applicability of national precedents are 'extraordinarily fluid in this respect, and in a state of considerable flux, not only between, but also within jurisdictions'.[85] Summers draws the very useful distinction between 'authority reasons', which regard a conclusion as correct because a previous court or judge so decided, and 'substantive reasons', which 'derive their justificatory force from moral, economic, political, institutional, or other social

[77] HRA, 1998 (UK) s 2(1).

[78] *Secretary of State for the Home Department v AF (No 3)* [2009] UKHL 28 (UK House of Lords).

[79] *Regina (Ullah) v Special Adjudicator; Do v Secretary of State for the Home Department* [2004] UKHL 26 (UK House of Lords).

[80] *R v Horncastle* [2010] 2 AC 373 (UK Supreme Court). [81] ibid. [82] ibid.

[83] *Al-Khawaja v UK* (2012) 54 EHRR 23 (European Court of Human Rights).

[84] N Bratza, 'The Relationship between the UK Courts and Strasbourg' [2011] EHRLR 505, 512.

[85] McCrudden (n 8) 515.

consideration'.[86] 'Authority reasons' cannot provide the only, or even the primary, source of justificatory reasons. Cases arise where precedents point in opposite directions, and there is always a significant number of cases which raise issues not covered by any precedent. In any event, as Summers points out, a judge cannot apply a precedent wisely without determining whether the application is consistent with the substantive reasons behind the precedent and indeed, behind the doctrine of precedent itself.[87] Precedents might also be wrong.[88]

The absence of strict rules of relevance for apex courts and the inevitable need for substantive reasoning lead us to question whether judges adjudicating complex human rights questions can ever be, or indeed should be, strictly neutral as to the background moral principles on which they are drawing. The deliberative approach does not eschew reasoning based on background moral principles: it accepts, at least in the human rights context, that value judgements need to be made. Indeed, many bills of rights, both internationally and domestically, explicitly incorporate terminology that invites value judgements, whether broadly in the preamble, or within different substantive rights. The concepts of 'fairness' in the right to a fair trial; of 'degrading' in the context of the right not to be subjected to inhuman or degrading treatment or punishment; of 'democracy' in many limitations clauses, are just a few that spring to mind. Instead of disguising such value judgements under the guise of technical legal interpretation or rules of relevance, the deliberative model requires judges openly to articulate their understanding of the background values they are adopting. It is the concealment of such value judgements which enables open-ended judicial discretion, risking that personal likes and dislikes will be the determining influence on conclusions. By requiring judges to account explicitly for the values they are using, personal interests which cannot qualify as valid reasons can be flushed out.[89] As Freund puts it, when precedents 'prove unavailing, as is more likely in the case of courts of last resort at the frontiers of the law, and most likely in a supreme constitutional court, the judge necessarily resorts to his [or her] own values. It may therefore be said that the most important thing about a judge is his [or her] philosophy; and if it be dangerous for him [or her] to have one, it is at all events less dangerous than the self-deception of having none'.[90]

This does not mean that the values judges can draw on in resolving human rights disputes are entirely at large. Human rights signal a commitment by a society to values such as freedom and equality, and, while the specific instantiation of those values requires evaluative decision-making, judges need to show, by their reasoning, that these instantiations further the broader commitments embodied in the human rights document. At the same time, the deliberative model expects that there will be room for

[86] RS Summers, 'Two Types of Substantive Reasons: The Core of a Theory of Common-law Justification' (1978) 63 Cornell L Rev 707, 716.

[87] ibid, 731.

[88] ibid, 716, 732.

[89] ibid, 739. He argues in relation to the common law that 'a judge in our system must give substantive reasons and must make law. Indeed, the most important attributes of a judge are his value system and his capacity for evaluative judgment. Only through the mediating phenomena of reasons, especially substantive reasons, can a judge articulately bring his values to bear': ibid, 710.

[90] PA Freund, 'Social Justice and the Law' in R Brandt (ed), *Social Justice* (Prentice Hall 1962) 93, 110.

legitimate disagreement: by rejecting the possibility of a universal 'right answer' to human rights questions, the deliberative model regards judicial decision-making in the human rights field as an ongoing process of contestation. As has been emphasized, substantive reasons can include institutional constraints, and it might be a good deliberative reason to state that the issue before the court is one that is better resolved by the legislature.[91] Summers also shows that substantive reasoning should include 'critical reasons', which are used by dissenting judges or council to disagree with the majority decision.[92] While there is a need for closure in the immediate decision, and while stability and settled expectations will generally militate against change, there is still scope for evolution of human rights law.

IV. Responding to the Critics

If we regard comparative human rights law as a deliberative resource, we can begin to answer some of the challenges posed to it. One of the most difficult methodological issues concerns the choice of comparators. What method should be used to select comparative jurisdictions and which judgments should be used? How do we avoid the charge of 'cherry-picking'? In the South African death penalty case *Makwanyane*,[93] Chaskalson P drew both on the concurring judgment of Brennan J in *Furman*,[94] and on his dissenting judgment in *Gregg*.[95] He expressly distanced himself from the more recent US majorities which had upheld the death penalty. On the other hand, the Indian Supreme Court in *Bachan Singh*[96] rejected Brennan's approach and preferred that of the majority. Do these examples simply confirm the suspicion that 'the foreign authorities were cited in the way courts always use comparative law; as a rhetorical flourish, to lend support to a conclusion reached on independent grounds'?[97]

Cram, in his analysis of the role played by human rights jurisprudence in judicial reasoning in relation to counter-terrorism measures, argues that 'until the methodology for selection of foreign norms is made much more explicit, the suspicion will linger that the court's selection of foreign judgments is purely results-driven'.[98] A deliberative approach does not require judges to conduct an empirical survey with strict sampling criteria in order to draw on comparative human rights law to reach their conclusions. Their function is deliberative, not binding. Therefore, comparative materials should be chosen for the force of their reasoning, regardless of their legal status in their country of origin. Relevant comparative jurisdictions are generally those with similarly worded human rights texts, and which have similar human rights commitments in that they have ratified international human rights documents. Relevant cases are those where judges have faced similar human rights questions. For some such

91 Summers (n 86) 722. 92 ibid, 726.
93 *S v Makwanyane* 1995 (3) SA 391 (CC) (South African Constitutional Court).
94 *Furman v Georgia* (1972) 408 US 238 (US Supreme Court).
95 *Gregg v Georgia* (1976) 428 US 153 (US Supreme Court).
96 *Bachan Singh v State of Punjab* (n 74).
97 L Hoffmann, 'Fairchild and After' in A Burrows, D Johnston, and R Zimmermann (eds), *Judge and Jurist: Essays in Memory of Lord Rodger of Earlsferry* (OUP 2013) 64.
98 Cram (n 6).

questions, there may be more contextual differences than others: the right to a fair trial, for example, is heavily dependent on domestic legal procedure and institutions. Part of the process of enriching decision-making in a deliberative manner is to demonstrate why outcomes reached on similar human rights questions should diverge.

Foreign judgments can even be referred to demonstrate why they should not be followed. A closer look at *Makwanyane* and *Bachan Singh* reveals that US case law was used for very different reasons. Chaskalson P in *Makwanyane* drew on Brennan J's dicta to support his view of the role of dignity in the South African Constitution. In *Bachan Singh*, the Indian Supreme Court was more interested in the balance of power between courts and elected representatives, holding that since Brennan's approach in *Furman* had been rejected by domestic electorates, the Indian Court should not make the mistake of intervening in the decisions of elected representatives. Inevitably, there will be an element of selectiveness, depending on which cases counsel bring to the court's attention. The deliberative model does not simply accept any citations; it requires the court to justify their relevance, identify their appropriate similarities and differences, and explain their role in reaching the decision at hand.

A second criticism of the use of comparative law is that it is used by judges as confirmatory, in the sense of simply buttressing their own value judgements, thereby giving apparent legitimacy to political decisions. Posner regards the search for a global consensus on an issue as 'an effort to ground controversial Supreme Court judgments in something more objective than the Justices' political preferences and thus to make the Court's political decision seem less political'.[99] For him, citation of foreign law is a fig leaf to cover 'naked political judgment'.[100] Scalia J shares this view, and this is implicit in Cram's suspicion that the court's selection of comparative materials is 'results-driven'.[101] However, it is hard to see why, if judges are looking for ways to hide their personal political beliefs, they should confine themselves to the use of foreign law to do so. Complex human rights cases are not likely to be resolved in a purely technical or formulaic manner. Decisions as to whether to use a particular precedent or to interpret a statute narrowly or broadly all require judicial value judgements. Domestic precedents could just as easily be manipulated to achieve a predetermined 'political judgement'. Such a cynical view of judges and the motives behind their decision-making must therefore surely undermine the legitimacy of much judicial decision-making.

Comparative law could be confirmatory or 'results driven' in a much more constructive and legitimate sense. It need not act as a subterfuge for other motives, but as a way of checking that the result reached on the basis of the legal reasons in the judge's own jurisdiction is one that is sound. This is how Kennedy J used foreign law in *Roper*, when he said: 'The opinion of the world community, while not controlling our outcome, does provide respected and significant confirmation for our own conclusions'.[102] On the other hand, a foreign authority might be rejected because of relevant textual differences, as with Dickson CJ's consideration of US law in the hate speech context; or because of substantive disagreement with the reasoning as in *Horncastle*; or for

[99] Posner (n 15) 85. [100] ibid. [101] Cram (n 6) 141.
[102] *Roper v Simmons* (n 4) 578.

institutional reasons, as we will see below in the context of the Australian court's approach to the prisoners' right to vote.

A different critique takes the view that comparative human rights law is anti-democratic, entailing a surrender of authority to a legal system which has no democratic accountability in the legal system in question.[103] Why should courts in one jurisdiction give legitimacy to the law of another jurisdiction, when it has none of the fundamental signals of legitimacy, such as constitutional or legislative endorsement? This assumes that referring to foreign legal materials entails a surrender of authority. However, the deliberative approach does not give foreign legal materials the same authority as domestic law. Instead, it regards them as a means to improve judicial reasoning. Indeed, judges using foreign legal material frequently stress that they do not regard it as controlling. Kennedy J argued that, while foreign materials are relevant, 'the task of interpreting the [Constitution] remains our responsibility'.[104] Perhaps the best articulation of this position is that of Sachs J in the SACC: 'If I draw on statements by certain United States Supreme Court justices', he stated, 'I do so not because I treat their decisions as precedents to be applied in our courts, but because their dicta articulate in an elegant and helpful manner problems which face any modern court dealing with what has loosely been called church/state relations. Thus, though drawn from another legal culture, they express values and dilemmas in a way which I find most helpful in elucidating the meaning of our own constitutional text'.[105]

It might still be asked where judges get the authority to refer to foreign legal materials, even if they are not binding. Cram argues that 'Parliament has not authorised the judges to go trawling through the decisions of foreign constitutional courts. At the very least, the practice is in need of a modicum of constitutional justification'.[106] Similarly, it could be asked whether the American people gave Kennedy J authority to seek confirmation for his views from the world community. This problem is not, however, confined to foreign sources. Beyond a very general authority for courts to interpret constitutions, it is hard to find explicit authorization for any particular mode of interpretation, even in the absence of foreign sources.[107] Bills of rights do not tend to specify precisely what authority apex courts can refer to, or whether apex courts should be bound by their own precedents. Even those who argue that courts are bound by the original intention of the drafters or the natural language of the text would find it difficult to find explicit authorization from 'the people' for remaining bound by drafters in an earlier generation. This is especially so for open-textured terms such as 'equality', 'fair', or 'cruel'. The US Constitution does not even expressly give the US Supreme Court power to strike down legislation: it was the Court itself, in *Marbury v Madison*,[108] which interpreted the Constitution in this way. But the reason that the legitimacy of this role has been broadly accepted ever since is because the Court took care to justify this conclusion in a thoroughly deliberative manner, drawing both on

[103] Waldron (n 5) 150, citing Roberts CJ at his confirmation hearings.

[104] *Roper v Simmons* (n 4) (Kennedy J).

[105] *Lawrence v State* (n 68) 141–42.

[106] Cram (n 6) 140.

[107] See further S Fredman, 'Living Trees or Dead-Wood' in N Barber et al (eds), *Essays for Lord Sumption* (forthcoming).

[108] *Marbury v Madison* 5 (US) (1 Cranch) 137 (1803) (US Supreme Court).

the logic of a written constitution which limited the powers of the legislature and the implications of the actual text of the US Constitution.[109]

This is the key too to the legitimacy of referring to foreign decisions, if done in a deliberative manner. Judges' accountability does not derive from elections, or even from their responsiveness to elected representatives. Instead, judges are accountable through the explanations they provide for their conclusions. Dyzenhaus argues that this role is inherently democratic: 'What justifies all public power is the ability of its incumbents to offer adequate reasons for the decisions which affect those subject to them'.[110] Where foreign materials are able to improve the quality of the reasoning process used by judges, this enhances their legitimacy in this sense. In the human rights field, this is particularly apt because there is at least a provisional acceptance amongst states of a common core of human rights, through ratification of international human rights instruments and broadly similar domestic human rights provisions. Reasoning used in other jurisdictions to interpret similarly worded human rights texts can enhance the reasoning of a judge facing a similar decision in a domestic context, provided its appropriateness to that context is carefully examined. Thus, it is not through express authorization that judges derive their legitimacy in referring to foreign sources, or indeed to any sources; it is through the persuasiveness of the reasons given.

A further criticism is based on the difficulty in fully understanding a foreign legal system. Since a different legal system can only be understood in its entirety, this argument goes, simply picking a single case or set of legal materials will inevitably be misleading and mistaken. This criticism certainly has validity. Failure to consider foreign materials can, however, also lead to serious errors. In *Bowers v Hardwick*,[111] the US Supreme Court referred in sweeping manner to the 'shared values' of a wider civilization to support its view that criminalizing sodomy was not a breach of fundamental human rights. In doing so, it omitted any reference to the seminal ECtHR case of *Dudgeon*,[112] which held that Northern Ireland's laws criminalizing sodomy breached the right to privacy in Article 8 ECHR. However, while this example shows some of the risks of comparative human rights law, it also demonstrates that the answer lies in more, rather than less, investment in this project. It was only because of increasing awareness of developments in other countries, and scholarly articles pointing this out, that the US Supreme Court could correct its perception.[113] Thus seventeen years later in *Lawrence v Texas*,[114] the Court rejected the *Bowers*' court's interpretation of shared values. Citing *Dudgeon*, Kennedy J stated:

[109] ibid, 178–79: noting that in the Constitution 'the powers of the legislature are defined and limited', the Court asked: 'To what purpose are powers limited, and to what purpose is that limitation committed to writing, if these limits may, at any time, be passed by those intended to be restrained?' The logical answer to this, in the Court's view, was that the Constitution would be worthless if its limits could be surpassed by legislative action.

[110] D Dyzenhaus, 'The Politics of Deference: Judicial Review and Democracy' in M Taggart (ed), *The Province of Administrative Law* (Hart 1997) 305.

[111] *Bowers v Hardwick* (1986) 478 US 186 (US Supreme Court).

[112] *Dudgeon v UK* [1982] 4 EHRR 149 (European Court of Human Rights).

[113] *Lawrence v Texas* (n 1). [114] ibid.

> To the extent Bowers relied on values we share with a wider civilization, it should be noted that the reasoning and holding in Bowers have been rejected elsewhere ... The right the petitioners seek in this case has been accepted as an integral part of human freedom in many other countries. There has been no showing that in this country the governmental interest in circumscribing personal choice is somehow more legitimate or urgent.[115]

V. Applying the Deliberative Method

This section tests the deliberative model by taking a brief look at two challenges for comparative human rights law: first, in developing an apparently common substantive conception such as that of dignity; and second, in formulating and applying justifiable limitations. In each case, the value lies in the nature of the reasoning rather than in the expectation of similar outcomes.

A. Interpreting substantive principles

A major challenge for comparative law is to determine its appropriate role in interpreting open-textured yet ubiquitous concepts in human rights law. One such concept is dignity.[116] While courts in these contexts rarely attempt to define dignity as such, they might look to each other's jurisprudence on the role of dignity in shaping an understanding of open-textured human rights or in evaluating the acceptability of limitations on the right. The apex courts in South Africa and Canada have tended to share insights on this issue. For example, in the South African prisoners' right to vote case of *August*, Sachs J stated, 'The vote of each and every citizen is a badge of dignity and of personhood. Quite literally, it says that everybody counts'.[117] In the Canadian case of *Sauvé No. 2*, McLachlan J referred several times to Sachs J's dictum to support the view that denial of prisoners' right to vote 'countermands the message that everyone is equally worthy and entitled to respect under the law—that everybody counts: see *August, supra*'.[118]

Conversely, the SACC frequently cites the Supreme Court of Canada to support its view of the centrality of the concept of dignity in determining the meaning of equality. In *Egan v Canada*, the Canadian Court emphasized that the equality guarantee in section 15 of the Charter

> means nothing if it does not represent a commitment to recognizing each person's equal worth as a human being, regardless of individual differences. Equality means

[115] ibid, 576. The risk of misunderstanding is enhanced when courts use social science evidence rather than legal materials: see *Chaoulli v Quebec (Attorney General)* (2005) SCC 35 (Supreme Court of Canada).

[116] For analyses of the concept of dignity in human rights, see C McCrudden, 'Human Dignity and Judicial Interpretation of Human Rights' 2008 EJIL 655; D Kretzmer and E Klein (eds), *The Concept of Human Dignity in Human Rights Discourse* (Kluwer 2002); D Feldman, 'Human Dignity as a Legal Value' [1999] PL 682.

[117] *August v Electoral Commission* (CCT8/99) [1999] ZACC 3 (South African Constitutional Court). See also *Haig v Canada* [1993] 105 DLR 4th 577, 613 (Supreme Court of Canada).

[118] *Sauvé v Canada (Chief Electoral Officer)* [2002] 3 SCR 519 (Supreme Court of Canada).

> that our society cannot tolerate legislative distinctions that treat certain people as second-class citizens, that demean them, that treat them as less capable for no good reason, or that otherwise offend fundamental human dignity.[119]

In *Prinsloo*, quoting at length from *Egan*, Ackerman, O'Regan, and Sachs JJ held that '[w]here discrimination results in treating persons differently in a way which impairs their fundamental dignity as human beings, it will clearly be a breach of [the equality guarantee]'.[120] Similarly, in striking down the criminalization of sodomy, Ackerman J cited the Supreme Court of Canada's dictum in *Vriend v Alberta*:[121]

> This is clearly an example of a distinction which demeans the individual and strengthens and perpetuates the view that gays and lesbians are less worthy of protection as individuals in Canada's society. The potential harm to the dignity and perceived worth of gay and lesbian individuals constitutes a particularly cruel form of discrimination.[122]

However, the two apex courts have not necessarily remained in step: the Canadian Court has now recalibrated dignity as a background value rather than a legal element in the definition of dignity,[123] whereas dignity arguably remains core to the South African conception.[124]

In the US courts, the role of comparative law in assisting in the determination of such substantive conceptions as dignity has been much more contested. In the early capital punishment case of *Furman v Georgia*, Brennan J identified dignity as the touchstone for determining whether punishments were in breach of the Eighth Amendment's prohibition of cruel and unusual punishments: 'A punishment is "cruel and unusual," therefore, if it does not comport with human dignity'.[125] The role of foreign materials in determining the meaning and applicability of dignity was not central to either his view or later judgments which rejected his conclusion.[126] However, this issue came to the fore in the 2005 case of *Roper v Simmons*,[127] which challenged the infliction of the death penalty on juvenile offenders between 15 and 18 years old. Kennedy J, delivering the opinion of the Court, reiterated that, 'by protecting even those convicted of heinous crimes, the Eighth Amendment reaffirms the duty of the government to respect the dignity of all persons'.[128] For him, 'the express affirmation of certain fundamental rights by other nations and peoples simply underscores the centrality of those same rights within our own heritage of freedom'.[129] In her dissenting opinion, O'Connor J also carefully considered the relevance of other countries' values in determining the applicability of dignity to this question:

119 *Egan v Canada* [1995] 2 SCR 513 (Supreme Court of Canada).
120 *Prinsloo v Van der Linde* (n 68).
121 *Vriend v Alberta* [1998] 1 SCR 493 (Supreme Court of Canada).
122 ibid, citing in *National Coalition for Gay and Lesbian Equality v Minister of Justice* 1998 (12) BCLR 1517 (South African Constitutional Court).
123 *R v Kapp* 2008 SCC 41 (Supreme Court of Canada).
124 L Ackermann, *Human Dignity: Lodestar for Equality in South Africa* (Juta & Company 2012); C McConnachie, 'Human Dignity, "Unfair Discrimination" and Guidance' (2014) 34(3) OJLS 417.
125 *Furman v Georgia* (n 94) 270.
126 *Gregg v Georgia* (n 95) 173.
127 *Roper v Simmons* (n 4).
128 ibid, 560.
129 ibid.

> This Nation's evolving understanding of human dignity certainly is neither wholly isolated from, nor inherently at odds with, the values prevailing in other countries. On the contrary, we should not be surprised to find congruence between domestic and international values, especially where the international community has reached clear agreement—expressed in international law or in the domestic laws of individual countries—that a particular form of punishment is inconsistent with fundamental human rights.[130]

However, for her, a global consensus was only relevant to confirm the reasonableness of an American consensus: 'The instant case presents no such domestic consensus, however, and the recent emergence of an otherwise global consensus does not alter that basic fact'.[131] Although reaching the opposite conclusion, her approach is equally deliberative.

It was Brennan J's understanding of dignity that the SACC drew on to support its decision that the death penalty was in breach of the South African Constitution. Nevertheless, Chaskalson P's use of the concept was carefully justified in a deliberative sense. Reiterating that under the South African constitutional order the right to human dignity is specifically guaranteed, he held: 'The weight given to human dignity by Justice Brennan is wholly consistent with the values of our Constitution and the new order established by it. It is also consistent with the approach to extreme punishments followed by courts in other countries'.[132]

Evaluating the use of comparative law by the Supreme Court of India in relation to dignity is more complex. The Delhi High Court decision in *Naz*[133] can be regarded as a model of the deliberative approach. In supporting its conclusion that the reference to 'sex' as a ground for discrimination in the Indian Constitution included 'sexual orientation', Murhalidur J drew on the use of dignity in the SACC case of *Prinsloo*. There the South African Court held that there would be discrimination on an unspecified ground if the impugned action were based on characteristics with the potential to impair the fundamental dignity of persons.[134] The Court in *Prinsloo* had in turn drawn on the Canadian Supreme Court's decision in *Egan v Canada*.[135] Murhalidur J also drew on the growing resource of comparative materials on decriminalization of homosexuality to support his finding that the impugned provision violated the right to full personhood implicit in the right to life in the Indian Constitution.[136] Importantly, too, he used these sources to underline similar themes in Indian law.[137]

However, the Supreme Court of India has been ambivalent about the value of drawing on understandings of dignity developed elsewhere. In the death penalty

[130] ibid, 604. [131] ibid, 605.

[132] *S v Makwanyane* (n 93) referring to [1977] 45 BVerfGE 187, 228 (*Life Imprisonment case*) (German Constitutional Court); *Kindler v Canada* (1992) 6 CRR (2d) 193 (Supreme Court of Canada).

[133] *Naz Foundation v Government of Delhi* WP (C) 7455/2001 (High Court of Delhi).

[134] *Prinsloo v Van der Linde* (n 68) 152. [135] *Egan v Canada* (n 119).

[136] Citing extensively from *National Coalition for Gay and Lesbian Equality v Minister of Justice* (n 122); *Vriend v Alberta Dudgeon v UK* (n 121); *Romer v Evans* 517 US 620, 634, 116 S Ct 1620, 134 LEd2d 855 (1996) (US Supreme Court); *Lawrence v Texas* (n 1); *Norris v Ireland* (1991) 13 EHRR 186 (European Court of Human Rights).

[137] *Naz Foundation v Government of Delhi* (n 133) 52.

case of *Bachan Singh*, the Court was reluctant to hold that 'the acceptance by India of the International Covenant on Civil and Political Rights ... makes any change in the prevailing standards of decency and human dignity by which counsel require us to judge the constitutional validity of the impugned provisions'.[138] Instead, it concluded that 'it cannot be said that the framers of the Constitution considered death sentence for murder ... as a degrading punishment which would defile "the dignity of the individual" within the contemplation of the Preamble to the Constitution'.[139] Similarly, in overturning the Delhi High Court's decision in *Naz*, the Court dismissed the use of comparative law, and therefore failed wholly to engage with the many dignity-based arguments put to it, preferring to focus on institutional reasons such as the presumption of constitutionality of statutes.[140] As we have seen, however, its reasons for dismissing the comparative dimension were less than convincing. A deliberative framework would not require the Court to adopt the arguments based on dignity; but it would, at the very least, require the Court to fully explain why such an approach, which had found favour in other courts, was not applicable to the status of Lesbian, Gay, Bisexual, Transgender, and Intersex people in India.

However, barely three months later, a different division of the Court, finding that discrimination against transgender people breached the Indian constitution, centred its decision on the principle of dignity, drawing on comparative law in the best deliberative sense. Beginning with the English case of *Corbett v Corbett*,[141] where the High Court held that the biological sex of a person is fixed at birth, the Court traced the development of a powerful alternative approach in a stream of cases and legislation from New Zealand, Australia, Malaysia, the UK, the EU, and the ECHR. The Court stated: 'We have referred exhaustively to the various judicial pronouncements and legislations on the international arena to highlight the fact that the recognition of "sex identity gender" of persons, and "guarantee to equality and non-discrimination" on the ground of gender identity or expression is increasing and gaining acceptance in international law and, therefore, be applied in India'.[142] Most importantly, the Indian Court drew on the ECtHR decision of *Goodwin v UK*, where the ECtHR reiterated that 'the very essence of the Convention is respect for human dignity and human freedom' in holding that the 'unsatisfactory situation in which post-operative transsexuals live in an intermediate zone as not quite one gender or the other is no longer sustainable'.[143] Reiterating that 'recognition of one's gender identity lies at the heart of the fundamental right to dignity', the Court followed these developments in rejecting the biological test in *Corbett*.[144]

[138] *Bachan Singh v State of Punjab* (n 74). The Court noted in any event that the International Covenant did not wholly outlaw capital punishment for murder.

[139] ibid, 136.

[140] *Suresh Kumar Koushal v Naz Foundation* (n 73).

[141] *Corbett v Corbett* [1970] 2 WLR 1306 (UK High Court).

[142] *NALSA v Union of India* (Writ Petition 604 of 2013) (April 2014) (Indian Supreme Court) 43.

[143] *Goodwin v UK* (2002) 35 EHRR 18 (European Court of Human Rights) cited in *NALSA v Union of India*, ibid, 32.

[144] *NALSA v Union of India* (n 142).

B. Justifying limitations of rights

While some human rights are absolute, many can be limited if the State can justify the limitation as necessary either to protect the rights of others, or for certain legitimate public interest objectives. The justifiability of any such limitation at first sight seems least apt for comparative scrutiny, since it involves a balancing of the proportionality of the interference with the right with the legitimacy of the aim in particular jurisdictions. Yet here, too, we can see how a deliberative approach to comparative materials can enhance courts' application of justification tests in different jurisdictions. This can be seen by considering one of the most active issues in comparative law in recent years, namely whether prisoners have the right to vote. The right to vote is generally not contested. Instead, the cases concern the justifiability of limiting the right. Nevertheless, courts in Canada, South Africa, Australia, and the UK, as well as the ECtHR and the United Nations Human Rights Committee (HRC), have drawn on each other's jurisprudence to determine this question. Particularly widely cited is the Canadian Supreme Court decision in *Sauvé No. 2*,[145] which struck down legislation denying the right to vote to prisoners serving prison sentences of two years or more. *Sauvé* has been cited both for the way in which the limitation test was framed and for its application to the State's claims of justifiability. For McLachlan CJ, the court's role in determining justification was centrally concerned with transparency and accountability. 'At the end of the day', she stated, 'people should not be left guessing about why their Charter rights have been infringed'. This dictum was quoted in full by Chaskalson CJ to support the SACC decision striking down a blanket ban on prisoners' right to vote in South Africa.[146] As Chaskalson CJ put it: 'In a case such as this where the government seeks to disenfranchise a group of its citizens and the purpose is not self-evident, there is a need for it to place sufficient information before the Court to enable it to know exactly what purpose the disenfranchisement was intended to serve'.[147] The *Sauvé* case was also influential in the decision of the Chamber of the ECtHR in *Hirst* when it held that the blanket ban on prisoners' voting rights in the UK was in breach of the Convention. According to the Chamber judgment: 'Taking due account of the difference in text and structure of the Canadian Charter, the Court nonetheless finds that the substance of the reasoning may be regarded as apposite in the present case'.[148] In this case, *Sauvé* was used not so much for its framing of the proportionality test, but for its application. In particular, the Chamber found 'much force in the arguments of the majority in *Sauvé* that removal of the vote in fact runs counter to the rehabilitation of the offender as a law-abiding member of the community and undermines the authority of the law as derived from a legislature which the community as a whole votes into power'.[149]

Merely referring to decisions does not, however, mean that they are used in a deliberative sense. When the Chamber decision in *Hirst* was appealed to the Grand

[145] *Sauvé v Canada (Chief Electoral Officer)* (n 118).

[146] *Minister of Home Affairs v National Institute for Crime Prevention and the Re-Integration of Offenders (NICRO) and others* 2004 (5) BCLR 445 (CC) (South African Constitutional Court).

[147] ibid.

[148] Cited in *Hirst v UK (No 2)* (2006) 42 EHRR 41 (European Court of Human Rights (Grand Chamber)).

[149] Cited in ibid, 46.

Chamber, the UK Government roundly criticized the Chamber decision for its use of foreign law.[150] In upholding the Chamber decision, the Grand Chamber cited these objections but did not address them directly.[151] Having considered the practice of Member States, where fewer than thirteen Member States imposed a blanket ban, it held that even if no common European approach could be discerned, this could not be determinative of the issue.[152] Instead, it simply held that '[s]uch a general, automatic and indiscriminate restriction on a vitally important Convention right must be seen as falling outside any acceptable margin of appreciation, however wide that margin might be'.[153] Similarly, in subsequent ECtHR decisions, such as that in *Scoppola*,[154] the Court stopped short of a deliberative approach, simply setting out the growing body of comparative material on this issue,[155] without expressly drawing on it to come to its conclusion. Nevertheless, the *Hirst* decision has been added to the growing resource of comparative law referred to by Courts facing the question of whether prisoners' right to vote can be curtailed. Thus, *Hirst* was referred to by the HRC to support its conclusion that 'the State party, whose legislation provides a blanket deprivation of the right to vote to anyone sentenced to a term of imprisonment, did not provide any arguments as to how the restrictions in this particular case would meet the criterion of reasonableness as required by the Covenant'.[156]

Deliberative consideration of foreign material does not necessarily entail that it should be accepted, as long as good reasons, based in textual or institutional differences, are provided. This can be seen in the judgments of the Australian High Court in the case of *Roach*,[157] in which a prisoner challenged the total prohibition on prisoners serving a sentence of imprisonment from voting in any Senate or House of Representatives elections.[158] The Court struck down the total ban but reinstated the previous formula, removing the right to vote from prisoners serving sentences of three years or more. Notably, however, although both *Sauvé* and *Hirst* were cited, the Australian justices were not convinced of their applicability in the Australian context. Gleeson CJ stressed that although the issues were similar, they arose under different legal regimes: 'There is a danger that uncritical translation of the concept of proportionality from the legal context of cases such as *Sauvé* or *Hirst* to the Australian context could lead to the application in this country of a constitutionally inappropriate standard of judicial review of legislative action'.[159] Nor does the judicial conversation necessarily lead to a convergence in outcomes. Although all the jurisdictions cited here have excluded a blanket ban, there is significant divergence as to the justifiability

150 ibid. 151 ibid. 152 ibid. 153 ibid.

154 *Scoppola v Italy (No 3)* [2013] 56 EHRR 19 (European Court of Human Rights (Grand Chamber)).

155 *Sauvé v Canada (Chief Electoral Officer)* (n 118); *August v Electoral Commission* (n 117); *Minister of Home Affairs v National Institute for Crime Prevention and the Re-Integration of Offenders (NICRO) and others* (n 146); *Roach v Electoral Commissioner* [2007] HCA 43 (High Court of Australia).

156 *Yevdokimov and Rezanov v Russian Federation* CCPR/C/D/1410/2005 (March 2011) (UN Human Rights Committee).

157 *Roach v Electoral Commissioner* (n 155).

158 The Commonwealth Electoral Act 1918 (Cth) s 93(8AA) (Australia). The total ban had been introduced in 2006; previously it had only applied to prisoners serving sentences of three years or more. The prohibition had been in place since 1902, but the minimum sentence had fluctuated over the years between one year and five.

159 *Roach v Electoral Commissioner* (n 155).

of curbs on prisoners with more serious sentences. Whereas the Supreme Court of Canada was unwilling to countenance any ban,[160] the Australian High Court accepted a ban for prisoners serving sentences above three years,[161] and the ECtHR in *Scoppola*[162] accepted the Italian regime, which applied to prisoners serving sentences above five years. What is important is not the divergence, but that these divergences themselves be justified in the light of comparative materials and good deliberative reasons be given for difference.

The powerful outlier in this picture is the US. US cases have been cited in both South Africa and the UK for opposite conclusions. Sachs J in *August* cited an early decision, *O'Brien*,[163] for the proposition that a state could not de facto deprive prisoners of the right to vote by refusing to register them or to apply appropriate polling stations. In *Hirst*, in the UK, by contrast, the UK court cited the US Supreme Court case of *Richardson v Ramirez*,[164] which upheld prisoner voting disqualification, to support the UK blanket ban on prisoner rights to vote. US Courts have not, for their part, ventured into the trans-jurisdictional discussion. One possible reason is the very real textual difference. In *Richardson*, the Supreme Court upheld prisoner voter disqualification on the grounds that this was set out expressly in the Fourteenth Amendment, which provides for the denial by states of the right to vote to persons 'for participation in rebellion, or other crime'.[165] However, as the dissent suggested, there is still room for discussion as to the meaning of 'or other crime'. Of course, *Richardson* pre-dated the current comparative interchange. But should similar facts come before the Court, a deliberative approach to the consideration of the comparative materials would certainly enhance the judgment.[166]

VI. Conclusion

This chapter has set the scene for the remainder of the book. Judges in different jurisdictions face the same demanding questions as to the meaning and application of human rights law. In this book, we are embarking on the journey of finding the commonalities and understanding the divergences. We are joining the incipient judicial conversations about the possibilities of cross-fertilization of principles in human rights law. The comparative law approach, which insists on public reasoning, deliberative justifications, and participation by affected parties, provides human rights lawyers with the possibility of engaging in this process by continually drawing attention to the range of substantive answers. Assessing human rights law from a comparative perspective opens up a vast array of new perspectives and insights. Basic preconceptions, assumed

[160] *Sauvé v Canada (Chief Electoral Officer)* (n 118).

[161] *Roach v Electoral Commissioner* (n 155).

[162] *Scoppola v Italy (No 3)* (n 154).

[163] *O'Brien v Skinner* 414 US 524 (1973) (US Supreme Court).

[164] *Richardson v Ramirez* 418 US 24 (1974) (US Supreme Court).

[165] ibid. See further *Romer v Evans* (n 136) where the Court describes principles that states may disenfranchise a convicted felon as 'unexceptionable'.

[166] In *Simmons v Galvin* 130 S Ct 2428 (2010) (US Supreme Court), the Supreme Court ordered the Solicitor General to 'express the views of the United States' on whether laws that take away the right to vote from people in prison or on parole can be challenged under the Voting Rights Act as racially discriminatory.

to be universal from within the confines of the jurisdiction's own legal system, are unsettled and require renewed justification. Throughout this book, the value of such a deliberative approach will be developed.

The first stage of the journey requires us to look in more abstract terms at what we mean by a human right. This is the subject of Chapter 2. As will be seen in that chapter, the paradigm case of human rights is frequently based on civil and political rights. Chapter 3 challenges the boundary between civil and political rights and socio-economic rights, demonstrating that they are indivisible and inter-dependent. Indeed, this is the approach of the book as a whole, which deals with both rights traditionally regarded as civil and political rights and those usually seen as socio-economic rights. Chapters 4 and 5 draw out the main elements of the analytic framework which will be applied to the substantive chapters that follow. Chapter 4 considers the role of courts and adjudication, the key focus of this book. It examines the democratic dilemma and considers the constraints and appropriate contributions courts should make. Chapter 5 turns to the role of the text and judicial interpretation. The starting point is the text of the human rights instrument before the court. While there have been, as we have seen, important constitutional borrowings and transplantations, each text has its own unique structure. But this in itself is not sufficient. Human rights language is necessarily open-textured and at a high level of abstraction. Judicial interpretation is therefore a key aspect of human rights adjudication. Here our comparative project requires attention to be paid both to the theories of interpretation different judges rely on to support the legitimacy of their position, and to the institutional constraints arising from different principles of separation of powers.

Also, of key importance are different social and political contexts. This book concentrates on jurisdictions which have sufficient similarities to make comparison meaningful, but enough differences to make comparative work interesting and challenging. The primary comparative sources are the US, Canada, South Africa, and India. They have the English language in common, as well as a colonial past, which continues to influence the present legal system; and all are liberal democracies which have a general commitment to human rights. At the same time, they span the global south and the global north, as well as including both developing and developed countries. The book also draws on the ECHR because of its important role in setting human rights standards in Europe and particularly in the UK, which does not have an entrenched constitution.

2

What Is a Human Right? Dealing with Disagreement

I. Introduction: Searching for Fundamentals?

> No matter who we are, we cannot establish the existence of a human right just by declaring it to be one. We can get it wrong, and we owe attention, therefore, to what are the criteria for right and wrong here. For example, the Universal Declaration contains a right to periodic holidays with pay, to which the overwhelming and cheering reaction has been that, whatever that supposed entitlement is, it is certainly not a human right.[1]
>
> (James Griffin)

Is there a human right to holidays with pay? For Griffin, the idea is preposterous. But how does he know? More generally, how do we go about establishing whether a claim is a human right? One seemingly obvious way is to look for universal consensus. The Universal Declaration of Human Rights (UDHR) seems to be a logical source: it was drawn up by a Commission from a wide variety of political, cultural, and religious backgrounds and was adopted by the United Nations General Assembly in 1948. For Griffin, however, such consensus is irrelevant. Indeed, he declares, the UDHR 'blunders at one point in asserting a right to periodic holidays with pay, which … is widely rejected'.[2] The criteria for right and wrong, on his view, can be discerned independently of such consensus. Not everyone agrees, however. Indeed, while the notion of fundamental human rights attracts general respect, there is little agreement on how we identify them. This is true both for the general question of what constitutes a fundamental human right, and the more specific question of its substantive content and application.

Several ways of addressing the foundational disagreements about human rights have been articulated. One, such as that of Griffin, is to formulate a basic, objective moral principle, from which human rights and their interpretation can be derived.[3] This means that some courts, thinkers, or human rights instruments have simply got it wrong. Section II briefly sketches some of the principles which have been proposed. The main candidates are autonomy, dignity, and basic interests, as well as a synthesis of some of these, such as the capability theory developed by Sen and Nussbaum. As

[1] J Griffin, *On Human Rights* (OUP 2009) 5.

[2] ibid, 16. He does not find it necessary to specify who he means when he describes the right as 'widely rejected'.

[3] Note that objectivity is not identical with truth. Objectivity requires a judgement based on relevant evidence which is not influenced by psychological or emotional factors.

will be seen, philosophers disagree on both the basic principle, and the rights that derive from it. These basic disagreements on the foundational principles have led some to reject the possibility of formulating universal principles at all. Instead, it could be argued, the values which inevitably inform human rights decision-making are wholly derived from the local legal, political, cultural, and social context. Some go even further and maintain that all values are relative, so that widespread and radical disagreement as to the basic human rights is incapable of rational resolution. Indeed, on this view, it is presumptuous of proponents of human rights to assume that their fundamentally Western values are an appropriate yardstick to judge the values of other cultures. Section III of this chapter critically assesses theories of pluralism and moral relativism in the context of human rights.

Section IV considers the liberal response to relativism. In particular, it assesses the implications for human rights of one of the fundamental dilemmas of liberal political theory, namely the role of tolerance. If one of the key tenets of liberalism is individuals' autonomy to choose their own values, how can this be reconciled with the imposition of particular human rights norms across different cultures? On the other hand, should intolerance be tolerated? Section V provides an outline of theories on ways to deal with disagreement on the meaning of human rights. It is suggested that there should be no aspiration to achieve absolute answers, which apply in all contexts over all time. Instead, drawing on the insights of deliberative democracy set out in Chapter 1, it is argued that the aim should be to engage in constant reasoned attempts to develop the understanding of human rights. Without losing the universality of the demands of human rights standards, we can make room for diversity or pluralism in their application.

The meaning of human rights has become a popular topic for philosophers and political theorists. For comparative human rights lawyers, however, the issue is not just one of theoretical debate. The meaning and extent of human rights raise intensely complex questions for individuals and the State, which courts are frequently called on to resolve. What assistance then can background philosophical and political theories be to these questions? It is from this angle that different theories are examined in this chapter. Can courts faced with an open-textured right, which could be interpreted in a range of plausible ways, resort to fundamental principles in order to determine the outcome? For example, if a court is asked to determine whether the right to life precludes abortion on the one hand, or capital punishment on the other, can judges turn to fundamental principles such as autonomy or dignity to inform their decision? Or should the judgment be based entirely on local or culturally relative values, which cannot be transplanted to other jurisdictions? Are political philosophers' theories on disagreement of any assistance?

II. Fundamental Values

A. Rationality and autonomy

The principles of rationality and autonomy are among the most commonly cited principles regarded as underpinning human rights. Griffin encapsulates this approach in his theory of normative agency. He argues that what distinguishes human beings from animals is our ability to deliberate, assess, and choose what we regard as a good life for ourselves, and take action to achieve it.[4] This he calls normative agency. Since the basic principle shaping human rights derives from the very fact of our humanity, he concludes that the function of human rights is to protect such normative agency. We can therefore determine whether a claim is a human right by considering whether it furthers our normative agency.

However, the implications of Griffin's approach are highly controversial. This is because he does not attribute normative agency to all human beings. 'Human', in his view, does not simply mean belonging to 'homo sapiens'. To be human, in Griffin's schema, requires being capable of agency, to choose paths through life, and to be at liberty to pursue them. Consequently, 'infants, the severely mentally retarded, people in an irreversible coma, are all members of the species, but are not agents'.[5] Moreover, since by 'human' in 'human rights' we mean a functioning human agent',[6] and since human rights are only there to protect normative agency, individuals without such agency do not count as rights-bearers in his schema. The paradoxical consequence is that the most vulnerable people, such as tiny babies, patients in a coma, or those who suffer from Alzheimer's disease, are not protected as bearers of human rights.

The view that rationality and autonomy are fundamental to what it means to be human has a long and pervasive history. But, as in Griffin's case, this role has been primarily to exclude some from human rights protection.[7] Thus, Aristotle argued that human beings only attain their purposes by exercising reason to make moral choices. Therefore, only rational beings could be the subject of rights.[8] However, not all human beings were capable of rationality, in his view. For Aristotle, women were less than rational—women's faculty of deliberation was inconclusive and lacking authority.[9] This exclusion of women from the highest goods of humanity, namely the exercise of reason, in turn justified their subordination in family and state.[10] Indeed, in Greek society, women were regarded as chattels. This was true too of slaves.

For early liberals, too, the value of being human lay in the capacity to be free to use one's rational capacities to exercise choice. Thus, Locke viewed the main function of human rights as being to protect individual autonomy from State interference.[11] Individuals entered society clothed in their natural rights, a protected space into which the State could not enter. However, although Locke regarded all men as equal because they all have an equal propensity for reason, this conception did not extend to women. This is because Locke regarded the need for protection against authority as being confined to the public sphere. Political power required justification. But power within the family did not. In the private sphere of the family, therefore, the

[4] Griffin (n 1) 32. [5] ibid, 34. [6] ibid, 36.

[7] For a detailed analysis of rationality in relation to women's rights, see S Fredman, *Women and the Law* (Oxford Monographs in Labour Law, OUP 1997) ch 1.

[8] Aristotle, *Politics* (Random House 1943).

[9] Aristotle, *The Politics of Aristotle* (translated by E Barker) (Clarendon Press 1946), 1260 a7. See further Fredman (n 7) 3–4.

[10] Aristotle (n 8) 1259 b1. [11] J Locke, *Two Treatises of Government* (CUP 1963).

husband was master over his wife, children, and servants.[12] As in Greek society, this simply legitimized the continuing legal subordination of women. This was epitomized by the law of coverture, according to which the woman's legal personality was obliterated on marriage, and husbands were given near-absolute control of both property and person of the wife. John Stuart Mill characterized marriage as the 'only legal bondage known to our law'. Indeed, he argued, the wife's position was worse in some respects than slaves: even a female slave could refuse to have intercourse with her master, a right denied to his wife.[13]

The development of human rights in the latter part of the twentieth century was premised on a decoupling of human rights from limiting notions of rationality. Indeed, the exclusion of women, black people, minorities, people with disabilities, and others from the protection of the law was one of the main motivating factors for the human rights movement. Griffin's emphasis on a less than all-encompassing concept of normative agency therefore reverses this crucial move towards an inclusive understanding of human rights.

Even if we accept normative agency as the basic principle, we might disagree about which rights it generates. Griffin regards it as necessary to autonomy to have the right to freedom of speech, assembly, and press. He sees the right not to be tortured as similarly following from the essence of normative agency. On the other hand, as we have seen, he is contemptuous of the possibility of a human right to periodic holidays with pay. Yet it is arguable that such a right is at least as important to individual autonomy as freedom of speech, assembly, and the press, let alone freedom of worship. This is because those whose existence depends on their paid work might find it impossible in practice to take time off without pay. This constitutes a grave interference with individual autonomy, coming close to the boundary with forced labour. On one view, then, rationality, for Griffin as much as for Aristotle and Locke, is arguably nothing but the rationality of those who live their lives under similar conditions as he does, having the good fortune both to exercise normative agency and to take holidays without himself or his family falling into absolute poverty.

B. Dignity

The above discussion demonstrates that regarding rationality and autonomy as the fundamental principles behind human rights generates as much disagreement as it aims to address. An alternative approach is to use the notion of human dignity as the foundational value. The UDHR begins by declaring that recognition of the inherent dignity and of the equal and inalienable rights of all members of the human family is the foundation of freedom, justice, and peace in the world. The International Covenant on Civil and Political Rights (ICCPR) and the International Covenant on Economic, Social and Cultural Rights (ICESCR) both begin with the ringing declaration that the inalienable rights of all persons derive from the inherent dignity of the human person. Many modern

[12] ibid, 'Second Treatise', 86; C Pateman, *The Sexual Contract* (Polity Press 1988) 21.

[13] JS Mill, *On Liberty* (Longman, Roberts, & Green 1869) 58.

constitutions also put dignity centre stage. The German Basic Law, strongly influenced by recent history, provides in its first and absolutely entrenched article that human dignity is unassailable and that it is the duty of all state authority to respect and protect it.[14]

Dignity is also central to the articulated values of the new South African Constitution. Addressing directly the history of humiliation and degradation to which the previous apartheid regime was dedicated, section 1 of the Constitution states that, amongst other things, the new South African state is founded on the values of 'human dignity, the achievement of equality, and the advancement of human rights and freedoms'. The general limitation clause in the South African Constitution also states that a right entrenched by the Constitution can only be limited to the extent that the limitation is 'reasonable and justifiable in an open and democratic society based on human dignity, autonomy and freedom'.[15] Most importantly, the South African Constitution requires every court, when interpreting human rights, to do so in a way that promotes the values of human dignity, equality, and freedom.[16] Notably too, the right to dignity is established in the first article of the European Union Charter of Fundamental Human Rights. Feldman concludes that 'dignity has been seen as underpinning what one might call "legal humanism", and has profoundly influenced the recent development of constitutional jurisprudence in a number of States'.[17] Moreover, as Waldron points out, dignity is used in two senses in the human rights canon: human rights are said to derive from the inherent dignity of the human person, while at the same time, dignity constitutes the specific content of some rights, such as the right not to be subjected to torture, or to inhuman or degrading treatment or punishment.[18]

Yet the meaning of dignity remains hotly contested. As Feldman puts it, 'The canon of fundamental rights and freedoms is controversial and indeterminate, but it is still more difficult to pin down the meaning of dignity'.[19] McCrudden, in his comprehensive survey of dignity in judicial interpretation of human rights, is more emphatic. For him, 'instead of providing a basis for principled decision-making, dignity seems open to significant judicial manipulation, increasing rather than decreasing judicial discretion'.[20] Indeed, he argues, 'That is one of its significant attractions to both judges and litigators alike'.[21] McCrudden does discern a basic minimum content: 'That each human being possesses an intrinsic worth that should be respected, that some forms of conduct are inconsistent with respect for this intrinsic worth, and that the state exists for the individual not vice versa'. However, there remains deep disagreement as to the meaning of each of these terms: 'what that intrinsic worth consists in, what forms of treatment are inconsistent with that worth, and what the implications are for

[14] Basic Law for the Federal Republic of Germany (Grundgesetz, GG), Article 1(1).

[15] South African Constitution, s 36(1).

[16] ibid, ss 39(1) and (2).

[17] D Feldman, 'Human Dignity as a Legal Value' [1999] PL 682 at 682.

[18] J Waldron, 'Dignity and Rank' in J Waldron and M Dan-Cohen (eds), *Dignity, Rank and Rights* (OUP 2012) 16.

[19] Feldman (n 17) 682.

[20] C McCrudden, 'Human Dignity and Judicial Interpretation of Human Rights' (2008) EJIL 655 at 655.

[21] ibid.

the role of the state'.[22] McCrudden's critique extends to both the decision as to whether something is a human right and the interpretation of the content of human rights. On both issues, he concludes: 'Rather than providing substantive meaning, a significant use is institutional: providing a language in which judges can appear to justify how they deal with issues such as the weight of rights, the domestication and contextualization of rights, and the generation of new or more extensive rights'.[23] It is this, he argues, which explains its popularity.

It is commonplace to refer to Kant to anchor the inclusive notion of dignity, and particularly, his principle that 'man does not exist as a mere means for any use or will but as an end in himself', and therefore 'each of them must treat itself and all others never merely as means, but in every case at the same time as ends in themselves'. Kant is also clear that all rational beings have dignity and therefore absolute worth. However, a closer look at Kant's work on dignity reveals a far more ambiguous picture. While Kant refers to dignity as a quality which is characterized by its pricelessness, its intrinsic value beyond any exchange,[24] the idea of dignity as the intrinsic worth of every person is not clearly delineated in his work. Other statements in his work reveal that his understanding of dignity was also based on 'autonomous moral capacity'. Thus, he stated, 'Autonomy then is the basis of the dignity of human and of every rational nature'.[25] This slippage from dignity as innate worth to dignity as conditional on rationality and autonomy can also be seen in Griffin's work. Indeed, Griffin regards his notion of 'normative agency' as a specification of dignity.[26]

Moreover, although dignity is now associated with the idea that all human beings should be valued simply as human beings, the concept of dignity originated in the valorization of hierarchy and rank. Thus, Eckert shows that in ancient philosophy, dignity referred on the one hand to the social rank of a person, and on the other to the distinction between human beings and other creatures.[27] Cicero, in particular, regarded dignity as based on rank, rather than as universal. A rival understanding of dignity posits quite the opposite: it sees dignity as inextricable from our very nature as human beings and therefore constitutes the best reason for according human rights to everyone regardless of rank, merit, or ability. Thus, Dworkin refers to 'the vague but powerful idea of human dignity, ... [which] supposes that there are ways of treating a man [*sic*] that are inconsistent with recognizing him as a full member of the human community, and holds that such treatment is profoundly unjust'.[28] This separation of dignity from rank can be dated back to the dismantling of feudal hierarchies, culminating in its explicit rejection by the French Revolution. As Eckert explains it: 'The events of the French Revolution led to the realization that the idea of dignity could only be justified by separating dignity from rank and acknowledging dignity as an

[22] ibid. [23] ibid.

[24] 'In the kingdom of ends everything has either value or dignity. Whatever has a value can be replaced by something else which is equivalent; whatever, on the other hand, is above all value, and therefore admits of no equivalent, has a dignity': I Kant, *Groundwork for the Metaphysics of Morals* (edited and translated by Allen W Wood) 1785 (Yale University Press 2008).

[25] ibid. [26] Griffin (n 1) 152.

[27] J Eckert, 'Legal Roots of Human Dignity in German Law' in D Kretzmer and E Klein (eds), *The Concept of Human Dignity in Human Rights Discourse* (Kluwer 2002) 43.

[28] R Dworkin, *Taking Rights Seriously* (Duckworth 1977) 198.

innate element of every human being. The universal and equal human dignity had to be inviolable and inalienable'.[29]

Nevertheless, it has been persuasively argued that there remain powerful residues in the modern use of dignity of the hierarchical notion of dignity as rank, or *dignitas*. On one view, the link is a progressive one: modern notions of dignity can be seen as a levelling up or generalization of the principles of respect and consideration which were previously reserved for those of higher rank. Waldron puts it vividly: dignity is 'nobility for the common man'.[30] However, Hennette-Vauchez questions 'whether the levelling-up process ever would have been—or if it ever has been—pushed to its logical conclusion, that is, the ultimate subversion of its own inegalitarian roots'. She argues instead that 'inegalitarian elements are still at play in contemporary dignity jurisprudence'.[31] Hennette-Vauchez takes this further and argues that dignity has been extended beyond the individual to the community, requiring individuals to uphold the broader *dignitas* of the communities they live in. Thus, the modern application of dignity is not simply about linking human rights to individuals because of their intrinsic worth; it also requires subjects of rights to regard themselves as complying with certain moral duties in order to maintain the *dignitas* of the whole of humanity or the societies in which they live. A different understanding of dignity sees it as incorporating a recognition of the social embeddedness of the individual, rather than requiring the individual to uphold the reputation of the community. As Van der Westhuizen J put it in the South African Constitutional Court case of *Barnard*:

> The individual, as the bearer of the right to dignity, should not be understood as an isolated and unencumbered being. Dignity contains individualistic as well as collective impulses. Its collectivist attributes, including that we are 'social beings whose humanity is expressed through ... relationships with others', find resonance in the South African idea of Ubuntu, which foregrounds 'interdependence of the members of a community'.[32]

These tensions within the conception of dignity can be seen playing themselves out in what has become known as the French 'dwarf-tossing case'. After the practice was prohibited in France, Wackenheim, who suffered from dwarfism, brought a claim for breach of his human rights. He had appeared in 'dwarf-tossing' events in which members of the audience competed to see how far they could throw him. Both sides relied on dignity to justify their position. The mayor who banned the events argued that the spectacle constituted a degrading affront to human dignity. Wackenheim, however, regarded the ban as an affront to his dignity by making it impossible for him to earn his livelihood. The French Conseil D'Etat held that dwarf tossing was an attraction that affronted human dignity;[33] and could be banned notwithstanding its consequences for freedom of employment because of its effect on public order, which included respect for human dignity. Wackenheim complained to the UN Human

[29] Eckert (n 27) 45. [30] Waldron (n 18) 22.

[31] S Hennette-Vauchez, 'A Human Dignitas? Remnants of the Ancient Legal Concept in Contemporary Dignity Jurisprudence' (2011) 9 I.CON 32, 55.

[32] *South African Police Service v Solidarity obo Barnard* [2014] ZACC 23 (South African Constitutional Court) para [174]. I am grateful to Nomfundo Ramalekana for pointing this out to me.

[33] Conseil d'Etat, Ass, 27 October 1995, Cne de Morsang-sur-Orge, Recueil Lebon 372.

Rights Committee. He argued that there was no work for dwarves in France and that the activity did not constitute an affront to human dignity since dignity consists in having a job. The Committee rejected his complaint.[34] It did not find that there had been discrimination, but even if there was, this could be justified as necessary to protect public order, bringing into play considerations of human dignity compatible with the objectives of the Covenant.

Hennette-Vauchez argues that the result is not to protect his individual dignity, but the *dignitas* of the community in which he lived. On a different view, it represents the imposition of a paternalistic concept of dignity on freedom of choice or autonomy—in this case, the autonomy of Wackenheim to participate in dwarf tossing. However, this ignores the constraints in which individual choices are exercised. In a world in which dwarves are denigrated and regarded as objects of humour, there might be few possibilities of employment open to people in this class. Seen in this light, prohibiting dwarf tossing simply removes one of the few sources of income available to dwarves and therefore interferes with their autonomy. An alternative approach, which furthers both dignity and autonomy, is to open up a wider range of genuine options. This would entail doing more than prohibiting dwarf tossing. It would require the stigma associated with dwarfism to be removed, and a range of dignified employment opportunities made available. This synthesis of dignity and autonomy is best encapsulated in the theory of capabilities in the work of Amartya Sen and Martha Nussbaum, to which we now turn.

C. The capabilities approach: a range of feasible options

Sen regards the individual's right to be and do what he or she chooses to be and do as central to his philosophy. But he differs from other autonomy-based theorists in his recognition of the constraints on genuine autonomy. For Sen, autonomy only matters within the context of a range of options which are actually available and feasible. Known as the capabilities approach, this concept was originally developed in order to measure the welfare of individuals in a way which went beyond aggregate welfare. Instead, Sen aimed to capture individuals' actual ability to 'be and do what they would wish to be and do'.[35] Nussbaum has developed a similar conception, which additionally clarifies the connection between autonomy in this substantive sense, and dignity. For Nussbaum, the core idea is 'that of the human being as a dignified, free being who shapes his or her own life in cooperation and reciprocity with others'.[36] This draws on the Kantian notion of the inviolability and dignity of the person. But it is supplemented by the Marxian insight that the major powers of a human being need material support and cannot be what they are without it. Thus, the aim is a society not just in which 'each person is treated as worthy of regard', but also 'in which each has been put in a position to live really humanly'.[37]

[34] *Manuel Wackenheim v France* Communication No 854/1999 UN Doc CCPR/C/75/D/854/1999 (2002) (UN Human Rights Committee).

[35] A Sen, *Development as Freedom* (OUP 1999).

[36] M Nussbaum, *Women and Human Development* (CUP 2000) 73.

[37] ibid.

Nussbaum identifies ten fundamental entitlements, or 'capabilities', which she argues are inherent in the very idea of a life worthy of human dignity. The items on her list are not simply read off from a factual observation of human nature but arise from an evaluation of the question of what opportunities are entailed by a life worthy of human dignity. To this extent, she attempts to give some determinate content to the meaning of dignity. Importantly, she sees sociability as a fundamental characteristic of human life, where flourishing depends on social relations with others, including relations of care and dependency. Because she subscribes to the liberal emphasis on choice, Nussbaum regards capabilities as giving individuals the potential to achieve a life of dignity but leaves the fulfilment of these capabilities to individual choice. She emphasizes, however, that dignity requires more than allowing the space to make those choices; it also requires the State to provide resources to promote the development of individual capabilities.[38]

These entitlements belong to people independently of their membership in a State: 'In other words, they belong to humans just on account of their human dignity, and would be there even if there were no political organization at all'.[39] Nevertheless, the key purpose of the State is to secure these central entitlements to people.[40] The connection with law and the State is straightforward. If a claim is required by a notion of a life worthy of human dignity, it ought to be enforced.[41] This, she acknowledges, is 'a type of human rights approach—but also one of both supplementation and critique'.[42]

The role of dignity in Nussbaum's work is, however, somewhat ambiguous. On the one hand, her ten central capabilities belong to individuals on account of their dignity; while at the same time, these capabilities are 'ways of realizing a life with human dignity'. Moreover, like Kant and Griffin, she seems to presuppose minimum levels of agency as a precondition for fundamental entitlements. This ambiguity can be seen in her argument that the basis of fundamental entitlements 'lies not in rationality, nor in any other specific human property, but, rather, in the bare fact of being a living human being: being born from human parents, and having a minimal level of agency or capacity for activity. That is enough to give a human being a dignity that is equal to that of every other human being'.[43] This suggests that the lives of some human beings, such as those in a persistent vegetative state, who are not able to achieve a minimum level of agency, do not have dignity in the sense she understands it.[44]

D. Basic interests

Rather than emphasizing a single value of dignity or autonomy, several philosophers have regarded rights as stemming from basic human interests. Most recently, this

[38] P Formosa and C Mackenzie, 'Nussbaum, Kant, and the Capabilities Approach to Dignity' (2014) 5 Ethical Theory and Moral Practice 875, 891.

[39] M Nussbaum, 'Capabilities, Entitlements, Rights: Supplementation and Critique' (2011) 12 Journal of Human Development and Capabilities 23, 25.

[40] ibid. [41] ibid. [42] ibid. [43] ibid.

[44] See further Formosa and Mackenzie (n 38) 879.

interest-based approach has been developed by Allen Buchanan as a way of delineating a universal core to human rights.[45] Thus, he argues, 'the implication of the phrase "human rights" is that there are some interests common to all persons that are of such great moral concern that the very character of our most important institutions should be such as to afford them special protection. These interests are shared by all persons because they are constitutive of a decent life—they are necessary conditions for human flourishing'.[46] In other words, human rights are rights whose 'violation poses the most serious threat to an individual's chances of living a decent human life; i.e. those interests that are most crucial for having a good human life'.[47]

As Tasioulas argues, a clear advantage of an interest-based approach over one that appeals exclusively to a single value is that it enables us to draw on the 'full spectrum of interests that underlie [human rights], not just some sub-set of interests specified ex-ante'.[48] Thus, a human right to health directly reflects the importance of health, rather than having to be related back to freedom or dignity. Similarly, the right not to be tortured is a response to the many human interests imperilled by torture, not just its consequences for our autonomy to make our own decisions, as Griffin suggests.[49] Most importantly, it avoids the exclusion from human rights protection of human beings who are not agents, or capable of autonomy, as Griffin, and even Nussbaum's theories do. Even if they are not able to utilize the full complement of human rights, such individuals will possess some rights, including the human right not to be tortured.[50]

The difficulty, of course, is to identify which basic interests are worthy of human rights protection. Buchanan begins with the premise that rights are universal in that they are ascribed to all human beings simply because they are human. However, the set of rights he derives from his principle of basic interests is highly parsimonious and restricted to a subset of traditional civil and political rights, to the exclusion of socio-economic rights. Thus he includes only the right not to be unjustly killed; the rights not to be tortured or subject to arbitrary arrest, detention, or imprisonment; rights against enslavement and involuntary servitude; the most fundamental rights of due process, freedom of expression, and association; and the right against persecution and at least the more damaging forms of discrimination on grounds of ethnicity, race, gender, or sexual preference.[51] Buchanan claims that his approach derives from a widely shared conception of human rights.[52] However, he is prepared to depart from that conception where widely agreed rights do not reflect his basic principle. Like Griffin, he takes aim at what he regards as the 'notorious right to holidays with pay', since in his view it is 'pretty obvious' that paid holidays are not necessary

[45] A Buchanan, *Justice Legitimacy and Self Determination: Moral Foundations for International Law* (OUP 2003) 78.

[46] ibid, 79.

[47] ibid, 81.

[48] J Tasioulas, 'Towards a Philosophy of Human Rights' (2012) 65 CLP 1, 14.

[49] Griffin (n 1) 52; see Tasioulas (n 48) 13.

[50] Tasioulas (n 48) 14.

[51] Buchanan (n 45) 81. Note that he concedes that his approach is consistent with different lists of basic rights.

[52] ibid, 75.

for a decent human life.[53] Again, it is difficult to see why this conclusion follows from his initial premise. Even if we concede that the consensus represented by the UDHR may have 'got it wrong', an individual's basic interest in not being subject to involuntary servitude could well suggest that they should not have to work without paid rest periods.

One of the reasons for the parsimonious approach of Buchanan and other philosophers is their concern at what they regard as the disorganized proliferation of rights. The discourse of human rights is finding its way into many fields previously reserved for public policy, development economics, and even charity. Some philosophers would argue that the adoption of human rights talk in all these new fields is simply a rhetorical flourish, or indeed a form of 'rights inflation'. Aiming to deflate what they regard as a populist expansion of the label of human rights, several thinkers are looking to pare down human rights to a basic minimum. Tasioulas takes a different approach. He concedes that potentially any combination of universal interests could lay claim to the status of a human right,[54] devaluing the notion of human rights as a whole. He addresses this by suggesting a threshold of generalizability. In other words, to qualify as the basis for a human right, a human interest should cross a threshold, 'the threshold that justifies the imposition of the self-same duties as being owed to all human beings'.[55] It is this that leads him from an approach which focuses entirely on the right-holder to one that also focuses on the implications of affirming the right for duty-bearers.[56] With this in mind, we turn to theories which are exclusively focused on duties, particularly that of Raz.

E. Obligations

For Raz, the distinctive feature of rights is that they are capable of creating correlative obligations in others. For example, Raz asserts that it is 'a truism ... that the right of one person limits the freedom of other people'.[57] This should lead, in his view, to a much greater focus on why others should be subject to duties correlative to the putative right. Thus, Raz argues, for a human right to exist, it is not enough to point to its importance to human beings. It is also necessary to establish a case for imposing a duty on others to secure the right-holder's enjoyment of the right. And yet, in his view, this central feature is too often neglected: 'That something is of value to someone does not even begin to establish that I or anyone else has a duty to secure or protect his possession or enjoyment of that thing. A special argument is needed here, and it is all too often missing, an argument which relies on the special character of the value that the right provides'.[58]

This focus has important consequences. Unless the duty can be enforced through reliable, efficient, and fair institutions, the correlative claim should not be regarded as a human right at all. Indeed, both Raz and Buchanan see the possibility of effective enforcement as an essential criterion in determining whether a claim is in fact a human

[53] ibid, 81. [54] Tasioulas (n 48) 13. [55] ibid. [56] ibid.
[57] J Raz, 'Human Rights in the Emerging World Order' (2010) 1 Transnational Legal Theory 31–47 at 35.
[58] ibid, 37.

right. In Buchanan's view, to be a human right, it must be shown, inter alia, that institutional arrangements necessary for protecting human rights exist and can be reasonably effective in doing so.[59] Raz puts it more strongly.

> First, if there is a human right to something, then there is also a duty to establish and support impartial, efficient and reliable institutions to oversee its implementation and protect it from violations. Second, until such institutions exist, normally one should refrain from attempts to use any coercive measures to enforce the right ... Third, if, given the prevailing circumstances, there is no possibility that impartial, efficient and reliable institutions may come into existence regarding a certain right, then that right is not a human right.[60]

The right to health is a good example. Thus, he argues, health is admittedly one of the most important values in anyone's life and might well be a right within the positive law of a particular country. However, it could not be effectively and reliably enforced internationally because each society must make its own decisions, consistently with its own values and political priorities, as to its meaning and relative importance. Thus, it should not qualify for the label of a human right.[61]

This approach potentially confuses enforcement with the substance of a right. It is true that some basic human values cannot be guaranteed. We cannot guarantee a person's health. On the other hand, this is not in itself a reason for rejecting the underlying right. There may still be duties on the State not to interfere with individual health; to protect individual health against interference by other individuals; and to make provision for access to health care. This has implications for the formulation of the right. As we will see in Chapter 8, it could be formulated as a right to the highest attainable standard of health as under the ICESCR, or the right to access health-care services, as in the South African Constitution. Tasioulas therefore argues for a two-stage process in setting a threshold for the recognition of a human right. The first stage is 'internal' in that it takes into account only the individual interests or status which potentially ground the right. The second stage functions 'externally', taking into account the implications of the right for other people, especially potential duty bearers.[62]

F. Justified interference

A further way of establishing a universal core to human rights is to focus on what makes them of international concern. In Beitz's view, whatever else is true of human rights, they are supposed to be of international concern in that 'a society's failure to respect its people's human rights on a sufficiently large scale may provide a reason for outside agents to do something'.[63] Thus he concludes that 'we should construe the doctrine so that appeals to human rights ... can provide reasons for the world community or its agents to act in ways aimed at reducing infringements or contributing to the satisfaction of the rights in societies where they are insecure'.[64]

[59] Buchanan (n 45) 80. [60] Raz (n 57) 44. [61] ibid, 46.
[62] Tasioulas (n 48) 15. [63] C Beitz, *The Idea of Human Rights* (OUP 2009) 105. [64] ibid.

Beitz derives this conclusion from what he regards as the existing doctrine and practice of human rights in international political life, an approach which he maintains is methodologically more defensible than that of analytic philosophers who attempt to derive human rights from an independent theoretical position: 'There is no assumption of a prior or independent layer of fundamental rights whose nature and content can be discovered independently of a consideration of the place of human rights in the international realm and its normative discourse and then used to interpret and criticize international doctrine'.[65] Beitz argues that the advantage of his approach is that it distinguishes between the international practice as to the purpose and functions of human rights, and their actual content. This allows for agreement as to the nature of international human rights law, but disagreement both about their content and about the kinds of considerations that ground them.[66] The practice of human rights law can then be evaluated according to whether it is suited to the public political role it is expected to play.

Beitz is one of several influential theorists, including Raz and Rawls, who delineate human rights according to whether it is justifiable to intervene in other States' affairs. Thus, for Rawls, human rights are only those rights which would fulfil the following three roles: first, their fulfilment is a necessary condition of a regime's legitimacy; second, their fulfilment is sufficient to exclude justified intervention by other peoples, whether by economic sanctions or military force; and third, they set a moral limit to pluralism among peoples.[67] Raz's approach leads him to a similar conclusion. For Raz, because 'we single out as human rights those rights respect for which can be demanded by anyone',[68] they are demands which can be addressed to governments of other countries, and therefore set limits to State sovereignty. The result is inevitably to prompt us to be circumspect in what we consider to be human rights.

This has drained much of the content from human rights as we know them: it is no accident that the list of rights of all these thinkers is far more limited than existing international human rights law, excluding some key civil and political rights and ignoring socio-economic rights. Moreover, specifying the role in this way creates an artificial divide between domestic and international human rights law, with the former being considered as constitutional rights rather than human rights per se. Yet, as the rest of this book demonstrates, it is the richness of the ongoing interaction, dialogue, and mutual influence of domestic human rights law in different jurisdictions, together with international human rights law, that contribute to the dynamism of the modern development of human rights. There seems no reason to remove these from sight by dint of definition.

[65] ibid. [66] ibid.

[67] J Rawls, 'The Law of Peoples' (1993) 20 Critical Inquiry 36–68, 59 (hereafter Rawls, 'The Law of Peoples').

[68] Raz (n 57) 42.

III. Relativism

The difficulty in finding agreement over a single, universal, and objective meaning of human rights might suggest that there is no such universal principle. On one view, widespread disagreement as to the meaning of human rights makes it doubtful that reasonable and well-informed people would ever tend to agree about their content or nature. MacIntyre takes this a step further, pointing out that even the question of what counts as a rational response is disputed: 'Disputes about the nature of rationality in general and about practical rationality in particular are apparently as manifold and intractable as disputes about justice'.[69]

Gowans points to three streams of non-objective theorists. First, a thoroughgoing moral sceptic would argue that although there exist moral truths, we can never know them. There are no modern proponents of this view and we need not pursue it.[70] The second, known as 'moral anti-realists' come in several forms, but the best known are those who regard moral beliefs as subjective attitudes or feelings, which can never be either true or false. Thus, Mackie states:

> People will judge that some things are good or right, and others are bad or wrong, not because ... they exemplify some general principle for which widespread implicit acceptance could be claimed, but because something about those things arouses certain responses immediately in them, though they would raise radically and irresolvably different responses in others. 'Moral sense' or 'intuition' is an initially more plausible description of what supplies many of our basic moral judgements than 'reason'.[71]

However, while it may be plausible that our moral judgements originate in intuitions, human rights law requires that such subjective beliefs be captured in norms which can have intersubjective application. Moral intuitions, at the very least, need to be capable of legally plausible explanation and elaboration. Indeed, to suggest that a judge is acting on her personal feelings and subjective attitudes is usually regarded as a severe criticism.

The third stream, which has been most influential in the human rights field, consists of the moral relativists, who argue that moral truths are always relative to a particular community or social context. Although morality is not entirely about subjective feelings, and intersubjectivity is possible, it is both wrong and misleading to claim that there are absolute moral truths to which all societies must be held to account. MacIntyre sums up the relativists' claim as denying the possibility of rational debate between rival traditions: 'If the only available standards of rationality are those made available by and within traditions, then no issue between contending traditions is rationally decidable'.[72] A slightly softer version of such relativism could take the form of

[69] A MacIntyre, *Whose Justice? Which Rationality?* (University of Notre Dame Press 1988) 1–2 reproduced in C Gowans (ed), *Moral Disagreements: Classic and Contemporary Readings* (Routledge 2000) 218 (hereafter MacIntyre, *Whose Justice?*).

[70] C Gowans, 'Debates about Moral Disagreements' in C Gowans (ed) *Moral Disagreements: Classic and Contemporary Readings* (Routledge 2000) 25 (hereafter Gowans, 'Debates and Moral Disagreements').

[71] J Mackie, *Ethics: Inventing Right and Wrong* (Penguin Books 1977) 37–38, reproduced in C Gowans (ed), *Moral Disagreements: Classic and Contemporary Readings* (Routledge 2000) 141–42.

[72] MacIntyre, *Whose Justice?* (n 69) 220.

what MacIntyre calls perspectivism: 'Instead of interpreting rival traditions as mutually exclusive and incompatible ways of understanding one and the same world ... let us understand them instead as providing very different, complementary perspectives for envisaging the realities about which they speak to us'.[73]

In the human rights field, theories of relativism have been particularly influential in the context of a challenge to the hegemony of the 'West', which is said to treat other cultures as if they were 'uncivilized' or 'primitive'. In this respect, the contribution of social anthropologists has been of great importance in unmasking the assumptions of dominant ideologies as to notions of right and wrong. In a statement published in the run-up to the process of drafting the UDHR in 1947, the American Anthropological Association issued a challenge to the drafters: 'How can the proposed Declaration be applicable to all human beings, and not be a statement of rights conceived only in terms of the values prevalent in the countries of Western Europe and America?'[74] The authors of the statement argued that Europe and America's assertions of absolute truth had been used to legitimate the colonization and oppression of millions of people all over the world, 'rationalized in terms of ascribing cultural inferiority to these peoples, or in conceptions of their backwardness in development of their "primitive mentality"'.[75] The Association argued instead that each individual 'can develop only in terms of the culture of his society'.[76] Standards and values are relative to the culture from which they derive, and there is no technique of qualitatively evaluating cultures. Thus 'what is held to be a human right in one society may be regarded as anti-social by another people, or by the same people in a different period of their history'.[77] The conclusion is that the only way to proceed is to incorporate into the proposed Declaration 'a statement of the right of men [*sic*] to live in terms of their own traditions'.[78]

More recently, the debate has focused on the claim that there exists a distinctive set of 'Asian values', to challenge the 'Western' hegemony over the understanding and interpretation of human rights. This tension can be seen in the Bangkok Declaration, adopted in 1993 by Ministers and representatives of Asian States in the context of the preparation for the World Conference on Human Rights. On the one hand, the Bangkok Declaration reaffirms the commitment to the principles contained in the UDHR and the full realization of all human rights throughout the world. On the other hand, it states: 'While human rights are universal in nature, they must be considered in the context of a dynamic and evolving process of international norm-setting, bearing in mind the significance of national and regional particularities and various historical, cultural and religious backgrounds'.[79]

[73] ibid, 221.

[74] The Executive Board, 'American Anthropological Association Statement on Human Rights' (1947) 49 New Series American Anthropologist 539.

[75] ibid. [76] ibid. [77] ibid. [78] ibid.

[79] Final Declaration of the Regional Meeting for Asia of the World Conference on Human Rights (The Bangkok Declaration) <https://www.hurights.or.jp/archives/other_documents/section1/1993/04/final-declaration-of-the-regional-meeting-for-asia-of-the-world-conference-on-human-rights.html> para 8 (accessed 12 July 2018).

In its most emphatic form, proponents of 'Asian values' argue that 'while Europe may have been the home ground of liberty and individual rights, "Asian values" cherish discipline and order'.[80] The propagation of 'universal' human rights is seen as an 'ideological complement to Western domination'.[81] Rights are a domestic matter: any attempt to impose human rights standards from outside is regarded as a type of modern colonialism.[82] Thus, the Bangkok Declaration reiterates that all countries should have the right to determine their political systems and emphasizes the principles of respect for national sovereignty, the non-interference in the internal affairs of States, and the 'non-use of human rights as an instrument of political pressure'.[83]

One of the key claims of this school of thought is that the individualism inherent in established understandings of human rights is alien to many cultures. Property ownership, for example, under many customary law systems is communal rather than individual. Those who 'inherit' property, usually the first-born male, do so in a position of responsibility rather than entitlement, being required to use the land to provide for the family. For example, under traditional customary law in South Africa, the 'heir' or 'indlalifa' holds the family property on behalf of and for the benefit of all family members. It therefore 'cannot be said that he is the owner of the family property or that he inherits it in the sense understood in common law'.[84] On one view, to regard male primogeniture as 'discriminatory' against daughters and younger sons is simply to impose individualistic notions of property ownership as if they were universal norms: 'Far from getting any property benefit, the indlalifa assumes the responsibilities of a family head. He is required to administer the family property for the benefit of the entire family'.[85]

The pre-eminence of the community over individuals is even more strongly stated by proponents of the 'Asian values' theory. The leading proponent of this approach was the former Prime Minister of Singapore, Lee Kuan Yew. In an interview in 1994, he declared that:

> the fundamental difference between Western concepts of society and government and East Asian concepts ... is that Eastern societies believe that the individual exists in the context of his family. He is not pristine and separate. The family is part of the extended family, and then friends and the wider society.[86]

By contrast, in his view, human rights are essentially individualist and therefore destructive of the social fabric.[87] A central consequence of the emphasis on community rather than the individual is disdain for what is regarded as the Western concept of

[80] A Sen, *Identity and Violence: The Illusion of Destiny* (Allen Lane 2006) 93.

[81] CY Hoon, 'Revisiting the "Asian Values" Argument Used by Asian Political Leaders and Its Validity' (2004) 32 The Indonesian Quarterly 154–74 at 155.

[82] This summary is taken from X Li, '"Asian Values" and the Universality of Human Rights' [2004] 102/103 Business and Society Review 81–87 at 82–83 and Hoon (n 81) 155.

[83] The Bangkok Declaration (n 79) paras 5 and 6.

[84] Per Ngcobo J in *Bhe v Khayelitsha Magistrate* 2005 (1) SA 580 (CC) (South African Constitutional Court).

[85] Per Ngcobo J in ibid. Ngcobo J did, however, hold that it was discriminatory against women.

[86] F Zakaria, 'Culture is Destiny—A Conversation with Lee Kuan Yew' (1994) 73 Foreign Affairs 109.

[87] See Li (n 82) 82–83 and Hoon (n 81) 155.

individual liberty. Individual freedom is seen as an invitation to behave or misbehave as the individual pleases: 'The liberal intellectual tradition that developed after World War II claimed that human beings had arrived at this perfect state where everybody would be better off if they were allowed to do their own thing and flourish. It has not worked out'.[88] On the other hand, 'In the East, the main object is to have a well-ordered society so that everyone can have maximum enjoyment of his freedoms'.[89] Similarly, it is more efficient for leaders to take the appropriate economic decisions to ensure development than to allow the instability associated with freedom of speech and democracy. Indeed, Lee is often attributed with managing 'the miraculous transformation in Singapore's economy while maintaining tight political control over the country'.[90]

Behind this unmasking of the culturally relative nature of individualistic human rights is the more far-reaching claim that the Western perspective blinkers its proponents, leading them to believe that their own culturally relative assumptions are universally valid. In its more sinister form, this argument suggests that this is a deliberate attempt to impose Western values and demean those of other cultures. Even the claim of 'rationality' is seen as a particular construct. The result is that there is no way of conducting a cross-cultural conversation about the meaning of human rights, still less of holding others to account, even in the minimal sense of providing a rational explanation, for departing from what are claimed to be essentially Western standards.

The challenges raised by cultural relativity for the possibility of universal human rights have thus far been dealt with as if they occur only in a geographic or inter-State dimension. Similar questions could also be raised from a temporal perspective. Do human rights apply across all time? This argument has more than theoretical importance. As we see in Chapter 5, courts in several jurisdictions take the view that a bill of rights is a 'living tree'. Does this mean that rights can evolve and change to reflect social developments? Buchanan states unequivocally that human rights, as moral rights, apply to all persons regardless of when they exist.[91] The fact that our understanding of the content of these rights changes over time is not, in his view, inconsistent with this principle: from the fact that we 'do not come into the world equipped with a fully adequate understanding of what human beings are entitled to, it does not follow that there is no correct answer to the question of what they are entitled to'.[92] Raz, however, regards the changing nature of human rights as a key objection to the possibility of universal human rights.[93] For example, it makes no sense to regard cavemen as having rights to education, since education is specific to more modern cultures. He uses this to reject the 'traditional' theory that everyone has human rights simply by virtue of being human. Once it is accepted that different people at different times can have different human rights, Raz argues, there is no principled reason in favour of synchronic universality—that is, the claim that all people alive today have the same rights: 'If people

[88] Zakaria (n 86) 112. [89] ibid. [90] ibid. [91] Buchanan (n 45) 76.
[92] ibid.
[93] Raz (n 57). Raz's rejection of universal human rights does not mean that he takes a morally relativist stance more generally.

can have different human rights at different periods, why can it not be the case that people who live today can have different human rights?'[94]

Nedelsky sees these changes over time in a different way. For her, they are part of a constant re-articulation of the values of a society, brought into focus once we acknowledge that rights structure and are structured by relationships. Thus, she argues, a 'focus on relationship automatically turns one's attention to context and makes sense of the commonly held belief that there are some basic human values *and* that how we articulate and foster those values varies significantly over time'.[95] Raz himself argues that even if it is conceded that a watertight claim of universality is difficult to sustain in principle, there may be good pragmatic reasons for regarding human rights as applicable to everyone, at least within any one time-frame. Because 'human rights are those rights respect for which can be demanded by anyone ... inhabitants of one country can address such demands to the governments of other countries regarding those governments' treatment of their own citizens'.[96] He also sees human rights as making two further crucial contributions to the emerging world order. One is to underpin a global commitment to the value of human life;[97] the other is to empower ordinary people, to create a new channel of political action, and thereby to function as 'a major corrective to the concentration of power in governmental and corporate hands'.[98]

IV. Responding to the Challenges of Relativism

How then do we respond to the challenges of relativism without undermining the human rights project as a whole? Relativism draws attention to different perspectives and therefore functions as an important corrective to an unquestioning assertion that the values of a particular group are 'normal' and universally valid. Attaching the label of universality to particular beliefs can obscure the way in which they function to sustain a particular set of power relations, which human rights should be in a position to challenge. This has been a key insight of feminist scholars, who have demonstrated the extent to which claims of truth and universality are covers for a male norm. These insights open the way to further challenges. On the one hand, white, Western feminists have been accused of replacing the male norm with an alternative set of ostensible truths which do no more than reflect their own position as white, middle class, and Western. On the other hand, cultural relativists who claim that feminism is a Western imposition may be using this position to legitimate serious breaches of women's human rights. As is seen in many places in this book, there is a constant tension between appropriate assertions of universal values and appropriate self-consciousness about the role of particular perspectives. How then do we address the need for sensitivity to a plurality of values while maintaining universal standards?

This section examines one of the chief internal contradictions of the relativist approach to human rights, namely its assertion of cultural homogeneity, as well as that of the liberal response to the relativist critique, namely its appeal to tolerance. It then turns

[94] ibid. Note that Raz nevertheless finds good pragmatic reasons to support synchronic universality.
[95] J Nedelsky, *Law's Relations: A Relational Theory of Self, Autonomy, and Law* (OUP 2011) 246.
[96] Raz (n 57) 42. [97] ibid. [98] ibid.

to more constructive ways of dealing with value pluralism and fundamental disagreements, which could be utilized as part of the project of comparative human rights.

A. Relativism and cultural homogeneity

The critique of human rights on the basis that it presents 'Western values' under the guise of universal human rights is itself based on a strong presumption of the homogeneity of cultures, and of a clear demarcation between 'Western' and other cultures. However, Western cultures are far from internally homogeneous; and although it may be true that dominant powers in the West have aimed to dominate other cultures, the same structures of dominance have frequently been replicated within Western countries themselves. Indeed, human rights standards have been developed internally to challenge the structures of dominance within 'Western' societies.

The converse of this is the claim of cultural homogeneity in other cultures. Yet cultural claims are often made by the dominant groups or individuals within a society, who claim to speak for the culture as whole. It is the very inability of subordinated groups to speak up for themselves that might require external criteria for evaluation and accountability. This is demonstrated clearly by the Canadian case of *Lovelace.*[99] Sandra Lovelace was born and registered as a Maliseet Indian but lost her rights and status after having married a non-Indian. Canadian legislation (The Indian Act) removed Indian status from Indian women marrying non-Indian men (but not vice versa). On her divorce, she attempted to return to her family home on the Tobique Reserve but was denied the right of abode because she was no longer regarded as an 'Indian'. She complained to the United Nations Human Rights Committee (HRC) that this breached her rights to enjoy her culture under the ICCPR. The Canadian Government argued that the Act was necessary to protect the right to culture of the indigenous Indian minority. A definition of who counted as Indian was indispensable in view of the rights of Indian communities to occupy reserve lands under treaties entered into between the Canadian Government and indigenous groups. Since reserve land was felt to be more threatened by non-Indian men than by non-Indian women, legal enactments provided that an Indian woman who married a non-Indian man would lose her status. It also maintained that any change in the legislation could only be sought in consultation with the Indian communities who, however, were divided on the issue of equal rights. The implication of these arguments was that Sandra Lovelace's voice should be discounted in favour of those of the dominant groups, both within the indigenous communities and in the Canadian political elite.

In the event, the HRC was more perceptive. Rather than accepting the Canadian Government's assertion of a right to culture to defeat Lovelace's claim, it held that she too had a right to enjoy her own culture in community with others.[100] It was this right which had been breached. Moreover, the fact that her identity as an Indian had been removed from her could not prevent her from 'belonging' to this minority and

[99] *Sandra Lovelace v Canada* Communication No R.6/24 UN Doc Supp No 40 (A/36/40) at 166 (1981) (UN Human Rights Committee).

[100] ICCPR Article 27.

from claiming the benefits of her right to enjoy her own culture. Thus, human rights functioned as an important vehicle to navigate between the assertion of universal values and the relative right to culture.

Nor is it correct to maintain that the values embodied in human rights are exclusively Western. Amartya Sen, for example, challenges Lee's generalizations about Asian values. He points out that support for ideas of liberty and public discussion have been articulated just as frequently in Asia as in Europe.[101] This is echoed by Nussbaum, who shows that human rights were often inserted into constitutions, such as the Indian Constitution, as a bulwark against the violations of human rights experienced at the hands of the colonials. Instead, she regards the idea of human dignity as having 'broad cross-cultural resonance and intuitive power'.[102] Similarly, the language of capabilities is a neutral and international language of what people are actually able to do and be.[103] Nevertheless, she recognizes that what is universal in the approach 'is only a starting point: each nation should describe the capabilities it pursues more concretely, using their own history and traditions as a guide'.[104]

This raises the further question of how we define the relevant 'group'. Lee Kuan Yew designates Korea, Japan, China, Vietnam, and Singapore as the 'East Asian' group he is referring to, and tends to equate the 'West' with the United States.[105] Others might refer to a different constellation. Moreover, individuals might be members of several groups, with potentially conflicting value systems. Lovelace was designated a non-Indian, but she regarded herself as a member of the Maliseet Indian community. She was also a Canadian and a member of the international community. This gave her the possibility of resorting to international human rights standards as a source of protection for her basic rights. On a culturally relative view, there is no way of creating a hierarchy between these different values.

B. The liberal dilemma: a critique of pure tolerance

Both the anthropological perspective and the 'Asian values' movement have played a crucial role in creating a self-consciousness among human rights thinkers of the need to avoid imposing culturally based perspectives under the guise of universality.[106] One response could be to extend the liberal principle of tolerance to address this critique. Many liberal philosophers regard it as a central tenet of political liberalism that different visions of the good should be permitted to flourish. But can such a principle be extended to encompass systems which are not committed to liberalism; and what effect does this have on the meaning of human rights? It is to this we now turn.

Tolerance stands for the principle that a person's beliefs should not be prohibited because others regard them as morally wrong. Translated into liberal political theory, it manifests as the principle that the State should not impose any particular version of the 'good' on its citizens. The right of individuals to make their own decisions as to

101 Sen (n 35) 94. 102 Nussbaum (n 36) 72. 103 ibid, 30. 104 ibid.
105 Zakaria (n 86) 113.
106 R Wolff, B Moore, and H Marcuse, *A Critique of Pure Tolerance* (Cape 1969).

the good life is seen to be fundamental to liberty.[107] It is here that liberalism makes its decisive break from the Aristotelian view that there is an objective 'good' discernible by the rational faculties. Aristotle saw the polis as not only a political entity but also a community based on a commitment to shared values.[108] By contrast, it is a central tenet of much liberal thought that the promotion of the good life is not a legitimate matter for governmental action. Instead, the State should remain neutral as between different ideals of the good.

Framed in this way, tolerance appears to be an appropriate vehicle to address the challenges of relativism, and particularly the charge that human rights are a Western imposition. Tolerance, however, brings with it its own paradoxes. As a start, it might be subject to the relativist challenge that tolerance itself is being held out as a universal value. For a relativist, tolerance can only be a value within the culture of the proponent. If my culture requires me to be tolerant of yours, and yours of mine, then all is well. But what if my cultural value system requires me to be intolerant of certain practices in your culture, and your cultural value system requires you to be intolerant of certain practices in my culture?[109] Without some overriding value framework, this simply resurrects the unresolvable disagreement.

This is, in fact, equally a problem at a domestic level. Human rights pit one form of tolerance against another. If a person's deeply held beliefs include a belief that she should not tolerate certain behaviour, then the liberal state has to take sides. For example, a recent case in the UK Supreme Court[110] concerned the refusal by the Christian owners of a bed-and-breakfast hotel to allow a same-sex couple to rent a double room on the grounds that this would promote what they regarded as sinful behaviour. Should the State tolerate the intolerance of the hotel owners? The UK Supreme Court held that the defendants had unlawfully discriminated against the complainants on grounds of their sexual orientation.[111] The Court defended this approach by arguing that tolerance was required on both sides. Lady Hale rejected the view that this risked replacing 'legal oppression of one community (homosexual couples) with legal oppression of another (those sharing the defendants' beliefs)'.[112] Instead, she held: 'If Mr Preddy and Mr Hall ran a hotel which denied a double room to Mr and Mrs Bull, whether on the ground of their Christian beliefs or on the ground of their sexual orientation, they would find themselves in the same situation that Mr and Mrs Bull find themselves today'.[113] Nevertheless, the difficulty of using tolerance on both sides of this equation shows its limited value in addressing deep social disagreement. The same is true for the wider question of tolerance of different cultures. If one society promotes tolerance,

[107] See further S Fredman, *Human Rights Transformed: Positive Rights and Positive Duties* (OUP 2008) ch 1.

[108] Aristotle (n 8) 1280–82, 1287, 1325 and see T Burns, '"Aristotle"' in D Boucher and P Kelly (eds), *Political Thinkers* (OUP 2003) 76–77.

[109] Gowans, 'Debates and Moral Disagreements' (n 70) 26–27.

[110] *Hall and Preddy v Bull and Bull* [2013] UKSC 73 (UK Supreme Court).

[111] ibid; and see also *Black and Morgan v Wilkinson* [2013] EWCA Civ 820 (UK Court of Appeal).

[112] Quoting from Rafferty LJ in the Court of Appeal.

[113] *Hall and Preddy v Bull and Bull* (n 110) 54. See further Chapter 12 (freedom of religion).

should it tolerate another society whose basic beliefs include intolerance of those with different values to its own?

Rawls has nevertheless developed the principle of tolerance to address the challenge of relativism. Rawls regards reasonable disagreement as being not just inevitable, but a positive characteristic of liberal societies.[114] Most of his work has been devoted to developing a carefully constructed theory of justice that supports disagreement while attracting co-operation and support for the basic institutions of society. Rawls does not, however, claim universality for his theory of justice, arguing that his political conception generates a consensus only within a particular Western tradition of political philosophy.[115] In *The Law of Peoples* he aims to find a way of developing a similar theory for the global community.

His acknowledgement that not all societies can be liberal leads him to explore the limits of his liberal theory of tolerance. Thus, he argues:

> Not all regimes can be reasonably required to be liberal; otherwise, the law of peoples itself would not express liberalism's own principle of toleration for other reasonable ways of ordering society nor further its attempt to find a shared basis of agreement among reasonable peoples. Just as a citizen in a liberal society is to respect other persons' comprehensive religious, philosophical, and moral doctrines, provided they are pursued in accordance with a reasonable political conception of justice, so a liberal society is to respect other societies organized by comprehensive doctrines, provided their political and social institutions meet certain conditions.[116]

Importantly, these conditions include honouring basic human rights. Thus, while 'any society must honour basic human rights, such a society need not be liberal'.[117]

Rawls deliberately frames his conception of human rights so that they 'could not be rejected as peculiarly liberal or special to our Western tradition'.[118] In that sense, he argues, 'they are politically neutral'.[119] They are only a subset of the wider group of liberal constitutional rights that are essential to a liberal conception of justice and therefore well suited to liberal democracies.[120] This, however, means that the catalogue of basic human rights Rawls generates cannot include the kind of principles that would guarantee a liberal society.

This has drastic consequences for our understanding of human rights, generating what Tasioulas calls a 'notoriously parsimonious set of rights'.[121] To be well ordered, Rawls suggests, a society needs to respect the following rights: 'at least certain minimum rights to means of subsistence and security (the right to life), to liberty (freedom from slavery, serfdom, and forced occupations), and (personal) property, as well as to formal equality as expressed by the rules of natural justice (for example, that similar cases be treated similarly)'.[122] A well-ordered society (such as a society organized by religious law) need not regard all its citizens as free and equal, as in a liberal society, nor do citizens need to have the right of freedom of speech, although there should be

[114] See further below (n 132).

[115] J Rawls, *Political Liberalism* (Columbia University Press 1993) 4–11.

[116] Rawls, 'The Law of Peoples' (n 67) 37. [117] ibid. [118] ibid. [119] ibid.

[120] ibid.

[121] J Tasioulas, 'Taking Rights out of Human Rights' in R Crisp (ed), *Griffin on Human Rights* (OUP 2014) 16.

[122] Rawls, 'The Law of Peoples' (n 67) 52.

opportunities for consultation, and leaders should take seriously expressions of dissent, albeit potentially voiced through associations and corporations, and not individuals.[123] As Buchanan points out, Rawls' frugal set of rights is consistent with societies which exclude women from education and political participation; which that require women to stay at home except if they are wholly covered; or which relegate some people to a lower caste systematically kept in poverty.[124]

But has Rawls conceded too much to the relativists in framing his principle of tolerance in this way? Rawls places great emphasis on respect for the reason of others, and therefore on tolerance of conclusions reached by conscientiously applying their reason. This assumes that his well-ordered but non-liberal society can be said to represent the views of everyone in the society. The paradox of this approach is that it takes no account of the reasonable disagreement of those within the society. Instead, he regards societies as equivalent to individuals in his laws of peoples. Although he makes provision for expression of dissent, which must be taken seriously, this need only be through corporations and associations. Yet human rights are often there to protect the very people whose interests are not accounted for and whose voice is extinguished or unheard. For the woman who is required by the 'common good conception' to remain covered or in the private sphere, tolerance of the reason of others simply means tolerance of the dominant group. The same is true for same-sex couples who are not permitted to marry.

V. Dealing with Disagreement

It is an over-reaction to the challenges of relativism to attempt to frame a principle of tolerance which saps human rights of much of their content. This section deals with some of the philosophical ways of dealing with the tension: Berlin's pluralist approach; Dworkin's 'overlapping consensus'; and Sunstein's 'incompletely theorised' agreement. The final part of the section considers legal responses.

A. Berlin's pluralist approach

In his essay 'The Pursuit of the Ideal', Berlin tracks his own intellectual journey: from his initial belief in the possibility of finding true answers to the central problems of life, to his realization that in reality 'not all the supreme values pursued by mankind now and in the past [are] necessarily compatible with one another'.[125] However, he rejects the charge that this view falls into the category of cultural or moral relativism. In his view, members of one culture can 'by the force of imaginative insight'[126] understand the values of another culture or society, even if they find those values unacceptable. For him, pluralism stands for the conception that there are many different ends that may be pursued by individuals, and yet individuals might still be fully rational, 'capable of understanding each other and sympathizing and deriving light from each

[123] ibid. [124] Buchanan (n 45) 100.

[125] I Berlin, 'The Pursuit of the Ideal' in H Hardy and R Hausheer (eds), *The Proper Study of Mankind: An Anthology of Essays* (Pimlico 1998), reproduced in Gowans (ed) (n 70) 196.

[126] ibid, 198.

other'.[127] There are some common values, which derive from what makes us human and which permit understanding. However, collisions of values, not just between cultures, but also between individuals, 'are of the essence of… what we are'.[128] Indeed, he sees the possibilities of a single seamless solution as an illusion, and a 'very dangerous one', for it leads its believers to attempt to pursue that solution at any cost to human lives.[129]

What then is to be done in a world in which values collide and are incompatible? He concedes that there is no clear reply. However, collisions can be softened through compromise and balancing, particularly in concrete situations, in which not every claim is of equal force. Crucially, 'priorities, never final and absolute, must be established'.[130] Since decisions must be made, 'all we can ask for is that none of the relevant factors be ignored',[131] and that the purposes people seek to realize should be seen as elements which can be enhanced or damaged by those decisions. At the same time, he recognizes that there is a great deal of broad agreement among people in different societies.

B. Rawls' overlapping consensus

Rawls, like Berlin, regards reasonable disagreement as being, not just inevitable, but a positive characteristic of liberal societies.[132] As we have seen above, he does not claim universality for his theory of justice, arguing that his political conception generates a consensus only within a particular Western tradition of political philosophy.[133] However, his approach to disagreement within liberal societies is valuable in enhancing our understanding of the many fundamental disagreements we find in the scope and application of human rights. Like Berlin, Rawls notes the diversity of opposing and irreconcilable religious, philosophical, and moral doctrines which always occur in the political culture of democratic societies. This diversity, he stresses, is the 'inevitable long-run result of the powers of human reason at work within the background of enduring free institutions'.[134] Moreover, like Berlin, he recognizes that this reasonable pluralism can be overcome only by the oppressive use of State power.[135] The consequence must be that a liberal society should accept a variety of reasonable comprehensive world views. Since it is logically impossible for all such doctrines to be foisted on society as true, everyone needs to accept that no single doctrine can be so foisted. Thus, Rawls concludes, 'it is unreasonable for us to use political power, should we possess it, or share it with others, to repress comprehensive views that are not unreasonable'.

It is important for our purposes to understand why Rawls regards disagreement as to comprehensive doctrines as being inevitable despite the fact that they are all a product of reason, because his account could make sense of how judges should approach human rights adjudication. In exercising our reason, we need to balance our various ends, while at the same time assessing the strength of other people's claims both as against our own and in relation to our common practices and institutions. A variety

[127] ibid. [128] ibid, 199. [129] ibid, 201. [130] ibid, 202. [131] ibid.
[132] Rawls (n 115) 4–11. [133] ibid. [134] ibid, reproduced in Gowans (ed) (n 70) 230.
[135] J Rawls, *Justice as Fairness* (Harvard University Press 2001) 34.

of reasonable conclusions to this balancing process is clearly possible. In addition, the empirical evidence might be conflicting and difficult to evaluate. Even if we agree about what kinds of considerations are relevant, we may disagree about their weight and so arrive at different judgements. Our concepts might be indeterminate to some extent, requiring interpretations on which reasonable people may differ. Moreover, Rawls recognizes that the perspective from which we make these judgements is shaped by our experience of life,[136] and often by the tradition of thought and doctrine we belong to.

The challenge then is to find principles which all citizens, as reasonable and rational, can endorse in light of their common human reason, but in the context of the enduring and inevitable existence of reasonable pluralism.[137] Rather than seek agreement on such divergent beliefs, Rawls argues that the political conception should be affirmed by a 'reasonable overlapping consensus'. In other words, it is 'supported by the reasonable though opposing religious, philosophical, and moral doctrines that gain a significant body of adherents and endure over time from one generation to the next'.[138] The overlapping consensus, importantly, should be founded on the basis of the norms drawn from their own religious, moral, and philosophical comprehensive view. In other words, it is affirmed on moral grounds, even if those moral grounds differ.[139] Moreover, the assent to the political conception endures through changes of political power.[140]

For Rawls, the most reasonable political conception of justice, which will attract an overlapping consensus, is one that 'protects the familiar basic rights and assigns them a special priority', and 'includes measures to ensure that all citizens have sufficient material means to make effective use of those basic rights'.[141] It also removes the most divisive issues from the political agenda.[142] He concedes that given the actual comprehensive views existing in society, there is no guarantee that any reasonable conception for a democratic regime would in practice gain the support of an overlapping consensus. Nevertheless, his principle of overlapping consensus is widely used to support particular conceptions. Nussbaum, for one, argues powerfully that her conception of capabilities is capable of attracting the support of an overlapping consensus. It is crucial to her theory that her list of central capabilities is one that can be endorsed 'for political purposes ... by people who otherwise have very different views of what a complete good life for a human being would be'.[143]

C. Sunstein's incompletely theorized agreement

Sunstein takes a different path to dealing with disagreement. Like Rawls, he takes it as given that comprehensive agreement will not be reached and therefore seeks a partial resolution by focusing on what agreement does exist. But whereas Rawls aims for the highest level of abstraction, Sunstein deliberately frames his approach to emphasize

[136] ibid. [137] ibid. [138] ibid.
[139] Rawls (n 115), reproduced in Gowans (ed) (n 70) 238.
[140] ibid, 239. [141] ibid, 240. [142] ibid, 44–45, 19.
[143] Nussbaum (n 36) 74.

agreement on particulars.[144] His theory is specifically aimed at judges (although it could be applicable to the broader political system) and is generated by the insight that participants in legal systems tend to agree on the result and on relatively narrow explanations for it. If people disagree about a high-level principle, they may be able to reach agreement by lowering the level of abstraction: 'They need not agree on fundamental principle. They do not offer larger or more abstract explanations than are necessary to decide the case. When they disagree on abstraction, they move to a level of greater particularity'.[145] In other words, participants in legal controversies try to produce 'incompletely theorised agreements on particular outcomes'.[146] Incompletely theorized agreements are about the result, but not about the general theory that accounts for it.

Because law nevertheless requires reasons, Sunstein formulates his theory to account both for agreement on the outcome of a case, and on what he calls a 'low-level' justification. He emphasizes that the 'lawyer's impulse is to offer reasons on which people can unite from widely diverse foundations'.[147] Therefore, in formulating their reasons, judges and other relevant actors seek to stay at the 'lowest level of abstraction necessary for the decision in the case'.[148] He illustrates this approach by reference to the controversy over *Roe v Wade*,[149] the US Supreme Court decision upholding abortion in certain circumstances. There are many who agree it should not be overruled but disagree on the reasons. One reason is that the Court should respect its own precedents; another is that the case was rightly decided to protect privacy or equality; a third is that the case was rightly decided because prohibiting abortion will not in practice protect foetuses.[150] There is no need to agree on these reasons in order to agree on the result.

Sunstein regards his approach as descriptive of a pervasive phenomenon in Anglo-American law, and in particular, of judge-made law. But he also regards his approach as having special advantages. In particular, in a heterogeneous society, incompletely theorized agreement promotes agreement where agreement is necessary, while at the same time making it unnecessary to obtain agreement where agreement is impossible.[151] Incompletely theorized agreements can enable people to live together, and to show each other mutual respect and reciprocity. A case may be decided on a lower level of abstraction, thereby avoiding challenging the most deeply held commitments of the parties. In particular, judges could decide a question on the basis of its own institutional limitations, or the importance of adherence to precedent, and therefore avoid making decisions on fundamental issues. Losers in such cases might have lost the particular decision but their abstract theory remains intact. The cost of enduring disagreement is therefore reduced.[152] Incompletely theorized agreements also permit moral evolution over time. More practically, but often most importantly, they are appropriate for people with limited time and capacities. Judges may not have the time, the desire, or the capacity to enter into complex philosophical arguments. Notably,

[144] C Sunstein, 'Incompletely Theorized Agreements' (1998) 108 Harv L Rev 1733 at 1736.
[145] ibid, 1736. [146] ibid, 1735. [147] ibid, 1741. [148] ibid, 1737.
[149] *Roe v Wade* (1973) 410 US 113 (US Supreme Court). [150] Sunstein (n 144) 1742–43.
[151] ibid, 1743. [152] ibid, 1748.

while Sunstein acknowledges that reason-giving is an essential part of adjudication, he cautions against their excessive use. Reasons might bind a court in a future unpredicted situation; and might interfere with well-honed judicial intuition. He thus argues in favour of reasons which are narrowly tailored to the case at hand. This does not mean that judges can never agree on a higher level of abstraction: if they do, this is a cause for celebration. Judges should therefore adopt 'a presumption rather than a taboo against high level theorization'.[153]

Sunstein's theory is helpful in justifying a descent from high levels of abstraction in order to reach closure on specific disputes. However, he arguably gives too little credence to the role of public reason in justifying decisions. For him, 'a key task for a legal system is to enable people who disagree on first principles to converge on outcomes in particular cases'.[154] In many human rights cases, however, the outcomes in particular cases may not attract agreement per se. Parties, judges, and broader society need to be persuaded that the outcome is legitimate because it is based on reasons which can be identified as reasonable, plausible, and based on sound evidence. Sunstein regards the giving of reasons as problematic because they could create more dissent than they dispel. This is to misunderstand the nature of the adjudicative process. The dynamism of human rights adjudication lies as much in the process of reasoning as in the substantive outcomes. Disagreement as to outcomes remains an inevitable and dynamic aspect of adjudication. But outcomes can be accepted if the standard of reasoning is persuasive. Conversely, unpersuasive reasoning, while leading to an acceptable result in the case in hand, might be the basis for future unacceptable outcomes.[155] Judges owe it both to the parties and to the overall development of the law to both give publicly justifiable reasons, and insist that government and legislators do the same.

D. Capturing theoretical insights in legal reasoning

These insights are helpful in addressing the tension between universal principles and cultural specificity, particularly from a legal reasoning perspective. As a start, it is unnecessary to make a rigid choice between universal and culturally relative values. Respecting the values of particular communities can itself be seen as a central human rights objective. Thus, the preamble to the African Charter on Human and Peoples' Rights declares that Member States should take 'into consideration the virtues of their historical traditions and values of African civilization which should inspire and characterize their reflection on the concept of human and peoples' rights'. One way of expressing this is through a right to culture, which is now found in the ICCPR, the ICESCR, and domestic constitutions such as the South African Constitution.[156] At the same time, some human rights values remain applicable across all cultures. This balance is epitomized by the South African Constitution. Both the right to culture and the right to participate in cultural life 'may not be exercised in a manner inconsistent

[153] ibid, 1767. [154] ibid, 1771.

[155] See eg *Suresh Kumar Koushal v Naz Foundation* (2014) 1 SCC 1 (Indian Supreme Court) discussed in Chapter 1.

[156] See eg ICCPR Article 27; ICESCR Article 15(2); South African Constitution, ss 30–31.

with any provision of the Bill of Rights'.[157] The same is true for customary or indigenous law. While customary law is protected by the Constitution in its own right, it is also subject to the Constitution.[158]

This leaves open the question of which rights can override the right to culture. Kymlicka, discussing this tension in relation to minorities within liberal societies, suggests that there are two specific constraints which apply universally: one group should not be allowed to dominate other groups, and a group should not be permitted to oppress its own members: 'In other words, liberals should seek to ensure that there is equality *between* groups, and freedom and equality *within* groups'.[159] Another, complementary way of navigating between universal principles and cultural claims is to use human rights themselves to facilitate genuine voice and participation by those actually affected. Where cultural relativism is used to suppress those voices, whether explicitly or through cultural norms, it is hard to see how it can be defended on the grounds of respect for difference. This is what was achieved for Lovelace.

The tension can also be managed by devolving certain kinds of decisions to local level, thus conceding that while the broad principles are universal, the specific application may be contextual. Lord Hoffman summed up this approach when he said:

> [O]f course we share a common humanity … Nevertheless … the specific answers, the degree to which weight is given to one desirable objective rather than another, will be culturally determined. Different communities will, through their legislature and judges, adopt the answers which they think suit them.[160]

As will be seen in later chapters, this approach is formalized through doctrines such as the margin of appreciation, used by the European Court of Human Rights (ECtHR) to signify aspects of decisions which it regards as better determined at local level. At the same time, it is far from easy to determine the boundary between the common standards and the specific answers. This is clearly demonstrated by the difficulty in discerning clear principles behind the ECtHR's use of its doctrine of the margin of appreciation. As Berlin so perceptively suggests, priorities must be established, and all relevant factors must be considered, but none of it is final and absolute. The dynamic interaction must continue.

VI. Conclusion: The Way Forward?

This chapter has demonstrated the difficulty in finding an all-encompassing approach to human rights, and the need for a dynamic balance between universal standards and context-specific applications. In the field of human rights law, there is a need to find a fair and acceptable way of dealing with disagreement, which takes into account the importance of different perspectives on what is fair and just, but also settles on basic standards which are applicable across cultures. Although from a philosophical

[157] South African Constitution, ss 30–31.

[158] *Bhe and Others v Khayelitsha Magistrate and Others* [2004] ZACC 17, 41; South African Constitution, s 39(3).

[159] W Kymlicka, *Multicultural Citizenship* (OUP 1995) 194.

[160] L Hoffman, 'Human Rights and the House of Lords' (1999) 62 MLR 159 at 165.

perspective this challenge is daunting, we discover that in practice there is a greater level of agreement than the above discussion might have suggested. As we have seen, the UDHR was endorsed in 1948 with no dissenting voices, and those who motivated for and drafted it were by no means mere spokespersons of the US or the 'West'. The Commission on Human Rights, tasked in 1947 by the United Nations to prepare an international bill of rights, consisted of representatives of eighteen Member States, including not just the Soviet Union, the UK, France, China, and the US, but also a range of other countries, including Australia, Belgium, Byelorussia, Chile, Egypt, India, Iran, Lebanon, Ukraine, Uruguay, and Yugoslavia.[161] Since then, binding international human rights instruments, foremost amongst them, the ICCPR and ICESCR, have been widely ratified. As many as 168 countries are parties to the ICESCR[162] and 171 to the ICCPR.[163] Many of them regard this as an expression of 'a transnational, even if not universal, rights culture [which] has developed in the world ... since the Universal Declaration of Human Rights'.[164] The starting point should therefore be the framework of human rights which has already attracted broad-based consent in international, regional, and domestic human rights instruments. There seems little sense in rejecting this basic consensus.

Nevertheless, human rights are inevitably formulated at a high level of generality. Even if there is agreement as to the broad principle, the interpretation and application of the principles remain contested. For example, while the right to life is almost invariably endorsed as a fundamental human right, there is little agreement on whether it precludes capital punishment, permits abortion, or extends to the right to basic subsistence such as food, healthcare, and housing. This is not just a problem for cross-cultural interaction. The problem of disagreement about establishing and interpreting human rights is intrinsic and inevitable.

But this can itself be seen as contributing to the dynamism and continuing vitality of human rights law. It is through the process of deliberation, consensus building, and accountability that human rights take on a dynamic role in society. In addition, as Nedelsky points out, it is important to determine who participates in standard forming:

> One need not reject the possibility of universal human values to recognize the real problem of who participates in the definition of the rights that are supposed to set limits to legitimate sovereign power. If human rights really are to attain universal legitimacy, then the processes by which they are defined must themselves be universally recognized as legitimate.[165]

This book is ultimately about human rights law rather than pure moral philosophy. The legal approach, which insists on public reasoning, deliberative justifications, and

[161] MA Glendon, *A World Made New: Eleanor Roosevelt and the Universal Declaration of Human Rights* (Random House 2002) 32.

[162] <https://www.ohchr.org/EN/professionalinterest/pages/CESCR.aspx> (accessed 16 July 2018).

[163] <https://www.ohchr.org/en/professionalinterest/pages/ccpr.aspx> (accessed 16 July 2018).

[164] S Kentridge, 'Comparative Law in Constitutional Adjudication: The South African Experience' (2005–6) 80 Tul L Rev 245 at 256.

[165] Nedelsky (n 95) 271.

participation by affected parties provides human rights lawyers with the possibility of engaging in this process by continually drawing attention to the range of substantive answers. But lawyers and judges are also subject to other constraints, concerned with constitutional, institutional, and practical issues. Having set the broad parameters of the debate, we now turn more specifically to the role of the constitutional or statutory text and theories of interpretation. Chapter 4 addresses the relationship between democracy, the judiciary, and human rights, while Chapter 5 examines the role of theories. But first we turn to a pressing question within human rights law—that is, the role of socio-economic rights within the canon of human rights law more generally.

3

Challenging the Divide: Socio-economic Rights as Human Rights

I. Introduction

> [A] world in which human beings shall enjoy freedom of speech and belief and freedom from fear and want has been proclaimed as the highest aspiration of the common people.

Thus spoke the preamble to the Universal Declaration of Human Rights (UDHR) adopted in 1948. Its vision of rights as encompassing both freedom of speech and assembly and freedom from fear and want spans the traditional divide between civil and political rights and socio-economic rights. Rights traditionally classed as civil and political rights, such as freedom of speech, association, religion, and the right to a fair trial sit side by side with rights generally regarded as socio-economic. These include the right to a standard of living adequate for the health and well-being of the individual and their family;[1] to just and favourable conditions of work;[2] to social security; and to the 'realization, through national effort and international co-operation in accordance with the resources of each State, of the economic, social and cultural rights indispensable for [their] dignity and the free development of [their] personality'.[3]

However, this commitment to a unified view of human rights was not sustained. The binding international human rights instruments adopted nearly two decades later entrenched a division between civil and political rights and socio-economic rights. The International Covenant on Civil and Political Rights (ICCPR) contains the familiar civil and political rights such as freedom of speech and belief; while the commitments to freedom from fear and want are found in the International Covenant on Economic, Social and Cultural Rights (ICESCR). This architecture is replicated at the European level, with the European Convention on Human Rights (ECHR) containing civil and political rights and the lesser known European Social Charter consisting of socio-economic rights. Nor do the two sets of rights have equal standing. It remains true today, as the Committee on Economic, Social and Cultural Rights (CESCR) stated in 1993: 'The shocking reality ... [is] that States and the international community as a whole continue to tolerate all too often breaches of economic, social and cultural rights which, if they occurred in relation to civil and political rights, would provoke expressions of horror and outrage and would lead to concerted calls

[1] Universal Declaration of Human Rights (adopted 10 December 1948 UNGA Res 217 A(III) (UDHR)) Article 25.

[2] UDHR Article 23.

[3] UDHR Article 22.

for immediate remedial action'.[4] It is increasingly common to find socio-economic rights enshrined in constitutions: Gauri found that, in 2004, of the 165 countries with available written constitutions, 116 referred to a right to education and 73 to a right to healthcare.[5] However, major western democracies, such as Canada, the US, and the UK, still do not explicitly include socio-economic rights in their human rights protection.

So why is it that socio-economic rights are still given only dubious credibility within the human rights corpus? And is there a valid distinction in the first place? Traditionally, civil and political rights have been understood to refer to rights which protect individuals against intrusion by the State, while socio-economic rights concern rights to State protection against want or need. In this chapter, however, it is argued that it is too simplistic to view civil and political rights as separate and distinct from socio-economic rights. It is more helpful to focus on the nature of the obligation generated by different rights.[6] As recent analysis has shown, both sets of rights give rise to a cluster of obligations: a primary duty to respect; a secondary duty to protect; and a tertiary duty to fulfil.[7] The challenges often attributed to socio-economic rights should instead focus on the nature of the obligation.

II. Divided or United? Civil and Political Rights versus Socio-economic Rights

There are several ways in which civil and political rights have traditionally been distinguished from socio-economic rights: the differing ideologies underpinning each kind of right; their differing subject matter; the differing obligations they give rise to; their resource implications; and whether or not they are justiciable. The following sections critically examine the viability of these distinctions.

A. Competing ideologies

Socio-economic rights have tended to be set apart from civil and political rights because they embody a different philosophy of the relationship between the individual and the State. Traditional human rights theory posits the State as a potential threat to liberty. The role of human rights, therefore, is to protect individuals against the State. By contrast, socio-economic rights are based on a more positive vision of the State. Instead of being a threat to liberty, the State is viewed as essential to the maintenance of liberty.

Underlying this difference are also two distinct versions of liberty. The traditional model posits liberty as freedom from interference. This is the approach endorsed by the US Supreme Court in *DeShaney* in 1988. According to Rehnquist J:

[4] Cited in HJ Steiner and P Alston, *International Human Rights in Context* (2nd edn, OUP 2000).

[5] V Gauri, 'Social Rights and Economics: Claims to Health Care and Education in Developing Countries' (2004) 32 World Development 465.

[6] S Fredman, *Human Rights Transformed: Positive Rights and Positive Duties* (OUP 2008).

[7] H Shue, *Basic Rights: Subsistence, Affluence, and US Foreign Policy* (2nd edn, Princeton University Press 1996).

> the Due Process Clause of the 14th Amendment was intended to prevent government from abusing [its] power, or employing it as an instrument of oppression, to secure the individual from the arbitrary exercise of the powers of government, and to prevent governmental power from being used for purposes of oppression. Its purpose was to protect the people from the State, not to ensure that the State protected them from each other. The Framers were content to leave the extent of governmental obligation in the latter area to the democratic political processes.[8]

Socio-economic rights are founded on a different vision of freedom, the attempt to secure freedom from want and fear. As President Roosevelt put it in 1941: 'True individual freedom cannot exist without economic security and independence ... We have accepted, so to speak, a second bill of rights, under which a new basis of security and prosperity can be established for all'.[9] Thus, instead of keeping the State at bay, the active participation of the State in moving towards this ideal is enlisted.

For some, these two notions of freedom are mutually exclusive. Kelley, for example, argues that liberty rights reflect a political philosophy that prizes freedom, while welfare rights reflect a philosophy that is willing to sacrifice freedom.[10] By contrast, there are many who argue that true freedom is impossible without social rights. The rights to freedom of speech, freedom of association, or freedom of religion are of little or no value to a starving or homeless person. In order to properly enjoy these freedoms, the basic needs of individuals must be met. This is particularly true for the right to life, as has been recognized by the Indian Supreme Court. As was stated in *Chameli Singh* in 1996: 'The right to life implies the right to food, water, decent environment, education, medical care and shelter, since no civil, political, social or cultural rights either in the Universal Declaration or the Indian constitution could be exercised without them'.[11] Similarly, without basic rights of access to justice or legal aid, those with few means will find it much harder to redress the violation of their rights to be free of State interference, including the right not to be detained without trial, the right not to be tortured, or the right to freedom of conscience or religion, than those who are well off.

The interrelationship between the two sets of rights works in both directions. Political and civil rights, including freedom of speech, might be highly instrumental in preventing or ameliorating poverty. Trade unions can only flourish in a climate of civil and political liberties. As Sen has argued, if leaders are not accountable to the population, and are insulated from the effects of famine or drought, they have no incentive to take action to protect the population from such disasters. Freedom of the press, free opposition, and freedom of information 'spread the penalty of famine to the ruling groups'. They also contribute greatly to the dissemination of information, which can assist in the prevention of such disasters. Moreover, he argues, the

[8] *DeShaney v Winnebago County Department of Social Services* 489 US 189 (1989) (US Supreme Court) 196.

[9] 11th Annual Message to Congress (11 January 1944) in J Israel (ed), *The State of the Union Messages of the Presidents* (Chelsea House Publishers 1966) vol 3, 2881, cited in Steiner and Alston (n 4) 243.

[10] D Kelley, *A Life of One's Own: Individual Rights and the Welfare State* (Cato Institute 1998) 1.

[11] *Chameli Singh and Others v State of UP and Another* (1996) 2 SCC 54 (Indian Supreme Court) para [8].

conceptualization of what constitutes a 'need' from the many deprivations we suffer in life is itself a product of debate, discussion, and the political process. 'Political rights, including freedom of expression and discussion, are not only pivotal in inducing political responses to economic needs, they are also central to the conceptualisation of economic needs themselves'.[12] Most importantly, measures taken to ameliorate need can only be legitimate and effective with democratic participation.

This interrelationship was recognized at the Vienna World Conference in 1993, which declared that all rights are 'indivisible and interdependent and interrelated'. It is reflected in the fundamental principles of the International Labour Organization (ILO), which declare that 'freedom of expression and of association are essential to sustained progress'.[13] Similarly, the preamble of the ICCPR states: 'The ideal of free human beings enjoying civil and political freedom and freedom from fear and want can only be achieved if conditions are created whereby everyone may enjoy his [or her] civil and political rights, as well as his [or her] economic, social and cultural rights'. A parallel provision is found in the ICESCR.

B. Content of the right

A second way of drawing the distinction might be to focus on the content of the right. Civil and political rights, it could be argued, refer to classic liberty rights against interference by the State, such as freedom of speech, freedom from arbitrary arrest, freedom of religion, the right to vote, and freedom from torture. Socio-economic rights, by contrast, refer to protection against the vicissitudes of life, such as poverty, ill health, old age, or other economic conditions, which are not directly a result of interference by the State, but capable of being corrected by the State. This classification largely follows the demarcation adopted by the ICCPR and the ICESCR, and, at first sight, might form a clear basis for distinction.

However, as is seen in subsequent chapters, there are many rights which are found in both lists and could be classified in either way. The right to education is found both in the ICCPR and the ICESCR, albeit with differing emphasis. The same is true for the right to belong to a trade union, which could be seen as an aspect of freedom of association, or a social right to collective action. The right to a home could be expressed as the right to respect for home and family or the right to be housed. Moreover, rights traditionally seen as civil and political have been interpreted by courts in some jurisdictions as giving rise to rights which could be seen as protecting against want as much as fear. We will see that the Indian Supreme Court has interpreted the right to life to include such rights as the right to livelihood, to health, and even to shelter. One right

[12] A Sen, 'Freedoms and Needs', The New Republic, 10 and 17 January 1994, 31, 32, cited in Steiner and Alston (n 4) 269.

[13] International Labour Organization (ILO), Declaration of Philadelphia, adopted by the International Labour Conference in 1944 and later incorporated into the ILO's constitution <http://www.ilo.org/wcmsp5/groups/public/---asia/---ro-bangkok/---ilo-islamabad/documents/policy/wcms_142941.pdf> (accessed 18 February 2018).

which clearly spans the divide is the right to equality and non-discrimination. In jurisdictions without socio-economic rights, it has been argued that the right to equality should entail equal benefit of the law, which in turn entails equal provision of benefits.

C. Rights and duties

The third way in which the distinction between civil and political rights and socio-economic rights is usually drawn focuses on the relationship between rights and duties. Civil and political rights are thought to give rise to duties on the State not to interfere with individual liberty, whereas socio-economic rights are said to give rise to positive duties on the State to take action. This is reflected in the wording of key human rights in domestic constitutions. For example, the Fourteenth Amendment of the US Constitution formulates the right in terms of a restraint on State interference: 'No State shall ... deprive any person of life, liberty, or property, without due process of law'. A bright-line distinction between such a negative duty and a positive duty on the State was underscored by the US Supreme Court in *DeShaney*. According to Rehnquist CJ:

> The Clause is phrased as a limitation on the State's power to act, not as a guarantee of certain minimal levels of safety and security. It forbids the State itself to deprive individuals of life, liberty, or property without 'due process of law,' but its language cannot fairly be extended to impose an affirmative obligation on the State to ensure that those interests do not come to harm through other means. Nor does history support such an expansive reading of the constitutional text.[14]

However, a closer look reveals that even paradigmatic civil rights, such as the right not to be tortured, carry with them some element of positive duty on the part of the State. As well as refraining from torturing individuals directly, the State must protect individuals against interference by other, non-State actors. Similarly, the right to vote requires sophisticated State machinery. As the South African Constitutional Court (SACC) put it:

> Unlike many other civil and political guarantees, the right to vote imposes an obligation upon the state not merely to refrain from interfering with the exercise of the right, but to take positive steps to ensure that it can be exercised. The right to vote necessitates an electoral system and the calling of elections.[15]

On the other hand, socio-economic rights do not necessarily impose positive duties. Examples of such rights are the rights to freedom of association, to strike, and to collective bargaining.

[14] *DeShaney v Winnebago County Department of Social Services* (n 8).

[15] *Richter v The Minister for Home Affairs and Others (with the Democratic Alliance and Others Intervening, and with Afriforum and Another as Amici Curiae)* [2009] ZACC 3 (South African Constitutional Court).

D. Resource-intensive and programmatic

A key difference between civil and political rights and socio-economic rights is often said to lie in the resource needs of each. Whereas the former simply require non-intervention by the State, and therefore in principle no budgetary allocation, the latter require the State to commit resources. With this comes a temporal dimension. In deference to the economic capacities of a State, socio-economic rights are often only realizable progressively and subject to available resources, while civil and political rights are immediately effective. Thus, the ICCPR requires State Parties to 'respect and ensure' the rights recognized therein to all individuals subject to its jurisdiction. By contrast, the ICESCR only requires State Parties to 'take steps ... to the maximum of its available resources, with a view to achieving progressively the full realization' of the rights recognized in that Covenant.[16]

However, here too it is difficult to draw a watertight distinction. In some circumstances, civil and political rights have resource implications. The right to a fair trial requires significant expenditure in setting up courts which are sufficiently resourced to avoid unreasonable delay. What amounts to a 'reasonable delay' and 'reasonable resources' may well depend on the total available resources of a country and its political priorities. Still more resources are required to provide interpreters and legal aid in criminal proceedings. The very basic civic right to vote would not take place unless a government committed public funds to create fair electoral machinery. Nor are all socio-economic rights programmatic. Some, such as the right to emergency health care, require a state to take immediate action.[17] The duty not to discriminate is also an immediate one.

E. Justiciability and the role of the courts

Critics of socio-economic rights frequently object, not to the ideal embodied in the right itself, but to the use of courts to interpret the right and provide remedies for individuals. The provision of socio-economic rights, on this argument, takes place through social policy delivery, in which the courts have an appropriately minor role. This is largely the approach in the UK, as reflected in its report to the UN Committee on its compliance with the socio-economic rights in the ICESCR.[18]

Relying on social policy delivery works well when the political forces are committed to providing social rights. However, as has been seen over decades of austerity measures in many countries, changed economic and political conditions, often driven by neoliberal economic theories, have undermined these commitments even in advanced social democratic regimes. It is in these circumstances that the role of fundamental

[16] ICCPR Article 2(1); ICESCR Article 2(1).

[17] See eg *Paschim Banga Khet Mazdoor Samity v State of West Bengal* AIR 1996 SC 2426, (1996) 4 SCC 37 (Indian Supreme Court); s 27(3) South African Constitution; *Soobramoney v Minister of Health, Kwa-Zulu-Natal* 1998 (1) SA 765 (CC) (South African Constitutional Court) para [20].

[18] UK report on Implementation of the ICESCR (4th periodic report submitted by States Parties under Articles 16 and 17 of the Covenant) 30 January 2001.

rights, which constrain political decision-making, comes into focus. As the Committee on Economic, Social and Cultural Rights (CESCR) has put it:

> Courts are frequently involved in decision making on a considerable range of matters which have important resource allocation implications. The adoption of a rigid classification of economic, social and cultural rights which puts them, by definition, beyond the reach of the courts would thus be arbitrary ... [and] drastically curtail the capacity of the courts to protect the rights of the most vulnerable and disadvantaged groups in society.[19]

The challenge is to define an appropriate role for the courts.

There are two sorts of criticism of courts in this context. The first questions the legitimacy of the courts to deal with essentially political decisions about allocation of resources. Judges interpreting open-textured social rights, it is argued, could well draw on personal or institutional value judgements which upset the political balance. This is a critique which could apply to all rights and is dealt with in Chapter 4. The second criticism of courts is concerned with their competence. While courts have expertise in interpreting relatively determinate rules of law, it is maintained, judges are not well equipped to deal with open-textured policy aims, to undertake cost–benefit analyses, to assess progress towards achieving objectives, or to examine spending priorities. Moreover, the litigation process is particularly ill-suited for such tasks. Litigation is a bipolar process. It is initiated by an individual complainant, focuses on an individual grievance, is based only on information presented by the litigants, and requires individual resolution. Polycentric decisions, having ripple effects over a wide area of interests, are not effectively dealt with by resolving individual complaints in a piecemeal and ad hoc manner in the judicial arena. However, as will be shown in Chapter 4, the litigation process could potentially be adapted to address these difficulties.

One way forward might be to establish a duty on the State to provide social rights, while reflecting concerns about the legitimacy and capability of the courts by excluding the possibility of judicial enforcement. Several constitutions make use of this approach in the form of 'directive principles', including the Irish, Namibian, and Indian Constitutions. Thus Part IV of the Indian Constitution, entitled 'Directive Principles of State Policy' specifically states: 'The provisions contained in this Part shall not be enforceable by any court, but the principles therein laid down are nevertheless fundamental in the governance of the country and it shall be the duty of the State to apply these principles in making laws'.[20] These are distinguished from the judicially enforceable 'fundamental rights', the demarcation largely tracking the familiar distinction between civil and political rights, contained in the fundamental rights provisions, and socio-economic rights, set out in the Directive Principles. For example, Article 39 provides that the State 'shall direct its policy towards securing', inter alia, that all citizens have the right to an adequate means of livelihood, that there is equal pay for equal work for men and women, and that children are given opportunities and facilities to develop in a healthy manner.

[19] CESCR, General Comment No 9 (1998), UN Doc E/1999/22, Annex IV, para 10.

[20] Indian Constitution, s 37.

However, without judicial enforcement of any kind, it is easy to ignore directive principles. Frustrated with the lack of serious commitment to these principles, individuals turned to the Indian Supreme Court to find a remedy. Although not directly enforcing the Directive Principles, the Court responded by drawing on the Directive Principles in order to interpret justiciable fundamental rights. Article 21, the right to life, has thus become the crucible of socio-economic rights in the Indian Constitution. These include rights to health, livelihood, and shelter. For example, in the seminal case of *Olga Tellis*,[21] thousands of pavement and slum dwellers challenged the attempt by the City of Bombay to evict and move them to areas far from the possibility of obtaining work. The right to life was interpreted, against the background of the Directive Principles, to include the right to livelihood, and the right to live in the vicinity of available work. Similarly, in a case in 1996, the Court stated: 'Article 21 [the right to life] imposes an obligation on the State to safeguard the right to life of every person ... Failure on the part of a Government hospital to provide timely medical treatment to a person in need of such treatment results in violation of his right to life guaranteed under Article 21'.[22]

F. Redrawing the boundaries: the nature of the obligation

The above discussion has shown that the traditional categories of civil and political rights on the one hand and socio-economic rights on the other are misleading. Far more useful is to consider each right as giving rise to a cluster of obligations, some of which require the State to abstain from interfering, and others which entail positive action and resource allocation. In his seminal work, Shue argues that there are no one-to-one pairings between kinds of duties and kinds of rights. Instead, 'the complete fulfilment of each kind of right involves the performance of multiple kinds of duties'. He therefore goes beyond the 'usual assumption that for every right there is a single correlative duty', and suggests instead that for every right, 'there are three types of duties, all of which must be performed if the basic right is to be fully honoured, but not all of which must necessarily be performed by the same individuals or institutions'. He classifies these three types of duty as duties to avoid, duties to protect, and duties to aid. Applied to the basic right of security, this would impose on the State the duties to avoid eliminating a person's security, duties to protect people against deprivation of security by other people, and duties to aid by providing for the security of those unable to provide for their own security.[23]

This three-fold classification has been adopted and developed in the ICESCR. Using the ICESCR terminology, all rights can be seen to give rise to at least three types of correlative duties: the duties to respect, protect, and fulfil. The duty to respect requires the State to refrain from interfering directly or indirectly with the enjoyment of the right. The duty to protect requires State parties to prevent third parties from interfering in any way with the enjoyment of the right. The duty to fulfil requires the State to either provide the right directly or to facilitate the provision by assisting individuals

[21] *Olga Tellis v Bombay Municipal Corp* AIR 1986 SC 180 (Indian Supreme Court).
[22] *Paschim Banga Khet Mazdoor Samity v State of West Bengal* (n 17).
[23] Shue (n 7).

and communities to make their own provision. Some formulations also include a duty to 'promote', which requires the State to promote the right by disseminating information and educating people as to their rights. This approach was endorsed by the African Commission on Human and People's Rights in the case of *SERAC v Nigeria*, where it stated: 'Internationally accepted ideas of the various obligations engendered by human rights indicate that all rights—both civil and political rights and social and economic—generate at least four levels of duties for a State that undertakes to adhere to a rights regime, namely the duty to respect, protect, promote, and fulfil these rights'.[24] It is also reflected in section 7 of the South African Constitution, which states: 'The state must respect, protect, promote and fulfil the rights in the Bill of Rights'.

The recognition of the whole cluster of duties triggered by a right opens up a much richer understanding of the right. Rather than confining civil and political rights to duties of respect, it can be seen that they also require duties to fulfil, protect, and promote. This will be seen throughout this book, but some examples from the avowedly civil and political instrument, the ECHR, make the point well. Thus Article 11, freedom of assembly, might be thought to give rise only to an obligation on the State to refrain from interfering with peaceful demonstrations. But even a quick glance reveals that this duty inevitably extends to the duty to protect participants in a peaceful demonstration from disruption by a violent counter-demonstration by other private individuals, as happened in the *Plattform* case. As the Court put it: 'Genuine, effective freedom of peaceful assembly cannot be reduced to a mere duty on the part of the state not to interfere … Article 11 sometimes requires positive measures to be taken, even in the sphere of relations between individuals, if need be'.[25] The duty to protect in such a context is, however, complex, since the other individuals also have rights to peaceful protest. Moreover, by requiring the State to protect marchers against other individuals, it inevitably also created a duty to fulfil, that is, to put in place and finance effective policing mechanisms. The Court navigated these tensions by formulating the duty as 'an obligation as to measures to be taken and not as to results to be achieved'. The duty was therefore only to 'take reasonable and appropriate measures to enable lawful demonstrations to proceed peacefully'. States are not expected to guarantee this absolutely and they have a wide discretion in the choice of the means to be used.[26]

Similar points can be made in respect of Article 3, the right not to be subjected to torture or inhuman or degrading treatment, again a right which has traditionally been thought to fall within the heartland of civil and political rights. Here too the European Court of Human Rights (ECtHR) has gone beyond the primary obligation of restraint to consider the secondary obligation to prevent others from infringing the right.[27] This was particularly evident in the child abuse case of *Z v UK*,[28] which concerned the extent of the responsibility of the State to protect children against abuse by their parents.

[24] *Social and Economic Rights Action Centre (SERAC) and Another v Nigeria* (2001) AHRLR 60 (ACHPR 2001) 44 (African Commission of Human and People's Rights).

[25] *Plattform 'Ärzte für das Leben' v Austria* (1988) 13 EHRR 204 (European Court of Human Rights) para [34].

[26] ibid.

[27] *Chahal v UK* Application 22414/93 (1996) 23 EHRR 413 (European Court of Human Rights).

[28] *Z and Others v UK* (2002) 34 EHRR 3 (European Court of Human Rights).

The Court emphasized that Article 3 requires States to take measures designed to ensure that individuals within their jurisdiction are not subjected to torture or inhuman or degrading treatment, including such ill-treatment administered by private individuals.[29] These measures should provide effective protection, in particular, of children and other vulnerable persons, and include reasonable steps to prevent ill-treatment of which the authorities had or ought to have had knowledge. The Court acknowledged 'the difficult and sensitive decisions facing social services and the important countervailing principle of respecting and preserving family life'.[30] The present case, however, left no doubt as to the failure of the system to protect these child applicants from serious, long-term neglect and abuse.

This contrasts starkly with the US Supreme Court's decision in *DeShaney*, which concerned very similar facts. In *DeShaney*,[31] as in *Z v UK*,[32] the mother of a child severely abused by his father brought an action on the basis that social workers, despite receiving complaints of the abuse, had not removed him from his father's custody. The claim was brought under the Due Process clause of the Fourteenth Amendment, which provides that '[n]o State shall ... deprive any person of life, liberty, or property, without due process of law'. As we have seen, the US Supreme Court refused to make the transition from the primary obligation of restraint to the obligations to protect or fulfil, except in special circumstances.[33] Not surprisingly, the Supreme Court has also refused to take the further step into creating an affirmative right to governmental aid.[34] 'Although the liberty protected by the Due Process Clause affords protection against unwarranted government interference ... it does not confer an entitlement to such [governmental aid] as may be necessary to realize all the advantages of that freedom'.[35]

Redrawing the boundaries between civil and political rights and socio-economic rights to reflect different sorts of obligations makes it possible to examine the difficult questions of justiciability in a more focused manner. It is not so much the nature of the rights, as the type of obligation, which gives rise to these problems. Duties to respect give rise to the fewest problems of this sort, whether they are triggered by civil and political rights or socio-economic rights. This is because they are generally negative, immediate, and determinate. But even in this area, there may be resource implications, as we have seen. More difficult questions arise in respect of duties to protect and fulfil. First, it may be argued that it is impossible to define a minimum core content, and therefore the duties are indeterminate and non-justiciable. Asserting rights to social security, to protection against poverty, to the protection of health, or to housing does not, on its own, tell us what standard of living is the minimum commensurate with human dignity and freedom. This leads Kelly to argue that there is no

[29] ibid, para [73]. [30] ibid, para [74].

[31] *DeShaney v Winnebago County Department of Social Services* (n 8).

[32] *Z and Others v UK* (n 28).

[33] *DeShaney v Winnebago County Department of Social Services* (n 8) 196.

[34] *Harris v McRae* 448 US 297, 317–18 (1980) (US Supreme Court) (no obligation to fund abortions or other medical services) (discussing Due Process clause of Fifth Amendment); *Lindsey v Normet* 405 US 56, 74, (1972) (US Supreme Court) (no obligation to provide adequate housing) (discussing Due Process clause of Fourteenth Amendment).

[35] *Harris v McRae*, ibid.

appropriate role for the courts. Since there is 'no universal and non-arbitrary standard for distinguishing need from luxury', it is for the political process to draw the line.[36] Second, many socio-economic rights are framed as progressively realizable, making it difficult to know at what point a breach has occurred. Does the 'right' then evaporate into a mere aspiration? Much has been written on how these challenges can be overcome, while preserving a role for justiciable positive duties and therefore a reassertion of the place of socio-economic rights in the canon of fundamental rights. It is to these ideas that we now turn.

III. Progressive Realization and Minimum Core

As we have seen, to take account of differing resource capacities in different States, many socio-economic rights are only realizable progressively and subject to available resources. Progressive realization is not always a feature of socio-economic rights. Thus, the right to a basic education in the South African Constitution is formulated as an immediately realizable right,[37] as the South African Constitutional Court has re-affirmed.[38] This contrasts with the right to further education, which is subject to progressive realization. Similarly, the Indian Supreme Court has interpreted the right to life to include several key socio-economic rights, including the rights to health and to education, without the added caveat of progressive realization.[39] However, many socio-economic rights are indeed so formulated. The ICESCR has framed the duty on contracting states as one to 'take steps ... to the maximum of its available resources, with a view to achieving progressively the full realization of the rights recognized in the present Covenant'.[40] In the South African Constitution, the rights of access to housing, health-care services, sufficient food and water, and social security are all correlated with a duty on the State to 'take reasonable legislative and other measures, within its available resources, to achieve the progressive realisation of this right'.[41]

It is these duties which are challenging. What is the substantive content of the right at the end of the road and what steps does the State need to take to show that it has fulfilled its duty of progressive realization of the right? Is the goalpost continually moving as technology develops and a country has more resources? For example, it could be argued that the 'highest attainable standard of health' in Article 12 ICESCR is continually rising so that a country might in fact never achieve the full realization of the right. Moreover, as Chapman shows, it is particularly difficult to evaluate compliance because 'progressive realization' within the context of 'maximum available resources' requires a multiplicity of performance standards for each right in the context of specific countries and their varied social, developmental, and resource contexts.[42]

36 Kelley (n 10) 1.

37 South African Constitution, s 29.

38 *Governing Body of the Juma Musjid Primary School and Others v Essay NO and Others* [2011] ZACC 13 (South African Constitutional Court).

39 See *Paschim Banga Khet Mazdoor Samity v State of West Bengal* (n 17) and *Mohini Jain v State of Karnataka* 1992 SCR (3) 658 (Indian Supreme Court) 667F.

40 ICESCR Article 2(1).

41 South African Constitution, ss 26(2), 27(2).

42 A Chapman, '"A Violations Approach" for Monitoring the International Covenant on Social, Economic and Cultural Rights' (1996) 18 Human Rights Quarterly 23, 23–66.

The acceptance that socio-economic rights can be progressively realized has led many to treat them as mere aspirations, rather than enforceable rights on a par with civil and political rights. Without a clear timetable for achievement, or even a clearly delineated substantive goal, socio-economic rights can easily be postponed indefinitely. The CESCR has countered this by stressing that the duty is in fact an immediate one: 'The fact that realisation over time ... is foreseen under the Covenant should not be misinterpreted as depriving the obligation of all meaningful content'. In order to demarcate the obligation more clearly, the Committee distinguishes between obligations of *conduct*, which are concrete and immediate, and obligations of *result*, which are more aspirational. The full realization of the relevant rights is an obligation of result. But the duty to take steps by all appropriate means is an unqualified obligation of conduct. The right therefore generates an immediate obligation to take steps towards the goal, and those steps should be 'deliberate, concrete and targeted as clearly as possible towards meeting the obligations recognised in the Covenant'.[43] Deliberately retrogressive measures would need 'the most careful consideration'.[44] In addition, some rights are immediate. The duty not to discriminate falls into this category.

However, this on its own might not be sufficient to give actual content to the right. It is for this reason that many have turned to the principle of a 'minimum core' of the right, which should be immediately attained. The CESCR has specified that the State has an obligation to ensure the satisfaction of 'at the very least, minimum essential levels of each of the rights'.[45] Chapman sees the specification of a minimum core as one of the key elements in finding an effective and feasible means of determining whether a State has violated its obligations under the ICESCR.[46] She identifies a set of such core requirements from the CESCR Concluding Observations over a period of years. The CESCR itself has begun the task of elaborating the minimum content of the rights in the Covenant in its General Recommendations.

However, the attempt to specify the content of the minimum core in this way encounters many difficulties, particularly if its aim is to provide a minimum across different countries with widely differing levels of development. It was this which led Yacoob J to find that it was inappropriate in the South African context. As he put it in *Grootboom*, the first case in South Africa on the right of access to adequate housing:[47] 'It is not possible to determine the minimum threshold for the progressive realisation of the right of access to adequate housing without first identifying the needs and opportunities for the enjoyment of such a right'.[48] These vary according to income, unemployment, availability of land and the circumstances of a country. 'All this', he concluded, 'illustrates the complexity of the task of determining a minimum core obligation for the progressive realisation of the right of access to adequate housing without having the requisite information on the needs and the opportunities for the enjoyment of this right'.[49]

[43] CESCR General Comment No 3: The Nature of States Parties Obligations (Fifth Session) (1990) UN Doc E/199123, Annex III.

[44] ibid, para 9. [45] ibid, para 10. [46] Chapman (n 42) 43–45.

[47] South African Constitution, s 26.

[48] *Republic of South Africa v Grootboom* 2001 (1) SA 46 (South African Constitutional Court) para [32].

[49] ibid.

Bilchitz counters this by suggesting that the minimum core should be characterized as a duty to realize the most urgent survival interests protected by the right. This is complemented by the duty to improve the level of provision by taking reasonable measures.[50] This approach insists that it is unacceptable for any human being to live without resources to survive and that this should therefore be the government priority. Although he accepts that millions of people might be living in poverty, requiring progressive improvement, his conception of the minimum core is unflinching in insisting on priority to those who would otherwise have no means of survival.[51] These survival needs can be determined locally on the basis of local information.

A common objection to both a content-based understanding of minimum core and Bilchitz's more principled view is that it would entitle everyone to claim the minimum core immediately, which is too demanding on the State. This is one of the recurrent objections of the SACC to the idea of a minimum core. In *Treatment Action Campaign*, the Court held that 'it is impossible to give everyone access even to a core service immediately. All that is possible and all that can be expected of the State, is that it act reasonably to provide access to the socio-economic rights ... on a progressive basis'.[52] This is countered by a different conception of the minimum core which does not focus on content so much as on priority. On this view, the minimum core consists of the most urgent aspects of the right, which need to be catered for first. It places a very high (although not impossible) burden on the State to justify failing to provide such a minimum. This is the more appropriate reading of the CESCR's approach to the minimum core. Thus, it states in General Comment No 3: 'In order for a State party to be able to attribute its failure to meet at least its minimum core obligations to a lack of available resources *it must demonstrate that every effort has been made* to use all resources that are at its disposition in an effort to satisfy, as a matter of priority, those minimum obligations'.[53] This means that the State is not required to do more than is possible given its resources; but it must be able to show that it could not do more than it has done, given its resources.[54] Thus, the minimum core is itself rephrased in temporal terms.

The decision of the SACC in *Grootboom* could be read in these terms. Although the Court rejected the idea of a content-based minimum core, it held that priority should be given to the worst off in any metropolitan housing plan. The housing programme in the area of the Cape Metropolitan Council failed to make reasonable provision within its available resources for people in the Cape Metropolitan area with no access to land, with no roof over their heads, and living in intolerable conditions or crisis situations. In this sense, it was found to be in violation of the Constitution. If the minimum core is interpreted as setting priorities for a State, which have to be fulfilled first, then this could be interpreted as a type of minimum core.

However, in later cases, the SACC has firmly set its face against the minimum core, taking the view that the role for judges in relation to progressively realizable rights

[50] D Bilchitz, 'Towards a Reasonable Approach to the Minimum Core' (2003) 19 SAJHR 1–26, 11.

[51] ibid, 16.

[52] *Minister of Health v Treatment Action Campaign (No 2)* (2002) 5 SA 721 (South African Constitutional Court) para [35].

[53] CESCR, General Comment No 3 (n 43) para 10 (emphasis added).

[54] ibid.

cannot include specifying the content of the right, or even the minimum core content. Instead its focus is on the duty to take reasonable measures to progressively realize the right. In *Treatment Action Campaign*, the Court made it clear that the Constitution should not be interpreted as providing for a minimum core as part of a self-standing right conferred on everyone. At most, it might be relevant to the reasonableness of the State's actions in discharging its duty to 'take all reasonable measures, within its available resources, to achieve the progressive realisation of the right'.[55] Thus, the Court declared, 'the socio-economic rights of the Constitution should not be construed as entitling everyone to demand that the minimum core be provided to them'.[56]

An even more emphatic rejection of the minimum core is found in the *Mazibuko* case, which concerned the right of access to sufficient water in section 27 of the Constitution.[57] The applicants argued that the Court should determine the content of the right by quantifying the amount of water sufficient for dignified life. They presented expert evidence that the appropriate amount was 50 litres per person per day. Having established the content of the right independently of the duty, the applicants contended, the Court should determine whether the State acted reasonably in seeking to achieve the progressive realization of this right. However, the Court rejected the claim that the content of the right, set out in section 27(1), could be determined independently of the State's duty to realize the right in section 27(2). The role for the Court, held O'Regan J, was to determine whether the State had taken reasonable measures. Thus, she stated:

> [Sections] 27(1) and (2) of the Constitution must be read together to delineate the scope of the positive obligation to provide access to sufficient water imposed upon the state. That obligation requires the state to take reasonable legislative and other measures progressively to achieve the right of access to sufficient water within available resources. It does not confer a right to claim 'sufficient water' from the state immediately.[58]

She therefore rejected the contention that the Court should establish 50 litres a day as the minimum content of the right.

Young is sceptical about the utility of the minimum core concept, for a different reason. For her, the various attempts to identify its content, whether through linking it to basic needs, deriving it from normative values such as dignity, equality, or freedom,[59] building it up from consensus based on the accumulated content of country reports,[60] or focusing on the obligations raised by the right and correlatively the role of the adjudicative body,[61] all encounter severe difficulties. This, in her view, undermines its utility.

Nevertheless, the SACC's conflation of the right and the duty is problematic. Bilchitz argues that rights should be recognized even if they are not capable of being fulfilled at present.[62] By recognizing them as rights, we retain the imperative to move

[55] South African Constitution, s 27(2).
[56] *Minister of Health v Treatment Action Campaign (No 2)* (n 52) para [44].
[57] *Mazibuko v City of Johannesburg* [2009] ZACC 28 (South African Constitutional Court).
[58] ibid, para [56]. [59] ibid, paras [133]–[138]. [60] ibid, paras [140]–[151].
[61] ibid, paras [151]–[164]. [62] Bilchitz (n 50) 20.

as expeditiously as possible to achieve this. Although an individual might not be able to claim a breach at this moment, the State might be held to account for failing to move towards the goal.

Perhaps the most helpful way to reconcile the need for progressive realization without giving up on the substantive content of the right draws on the concept of 'principles', developed by Alexy. According to Alexy, a principle is a norm which must be realized to the greatest extent possible given the legal and factual possibilities. Principles are not binary in the sense of being fulfilled or breached, but instead can be satisfied to varying degrees.[63] Their normative force lies in the requirement to realize their content to the greatest extent possible, given the legal and factual possibilities. In Alexy's terminology, principles are 'optimisation requirements'. Principles do not lose their prima facie binding force when they are outweighed in particular circumstances by other principles. This clearly demonstrates why it is important to keep the right and the duty separate. The right is the goal; the duty is to realize the goal. The right may not be capable of immediate fulfilment, either because other principles have priority or because the resources are not available. This does not, however, reduce the right to a mere aspiration. There is still a duty to realize the right: the fact that the duty is complex and subject to competing factors is not a reason for downgrading the right. In Alexy's terms, the principle remains prima facie binding. The task is to optimize it to the extent legally and factually possible.[64]

Alexy's approach casts light both on the issues of minimum core and of progressive realization. In some contexts, the right must be fulfilled immediately because there are no competing principles with sufficient weight to displace them. Duties to fulfil civil and political rights are often of this nature; but this might be true too of duties to fulfil socio-economic rights. Thus, the South African Constitution gives every child the right to basic nutrition, shelter, basic health-care services, and social services.[65] This gives rise to a duty to immediately realize the right. No other principles, nor demands on resources, have sufficient weight to displace it. Similarly, the duty might not require extra resources, so that there are no factual impediments to its immediate fulfilment. A better allocation of existing resources might make the right immediately available.[66]

Even where the duty to optimize the right is progressive, it is not the case that the whole obligation is postponed.[67] First, the State is under an immediate obligation to take action towards achieving the goal so far as current circumstances permit, striving to ensure the widest possible enjoyment of the relevant rights under the prevailing circumstances even where the available resources are demonstrably inadequate.[68] In particular, resource constraints have no effect on the duty to devise strategies and programmes for the fulfilment of the duty. Clearly retrogressive steps should not be taken except where fully justified and in the context of full use of maximum available resources. Second, there is an immediate obligation to monitor the extent of the

[63] R Alexy, *A Theory of Constitutional Rights* (OUP 2004) 45–57, 348.

[64] See Fredman (n 6) 71–72.

[65] South African Constitution, s 28 (1)(c).

[66] See A Chapman, 'The Status of Efforts to Monitor Economic, Social and Cultural Rights' in *Economic Rights: Conceptual, Measurement, and Policy Issues* (University of Connecticut 2005) 143–63.

[67] CESCR, General Comment No 3 (n 43).

[68] ibid, para 9.

realization.[69] Third, there is an immediate duty to guarantee that the relevant rights will be exercised without discrimination. This entails extending existing provision to excluded groups, whether in the form of housing,[70] social security,[71] or healthcare.

This has particular bearing on the minimum core. The minimum core could be said to constitute those conditions which are so important that they will almost invariably trump other principles, such as State resources. The minimum core principle in this form requires the State to do everything possible to optimize the basic right of survival of the most destitute and disadvantaged in society, because there is very little that can take priority over the basic right of survival.[72] This can be explained as a failure to value the fundamental dignity of the most deprived,[73] or developed as a principle in its own right.[74] The State's duty to optimize the principle therefore requires this aspect of the duty to be fulfilled unless there are extremely weighty principles which justify delaying its full implementation. The Committee has not defined a minimum core content to all the rights, but it is not difficult to identify the most blatant aspects. For example, the very first goal in the 2030 Sustainable Development Goals Agenda states that the world has committed itself, by 2030, to eradicate extreme poverty for all people everywhere, currently measured as people living on less than $1.25 a day.[75] A State which is unable to provide this very basic income for all of its people would need to justify its omission with clear, weighty evidence, including the extent to which it has sought international assistance, also a binding requirement of the ICESCR.

IV. Maximum Available Resources

This leads to the next challenge, namely, how to assess 'maximum available resources'. What resources are available, and are the resources used to the maximum extent? Do resources include private resources, which could be accessed through more progressive tax regimes? This also raises the question of whether 'available resources' refers only to budgets or, as Elson argues, also to wider decisions such as monetary policy.[76]

Some general principles were elaborated in 1986 in the form of the Limburg Principles. The principles provide that resources must be used equitably, effectively, and accessibly; and priority should be given to the need to assure to everyone the satisfaction of subsistence requirements as well as the provision of essential services.[77] But

[69] ibid, para 11. [70] *Ghaidan v Godin-Mendoza* [2004] UKHL 30 (UK House of Lords).

[71] *Khosa and Others v Minister of Social Development and Others; Mahlaule and Another v Minister of Social Development* 2004 (6) SA 505 (CC) (South African Constitutional Court).

[72] Fredman (n 6) 86.

[73] S Liebenberg, 'The Value of Human Dignity in Interpreting Socio-economic Rights' (2005) 21 SAJHR 1.

[74] Bilchitz (n 50).

[75] UN General Assembly, 'Transforming our world: the 2030 Agenda for Sustainable Development' 21 October 2015, A/RES/70/1 <https://sustainabledevelopment.un.org/index.php?page=view&type=111&nr=8496&menu=35> (accessed 17 February 2018).

[76] D Elson, 'Are Some Varieties of Economics More Congruent with Human Rights Budget Analysis than Others?', presentation at Oxford Martin Programme on Human Rights for Future Generations Workshop: Human Rights Budget Analysis (29 January 2015).

[77] Limburg Principles on the Implementation of the International Covenant on Economic, Social and Cultural Rights, UN Doc E/CN.4/1987/17, para 27.

this too begs some questions. How do we determine whether resources have been used effectively? Harvey and Rooney point to several alternative techniques. One is to apply a cost–benefit analysis to assess effectiveness. But since many of the benefits, particularly health care and education, are not appropriately measured by market prices or 'willingness to pay', this is not a straightforward formula. In any event, publicly provided benefits are specifically aimed at overcoming market-based valuations, where poorer people might be inevitably willing to pay for far less than wealthier people. Instead of a broad cost–benefit analysis, it may be preferable to use cost-effectiveness, which focuses more closely on a specific issue. A well-known example in the healthcare context is that of Quality Adjusted Life Years. Harvey and Rooney warn, however, that, while much is to be learned from other disciplines, it is essential to develop a distinctive human rights-based approach. Ultimately, a policy decision must be taken, which should not be obscured by apparently technical formulae.[78]

In a valuable additional perspective on this question, Skogly argues that there has been an undue emphasis on the financial aspects of resources. She suggests that a great deal might be achieved, without necessarily increasing financial commitments, by including the resources which can be made available in society through applying natural, human, educational, and regulatory resources. For example, through managing its natural resources in the public interest, a State might release more resources to fulfil basic subsistence rights. Conversely, a State which allows business to pollute the local geography will be failing to enhance existing resources through environmental regulation; and a State which permits tax avoidance would be failing to increase its financial resources through adequate taxation.[79] Aspects of Skogly's qualitative perspective, however, are somewhat circular. She argues, for example, that legislation should be used to implement minimum wage schemes and protect against unhealthy and dangerous workplaces, 'thus protecting the human resources available for human rights implementation in society'.[80] Similarly, she argues for qualitative investment in human resources through education.[81] Yet the duty to use maximum resources is intended to secure the rights to education, fair conditions at work, and personal security, rather than that fair conditions at work, personal security, and education constitute resources for the realization of the rights. It is true, as she argues, that there are choices in educational policy where the same amount of financial spending may be used in different ways, but this is a question of substance for the right to education rather than a means of augmenting resources, whether personal or other.

One of the most challenging aspects of the 'maximum available resources' standard under the ICESCR is that available resources should include international assistance and co-operation. Under Article 2(1) ICESCR, each State party undertakes to take steps 'individually and through international assistance and co-operation, especially economic and technical, to the maximum of its available resources' to progressively fulfil

[78] C Harvey and E Rooney, 'Integrating Human Rights? Socio-economic Rights and Budget Analysis' (2010) European Human Rights Law Review 3, 266–79, 274.

[79] S Skogly, 'The Requirement of Using the "Maximum of Available Resources" for Human Rights Realisation: A Question of Quality as Well as Quantity?' (2012) Human Rights Law Review 12(3) 393–420, 405–10.

[80] ibid, 412. [81] ibid, 408.

the rights in the Covenant. At first sight, international assistance and co-operation might seem to refer primarily to aid and technical assistance. Sepúlveda instead helpfully examines the nature of the duty on developed countries through the prism of the three-fold characterization of duties: to respect, protect, and fulfil.[82] The duty to respect—that is to avoid measures which hinder or obstruct socio-economic rights in another State—can be surprisingly far-reaching. For example, States should avoid participation in decision-making in international financial institutions which obstruct or hinder rights. They should also avoid interfering with basic socio-economic rights such as the right to education and health, when imposing conditions when granting aid. The duty to protect can be similarly wide-reaching, requiring the State to regulate corporations to prevent them from interfering with socio-economic rights in third countries in which they operate, and to ensure that trade liberalization measures respect such rights, especially fair conditions at work. Finally, the duty to fulfil requires developed States to facilitate and promote as well as to provide. Both aid and financial investment should be required to advance the rule of law and democracy and promote and fulfil socio-economic rights.

The introduction of an individual and collective complaints procedure under the Optional Protocol to ICESCR raises the interesting possibility of adjudicating on violations of the duty of international assistance and co-operation, explored too by Sepúlveda.[83] This would require a clearer specification of the duty than we have seen so far. Notably, however, an individual cannot claim that another State has failed to co-operate: Article 2 only allows individuals to bring a complaint in relation to her State. Also challenging is the need to establish a causal link between harm to the individual complainant, the alleged violation, and the State's failure to co-operate. This is particularly difficult as there is no definitive framework for assessing when a State is required to seek or provide co-operation and assistance. The Sustainable Development Goals (SDG-17) call on States to strengthen the means of implementation and revitalize the global partnership for sustainable development. Coupled with the increasing recognition that gross violations of socio-economic rights are not captured by a traditional State-centred lens, it is imperative that human rights mechanisms evolve to hold States accountable for a duty of co-operation and assistance.[84]

V. Conclusion

Despite important progress, the commitment to indivisibility of human rights is still only partially realized. A thoroughgoing acceptance of socio-economic rights requires more than just the label of 'human right'. It also entails a re-characterization of the values behind human rights, and in particular of the relationship between the individual, the community, and the State, which emphasizes inter-connectedness and

[82] M Sepúlveda Carmona, 'The Obligations of "International Assistance and Cooperation" under the International Covenant on Economic, Social and Cultural Rights. A Possible Entry Point to a Human Rights Based Approach to Millennium Development Goal 8' (2009) International Journal of Human Rights 13(1) 86–109.

[83] ibid.

[84] M Campbell, *Women, Poverty, Equality: The Role of CEDAW* (Hart 2018) 130–33.

mutual dependence. The familiar values of freedom and dignity need to be refashioned to ensure that individuals have genuine and feasible choices, which in turn requires the State to make sure that everyone has the basic means of subsistence and a range of valuable options. This is allied with a substantive conception of equality; and a commitment to deliberative democracy, which stresses deliberative participation within a framework of shared values.

Nevertheless, there remain many challenges. It is now generally accepted that all rights give rise to a cluster of duties: to respect, protect, and fulfil. As the above discussion has shown, it is the duty to fulfil which is most challenging, especially when explicitly framed as a duty of progressive realization subject to maximum available resources. The many debates as to how to specify a minimum core remain largely unresolved, but a great deal of constructive work has been done on indicators and benchmarks, particularly in the field of the right to health.[85] Equally, more attention is being paid on how to approach the question of the appropriate deployment of resources, especially through budgeting processes. Ultimately, however, the experience of recent decades has shown that specifying the duty should not aim for a definitive answer. Instead, it is an iterative process, which requires collaboration and participation of a variety of different institutions and civil society actors, within a framework of accountability, transparency, non-discrimination, and purpose-oriented planning.

This too casts important light on the role of courts. Difficulties arise when socio-economic rights are regarded as giving rise to entitlements to specific objects, with distributive implications which risk inequitable outcomes for those not appearing before the court. Instead, rights should be regarded as structuring relationships to mitigate imbalances of power, triggering duties to act rather than entitlements to particular benefits. As will be argued in Chapter 4, courts contribute to the iterative process of specifying the right by demanding a deliberative justification for a State's actions or inactions in progressively realizing a right, thereby strengthening democratic accountability. But courts are one actor in a wider set of democratic participatory structures. As Karl Klare concludes:

> Numerous jurisdictions around the world are engaged in remarkable experimentation to develop flexible and nuanced technologies of judicial review responsive to new thinking about self-governance and self-determination and designed to encourage public engagement and social dialogue ... Despite imperfections, [socio-economic rights] enforcement offers a promising arena for social justice struggle in the context of a broad project to reimagine democracy and distributive justice.[86]

[85] See the report of the UN Special Rapporteur on the right of everyone to the enjoyment of the highest attainable standard of physical and mental health UN Doc E/CN.4/2006/48 (2006).

[86] K Klare, 'Critical Perspectives on Social and Economic Rights, Democracy and Separation of Powers' in H Alviar Garcia, K Klare, and L Williams (eds), *Social and Economic Rights in Theory and Practice: Critical Inquiries* (Routledge 2015) 3–22.

4

Allies or Subversives? Adjudication and Democracy

I. Introduction

There are many who have no difficulty with human rights from a moral perspective. However, they argue that human rights should not be the responsibility of courts, but of the political process. Courts, it is argued, are unaccountable and unelected, and therefore should not have the right to overturn decisions of the democratically elected legislature. Given that the State is accountable to the electorate, the nature and extent of intervention in society by the State should be determined by political processes and not human rights pre-commitments in legal instruments.

The principle that in a democracy it is for the people to decide fundamental issues is an immediately appealing one. On the other hand, unconstrained decision-making by elected representatives may invade the basic human rights of individuals and minorities. Majority voting may even be used to disenfranchise individuals or groups. Instead, it could be argued that the chief rationale of human rights law is to function as a counter-majoritarian force and that democracy is more than majoritarianism. But this assumes that courts can be trusted with this task. Who will police the police?

This chapter examines the apparent paradox behind justiciable human rights. If it is entirely left to elected representatives to interpret and apply human rights on the basis of majority voting, perpetual minorities may be perpetually subordinated. But leaving judges to make the final decision flies in the face of the basic principle that all fundamental decisions in society should be taken by the people themselves. The question is whether we can create a role for justiciable human rights which reinforces democracy rather than detracts from it. Section II considers the democratic objections to justiciable human rights, and some of the responses. Section III examines ways in which the role of courts could be reconciled with democracy. It considers three possible approaches: representation-reinforcing; dialogic theories; and deliberative theories. These two sections deal with the issue from the perspective of judicial legitimacy. Section IV considers objections based on lack of judicial competence to address complex, often polycentric issues raised by human rights. Using the example of India's public interest litigation, it examines ways in which the court structure might be adapted to address these concerns. Finally, section V takes a very brief look at remedies and implementation.

II. The Democratic Objection and Its Responses

A. The democratic objection

Perhaps the most cogent articulation of the democratic objection is that put forward by Jeremy Waldron. For Waldron, the right to participate on equal terms in social decisions is the most fundamental right, the right of all rights. It is not sufficient to afford the right of participation to decisions in relation to interstitial matters of social and economic policy. The crucial role of the right to participate should extend to all issues of high principle, and especially those addressed by human rights.[1] Giving judges the power to decide the content of human rights, on this view, entails a profound disrespect for people in their democratic and representative capacities. It implies that any conception of human rights and their content 'concocted by elected legislators next year or in ten years' time is so likely to be wrong-headed or ill-motivated that [the judge's] conception should be elevated immediately beyond the reach of ordinary legislative revision'.[2] To the contrary, Waldron maintains, the reasons why we think of individuals as bearers of rights are the very reasons why we should trust them as the bearer of political responsibilities.[3] There is no reason why a decision by a majority of nine judges should be given more weight than a decision by a majority of the electorate.[4] This objection is particularly strong in relation to socio-economic rights, or other rights giving rise to positive duties. Distributive decisions about allocation of resources or other social benefits, it is argued, are quintessentially for legislatures and the executive. Giving courts powers to adjudicate such rights, on this view, unacceptably infringes on constitutional separation of powers.

B. Responding to the democratic objection

Waldron's approach is based on two assumptions. The first is that justiciability means that judges have the last word on the matter. The second is that the right of participation is alive and well in the political system. It is argued here that re-examining both these premises makes it possible to fashion a role for judges which augments and reinforces democratic participation rather than undermining it.

1. *The judicial role*

The first assumption behind Waldron's democratic objection to human rights is that justiciability gives judges a non-revisable power, or the last word. But this generalizes from the US constitutional model,[5] according to which the Supreme Court can strike down decisions of the legislature on the basis of an interpretation of a broad, open-textured document formulated centuries earlier. However, human rights can be justiciable in a meaningful way without judges having the last word. This has been achieved in various ways in different jurisdictions. One way is to allow Parliament to override

[1] J Waldron, *Law and Disagreement* (OUP 1999) 213 (hereafter Waldron, *Law and Disagreement*).
[2] ibid, 222. [3] ibid, 251. [4] ibid, 15. [5] ibid, 213.

judicial strike-down of legislation. This is the approach taken in the Canadian Charter of Rights and Freedoms. Although Canadian courts have the power to strike down legislation, section 33 of the Charter states that Parliament may expressly declare that an Act of Parliament or one of its provisions will operate notwithstanding the Charter. Such a declaration must be renewed every five years. Although rarely used, this provision was invoked in 2017 by the Saskatchewan legislature to override a judicial decision striking down legislation.[6] A much more auxiliary role for the courts is found in New Zealand. Under the New Zealand Bill of Rights Act 1990, judges merely have an interpretive power. Thus, courts are required to prefer any interpretation of an enactment which is consistent with the rights and freedoms contained in the Bill.[7] If there is no such interpretation, the courts do not have the power to strike down legislation which is incompatible with the Bill.

The UK Human Rights Act 1998 (HRA) establishes a different relationship. Under the HRA, judges do not have the power to override legislation; but nor are they limited to an interpretive role. Instead, judges faced with a successful human rights challenge to legislation can do one of two things. They can interpret the legislation so far as possible to comply with the courts' understanding of the right at issue,[8] in which case the amended legislation may be repealed or further amended by Parliament. This is stronger than the New Zealand courts' interpretive power, because of the reference to 'as far as possible' rather than the usual interpretive approaches. Alternatively, they can issue a declaration of incompatibility.[9] Such a declaration does not itself alter the law but gives a powerful signal to the legislature that the law ought to be altered. This shows how adjudication can be seen as feeding into the political process, while leaving the ultimate decision-making power to the democratically elected representatives. By making a declaration of incompatibility, the courts can reopen the political debate, as well as enriching it by the insights uniquely generated through the process of judicial deliberation. In this sense, as Lord Scott recognized,[10] the import of the declaration of incompatibility is political, not legal. There are those who have argued that legislatures would find it so difficult to gainsay the court that this amounts to a power of veto. However, this misunderstands the difference between legally binding decisions and those which enter the political process as a factor, albeit weighty, which legislators consider. The HRA operates as an input into the political process, not as a point of closure. This expands rather than contracts democratic participation.

Even where judges do in principle have the power to strike down legislation, this does not generally mean, as Waldron suggests, that the decision is permanent and non-revisable. As a start, not all constitutions are as difficult to amend as the US Constitution. For example, the Indian Constitution was amended by Parliament after a series of early cases in which the Indian Supreme Court struck down social legislation in the name of

[6] *Good Spirit School Division No 204 v Christ the Teacher Roman Catholic Separate School Division No 212 and The Government of Saskatchewan*, 2017 SKQB 109 (Court of Queen's Bench for Saskatchewan); M Campbell, 'Reigniting the Dialogue: The Latest Use of the Notwithstanding Clause in Canada: *Good Spirit School Division v Christ the Teacher Roman Catholic Separate School Division No. 212 and The Government of Saskatchewan*' (2018) Jan *Public Law* 1.

[7] New Zealand Bill of Rights Act 1990, s 6. [8] HRA 1998, s 3. [9] HRA 1998, s 4.

[10] *A v Secretary of State for the Home Department* [2004] UKHL 56 (UK Supreme Court) 143.

the right to property.[11] Although the Court reasserted jurisdiction so that the 'basic structure' of the Constitution could not be amended, the possibility of legislative override nevertheless acted as a constraint on the Court.[12] In other contexts, courts have revised their interpretations according to changing contexts and different arguments put before them. In any event, judges, conscious of their position relative to accountable decision-makers, have often been quick to carve out areas of autonomy for decision-makers. As we will see in subsequent chapters, there are many strong judicial statements deferring to democratic decision-making. In addition, concepts such as 'reasonableness' permit ongoing interaction between judges and elected officials even in the context of a binding constitution.

2. *Participation in the democratic sphere*

The second assumption behind Waldron's democratic objection to human rights adjudication is that the right of participation is alive and well in the political system. But in what sense can it be said that democracy means decision-making by the people? The concept of participation in democracy is a complex topic for political theory, and there have been many ways in which democracy has been described and defended. It is worth having a quick glance at these, if only to reveal the complexities behind bland references to democracy and participation by judges and opponents of justiciable human rights.

At first sight, the closest to the ideal behind Waldron's participative right is the model of direct democracy, derived from the Athenian paradigm, according to which all decisions are directly made by the people, through a majority vote. However, although there is sporadic use of referenda to decide important issues, no one would nowadays consider this to be a feasible approach for all decision-making. Apart from its impracticality, it could be asked whether it is appropriate to have decision-making by the people with no rights-based constraints. Critics dating as far back as Plato and Aristotle argued that decision-making by the demos is undesirable without further constraints, since the crowd is easily swayed by the passion of the moment, manipulated by opinion-formers and lacking the expertise necessary to make consistent and sustained decisions.[13] Illustrations from ancient Greece to fascist Germany support this view, and this critique has a strikingly modern hue. As MacLennan puts it, '[C]lassical democratic theory never did provide a utopian scenario in which equal citizens actively, knowledgeably and collectively decide upon the rational course of action for their society'.[14]

The modern State in any event necessarily requires representative government. So how much real participative power does modern democracy give individuals? On one view, the reality of modern democracy is that casting a vote in periodic elections gives

[11] *State of Madras v Champakam Dorairajan* AIR 1951 SC 226 (Indian Supreme Court).

[12] *Golaknath v State of Punjab* AIR 1967 SC 1643 (Indian Supreme Court); *Kesavananda Bharati v State of Kerala* (1973) 4 SCC 225 (Indian Supreme Court).

[13] See Plato, *The Republic* (Penguin 1974) 282; D Held, 'Central Perspectives on the Modern State' in G McLennan, D Held, and S Hall (eds), *The Idea of the Modern State* (Open University Press 1984) 19–27.

[14] G McLennan, 'Capitalist State or Democratic Polity?' in McLennan, Held and Hall (eds), ibid, 82.

barely any real participative power to individual voters. Instead, Schumpeter argues, democracy is better viewed as a process of elite teams seeking popular endorsement by any means at their disposal.[15] Power is exercised by a coalition of elites, with relative autonomy of decision-making between elections. Participation of ordinary people is necessarily tenuous, and even accountability is attenuated, since 'popular opinion' is as much shaped by political representatives as a response to it. The voices of the media, big business, and other powerful bodies drown out that of ordinary people.

One potential alternative to Schumpeter's avowedly pessimistic view of the possibility of participation is that of political pluralists.[16] Pluralists agree that individuals on their own cannot exercise real power in modern democracies. Nevertheless, individuals can effectively augment their power and achieve real political participation by combining into interest groups. Democracy is characterized as a process of negotiation and contest between organized interest groups for power. It is democratic in that any group should be able to protect itself by entering into the give-and-take of the political marketplace. Oligarchy and rule by elite is avoided because alliances are continually reconfigured, ensuring that power is not concentrated for too long in any particular set of elites.

Political pluralism assumes that individuals have the capacity to organize around common interests, and if they are so organized, that different interest groups have equal access to the pluralist political marketplace. However, the tendency to reinforce concentrations of power and inequalities among various competing groups is now readily acknowledged.[17] Even when blatant exclusionary practices are not in place, it is clear that, as Rawls acknowledged, social and economic inequalities in a modern democratic State are so large that those with greater wealth and position usually control political life and enact legislation and social policies that advance their interests.[18] Concentrations of wealth and power inevitably skew the decision-making process in favour of interest groups made up of those with power in society. It is a short distance between this and Schumpeter's description of rule by elites. For a pluralist model to be democratic, the background requirements for fair bargaining require that all parties should have equal opportunities to influence each other. It is precisely here that human rights, enforced by a body outside of the political process, are required. TH Marshall's approach takes this further and argues that political citizenship is not sufficient. To ensure full and democratic citizenship, it is necessary to go beyond liberal and political rights, to the granting of social rights.[19]

A different, more frankly normative approach is that of deliberative democracy. Deliberative democrats argue that not all political co-operation should be based on interest bargaining, where the outcome depends on relative economic, material, political, or numerical strength. Habermas distinguishes between 'interest-governed' and

[15] J Schumpeter, 'Two Concepts of Democracy' in A Quinton (ed), *Political Philosophy* (OUP 1967) 153–88.

[16] D Held, *Models of Democracy* (3rd edn, Stanford University Press 2006) 158–85.

[17] JH Ely, *Democracy and Distrust: A Theory of Judicial Review* (Harvard University Press 1980) 135.

[18] J Rawls, *Justice as Fairness* (Harvard University Press 2001) 148–50.

[19] TH Marshall, 'Citizenship and Social Class' in TH Marshall and T Bottomore (eds), *Citizenship and Social Class* (Pluto 1992) 7.

'value-oriented' co-ordination. Interest bargaining is communication for the purpose of forcing or inducing the opponent to accept one's claim. Success depends on factual power rather than on good reasons or the power of the better argument. Interest bargaining presupposes that each person's or group's interests are fixed and unchangeable; and the solution is either victory, surrender, or compromise. This contrasts with co-ordination based on values. Instead of factual power, such co-ordination is based on the ability to adduce reasons which can convince all the parties. The parties enter the process aiming to justify their position by appeal to reasons that all parties can accept, and willing to be persuaded by arguments put forward by other parties. In place of defeat or victory, therefore, co-ordination takes place through rationally motivated consensus.[20]

The desire to increase the role of value co-ordination relative to interest bargaining in modern democracies is reflected in the recent surge of interest in deliberative democracy. Democratic decision-making, on this view, is a situation in which citizens 'share a commitment to the resolution of problems of collective choice through public reasoning'.[21] Deliberative democracy contests the assumption that preferences are fully formed prior to the political process. Arguing that preferences are heavily influenced by social circumstances, theorists in this school conclude that the process of decision-making can itself play a central part in shaping those premises. This in turn means that initial preferences may be revised in the course of deliberation in a way which encompasses not only one's own perspective, but also those of other members of an association. Deliberation enables participants to see the extent to which their preferences are adaptations to their own limited circumstances.[22]

Nor is the aim of the process simply to reach a compromise or to aggregate those preferences. Instead, the aim is to arrive at a decision which is capable of being justified by reasons which participants sincerely expect to be persuasive to others. Attempting to justify a position by resorting to self-interest alone is unlikely to be successful. In addition, taking the deliberative commitment seriously requires a willingness to revise one's own preferences and convictions.[23] This is particularly true for preferences which a participant discovers cannot be justified. The result is to open up the possibility of resolving disagreements by reasoned persuasion. Moving from a bargaining model to a deliberative model therefore requires a substitution of interest-governed action by value-oriented action. Particularly important is the function of disciplining political representatives, by requiring them to justify decisions by reference to the public interest, not to preferences (their own or voters') which could be distorted or self-seeking.[24] At the same time, deliberative democracy is postulated as being a pluralistic association, whose members have diverse preferences, convictions, and ideals. Apart from sharing a commitment to deliberative democracy itself, participants need

[20] J Habermas, *Between Facts and Norms* (Polity Press 1997) 139–40, 165.

[21] J Cohen, 'Deliberation and Democratic Legitimacy' in A Hamlin and P Pettit (eds), *The Good Polity* (Blackwell 1989).

[22] ibid, 27. [23] ibid, 25–26.

[24] CR Sunstein, 'Beyond the Republican Revival' (1998) 9 Yale L J 1539.

not share a conception of the good.[25] This in turn necessitates explicit discussion of what values should be the basis of community aspirations.[26]

The deliberative democracy approach is not without its difficulties, both in principle and in practice. In particular, it is difficult to see how consensus can always be achieved through deliberation, and at what point closure is declared. One way forward is to use Sunstein's notion of incompletely theorized agreements, discussed in Chapter 2. As will be recalled, Sunstein argues that people might disagree at one level of abstraction but agree on a more particular application. This allows agreement on outcomes without agreeing on the most general theory that accounts for it.[27] Incompletely theorized agreement modifies deliberative democracy to the extent that, in putting forward their reasons, participants are not aiming to convince others of the soundness of their reasons, but only of their plausibility, so that the background value of mutual respect permits agreement to be reached.

Even in this form, however, it is clearly unrealistic to expect that all decision-making satisfies the criteria of deliberative democracy. Instead, the insights of deliberative democracy could be used to fulfil the more partial function of acting as a discipline on decision-makers. Deliberative democracy requires decision-makers to justify their decisions by reference to reasons that all can regard as sound, even if they cannot command a consensus.[28] At the same time, deliberative procedures will always co-exist alongside interest bargaining. Habermas concedes that in complex societies it is often the case that interests are sufficiently diverse that consensus is not possible.[29] In such cases, resort must be had either to majority voting or to bargaining between success-oriented parties who are willing to co-operate. Similarly, Sunstein describes the legislative process as a continuum, at one pole of which interest group pressures are determinative, while at the other end, legislators engage in deliberation in which interest group pressures play little or no role. Along the continuum, outcomes depend on an amalgam of pressure, deliberation, and other factors.[30] Even for those decisions in which interest bargaining is unavoidable, deliberative procedures are necessary to ensure that all interested parties are provided with equal opportunities to influence one another.[31]

In any event, as with other models of democracy, deliberative democracy requires background rights to function. To secure the conditions for effective exercise of deliberative democracy, participants must be both formally and substantively equal. This in turn means that the distribution of power and resources should not obstruct their chances to contribute to deliberation.[32] To the extent that deliberative democracy is thought to be desirable, there is a clear role for human rights duties to facilitate deliberation and thereby both to reinforce existing deliberative democratic arenas and to channel decision-making away from interest bargaining towards deliberation.

The above has discussed participation in democracy in what Held calls its 'protective' sense, that is, aiming to prevent domination by a single group or ruler. Recently, there

[25] Cohen (n 21) 23. [26] ibid, 24.
[27] CR Sunstein, *Designing Democracy: What Constitutions Do* (OUP 2001) 50–65.
[28] Sunstein (n 24). [29] Habermas (n 20) 166.
[30] CR Sunstein, 'Interest Groups in American Public Law' (1985) 38 Stanford Law Review 29, 48–49.
[31] Habermas (n 20) 166. [32] Cohen (n 21) 23.

has been a renewed focus on democracy from a 'developmental' perspective, where participation is not just a means to an end but is part of the self-fulfilment of citizens. This has reawakened interest in the developmental perspective of the republican tradition, which regards rule by the people as the fulfilling of civic virtue through taking part in the activities of the State. On a developmental view, the key aim of participation is to revitalize the public sphere,[33] reversing the trend towards, in Arendt's words, the drab 'substitution of [politics by] bureaucracy, the rule of nobody, for personal rulership'.[34] Freedom is not the same as licence; freedom consists as much in not dominating others as in not being subject to others.

III. Adjudication as Democratic: Legitimacy and the Role of Courts

The discussion above has revealed that, whatever model of political participation we subscribe to, it cannot be taken for granted that individuals have a real possibility of participation. Nevertheless, opponents of justiciability insist that if the political system is defective in the extent to which ordinary people participate, the answer is to improve the political system rather than taking away more power from the people and giving it to the courts. But is this a false dichotomy? Can human rights litigation in fact reinforce democracy? The above discussion has shown that modern democracies are a complex amalgam of individual representation, interest-group bargaining, and deliberative procedures. For these to function well, there is a need to ensure background human rights. Moreover, it is not clear why participation should be confined to the political process. Courts adjudicating on human rights might be both an arena for participation and a means to underpin participation in the political process. However, this requires closer attention to the converse questions: how to achieve judicial accountability, and how to address limitations in judicial competence. This section deals first with the question of judicial legitimacy, while section IV addresses judicial competence.

There have been numerous attempts to demarcate the legitimate role of courts as against the role of policy-makers or legislators. Some distinguish between 'law' and 'policy'. Some draw the lines on the basis of 'justiciability', 'deference', or 'comity'. Others simply rely on judges' good sense, on a case-by-case basis. The most promising way out of this dilemma is to move away from a polarization between courts and legislatures, and instead regard both as contributing to a democratic resolution of human rights disputes. This section deals with three potentially promising approaches: one drawing on the notion of adjudication as reinforcing representation of under-represented groups; one based on dialogue between courts and legislatures; and one on deliberative democracy. The analysis is brief but intended as a pointer towards ways of analysing the comparative jurisprudence in forthcoming chapters.

[33] Habermas (n 20) 300.

[34] H Arendt, *The Human Condition* (2nd edn, University of Chicago Press 1998) 45.

A. The representation-reinforcing theory

The 'representation-reinforcing' theory[35] builds in human rights to a pluralist model by arguing that the function of judicial review is to correct the defects in pluralism.[36] When minorities are excluded from the political process, or their voice is systematically silenced, representative democracy is not functioning properly. It is here that judicial review comes into its own. On this view, the role of the judiciary is to remedy this deficit, and it is this which gives the judicial function its legitimacy. The representation-reinforcing theory originates in the famous *Carolene Products* case, in which the Supreme Court of the United States noted that judges should scrutinize particularly carefully laws which, inter alia, restrict 'those political processes which can ordinarily be expected to bring about repeal of undesirable legislation'; laws 'directed at particular religious ... or national ... or racial minorities'; or laws reflecting 'prejudice against discrete and insular minorities'.[37] Taking his cue from the *Caroline Products* case, John Hart Ely has argued that judicial review can make it possible for representative democracy to function properly by creating procedural means to free up the process of representation, and make sure that all are in fact accorded equal regard and respect. By demarcating the judicial role as 'representation-reinforcing', courts can be harnessed to buttress democracy without overstepping their legitimate bounds.

Ely recognizes that, left to its own devices, interest-group bargaining favours the powerful, so that some groups are permanently excluded from the possibility of sharing power. This constitutes a serious malfunction in the process of democracy. In his words, this occurs when: '(1) the ins are choking off the channels of political change to ensure that they will stay in and the outs will stay out or (2) though no-one is actually denied a voice or a vote, representatives beholden to an effective majority are systematically disadvantaging some minority out of simple hostility or a prejudiced refusal to recognize commonalities of interest and thereby denying that minority the protection afforded other groups by a representative system'.[38] It is precisely in this context that judicial review is legitimate.

The representation-reinforcing theory is valuable in that it sees justiciable human rights as enhancing democracy rather than detracting from it. However, in the form Ely presents it, it is subject to several drawbacks. As a start, it is limited by his assumption that judicial review is only legitimate if it is value neutral or impartial. For Ely, it remains fundamental to representative democracy that 'value determinations are to be made by our elected representatives, and if in fact most of us disapprove, we can vote them out of office'. This leads him to argue that the representation-reinforcing function is only a procedural rather than a substantive one. Judicial review should be aimed at freeing up the process of representation, but not at dictating any particular outcome, since the latter would constitute an illegitimate usurpation of the function of democratic decision-makers. This is particularly so in respect of distributive justice.

[35] This section is taken from S Fredman, *Human Rights Transformed: Positive Rights and Positive Duties* (OUP 2008).
[36] Ely (n 17).
[37] *United States v Carolene Products Co* 304 US 144 (1938) (US Supreme Court).
[38] Ely (n 17) 103.

Ely argues that the only concern of judicial review in the context of distributive justice should be to ensure that the procedure whereby benefits and burdens are distributed is fully representative. The actual distribution should remain with the political process. 'Benefits—goods, rights, exemptions or whatever—that are not essential to political participation or explicitly guaranteed by the language of the constitution, ... we can call constitutionally gratuitous—though obviously they may be terribly important—and malfunction in their distribution can intelligibly inhere only in the process that effected it'.[39]

However, the distribution of resources may themselves be key to the possibility of effective participation in politics and society more generally. If judicial review is to play a genuine role in reinforcing representation, the distribution of benefits must be seen as essential to political participation and not left entirely to the political process. This demonstrates that for judicial review to be legitimate in a democratic sense, it is neither possible nor necessary to sterilize its role of all evaluative content. Human rights represent a value pre-commitment to which society as a whole is bound; and judicial review should reflect that. Indeed, democracy itself is one of the values to which human rights are committed. This does not, of course, mean that all values are legitimate for judicial determination. It is only those specific values which promote democracy that are within the range of judicial legitimacy.

Ely's theory is also limited by the model of pluralism on which it is based. In order to distinguish between minorities who are systematically excluded and those who are simply the transient losers in any majority voting system, Ely argues that the representation-reinforcing function of judicial review is specifically aimed at 'discrete and insular minorities'. Drawing on *Carolene Products*,[40] Ely argues that it is 'discrete and insular minorities' who are thus 'barred from the pluralist's bazaar ... for reasons that are in some sense discreditable'[41] and to 'whose needs and wishes elected officials have no apparent interest in attending'.[42] This assumes that all groups are able to organize around common interests and thereby achieve an effective bargaining position. Deficiencies in representation are also characterized as group based. However, as Ackermann shows, those who are in fact least likely to succeed in the 'pluralists' bazaar' are those who are neither discrete nor insular. It is precisely because they are diffuse that certain groups find it difficult or impossible to organize themselves sufficiently to compete. Those who have the least access to resources are possibly the most diffuse, and it is they who should have the greatest claim to judicial concern with the fairness of the political process.[43] As Ackerman concludes, once the focus on interest groups is undermined, it becomes evident that it is not truly possible to 'perfect the pluralist process of democracy'.[44]

Nor is Ely's theory capable of taking us beyond the pluralist characterization of democracy as consisting of no more than interest bargaining. Interest bargaining is clearly an important part of decision-making in a democracy; but if it is the only form of co-ordination, then those without factual power will never have their

[39] ibid, 136. [40] *United States v Carolene Products Co* (n 37). [41] Ely (n 17) 152.
[42] ibid, 151. [43] B Ackerman, 'Beyond Carolene Products' [1985] 98 Harv L Rev 713, 718.
[44] ibid, 741.

interests given appropriate weight. In addition, the characterization of decision-making as entirely interest governed gives no weight to the collective values or aspirations which transcend interest group accommodation. Nor is there a principled yardstick by which judges can correct the imbalance in interest bargaining, since by definition it depends on the power of the parties. Instead, if there is to be a real commitment to equality in decision-making, justiciable duties must be based on substantive values, principles which 'pluralist politicians are simply not allowed to bargain over'.[45]

Representation-reinforcing theories are also ambiguous as to how exclusion from democratic decision-making should be addressed. Should minorities be given a voice, or should they be allowed to win the argument? The first option requires the majority to take excluded groups' interests into account ('virtual representation' in Ely's sense). But this could mean no more than that the majority, having considered minority interests, reaches the same decision. The second option in effect permits the judiciary to withdraw the issue wholly from democratic decision-making.[46] But this may risk subverting democracy.

Nevertheless, the representation-reinforcing approach is an essential element in the potential of the courts to contribute to democracy. The difficulties with Ely's approach can be avoided in two ways. The first is to move beyond the attempt at neutrality inherent in his focus on procedure. Instead, it is necessary openly to endorse the substantive value of equality in protecting minorities. As Baroness Hale has emphasized in the British House of Lords: 'It is a purpose of all human rights instruments to secure the protection of the essential rights of members of minority groups, even when they are unpopular with the majority. Democracy values everyone equally even if the majority does not'.[47] Equality also serves democracy generally: in the famous words of Justice Jackson of the US Supreme Court:

> There is no more effective practical guarantee against arbitrary and unreasonable government than to require that the principles of law which officials would impose upon a minority must be imposed generally ... Courts can take no better measure to assure that laws will be just than to require that laws be equal in operation.[48]

The second is to move beyond his attempt to perfect the pluralist approach to a recognition that interest bargaining will always reflect inequalities of power.[49] Instead, the role of the court could be characterized as augmenting deliberative democracy. This possibility is expanded below.

[45] Ackermann (n 43) 741.

[46] WN Eskridge, 'Pluralism and Distrust: How Courts Can Support Democracy by Lowering the Stakes of Politics' (2005) 114 Yale L J 101–49.

[47] *Ghaidan v Godin-Mendoza* [2004] UKHL 30 (UK Supreme Court) 132; and see also *A v Secretary of State for the Home Department* (n 10) 108, 237; and *West Virginia State Board of Education v Barnette* 319 US 624 (1943) (US Supreme Court) 3.

[48] *Railway Express Agency Inc v New York* 336 US 106 (1949) (US Supreme Court) 112–13.

[49] D Held, *Models of Democracy* (Polity Press 1987) 186–220.

B. Dialogue theory

The second theory of the role of justiciable human rights focuses on the potential of courts to participate in a dialogue with governments so that human rights concerns can be addressed by legislatures while still achieving the original purposes the latter aimed to achieve. In this way, the risk that courts cut across democratic outcomes is averted, while at the same time protecting human rights. The dialogic approach originated in a highly influential article by Hogg and Bushell,[50] who argued that the record of decisions under the Canadian Charter demonstrated that judges did not in fact have the last word on the matter. Instead, the legislature was generally able to respond to judicial invalidation of legislation in ways that preserved the basic legislative objective. 'While the Charter would often influence the design of legislation that encroached on a guaranteed right', legislatures 'would usually be able to accomplish what they wanted to do while respecting the requirements of the Charter'.[51] Having examined the aftermath of every case in which a law had been declared contrary to the Charter by the Supreme Court of Canada, they found that, of sixty-six cases, all but thirteen had elicited some response from the legislature. In seven cases, the legislation was simply repealed; but in the remaining forty-six, a new law was substituted for the old one. Although the legislature re-enacted the same law in two cases (in effect defying the court), in all the other cases the legislature 'respected the judicial decision by adding some civil libertarian safeguards in the new version of the law, but maintained the legislative purpose'.[52] The result was that, in the Canadian context, judicial review did not mean that judges had the last word.

Although these claims were primarily empirical, they quickly formed the basis for normative arguments in favour of a dialogic model. Thus, Iacobucci J enthusiastically embraced the dialogic model in *Vriend v Alberta*.[53] It also seems apt to describe the HRA, which gives courts the power to issue a declaration of incompatibility but not to strike down legislation, as following a dialogic model.

The dialogic model is an attractive one. Rather than taking the side of either an unadulterated parliamentary sovereignty or a robust judicial supremacy, it characterizes the process of decision-making as collaborative. However, a closer look reveals a deep ambiguity as to the role of the judiciary. Can judges ultimately make authoritative decisions on the meaning of human rights or should they defer the authoritative decision to the legislature? The dialogic approach is compatible with either. Tushnet takes the view that the task of the court should be 'to bring constitutional values … into focus in the legislative forum' but leave the final decision to the legislature.[54] Similarly, for Roach, the courts' expertise in interpreting rights justifies their drawing 'the attention of the legislature to fundamental values that are likely to be ignored or finessed in the legislative process', but not in their attempting to 'end the conversation or conduct a

[50] P Hogg and A Bushell, 'The Charter Dialogue Between Courts and Legislatures (or Perhaps the Charter of Rights Isn't Such a Bad Thing After All)' (1997) 35 Osgoode Hall L J 75.

[51] P Hogg, A Thornton, and W Wright, 'Charter Dialogue Revisited: Or Much Ado about Metaphors' [2007] 45 Osgoode Hall L J 1, 3.

[52] ibid, 4.

[53] *Vriend v Alberta* [1998] 1 SCR 493 (Supreme Court of Canada).

[54] M Tushnet, 'Dialogic Judicial Review' (2009) 61 Ark L Rev 205, 212.

monologue in which [their] ... Charter rulings are the final word'.[55] By contrast, Hogg et al argue that the 'final authority for interpreting the Charter rests properly with the judiciary'.[56] Similarly, Hickman's preferred 'strong form' dialogue reflects a belief that 'courts have a vital constitutional role in protecting fundamental principles from the sway of popular sentiment'.[57] Courts should not simply impose these principles, but work with the executive and legislature in 'evolving them and in fostering their acceptance'. In doing so courts should have the capacity for compromise in the interests of expediency, while at the same time 'insulating fundamental principles even in the face of such compromises'.[58]

C. Bounded deliberative democracy

The third model, described here as 'bounded deliberative democracy', aims to find a role for courts in human rights adjudication which strengthens the deliberative potential of democracy, displacing interest bargaining in the context of human rights.[59] To do so, it draws on Habermas' distinction between 'interest-governed' and 'value-oriented' co-ordination, set out above.[60] While, as we have seen, interest-based bargaining is an inevitable and often an appropriate component of democracy, the possibility of deliberation stands out as an alternative which can transcend inequalities in bargaining power. Most importantly, on this view, human rights should not be addressed on the basis of interest bargaining.[61] If they were, those with superior numerical, political, or financial power might always trump the rights of those without power. The power of the principle must itself be the reason for adopting it, rather than the numbers of those who back it. It is here that courts can potentially fulfil a democratic role. When human rights are at issue, courts should augment democratic participation by steering decision-making away from interest bargaining towards value-oriented deliberation, or indeed, by functioning as a forum for deliberation.

To what extent, then, can courts contribute to a deliberative resolution of human rights issues? At first sight, they are an unlikely option. Adversarial litigation appears to be a paradigm interest-bargaining framework. Litigation is arguably bipolar, retrospective, and sufficiently expensive to serve only elites. However, on closer inspection, it is clear that judicial decision-making is essentially deliberative. It is not the parties' political, numerical, or economic strength that persuades courts, but the strength of their reasoning. Judges are required to come to the process open to the possibility of being persuaded by one side or the other, and the outcome is often a synthesis of the arguments of both sides. Thus, while the primary responsibility for articulating

[55] K Roach, *The Supreme Court on Trial: Judicial Activism or Democratic Dialogue* (Irwin Law Books 2001) 530–31.

[56] Hogg, Thornton, and Wright (n 51) 3.

[57] T Hickman, 'Constitutional Dialogue, Constitutional Theories and the Human Rights Act 1998' (2005) PL 306, 316.

[58] ibid.

[59] For an expanded version of this argument, see Fredman, *Human Rights Transformed* (n 35) ch 4; S Fredman, 'From Dialogue to Deliberation: Human Rights Adjudication and Prisoners' Right to Vote' (2013) PL 292 (hereafter Fredman, 'Dialogue to Deliberation').

[60] Habermas (n 20) 139–41.

[61] Fredman, 'Dialogue to Deliberation' (n 59).

and delivering human rights responsibilities lies with Parliament, decision-makers must be in a position to justify their decisions in a deliberative sense. This builds on Mureinik's influential conception of a 'culture of justification'.[62] Judges are often referred to as 'unelected and unaccountable'. However, accountability means more than removing representatives from power when they fall out of favour with a majority of the electorate. Accountability also means that both elected representatives and judges have the duty to explain and justify their decisions in ways which are capable of convincing. Courts should not prescribe to elected representatives exactly what decisions should be taken, but instead should require them to justify why those decisions have been made in the light of other competing principles. Dyzenhaus argues that this role is inherently democratic: 'What justifies all public power is the ability of its incumbents to offer adequate reasons for the decisions which affect those subject to them ... The courts' special role is as an ultimate enforcement mechanism for such justification'.[63]

Courts are in a position to augment deliberative democracy in human rights adjudication in two complementary ways. First, the court functions as a deliberative forum in its own right. Moreover, the arguments of the parties, as well as both majority and dissenting judgments, feed into the wider deliberative process. Second, courts can steer legislative and executive decision-making away from interest bargaining and towards deliberation. They do this by insisting that decision-makers justify their decisions on the interpretation or limitation of human rights in a deliberative manner. By requiring decision-makers to lay out and substantiate their reasons, with evidence where appropriate, judicial decisions can constitute an incentive for decision-makers to make decisions in a deliberative way even outside of the courtroom. This process can also give greater weight and legitimacy to parliamentary processes such as cross-party select committees, which are also capable of conducting rights-based debates in a deliberative manner. The UK Joint Committee on Human Rights is a particularly good example of such a mechanism.[64]

It could be argued, however, that a deliberative approach is incompatible with the very essence of human rights adjudication. Deliberative models assume an open-ended approach, allowing the process to produce a solution with no preconditions. Thus, Cohen argues that, apart from sharing a commitment to deliberative democracy itself, participants need not share a conception of the good.[65] Human rights, by contrast, require a prior commitment to the observation of human rights. Moreover, court proceedings themselves suggest closure, precluding the possibility of further deliberation. This is precisely why many might oppose judicial intervention.

However, the issue is more complex than this. Human rights pose particularly difficult challenges because they are neither fully determined nor open to thoroughgoing

[62] E Mureinik, 'A Bridge to Where? Introducing the Interim Bill of Rights' (1994) 10 SAJHR at 32; see also D Dyzenhaus, 'Law as Justification: Etienne Mureinik's Conception of Legal Culture' (1998) 14 SAJHR 11.

[63] D Dyzenhaus, 'The Politics of Deference: Judicial Review and Democracy' in M Taggart (ed), *The Province of Administrative Law* (Hart 1997) 305.

[64] See eg *Monitoring the Government's response to court judgments finding breaches of human rights*, Sixteenth report of the House of Commons and House of Lords Joint Committee on Human Rights (HL 128, HC 728, 2006–7).

[65] Cohen (n 21) 23.

deliberative solutions. If they were fully determined, then both courts and legislatures could simply apply formulaic responses. Both institutions would be bound by the same mandatory norms and neither would be superior. However, human rights are open to a range of interpretations in particular contexts. Similarly, the question of whether human rights have justifiably been limited inevitably requires a judgement. On the other hand, human rights are not simply open moral questions. They are based on a consensus which has developed over time and is universally accepted as to what the fundamentals of being human in a political society require. It is within the framework set by this prior deliberative consensus that current decision-making must take place. Thus, human rights place real constraints on both judicial and legislative decision-making, while at the same time being open to interpretation.

It is in this interpretative space that the deliberative approach functions. Human rights decisions should be taken in a deliberative rather than an interest-based mode. The primary deliberative role belongs with the legislature, as Waldron suggests. However, one cannot assume, as Waldron does, that there is necessarily a commitment on the part of most members of the society to the idea of individual and minority rights.[66] There may be a very high-level commitment, for example in the simple fact of having a bill of rights. But it is hard to maintain that all human rights disputes are about good faith disagreements about the meaning of rights, as has been seen in relation to prisoners' voting rights.[67] It is here that courts can make a unique contribution to the democratic resolution of human rights disputes. Courts should enhance the democratic accountability of decision-makers by insisting on a deliberative justification for the interpretation or limitation of rights. Although ideally this should trigger deliberative justification in the legislature itself, whether on the floor of the house or in select committees, courts can also function as a forum of accountability. This is particularly true for decisions taken which affect groups without the political power to influence the decision.

At the same time, courts are not entitled to impose their views on open-ended moral grounds. The deliberative approach is bounded in that it operates within the constraints of human rights, which are themselves a product of prior deliberative consensus. The role of the court is not to exercise a conclusive veto or to prescribe an authoritative interpretation, but nor is justification measured against an open-ended standard of rationality or reasonableness, as in administrative law. Decision-makers must be in a position to persuade the court that they have fulfilled their human rights obligations, account being taken both of the pre-existing deliberative consensus and of the fact that there is room for reasonable disagreement. The model I propose is therefore not one of pure deliberative democracy, but of 'bounded deliberation'.

Waldron regards the fact that courts do not have a mandate to reason in an open-ended moral manner but are bound by a pre-existing legal framework as a reason why they are unsuitable for human rights adjudication. He argues that the institutional setting in which judges act and the role they adopt 'require them to address questions about rights in a particular legalistic way—indeed, in a way that, sometimes, makes it

[66] J Waldron, 'The Core of the Case Against Judicial Review' (2006) 115 Yale L J 1346, 1359.
[67] Fredman, 'Dialogue to Deliberation' (n 59).

harder rather than easier for essential moral questions to be identified and addressed'. He contrasts this with 'legislative approaches, which proceed by identifying all the issues and all the opinions that might be relevant to a decision, rather than artificially limiting them in the way that courts do'.[68] As the debates on prisoners' voting rights show, this idealizes legislative decision-making.[69] Indeed, much relevant evidence and opinion is frequently omitted from legislative consideration. More importantly, it is paradoxical to valorize the output of legislative deliberation while at the same time regarding legal materials as irrelevant to judicial decision-making. A Bill of Rights makes judges more rather than less accountable, because they too have to justify their own decisions against a background of values reached by a process of prior consensus. In this way, a Bill of Rights acts as a mechanism for accountability for both the legislature and the judiciary.

At the same time, the court hearing itself should not be seen as comprising the whole of the participative opportunity. Participation can occur throughout the process, stretching from the decision to file the docket, through the process of preparation, to the hearing, and then to the response. Triggering a deliberative process in the courts might also give individuals a more emphatic voice in the policy field, through re-articulating an aspiration as a right. All of these mechanisms augment the public reasoning regarded by Sen, Michelman, and Klare as central to the legitimacy of constitutionalized socio-economic rights.

The bounded deliberative model retains some of the valuable aspects of Ely's representation-reinforcing theory but addresses some of its difficulties. This is because it moves beyond his attempt to perfect the pluralist approach to a recognition that interest bargaining will always reflect inequalities of power. Pluralist democracy characterizes the political process as one in which groups vie for power to further their own interests, with the majority principle playing an indispensable role in determining whose interests count.[70] Instead, the role of the court, as argued here, should be to augment deliberative democracy. While interest groups will always be unequal, deliberative democracy should foster equality of participation. But this too requires intervention. Not all participants will have the same level of articulacy, nor the same skills in expressing a perspective and convincing others. Not all will even find their way into the deliberative forum. Courts in human rights litigation can only play a legitimate role if they make it possible for even the weakest voice to be heard and give equal persuasive power to all. Thus, Michelman has argued that the Constitutional Court should 'reach for the inclusion of hitherto excluded voices of emergently self-conscious social groups'.[71]

Placing litigation in a deliberative context also resolves the problem of the weight to be given to a minority group. A judicial decision should not necessarily give a veto power to a minority. But neither should it simply require the interests of a weaker group to be considered. Instead, the process of articulating the case and its endorsement by the judiciary amplifies the voice of the minority and annexes to it the authority and

[68] J Waldron, 'Judges as Moral Reasoners' (2009) 7 I.CON 2.
[69] Fredman, 'Dialogue to Deliberation' (n 59). [70] Held (n 16) 186–220.
[71] FI Michelman, 'Law's Republic' (1988) 97 Yale L J 1493, 1529.

persuasiveness of judicial reasoning. This fundamentally changes the political, if not the legal, power of the litigants. As is seen in section IV, the Indian courts have deliberately taken the view that the function of the court is to give a voice to the most disadvantaged. It is in this context that the deliberative model can achieve the primary aim of representation-reinforcing theories.

IV. Judicial Competence: The Challenge of Polycentricity

Even if the democratic concerns are met, many would argue that courts have limited competence. Courts are focused on the dispute before them, and therefore are said to lack the competence to deal with complex social and economic issues. Legitimacy and competence concerns are, of course, closely intertwined. Courts' competence might be able to be adapted to reflect their legitimate sphere of action; and conversely, legitimacy might be tempered by courts' structural limitations. Socio-economic rights are regarded as posing particular challenges, largely because they tend to impose positive duties on States to fulfil such rights rather than simply restraining the State from interfering with rights. As we have seen in Chapter 3, this distinction is misleading. Many civil and political rights impose positive duties on the State, the rights to vote and to a fair trial being two central examples, and courts regularly adjudicate on such issues.[72] Conversely, some socio-economic rights give rise only to duties of restraint. The better view is to regard all rights as giving rise to a cluster of obligations: duties to respect, protect, and fulfil.[73] Nor is it appropriate to see these duties as insulated from one another. A single right can give rise to a nest of obligations. For example, in relation to the right to housing, the negative duty not to evict a person can go hand in hand with the positive right to re-house her. Where housing is privately owned, the right not to be evicted takes the form of a duty on the State to protect. The real challenge for justiciable human rights is not therefore the division between socio-economic rights and civil and political rights, but the need to adjudicate positive duties.

The challenges faced by courts adjudicating social issues with implications well beyond the parties before them are encapsulated by Fuller's notion of 'polycentricity'. In his ground-breaking work, Fuller used the metaphor of a spider's web to describe the concept of polycentricity.

> A pull on one strand will distribute tensions after a complicated pattern throughout the web as a whole. Doubling the original pull will, in all likelihood, not simply double each of the resulting tensions but will rather create a different complicated pattern of tensions ... This is a 'polycentric' situation because it is 'many centred'—each crossing of strands is a distinct centre for distribution tensions.[74]

[72] See eg on prisoners' right to vote: *August v Electoral Commission* (CCT8/99) [1999] ZACC 3 (South African Constitutional Court).

[73] H Shue, *Basic Rights: Subsistence, Affluence, and US Foreign Policy* (2nd edn, Princeton University Press 1996); South African Constitution, s 7; Committee on Economic, Social and Cultural Rights (CESCR), General Comment No 3: The Nature of States Parties Obligations (Fifth Session) (1990) UN Doc E/199123, Annex III.

[74] L Fuller, 'The Forms and Limits of Adjudication' (1978) 92 Harv L Rev 353, 395.

Fuller argued that there are polycentric elements in almost all problems submitted to adjudication, even if only by setting precedents which are then applied in unforeseen situations. The extent to which judges can handle polycentricity is therefore a matter of degree. The challenge this poses for human rights adjudication is to determine when polycentric elements become so significant that the proper limits of adjudication are reached.

On the face of it, courts are particularly maladapted to deal with positive duties when resource implications arise. This is because, under the familiar adversarial procedure, the dispute is bipolar. The court is passive, responding to the case as it is formulated by the two opposing parties before it and dependent on the evidence they have gathered. This is problematic in a polycentric situation, since not all interests are represented, and the court does not have access to information beyond that which concerns the parties before it. Furthermore, the adversarial procedure leads to a win or lose outcome. The court's role is to determine which party has won, and which has lost. Yet polycentric situations require complex trade-offs between different interests. Moreover, the remedy is focused on the individual, and the court is unaware of and unconcerned with the ripple effects it may cause.

However, this assumes a rigid structure of court procedure, based essentially on a private law model of dispute resolution. As Chayes demonstrates, legislation which explicitly modifies and regulates basic social and economic realities challenges the traditional adversarial model of adjudication.[75] He argues that the bipolar structure is particularly inappropriate for public and private interactions which are not bilateral transactions between individuals but have wide social implications. This in turn requires a transformation of the adjudicative structure from what Owen Fiss calls a 'dispute-resolution' model to a model of 'structural reform'.[76] In the dispute-resolution model, the defendant is both the wrongdoer and the provider of a remedy. Moreover, the victim, spokesperson, and beneficiary are automatically combined in one plaintiff. However, in the model of structural reform, the wrongdoer disappears, and instead the focus is on the body able to achieve reform. Equally importantly, the structural model does not require the individual to bear the burden of enforcing her own rights.[77] Structural changes can include wide standing rules; inquisitorial functions for the court; wider rules of evidence and ongoing supervisory remedies. Particularly helpful in the case of polycentric decisions is the possibility of intervenor roles, allowing more interests to be represented and different perspectives articulated.

Probably the most innovative examples of such foundational institutional reform can be found in the Indian Supreme Court's public interest litigation. From the early 1980s, the Indian Supreme Court began initiating institutional changes to give greater accessibility to poor litigants and to adapt the Court better to social rights litigation.[78] Recognizing that deep inequalities in society should not be replicated in relation to access to justice, the Court stated in the seminal case of *Gupta*: 'Where one of the

[75] A Chayes, 'The Role of the Judge in Public Law Litigation' (1976) 89 Harv L Rev 1281.

[76] O Fiss, 'The Forms of Justice' (1979) 93 Harv L Rev 1, 16–28.

[77] See further, S Fredman, 'Breaking the Mold: Equality as a Proactive Duty' (2012) 60 American Journal of Comparative Law 265.

[78] For a full discussion, see Fredman (n 35) ch 5.

parties belongs to a poor and deprived section of the community and does not possess adequate social and material resources, he is bound to be at a disadvantage as against a strong and powerful opponent under the adversary system of justice, because of his difficulty in getting competent legal representation and inability to produce relevant evidence before the Court'.[79] In recognition of the social reality, the Court declared: 'When the poor come before the Court, particularly for enforcement of their fundamental rights, it is necessary to depart from the adversarial procedure and to evolve a new procedure which will make it possible for the poor and the weak to bring the necessary material before the court'.[80]

This recognition has led the Court to initiate radical changes in court procedure, now widely known as 'public interest litigation' or PIL. Insisting that 'only the Anglo-Saxon juridical heritage makes the adversarial system appear sacrosanct', the Court has opened up standing rules so that any member of the public can approach the court on behalf of socio-economically disadvantaged people. Indeed, the Court itself can initiate cases on the basis of information it has itself received. Thus, in a case in Karnataka,[81] the High Court, having read newspaper reports of large numbers of out-of-school children, initiated a case against the State government on their behalf in relation to breach of the right to education. As part of the litigation, the Court required the State government to constitute a high-powered committee, consisting of all State government departments and members of civil society movements, to come up with a plan to bring the out-of-school children back to school.[82] As well as very wide standing rules and court-initiated litigation, the Court takes on itself the responsibility of gathering and testing facts through the appointment of fact-finding Commissioners. In the Karnataka out-of-school case, the first stage of the process required collaborative fact-finding of the scale of the problem and its causes, as well as both producing and implementing a plan to address the problem.

Possibly the most effective and far-reaching case following this procedure was the ground-breaking 'Right to Food' case. Although India has a plethora of food distribution schemes, there was little impetus to implement them until the People's Union of Civil Liberties (PUCL) moved the Court to transform the right to food into a fundamental human right.[83] In 2001, the PUCL filed a public interest writ in the Indian Supreme Court, seeking legal enforcement of the right to food as an aspect of the right to life in Article 21 of the Indian Constitution. The case was prompted by the stark paradox whereby stocks of food accumulated by the Food Corporation of India were overflowing and rotting, while at the same time people were dying of starvation. For example, in the state of Rajasthan, as many as 50 million tons of grain were lying

[79] *PG Gupta v State of Gujarat* (1995) Supp 2 SCC 182 (Indian Supreme Court). [80] ibid.

[81] Writ Petition No 15768/2013.

[82] Jayna Kothari and Gaurav Mukherjee, 'The Out of School Children Case: A Model for Court-Facilitated Dialogue?' (OxHRH Blog, 18 September 2015) <http://ohrh.law.ox.ac.uk/the-out-of-school-children-case-a-model-for-court-facilitated-dialogue/> (accessed 22 January 2018) (hereafter Kothari and Mukherjee, 'Out-of-School Children Case').

[83] The information in this and subsequent paragraphs on the 'Right to Food' case are taken from material on the website of the Right to Food Campaign (<http://www.righttofoodcampaign.in/>) and in particular the booklet 'Supreme Court Orders on the Right to Food, October 2005' <http://www.righttofoodindia.org/orders/interimorders.html> (accessed 22 January 2018) (hereafter *Right to Food*).

unused in government storage, much of it deteriorating beyond use. At the same time, half the rural population in that state were living below the poverty line. As the Court commented:

> In case of famine, there may be shortage of food, but here the situation is that amongst plenty there is scarcity. Plenty of food is available, but distribution of the same amongst the very poor and the destitute is scarce and non-existent leading to mal-nourishment, starvation and other related problems.[84]

The Court affirmed that the right to food was a necessary element of the right to life in Article 21 of the Indian Constitution. Equally importantly, it ordered the Food Corporation of India to ensure that food grains did not go to waste and that the plethora of distribution systems and poverty alleviation programmes be properly administered.[85] Possibly the most far-reaching order was the Court's insistence that the scheme requiring mid-day meals at schools be properly implemented and strengthened by requiring not just a supply of food, but a proper cooked meal.

What is striking about the case is that, instead of abstaining from adjudicating a right with complex polycentric implications, the Court adapted its procedure to address these limitations. In 2002, the Supreme Court adopted the wholly novel measure of appointing two Commissioners to monitor the implementation of the orders. The Commissioners were empowered to enquire into any violations of the interim orders and had the full authority of the Court to demand redress. The role was subsequently broadened to include scrutiny of any aspect of food-related measures and schemes, even if not the object of any specific order. This meant that the Commissioners could analyse data, seek responses from State governments on specific issues, take up complaints from grassroots organizations, and set up committees to verify particular issues. The case was highly unusual too in that, from 2002 until it was discharged in 2013, it progressed through a series of interim orders, many of them consisting of a remedy of interim mandamus addressed to government departments or State governments. This permitted the Court to remain cognizant of the case, to issue further orders requiring monitoring of the previous orders, and to expand the reach of the original case.

Although the work of the Commissioners, assisted by a network of advisors at state level, was not always successful, they did make important strides in implementing food security and distribution programmes. Notably, the Court was not required to design these programmes, which already existed. Instead, the Court's intervention had the effect of transforming policies into fundamental entitlements, which in turn meant it could require them to be implemented reasonably, fairly, and effectively. This was reinforced by the close alliance between the plaintiffs in the case and a large public campaign around the right to food, where activists on the ground were able to rely on the vocabulary of entitlement to demand compliance. The Court's continuing

[84] *People's Union for Civil Liberties v Union of India and Others*, Writ Petition (Civil) 196 of 2001 (Indian Supreme Court).

[85] Human Rights Law Network, 'PUCL v Union of India & Others' <http://www.hrln.org/hrln/right-to-food/pils-a-cases/255-pucl-vs-union-of-india-a-others-.html> (accessed 28 January 2018); see further Fredman (n 35) ch 5.

involvement was both a response to and a catalyst for a well-organized, grass-roots activist campaign of fact-finding, compliance-monitoring, and strategic litigation.[86] In their last major report in 2012, the Commissioners reported that the picture that emerged from most states was encouraging, but still not fully satisfactory. The highest levels of compliance were in respect of the school mid-day meal scheme, where the Supreme Court orders had been backed up by lively campaigns for mid-day meals all over the country.[87] Other programmes had a far poorer implementation record.

On the face of it, the purpose of the litigation was achieved with the passing of the Food Security Act in 2013. The Act's stated aim was to provide food and nutritional security by ensuring adequate quantities of quality food at affordable prices to people 'to live a life with dignity'. Regarding its work as having been completed with the passing of the Act, the Court finally discharged the case in 2013.[88] However, this proved optimistic, and it was not long before the Court's intervention was again needed. This was because of the lack of political commitment, resulting in poor implementation. Most problematic was the failure of states to set up the cornerstone institutional compliance mechanisms, namely State Food Commissions. This prompted further litigation and further Court orders requiring states to do so. As Justice Madhan Lokhur stated in a 2017 petition by Swaraj Abhiyan, almost four years had gone by and the main authorities mandated to operationalize the Act had not been established: 'It is a pity that legislation enacted by Parliament for the benefit of the people should be kept on the backburner by some of the State Governments before us. It was submitted that this apathy is pervasive'.[89] The lack of implementation, he held, is the 'bane of our society'.[90] The Court therefore gave orders for the relevant minister to convene meetings with all concerned secretaries of all state governments and union territories 'to brainstorm over finding ways and means to effectively implement the provisions of the NFS Act in letter and spirit. A law enacted by Parliament as a part of its social justice obligation must be given its due respect and must be implemented faithfully and sincerely and positively before the end of this year'.[91] Further hearings have taken place, the most recent at the time of writing having been in December 2017, to call state governments to account for progress in establishing the relevant commissions.[92]

Similarly, the impact of the Court action in the Karnataka out-of-school case has been largely positive, with the state reporting in 2014 that the absolute number of out-of-school children had dropped by 75 per cent. Kothari and Mukherjee comment that the deliberation facilitated by the Court in this case presented some strategic advantages due to the involvement of stakeholders in the formulation and implementation of the policy. However, they note that it also highlighted the limitations of working with State authorities, in this case manifested as a reluctance to monitor its welfare schemes.[93]

[86] I am indebted to Colin Gonsalves for providing me with a rich perspective on this case.
[87] *Right to Food* (n 83) 18.
[88] *People's Union for Civil Liberties (PDS Matters) v Union of India* (2013) 2 SCC 688.
[89] *Swaraj Abhiyan v Union of India Writ Petition (C) No 857 of 2015*, 21 July 2017 (Indian Supreme Court) 31.
[90] ibid, 42 [91] ibid.
[92] ibid, Interlocutory Application 5 December 2017 (Indian Supreme Court).
[93] Kothari and Mukherjee, 'Out-of-School Children Case' (n 82).

The radical changes in court procedure to address polycentric social problems bring with them their own problems. There are various aspects to these challenges, which I explored in detail in *Human Rights Transformed*.[94] These are briefly recounted below.

A. Litigation as a 'social conversation'

In its early decades of development, the PIL procedure, together with progressive constitutional interpretation, gave the Indian Supreme Court a central role in social transformation on behalf of those who were oppressed and marginalized. As Baxi describes it, a novel conception of judicial power and process developed.

> Adjudication emerges as a form of social conversation among the activist judicial and social/human rights movements ... Social conversation on issues of law, rights and justice is no longer a matter of cultivated discourse by, of and for the professional managerial classes (planners, policymakers, judges, lawpersons and related learned professionals). It now becomes a form of conversation among multitudinous narrative voices.[95]

The notion of litigation as social conversation de-centres the judicial role itself, portraying litigation not as a transfer of hierarchical power to the court but as a trigger for democratic interaction between judges, government actors, and different social and political groups. Groups without a voice in the political process are able to enter into the conversation and shape its outcome. This in turn highlights the role of social groups themselves in setting the litigation agenda, and therefore shaping the pattern of judicial intervention, not just in terms of the issues that come to court, but also in terms of the perspectives through which the judicial conversation is filtered. Of central importance has been the availability within civil society of activist groups and lawyers willing to commit themselves to participating, who work with their constituents, not as charitable benefactors, but as equal partners. The notion of judicial conversation also highlights the need to achieve governmental co-operation. Coercive remedies such as contempt might have a background impact in spurring on action, but judges can only make good the inactivity of government with the compliance of the same government.

While the notion of a social conversation has great potential for a participative model of adjudication, it potentially underestimates the extent to which louder voices can frame the terms of the litigation as well as silencing others. There is always the risk of capture by more articulate and powerful groups, marginalizing the voices of the poorest. This has been clearly seen in more recent decades in India, where middle-class groups, ostensibly furthering environmental causes, have used the PIL mechanism to spur the Court into ordering wholescale removal of poor people from their housing. This is partly because, far from remaining within its original function of serving the poor and disadvantaged who would not otherwise have access to the Court, PIL is now

[94] Fredman (n 35) ch 5.

[95] U Baxi, 'The Avatars of Indian Judicial Activism' in SK Verma and Kusum (eds), *Fifty Years of the Supreme Court of India: Its Grasp and Reach* (OUP 2000) (hereafter Baxi, 'Indian Judicial Activism').

widely available to anyone claiming the public interest. The result is that procedural safeguards are circumvented even when the normal writ procedure would not render the Court inaccessible. Cases contesting the treatment of wild monkeys in Delhi jostle with cases contesting the right of private schools to conduct admissions interviews for very young children. Widening access beyond the original constituency of the poor and disadvantaged has resulted in a crucial change in the perspective from which the case is presented to the Court. Since those who initiate the case have the power to frame the issues for the Court, widening access runs the risk that those who already have political and economic power will drown or even silence the voices of the poor and disadvantaged. In this context, as Baxi puts it, the social conversation easily moves along an 'axis of discursive inequality'.[96]

The power of the litigants to frame the perspective can be illustrated by contrasting cases initiated by slum-dwellers asserting rights to livelihood with those initiated by environmentalists or middle-class property owners asserting rights to a cleaner city. Thus, it was in response to petitions by pavement-dwellers themselves that the Court in the seminal case of *Olga Tellis* articulated the rights of slum-dwellers to livelihood and therefore to remain in the city.[97] The role of the litigants is apparent from the opening paragraphs of the case, which clearly present the petitioners' perspective. The Court not only describes their plight with great sympathy, narrating the conditions of appalling squalor in which they, together with nearly half the population of Bombay, lived; it also stresses their 'respectability': they were in employment and had paid rent (to local slumlords) for their shelters. 'It is these men and women who have come to the Court to ask for a judgement that they cannot be evicted from their squalid shelters without being offered alternative accommodation'. By 1996, when cases were increasingly initiated by environmentalists and middle-class property owners, slum-dwellers were no longer characterized as rights-bearing citizens. In the waste-disposal case of *Almitra*,[98] initiated by a public-interest litigant committed to the improvement of the urban environment, the Court characterized the provision of alternative accommodation as rewarding wrongdoers. According to the Court: 'The promise of free land, at the taxpayers cost, in place of a jhuggi, is a proposal which attracts more land grabbers. Rewarding an encroacher on public land with free alternate site is like giving a reward to a pickpocket'.[99]

From this, it can be seen that although the PIL was originally intended to give access to those who would otherwise not have a voice, it is easily captured by articulate and well-organized interest groups. Indeed, the partial reversal in the Court's attitude to the poor and disadvantaged reflects, at least in part, the change in the character of the public-interest litigant. How then can this dilemma be addressed? One way is through intervenors, who can represent the interests of the poor and disadvantaged regardless of who initiates the case. However, this is an empty promise for those who are insufficiently organized or who do not have the resources to keep in touch with

[96] ibid, 173.

[97] *Olga Tellis v Bombay Municipal Corporation* AIR 1986 SC 180 (Indian Supreme Court), initiated by two pavement-dwellers and a journalist.

[98] *Almitra Patel v Union of India* (16 January 1998) [1998] INSC 35 (Indian Supreme Court).

[99] ibid.

Court developments. More frequently, they will be drawn into the litigation after the original orders have been passed, to redress the implications of judicial intervention to which they suddenly find themselves exposed.[100] Alternatively, the Court itself could raise relevant issues, but this is no substitute for participation. Ultimately, a conversation between equal participants is premised on the ability of the poor and disadvantaged to make themselves heard. This is frequently not the case.

A different approach is through reconsidering what constitutes the public interest and also who can legitimately represent it. Early cases held that standing would not be granted to those pursuing private interests. It is open to state governments to contest the bona fides of PIL petitioners, and they regularly do so, sometimes successfully. Beyond that, however, as the range of litigated cases demonstrates, the definition of public interest is wide and inclusive. Perhaps this is inevitable, given the impossibility of a single public interest in a highly diverse and complex society such as India. This moves the focus onto who can be said to 'represent' the public interest. Baxi argues that the meaning of representation is itself contested. While representation usually entails 'speaking for others', deliberative democracy aims to 'speak with others'. Viewed in this light, for the court to impose criteria of representation might only detract from the ability of PIL to redefine representativity as a conversation between and among co-equal citizens.[101] At the same time, it must be recognized that the conversation between co-equal citizens can only take place if the participants can in reality participate on equal terms. The court also has a role to play in ensuring that the voice of all is actually heard, not just in response to a question already framed but in the framing of the question itself.

These dilemmas are well illustrated in the Narmada dam litigation, where the problems raised by allowing the Court to determine the representativity of the plaintiff are highlighted. In this case, an environmental group brought a PIL to ask the Court to restrain the government from proceeding with the construction of the dam on the Narmada River, which would displace tens of thousands of people. Here the Court refused to accept the petitioner's credentials in representing the weaker sections of society. The petitioner was an organization which had campaigned against the dam largely for environmental reasons, and although this included a concern for the interests of those ousted by the project, the Court did not regard the petitioner as an authentic representative of those interests. Instead, it accepted the government's view that ousted tribals and people of weaker sections would in fact gain from resettlement, since many of them were living as labourers or marginal farmers and would be given a house and land of their own. Indeed, it was contended that opponents of the dam were simply 'playing the card of tribals and weaker sections' on behalf of the land-owning class, who were opposing the project because it would deprive them of cheap labour. In coming to the conclusion that the oustees would in fact be better off as a result of the project, the Court gave no indication that it had made any attempt to find a means

[100] eg an interlocutory order was passed on 5 April 2006 ordering removal of slum dwellers from the Nangla Machi slum in Delhi without hearing the people affected (SP (C) No 3419/1999). The affected people then brought a special petition requesting that they be heard. See *Ram Rattan et al v Commissioner of Police*, Special Petition, 9 May 2006.

[101] U Baxi, oral communication.

whereby these groups could articulate their own position. It was again only in subsequent hearings that these groups were able to articulate their concerns as interveners, and this was only after the Court had allowed construction to proceed *pari passu* with rehabilitation measures.

One possibility is to attempt to confine PIL to those who would not otherwise have a voice, thus returning PIL to its original constituency of the poor and disadvantaged. It is arguable that where litigants do not speak for those whose poverty or other social disadvantage is a bar to access to justice, they should be bound by the rigours of normal civil procedure, including narrow rules of standing, rigorous fact-finding, and limited remedial powers. For example, middle-class environmental groups agitating for slum clearance would need to bring a claim in nuisance and follow the regular court procedure to do so. However, this may present practical problems in screening out the appropriate cases, and may in any event simply transpose the problem of identifying appropriate litigants to an earlier phase of the process. The power of the court to define who speaks would thereby be unnecessarily enhanced. An alternative might be an approach which gives greater emphasis to opening up the procedure to all concerned, from the very beginning of the litigation. The claim to represent the public interest in cases such as environmental litigation should be scrutinized, and avenues opened up from the very beginning of the litigation to ensure representation for diverse parts of the public.

B. Overstepping the mark: mimicking the executive?

The extent of the transformation in the judicial role necessitated by the PIL jurisdiction and the continuing mandamus remedial structure have raised deeply controversial questions about the proper role of the Court, particularly where positive duties to provide and promote have been at issue. What then is the appropriate role for a court in polycentric decisions? One way forward is to regard the court's role as intervening when government fails. In the context of a highly malfunctioning State, there are a wide range of situations in which judicial prompting does no more than require the government to act in ways it has already committed itself to, but which it has simply failed to honour. Thus, when the Indian Supreme Court required the State to build a road to an isolated hill community in order to fulfil the residents' right to life,[102] it was in fact only requiring the proper implementation of a scheme already instituted by the relevant authority, but one which had never been brought to fruition.

PIL does indeed appear to be most successful when the Court intervenes to require implementation of policies which have already achieved broad consensus but, through apathy, disorganization, or failure to prioritize, have not been put into action. The 'Right to Food' case, as we have seen, turned existing policies into fundamental rights and elaborated on them. The Court can also be effective in its intervention in cases where there is a conspicuous gap in policy-making in areas affecting the most fundamental rights, such as the right to dignity and equality of mentally disabled

[102] *State of Himachal Pradesh v Umed Ram Sharma* AIR 1986 SC 847 (Indian Supreme Court).

people. A particularly important area in which the Indian Supreme Court has been instrumental in filling a gap in legislation is that of sexual harassment. In response to a PIL, the Court held that sexual harassment constitutes a violation of women's constitutional right to dignity, and drafted quasi-legislative guidelines, drawing on internationally recognized norms.[103] Here, however, the institutional limitations of a court taking on a legislative role quickly became apparent. The process of drafting a statute in line with the Court's prescriptions has proved very difficult, because of the diversity of situations the law needs to address. This is exacerbated by the Court's delineation of the issue as one for the public sector only.[104] Nevertheless, the guidelines formulated by the Court remained the only legal source of regulation of sexual harassment at the workplace until legislation was finally passed in 2013.[105]

The role of the Court in stepping in where government fails is more complex than it seems at first sight. Appointment of commissions can, in some cases, create a parallel structure of decision-making deep within the area of executive competence. Court-appointed commissions have a wide-ranging remit not just to find facts, but also to consider possible solutions as a basis for positive duties to be imposed by the Court. Judicial commissions then parallel and mirror executive structures which should have been in place. For example, in a case challenging the failure of the Delhi authorities to deal with waste and pollution in the city, the terms of reference of a judicially appointed committee took commissioners to the centre of executive policy-making. Its remit covered formulating proposals for economically feasible, safe, and eco-friendly hygienic processing and waste disposal practices; suggesting necessary modifications to municipal by-laws; and formulating standards and regulations for management of urban solid waste.[106] There are many who consider that the Court has had the effect of perpetuating government inactivity. The prospect of a Court-appointed commission either gives the executive a pretext for further inaction, or makes action seem futile because judges will decide in any event.

Empirical work would be needed to establish the proof of this claim, but certainly the impression given by the Court to many of those affected by its actions is as often one of unhelpfully suffocating government initiative as of constructively spurring recalcitrant executives into action. Questions are also raised as to the fact that the appointment of commissioners is entirely in the gift of the Court. The Court selects commissioners on the basis of its own views of who would have the appropriate standing or expertise, without being required to follow any procedure or open application process. Although the commissioners generally serve the Court very well, some safeguards in terms of transparency and accountability should be in place. In addition, it may be necessary to ensure that the commissioners are drawn from a wider section of society than the limited pool the Court tends to draw from.

[103] *Vishaka v State of Rajasthan* (1997) 6 SCC 241 (Indian Supreme Court); and see I Jaising, 'Gender Justice and the Supreme Court' in B Kirpal and others (eds), *Supreme but not Infallible* (OUP 2000) 312–15.

[104] I am grateful to Indira Jaising for this insight.

[105] Sexual Harassment of Women at Workplace (Prevention, Prohibition and Redressal) Act 2013.

[106] *Almitra Patel v Union of India* (n 98).

C. Straying too far: relaxing the criteria

A further source of criticism of the Court concerns the rigour of its fact-finding procedures in PIL cases.[107] Commissioners are able to pursue their investigative function in any way they please and will often visit the contested area and hear representations from a wide range of interested parties on the ground. Their report and any other evidence are presented by affidavit, without the facility for cross-examination. On one level, this is an appropriate response to cases with wide social implications. Inquisitorial fact-finding of this nature is likely to elicit a greater appreciation of the complex polycentric matters at issue than a bipolar adversarial system and cross-examination, which encourage defensiveness rather than co-operation. On another level, there is a risk that evidence gathered through affidavits alone does not give a sufficiently rigorous foundation for the highly complex orders promulgated by the Court. Commissioners are part-time and temporary appointments, required to take time out of their busy, and usually highly paid, jobs to serve the Court for a small consideration, and this might make it difficult for them to achieve the highest standard of fact-finding necessary to ground a PIL.[108] It is arguable that PIL is best suited to cases where the facts are reasonably straightforward or uncontested. Alternative means of accessible justice, such as tribunals, might fill the gap thus created. Such specialist tribunals could well deal with complex situations without relying only on affidavit evidence. Environmental tribunals have in fact frequently been proposed in India, but they have not yet been established.

The relaxation of rules of procedure can also lead to a loss of the protections at the basis of fair procedure. Thus, in his recent book, Bhuwania is highly critical of the Indian Court for descending into informality and breaching the bounds of judicial competence. He focuses in particular on the role of Court-appointed commissioners, monitoring committees, and amicus curiae in turning PIL into a 'highly effective slum demolition machine', claiming that the result was to make almost a million people in Delhi homeless in the first decade of the twenty-first century.[109] He also argues that the wide rules of standing mean that the real plaintiff has disappeared, and therefore the interests of the disadvantaged ignored. Notably, however, he acknowledges that in this case the procedural departures of PIL were taken by the Delhi High Court to its *reductio ad absurdum*.[110]

Also problematic is the fact that the PIL procedure brings polycentric cases before the Court, without necessarily giving it the tools to deal with the range of issues implicated in a complex policy field. In making the transition from immediate relief, as is frequently the case in imposing merely a duty of restraint, to structural change which requires the design, institution, and implementation of complex policies, positive duties can overtax the resources of the Court.

[107] I am indebted to Justice Madan Lokur for many of the insights in this and subsequent paragraphs.

[108] Alternatively, the Supreme Court of India has deputed District Justices to perform similar functions as permanent commissions with routine reporting obligations.

[109] A Bhuwania, *Courting the People* (CUP 2017) 13.

[110] ibid, 81.

D. The Court as a social actor: risks and rewards

As we have seen, the Court acting under the PIL procedure is most successful when it prods the government to implement policies which have already been given some backing. Where, however, the PIL challenges an existing policy backed by powerful political forces, and established in the name of economic development, the Court's grasp of its fundamental rights mission becomes more unsteady. This has been painfully clear in an era in which the forces of globalization and the rhetoric of economic development have permeated Indian policy-making. In such cases, the public interest is easily transmuted to exclude the fundamental rights of the most disadvantaged, either through a utilitarian calculus or through equating the benefit to some parts of the population with the public interest as a whole. Using familiar legal formulae, such as separation of powers, legality, and deference, courts have in several dramatic cases endorsed the position of the powerful and the privileged at the expense of the poor and marginal. Indeed, some would argue that the deference to globalization and multinational capital makes sense of the Court's simultaneous assault on pollution, corruption, and labour rights.[111] This can be particularly marked in urban development and protection of the environment.

Although India has had severe housing shortages and chaotic urban planning for many years, urban development comes into focus in a different way when the aim is to create cities which are attractive to inward investment and global capital. In this light, urban development requires orderly planning, effective services, anti-pollution measures, and public spaces—all of which immediately undermine the claim to urban citizenship of the slum- and pavement-dwellers, the hawkers and the homeless, who now constitute as much as 17.4 per cent of the urban population in India.[112] Instead of aiming for integration, through housing, services, and schools, the focus is on removal. The Indian Supreme Court, faced with powerful demands for eviction and displacement, has taken refuge in a narrow concept of legality which relies on absence of proprietary rights to shut down any claims at the threshold. The result is to characterize all those without property rights as encroachers, trespassers, and even petty criminals. Yet the guiding principle behind human rights is to challenge legality when it deprives people of their rights. By failing to regard slum-dwellers as urban citizens with equal rights, the courts have strayed from their human rights role.

This can be seen in the string of cases concerned with eviction of slum-dwellers. Constituting a massive 65.49 million people in India's 2,613 statutory towns,[113] slum-dwellers have found themselves pitted against pedestrians, town-planners, middle-class homeowners, environmentalists, and local authorities in their struggle for minimum human rights. While lip service is often paid to the duty to rehabilitate, relocation is frequently to unserviced sites inaccessible to schools or work, where displaced people are required to pay for a piece of land with little real utility to themselves.

[111] U Baxi, oral communication (n 101).

[112] Government of India Ministry of Housing and Urban Poverty Alleviation, *Slums in India: A Statistical Compendium* 21 <http://nbo.nic.in/Images/PDF/SLUMS_IN_INDIA_Slum_Compendium_2015_English.pdf> (accessed 15 February 2018).

[113] ibid.

In such cases, the Court has neither imposed a duty of restraint (against eviction) nor used its extensive remedial powers to insist on implementation of positive duties to provide housing and infrastructure. The result is that evicted slum-dwellers are forced back into the illegal settlements as their only means of making a living. As is seen in Chapter 9, the Court in the famous case of *Olga Tellis*, although using the vocabulary of a right to livelihood, in fact imposed only a duty to consult those facing eviction. Particularly serious was the refusal to insist that alternative pitches with proper infrastructure be provided as a condition precedent to removals.[114] In one sense, the Court's reluctance to enforce such positive duties is difficult to explain, since the Court could have followed its own example in the 'Right to Food' case and insisted on the implementation of existing policy documents, thus turning a policy commitment into a fundamental right to livelihood and shelter. In particular, the Delhi Master Plan aims to deal systematically with Delhi's housing problems through the integration of slum-dwellers into housing with the necessary infrastructure and accessibility to sources of work.[115] The plan, which includes a significant land allocation, has been consistently ignored.

Overlapping with housing issues, and similarly caught between a fundamental rights approach and the utilitarianism of global capitalism, are environmental concerns, an arena in which the Court has been a major player.[116] Many of the environmental cases upheld by the Court have of course benefited the poor as well as the middle classes. The Court's intervention after public-spirited individuals drew its attention to the dangerous leak of oleum gas from factory premises in Delhi,[117] and the discharge of toxic effluents into the soil in Udaipur,[118] are good examples. In the famous *Vehicular Pollution* cases,[119] the Court was faced with government statistics showing that vehicles contributed to 70 per cent of the air pollution in Delhi and other major cities. In response, it ordered strict measures to decrease such pollution, including the conversion of all public transport in Delhi to use Compressed Natural Gas rather than petrol. The resulting drop in pollution clearly benefits all. Such cases are, however, consistent with a judicial approach which views cleaner cities as an essential way of attracting global capital.

Other aspects of the environment raise more complex conflicts of interest. A particularly ferocious instance of the Court privileging environmental issues over people was the action in May 1997 of the Bombay High Court in ordering the eviction of informal settlement dwellers adjacent to the Sanjay National Park. The Court was responding to a petition filed in 1995 by the Bombay Environmental Action Group,

[114] *Olga Tellis v Bombay Municipal Corporation* (n 97) 586.

[115] The most recent being the Delhi Development Authority, 'Master Plan of Delhi 2021' <https://dda.org.in/ddanew/pdf/Planning/reprint%20mpd2021.pdf> (accessed 18 February 2018).

[116] M Lokur, 'Environmental Law: Its Development and Jurisprudence', Greenlaw Lecture IX, Greenlaw Lecture Series, World Wide Fund for Nature, India 1.

[117] *MC Mehta v Union of India* (1986) 2 SCC 176; (1986) 2 SCC 325; (1987) 1 SCC 395 (Indian Supreme Court).

[118] *Indian Council for Enviro-legal Action v Union of India* (1996) 3 SCC 212 (Indian Supreme Court).

[119] *MC Mehta v Union of India* (1998) 6 SCC 60; (1998) 8 SCC 648; (1999) 6 SCC 14; (2000) 9 SCC 519; (2001) 3 SCC 756; (2001) 3 SCC 763; (2001) 3 SCC 767; (2002) 4 SCC 352; (2002) 4 SCC 356; (2003) 10 SCC 560 (Indian Supreme Court).

asking the Court to 'remove forthwith' the 'encroachers' in order to ensure protection of 'the environment and all its aspects'. Not only did the Bombay High Court direct the relevant authorities to evict persons from their homes, it also specifically ordered the demolition of shelters and the destruction of all belongings and construction materials.[120] As many as half a million slum-dwellers were potentially affected. A similar pattern can be seen in the decision to clear one of the biggest and oldest slums in Delhi, housing 150,000 people in 40,000 homes, which had existed for many years on the banks of the Yamuna River. The slum was demolished in 2004 by order of the High Court of Delhi, in response to a petition brought by citizens concerned at the pollution and encroachment on the river. About one-fifth of the residents were resettled on the outskirts of Delhi, without local services or transport into the city. The rest were left to their own devices. Although the High Court directed that proper basic amenities (including power, water, sewerage), schools, and transportation be provided in the rehabilitation colonies, it refused to stay the eviction until these has been provided. By 2006, little had been done to implement the Court's directions. While no one is in any doubt that the Yamuna is seriously polluted, the extent to which the slums contribute is controversial. One study puts the contribution of slums to such pollution at less than 1 per cent.[121]

V. Remedies and Implementation

Discussions of justiciable human rights often end with the court judgment. Yet the remedies and ongoing implications are of crucial importance. Indeed, judges might well approach the substantive interpretation of the right with the remedies in mind and limit their judgments accordingly. As in other respects, the challenges are enhanced in relation to duties to fulfil, particularly when the duty is subject to progressive realization and depends on available resources. How should courts fashion remedies which can achieve the realization of a right, and what ongoing role should they have in supervising implementation? This section gives a brief account of some of the main challenges, without attempting to be comprehensive.

A wide range of remedies is available to judges in human rights cases, and there is often a significant degree of discretion left to judges to frame these remedies.[122] The challenges of backward-looking remedies, such as the award of individual damages, are familiar to courts, and adjudicative systems are as well equipped to handle them as in any other cases. It is the forward-looking remedies which are potentially most problematic for proponents of justiciable human rights. These challenges are intensified when human rights remedies are caught up in complex social and political cross-currents.

[120] Writ Petition No 305 of 1995 in the Bombay High Court; see U Ramanathan, 'Illegality and Exclusion: Law in the Lives of Slum Dwellers', International Environmental Law Research Centre Working Paper 2004-2, 9.

[121] RN Barucha, *Yamuna Gently Weeps* <http://www.yamunagentlyweeps.com> (accessed 18 February 2018).

[122] See eg South African Constitution, s 172.

The difficulty in fashioning appropriate remedies for human rights violations in conditions of deep social conflict was highlighted in the famous case of *Brown v Board of Education*.[123] As is seen in Chapter 11, the US Supreme Court in *Brown* famously held that racially segregated schools were in violation of the Fourteenth Amendment of the US Constitution, which forbids States from denying the equal protection of the law to anyone within their jurisdiction. Cognizant of the social resistance the decision faced, the Court delayed its remedial decision for a whole year. Even then, its final remedial approach took place against the background of President Eisenhower's failure to signal support for prompt aggressive enforcement. Instead, the US President urged moderation and local decision-making.[124] Taking its cue from the President, the Court in *Brown II* held that the full implementation of the constitutional principles might require varied local solutions. Whereas 'school authorities have the primary responsibility for elucidating, assessing, and solving these problems', held Warren CJ, the role of courts was 'to consider whether the action of school authorities constitutes good faith implementation of the governing constitutional principles'.[125] This, in the Court's view, was best performed by local district courts, because of their proximity to local conditions and the possible need for further hearings. In his guidance to these courts, Warren CJ stressed the need for practical flexibility in shaping remedies and the importance of adjusting and reconciling public and private needs. In an approach remarkably like the progressive realization standard, the Court held: 'While giving weight to these public and private considerations, the courts will require that the defendants make a prompt and reasonable start toward full compliance'.[126]

The cases were remanded to district courts to take such proceedings and enter such orders and decrees as were necessary and proper to admit the plaintiffs to public schools on a racially non-discriminatory basis 'with all deliberate speed'.[127] Minow regards what she calls the incongruous notion of 'all deliberate speed' as the compromise offered by a Court deeply concerned at the widespread nature of white resistance to racial equality.[128] Importantly, however, district courts were required to retain jurisdiction during the implementation period, scrutinizing the adequacy of plans drawn up by the defendants to meet the obstacles they identify in effecting integration. This meant that district courts continued to play a crucial role in either accelerating change or putting a brake on implementation, depending on the way they positioned themselves relative to local groups.

As Minow points out, '[T]he Court-supervised remedial process produced protracted and sometimes violent conflicts over the succeeding decades and decreasing success in advancing either the ideal or the reality of the integration or even simply racially mixed schools'.[129] The depth of social resistance was immediately witnessed when the Governor of Arkansas brought out the Arkansas National Guard to prevent nine black students from enrolling in Little Rock's central high school. The President, albeit reluctantly, sent in national troops. This was the start of a protracted struggle

[123] *Brown v Board of Education* 347 US 483 (1954) (US Supreme Court).
[124] M Minow, *In Brown's Wake* (OUP 2010) 20.
[125] *Brown v Board of Education (Brown II)* 349 US 294 (1955) (US Supreme Court) 299.
[126] ibid, 300. [127] ibid, 301. [128] Minow (n 124) 20. [129] ibid, 7.

between white supremacist groups resisting school desegregation, and court orders implementing the constitutional rights of black people. Resistance in some locations was so strong that in some states governors and local school boards closed public schools rather than permit them to be integrated.[130]

It was not until the Civil Rights Act 1964 that the *Brown* case received the full backing of the federal government. The Act gave the Federal Department of Justice the power to enforce *Brown* through litigation as well as to withhold federal funds from school systems that continued to discriminate against African-Americans. This in turn emboldened the US Supreme Court, in a bench reinforced by justices appointed by Democratic presidents, to reject delaying tactics of school authorities, many of which had been backed by district courts. Even this, however, proved short-lived. As we see in Chapter 11, residential segregation, which perpetuated and entrenched racial segregation in schools, was not regarded by the Court as within the legitimate bounds of judicial remedy. Instead, a Court now increasingly dominated by Republican appointments limited its intervention to officially sanctioned segregation, and terminated judicially supervised desegregation plans even when confronted with increasingly racially separate schools.[131] Any attempts to achieve a balance in schools by local schools were even held to be racially discriminatory.[132]

This suggests that Court remedies should not be considered in isolation from the institutional and social barriers they face. Regulation theorists have stressed the limits of traditional 'command-and-control' legal remedies in inducing changes of behaviour and in achieving sustained action by bureaucracies towards a predefined goal.[133] Organizations are likely to have their own internal logic, interpreting messages from legislation or other external stimuli according to their own 'language' or organizational system.[134] Regulation theorists therefore stress the importance of understanding the internal workings of organizations in order to find the triggers for change as well as to avoid obstacles and misunderstandings. Otherwise, attempting to impose change through simple 'command-and-control' remedies might have contradictory consequences. Teubner characterizes this process as giving rise to a 'regulatory trilemma'.[135] First, prescriptive legal remedies might encounter token compliance without real change. A familiar manifestation consists of the generation of policies, committees, or inquiries which create the appearance of activity but without producing any real change. Second, command-and-control remedies may be openly flouted, damaging the credibility of the legal system. The continuing non-response and evasion of the provincial government to the right-to-education litigation in the Eastern Cape in South Africa is a good example. Third, prescriptive legal solutions might be accepted, but at the cost of damaging the capacity of the organization to function properly. Teubner uses the example of juridification of collective bargaining as an instance of

[130] ibid, 21. [131] ibid, 25.

[132] *Parents Involved in Community Schools v Seattle School District* 127 S Ct 2738 (2007) (US Supreme Court).

[133] Fredman (n 35).

[134] G Teubner, 'Substantive and Reflexive Elements in Modern Law' (1983) 17 Law and Society Review 239.

[135] ibid.

the third aspect of the regulatory trilemma. It is possible to point too to India, where judges are accused of creating paralysis in the civil service and bureaucracy as a result of their intervention in socio-economic rights cases. The empirical case for the latter has not, however, yet been made out.

Roach and Budlender take this forward by suggesting that the remedy should be geared to addressing the reason why governments have failed to respect constitutional rights. Drawing on Hansen's work, they identify three broad reasons for governmental non-compliance with constitutional standards: *inattentiveness, incompetence*, and *intransigence*. Each of these calls for different remedial responses.[136] *Inattentiveness* can arise because the executive fails to understand its constitutional commitments, or because the disadvantaged are not sufficiently powerful as to make their voices heard. In such situations, it might be sufficient for a court to issue a declaratory remedy, declaring the rights of the parties without expressly requiring anything to be done. A declaratory remedy, however, only works where there is governmental goodwill. Experience in both Canada and South Africa have shown that more might be needed in cases of inattentive government to ensure compliance. Roach and Budlender therefore suggest public reporting requirements, to achieve transparency and public accountability. The second reason, *incompetence*, which in practice is the most common cause of lack of compliance, gives rise to a strong case for the court to assume a supervisory jurisdiction. This should include the requirement to submit a plan and subsequent progress reports for the court's approval, possibly including interveners or court-appointed experts to comment on such plans. Where *intransigence* is encountered, the supervisory jurisdiction needs to include a credible threat of punishment through contempt proceedings.

Rather than matching remedies to particular reasons for lack of governmental responsiveness, as Budlender and Roach suggest, Braithwaite's work on 'responsive regulation' suggests an escalating approach. Described as a regulatory pyramid, this begins with an attempt at persuasion and voluntary compliance and escalates through threats of coercive intervention (deterrence) to actual coercion or punishment.[137] Braithwaite stresses that this is a dynamic model. It begins with dialogue regardless of the reason for the lack of compliance, both in order to achieve a better outcome and because this gives greater legitimacy to subsequent more punitive approaches. At the same time, he is mindful that persuasion is not likely to be effective unless there is a credible option of escalation into coercive remedies. Conversely, when reform and repair are forthcoming, it is important to de-escalate down the pyramid in order to reward change. Braithwaite identifies a number of reasons why the first level (restorative justice) and the second level (deterrence) might fail, requiring resort to the top level of punitive remedies. One of these is that it might always be cheaper for the regulated body to pay fines or absorb the costs of other punitive remedies than to comply. This he calls the 'deterrence trap'.[138] Nevertheless, he suggests that in practice, failure to comply is not due to lack of goodwill nor a rational calculation that

[136] C Hansen, 'Inattentive, Intransigent and Incompetent' in SR Humm (ed), *Child, Parent and State* (Temple University Press 1994) 232.

[137] J Braithwaite, *Restorative Justice and Responsive Regulation* (OUP 2002).

[138] ibid, 32.

cheating is more profitable. Instead, it is simply that management lack the competence to comply. His suggested response is more far-reaching, however, than that of Budlender and Roach. For him, the ultimate coercive remedy for incompetence ought to be incapacitation: the removal of incompetent managers, or, failing that, the removal of a company's licence to operate.

Hepple, Coussey, and Choudhury drew on this regulatory pyramid in their proposals for an effective and fair framework of equality law. Their enforcement pyramid harnesses three interlocking mechanisms: internal scrutiny to ensure self-regulation, the participation of interest groups, and external enforcement in the form of a commission which can both assist in voluntary change and employ coercive sanctions where necessary. The process begins from a base of persuasion, information, and voluntary actions. If these fail, more stringent compliance mechanisms are progressively triggered, through investigation by an equality commission, issuing of compliance notices, and then judicial enforcement with the potential of direct sanctions, and also withdrawal of contracts or subsidies.[139]

VI. Conclusion: Assessing Justiciable Human Rights—A Peril and a Promise

To what extent then does giving courts a more prominent role in human rights adjudication make governments more accountable in responding to extreme poverty and deprivation, or do legal processes inevitably favour the better off?[140] Similarly, are classical objections to justiciable positive duties well founded: do courts usurp the policy-making power of more representative branches of government, yet lack the skills to make policy in such polycentric areas? Gauri and Brinks' valuable study of five developing countries attempts to offer empirically grounded answers to some of these difficult questions. Based on these studies, they reject the popular dichotomy between judicial and legislative action. Such a dichotomy portrays courts as following only the deontological logic drawn from legal precedents and the parties before them. By contrast, legislatures are described as capable of representing and aggregating the preferences of the voting public, taking into account the wider interests of the polity and even of future generations.[141] Gauri and Brinks instead argue that courts are just one actor in the 'deeply strategic and iterative process of legalization'.[142] This means that courts incorporate a wider set of concerns: responding to popular demands, taking account of infrastructural limitations, anticipating legislative and executive priorities, and engaging in an ongoing dialogue in the process of adjudication. This in turn

[139] B Hepple, M Coussey, and T Choudhury, *Equality: A New Framework Report of the Independent Review of the Enforcement of UK Anti-Discrimination Legislation* (Hart 2000) xv.

[140] V Gauri and D Brinks (eds), *Courting Social Justice: Judicial Enforcement of Social and Economic Rights in the Developing World* (CUP 2008) 3.

[141] V Gauri and D Brinks (eds), 'Introduction: The Elements of Legalization and the Triangular Shape of Social and Economic Rights' (2009) in ibid, 1–37 (hereafter Gauri and Brinks, 'The Triangular Shape of Social and Economic Rights').

[142] They define 'policy legalization' as the extent to which courts and lawyers, and categories of law and rights become relevant in the design of public policy.

pushes legislatures towards special solicitude for rights-protected interests and therefore introduces some deontological reasoning into legislative decision-making. On the other hand, their notion of 'legalization' differs from political demands in the kinds of resources needed to make such claims, the avenues of access for claims, and the way in which claims are articulated. Because of these differences, 'legalization' tends to prioritize a different set of social demands than the political process does. Bearing out the discussion above, they see legalization as capable of benefitting the disempowered. But it also might serve the interests of elites and middle-class interests, dependent on the legal and political context.[143]

Gauri and Brinks' rich empirical research also bears out the insights gained from the discussion above. They found that courts can help overcome political blockages, challenge lack of implementation of existing policies, and hold governments to account for 'incomplete commitments', that is, announced projects of social transformation which have imparted great legitimacy to a government, but which have not been implemented. Courts can also create spaces of deliberation and compromise between competing interests and channel important information to political and bureaucratic actors; and they can reprioritize claims so that access to social and economic goods is extended. On the other hand, litigation can be very resource intensive, and this might prevent socio-economic rights claims from benefiting the neediest, at least directly. But they also found that socio-economic rights litigation might ultimately produce indirect benefits for those who do not have the resources to litigate on their own account. In the end, their findings suggest that 'courts can become important actors in the policy arena while benefiting, or at least without making matters worse for, the underprivileged'.[144] Particularly interestingly, their research shows that courts are most effective when they act well within the political mainstream and with support from other actors in the political realm. They conclude that courts can advance socio-economic rights under the right conditions 'precisely because they are never fully independent of political pressures'.[145]

This is supported by Baxi's appraisal of the Indian PIL record. Baxi argues that 'the growth in constitutional faith overloads adjudicatory power with great expectations, which it does not quite efficiently manage and which it may not always fulfil'.[146] The result has been that 'judicial activism is at once a peril and a promise, an assurance of solidarity for the depressed classes ... as well as a site of betrayal'.[147] However, he concludes: 'Courts are, at the end of the day, never an instrument of total societal revolution: they are, at best, ... instruments of piecemeal social engineering ... never a substitute for direct political action'.[148] This suggests that courts' role in adjudicating human rights should not be judged by expectations it cannot fulfil, but instead be tailored to achieve what it was intended for. A central aspect of this mission is to step in when government fails to act to achieve positive freedom and fulfil human rights. At the same time, there is no reason to believe that courts will always succeed where government has failed. Even when restructured along the lines Fiss suggests, courts have

143 Gauri and Brinks, 'The Triangular Shape of Social and Economic Rights' (n 141).
144 ibid, 6. 145 ibid, 28. 146 Baxi, 'Indian Judicial Activism' (n 95) 159.
147 ibid, 161. 148 ibid, 164.

limited fact-finding facilities, and appointed committees do not in themselves have the resources to ensure that court decrees are fulfilled. In that sense, courts cannot substitute for recalcitrant governments. Nor can they replace political activity. What courts can do, however, is to act as a catalyst for the democratic pressures which ultimately make recalcitrant governments act. Courts in adjudicating human rights should enable ordinary people to require governments to be accountable, that is, to come to court and explain and justify their actions or inactivity. Beyond that, human rights adjudication should facilitate deliberative reasoning rather than pure interest bargaining, which in turn requires governments to listen and interact with civil society, and groups within civil society to listen and interact with each other. Most importantly, human rights adjudication should require deliberation to take place on equal terms.[149] To maintain this, courts should take care to avoid capture by those who already have political power in society, remaining true to their original mission of ensuring that everyone should be given an equal voice within judicial proceedings. This is true too for remedies and implementation structures. Energizing the political process requires the creation of structures which can themselves manage implementation, which are responsive to the range of interests, and which can deal with polycentric implications, with judicial supervision acting as a facilitator rather than a substitute. This is of course a delicate tightrope to walk, but is nevertheless a goal to be aspired to.

[149] Baxi, oral communication (n 101).

5

Interpreting Human Rights Law

I. Introduction

Bills of Rights, like other constitutional documents, are by their nature open-textured and general. As US Chief Justice Marshall put it as long ago as 1819:

> A constitution, to contain an accurate detail of all the subdivisions of which its great powers will admit, and of all the means by which they may be carried into execution, would partake of the prolixity of a legal code, and could scarcely be embraced by the human mind. It would, probably, never be understood by the public. Its nature, therefore, requires, that only its great outlines should be marked, its important objects designated, and the minor ingredients which compose those objects, be deduced from the nature of the objects themselves.[1]

The same is true of Bills of Rights.

However, this creates acute interpretive challenges for judges called on to resolve disputes as to the meaning of human rights. For example, the words 'cruel and unusual punishment' date back to the English Bill of Rights of 1689 and are now found in the Eighth Amendment of the US Constitution, and more recently in the Canadian Charter.[2] But what do these words mean? Do they outlaw the death penalty completely? If not, do they forbid inflicting capital punishment on juveniles, pregnant women, or people with mental disabilities? In answering these difficult questions, should judges look to standards of cruelty when the provision was first promulgated, or should they rely on prevailing mores? A similar set of questions can be asked about the right to 'equality' or 'non-discrimination'. When a constitution guarantees 'equal protection of the laws', does it preclude segregated schools? Does it prohibit affirmative action?

Even apparently straightforward terms like 'person' and 'marriage' are deeply contested. Thus, in *Edwards v AG for Canada*,[3] it was argued before the Privy Council that the word 'persons' in the British North America Act 1867[4] referred only to men, thus precluding women from standing for public office. Did the fact that 'persons' was understood as only applying to men in the nineteenth century mean that women should be excluded from standing for office in 1929? More recently, the Supreme Court of Canada was asked to decide whether the word 'marriage' applied

[1] *McCulloch v Maryland* 17 US 157 (1819) (US Supreme Court) 200.

[2] Canadian Charter, s 12. See also European Convention on Human Rights (ECHR), Article 3, which prohibits 'inhuman or degrading treatment or punishment'.

[3] *Edwards v Attorney General for Canada* [1930] AC 124 (Judicial Committee of the Privy Council (Canada)).

[4] The equivalent of the Canadian Constitution. There are now two constitutional documents: the British North America Act (which mostly has to do with the division of power between the federal government and the provinces) and the Charter.

only to opposite-sex couples,[5] an issue which has come before many courts in recent decades. Even if questions such as these can be resolved, words such as 'unreasonable',[6] the right to a 'fair trial',[7] the principles of 'fundamental justice',[8] or 'due process of law'[9] are both ubiquitous and indeterminate. Human rights limitations clauses are even more challenging, requiring the court to balance competing individual and communal interests. Human rights cases before apex courts are almost by definition the most contested; otherwise they would have been settled long before reaching the highest courts.

On the face of it, judges are tasked with applying the law, not making it. Yet such general and open-textured terms inevitably require a value judgement. This raises the crucial question of what values judges may draw on to give substance to human rights guarantees. Most would argue that judges should not draw on their own values, but is it possible for them truly to leave their values at the door of the Court? Others regard judicial interpretation as gaining legitimacy only when it is true to the original intention of the drafters, or the natural meaning of the text. By contrast, many judges regard the Bill of Rights as necessarily responsive to changing times. This is the 'living tree' or purposive approach. Most recent, and particularly in the context of South Africa, has been the notion of transformative constitutionalism, which suggests that in some contexts the Bill of Rights should be interpreted expressly to bring about social change.

On closer inspection, the contrast between these approaches often proves to be more one of polemic than practical reality. This is particularly true of the contest between original intent and 'living tree' approaches. The open-textured nature of many human rights concepts makes it impossible in some contexts to rely on the intent of framers, who could not have envisaged the issue in the current context. At the same time, even under the 'living tree' approach, text and history are factors which need to be considered to avoid free-floating, unaccountable value judgements. Judgements on human rights issues in practice land up considering a variety of factors before coming to a conclusion. Possibly the major difference lies in the extent to which this is acknowledged. It is argued here that the crucial issue is for judges to acknowledge, explain, and convincingly defend both their interpretive philosophy and the way it is applied to the human rights dispute they face. This chapter explores different approaches to interpretation of human rights in a comparative context. It begins in section II with a brief look at the role of judges' own values, before moving to the main rival approaches. Section III discusses originalism or the intention of the drafters; section IV considers the natural meaning of the text; while section V examines the 'living tree' or purposive approach. Section VI explores the notion of transformative constitutionalism; and the chapter concludes with the approach which will guide the remaining chapters in this book.

[5] *Re Same Sex Marriage* [2004] SCC 79 (Supreme Court of Canada).
[6] See eg the prohibition on 'unreasonable' searches and seizure in s 8 of the Canadian Charter.
[7] ECHR, Article 6. [8] Canadian Charter, s 7.
[9] US Constitution, Fourteenth Amendment.

II. Personal Values

Many jurists are adamant that it is not constitutionally legitimate for judges to draw on their personal values. As US Justice Burger CJ emphasized: 'It is essential to our role as a court that we not seize upon the enigmatic character of the guarantee as an invitation to enact our personal predilections into law'.[10] A chorus of judicial voices in different jurisdictions regularly reiterates this view.

However, is it possible to genuinely avoid relying on personal values, or are apparent legal formulae simply disguises for judges' own preferences? Certainly, US judges are fond of accusing each other of dissembling in this way. Thus, Scalia J has written extra-judicially:

> It would be hard to count on the fingers of both hands and the toes of both feet, yea, even on the hairs of one's youthful head, the opinions that have in fact been rendered not on the basis of what the Constitution originally meant, but on the basis of what the judges currently thought it desirable for it to mean ... But in the past, non-originalist opinions have almost always had the decency to lie, or at least to dissemble, about what they were doing.[11]

One school of thought would argue that such dissembling is inevitable and that judges regularly hide their personal political decisions behind technical, legal formulae.[12] At the other extreme, judges might attempt to deduce the meaning from natural or moral law. The difficulty with this, as we saw in Chapter 2, is that there is no easy way of checking that judges' view of what natural law requires is correct.

This in turn challenges the very possibility of a value-neutral Bill of Rights or method of adjudication. The traditional understanding of the liberal constitution is premised on a strict divide between law and politics, where it is only in the realm of politics that value judgements should be made. As Klare describes it, '[T]he rule-of-law ideal enjoins judges to check their politics at the courthouse door ... They are supposed to provide legal interpretations of texts, which means filtering out, as best they can, their "personal" or "subjective" views, or, what is taken to be the same thing, their "political values" and "ideological preconceptions."'[13] However, given the indeterminacy of legal texts, there is no simple 'rule of law' answer. 'Judges' personal/political values and sensibilities *cannot be* excluded from interpretive processes or adjudication. Not because judges are weak and give in to political temptation, but because the exclusion called for by the traditional rule-of-law ideal is quite simply impossible'.[14] The conclusion is that, since 'we have no solely legal criteria of correctness for resolving contested cases ... then there is nothing legal practitioners can do but acknowledge their political and moral responsibility in adjudication and share the secret with their publics in the interests of transparency'.[15] The question then becomes, not so much whether the

[10] *Furman v Georgia* 408 US 238 (1972) (US Supreme Court) 375–76; for another example, see *Bachan Singh v State of Punjab* 1983 SCR (1) 145 (Indian Supreme Court) 176.

[11] A Scalia, 'Originalism: The Lesser Evil' (1988–1989) 57 U Cinn L Rev 849, 852.

[12] J Griffiths, *The Politics of the Judiciary* (5th edn, Fontana Press 1997).

[13] K Klare, 'Legal Culture and Transformative Constitutionalism' (1998) 14 SAJHR 146, 157.

[14] ibid, 163 (italics in the original). [15] ibid.

decision is based on judges' personal values, but whether the reasons given are persuasive, both in terms of their substantive reasons, and for their consistency with specific constraints of legal reasoning, such as their relationship with the constitutional text, previous decisions, and institutional factors.

To avoid the Scylla of natural law and the Charybdis of personal preference, judges have used a variety of techniques, ranging from seeking the original intention of the drafters, to focusing on the language of the text itself, to regarding the Bill of Rights as a 'living tree', or searching for the most coherent underlying theory or the purpose of the provision. However, it should be borne in mind in the following discussion that adjudicating human rights inevitably involves value judgements: even the choice as to whether to defer to other decision-makers, be they the current legislature or the original drafters, is value-laden. It is important for judges to be open about this. Moreover, judges should be able to explain and defend their choice of values and show that they are drawn from a recognized store of possibilities. Some of these are institutional (sometimes known as 'second-order' decisions), including principles of separation of powers, legitimacy, and competence. Others are based on adjudicative issues such as *stare decisis* and interpretive theories of how texts should be construed. Others are philosophical, historical, or social. The danger lies in disguising value judgements rather than acknowledging them.

III. Originalism or the Intention of the Drafters

Given that the task of judges is not to answer fundamental moral questions, but to apply the law, one way of resolving contested questions about the meaning of human rights instruments is to ask what the drafters intended them to mean. This is a well-known approach to statutory construction: since judges are said to be responsible for interpreting rather than drafting laws, they will frequently justify their interpretation of an enactment by reference to parliamentary intention. It seems to make sense to do the same for the interpretation of constitutional human rights. Rather than rely on judges' own values or predilections, the argument goes, the intentions of the framers of the document should be determinative. An analogous argument might be made in relation to international or regional human rights instruments and the role of preparatory documents or *travaux préparatoires*. On one view, since international treaties are potentially an incursion on the sovereignty of states, signatory states cannot be bound beyond the extent to which they actually agreed, and these original intentions should be sought in the *travaux préparatoires*.

Several advantages are claimed for this approach. The first and most important is concerned with legitimacy, an issue which US Supreme Court Justice Antonin Scalia, one of its main modern proponents, urges us to take seriously. For him, originalism is more compatible with the nature and purpose of a constitution in a democratic system than its alternatives. He argues that it is not the function of constitutional guarantees of human rights to ensure that they reflect current values. This is the function of elections. To the contrary:

> The purpose of constitutional guarantees—and in particular those constitutional guarantees of individual rights that are at the centre of this controversy—is precisely to prevent the law from reflecting certain changes in original values that the society adopting the Constitution thinks fundamentally undesirable. Or, more precisely, to require the society to devote to the subject the long and hard consideration required for a constitutional amendment before those particular values can be cast aside.[16]

The second advantage of originalism, as Scalia puts it, is to insulate judges from the temptation to

> mistake their own predilections for the law. Avoiding this error is the hardest part of being a conscientious judge; perhaps no conscientious judge ever succeeds entirely. Non-originalism, which, under one or another formulation invokes 'fundamental values' as the touchstone of constitutionality, plays precisely to this weakness. It is very difficult for a person to discern a difference between those political values that he personally thinks most important, and those political values that are 'fundamental to our society'. Thus, by the adoption of such a criterion, judicial personalization of the law is enormously facilitated.[17]

Dworkin frames the argument thus:

> Suppose judges can discover how the Framers intended uncertain provisions of the Constitution to be understood. If judges follow that original intention, they would not be making substantive choices themselves but only enforcing choices made long ago by others, choices that have been given authority by the people's ratification and acceptance of the Constitution.[18]

The third advantage is, in Scalia's view, a negative one: the absence of any constructive alternatives, or rather 'the impossibility of achieving any consensus on what, precisely, is to replace original meaning once that has been abandoned'.[19] Although he regards this last defect as 'fundamental and irreparable', Scalia himself admits to being only a 'faint-hearted originalist'.[20] He acknowledges that, even though public flogging might not have been considered a 'cruel and unusual' punishment by the framers of the US Constitution, he would not, as a judge of the US Supreme Court, uphold a statute which imposes public flogging.[21] However, it is hard to see how he can sustain his originalist stance in the face of this concession. For if he rejects both the values of the framers and the values of those who passed public flogging legislation, where does he get his 'values' from? It is not enough to say, as he does, that he cannot imagine being faced with such a statute or that the practical defects of originalism are less corrosive than those of non-originalism. This is because as soon as he allows other values to enter into the discussion, he needs to be able to find a plausible way of defending them. If not, he falls foul of his own criticism of those who disguise their value judgements behind apparently objective legal techniques.

[16] Scalia (n 11) 862. [17] ibid, 863.
[18] R Dworkin, *A Matter of Principle* (OUP 1985) 34 (hereafter Dworkin, *A Matter of Principle*).
[19] Scalia (n 11) 862–63. [20] ibid, 863. [21] ibid, 864.

There are several other difficulties with an originalist position. First, parliamentary intention is notoriously difficult to gauge. How much more so, the intention of the original founders? In the death penalty case of *Furman v Georgia,* several of the Supreme Court Justices looked to the debates in the First Congress in 1789 in an attempt to ascertain the meaning of the 'cruel and unusual punishment clause' in the Eighth Amendment. However, they found that this clause received very little attention in these debates, being confined to comments by two opponents of the Clause in the House of Representatives, one of whom regarded its meaning as simply too indefinite.[22] The conclusion, as Brennan J acknowledged, was that 'we have very little evidence of the Framers' intent in including the Cruel and Unusual Punishments clause ... in the Bill of Rights'.[23] Dworkin takes this one step further: 'There is no such thing as the intention of the framers waiting to be discovered, even in principle. There is only some such thing waiting to be invented'.[24]

A similar approach can be seen in relation to international human rights law. Preparatory documents are considered 'notoriously unreliable'[25] in relation to treaty interpretation generally and therefore given only a supplementary role by the Vienna Convention on the Law of Treaties.[26] This approach was accepted by the European Court of Human Rights (ECtHR) in the seminal case of *Golder,*[27] when the Court was asked to decide whether the right to a fair trial in Article 6 of the Convention included a right of access to court. Even the strongly worded dissent in that case acknowledged that '[i]t is hardly possible to establish what really were the intentions of the Contracting States under this head',[28] and that 'to go into the drafting history of Article 6(1) ... would be both tedious and unrewarding because, like so many drafting histories, the essential points are often obscure and inconclusive'.[29] The drafters' intentions in omitting poverty from the Convention on the Elimination of All Forms of Discrimination Against Women (CEDAW) are similarly inconclusive.[30]

This problem might seem easier to confront when a Bill of Rights has been drafted within living memory of adjudicators, as has been the case with the Canadian Charter and the South African Constitution. Yet the Supreme Court of Canada has emphatically rejected the originalist approach, partly because the records left by the drafters were intrinsically unreliable. Thus, in one of its earliest Charter cases, the Court stated that although it was prepared to admit in evidence the Minutes of Procedure of the Special Joint Committee tasked with drafting the Charter, these should be given minimal weight. This is because they were inherently unreliable.[31] 'Were this Court to accord any significant weight to this testimony, it would in effect be assuming a fact

[22] See *Furman v Georgia* (n 10) per Brennan J at 261–62; Douglas J at 244. Nevertheless, the Eighth Amendment was passed by a considerable majority: see Brennan J at 262, citing 1 Annals of Cong 754 (1789).

[23] *Furman v Georgia*, ibid.

[24] Dworkin, *A Matter of Principle* (n 18) 39.

[25] C Ovey and R White, *Jacobs & White European Convention on Human Rights* (4th edn, OUP 2006) 40.

[26] Article 32.

[27] *Golder v UK* (1979–80) 1 EHRR 524 (European Court of Human Rights).

[28] ibid, para [40].

[29] ibid, para [41].

[30] M Campbell, *Women, Poverty, Equality: The Role of CEDAW* (Hart 2018).

[31] *Re BC Motor Vehicle Act* [1985] 2 SCR 486 (Supreme Court of Canada) 508.

which is nearly impossible of proof, i.e. the intention of the legislative bodies which adopted the Charter'.[32]

The same dilemma was thrust before the South African Constitutional Court almost immediately after its inception. In *Makwanyane*,[33] the second case that came before the newly constituted Court, the Court was faced with the explosive question of whether the death penalty remained lawful under the Interim Constitution. In its argument, the Government wished to refer to the records of the Multi-Party Negotiating Process responsible for drafting the Constitution. The relevance of the drafters' intentions immediately arose. Chaskalson P agreed that the reports of the technical committees which advised the Multi-Party Negotiating Process could provide a context for the interpretation of the Constitution.[34] However, taking his cue from the Canadian Supreme Court, he emphasized that the Constitution was a product of a multiplicity of persons, and therefore the comments of individual actors should be regarded with great caution, no matter how prominent a role they might have played.[35] For the case in hand, he held, they could only be relied on if the record on this point was clear, not in dispute and relevant.

In *Makwanyane* itself, however, the drafting materials did not assist the Court. What they did indicate was that no agreement had been reached on the lawfulness of the death penalty. In essence, the baton had been passed to the Court. As Chaskalson P put it:

> Capital punishment was the subject of debate before and during the constitution-making process, and it is clear that the failure to deal specifically in the Constitution with this issue was not accidental. In the constitutional negotiations which followed, the issue was not resolved. Instead, the 'Solomonic solution' was adopted. The death sentence was, in terms, neither sanctioned nor excluded, and it was left to the Constitutional Court to decide whether the provisions of the pre-constitutional law making the death penalty a competent sentence for murder and other crimes are consistent with ... the Constitution.[36]

One way forward is to widen original intent by arguing that the framers deliberately chose to use standards which could reflect changing mores. US Supreme Court Justice Brennan J, although generally eschewing original intent, still felt moved to support his conclusion in *Furman* by stating: '[T]he Framers ... [did not] intend simply to forbid punishments considered "cruel and unusual" at the time. The "import" of the Clause is, indeed, "indefinite," and for good reason'.[37] Scalia J, by contrast, takes the view that there is little evidence that the framers intended to leave the interpretation of 'cruel and unusual' in the Eighth Amendment to later generations. On the other hand, he argues, the clear words of Article 14, which declares that the state shall not 'deprive any person of life, liberty, or property, without due process of law',[38] are evidence the death penalty was specifically permitted by the framers of the US Constitution.[39]

[32] ibid. [33] *S v Makwanyane* 1995 (3) SA 391 (CC) (South African Constitutional Court).
[34] ibid, para [17]. [35] ibid, para [18]. [36] ibid, para [20] per Chaskalson P.
[37] *Furman v Georgia* (n 10) 264.
[38] For further discussion on whether 'due process of law' can be interpreted to limit the applicability of the death penalty, see Chapter 6.
[39] Scalia (n 11) 863.

A similar resort to original intention to justify evolving norms can be seen in the jurisprudence of the ECtHR. In the recent case of *Markin v Russia*,[40] the concurring opinion stated: 'The petrification of the Convention would not only depart from the common rules of treaty interpretation, ... it would also ultimately disregard the true intention of the founding fathers, namely to create an instrument for the guarantee of rights that are practical and effective, not theoretical and illusory'.[41] However, here too, the resort to original intention to justify evolving norms is risky; it could quite easily be argued that the framers meant to limit the right to its original meaning. The dissenting opinion in the earlier case of *Golder* made this kind of point in response to the argument that, although the Convention had no explicit provision for a right of access to courts, the drafters intended it be included. According to Judge Sir Gerald Fitzmaurice, 'It is hardly possible to establish what really were the intentions of the Contracting States under this head; but that of course is all the more reason for not subjecting them to obligations which do not result clearly from the Convention'. Indeed, it was 'quite inconceivable that governments intending to assume an international obligation to afford access to their courts, should have set about doing so in this roundabout way—that is to say . . ., without stating the right explicitly. . . '.[42]

A second and more far-reaching objection to original intent questions its very foundations in legitimacy. For Dworkin, the problem is not the difficulty in determining the framers' own interpretive theory. It is 'to think the interpretive intention of the Framers matters one way or the other'.[43] Why then should the intentions of the drafters be given such significance? One way of responding would be to argue that democracy requires that those who have been selected by the people to draft a constitution should determine its meaning. However, as Dworkin points out, the framers of the US Constitution were 'remarkably unrepresentative of the people as a whole'.[44] The majority of the population, including women, slaves, and the poor, were excluded from the selection and ratification process. And even if they had been included, it is difficult to explain 'why people now should be governed by the detailed political convictions of officials elected long ago'.[45] The result is that even if the intention of the drafters is clear from the legislative history, this may not be a relevant issue for later generations. Thus, in the famous US case of *Brown v Board of Education*,[46] the US Supreme Court was required to decide whether state-imposed racial segregation in schools was a breach of the Fourteenth Amendment's command that no state shall 'deny to any person within its jurisdiction the equal protection of the laws'. It was clear from the legislative history that the congressmen who proposed the Fourteenth Amendment did not regard state-imposed racial segregation as unconstitutional.[47] As Vicki Jackson points out, 'Not only did the 1789 US Constitution contemplate the continued existence of slavery

[40] *Markin v Russia* (2013) 56 EHRR 8 (European Court of Human Rights). [41] ibid, at OI-7.

[42] *Golder v UK* (n 27) paras [40]–[41]. [43] Dworkin, *A Matter of Principle* (n 18) 53.

[44] R Dworkin, *Law's Empire* (Fontana 1986) 364 (hereafter Dworkin, *Law's Empire*); see also J Waldron, *Partly Laws Common to Mankind: Foreign Law in American Courts* (Yale University Press 2012) 151 (hereafter Waldron, *Partly Laws Common to Mankind*).

[45] Dworkin, *Law's Empire* (n 44), 364.

[46] *Brown v Board of Education* 347 US 483 (1954) (US Supreme Court).

[47] Dworkin, *Law's Empire* (n 44) 389.

and a voting structure favouring slave states, but there is evidence that the Framers and ratifiers of the Fourteenth Amendment did not necessarily understand the Equal Protection Clause to prohibit state imposed segregation of the races'.[48] However, this fact was no longer relevant, opening the way for the Court in *Brown* to strike down official segregation in schools.

The ECtHR faced a more complex situation when faced with the question of whether the right to freedom of association in Article 11 of the European Convention on Human Rights (ECHR) also included the right not to join an association. This had been a highly controversial issue when the Convention was drafted, due to the prevalence in the UK of the 'closed shop' or a system of compulsory trade union membership. In *Young, James and Webster v UK*,[49] three workers who had been dismissed because they did not belong to a union claimed that this breached their right of freedom of association. The Court's attention was drawn to the following paragraph in the *travaux préparatoires*: 'On account of the difficulties raised by the "closed-shop system" in certain countries, the Conference in this connection considered that it was undesirable to introduce into the Convention a rule under which "no one may be compelled to belong to an association" which features in the United Nations Universal Declaration'.[50] The Court nevertheless held that the applicants' rights had been breached by the requirement to join the union. Even if such a general rule had been deliberately omitted from the Convention, it held, this did not mean that every compulsion to join a union was compatible with the intention of Article 11.[51]

The Canadian courts have been even more emphatic. For them, the opinion of senior public servants, however well respected, cannot be determinative.

> The simple fact remains that the Charter is not the product of a few individual public servants, however distinguished, but of a multiplicity of individuals who played major roles in the negotiating, drafting and adoption of the Charter. How can one say with any confidence that within this enormous multiplicity of actors ... the comments of a few federal civil servants can in any way be determinative?[52]

The Indian Supreme Court has been more equivocal. In the early case of *Gopalan*,[53] decided in 1950, the Court was required to construe Article 21, which provides: 'No person shall be deprived of his life or personal liberty except according to procedure established by law'. It was argued that the words 'procedure established by law' included principles of natural justice. The Court was referred to the proceedings of the Constituent Assembly, which demonstrated that the Article as originally drafted contained the words 'without due process of law', but these words were subsequently replaced by the words 'except according to procedure established by law'. The Court was careful to say that great caution should be exercised in relation to Constitutional

[48] V Jackson, 'Constitutions as "Living Trees"? Comparative Constitutional Law and Interpretive Metaphors' (2006) 75 Fordham L Rev 921–60 at 955.

[49] *Young, James and Webster v UK* (1982) 4 EHRR 38 (European Court of Human Rights).

[50] Report of 19 June 1950 of the Conference of Senior Officials, Collected Edition of the 'Travaux Préparatoires', vol IV, 262.

[51] *Young, James and Webster v UK* (n 49) para [52].

[52] *Re BC Motor Vehicle Act* (n 31) 508.

[53] *Gopalan v State of Madras* (1950) SCR 88 (Indian Supreme Court).

Assembly proceedings, and resort should be had to such sources only when needed to resolve latent ambiguities.[54] Nevertheless, it was held that the records did show that the Assembly intended to avoid the use of the expression 'due process of law'.[55] Instead, by using 'procedure established by law', the drafters set out a clear standard which could not include the vague principles of natural justice.[56] This was one of the reasons which led the Court to conclude that deprivation of life or personal liberty by the State would be legitimate as long as it was supported by a statutory procedure, even if the latter was unreasonable or in breach of natural justice. This effectively gave free rein to the legislature: indeed, one former Chief Justice of India declared that *Gopalan* had 'in effect destroyed one of the greatest of the fundamental rights, i.e. personal liberty'.[57]

This approach, however, changed radically in the 1977 case of *Menaka Gandhi*,[58] representing 'a metamorphosis after the traumatic experiences under the internal emergency imposed in 1975 and which was lifted in 1977'.[59] In holding that the word 'procedure' in Article 21 meant 'right and just and fair' procedure, and that the expressions 'life' and 'personal liberty' should be given a broad and liberal interpretation, the Court made no further reference to the debates in the Constituent Assembly. Instead, Beg CJ preferred to look to 'the idea of a natural law as a morally inescapable postulate of a just order, recognizing the inalienable and inherent rights of all men (which term includes women) as equals before the law . . . It is, I think, embedded in our own Constitution'.[60] The result has been that, as commentators have noted, 'Article 21 has emerged as the Indian version of the American concept of due process of law'.[61]

Nevertheless, the Supreme Court of India will on occasion still look to the report of the Drafting Committee on the Constitution where the language of the text is ambiguous. Thus, in *Bachan Singh*,[62] in determining the constitutionality of the death penalty, the Court held that it was not appropriate to consider evolving norms of public opinion. Instead, it held that Article 21 clearly showed that 'the Founding Fathers recognised the right of the State to deprive a person of his life or personal liberty in accordance with fair, just and reasonable procedure established by valid law'. It also pointed to several indications showing that the Constitution-makers were fully cognizant of the fact that, at the time, the Indian Penal Code included the death penalty for murder and certain other offences. In view of these indications, the Court concluded that 'it cannot be said that the framers of the Constitution considered death sentence for murder or the prescribed traditional mode of its execution as a degrading punishment which would defile "the dignity of the individual" within the contemplation of the Preamble to the Constitution'.[63]

However, the equivocation continues. In a case as recent as 2001, the Court stated that '[i]t is a settled position that debates in the Constituent Assembly may be relied

[54] ibid, 111–12. [55] ibid, 158. [56] ibid, 111–12.

[57] K Subba Rao, *Some Constitutional Problems* (University of Bombay 1970) 115, cited in M Jain, 'The Supreme Court and Fundamental Rights' in S Verma and Kusum (eds), *Fifty Years of the Supreme Court of India* (OUP 2000) 23.

[58] *Maneka Gandhi v Union of India* AIR 1978 SC 597 (Indian Supreme Court).

[59] Jain (n 57) 23. [60] *Maneka Gandhi v Union of India* (n 58) 649. [61] Jain (n 57) 25.

[62] *Bachan Singh v State of Punjab* (n 10). [63] ibid, para [163].

upon as an aid to interpret a constitutional provision because it is the function of the Court to find out the intention of the framers of the Constitution'. At the same time, it went on to say, 'We must remember that a Constitution is not just a document in solemn form, but a living framework for the Government of the people exhibiting a sufficient degree of cohesion and its successful working depends upon the democratic spirit underlying it being respected in letter and in spirit'.[64]

Dworkin concludes that searching for intention is a 'mischievous' idea because it covers up the substantive decisions which judges inevitably make and pretends that this has not occurred.[65] The content of the framers' intention cannot be regarded as 'just a matter of historical, psychological or other fact'. It can only be resolved through political theory. That 'judges can make apolitical constitutional decisions by discovering and enforcing the intention of the Framers' is a promise that cannot be redeemed. Judges can only discover that intention by 'making the decisions of political morality they were meant to avoid'.[66]

IV. Textualism

Closely related to theories of original intent are those that focus on the language of the constitutional provision or Bill of Rights as the primary source of meaning. Textualism comes close to originalism in that its rationale is often stated to be in originalist terms—that is, that the text is the surest guide to the intentions of those who framed it.[67] It resolves the difficulty of ascertaining the framers' intentions, however, by resort to the 'plain meaning rule'. This assumes that the framers must have intended words to have the plain meaning that words bear. This in turn permits textualism to go beyond some of the strictures of originalism. Textualists are not concerned with the subjective intentions of the framers, nor with idiosyncratic use of language, but rather with the way in which such language is understood.

However, this introduces a crucial ambiguity which could undermine the *raison d'être* of textualism. If the 'plain meaning of words' is impossible to gauge without the linguistic and social contexts in which they are used,[68] should this meaning be sought by reference to that of the society in which the framers found themselves, or the current social context? Brest argues that the interpreter of a constitutional text 'cannot assume that a provision adopted one or two hundred years ago has the same meaning as it had for the adopters' society today. She must immerse herself in their society to understand the text as they understood it'.[69] For example, she needs to ask what words like the 'equal protection of the laws' meant to those who adopted the Fourteenth Amendment in 1868.[70]

The difficulty with this is that, like originalism, such an approach turns judges into historians, and even then, might not yield sufficiently determinate results. As Easterbrook points out, the interpretive community of 1791 or 1868 might not have

[64] *SR Chaudhuri v State of Punjab* AIR 2001 SC 2707 (Indian Supreme Court) 2717.
[65] Dworkin, *A Matter of Principle* (n 18) 34. [66] ibid, 55–66.
[67] P Brest, 'The Misconceived Quest for the Original Understanding' (1980) 60 *BUL Rev* 204, 205.
[68] ibid, 206. [69] ibid, 208. [70] ibid, 209.

thought about the issues that arise in the application of constitutional terms in later eras. For example, 'because official action favouring racial minorities was unheard of in 1871, we do not know (and cannot reconstruct) how the interpretive community of that era would have understood the Fourteenth Amendment'.[71] In particular, we cannot know whether the phrase 'equal protection of the laws' means 'no official use of race', therefore precluding affirmative action in favour of minorities; or only 'no use of race to harm minorities', which would permit affirmative action.[72] In any event, as Brest argues, we may be too hopelessly imprisoned in our current perspectives even to appreciate that our view of previous social understandings is tempered by our own conceptual framework.[73]

Should we then be looking for the 'plain meaning' of the text as we currently understand it? It can quickly be seen that here too, there may be well-founded disagreements as to the meaning of key terms such as 'reasonable' and 'cruel'. In choosing between these meanings, judges are inevitably making a value judgement, undermining the *raison d'être* of the textualist approach. This leads the critics of the role of courts in adjudicating human rights to question why the arbiter of such meaning should be the judge. Disagreements of this sort, they argue, should be addressed through the political sphere, where disagreements are resolved through democratic elections and accountability to the public. Thus, Easterbrook maintains that the interpretive task should be limited to reflect a narrow view of courts' institutional legitimacy and capability. Only if there is a strong textual claim, should judges interfere with legislative majorities. 'If the age or generality of the text frustrates the statement of a rule, then it also defeats the claim of judicial power. If the living must indeed chart their own course, then the question is political, outside the domain of judicial review ... Judicial review depends on the belief that decisions taken long ago are authoritative'.[74] The conclusion he draws is that judges should enforce, 'against the contrary views of other governmental actors, only the portion of the text or rule sufficiently complete and general to count as law'.[75]

Easterbrook's approach in the human rights context leads to a highly restrictive judicial approach, potentially leaving human rights exposed to executive or legislative override. This can be seen in the early history of the Indian Supreme Court, which took a narrow textualist approach, very similar to that advocated by Easterbrook. Thus, the Court stated in an early case: 'In interpreting the provisions of our Constitution, we should go by the plain words used by the constitution-makers'.[76] This led to a series of highly restrictive cases, including the notorious *Habeas Corpus* case, in which the Court refused to issue writs of habeas corpus during the emergency imposed by Indira Gandhi.[77] Basing his decision on the Constitutional provision permitting the President to suspend fundamental rights in a time of emergency,[78] Baghwati J stated: 'I

[71] F Easterbrook, 'Abstraction and Authority' (1992) 59 University of Chicago Law Review 349–80 at 361.

[72] ibid. [73] Brest (n 67) 221–22. [74] Easterbrook (n 71) 375. [75] ibid, 376.

[76] *Chiranjit Lal Chowdhuri v Union of India* AIR 1951 SC 41 (Indian Supreme Court).

[77] *ADM Jabalpur v Sivkanth Shukla* (1976) SCR 172 (Indian Supreme Court).

[78] Article 359(1). 'Where a Proclamation of Emergency is in operation, the President may by order declare that the right to move any court for the enforcement of such of the rights conferred by Part III (except Article 20 and 21) as may be mentioned in the order and all proceedings pending in any court

do not think it would be right for me to allow my love of personal liberty to cloud my vision or to persuade me to place on the relevant provision of the Constitution a construction which its language cannot reasonably bear'.[79] Although the Court dramatically reversed its position in the later *Maneka Gandhi*[80] case, this approach reappeared in a disturbing form in 2013 in *Koushal* when the Court refused to strike down legislation criminalizing homosexuality. According to the Court, 'unless a clear constitutional violation is proved, the Court is not empowered to strike down a law merely by virtue of its having fallen into disuse or the perception of society having changed as regards the legitimacy of its purpose and its need'.[81] The Court defended its position by maintaining that any change should be brought about by the legislature, not the courts. However, such an approach, concerning a minority with no chance of gaining the favour of a majority in the political sphere, throws into question the very role of a human rights instrument.

Waldron takes a very different view. He regards himself as a textualist, particularly in relation to statute, but also on constitutional matters.[82] However, he is concerned that constitutional textualism sometimes veers into originalism in an indefensible way.[83] Indeed, he regards Scalia as a textualist who lapses into an appeal to the historic intent of the framers whenever politically convenient.[84] Waldron's defence of textualism is based on the authority given to the text by the laborious processes of enactment rather than on fidelity to original intention.[85] He argues that 'textualism requires a judge to focus his [*sic*] interpretive energies on a particular piece of constitutional text, binding on him and his society on account of the circumstances of its framing and ratification in that country'.[86] Moreover, the main reason for textualists' emphasis on natural language is the constancy of language, which can be used to co-ordinate understanding among diverse communities in a given culture.

This leads him to take a very different view of how to discern the plain meaning of words from that portrayed by Brest and Easterbrook. While Waldron acknowledges that language can change over time, he argues that most of the words in current bills of rights mean what they used to mean. The words 'cruel and unusual', for example, mean the same now as they did when they were first used in the English Bill of Rights in 1689. 'Cruel' means 'causing or characterized by great suffering'; 'unusual' still means 'uncommon', all in use since 1630.[87] The application of the term may have changed—people today apply the term 'cruel' to practices which previously were not considered to cause considerable pain and suffering—without changing the meaning of the word.[88]

Waldron's approach is important for our purposes because of its implications for the study and use of comparative human rights law. He argues that textualism requires a

for the enforcement of the rights so mentioned shall remain suspended for the period during which the Proclamation is in force or for such shorter period as may be specified in the order'. This Article has subsequently been repealed.

[79] *ADM Jabalpur v Sivkanth Shukla* (n 77) para [585].
[80] *Maneka Gandhi v Union of India* (n 58).
[81] *Suresh Kumar Koushal v Naz Foundation* (2014) 1 SCC 1 (Indian Supreme Court) para [33].
[82] Waldron, *Partly Laws Common to Mankind* (n 44) 155. [83] ibid. [84] ibid, 167.
[85] ibid, 155. [86] ibid, 156. [87] ibid, 165. [88] ibid.

preoccupation with the natural meaning of the text. A textualist judge can learn a lot from what others have said about the natural meaning of the text, and this includes what judges in other jurisdictions might have to say, particularly where the same text has been transposed from one human rights instrument to another (such as 'cruel and unusual') or where domestic bills of rights also aim to fulfil international human rights obligations or where similar words in different configurations are used.[89] This marks a decisive break with originalism, unless, as in the South African Constitution, there is a clear mandate to consider comparative law through interpretive mechanisms.

Balkin develops a similar approach. For him, interpreters ought to be faithful to the original meaning of the constitutional text and its underlying principles. Importantly, like Waldron, he uses 'meaning' in this context only to refer to the concepts the words in a clause point to, and not their application or purpose, nor the specific intentions behind them nor what the clause is generally associated with in our culture. Retaining the original meaning of words is necessary to preserve the constitution's legal meaning over time: 'If the dictionary definitions of words changed over time, their legal effect would also change, not because of any conscious act of law-making (or even political mobilization), but merely because of changes in language'.[90] However, fidelity to original semantic content does not require us to apply a constitutional text in the way people at the time of its enactment would expect it to be applied, or to articulate its purposes as the framers would have, or to apply it only in ways which are consistent with their intentions. Instead 'every generation is charged with the obligation to flesh out and implement text and principle in their own time'.[91]

Balkin's approach signals an important step towards convergence with theories which regard constitutional interpretation as dynamic and evolving, albeit within the framework of the text, context, and history. Indeed, he expressly regards what he calls 'original meaning originalism' and 'living constitutionalism' as two sides of the same coin. So, what is 'living constitutionalism'? It is to this that we now turn.

V. The 'Living Tree' or Purposive Approach

Rather than search for meaning in the original intention of the framers, several jurisdictions, such as Canada and the ECHR, prefer to regard the Bill of Rights as an evolving document, a 'living tree', capable of growing and changing to reflect current values. Canada has been at the forefront of the development of the organic metaphor of the living tree; while other jurisdictions use the less graphic terms of 'living instrument' or 'living constitution'. This approach is highly challenging: once the veneer of legitimacy achieved by referring to text or original intent is finally abandoned, the source of human rights values is laid bare. As Sharpe and Roach point out, 'The judges are called upon to delve deeply into the very foundations of our legal system and political culture to answer questions of the most fundamental nature, and many

[89] ibid, 157–63.

[90] J Balkin, 'Framework Originalism and the Living Constitution' (2009) 103 Northwestern University Law Review 549, 553.

[91] ibid, 252.

of these questions cannot be answered adequately by reference only to traditional legal sources'.[92]

The 'living tree' metaphor was first used in the oft-cited Privy Council case of *Edwards v AG for Canada*.[93] The context was auspicious, concerning as it did the question of whether the word 'persons' in the British North America Act 1867 referred only to men, thereby perpetuating the long-standing prohibition on women's right to vote and stand for public office. Rather than seeking out the original meaning or intent of the relevant provision, the Court made it clear that

> the British North America Act planted in Canada a living tree capable of growth and expansion within its natural limits ... Their Lordships do not conceive it to be the duty of this Board—it is certainly not their desire—to cut down the provisions of the Act by a narrow and technical construction, but rather to give it a large and liberal interpretation so that the Dominion to a great extent, but within certain fixed limits, may be mistress in her own house.[94]

The Court rejected an originalist approach, regarding it as impossible to speculate whether the framers of the Act purposely followed one or other of the existing models of legislative composition. Even more importantly, the Court recognized that 'customs are apt to develop into traditions which are stronger than law and remain unchallenged long after the reason for them has disappeared'.[95] Whatever 'persons' meant at the time the Act was passed, in the present there was no reason to hold that it excluded women. This principle has been consistently followed by the Supreme Court of Canada in interpreting the Canadian Charter.[96] Thus, in the *Same-Sex Marriage* case, it described as 'one of the most fundamental principles of Canadian constitutional interpretation: that our Constitution is a living tree which, by way of progressive interpretation, accommodates and addresses the realities of modern life'.[97]

The Canadian Court has robustly defended this evolutionary approach. Most importantly, whereas originalists and textualists regard the legitimacy of constitutional interpretation as deriving from the document's history, the Canadian Supreme Court views the document as intrinsically future-oriented. Unlike a statute, which is 'easily enacted and easily repealed', a constitution

> is drafted with an eye to the future. Its function is to provide a continuing framework for the legitimate exercise of Governmental power, and when joined by a Bill or a Charter of Rights, for the unremitting protection of individual rights and liberties. Once enacted, its provisions cannot easily be repealed or amended. It must, therefore,

[92] R Sharpe and K Roach, *The Charter of Rights and Freedoms* (5th edn, Irwin Law Inc 2013) 55.

[93] *Edwards v Attorney General for Canada* (n 3). [94] ibid. [95] ibid.

[96] *Hunter v Southam* [1984] 2 RCS 145 (Supreme Court of Canada) (hereafter *Hunter*); *Law Society of Upper Canada v Skapinker* [1984] 1 SCR 357 (Supreme Court of Canada) (hereafter *Skapinker*); *R v Big M Drug Mart Ltd* [1985] 1 SCR 295 (Supreme Court of Canada) (hereafter *Drug Mart*); *Blais v Her Majesty the Queen* (2003) SCC 44 (Supreme Court of Canada); *United States v Burns* (2001) SCC 7 (Supreme Court of Canada); *Reference re Same-Sex Marriage* (2004) SCC 79 (Supreme Court of Canada); *Reference Re Prov Electoral Boundaries (SASK)* (1991) 2 SCR 158 (Supreme Court of Canada) (hereafter *Reference Re Prov Electoral Boundaries*).

[97] *Reference re Same-Sex Marriage* (n 96) paras [22]–[23].

> be capable of growth and development over time to meet new social, political and historical realities, often unimagined by its framers.[98]

Nor is its evolving interpretation therefore left to the political process, as Easterbrook would have it. The Canadian Supreme Court has been unabashed in its readiness to assume responsibility for such interpretation. Thus, in another of the early cases, Estey J stated: 'The fine and constant adjustment process of these constitutional provisions is left by a tradition of necessity to the judicial branch'.[99]

However, abandoning original intent is not sufficient to create a coherent theory of interpretation. Scalia's challenge of finding a plausible alternative source of values, short of judges' personal preferences, must still be faced. The Canadian Court has sought these values through a purposive approach. By determining the purpose of a provision, guidance as to its meaning may be found. This is an avowedly complex and value-laden approach. An early example of its application is in *Hunter v Southam*,[100] where the Court was required to determine the meaning of the right to 'be secure against unreasonable search or seizure' in section 8 of the Charter, a guarantee which the Court acknowledged was 'vague and open'.[101] Dickson J noted that the meaning of 'unreasonable' could not be determined by recourse to a dictionary; nor was there any particular historical, political, or philosophical context capable of guiding the court as to the meaning of the section.[102] Instead he reaffirmed what he regarded as obvious: 'The *Canadian Charter of Rights and Freedoms* is a purposive document. Its purpose is to guarantee and to protect, within the limits of reason, the enjoyment of the rights and freedoms it enshrines'.[103] But how is purpose assessed? The first step is to delineate the nature of the interests the right is meant to protect. These, the Court held, were wider than had been the case at common law,[104] where only property interests were protected. Instead, it was held, the underlying purpose was to protect individuals from unjustified state intrusions on their privacy. Equally important, the assessment of reasonableness must focus on the 'impact on the subject of the search or the seizure, and not simply on its rationality in furthering some valid government objective'.[105]

The search for the purpose of the provision means that history plays a very different role to that under the doctrine of original intent. As McLachlan CJ put it:

> The doctrine of the constitution as a living tree mandates that narrow technical approaches are to be eschewed. It also suggests that the past plays a critical but non-exclusive role in determining the content of the rights and freedoms granted by the Charter. The tree is rooted in past and present institutions, but must be capable of growth to meet the future.[106]

In relation to the right to vote, as much as in the right to freedom of religion, 'while rooted in and hence to some extent defined by historical and existing practices, [the right] cannot be viewed as frozen by particular historical anomalies. What must be sought is the broader philosophy underlying the historical development of the right

98 *Hunter* (n 96). 99 *Skapinker* (n 96), 366. 100 *Hunter* (n 96). 101 ibid, 154.
102 ibid, 155. 103 ibid, 156.
104 *Entick v Carrington* (1765) 19 St Tr 1029, 1 Wils KB, 275 (House of Lords) at 1066.
105 *Hunter* (n 96) 157–59. 106 *Reference Re Prov Electoral Boundaries* (n 96).

to vote—a philosophy which is capable of explaining the past and animating the future'.[107]

Thus, the purposive approach signified by the metaphor of the living tree is a complex one. It draws together multiple factors, from 'the character and the larger objects of the Charter itself, to the language chosen to articulate the specific right or freedom, to the historical origins of the concepts enshrined, and where applicable, to the meaning and purpose of the other specific rights and freedoms with which it is associated within the text of the Charter'.[108] The interpretation should be:

> a generous rather than a legalistic one, aimed at fulfilling the purpose of the guarantee and securing for individuals the full benefit of the Charter's protection. At the same time, it is important not to overshoot the actual purpose of the right or freedom in question, but to recall that the Charter was not enacted in a vacuum, and must therefore ... be placed in its proper linguistic, philosophic and historical contexts.[109]

A similar set of issues has been played out before the ECtHR. Early on in its jurisprudence, the Court, like its counterparts in other jurisdictions, found itself confronted with the application of open-textured terms in contexts possibly not envisaged by the original drafters. Thus in *Golder*, the Court was asked to decide whether the right to a fair trial in Article 6 of the Convention included a right of access to court.[110] In the face of a strongly worded dissent,[111] the Court decided to be guided by the Vienna Convention on the Law of Treaties,[112] and in particular, Article 31(1) of the Treaty, which states: 'A treaty shall be interpreted in good faith in accordance with the ordinary meaning to be given to the terms of the treaty in their context and in the light of its object and purpose'.

This paved the way to the development of a contextual approach, which regards the Convention as a 'living instrument'. The earliest mention of this approach arose in the context of the interpretation of the right in Article 3 not to be subjected to 'inhuman and degrading treatment or punishment'. As in other jurisdictions, this right invokes the evolutionary dilemma in its starkest form. In *Tyrer*,[113] the Court was asked to determine whether sentences of 'birching', or judicially imposed corporal punishment for crimes committed by juveniles, constituted a breach of Article 3. The Court, in an oft-cited phrase, held that:

> the Convention is a living instrument which ... must be interpreted in the light of present-day conditions. In the case now before it the Court cannot but be influenced by the developments and commonly accepted standards in the penal policy of the member States of the Council of Europe in this field.[114]

[107] ibid. [108] *Drug Mart* (n 96) para [344]. [109] ibid, paras [180]–[181].

[110] *Golder v UK* (n 27).

[111] The dissent held that the absence of express mention of such a right should be regarded as strong evidence against its implication: see above.

[112] Although it was not yet in force.

[113] *Tyrer v UK* (1979–80) 2 EHRR 1 (European Court of Human Rights).

[114] ibid, para [31].

Here too, the question immediately arises as to how to determine the appropriate context, and in particular, how to distinguish between judges' personal values and the values of the Convention. For the majority of the Court, 'his punishment—whereby he was treated as an object in the power of the authorities—constituted an assault on precisely that which it is one of the main purposes of Article 3 to protect, namely a person's dignity and physical integrity'.[115] The dissenting judge, Sir Maurice Fitzgerald, by contrast, held that judicially imposed corporal punishment could not be considered degrading. He admitted that

> my own view may be coloured by the fact that I was brought up and educated under a system according to which the corporal punishment of schoolboys (sometimes at the hands of the senior ones—prefects or monitors—sometimes by masters) was regarded as the normal sanction for serious misbehaviour, and even sometimes for what was much less serious. Generally speaking, and subject to circumstances, it was often considered by the boy himself as preferable to probable alternative punishments … They also not infrequently took place under conditions of far greater intrinsic humiliation than in his case. Yet I cannot remember that any boy felt degraded or debased.[116]

The living-instrument approach has allowed the ECtHR to develop the Convention to respond to important new challenges not envisaged at the time of its adoption, and to change its mind when it appeared that society had evolved. Possibly the clearest manifestation of this evolutionary approach has been in relation to discrimination on grounds of sexual orientation. The case of *Dudgeon*[117] was the Court's first robust intervention in this area, holding that criminalization of sodomy in Northern Ireland was a breach of the right to respect for privacy and family life in Article 8 of the Convention. Since then, there has been a series of cases challenging many aspects of inequality for same-sex couples, which Contracting States have regularly attempted to justify by arguing that the aim was to protect the traditional family. In responding to these cases, the Court has consistently reaffirmed the evolutionary nature of the Convention. Thus, it has repeatedly stated, most recently in *X v Austria* in 2013:

> Given that the Convention is a living instrument, to be interpreted in the light of present-day conditions, the state, in its choice of means designed to protect the family and secure, as required by art. 8, respect for family life must necessarily take into account developments in society and changes in the perception of social, civil-status and relational issues, including the fact that there is not just one way or one choice in the sphere of leading and living one's family or private life.[118]

This raises the same dilemma encountered in Canada and the US: how does the Court determine relevant social developments from which it can draw its conclusions as to

[115] ibid, para [33]. [116] ibid, paras [23]–[24].

[117] *Dudgeon v UK* [1982] 4 EHRR 149 (European Court of Human Rights).

[118] *Kozak v Poland* (2010) 51 EHRR 16 (European Court of Human Rights) para [98]; *X v Austria* (2013) 57 EHRR 14 (European Court of Human Rights) para [139]. For a similar use of the living instrument argument, see *Vallianatos and Others v Greece* (2014) 59 EHRR 12 (European Court of Human Rights) para [84] and *Oliari v Italy* (2017) 65 EHRR 26 (European Court of Human Rights) para [189].

the changing meaning of the Convention? One important source is the common traditions and values of the Member States which make up the Council of Europe. The Court will regularly require a comparative survey of the laws of the Member States in order to discover a common tradition, and consensus has frequently been invoked to justify a dynamic interpretation of the Convention.[119] Thus in *Dudgeon*, the Court stated:

> As compared with the era when that legislation [criminalizing sodomy] was enacted, there is now a better understanding, and in consequence an increased tolerance, of homosexual behaviour to the extent that in the great majority of the member States of the Council of Europe it is no longer considered to be necessary or appropriate to treat homosexual practices of the kind now in question as in themselves a matter to which the sanctions of the criminal law should be applied; the Court cannot overlook the marked changes which have occurred in this regard in the domestic law of the member States.[120]

But consensus is a problematic criterion. Is the Court a norm-setter? Or is it a norm-reflector, doing no more than making sure that outliers are keeping pace with the dominant position within Europe? Certainly, in *X v Austria*, the dissenting judges thought the majority were moving too fast. They protested that 'the point of the evolutive interpretation, as conceived by the Court, is to accompany and even channel change; it is not to anticipate change, still less to try to impose it'.[121] Simply reflecting existing norms might assist the Court in its relationships of comity with Member States. However, the mere fact that a majority of countries do not agree that their practices are a breach of fundamental human rights should not itself be a reason for holding that no breach has occurred. Conversely, is the existence of a consensus sufficient to require outliers to change their practices?

The Court has attempted to address this tension by delineating principles which it regards as impervious to a lack of European consensus. In particular, 'where a particularly important facet of an individual's existence or identity is at stake', such as in relation to discrimination on grounds of sex or sexual orientation, the Court will give little latitude to Member States to make their own decisions.[122] However, it will be reluctant to intervene where 'there is no consensus within the member States of the Council of Europe, either as to the relative importance of the interest at stake or as to the best means of protecting it, particularly where the case raises sensitive moral or ethical issues'.[123] This is because 'by reason of their direct and continuous contact with the vital forces of their countries, the State authorities are, in principle, in a better

[119] *A, B and C v Ireland* (2011) 53 EHRR 13 (European Court of Human Rights) paras [23]–[24]; *Marckx v Belgium* (1979–80) 2 EHRR 330 (European Court of Human Rights); *Dudgeon v UK* (n 117); *Soering v UK* (1989) 11 EHRR 439 (European Court of Human Rights); *L and V v Austria* (2003) 36 EHRR 55 (European Court of Human Rights); and *Goodwin v UK* (2002) 35 EHRR 18 (European Court of Human Rights).

[120] *Dudgeon v UK* (n 117) para [60]; see also *Smith and Grady v UK* (2000) 29 EHRR 493 (European Court of Human Rights) para [104].

[121] *X v Austria* (n 118) OII-23 (Joint Partly Dissenting Opinion of Judges Casadevall, Ziemele, Kovler, Jočienė, Šikuta, De Gaetano, and Sicilianos).

[122] ibid, para [149]. [123] ibid.

position than the international judge to give an opinion, not only on the "exact content of the requirements of morals" in their country, but also on the necessity of a restriction intended to meet them'.[124] As we see in more detail in later chapters, the Court uses the concept of a 'margin of appreciation' to calibrate the extent to which it will insist on a common standard on the one hand, or permit Member States to determine their own standards on the other.

However, a closer look at the formulae used by the Court reveals their malleability. The category of 'sensitive moral or ethical issues' is not self-defining: it is not clear why issues of individual identity, such as sex and sexual orientation discrimination, have been held to fall outside of this category, warranting a robust human rights standard, while others, such as abortion, have been held to be issues solely for the Member State. Even the concept of consensus can be malleable. In *X v Austria*, the Court found only ten relevant comparators within the Council of Europe, of which six treated heterosexual couples and same-sex couples alike, while four adopted the same position as Austria. It held that the narrowness of this sample meant that no conclusions could be drawn as to the existence of a possible consensus.[125] Nevertheless, the Court held that the right to equality for same-sex couples should be upheld. On the other hand, in *A, B and C v Ireland*,[126] the existence of a strong European consensus in favour of abortion was not sufficient for the Court to reject Ireland's justification for prohibiting abortion.[127] It did this by shifting the focus from whether Member States afforded a right to abortion to the question of when the right to life begins. Because it found no consensus on this issue, it held that it was up to Ireland to balance the rights of the mother against the rights of the unborn.[128]

Even more complex is to determine the tipping point for the Court to consider that values have changed enough for it to reverse its previous position. This dilemma has been faced in relation to the right of lesbian and gay people to adopt children, and in relation to the right of fathers to paternity leave, both issues which have seen rapid change in recent years. Thus, in *Fretté v France*,[129] the Court found that the French authorities' decision not to allow a gay man to adopt a child was not discriminatory within the meaning of Article 14 of the Convention. The Court noted that the law appeared to be going through a transitional phase and that there was little common ground between Member States of the Council of Europe. Moreover, the scientific community was divided over the possible consequences of children being brought up

[124] *A, B and C v Ireland* (n 119) para [232].

[125] *X v Austria* (n 118) para [149]. Contrast *Vallianatos and Others v Greece* (n 118), where the Court found a violation of Article 14 taken together with Article 8 where a law barred same-sex couples from entering into civil unions, noting that of the nineteen State parties to the Convention which authorized some form of registered partnership other than marriage, only two States reserved it exclusively to different-sex couples.

[126] *A, B and C v Ireland* (n 119).

[127] The first applicant could have obtained an abortion justified on health and well-being grounds in approximately forty Contracting States and the second applicant could have obtained an abortion justified on well-being grounds in some 35 Contracting States. Only three States have more restrictive access to abortion services than in Ireland, namely a prohibition on abortion regardless of the risk to the woman's life (*A, B and C* v Ireland (n 119) para [235]).

[128] *A, B and C v Ireland* (n 119) para [237].

[129] *Fretté v France* (2004) 38 EHRR 21 (European Court of Human Rights).

by one or more homosexual parents. However, the Grand Chamber reversed its position only four years later, in *EB v France*.[130] It concluded that in refusing authorization to adopt a child to the applicant, who was living with another woman in a stable relationship, the French authorities had made a distinction on the basis of her sexual orientation which was not acceptable under the Convention and constituted a breach of Article 14 in conjunction with Article 8, the right to respect for family life.

A similar shift occurred in relation to the right to paternity and family leave and allowances. In *Petrovic v Austria*[131] in 2001, the Court was faced by a claim that it was discriminatory to make parental leave allowances available only to mothers and not fathers. The Court rejected the claim, holding that as the majority of Contracting States did not provide for parental leave or related allowances for fathers, there was no European consensus on this issue. However, in 2012 it was able to discern a sufficient evolution in social attitudes in Europe to uphold a similar claim.[132] By that time, an absolute majority of European countries provided for parental leave for both mothers and fathers, indicating that 'contemporary European societies have moved towards a more equal sharing between men and women of responsibility for the upbringing of their children and that men's caring role has gained recognition'. According to the judgment, 'the Court cannot overlook the widespread and consistently developing views and associated legal changes to the domestic laws of Contracting States concerning this issue'.[133] On the other hand, as we have seen, it refused to shift ground in relation to abortion. It justified its position on the basis that this was a highly contentious issue within Ireland, and that the people of Ireland had recently voted in a referendum in favour of a continuation of the prohibition.

While the metaphor of a living constitution has become orthodoxy in Canada and under the ECHR, it remains highly controversial in the interpretive community in the US. As Vicki Jackson puts it:

> Interpretive battles in the United States pitch the 'living constitution,' whose content can change not only through amendment but through interpretation, against an unmovable 'original' Constitution ... Poised as polar opposites in American legal culture today, the 'original constitution' seems to have significant appeal over the 'living constitution'.[134]

A central arena for such contestation remains the interpretation of the elusive phrase 'cruel and unusual punishment' in the Eighth Amendment. Textualism may give us the meaning of the words 'cruel' or 'unusual' but says little about their application. On the other hand, original intent gives answers which, although clear, are often unpalatable. Faced with the question whether it was cruel and unusual to impose the death penalty on juveniles, even Scalia J acknowledged that original intent was a questionable guide: at the time the Bill of Rights was adopted, the common law permitted capital punishment to be imposed on anyone over the age of seven.[135] Instead, in a clear

[130] *EB v France* (2008) 47 EHRR 21 (European Court of Human Rights); see *X v Austria* (n 118) para [102].
[131] *Petrovic v Austria* (2001) 33 EHRR 14 (European Court of Human Rights).
[132] *Markin v Russia* (n 40). [133] ibid, para [130]. [134] Jackson (n 48) 941–42.
[135] *Stanford v Kentucky* (1989) 492 US 361 (US Supreme Court).

manifestation of living constitutionalism, it is now well established that the phrase 'cruel and unusual' 'must draw its meaning from the evolving standards of decency that mark the progress of a maturing society'.[136] As Stevens J emphasized in *Atkins v Virginia*, 'A claim that punishment is excessive is judged not by the standards that prevailed in 1685 when Lord Jeffreys presided over the "Bloody Assizes" or when the Bill of Rights was adopted, but rather by those that currently prevail'.[137]

This, however, is a formula easier to state than to apply. In searching for 'objective indicators from which a court can conclude that contemporary society considers a severe punishment unacceptable',[138] justices on the Court have faced similar dilemmas to their counterparts in Canada and the ECHR. Should the Court attempt to gauge public opinion, or should it exercise its own independent judgement? If the former, what reliable means are available to a court to determine evolving standards of decency? The jurisprudence on the death penalty shows vehement disagreement among members of the Court. When *Furman v Georgia* was decided in 1972, Brennan J looked to the fact that the death penalty had been inflicted so rarely as constituting compelling evidence of a deep-seated reluctance to inflict it.[139] For Marshall J, however, values were not gauged by what people actually did or thought, but by whether 'people who were fully informed as to the purposes of the penalty and its liabilities would find the penalty shocking, unjust, and unacceptable'.[140] He held that 'the great mass of citizens would conclude on the basis of the material already considered that the death penalty is immoral and therefore unconstitutional'.[141] But Burger J, dissenting, thought that it was much more appropriate to refer to legislatures as a source of current social values: 'In looking for reliable indicia of contemporary attitude, none more trustworthy has been advanced'.[142]

In the event, Brennan J's assumptions about public opinion were soon shown to be misplaced. By the time the *Gregg*[143] case came before the Court four years later, at least thirty-five States had enacted new death penalty statutes; by the end of March 1976, more than 460 persons were subject to death sentences.[144] Stewart J, speaking for the majority, made it clear that in assessing contemporary standards, the legislative judgment weighed heavily. Clearly, it was now 'evident that a large proportion of American society continues to regard it as an appropriate and necessary criminal sanction'.[145]

Resort to State legislatures as a source of current values is, however, problematic, for at least three reasons. One is that the results can be read in different ways, supporting whatever conclusion the author wishes. Thus, in *Atkins v Virginia*[146] in 2002, the question arose whether the execution of persons with intellectual disabilities was 'cruel and unusual'. Stevens J stated: 'The large number of States prohibiting the execution of mentally retarded persons (and the complete absence of States passing legislation reinstating the power to conduct such executions) provides powerful evidence that today our society views mentally retarded offenders as categorically less culpable than the average criminal'.[147] Rehnquist J, dissenting, interpreted the data in the opposite direction.

[136] *Trop v Dulles* (1958) 356 US 86 (US Supreme Court) 100–01.
[137] *Atkins v Virginia* (2002) 536 US 304 (US Supreme Court) 311.
[138] *Furman v Georgia* (n 10) 278. [139] ibid, 299. [140] ibid, 361. [141] ibid, 363.
[142] ibid, 385. [143] *Gregg v Georgia* (1976) 428 US 153 (US Supreme Court).
[144] ibid, 180–81. [145] ibid, 179. [146] *Atkins v Virginia* (n 137). [147] ibid, 136.

'The Court pronounces the punishment cruel and unusual', he argued, 'primarily because 18 States recently have passed laws limiting the death eligibility of certain defendants based on mental retardation alone, despite the fact that the laws of 19 other States besides Virginia continue to leave the question of proper punishment to the individuated consideration of sentencing judges or juries familiar with the particular offender and his or her crime'.[148]

A similar division can be seen in relation to the question of whether it is cruel and unusual to impose the death penalty on defendants who were between the ages of fifteen and eighteen when they committed a capital crime. In *Stanford v Kentucky*,[149] a divided court held that it is not. Scalia J was adamant that the most important of the objective indicia that reflect the public attitude 'are statutes passed by society's elected representatives', not the 'uncertain foundations' of public opinion polls, the views of interest groups, and the positions of professional associations.[150] However, in determining that there was an insufficient degree of national consensus to label a punishment cruel and unusual, the plurality looked only to the thirty-seven States whose laws already permitted capital punishment, of which a minority (fifteen) excluded sixteen-year-old offenders. A different majority in the later case of *Roper v Simmons*[151] took issue with this selection. Instead, the Court declared that the relevant sample should have included States which prohibited capital punishment for all ages, which would have demonstrated a clear national consensus against the death penalty for this age group.

The second difficulty with reliance on current legislative consensus is that it is liable to change. We can immediately see similar dilemmas in the US to those faced in jurisdictions that have adopted the living-tree approach. In particular, is the Court a norm-reflector or a norm-setter? At what point can it determine whether social attitudes have changed sufficiently to warrant a change in interpretation? Balkin argues that 'Courts have taken on the task of articulating and applying the values of the dominant national coalition', so that many disputes turn on whether the 'Court has adequately recognized a genuine trend, and whether the trend marks a truly enduring constitutional value or merely reflects a temporary and revisable policy preference'.[152] We have already seen that in *Furman*, the direction of change was in favour of the death penalty. The movement was in the opposite direction in the case of the death penalty for juveniles between fifteen and eighteen. In 2005, the Court in *Roper* found that the consensus relied on in *Stanford* sixteen years before had changed. Instead, 'the objective indicia of consensus in this case—the rejection of the juvenile death penalty in the majority of States; the infrequency of its use even where it remains on the books; and the consistency in the trend toward abolition of the practice—provide sufficient evidence that today our society views juveniles as "categorically less culpable than the average criminal"'.[153] It regarded this as a strong reason to reverse the decision in *Stanford*.

However, this assumes that legislation is the appropriate source of values, raising the third source of criticism of reliance on public opinion as evidence of constitutional

[148] ibid, 322. [149] *Stanford v Kentucky* (n 135). [150] ibid, 377.
[151] *Roper v Simmons* (2005) 543 US 551 (US Supreme Court). [152] Balkin (n 90) 571.
[153] *Roper v Simmons* (n 151) 567.

meaning. Given that a constitution is a signal of certain fundamental values, which endure beyond volatile majorities, perhaps courts should be developing their own independent judgement as to the meaning of those values. One such candidate is the value of human dignity. Indeed, in the seminal case of *Trop v Dulles,* Warren CJ declared that '[t]he basic concept underlying the Eighth Amendment is nothing less than the dignity of man'.[154] Certainly, there has been much contestation in the death penalty jurisprudence as to the appropriate balance between the Court's independent judgement and legislative trends. In *Gregg v Georgia,* Stewart J, although regarding the legislative judgement as a weighty source of evidence, was moved to seek more enduring values: 'Our cases also make clear that public perceptions of standards of decency with respect to criminal sanctions are not conclusive. A penalty also must accord with "the dignity of man," which is the "basic concept underlying the Eighth Amendment"'.[155] By contrast, in *Stanford v Kentucky,*[156] Scalia J, for the plurality, 'emphatically reject[ed] petitioner's suggestion that the issues in this case permit us to apply "our own informed judgement"'.[157] The Court's role was to identify evolving standards, not determine what they should be; to look 'not to our own conceptions of decency, but to those of modern American society as a whole'.[158] The most important of the objective indicia that reflect the public attitude, he stressed, 'are statutes passed by society's elected representatives', not the 'uncertain foundations' of public opinion polls, the views of interest groups, and the positions of professional associations.[159] The difficulty with this approach is that it ignores the fact that elected majorities might not include the voices of the very persons for whom human rights are formulated.

In *Roper,* however, the Court reaffirmed its right to bring its independent judgement to bear on the proportionality of the death penalty.[160] 'Instead we return to the rule, established in decisions predating *Stanford,* that "the Constitution contemplates that in the end our own judgment will be brought to bear on the question of the acceptability of the death penalty under the Eighth Amendment"'.[161] The result is that the objective indicia of consensus, as expressed by the enactments of State or Federal legislature, give 'essential instruction' but, having considered these, the Court should determine 'in the exercise of our own independent judgment' whether the death penalty was a disproportionate punishment for juveniles.[162] This too supported the decision in *Roper* to reverse *Stanford,* holding that imposing the death penalty on juveniles in this age group did indeed breach the Eighth Amendment's prohibition of cruel and unusual punishment.

Perhaps the most vivid manifestation of living constitutionalism in the US interpretive canon concerns the Equal Protection clause in the Fourteenth Amendment. Here too, original intention is an awkward guide, given that there is evidence that the framers and ratifiers of the Equal Protection clause of the US Constitution did not necessarily regard State-imposed segregation as unconstitutional.[163] This was reaffirmed by the Court in 1896 in the notorious case of *Plessy v Fergusson,*[164] which

154 *Trop v Dulles* (n 136) 99.
155 *Gregg v Georgia* (n 143) 173.
156 *Stanford v Kentucky* (n 135).
157 ibid, 378.
158 ibid, 369.
159 ibid, 377.
160 *Roper v Simmons* (n 151) 574.
161 ibid, 597.
162 ibid, 564.
163 See above (n 48).
164 *Plessy v Ferguson* 163 US 537 (1896) (US Supreme Court).

held that State-imposed segregation on public transport was constitutional. It was not until 1954, in the watershed case of *Brown v Board of Education*,[165] that the Court was prepared to dislodge this precedent. Much of the argument before the Court was devoted to the circumstances surrounding the adoption of the Fourteenth Amendment in 1868. Warren CJ, delivering the opinion of the Court, concluded that, at best, these sources were inconclusive.[166] He was therefore adamant that:

> we cannot turn the clock back to 1868 when the Amendment was adopted, or even to 1896 when Plessy v. Ferguson was written. We must consider public education in the light of its full development and its present place in American life throughout the Nation. Only in this way can it be determined if segregation in public schools deprives these plaintiffs of the equal protection of the laws.[167]

The Court in *Brown* did not give any detailed exegesis of the role of statute, public opinion, or the Court's own objective values, in the way we have seen in the Eight Amendment cases. Instead, in a judgment characterized by its extreme brevity, the Court held that the function of education had changed drastically since the nineteenth century, so that it was now 'doubtful that any child may reasonably be expected to succeed in life if he is denied the opportunity of an education'.[168] Whereas the *Plessy* court had made it clear that segregation was not a 'badge of inferiority',[169] the *Brown* Court wholeheartedly accepted evidence in the lower courts demonstrating that a policy of separation is usually interpreted as denoting the inferiority of the African-American group, tending to retard their educational and mental development: 'Any language in Plessy v. Ferguson contrary to this finding is rejected'.[170] The Court concluded that separate educational facilities are inherently unequal.

A similar pattern is unfolding in relation to sexual orientation. In 1986 in the case of *Bowers v Hardwick*,[171] a majority of the Supreme Court held that a Georgian statute criminalizing sodomy was constitutional. This was because the majority regarded the claim as requiring the Court to proclaim a 'fundamental right to commit homosexual sodomy', which they refused to do.[172] Only seventeen years later, *Lawrence v Texas*[173] decisively overturned this decision. The search for a fundamental right to commit sodomy was misconceived. Instead the Court held that Texan legislation criminalizing sodomy between persons of the same sex was in breach of the right to liberty under the Due Process clause of the Fourteenth Amendment. It was only twelve years later, in 2015, that the Court took a further decisive step in this direction. In *Obergefell v Hodges*, by a slim five–four majority, the Court held that it was unconstitutional for States to refuse to license same-sex marriages.[174] This time the Court relied on the

[165] *Brown v Board of Education* (n 46). [166] ibid, 489. [167] ibid, 492–93.

[168] ibid, 494.

[169] 'We consider the underlying fallacy of the plaintiff's argument to consist in the assumption that the enforced separation of the two races stamps the colored race with a badge of inferiority. If this be so, it is not by reason of anything found in the act, but solely because the colored race chooses to put that construction upon it' (*Plessy v Ferguson* (n 164) 551).

[170] *Brown v Board of Education* (n 46) 497.

[171] *Bowers v Hardwick* (1986) 478 US 186 (US Supreme Court). [172] ibid.

[173] *Lawrence v Texas* (2003) 123 S Ct 2472 (US Supreme Court).

[174] *Obergefell v Hodges* 2015 WL 1041665 (US Supreme Court).

values of liberty and equality to recognize a fundamental right to marriage, a step the dissenters refused to take.

Three important themes vividly demonstrate the commitment of the majorities in *Lawrence* and *Obergefell* to living constitutionalism. The first is the way in which the Court dealt with original intent. According to Kennedy J in *Lawrence*:

> Had those who drew and ratified the Due Process Clauses of the Fifth Amendment or the Fourteenth Amendment known the components of liberty in its manifold possibilities, they might have been more specific. They did not presume to have this insight. They knew times can blind us to certain truths and later generations can see that laws once thought necessary and proper in fact serve only to oppress. As the Constitution endures, persons in every generation can invoke its principles in their own search for greater freedom.[175]

More specifically, he declared in *Obergefell*, the drafters of the Constitution specifically entrusted future generations with the ongoing responsibility to develop the meaning of liberty. Thus, he stated, 'the generations that wrote and ratified the Bill of Rights and the Fourteenth Amendment did not presume to know the extent of freedom in all of its dimensions, and so they entrusted to future generations a charter protecting the right of all persons to enjoy liberty as we learn its meaning'.[176]

This, as in all instances of evolutionary interpretation, raises the question of which values the Court can legitimately draw on to give content to an evolving constitution. For Kennedy J in *Obergefell*, the source of such values lay in the bedrock principles of the Constitution: liberty and equality. He held that there has been an abiding connection between marriage and personal choice in the Court's precedents, and the fundamental right to marry is part of the liberty promised by the Fourteenth Amendment. The right of same-sex couples to marry is also derived from the principle of equality in the Fourteenth Amendment. Here too 'in interpreting the Equal Protection Clause, the Court has recognized that new insights and societal understandings can reveal unjustified inequality within our most fundamental institutions that once passed unnoticed and unchallenged'.[177]

The second theme demonstrating the evolutionary approach of the *Lawrence* and *Obergefell* courts is the way in which Kennedy J dealt with the role of history, on which the *Bowers* court had heavily relied. Not only did he contest the veracity of the historical evidence relied on in *Bowers*. Kennedy J went further and downplayed its relevance in favour of current understandings. Thus, he stated in *Lawrence*: '[H]istory and tradition are the starting point but not in all cases the ending point of the substantive due process inquiry'. In this context, 'our laws and traditions in the past half century are of most relevance here. These references show an emerging awareness that liberty gives substantial protection to adult persons in deciding how to conduct their private lives in matters pertaining to sex'.[178] In *Obergefell*, Kennedy J developed his understanding of the relationship of history to social realities in more detail. Thus, he stated, 'the identification and protection of fundamental rights is an enduring part of the

[175] *Lawrence v Texas* (n 173) 579. [176] *Obergefell v Hodges* (n 174). [177] ibid.
[178] *Lawrence v Texas* (n 173) 572.

judicial duty to interpret the Constitution'.[179] Crucially, 'history and tradition guide and discipline this inquiry but do not set its outer boundaries. That method respects our history and learns from it without allowing the past alone to rule the present'.[180] In interpreting the Constitution, he held, it was necessary for the court to respond to changing social realities. Marriage had developed and changed in many ways over the past century, and these changed understandings of marriage 'are characteristic of a Nation wherein new dimensions of freedom become apparent to new generations'.[181] Such changes should feature in the nature of judicial interpretation.

The third theme demonstrating the commitment to living constitutionalism is the Court's attitude to the role of legislation. In *Lawrence*, Kennedy J pointed out that one way of verifying this change was to point out that since *Bowers*, the number of States proscribing sodomy had dropped from twenty-five to thirteen; and even in those, there was a pattern of non-enforcement against consenting adults acting in private. More importantly, however, the Court endorsed Justice Stevens' dissenting opinion in *Bowers*: 'The fact that the governing majority in a State has traditionally viewed a particular practice as immoral is not a sufficient reason for upholding a law prohibiting the practice; neither history nor tradition could save a law prohibiting miscegenation from constitutional attack'.[182] The departure from legislation as a gauge of constitutional values in turn required a robust assertion of the judicial role in discerning and applying such values. Here too Kennedy J had no doubt of the role of the Court. 'Of course,' he stated in *Obergefell*, 'the Constitution contemplates that democracy is the appropriate process for change, so long as that process does not abridge fundamental rights'. However, 'the dynamic of our constitutional system is that individuals need not await legislative action before asserting a fundamental right ... An individual can invoke a right to constitutional protection when he or she is harmed, even if the broader public disagrees and even if the legislature refuses to act'. Citing the 1943 case of *West Virginia v Barnette*,[183] he reiterated that '[t]he idea of the Constitution "was to withdraw certain subjects from the vicissitudes of political controversy, to place them beyond the reach of majorities and officials and to establish them as legal principles to be applied by the courts"'.[184]

It was this last point which provoked the most vigorous response from the dissent. Roberts CJ insisted that 'this Court is not a legislature. Whether same-sex marriage is a good idea should be of no concern to us. Under the Constitution, judges have power to say what the law is, not what it should be'. As in many such dissents, Roberts CJ regarded the evolutionary approach of the majority as a pretext or cover for personal value judgements: 'It can be tempting for judges to confuse our own preferences with the requirements of the law'. For him, the key question was not about his own opinion on gay marriage but 'whether in our democratic republic, that decision should rest with the people acting through their elected representatives, or with five lawyers who happen to hold commissions authorizing them to resolve legal disputes according to

179 *Obergefell v Hodges* (n 174). 180 ibid. 181 ibid.
182 *Lawrence v Texas* (n 173) 578.
183 *West Virginia Board of Education v Barnette* 319 US 624 (1943) (US Supreme Court).
184 *Obergefell v Hodges* (n 174).

law'. For him, the answer was clear. Because the Constitution itself says nothing about marriage, this must mean that the framers entrusted the States with the definition of marriage. Scalia's dissent was on the same lines, but characteristically scathing. For him, the majority opinion was 'a naked judicial claim to legislative ... power; a claim fundamentally at odds with our system of government'.[185]

The difference in the interpretive philosophy of the minority and the majority respectively is stark. For Roberts CJ and Scalia J, the absence of an express mention in the Constitution implies it was left to State legislatures to address. For Kennedy and the majority judges, the judicial role was precisely to identify and protect fundamental rights, not on the basis of a fixed formula, but through the exercise of reasoned justice to identify interests of the person 'so fundamental that the State must accord them its respect'. Through the lenses of liberty and equality, they were able to identify marriage as a fundamental right in this sense.

The Indian Court has faced similar dilemmas. As we have seen, in its early jurisprudence, it took a narrow textualist approach, with highly restrictive consequences.[186] Since then, however, the Supreme Court of India has adopted a robustly purposive approach to the interpretation of the Constitution. In the watershed *Maneka Gandhi* case, Bhagwati J emphasized that 'the attempt of the Court should be to expand the reach and ambit of the fundamental rights rather than attenuate their meaning and content by a process of judicial construction'.[187] The metaphor of a 'living organ' joins that of the living tree and the living instrument. It is now taken as read that 'our Constitution is organic in nature. Being a living organ, it is ongoing and with the passage of time, law must change. Horizons of constitutional law are expanding'.[188] Strikingly, as we will see, Article 21 has been the fastest growing branch of the living tree. 'Unshackled from the restrictive meaning placed upon it in *Gopalan*, [i]t came to acquire a force and vitality hitherto unimagined'.[189]

As in the other jurisdictions, this opens up the question of where the Court derives its values from. One possibility is to look to contemporary standards of public morality. However, the experience of the US Court in *Furman* has been seen as salutary. In the Indian case of *Bachan Singh*,[190] the Indian Supreme Court stated as follows: 'In *Furman*, the Hon'ble Judges claimed to articulate the contemporary standards of morality among the American people. But speaking through public referenda, Gallup polls and the state legislatures, the American people sharply rebuffed them. We must draw a lesson from the same'.[191] For the Indian Supreme Court, this was a reminder that 'judges should not take upon themselves the responsibility of becoming oracles or spokesmen of public opinion', a role better left to the legislature.[192] At the same time, judges must resist the temptation to substitute their own values.[193] The conclusion was, however, that rather than seeking an objective system of values, the Court resorted to looking to original intent: in this case, that 'the Founding Fathers recognised the right

[185] ibid, 2–3, 6 (Roberts J dissenting opinion), 5 (Scalia J dissenting opinion).
[186] *Chiranjit Lal Chowdhuri v Union of India* (n 76).
[187] *Maneka Gandhi v Union of India* (n 58) 628.
[188] *Saurabh Chaudri v Union of India* (2003) 11 SCC 146 (Indian Supreme Court).
[189] *Abdul Rehman Antulay v Rs Naik* AIR 1992 SC 1701, 1717 (Indian Supreme Court).
[190] *Bachan Singh v State of Punjab* (n 10). [191] ibid, para [176]. [192] ibid, para [125].
[193] ibid, para [176].

of the State to deprive a person of his life or personal liberty in accordance with fair, just and reasonable procedure established by valid law'.[194] Nevertheless, as we will see, the Court in *Bachan Singh* held that the death penalty should only be imposed in the 'rarest of rare cases when the alternative option is unquestionably foreclosed'.[195]

A second way forward is to regard the 'living tree' as having its roots in the underlying values which inform the constitution. An example of such an approach can be seen in the lone dissenting opinion of Khanna J in the notorious *Habeas Corpus* cases in the Indian Court. It will be recalled that the Constitution itself gave the President the power to override fundamental rights such as the right to life and liberty in times of emergency. Khanna J was able to preserve habeas corpus by arguing that the right not to be deprived of one's life or liberty without the authority of law could not be extinguished by the use of a constitutional power because it pre-dated the Constitution.[196] Indeed, it was an 'essential postulate and basic assumption of the rule of law in every civilised society' that the State has no power to deprive a person of life or personal liberty without the authority of law.[197]

There are several other sources of values within the Constitution itself. Of particular importance are the Directive Principles of Social Policy. The Directive Principles play an unusual role within the Constitution because they impose duties on the State to fulfil specified human rights but are explicitly declared to be non-justiciable.[198] Nevertheless, the Indian Supreme Court has explicitly drawn on the values in the Directive Principles in interpreting the fundamental rights, and in particular the right to life in Article 21. This is expressed clearly in the seminal case of *Olga Tellis*,[199] where the Court interpreted the right to life to include the right to livelihood. Two Directive Principles were directly in point. Article 39(a) provides that the State shall direct its policy towards securing that the citizens, men and women equally, have the right to an adequate means of livelihood and Article 41 provides, inter alia, that the State shall, within the limits of its economic capacity and development, make effective provision for securing the right to work in cases of unemployment and of undeserved want. The Court held that, although not enforceable by any court, the Directive Principles were fundamental both in the governance of the country and, crucially, in the understanding and interpretation of the fundamental rights. 'If there is an obligation upon the State to secure to the citizens an adequate means of livelihood and the right to work, it would be sheer pedantry to exclude the right to livelihood from the content of the right to life'.[200] The Directive Principles could not be directly enforced, for example by attempting to compel the State to provide adequate means of livelihood or

[194] ibid, para [136]. Article 21 of the Indian Constitution reads: 'No person shall be deprived of his life or personal liberty except according to procedure established by law'. This has been interpreted as meaning 'except according to fair, just and reasonable procedure established by valid law'.

[195] ibid, para [207]. See also *Santosh Kumar Satishbhushan v State of Maharashtra* Criminal Appeal No 1478 of 2005 (Indian Supreme Court), holding that public opinion should not be determinative in the decision as to when the death penalty should be applied. See further Chapter 6 (capital punishment).

[196] *ADM Jabalpur v Sivkanth Shukla* (n 77) para [169].

[197] ibid, para [168].

[198] Constitution of India, Article 37.

[199] *Olga Tellis and Others v Bombay Municipal Corporation* AIR 1986 SC 180; 1985 SCR Supl (2) 51 (Indian Supreme Court).

[200] ibid, 80.

work to the citizens. 'But, any person, who is deprived of his right to livelihood except according to just and fair procedure established by law, can challenge the deprivation as offending the right to life conferred by Article 21'.[201]

A further potential source of values is the preamble of the Constitution. As amended in 1976, the preamble affirms the resolve of the people of India to constitute India into a 'Sovereign, Socialist, Secular, Democratic Republic and to secure to all its citizens: Justice, social, economic and political; liberty of thought, expression, belief, faith and worship; equality of status and of opportunity; and to promote among them all fraternity assuring the dignity of the individual and the unity and integrity of the nation'. Referring to the preamble as 'the floodlight illuminating the path to be pursued by the State', the Court declared in *DS Nakara*[202] that it was well established that 'while interpreting or examining the constitutional validity of legislative/administrative action, the touchstone of Directive Principles of State Policy in the light of the Preamble will provide a reliable yardstick to hold one way or the other'. On this basis, and in particular on the basis of the socialist ideal to provide a welfare State, the Court held that a liberalized pension scheme which excluded people who had retired before 1979 was a breach of the right to equality.

VI. Transformative Constitutionalism

The metaphor of the living tree connotes an organic connection between past, present, and future. The South African Constitution, however, is deliberately and expressly a break from the past, a framework for a transformed society which can 'heal the scars of apartheid'. It is also expressly value-driven. In its powerful preamble, the Constitution declares that its aim is to 'heal the divisions of the past and establish a society based on democratic values, social justice and fundamental human rights' as well as to 'lay the foundations for a democratic and open society', to 'improve the quality of life of all citizens and free the potential of each person', and to 'build a united and democratic South Africa'.[203] Section 7 again affirms the 'democratic values of human dignity, equality and freedom', while section 10 states that 'everyone has inherent dignity and the right to have their dignity respected and protected'. In *Makwanyane*, referring to the interim constitution, Mahomed DP expressed it thus: 'The South African Constitution is different: it ... represents a decisive break from, and a ringing rejection of, that part of the past which is disgracefully racist, authoritarian, insular, and repressive and a vigorous identification of and commitment to a democratic, universalistic, caring and aspirationally egalitarian ethos, expressly articulated in the Constitution'.[204]

Whereas the 'living tree' metaphor is a judge-made response to the challenge of applying open-textured terms to evolving societies, the South African Constitution itself invites judges to use an evolving interpretive method. Most importantly for our purposes, section 39 states that 'when interpreting the Bill

[201] ibid, 80–81.
[202] *DS Nakara and Others v Union of India* (1983) SC (2) 165 (Indian Supreme Court).
[203] Preamble, South African Constitution.
[204] *S v Makwanyane* (n 33) para [262].

of Rights, a court, tribunal or forum must promote the values that underlie an open and democratic society based on human dignity, equality and freedom'.[205] In this sense, in the memorable words of Karl Klare, it sets South Africa on the path of 'transformative constitutionalism'. Unlike classic liberal constitutions, the South African Constitution:

> does not even purport to present itself as timeless and metahistoric, coming down from on high. It rejects the fiction that the political community is founded at a single magic moment of 'social contract,' thereby ratifying the pre-existing hierarchy and distribution of social and economic power. It evinces an understanding that legal and political institutions are chosen, not given, that democracy must be periodically reinvented, and that the Constitution itself is the contingent (even fragile) product of human agency.[206]

Transformative constitutionalism has proved challenging for judges, who were from the start acutely conscious of the risk of inappropriate judicial incursion on the new democratic order which had been so carefully constructed. At the same time, the development and protection of human rights through the Constitutional Court were clearly envisaged as a central tenet of democracy. These challenges were articulated in the first two cases to reach the Constitutional Court: *Zuma*[207] and *Makwanyane*.[208] In the *Zuma* case, the Court was required to interpret the meaning of the right to a fair trial in section 25(3) of the Interim Constitution. Kentridge AJ attempted to reconcile the transformative push with the pull of judicial constraint. On the one hand, he stressed that the right to a fair trial in the newly adopted Constitution 'embraces a concept of substantive fairness which is not to be equated with what might have passed muster in our criminal courts before the Constitution came into force'.[209] On the other hand,

> while we must always be conscious of the values underlying the Constitution, it is nonetheless our task to interpret a written instrument. I am well aware of the fallacy of supposing that general language must have a single 'objective' meaning. Nor is it easy to avoid the influence of one's personal intellectual and moral preconceptions. But it cannot be too strongly stressed that the Constitution does not mean whatever we might wish it to mean.[210]

He addressed the clear difficulty with adhering to a text which was itself value-laden and substantive by extensive resort to values articulated in other jurisdictions, particularly Canada and the UK.

More difficult, however, was the second case to come before the Court, *S v Makwanyane*,[211] which required the Court to determine whether the death penalty, extensively used almost entirely against black people during the apartheid era, should remain lawful in the new constitutional dispensation. Even if the Court had wished to resort to original intention, it would have found none: as we have seen, no agreement

[205] South African Constitution, s 39(1). [206] Klare (n 13) 155.
[207] *S v Zuma* [1995] ZACC 1 (South African Constitutional Court).
[208] *S v Makwanyane* (n 33). [209] *S v Zuma* (n 207) para [16]. [210] ibid, para [17].
[211] *S v Makwanyane* (n 33).

was possible in the Constitution-making process, an open invitation to the Court to determine the issue itself. The narrow textualism of the apartheid era, where 'courts engaged in simple statutory interpretation, giving effect to the clear and unambiguous language of the legislative text—no matter how unjust the legislative provision',[212] was also decisively rejected. Instead, the judges on the Court were prepared to openly embrace the value-laden nature of the adjudication process. Thus, Mokgoro J stated:

> [T]he interpretive task frequently involves making constitutional choices by balancing competing fundamental rights and freedoms. This can often only be done by reference to a system of values extraneous to the constitutional text itself, where these principles constitute the historical context in which the text was adopted and which help to explain the meaning of the text. The constitution makes it particularly imperative for courts to develop the entrenched fundamental rights in terms of a cohesive set of values, ideal to an open and democratic society.[213]

However, as in *Zuma*, there was also a recurring articulation of the legal rather than personal or political nature of the judicial approach. This was most strongly emphasized by Kriegler J. For him, the issue was not

> whether I favour the retention or the abolition of the death penalty, nor whether this Court, Parliament or even overwhelming public opinion supports the one or the other view. The question is what the Constitution says about it. In answering that question the methods to be used are essentially legal, not moral or philosophical. To be true the judicial process cannot operate in an ethical vacuum ... And it would be foolish to deny that the judicial process, especially in the field of constitutional adjudication, calls for value judgments in which extra-legal considerations may loom large. Nevertheless, the starting point, the framework and the outcome of the exercise must be legal.[214]

For Didcott J, this tension should be navigated by distinguishing between subjective and objective value judgements:

> Whether execution ranks also as a cruel, inhuman or degrading punishment is a question that lends itself to no precise measurement. It calls for a value judgment in an area where personal opinions are prone to differ, a value judgment that can easily become entangled with or be influenced by one's own moral attitude and feelings. Judgments of that order must often be made by courts of law, however, whose training and experience warns them against the trap of undue subjectivity. Such a judgment is now required from us, at all events, and would have been inescapable whichever way the question was answered.[215]

This leaves open the difficult question of where 'objective' values are drawn from, if not from the judges' personal predilections, the text itself, or the original intentions of the drafters. Or, as Klare suggests, does this question itself assume falsely that clear lines can be drawn between these categories? Reference to prevailing standards was

[212] ibid, para [301] per Mokgoro J. [213] ibid, para [302]. [214] ibid, paras [206]–[207].
[215] ibid, para [177].

convincingly rejected in *Makwanyane*. Distancing himself from the fruitless quest in the US Court for appropriate evidence of prevailing standards, Chaskalson P stressed:

> Public opinion may have some relevance to the enquiry, but, in itself, it is no substitute for the duty vested in the Courts to interpret the Constitution and to uphold its provisions without fear or favour. If public opinion were to be decisive there would be no need for constitutional adjudication. The protection of rights could then be left to Parliament, which has a mandate from the public, and is answerable to the public for the way its mandate is exercised, but this would be a return to parliamentary sovereignty, and a retreat from the new legal order established by the 1993 Constitution. By the same token the issue of the constitutionality of capital punishment cannot be referred to a referendum, in which a majority view would prevail over the wishes of any minority. The very reason for establishing the new legal order, and for vesting the power of judicial review of all legislation in the courts, was to protect the rights of minorities and others who cannot protect their rights adequately through the democratic process.[216]

Davis argues that the original intention and the text of the South African Constitution contain a very clear set of values, namely a form of social democracy built upon a transformed legal system.[217] For him, 'the constitutional text promised the development of the existing legal system into a body of law which would, as coherently as possible, reflect the core values of the Constitution'.[218] Yet, turning the 'living tree' argument on its head, he argues, the political and legal culture within society will too often influence the developing jurisprudence away from what the drafters might have had in mind. He characterizes judicial interpretation as itself a form of constitutionalism, rewriting the Constitution significantly as time passes. This means that it is crucial to check whether such rewriting remains faithful to the spirit of the Constitution. It is therefore a serious criticism on his behalf when he concludes that 'the democratic society promised by the Constitution which, in part at least, would have required a radical transformation of the legal concepts which underpinned the entire society, was replaced by a narrow vision'.[219]

Chaskalson, the first President of the South African Constitutional Court, takes a different position. For him too, the South African Constitution is plainly a moral document, which contains an objective normative value system which should permeate all aspects of the law and which demands a moral reading of its provisions.[220] But he would not concur with the view that constitutional interpretation has replaced the transformative essence with a narrow vision. This is because his articulation of constitutional values is consistent with the way in which the Court has applied them. For him, the central guiding principle is the Dworkinian conception of equal concern and respect, which he regards as underpinning both the Constitution and the Court's case-law. This issue is particularly important in attempts to construe the meaning of

[216] ibid, para [88].

[217] D Davis, 'Transformation: The Constitutional Promise and Reality' (2010) SAJHR 85.

[218] ibid, 85. [219] ibid, 101.

[220] A Chaskalson, 'From Wickedness to Equality: The Moral Transformation of South African Law' (2003) 1 Int'l J Const L 590.

the open-textured term 'reasonably', which is used in socio-economic rights cases to prescribe the government's obligations to fulfil socio-economic rights.

By contrast, Roux suggests that the Court has been successful in maintaining its institutional legitimacy because of its ability to synthesize principle and pragmatism. It was able to strike down the death penalty in *Makwanyane*[221] despite widespread public support for capital punishment because the outcome was favoured by the ruling African National Congress (ANC) elite who were so dominant in the political field as to feel immune from the possibility of losing votes on this issue.[222] On the other hand, the Court's decision to require the legalization of gay marriage in *Fourie* was taken in full awareness that the ANC elite was divided on the issue of gay and lesbian rights. The Court therefore mediated the result by deferring the task of rewriting the relevant legislation to the legislature rather than doing so itself. By contrast, in the *Treatment Action Campaign* decision, the Court's decision to order the Government to make nevaripine widely available to prevent mother–child transmission of HIV/AIDS, although going strongly against government policy, in fact had very wide public support.[223]

VII. The Way Forward?

Much of the difficulty in the above discussion stems from an attempt to find an interpretive theory which does not require judges to make substantive decisions on the basis of their own personal or political values. The only way forward is to accept that judges do in fact make value-laden decisions. Dworkin argues that the common distinction between 'conservative' judges, who 'obey' the Constitution, and 'liberal' judges, who try to reform it according to their personal convictions, is a fallacy. All judges are engaged in an interpretive exercise: they all agree on which text they are interpreting; but disagree on how to interpret it.[224] 'The issue is rather what reasons are, in [a court's] hands, good reasons'.[225] Thus while it is unavoidable and even desirable that judges do in fact make political decisions, Dworkin argues that there are some kinds of political arguments which are appropriate for judges to rely on, and some which are not. Judges can and do rely on arguments of political *principle*, which concern the political rights of individual citizens. They should not, however, rely on arguments of political *policy*, or arguments which seek to promote 'some conception of the general welfare or public interest'.[226]

How then do they determine which principles they should apply in interpreting the Constitution to decide a hard case? For Dworkin, the best way to describe appropriate judicial interpretation is through his theory of integrity.

> Judges who accept the interpretive ideal of integrity decide hard cases by trying to find, in some coherent set of principles about people's rights and duties, the best

[221] *S v Makwanyane* (n 33).
[222] T Roux, 'Principle and Pragmatism on the Constitutional Court of South Africa' (2009) 7 Int'l J Const L 106, 120.
[223] ibid, 119–25.
[224] Dworkin, *Law's Empire* (n 44) 359.
[225] Dworkin, *A Matter of Principle* (n 18) 69.
[226] ibid, 11.

> constructive interpretation of the political structure and legal doctrine of their community. They try to make that complex structure and record the best these can be.[227]

This approach imposes important constraints on the extent to which judges' personal convictions of justice can play a role in their decisions. This is because of the requirement of 'fit': the decision should be consistent with the political structure and legal doctrine of their community. Where there are two possible plausible interpretations, the judge must choose between them by asking 'which shows the community's structure of institutions and decisions—its public standards as a whole—in a better light from the standpoint of political morality'.[228] This is not in itself a mechanical exercise: judges will need to exercise their political judgement as to which decision constitutes the best 'fit', and judges are likely to disagree on the outcome. However, in US society at least, Dworkin discerns a central or root principle of political morality which he believes makes best sense of that community's political culture. For him, decisions of principle should be taken from 'the root principle that government must treat people as equals'.[229] In this way, some issues are called 'from the battleground of power politics to the forum of principle'.[230] As we have seen, this was the approach too of Chaskalson P to the interpretive task in the South African Constitutional Court.

This is a powerful theory, especially in its ability to recognize both the importance of judicial value judgements and the role of the Constitutional text and history in giving consistency and legitimacy to such value judgements. However, in the human rights context, it is less helpful in its distinction between principle and policy. This is because most human rights can be limited, or justified, on the basis of arguments about the public interest. For example, the ECHR permits rights such as freedom of speech, religion, assembly, and association to be limited where necessary in the interests of a democratic society for a range of public-interest goals. It will be seen in later chapters that the balancing of these public-interest arguments against individual human rights constitutes one of the knottiest dilemmas in human rights adjudication.

The above discussion has shown that judges in fact use an eclectic mix of approaches to interpretation. An unadulterated adherence to original intent, text, or other historical sources will often be inconclusive or implausible. Instead, history and text are often dealt with as part of the context, which also includes prevailing understandings and objective values. There are thus significant convergences between the different approaches. Balkin, for example, presents this convergence as part of an understanding of the Constitution, not as a finished product, but as a framework for governments.

> We look to original meaning to preserve this framework over time, but it does not preclude us from a wide range of future constitutional constructions that implement the original meaning ... In this model of originalism, the Constitution is never finished, and politics and judicial construction are always building up and building out new features.[231]

[227] Dworkin, *Law's Empire* (n 44) 255. [228] ibid, 256.
[229] Dworkin, *A Matter of Principle* (n 18) 69. [230] ibid, 71. [231] Balkin (n 90) 557.

He therefore sees the goal as 'creating a set of key values and commitments that set the terms of political discourse, and that future generations must attempt to keep faith with'.[232]

How these key values are shaped and determined remains a source of both the challenge and the dynamism of comparative human rights law. This suggests that, contrary to Sunstein's defence of incompletely theorized agreement, it is not merely the outcome that matters, but the process of reasoning leading to the outcome. This process needs to be clear and transparent: it is the temptation to manipulate ostensibly mechanical legal doctrines that constitutes the most serious risk for the development of human rights jurisprudence. It has also been clearly demonstrated that the values that judges bring to bear cannot easily be divided into personal and legal: even the choice of interpretive theory requires a judgement which depends to some extent on the judge's own values. But, confirming the conclusions in Chapter 4, this chapter has shown that these choices need to be convincingly defended as furthering the human rights standards committed to judicial oversight. Such defences might lead to different conclusions, at different times, or even among different members of a court. But that is itself a source of dynamism, allowing human rights law to retain its energy and to progress.

VIII. Conclusion

The first five chapters of this book have set out the main cross-cutting themes in comparative human rights law: the role of comparative materials; the meaning of human rights; the relationship between civil and political rights and socio-economic rights; the role of adjudication; and different approaches to judicial interpretation. The following chapters apply these themes to some of the most challenging issues in comparative human rights law. Chapters 6–9 consider aspects of the right to life: capital punishment, abortion, health, and housing. Chapters 10–12 consider freedom aspects of human rights: speech, education, and religion. The coverage is not intended to be comprehensive, but to be challenging and thought-provoking. By considering the same topics over five different jurisdictions, many of the themes in the first part are illuminated; and in turn cast light on these difficult issues. It is in this spirit that we turn to consider comparative human rights law on the death penalty.

[232] ibid, 554–5.

PART II

6

Capital Punishment

I. Introduction

> It seems absurd to me that the laws, which are the expression of the public will, and which hate and punish murder, should themselves commit one, and that to deter citizens from murder, they should decree a public murder.
>
> (Cesare Beccaria, *On Crimes and Punishments* 1764)

> Capital punishment presents moral questions that philosophers, theologians, and statesmen have grappled with for millennia. The Framers of our Constitution disagreed bitterly on the matter. For that reason, they handled it the same way they handled many other controversial issues: they left it to the People to decide.
>
> (Scalia J, *Glossip v Gross* (2015) 35 S Ct 1885 (US Supreme Court))

Does the death penalty breach human rights? The answer to this question remains contentious. There are now a growing number of jurisdictions which have abolished the death penalty. By the end of 2014, a majority of countries had either removed the death penalty from their laws or were abolitionist in practice. As many as ninety-eight countries had abolished the death penalty for all crimes, a steep rise in only three decades. Nevertheless, the minority of countries which retain the death penalty are also among the most populous, including India, China, Indonesia, and the US. In practice, then, the majority of people in the world are potentially subject to the death penalty.[1] In the US, although the number of executions actually carried out in 2015 was the lowest since 1991, there were still twenty-eight executions in six States. And even though the number of death sentences handed down decreased by one-third, there were still forty-nine new death sentences imposed in 2015.[2]

Are countries which have not abolished the death penalty therefore in breach of human rights? Judicial responses to this question vary widely, not just between jurisdictions, but between judges in the same jurisdiction and over differing periods of time. In 1972, the US Supreme Court, by a narrow majority, held that the imposition of the death penalty constituted cruel and unusual punishment in violation of the US Constitution.[3] However, only four years later, with the dissenters now in the majority, this decision was reversed.[4] By contrast, the South African Constitutional

[1] 'Law Commission of India Report No 262: The Death Penalty' (Government of India, August 2015) paras 3.5 and 3.6 (hereafter 'Indian Law Commission 2015').

[2] Death Penalty Information Centre, 'The Death Penalty Year End Report 2015' 1 <http://www.deathpenaltyinfo.org/> (accessed 24 February 2018).

[3] *Furman v Georgia* 408 US 238 (1972) (US Supreme Court).

[4] *Gregg v Georgia* (1976) 428 US 153 (US Supreme Court).

Court, having surveyed the earlier US jurisprudence, struck down the death penalty in one of its first decisions under the new democratic constitution.[5] On the other hand, the Indian Supreme Court, similarly conscious of the earlier US jurisprudence, upheld the validity of capital punishment in the *Bachan Singh* case in 1980, albeit for the 'rarest of the rare' cases.[6]

Such contestations have spilled over into the twenty-first century. From the beginning of the century, differing majorities of the US Supreme Court, against vitriolic dissents, began to limit the reach of the death penalty for particular groups, such as those under eighteen at the time of the commission of the crime[7] or people with learning difficulties or mental illness.[8] However, as recently as 2015, five justices of the Court upheld the use of lethal injection, although it contained drugs which risked causing severe suffering, on the basis that the prisoner had not been able to prove that a different drug could be administered with a lower risk.[9] This came against a powerful dissent by Breyer J, with whom Ginsburg J agreed, arguing that the time had come for abolition. The Indian courts have witnessed similar turbulence. Several judgments of the Indian Supreme Court have expressed disquiet at the unpredictable ways in which the 'rarest of the rare' test laid down in *Bachan Singh* has been applied.[10] As the Court stated in *Bariyar*: 'There is no uniformity of precedents, to say the least. In most cases, the death penalty has been affirmed or refused to be affirmed by us, without laying down any legal principle'.[11] Indeed, as the Indian Law Commission pointed out, the 'Supreme Court itself has come to doubt the possibility of a principled and consistent implementation of the "rarest of rare" test'.[12] This in turn led the Commission to recommend that the death penalty be abolished for all crimes other than terrorism-related offences and waging war.[13] However, by 2017, it seemed unlikely that there would be legislation to this effect.

How then can we explain these divergent responses? The starting point is, of course, the text of the relevant human rights instrument. It will be seen that in several constitutional and international instruments, the State is prohibited from taking life except by due process of law, or similarly phrased caveat. This appears to mandate the death penalty. On the other hand, human rights instruments also contain a separate right not to be subjected to cruel or inhuman punishment, variously phrased. There is therefore much space for judicial interpretation. Divergent judicial approaches have focused on three main issues. The first is procedural. Is it possible to find a way of deciding whether to impose the death penalty which is not arbitrary, random, or

[5] *S v Makwanyane* 1995 (3) SA 391 (CC); 1995 (6) BCLR 665 (CC) (South African Constitutional Court).

[6] *Bachan Singh v State of Punjab* 1983 SCR (1) 145 (Indian Supreme Court): see Chapter 1 and S Fredman, 'Foreign Fads or Fashions? The Role of Comparativism in Human Rights Law' (2015) 64 ICLQ 631.

[7] *Roper v Simmons* (2005) 543 US 551 (US Supreme Court).

[8] *Atkins v Virginia* (2002) 536 US 304 (US Supreme Court).

[9] *Glossip v Gross* (2015) 135 S Ct 1885 (US Supreme Court).

[10] *Santosh Kumar Satishbhushan Bariyar v State of Maharashtra* (2009) 6 SCR 498 (Indian Supreme Court); *Shankar Kisanrao Khade v State of Maharashtra* (2009) 6 SCC 498 (Indian Supreme Court).

[11] *Santosh Kumar Satishbhushan Bariyar v State of Maharashtra*, (n 10) para [104].

[12] Indian Law Commission 2015 (n 1) para 1.3.13.

[13] Indian Law Commission 2015 (n 1) para 7.2.4.

discriminatory? While varying majorities of the US Court have held that it is possible to do so, the South African Court has been unequivocal in its rejection of this route. The second asks whether the death penalty can be justified by reference to penological goals, such as deterrence, retribution, and rehabilitation. Can the death sentence be said to be a proportionate punishment so as to satisfy the strict standards required to justify overriding the right to life? The third is substantive. Even if there is an affirmative answer to the first and second questions, can the death penalty be reconciled with human rights standards of dignity, humanity, and equality?

Each of these points is elaborated below. Although they are discussed separately, many of them are contested within a single case.[14] It will be seen that judges' choice of answers to these questions further depends on their background positions on the cross-cutting issues identified in the first five chapters of this book. Particularly influential are judges' theory of constitutional interpretation, their view of the proper role of the court, and their approach to comparativism. Some judges have clearly articulated a value-based view, derived from human rights or constitutional values such as dignity and equality. For others, the issue is firmly one for the legislature, regardless of the judges' own personal opinion. Alternatively, procedural safeguards might be perceived to be an approach more compatible with the judicial role than a substantive position.

A further theme running through this analysis concerns the role of comparative law. Judges increasingly refer to decisions in other jurisdictions, but the way they do so depends on their background theory of comparativism. As we saw in Chapter 1, the case of *Roper v Simmons*[15] was the scene of one of the fiercest disagreements between the majority of the US Court, which favoured reference to foreign and international law, and the dissenters, who saw this as a betrayal of the judicial role of upholding domestic law. At the same time, it is no longer possible for courts to have a purely parochial approach to the death penalty. Judges in one jurisdiction have to co-operate with other jurisdictions in an increasing number of circumstances. This is particularly so in relation to decisions about extradition of offenders to a country where they might face capital punishment. The interaction between jurisdictions has also become a central issue in relation to drugs used for lethal injection, since European countries have prohibited their export, primarily affecting the ability of US States to carry out the death penalty.

This chapter begins by considering the role of constitutional texts and international human rights law, as well as global interconnectedness. It then turns to the three main areas of contestation: procedure; penological justifications; and substantive values. Running through the discussion on each issue are the cross-cutting themes: separation of powers; interpretive theory; use of comparative material; and the extent to which decisions in one jurisdiction can affect others.

[14] See eg the plurality judgment in *Furman v Georgia* (n 3).

[15] *Roper v Simmons* (n 7).

II. Constitutional Texts and International Human Rights Instruments

The textual basis for the legitimacy or otherwise of the death penalty generally revolves around the interpretation of three key rights: the right to life; the right to due process of law; and the right not to be subjected to cruel or inhuman punishment or torture. Although constitutional texts differ in the wording of these rights, it is through the stormy waters at the confluence of these rights that judges have had to steer.

This tension is particularly explicit in the US Constitution. The Fourteenth Amendment states that no State shall 'deprive any person of life, liberty, or property, without due process of law'. Also relevant is the Fifth Amendment, which states: 'No person shall be held to answer for a capital, or otherwise infamous crime, unless on a presentment or indictment of a Grand Jury' except in relation to those serving in the armed forces. Both these provisions have been relied on by judges in the US Supreme Court to support the view that the death penalty is permitted. On the other hand, the death penalty must conform with the Eighth Amendment's prohibition on the infliction of 'cruel and unusual punishment'. It is in an attempt to reconcile these two provisions that the major divergences between different justices in the US Supreme Court arise.

Other constitutional provisions for the right to life, while modelled on the Fourteenth Amendment, include conscious differences. The Indian Constitution, in Article 21, states that '[n]o person shall be deprived of his life or personal liberty except according to procedure established by law'. On the face of it, this would permit any law, as long as it was duly passed by the legislature. However, in *Maneka Gandhi* the Court held that the procedure established by law must be 'fair, just and reasonable, not fanciful, oppressive or arbitrary'.[16] In the death penalty context, this means that no person should be deprived of life or liberty 'except according to fair, just and reasonable procedure established by a valid law'.[17] The Indian Supreme Court has relied on this formulation to underpin its finding of the constitutionality of the death penalty with a scrupulous attention to fair procedure.[18]

Somewhat surprisingly, the Indian Constitution does not contain a separate provision prohibiting torture or cruel and inhuman punishment. However, the Indian Supreme Court has held unequivocally that the right to life includes the right not to be tortured. In *Francis Coralie Mullin* in 1981, Bhagwati J stated:

> Now obviously, any form of torture or cruel, inhuman or degrading treatment would be offensive to human dignity ... No law which authorises and no procedure which leads to such torture or cruel, inhuman or degrading treatment can ever stand the test of reasonableness and non-arbitrariness: it would plainly be unconstitutional and void as being violative of Articles 14 and 21.[19]

[16] *Maneka Gandhi v Union of India* AIR 1978 SC 597 (Indian Supreme Court) 48.

[17] *Bachan Singh v State of Punjab* (n 6). [18] ibid.

[19] *Francis Coralie Mullin v The Administrator, Union Territory of Delhi* (1981) SCR (2) 516 (Indian Supreme Court) 529 B–F.

The right to life in section 11 of the South African Constitution does not include the caveat found in other constitutions. Instead, it states simply that 'everyone has the right to life'. Only the general limitation clause in section 36 applies, and this expressly requires a limitation which is reasonable, proportionate, and justifiable in an open and democratic society based on human dignity, equality, and freedom. At the same time, section 12 gives an express right not to be treated or punished in a cruel, inhuman, or degrading way.[20] Moreover, the right to dignity is express and self-standing. Under section 10, '[e]veryone has inherent dignity and the right to have their dignity respected and protected'. The South African Constitutional Court, in one of its very first decisions, struck down the death penalty on the basis that it infringed all these provisions.[21]

The tension between permitting the State to take life with due process of law and forbidding cruel and inhuman punishment is similarly evident in the international and European human rights instruments. Both the European Convention on Human Rights (ECHR) and the International Covenant on Civil and Political Rights (ICCPR) include an exception for the death penalty while at the same time prohibiting cruel, inhuman, or degrading punishment. Article 2(1) of the ECHR states that '[n]o one shall be deprived of his life intentionally save in the execution of a sentence of a court following his conviction of a crime for which this penalty is provided by law'. At the same time, Article 3 prohibits inhuman or degrading punishment. Similarly, Article 6(2) of the ICCPR provides that 'in countries that have not abolished the death penalty, sentence of death may be imposed only for the most serious crimes in accordance with the law in force at the time of the commission of the crime'. Yet Article 7 prohibits 'cruel, inhuman or degrading treatment or punishment'.

However, recognition of the unacceptability of the death penalty has been gathering momentum in Europe. In December 1982, the ECHR adopted Protocol 6, which provided for the abolition of the death penalty in peacetime. States could, however, make provision for the death penalty in time of war or of imminent threat of war. Just over a decade later, this was followed by Protocol 13, abolishing the death penalty in all circumstances. Protocol 13 entered into force in 2003. By May 2016, Protocol 13 had attracted forty-four ratifications and one signatory, with only Russia and Azerbaijan declining to sign. In 2005, the European Court of Human Rights (ECtHR) felt able to declare Europe a 'zone free of capital punishment'.[22] This was followed by a similar move by the Organization of American States, which adopted a Protocol to the American Convention on Human Rights which calls on States to abstain from the use of the death penalty and prevents States from reintroducing the death penalty.[23] This is less widely accepted: thirteen States have ratified the protocol, while twenty have not.[24]

[20] South African Constitution, s 12.

[21] *S v Makwanyane* (n 5); see further below.

[22] *Öcalan v Turkey* (2005) 41 EHRR 45 (European Court of Human Rights) para [163].

[23] Organization of American States, *Protocol to the American Convention on Human Rights to Abolish the Death Penalty ('Pact of San Jose')*, 8 June 1990, OAS Treaty Series, No 73 <http://www.oas.org/juridico/english/treaties/a-53.html> (accessed 24 February 2018).

[24] Department of International Law, OAS, Signatories and Ratifications <http://www.oas.org/juridico/english/sigs/a-53.html> (accessed 24 February 2018).

The ICCPR has similarly been augmented by the Second Optional Protocol, adopted in 1989, which states that '[n]o one within the jurisdiction of a State Party … shall be executed'. Reservations for time of war can only be made at the time of ratification or accession. In the decades since then, the Office of the UN High Commissioner for Human Rights (OHCHR) has been expressly advocating for the universal abolition of the death penalty. It has clear answers to all three of the main issues set out above, namely procedural fairness, penological justifications, and substantive values. According to the UN High Commissioner, there is no procedure which mitigates the unacceptable risk of executing innocent people; there is no proof that the death penalty serves as a deterrent to crime; and the right to life is fundamental.[25] Indeed, UN Secretary-General Ban Ki-moon made it clear that 'the death penalty has no place in the twenty-first century'.[26] This has been supported by a series of five resolutions adopted by the UN General Assembly between 2007 and 2013,[27] urging States to respect international standards that protect the rights of those facing the death penalty, to progressively restrict its use, and to reduce the number of offences which are punishable by death. Nevertheless, in May 2016, although there were eighty-one State Parties and one signatory to the Optional Protocol, as many as 132 countries in the world had not signed or ratified it.[28] Most of Africa and Asia, as well as the US, fell within this camp.

In both the UK and Canada, the death penalty was abolished through legislation. In the UK, a long and tortuous campaign for abolition culminated in a private member's bill introduced by Sydney Silverman in 1965, which passed in both houses. Entitled the Murder (Abolition of Death Penalty) Act 1965, it suspended the operation of capital punishment for an initial period of five years, which was repeatedly renewed despite at least thirteen attempts in subsequent years to reintroduce the death penalty. The 1965 Act therefore amounted to de facto abolition. Nevertheless, it was not until 1999 that the UK ratified Protocol 6 to the ECHR and Protocol 2 to the ICCPR.[29] In Canada, capital punishment was progressively restricted until it was abolished for all ordinary crimes in 1976. The remaining provisions referring to the death penalty for military offences and treason were removed from the National Defence Act in 1998 and Canada ratified the Second Optional Protocol to the ICCPR in November 2005.[30]

III. Global Interconnectedness

Even for abolitionist countries, the death penalty issue remains live in relation to the question of whether extradition to a death penalty country is permissible. There has

[25] OHCHR, 'Death Penalty' <http://www.ohchr.org/EN/Issues/DeathPenalty/Pages/DPIndex.aspx> (accessed 24 February 2018).

[26] ibid.

[27] UN General Assembly Resolutions 62/149 (adopted on 18 December 2007); 63/168 (adopted on 18 December 2008); 65/206 (adopted on 21 December 2010); 67/176 (adopted on 20 December 2012); and 69/186 (adopted in 18 December 2014) on a moratorium on the use of the death penalty.

[28] OHCHR, 'Status of Ratification Interactive Dashboard' <http://indicators.ohchr.org/> (accessed 24 February 2018).

[29] R Hood and C Hoyle, *The Death Penalty: A Worldwide Perspective* (5th edn, OUP 2015) 54–56.

[30] ibid.

been a growing acceptance that the legitimacy of the use of the death penalty is not simply a domestic matter, left to the sovereign decision of individual states. In Europe, including the UK, as well as in Canada and South Africa, the commitment to eradicating the death penalty extends beyond abolition at home to a refusal to be complicit in executions abroad. This manifests itself in particular in a refusal to extradite offenders wanted for trial on a charge which might carry the sentence of death in the requesting country, without assurances that the death penalty will not be applied. In the seminal case of *Soering*,[31] the ECtHR held that it would be a breach of the prohibition on inhuman or degrading treatment or punishment in Article 3 ECHR for the UK to extradite Soering to the US State of Virginia without assurances that he would not face the death penalty.

The Supreme Court of Canada appeared to take the opposite view in *Kindler*,[32] when it held that extraditing a person who had committed the worst sort of crime to face capital punishment did not 'shock the conscience of the Canadian people'. This was somewhat surprisingly upheld by the United Nations Human Rights Committee as consistent with the ICCPR.[33] However, a decade later, the Supreme Court of Canada reversed its position. In the 2001 case of *Burns*,[34] it decided that the extradition of the fugitive to the US State of Washington without any assurance that he would not face capital punishment constituted a breach of the Canadian Charter. Notably, the Court did not regard this as a breach of the right not to be subjected to 'cruel and unusual treatment or punishment' in section 12 of the Charter,[35] since it would be the State of Washington and not the government of Canada that would impose the death penalty. To this extent it followed *Kindler*, which was wary of giving extraterritorial effect to this section.[36] Instead, the Court addressed the question under section 7 of the Charter, which states: 'Everyone has the right to life, liberty and security of the person and the right not to be deprived thereof except in accordance with the fundamental principles of justice'. The Court concluded that in the absence of exceptional circumstances, the 'fundamental principles of justice' referred to in section 7 would be breached if a fugitive was extradited without assurances in a death penalty case. And this too was followed by a reversal on the part of the HRC, which, detecting a growing international consensus in favour of abolition, held that abolitionist states had a duty not to expose a person to the risk of the death penalty.[37]

Similarly, the South African Constitutional Court in *Mohammed v President of the Republic of South Africa*[38] held that it would be in breach of the right not to be subjected to degrading and inhuman treatment or punishment to extradite an offender to the US without an assurance that he would not be subject to the death penalty. In

[31] *Soering v UK* (1989) 11 EHRR 439 (European Court of Human Rights).
[32] *Kindler v Canada (Minister of Justice)* (1991) 2 SCR 779 (Supreme Court of Canada).
[33] *Roger Judge v Canada*, CCPR/C/78/D/829/1998 (UN Human Rights Committee).
[34] *Minister of Justice v Burns* [2001] RSC 283 (Supreme Court of Canada).
[35] Canadian Charter, s 12.
[36] *Minister of Justice v Burns* (n 34) at 55; see *Kindler v Canada (Minister of Justice)* (n 32) 845–46.
[37] *Roger Judge v Canada* (n 33).
[38] *Mohammed v President of South Africa* (2001) 3 SA 893 (South African Constitutional Court).

coming to this conclusion, it cited the European and Canadian authorities of *Soering* and *Burns*. But it also reaffirmed the values within the South African Constitution itself that left it in no doubt that the death penalty was in breach of the rights to life and to dignity, as well as the right not to be subjected to inhuman and degrading punishment or torture.

> For the South African government to cooperate with a foreign government to secure the removal of a fugitive from South Africa to a country of which the fugitive is not a national and with which he has no connection other than that he is to be put on trial for his life there, is contrary to the underlying values of our Constitution. It is inconsistent with the government's obligation to protect the right to life of everyone in South Africa, and it ignores the commitment implicit in the Constitution that South Africa will not be party to the imposition of cruel, inhuman or degrading punishment.[39]

This refusal to co-operate has extended to the export of drugs used for lethal injections in executions in the US. In 2005, the EU prohibited trade in goods which could be used for capital punishment, torture, or other cruel, inhuman, or degrading treatment or punishment.[40] This was further strengthened in 2009 by a regulation prohibiting any export of goods which have no practical use other than for the purpose of capital punishment, regardless of their origin.[41] American pharmaceutical companies have also responded to increasing public distaste for the death penalty by refusing to supply key lethal drugs. This has had a considerable effect on the availability of these drugs for carrying out executions in the US. Some States have reacted by expediting the abolition of the death penalty. The Connecticut legislature passed legislation prospectively outlawing capital punishment for all crimes committed after 25 April 2012. The Connecticut Supreme Court held in 2015 that, following its prospective abolition, the State's current death penalty no longer comported with contemporary standards of decency and no longer served any penological purpose. It would therefore be unconstitutional to execute those offenders who committed capital felonies prior to 25 April 2012.[42] Other US States, however, have defiantly sought alternatives. In 2015, Utah voted to reinstate the firing squad as a method of executing, given the difficulty of obtaining reliable drugs for lethal injection. Shortly afterwards, Oklahoma passed legislation allowing the death penalty to be administered through asphyxiation with nitrogen gas.[43] Most recently, in *Glossip v Gross*,[44] the US Supreme Court upheld the use of alternative drugs to carry out executions, despite evidence of the considerable physical pain and suffering inflicted on the offender.

[39] ibid, para [56]. [40] Council Regulation 1236/2005. [41] Council Regulation 428/2009.

[42] *State of Connecticut v Eduardo Santiago* 122 A 3d 1 2015 (Connecticut Supreme Court).

[43] Death Penalty Information Center, 'The Death Penalty in 2015: Year End Report' <https://deathpenaltyinfo.org/documents/2015YrEnd.pdf> (accessed 18 February 2018) 12.

[44] *Glossip v Gross* (n 9); see further below.

IV. Judicial Interpretation

A. Procedural fairness

1. *No room for error: the paradox of fair procedures*

Most of the jurisdictions examined here have not moved towards express prohibition. The extent to which the death penalty breaches human rights has therefore rested on judicial interpretation of relatively open-textured provisions such as 'due process of law', 'cruel and unusual', 'inhuman and degrading'. In the tense history of judicial treatment of challenges to the death penalty, a consistent theme has been to focus on the question of fair procedures. Is it possible to find a way of administering the death penalty which is not arbitrary, random, or discriminatory? While varying majorities of the US Supreme Court have held that it is possible to do so, the South African Constitutional Court has been unequivocal in its rejection of this route. Because this approach deals with legal process, courts have not had qualms about regarding it as falling within their legitimacy and competence. However, the difficulties in establishing a fair process have inevitably triggered more substantive issues which do challenge these boundaries.

Fair procedures gain unparalleled significance in the context of capital punishment. Unlike other punishments, the death penalty is 'unique in its total irrevocability'.[45] This puts a great premium on fair procedure. As Hood and Hoyle argue, the ultimate test of good procedure is that innocent people should never be executed.[46] Equally, given the mental anguish and physical suffering on death row, innocent people should not be wrongly convicted and sentenced to death in the first place because of lack of due process.[47] Procedures are known to be flawed in many cases, due to such factors as mistaken eyewitness identifications, false confessions, unreliable expert evidence, and failure of police and prosecutors to bring evidence of innocence before the court, often combined with weak or incompetent legal representation on behalf of the defence.[48] The 'Innocence List' published by the American Death Penalty Information Center shows that between 1973 and October 2017, as many as 161 people who had been sentenced to death had subsequently had their conviction overturned, or had all charges dropped, or been given an absolute pardon based on new evidence of innocence. Six of these cases occurred in 2015 alone.[49] This is reinforced by a study of every capital conviction between 1973 and 1995 in the US, which found that there had been an error sufficient to overturn the original conviction in as many as 68 per cent of cases which reached the final stage of appeal.[50] The authors point out that 'capital trials produce so many mistakes that it takes three judicial inspections to catch them—leaving grave doubt whether we do catch them all. After state courts threw out 47 per cent of death sentences due to serious flaws, a later federal review found 'serious error'—error

[45] *Furman v Georgia* (n 3) 306, per Stewart J. [46] Hood and Hoyle (n 29) at 323.
[47] ibid. [48] ibid.
[49] Death Penalty Information Center, *Innocence: List of Those Freed from Death Row* <http://www.deathpenaltyinfo.org/innocence-list-those-freed-death-row> (accessed 24 February 2018).
[50] J Liebman et al, 'Capital Attrition: Error Rates in Capital Cases, 1973– 1995' (2000) 78 Tex L Rev 1839.

undermining the reliability of the outcome—in 40 per cent of the remaining sentences'.[51] The figures from the 2015 Indian Law Commission on the Death Penalty are even more disturbing. According to these figures, the death penalty imposed by trial courts was confirmed by appellate courts in only 4.3 per cent of cases. In other words, trial judges erroneously impose the death penalty in a staggering 95.7 per cent of cases.[52] Yet, as we see below, there are many people who cannot afford or may not have access to appeals.

There has been fierce judicial disagreement, especially in the US, on the extent to which it is possible to find a procedure which is sufficiently fair to avoid convicting the innocent. This is partly because of the central tension in relation to fair procedure: there needs to be sufficient discretion for judges to respond to individual circumstances, while at the same time, there must be sufficient consistency as between cases. If the death penalty is issued in only a small and relatively random set of cases, and of these the number executed is even fewer and even more unpredictable, it is difficult to say that the procedure is either fair or fulfils socially useful purposes. This was the approach of Justices White and Stewart concurring in the majority judgment in *Furman v Georgia*, which struck down the death penalty in the case before the Court.[53] Whereas Justices Brennan and Marshall held that the death penalty was unconstitutional per se, Justices White and Stewart focused on the arbitrariness of the procedure. For Stewart J, the petitioners before the court were 'among a capriciously selected random handful upon whom the sentence of death has in fact been imposed'.[54] This arbitrariness in itself made it cruel and unusual: 'the Eighth and Fourteenth Amendments cannot tolerate the infliction of a sentence of death under legal systems that permit this unique penalty to be so wantonly and so freakishly imposed'.[55] The problem, as White J saw it, lay in the breadth of the discretion left to juries to impose sentences. The result of such open-ended discretion was that 'there is no meaningful basis for distinguishing the few cases in which it is imposed from the many cases in which it is not'. However, like Stewart J, he would not conclude from this that there was no system of capital punishment consistent with the Eighth Amendment's prohibition on cruel and unusual punishment.[56]

This left open the possibility of fashioning a procedure with less discretion, an approach which Georgia and several other States adopted. Only four years later, in *Gregg v Georgia*,[57] Stewart J was now convinced that a fair procedure had been found. For him, the concerns about arbitrary or capricious imposition of the death penalty could be met by drafting a statute giving adequate information and guidance to the judge or jury. Unlike the open-ended discretion at issue in the *Furman* case, the new Georgia sentencing procedure required the jury to pay attention to the particular nature of the crime and the particular characteristics of the defendant: 'No longer can a jury wantonly and freakishly impose the death sentence; it is always circumscribed by the legislative guidelines'.[58] White J took a similar view, and he was joined by the dissenters

[51] ibid; J Fagan and V West 'A Broken System' (2000) <http://www.ncadp.org/page/-/resources/A%20broken%20system-Error%20rates%20in%20capital%20cases%201973-1995,%20Liebman.pdf> (accessed 24 February 2018).

[52] India Law Commission 2015 (n 1) para 5.2.7.

[53] *Furman v Georgia* (n 3).

[54] ibid, 310.

[55] ibid.

[56] ibid, 311.

[57] *Gregg v Georgia* (n 4).

[58] ibid, 207.

in *Furman* so that a differently constituted majority was now in a position to uphold the death penalty. White J was adamant in his rejection of the petitioners' claim that government, created and run by humans, must be inevitably incompetent to administer the death penalty. While admitting that 'mistakes will be made and discriminations will occur which will be difficult to explain',[59] he insisted that enforcement of criminal law against murder was a basic function of the State: 'I decline to interfere with the manner in which Georgia has chosen to enforce such laws on what is simply an assertion of lack of faith in the ability of the system of justice to operate in a fundamentally fair manner'.[60]

However, experience since *Gregg* makes it questionable as to whether a procedure can indeed be devised which gives sufficient discretion to ensure that personal circumstances are fairly considered, while at the same time ensuring consistency as between cases. Indeed, in 1994, in *Callins v Collins*, Blackmun J, who had dissented in *Furman* and supported the majority in *Gregg*, came to the conclusion that it was impossible to achieve both fairness and consistency.[61] Dissenting in the decision not to grant certiorari, he declared:

> It seems that the decision whether a human being should live or die is so inherently subjective—rife with all of life's understandings, experiences, prejudices, and passions—that it inevitably defies the rationality and consistency required by the Constitution ... In my view, the proper course when faced with irreconcilable constitutional commands is not to ignore one or the other, nor to pretend that the dilemma does not exist, but to admit the futility of the effort to harmonize them. This means accepting the fact that the death penalty cannot be administered in accord with our Constitution.[62]

This conclusion was borne out by a review of the administration of the death penalty commissioned by the American Law Institute in 2009, thirty-three years after its recommendations on how to make the death penalty less arbitrary were adopted by the Supreme Court in *Gregg*. The authors of the study concluded that 'the preconditions for an adequately administered regime of capital punishment do not currently exist and cannot reasonably be expected to be achieved'. As a result, the American Law Institute withdrew the capital punishment provisions of its Model Penal Code 'in light of the current intractable institutional and structural obstacles to ensuring a minimally adequate system for administering capital punishment'.[63]

The South African Constitutional Court took a similar view in its carefully reasoned decision in *Makwanyane*,[64] when it refused to embark on the same road as that in *Gregg v Georgia*. Referring in detail to the complex contortions of US jurisprudence, it held that any attempt to devise a fair procedure for capital punishment was futile.[65] In addition to the difficulty of achieving both consistency and individualized sentencing,

[59] ibid, 226. [60] ibid. [61] *Callins v Collins* 510 (US) 1141 (1994) (US Supreme Court).
[62] ibid, 36 and 39.
[63] American Law Institute, 'Model Penal Code: Sentencing' <https://www.ali.org/projects/show/sentencing/> (accessed 24 February 2018).
[64] *S v Makwanyane* (n 5). [65] ibid, para [56].

there was the inevitability of long delays in making sure the procedure was correct. As Chaskalson P put it:

> The acceptance by a majority of the United States Supreme Court of the proposition that capital punishment is not per se unconstitutional, but that in certain circumstances it may be arbitrary, and thus unconstitutional, has led to endless litigation. Considerable expense and interminable delays result from the exceptionally-high standard of procedural fairness set by the United States courts in attempting to avoid arbitrary decisions. The difficulties that have been experienced in following this path ... persuade me that we should not follow this route.[66]

The death penalty was unique in this respect because it was irreversible: 'Unjust imprisonment is a great wrong, but if it is discovered, the prisoner can be released and compensated; but the killing of an innocent person is irremediable'.[67]

Nevertheless, the Indian Supreme Court has continued with the quest for a procedure which is both consistent and individualized. In *Bachan Singh*,[68] the Court upheld the constitutionality of the death penalty, but only for the 'rarest of rare' cases. The majority opinion paid close attention to the approach to fair procedure in the US Supreme Court cases of *Furman* and *Gregg*. However, it differed from the *Gregg* majority in that it regarded the emphasis on sentencing guidelines as constituting too great a sacrifice of judicial discretion, which it considered essential to ensure that the individual circumstances of the offender were taken into account. (Notably, neither South Africa nor India uses jury trials.) The optimism of the Court in *Bachan* that a fair, consistent approach to the death penalty could be found has not, however, matched the unfolding reality. So much so that by 2008, the Court was expressing its anxiety that sentencing, far from being principled, was dependent on the 'personal predilection of the judges constituting the Bench'.[69] This bears out the recognition by Bhagwati J in his powerful dissent in *Bachan Singh* that the quest for a fair procedure is ultimately futile: 'Howsoever careful may be the procedural safeguards erected by the law before death penalty can be imposed, it is impossible to eliminate the chance of judicial error'.[70] Notably, however, unlike the US Supreme Court in *Glossip v Gross*,[71] the Indian Supreme Court had no doubt that the burden lay on the State to prove that the deprivation of life or liberty is according to a just, fair, and reasonable procedure: 'The burden is never on the petitioner to prove that the procedure prescribed by law which deprives him of life or personal liberty is unjust, unfair or unreasonable'.[72]

The ECtHR, by contrast, has thus far relied on unfair procedures to avoid expressly finding that capital punishment in itself constitutes a breach of the right not to be subjected to cruel and inhuman punishment in Article 3 of the Convention. This issue does not frequently arise in Europe because, as we have seen, the vast majority of Member States have signed and ratified Protocol 13, which constitutes a blanket prohibition of the death penalty. However, it remains relevant for the small number of Contracting

[66] ibid. [67] ibid. [68] *Bachan Singh v State of Punjab* (n 6).

[69] *Swamy Shraddananda v State of Karnataka* (2008) 13 SCC 767 (Indian Supreme Court) para [33].

[70] *Bachan Singh v State of Punjab* (n 6) 283 D–E, G–H. [71] *Glossip v Gross* (n 9).

[72] *Deena @ Deena Dayal v Union of India* AIR 1983 SC 1155 (Indian Supreme Court).

States who have not yet signed the Protocol. In *Öcalan v Turkey*,[73] the applicant, who had been sentenced to death in Turkey, maintained that the imposition of the death penalty constituted a violation of Article 2 of the Convention (the right to life) as well as constituting an inhuman and degrading punishment contrary to Article 3 of the Convention. Although, as we have seen, Article 2 appears to permit the intentional taking of life 'in the executing of a sentence of a court following … conviction for a crime for which this penalty is provided by law', the applicant argued that Article 2 should no longer be interpreted as permitting capital punishment. The Court, however, refused to deal with this argument in the light of the fact that the death penalty had subsequently been abolished in Turkey and the applicant's sentence had been commuted to life imprisonment.[74] However, it did find that even if Article 2 were to be construed as still permitting the death penalty, it would be contrary to the Convention to implement such a sentence following an unfair trial.[75] For the deprivation of life to be pursuant to the 'execution of a sentence of a court', the adjudicator should be independent and impartial and the most rigorous standards of fairness should be observed. In the applicant's case, the imposition of the death sentence following an unfair trial itself amounted to inhuman treatment in violation of Article 3 of the Convention.[76]

With the near-universal ratification of Protocol 13 abolishing the death penalty under the ECHR, this issue might seem to be of little importance. However, it remains a central issue in relation to deportation. In the subsequent *Bader* case,[77] the applicant Syrian family challenged the decision by Sweden to deport them to Syria where the father faced the death penalty imposed in absentia by a Syrian court. The ECtHR held that an issue may arise under Articles 2 and 3 of the Convention if a 'contracting state deports an alien who has suffered or risks suffering a flagrant denial of a fair trial in the receiving State, the outcome of which was or is likely to be the death penalty'.[78] It found that in this case these conditions were made out, and the Court found in favour of the applicants.

2. *Delays and the death row phenomenon*

An insistence on fair procedures brings with it its own paradoxes, adding weight to the argument that a procedural emphasis cannot solve the substantive issues concerning the death penalty. This is clearly evidenced in relation to delays between sentencing and execution. While such delays are necessary to allow for appeals, reviews, and clemency, they also increase the mental anguish experienced by those awaiting the sentence of death. Can delay on its own constitute cruel and inhuman punishment even if the death penalty itself is held to be constitutionally mandated? On the one hand, it is an essential aspect of procedural fairness that those under sentence of death should be able to appeal against that sentence as well as apply for clemency or approach international committees. A speedy execution after sentence risks sending

[73] *Öcalan v Turkey* (2005) 41 EHRR 45 (European Court of Human Rights).
[74] ibid, paras [154]–[155]. [75] ibid, para [165]. [76] ibid, para [175].
[77] *Bader v Sweden* (2008) 46 EHRR 13 (European Court of Human Rights).
[78] ibid, para [42].

innocent people to their death where there might have been a reason for commutation. On the other hand, the mental anguish caused by long periods on death row awaiting execution has been widely recognized as cruel and inhuman. As the Privy Council put it in *Pratt v Attorney General for Jamaica*:[79]

> There is an instinctive revulsion against the prospect of hanging a man after he has been held under sentence of death for many years. What gives rise to this instinctive revulsion? The answer can only be our humanity; we regard it as an inhuman act to keep a man facing the agony of execution over a long extended period of time.[80]

This inevitable paradox is reflected in the well-known 'Death Row' phenomenon. In the US, long delays between sentence and execution are chronic. In the US, the average time spent on death row has been steadily increasing, reaching 198 months in 2011 and 190 months in 2012.[81] Typically, death row inmates in the US spend over a decade awaiting execution and some have been on death row for over twenty years. Not only are they generally isolated from other prisoners, excluded from educational programmes, and given very limited visitation and exercise rights, but they also live in a state of constant uncertainty over when they will be executed.[82]

A similar pattern is evident in India, where death row convicts spend many years exhausting their criminal appeals. In their report in 2016, Surendrenath et al found that the median incarceration for prisoners sentenced to death whose appeals were pending to the Supreme Court was six years and seven months, with one prisoner waiting as long as 21.5 years.[83] Once the death penalty is confirmed by the Indian Supreme Court, they wait for many more years to hear whether their petition for mercy has been upheld. Surendrenath et al found that the median number of years in incarceration for prisoners whose mercy petitions had been rejected was sixteen years and nine months, while the median for those whose mercy petitions were pending was twelve years. One prisoner had spent as long as twenty-five years in prison, over twenty-one of which were under sentence of death before his death sentence was commuted to life imprisonment by the Indian Supreme Court on the ground that the executive had caused inordinate delay in determining his mercy petition.[84] In the majority of cases, prisoners are moved to solitary confinement as soon as the death penalty is awarded by the trial court and are exposed to multiple warrants for their execution.[85] The Indian Law Commission graphically describes the 'extreme agony, anxiety and debilitating fear of an impending execution and uncertainty' which is experienced by a prisoner who 'ekes out an existence under the hangman's noose',[86] producing conditions of near-torture for the death row convict. Given that in practice there is an extremely low number of actual executions, with only four prisoners being executed in India between 2000 and 2015, Surendrenath et al rightly urge that the focus of the

[79] *Pratt v AG for Jamaica* (1994) 2 AC 1 (Privy Council (Jamaica)).

[80] ibid, 29 H.

[81] Death Penalty Information Center, 'Time on Death Row' <http://www.deathpenaltyinfo.org/time-death-row> (accessed 24 February 2018) (figures derived from US Department of Justice statistics).

[82] ibid.

[83] A Surendrenath et al, *Death Penalty India Report* (National Law University 2016) Vol 1, 50.

[84] ibid, 49.

[85] Indian Law Commission 2015 (n 1) para 6.7.1.

[86] ibid, para 6.7.2.

human rights debate should be on the tremendous mental and physical suffering inflicted on death row prisoners.[87]

The question of whether delay can itself constitute cruel and inhuman treatment has come before courts in several jurisdictions, with differing responses. On one view, the fact that a prisoner takes advantage of every possibility of having the death penalty commuted means that any delay should be considered to be the responsibility of prisoners themselves. This approach was endorsed by La Forest J in the Canadian case of *Kindler v Canada*, when he stated: 'It would be ironic if delay caused by the appellant's taking advantage of the full and generous avenue of the appeals available to him should be viewed as a violation of fundamental justice'.[88] There are dicta from the UK courts to similar effect.[89] While both these jurisdictions have now reversed this position, the US Supreme Court has firmly set its face against regarding delay as in itself a reason to commute a death penalty. In 2011, in *Valle v Florida*,[90] a prisoner who had spent thirty-three years on death row argued that execution following decades of incarceration on death row violated the Constitution's prohibition of 'cruel and unusual punishment'. The US Supreme Court, over a strong dissent by Breyer J, refused certiorari for an application for stay of execution.

In India, the effect of delay has been contentious. A two-judge bench of the Indian Supreme Court held in *Vatheeswaran*'s case in 1983 that any delay of more than two years would entitle the condemned prisoner to ask for a commutation of his sentence of death to life imprisonment.[91] But this was almost immediately over-ruled by a three-judge bench which held that delay alone was not sufficient for commutation.[92] The guiding authority is now *Smt Treveniben v State of Gujarat*,[93] where a five-judge bench held that delays in the process of the trial itself were for the benefit of the accused, and the good administration of justice. Such delay constituted a 'ray of hope' for prisoners and therefore could not be said to constitute the mental torture experienced once final sentence has been passed. Undue and prolonged delays in determining petitions of mercy could attract the jurisdiction of the Court, but only where the delay occurred at the instance of the executive, rather than the convicted person.[94] Even then, the jurisdiction of the court to commute the sentence was extremely limited, namely to consider whether the State was guilty of dilatory conduct, causing undue delay in disposing of the mercy position, and while this might be a significant factor, it could not itself render the execution unconstitutional.[95]

The opposite view has, however, gained momentum in a series of powerful judgments in the ECtHR, the Privy Council, and the Supreme Court of Canada, as well as the opinion of the Indian Law Commission on the Death Penalty. In *Soering*, the ECtHR held that, even though the death penalty could not itself amount to a breach of

[87] Surendrenath et al (n 83) 53. [88] *Kindler v Canada (Minister of Justice)* (n 32) 81.

[89] *Abbott v Attorney General for Trinidad and Tobago* (1979) 1 WLR 1342 (Privy Council) 1345; *Riley v Attorney General of Jamaica* (1983) 1 AC 719 (Privy Council) 724.

[90] *Valle v Florida* 132 S Ct 1 (2011) (US Supreme Court).

[91] *TV Vatheeswaran v State of Tamil Nadu* (1983) 2 SCC 68 (Indian Supreme Court).

[92] *Sher Singh v State of Punjab* (1983) 2 SCC 344 (Indian Supreme Court).

[93] *Smt Treveniben v State of Gujarat* [1989] 1 SCJ 383 (Indian Supreme Court).

[94] ibid, 528 F, G, 529 A, 529 B. [95] ibid, 550 D–G.

the prohibition on inhuman or degrading treatment or punishment in Article 3 of the Convention, the manner in which it is imposed or executed, as well as the conditions of detention, are factors capable of bringing the treatment of the condemned person within its proscription.[96] The applicant challenged his extradition by the UK to the US State of Virginia to face a murder trial on the grounds that the circumstances to which he would be exposed would constitute such serious treatment as to contravene Article 3. A condemned prisoner could expect to spend an average of six to eight years on death row in the State of Virginia. The Court accepted that the length of time awaiting death was 'in a sense largely of the prisoner's own making' in taking advantage of all avenues of appeal open to him. Nevertheless,

> just as some lapse of time between sentence and execution is inevitable if appeal safeguards are to be provided to the condemned person, so it is equally part of human nature that the person will cling to life by exploiting those safeguards to the full. However well-intentioned and even potentially beneficial is the provision of the complex of post-sentence procedures in Virginia, the consequence is that the condemned prisoner has to endure for many years the conditions on death row and the anguish and mounting tension of living in the ever-present shadow of death.[97]

The Court recognized that some delay between imposition and execution of a sentence was inevitable, and emphasized that the machinery of justice in the US respected the rule of law and provided considerable procedural safeguards. However, 'the very long period of time spent on death row in such extreme conditions, with the ever-present and mounting anguish of awaiting execution of the death penalty', together with the personal circumstances of the applicant (his youth and mental state), meant that extradition would expose him to a real risk of treatment going beyond the threshold of Article 3. Therefore, it held that the extradition would breach Article 3.[98]

The Privy Council took an even clearer stand in *Pratt v AG for Jamaica*. The Jamaican Constitution provided that any punishment which had been in force at the time the Constitution was passed (which included the death penalty) could not be regarded as falling foul of the prohibition on inhuman and degrading treatment or punishment in section 17(1) of the Constitution.[99] The only avenue for challenge was therefore on grounds of procedure. Importantly, the Privy Council held that the preservation of pre-existing punishments only applied to the sentence itself, not to the manner in which the sentence was carried out.[100] Delay could, therefore, in principle, constitute inhuman and degrading punishment. A much more difficult question was whether this would include a situation in which the delay was a result of the accused resorting legitimately to all available appellate procedures. The Privy Council, having canvassed the conflicting approaches of courts in different jurisdictions, was emphatic that it was

> part of the human condition that a condemned man will take every opportunity to save his life through use of the appellate procedure. If the appellate procedure enables

[96] *Soering v UK* (n 31) paras [103]–[104]. [97] ibid, para [111].
[98] ibid. Note that there was an alternative of extradition to Germany.
[99] Jamaican Constitution, s 17(1). [100] *Pratt v AG for Jamaica* (n 79) 29 F.

> the prisoner to prolong the appellate hearings over a period of years, the fault is to be attributed to the appellate system that permits such delay and not to the prisoner who takes advantage of it.[101]

To execute the prisoners after holding them in custody 'in an agony of suspense for so many years would be inhuman punishment'.[102] The Court therefore held that in any case in which execution was due to take place more than five years after sentence, there would be strong grounds for believing that the delay would constitute 'inhuman or degrading punishment'.[103] In the case before it, in which the applicants had been on death row for over fourteen years, there was no doubt that the sentence should be commuted.

Picking up the cue from *Soering* and *Pratt*, the Supreme Court of Canada in the more recent case of *Burns*[104] revisited its approach to the death row phenomenon. In extradition proceedings against two fugitives wanted for murder charges in the US, the Court held that while the death row phenomenon was not a controlling factor in determining whether the extradition would infringe the individual rights under section 7, 'even many of those who regard its horrors as self-inflicted concede that it is a relevant consideration'.[105] The death row phenomenon was a factor that weighed against extradition without assurances. Similarly, the Indian Law Commission cited extensively from the Privy Council decision in *Pratt* to argue that the extensive delays between sentence and execution in India and the appalling conditions of 'what can only be called a living death'[106] should be viewed as reaching the standard of impermissible cruel and degrading punishment.[107] It proposed that the two-year limit in *Vatheeswaran* should be resurrected, particularly in that it rightly did not distinguish between judicial delay and executive delay in the consideration of mercy petitions. Nor did it consider it relevant whether the delay was on account of litigation efforts of the prisoner.[108]

The response to such an approach could itself be paradoxical, namely to shorten the time between sentence and execution. Indeed, even in *Pratt*, the Privy Council took the view that where a State wishes to retain capital punishment, it should accept the responsibility of ensuring that the execution followed swiftly after sentence, allowing a reasonable time for appeal and consideration of reprieve.[109] But this brings with it the risk that appeals will not be properly dealt with. Clemency powers also take time to exercise properly. In India, for example, the President and Governor can look afresh at the evidence, can consider new evidence, and can take into account issues outside the judicial ken. Delay also undermines any penological justifications for the death penalty. In the end, the conflicting tensions cannot be reconciled. As Breyer J recognized it in his dissenting opinion in *Valle v Florida*,[110] procedures necessary to assure that the wrong person is not executed will inevitably cause the inhuman suffering of death row. In the powerful words of Bhagwati J, dissenting in *Bachan Singh* in the Indian Supreme Court: 'It is indeed a very live possibility and it is not at all unlikely

[101] ibid, 33 C. [102] ibid, 33 E. [103] ibid, 33 G.
[104] *Minister of Justice v Burns* (n 34). [105] ibid, para [123].
[106] Indian Law Commission 2015 (n 1) para 6.8.5. [107] ibid, para 6.7.13.
[108] ibid, para 6.7.14. [109] *Pratt v AG for Jamaica* (n 79). [110] *Valle v Florida* (n 90).

that so long as death penalty remains a constitutionally valid alternative, the court or the State acting through the instrumentality of the court may have on its conscience the blood of an innocent man'.[111]

B. Penological justifications

The above discussion concerned attempts to bring the death penalty within the human rights canon by attempting to achieve fair procedures. A second way of attempting to reconcile the death penalty with the prohibition on cruel and inhuman punishment focuses on penological justifications.[112] As US Supreme Court Justice Breyer stated in his dissenting opinion in *Glossip v Gross*:

> The rationale for capital punishment classically rests upon society's need to secure deterrence, incapacitation, retribution, or rehabilitation. Capital punishment by definition does not rehabilitate. It does, of course, incapacitate the offender. But the major alternative to capital punishment—namely, life in prison without possibility of parole—also incapacitates. Thus, ... the death penalty's penological rationale in fact rests almost exclusively upon a belief in its tendency to deter and upon its ability to satisfy a community's interest in retribution.[113]

This section considers the role of deterrence and retributory justifications.

1. *Deterrence*

The evidence relating to the deterrent effect of the death penalty has been used by judges to support opposite conclusions. Dissenting in *Glossip v Gross*,[114] Breyer J referred to a review of thirty years of empirical evidence by the US National Research Council, which concluded that 'research to date on the effect of capital punishment on homicide is not informative about whether capital punishment decreases, increases, or has no effect on homicide rates. Therefore, the committee recommends that these studies not be used to inform deliberations requiring judgments about the effect of the death penalty on homicide'.[115] This led Breyer J to conclude that deterrence could not be a sufficient justification for the death penalty. On the other hand, Scalia J, concurring with the majority in the same case, was scathing about this conclusion. Citing research which estimated that each state execution deterred between fourteen and eighteen murders on average per year, he thought that it was likely the death penalty did have a deterrent effect.[116] By contrast, in *Makwanyane*, Chaskalson P canvassed in

[111] *Bachan Singh v State of Punjab* (n 6) at 283 G–H.

[112] See eg the State's arguments in *S v Makwanyane* (n 5) para [27].

[113] *Glossip v Gross* (n 9). [114] ibid.

[115] D Nagin and J Pepper (eds), *National Research Council, Deterrence and the Death Penalty*, cited by Breyer J in *Glossip v Gross* (n 9).

[116] Citing Zimmerman, 'State Executions, Deterrence, and the Incidence of Murder', 7 J Applied Econ 163, 166 (2004) ('[I]t is estimated that each state execution deters approximately fourteen murders per year on average'); H Dezhbakhsh, P H Rubin, and J M Shepherd, 'Does Capital Punishment Have a Deterrent Effect? New Evidence from Postmoratorium Panel Data', 5 Am L & Econ Rev 344 (2003) ('[E]ach execution results, on average, in eighteen fewer murders [per year]'): Scalia J in *Glossip v Gross* (n 9).

detail all the evidence for the efficacy of the death penalty for the purposes of deterrence and prevention. His conclusion was that it had not been shown that the death sentence would be materially more effective to deter or prevent murder than life imprisonment.[117] On the other hand, in *Bachan Singh*, the Supreme Court of India was persuaded by the fact that 'in most of the countries in the world, including India, a very large segment of the population, including notable penologists, judges, jurists, legislators and other enlightened people still believe that death penalty for murder and certain other capital offences does serve as a deterrent, and a greater deterrent than life imprisonment'.[118] Although it recognized that there was evidence against this view, it found that the pattern was too inconclusive for the Court to reject the legislature's support for the death penalty. Meanwhile, in their authoritative study, Hood and Hoyle make it clear that evidence stands fully behind the view that the death penalty cannot be credited with a deterrent effect. Indeed, some of the research which is commonly placed before courts, such as that of Ehrlich,[119] to which the Court in *Bachan Singh* paid specific attention,[120] has been shown to have significant weaknesses in its purported proof of deterrent effects.[121]

The difficulty courts find in handling social science evidence of this sort pushes the issue back to questions of who bears the burden of justification, and how strict the standard of proportionality should be. The Indian Supreme Court in *Bachan Singh* placed the burden squarely on opponents of the death penalty to prove that there were no deterrent effects. Provided that a rational person could believe that this penological purpose might be served, the Court was prepared to uphold legislation permitting the death penalty, albeit only for the rarest of rare cases. Behind this low standard of proof was the Court's view that capital punishment was clearly envisaged in the Indian Constitution and therefore the Court should be slow to displace the legislative judgment. 'The very fact that persons of reason, learning and light are rationally and deeply divided in their opinion on this issue, is a ground among others, for rejecting the petitioner's argument that retention of death penalty in the impugned provision, is totally devoid of reason and purpose'.[122]

By contrast, the South African Constitutional Court in *Makwanyane* emphasized that any incursion on the fundamental right to life needed to be strictly justified, with the burden on the State to provide positive proof, not just of a deterrent effect per se, but of a greater deterrent effect than feasible alternatives, bearing in mind the arbitrariness and possibility of error.[123] From this perspective, the lack of conclusive evidence of deterrence indicated that the death penalty had not been justified and therefore could not be upheld. Ultimately, from a human rights perspective, it is incontestable that the strict approach to proportionality must be preferred. As Wright

[117] *S v Makwanyane* (n 5) paras [121]–[127].

[118] *Bachan Singh v State of Punjab* (n 6) para [77].

[119] I Ehlrich, 'The Deterrent Effect of Capital Punishment: A Question of Life and Death' (1975) 65 American Economic Review 397.

[120] *Bachan Singh v State of Punjab* (n 6) para [92].

[121] P Passell and J Taylor, 'The Deterrent Effect of Capital Punishment: Another View' (1977) 67 American Economic Review 445.

[122] *Bachan Singh v State of Punjab* (n 6) 221 B–H.

[123] *S v Makwanyane* (n 5) para [181].

CJ put it in the Supreme Court of California as early as 1972, 'A punishment as extreme and as irrevocable as death cannot be predicated upon speculation as to what the deterrent effect might be'.[124]

Nor are procedural and penological considerations unconnected. As Breyer J pointed out in *Glossip v Gross*, lengthy delays can undermine any possible deterrent value of the death penalty. Very few of those sentenced to death are actually executed, and many can spend up to two decades on death row. This, he concluded, 'makes it difficult to believe (given the studies of deterrence cited earlier) that such a rare event significantly deters horrendous crimes'.[125]

2. Retribution

Retribution is an even more difficult pillar on which to rest the claim that the death penalty can be justified as a proportionate limit on the right to life, or that it is not a cruel and inhuman punishment. As Chaskalson P put it in *Makwanyane*:

> The state does not need to engage in the cold and calculated killing of murderers in order to express moral outrage at their conduct. A very long prison sentence is also a way of expressing outrage and visiting retribution upon the criminal.[126]

Concluding that revenge was not compatible with the foundational values of the South African Constitution, he cited Brennan J in *Furman* that society should be one which 'wishes to prevent crime ... [not] to kill criminals simply to get even with them'.[127]

The approach of the Indian Supreme Court is more complex. It has recognized that retribution in the form of revenge (or 'an eye for an eye') does not pass constitutional muster.[128] On the other hand, 'society's cry for justice' has been regularly used by the Supreme Court as a justification for imposing the death penalty.[129] In *Bachan Singh*, the Court stated that retribution, not in the sense of an 'eye-for-an-eye' approach, but 'in the sense of society's reprobation for the worst of crime is not an altogether outmoded concept'.[130] The Indian Commission nevertheless came to the conclusion that cases justifying the death penalty on the basis of 'society's cry for justice' were highly problematic in that they did not properly analyse individual aggravating and mitigating circumstances and therefore departed from any principle of just desert.[131] Even within the retributive framework, the death penalty might be disproportionate: first, by not giving the offender the opportunity to express remorse; and second, due to its 'brutalization effect', in justifying the taking of life and therefore giving legitimacy to the devaluation of life.[132]

Like the Indian Supreme Court, the US Supreme Court has not given up the adherence to retribution as a justification for the death penalty. Scalia J, concurring with the

[124] *People v Anderson* 493 P 2d 880, 886 (Cal 1972) (Wright, CJ.); endorsed by Chaskalson P in *S v Makwanyane* (n 5) para [127].

[125] *Glossip v Gross* (n 9).

[126] *S v Makwanyane* (n 5) para [129].

[127] Chaskalson P in ibid, para 131, citing Brennan J in *Furman v Georgia* (n 3) 305.

[128] Indian Law Commission 2015 (n 1) para 4.7.5.

[129] ibid, para 4.7.7.

[130] *Bachan Singh v State of Punjab* (n 6) para [102].

[131] Indian Law Commission 2015 (n 1) para 4.7.8.

[132] ibid, paras 4.8.6 and 4.8.7.

majority in *Glossip*, was scornful about the idea that retributive aims could equally be fulfilled by life imprisonment:

> With all due respect, whether the death penalty and life imprisonment constitute more-or-less equivalent retribution is a question far above the judiciary's pay grade. Perhaps [his learned brethren] is more forgiving—or more enlightened—than those who, like Kant, believe that death is the only just punishment for taking a life. I would not presume to tell parents whose life has been forever altered by the brutal murder of a child that life imprisonment is punishment enough.[133]

It was left to Breyer J's dissent in *Glossip v Gross* to suggest that 'whatever interest in retribution might be served by the death penalty as currently administered, that interest can be served almost as well by a sentence of life in prison without parole'.[134] Here too, very long delays were relevant: in his view, the 'community's sense of retribution' must be diluted if the punishment comes decades after the crime:

> By then the community is a different group of people. The offenders and the victims' families have grown far older. Feelings of outrage may have subsided. The offender may have found himself a changed human being. And sometimes repentance and even forgiveness can restore meaning to lives once ruined. At the same time, the community and victims' families will know that, even without a further death, the offender will serve decades in prison under a sentence of life without parole.[135]

All these cases assume without question that life without parole is the appropriate alternative to the death penalty, capable of answering critics' concerns that the retributive and deterrent functions of the death penalty need to be met. Yet there is increasing concern that whole life sentences also overstep the boundaries of the injunction against cruel and inhuman punishment. Indeed, the Council of Europe declared in 1972 that 'it is inhuman to imprison a person for life without the hope of release'.[136] In *Vinter v UK*,[137] the Grand Chamber of the ECtHR held that the penological justifications for continued detention of a prisoner could only be sustained if there was a possibility of review at an appropriate point in the sentence. It stressed that there was now clear support in European and international law for the principle that 'all prisoners, including those serving life sentences, be offered the possibility of rehabilitation and the prospect of release if that rehabilitation is achieved'.[138] In the context of life sentences, it held, Article 3 requires that there should be a review which allows the authorities to decide whether any changes are sufficiently significant, and in particular whether such progress towards rehabilitation has been made, that continued detention can no longer be justified on legitimate penological grounds.[139] Importantly, the prisoner should know at the start of the sentence that such a review would take place, and when it would take place, so that they have the incentive to rehabilitate.[140] This, of course,

[133] *Glossip v Gross* (n 9). [134] ibid. [135] ibid.

[136] European Committee on Crime Problems, 'General Report on the Treatment of Long-Term Prisoners' (Council of Europe 1975) para [77].

[137] *Vinter v UK* 34 BHRC 605 (European Court of Human Rights (Grand Chamber)).

[138] ibid, para [141]. [139] ibid, paras [119]–[121].

[140] ibid, para [119]. But see *R v McLoughlin and Newell* [2014] EWCA Crim 188, where the Court of Appeal held that the procedure in place in the UK fulfilled these requirements. For a critique, see Hood and Hoyle (n 29) 489.

did not preclude the possibility that a decision could be taken to prolong the detention on public safety or other grounds.

C. Substantive values: dignity and equality

The futile quest for procedurally fair means of applying the death penalty, together with its shaky penological foundations, opens the question of whether substantive, value-driven decision-making is unavoidable and indeed required. The key question becomes whether the prohibition on cruel, inhuman, or degrading punishment should be interpreted to override any textual basis for upholding the death penalty in human rights instruments. Because any response to such a question propels judges into openly substantive judgments, there has been fierce contestation between judges, even within the same jurisdiction, as to whether this is a legitimate area for judges to enter into. Some judges have expressly eschewed any such role, arguing that these are decisions which should be left to the democratic will of the 'people'. As we saw in Chapter 4, however, this is itself a value judgement, especially because those who are affected are unlikely to have any political voice. A different approach is to attempt to gauge the intention of the drafters. As we saw in Chapter 5, even if such an intention can be discovered (which has generally not been possible), it is questionable whether such an approach gives any greater legitimacy to judges.

The alternative, which is explored in this section, is to be openly substantive, drawing on constitutional values such as dignity, equality, and basic humanity. The South African Constitutional Court has been at the forefront of such an approach. The US jurisprudence on substantive decision-making is more complex. On the one hand, the Eighth Amendment prohibition of 'cruel and unusual punishment' invites value judgements to give meaning to its central concept. On the other hand, judges aim to avoid the accusation of relying on their own personal predilections or values. This has led to fierce disagreements between judges in capital punishment cases about the role of substantive decision-making. Although, since *Furman*, the substantive approach has not won the day in striking down the death penalty in its entirety, fluctuating majorities in the US Supreme Court have nevertheless relied on values such as dignity to limit its scope in relation to either the offender or the offence. These points are elaborated below.

1. *Dignity and its detractors*

The scene was set for a value-based approach to the meaning of 'cruel and unusual punishment' in the US Constitution by Chief Justice Warren in *Trop v Dulles*[141] when he said: 'The basic concept underlying the Eighth Amendment is nothing less than the dignity of man ... The Amendment must draw its meaning from the evolving standards of decency that mark the progress of a maturing society'. Changing majorities of judges have attempted to pin the meaning of 'evolving standards of decency'

[141] *Trop v Dulles* (1958) 356 US 86 (US Supreme Court) 100–101; and see also *Roper v Simmons* (n 7) 561.

to State legislation, but also opinion polls. The difficulty with this approach is that human rights would not be necessary if majoritarian politics or public opinion, however determined, simply supported them. This paradox has led some judges to insert substantive values into the determination of evolving standards of decency. At the forefront of this approach are the dicta of Justices Brennan and Marshall in *Furman*. Indeed, Brennan J's formulation has become the lodestone of a value-based approach to capital punishment. 'The State, even as it punishes,' he stated, 'must treat its members with respect for their intrinsic worth as human beings'.[142] Since 'the calculated killing of a human being by the State involves, by its very nature, a denial of the executed person's humanity',[143] he had no doubt that 'in comparison to all other punishments today ... the deliberate extinguishment of human life by the State is uniquely degrading to human dignity'.[144] Marshall J was similarly forthright in his embrace of substantive principles.

Although Brennan J's judgment in *Furman* was rejected by later majorities in the US Supreme Court, his focus on dignity resonated with the South African Constitutional Court in *Makwanyane*.[145] Indeed, Chaskalson P expressly cited Brennan J's dicta in *Furman* in support of his view that the death penalty was irreconcilable with the values behind the South African Constitution, and particularly the right to dignity in section 10.[146] For Chaskalson P: 'The rights to life and dignity are the most important of all human rights ... By committing ourselves to a society founded on the recognition of human rights we are required to value these two rights above all others'.[147] Dignity is not only about the offender. The death penalty degrades and dehumanizes all who participate in its processes.[148] This, of course, raises the question of the rights to life and dignity of the victim of murder at the hands of the accused. But the life and dignity of the victim would only be protected if the death penalty would have prevented the murder. As we have seen, the deterrent value of the death penalty has not been established.[149] Moreover, as Kentridge AJ put it in *Makwanyane*, it cannot be denied that offenders subject to the death penalty have committed unspeakably cruel acts of violence on their victims. However, 'that does not mean that the State should respond to the murderer's cruelty with a deliberate and matching cruelty of its own'.[150] The Hungarian Constitutional Court has similarly held that the death penalty is inconsistent with the inherent rights to life and human dignity enshrined in its Constitution.[151] There have also been powerful dicta in other courts, albeit in dissent. Thus, in the Supreme Court of Canada in *Kindler*, Cory J in his dissenting opinion described the death penalty as 'the ultimate desecration of human dignity'.[152]

Brennan and Marshall JJ in *Furman*, however, were not unaffected by concerns as to how legitimate it is for judges to enter the arena of value-based decision-making. It was their attempt to locate these values, not in the Constitution itself, but in what

[142] *Furman v Georgia* (n 3) 270. [143] ibid, 290. [144] ibid, 291.
[145] *S v Makwanyane* (n 5). [146] ibid, para [26]. [147] ibid, para [144].
[148] ibid, per Didcott J, para [189]. [149] ibid, per Didcott J, para [181].
[150] ibid, per Kentridge AJ, para [197].
[151] Hungarian Constitution, s 54; see Hungarian Constitutional Court (Decision 23/1990 (X31) AB).
[152] *Kindler v Canada (Minister of Justice)* (n 32) (per Cory J, dissenting with Lamer CJC concurring); see also La Forest J at 833.

they discerned to be the 'evolving standards of decency' of contemporary US society that led to the downfall of their approach. Thus, Marshall J stated: 'Even if capital punishment is not excessive, it nonetheless violates the Eighth Amendment because it is morally unacceptable to the people of the United States at this time in their history'.[153] However, the rapid resurrection of the death penalty in a significant number of US States after *Furman* belied the view that these values were grounded in current social norms. In *Makwanyane*, on the other hand, Chaskalson P was forthright in his embrace of substantive decision-making by courts in the human rights field, even if it conflicted with public opinion. Thus, he stated:

> I am prepared to assume that the majority of South Africans agree that the death sentence should be imposed in extreme cases of murder. The question before us, however, is not what the majority of South Africans believe a proper sentence for murder should be. It is whether the Constitution allows the sentence.[154]

Deliberately eschewing a majoritarian approach, he declared: 'It is only if there is a willingness to protect the worst and the weakest amongst us, that all of us can be secure that our own rights will be protected'.[155]

The Indian Supreme Court came to the opposite conclusion, relying on their originalist approach to constitutional interpretation. Thus, in *Bachan Singh*, the Court held:

> It cannot be said that the framers of the Constitution considered death sentence for murder or the prescribed traditional mode of its execution as a degrading punishment which would defile 'the dignity of the individual' within the contemplation of the Preamble to the Constitution.[156]

The Court was highly dismissive of Brennan and Marshall's approach in *Furman*, on the basis that it misjudged the opinion of the American people. The lesson the Indian Supreme Court drew was one of deference:

> The rejection by the people of the approach adopted by the two learned Judges in Furman, furnishes proof of the fact that judicial opinion does not necessarily reflect the moral attitudes of the people. At the same time, it is a reminder that Judges should not take upon themselves the responsibility of becoming oracles or spokesmen of public opinion: Not being representatives of the people, it is often better, as a matter of judicial restraint, to leave the function of assessing public opinion to the chosen representatives of the people in the legislature concerned.[157]

This indeed echoed the stance of Brennan and Marshall's opponents on the US Supreme Court, who took the view that substantive value judgements were for legislatures, not for judges, however reprehensible they found the death penalty within their own moral compass. This was vividly expressed by Chief Justice Burger, dissenting in *Furman*:

[153] *Furman v Georgia* (n 3) 360. [154] *S v Makwanyane* (n 5) para [87].
[155] ibid, para [88]. [156] *Bachan Singh v State of Punjab* (n 6) para [136].
[157] ibid, para [125].

> If we were possessed of legislative power, I would either join with Mr. Justice Brennan and Mr. Justice Marshall or, at the very least, restrict the use of capital punishment to a small category of the most heinous crimes. Our constitutional inquiry, however, must be divorced from personal feelings as to the morality and efficacy of the death penalty, and be confined to the meaning and applicability of the uncertain language of the Eighth Amendment. The highest judicial duty is to recognize the limits on judicial power and to permit the democratic processes to deal with matters falling outside of those limits.[158]

For Blackmun J, the dilemmas were even more acute:

> Cases such as these provide for me an excruciating agony of the spirit. I yield to no one in the depth of my distaste, antipathy, and, indeed, abhorrence, for the death penalty, with all its aspects of physical distress and fear and of moral judgment exercised by finite minds. That distaste is buttressed by a belief that capital punishment serves no useful purpose that can be demonstrated . . .[159]

However, the task for judges was not the same as that of legislators.

> Our task here, as must so frequently be emphasized and re-emphasized, is to pass upon the constitutionality of legislation that has been enacted and that is challenged. This is the sole task for judges. We should not allow our personal preferences as to the wisdom of legislative and congressional action, or our distaste for such action, to guide our judicial decision in cases such as these.[160]

In the Indian Supreme Court, it was only Bhagwati J dissenting in *Bachan Singh* who was prepared to be frank in his embrace of substantive judicial value judgements. Judges must 'take care to see that they are guided by "objective factors to the maximum possible extent"'. But ultimately,

> it must be realized that the question of constitutional validity of death penalty is not just a simple question of application of constitutional standards by adopting a mechanistic approach ... it is a problem which raises profound social and moral issues and the answer must therefore necessarily depend on the judicial philosophy of the Judge.[161]

Bhagwati J acknowledged that the Indian Constitution recognized the death sentence as one of the penalties which may be imposed by law. But that did not mean that 'the infliction of death penalty is blessed by the Constitution or that it has the imprimatur or seal of approval of the Constitution'.[162] Instead, 'the entire thrust of the Constitution is in the direction of development of the full potential of every citizen and the right to life along with basic human dignity is highly prized and cherished and torture and cruel or inhuman treatment or punishment which would be degrading and destructive of human dignity are constitutionally forbidden'.[163]

[158] *Furman v Georgia* (n 3) 375. [159] ibid, 405. [160] ibid, 411.
[161] *Bachan Singh v State of Punjab* (n 6) at 302 A–B. [162] ibid, 276 D–H, 277 A–B.
[163] ibid.

2. *Dignity as a restraining principle*

Despite the refusal to use dignity to mount a full-scale offensive against the death penalty, judges in various jurisdictions have felt able to resort to it in order to limit the reach or scope of capital punishment. This can be seen in *Bachan Singh*, where the Indian Supreme Court relied on dignity to confine the applicability of the death penalty to the 'rarest of the rare' cases. Thus, it declared: 'A real and abiding concern for the dignity of human life postulates resistance to taking a life through law's instrumentality. That ought not to be done save in the rarest of rare cases when the alternative option is unquestionably foreclosed'.[164]

In the US, substantive decision-making has instead emerged in relation to specific classes of offence or offender. Here the struggle has been between those judges who assert that it is legitimate for them to bring their own independent judgement to bear in determining evolving standards of decency, and those who continue to maintain that this merely disguises personal predilections. The contestation is clearly seen in *Coker v Georgia*,[165] in which the death penalty for rape of an adult woman was struck down. Giving the opinion of the Court, White J stated: 'The attitude of state legislatures and sentencing juries do not wholly determine this controversy, for the Constitution contemplates that in the end our own judgement will be brought to bear on the question of the acceptability of the death penalty under the Eighth Amendment'.[166] The case, coming as it did after *Gregg v Georgia*,[167] could not revisit the question of whether the death penalty per se was inevitably cruel and unusual. Nevertheless, White J reiterated that even under *Gregg*, a punishment which was excessive would breach the Eighth Amendment: the death penalty for the rape of an adult woman was grossly disproportionate and excessive and therefore forbidden by the Eighth Amendment. The dissenters, however, saw this as an illegitimate imposition of judicial values. According to Burger CJ, with whom Rehnquist J agreed: 'The Cruel and Unusual Punishments Clause does not give the Members of this Court license to engraft their conceptions of proper public policy onto the considered legislative judgments of the States'.[168] The approach in *Coker* was nevertheless reinforced in the later case of *Enmund*,[169] where the Court concluded that it was an impermissible breach of the Eighth and Fourteenth Amendments to impose the death penalty on an offender whose involvement in the crime was no more than to wait in the getaway car, and who had not intended or anticipated that lethal force would be used to effectuate the planned burglary. Here too the Court followed *Coker* in looking at various objective sources, including legislative judgment, international opinion, and juries' sentencing decisions before bringing its own judgement to bear on the matter.[170]

This contestation continues apace. In *Thomson v Oklahoma*,[171] a plurality of the Court decided that evolving standards of decency did not permit the execution of an offender who was under sixteen at the time of the crime. Here too the plurality reiterated that '[a]lthough the judgments of legislatures, juries, and prosecutors weigh

[164] ibid, para [207]. [165] *Coker v Georgia* 433 (US) 584 (1977) (US Supreme Court).
[166] ibid, 597. [167] *Gregg v Georgia* (n 4). [168] *Coker v Georgia* (n 165) 604.
[169] *Enmund v Florida* 458 US 782 (1982) (US Supreme Court). [170] ibid, 788–89.
[171] *Thompson v Oklahoma* 417 US 815 (1988) (US Supreme Court).

heavily in the balance, it is for us ultimately to judge whether the Eighth Amendment permits imposition of the death penalty'.[172] Notably, the plurality observed that its conclusion was consistent with views expressed by 'other nations that share our Anglo-American heritage, and by the leading members of the Western European community'.[173] However, the extent to which the Court could bring its own judgement to bear on the acceptability of the death penalty was rejected by a differing majority in two important cases in 1989. In *Stanford v Kentucky*, a narrow majority referred to contemporary standards of decency to conclude that executing offenders over the age of fifteen but younger than eighteen at the time of committing the crime did not breach the Eighth Amendment. A plurality of the Court 'emphatically rejected' the suggestion that the Court should bring its own judgement to bear on the acceptability of the death penalty for juveniles.[174] For similar reasons, and on the same day, the Court decided in the *Penry* case that the Eighth Amendment did not require a categorical exemption from the death penalty for offenders with intellectual disabilities who were otherwise competent to stand trial.[175]

The pendulum swung again in the opposite direction in the first decade of the twenty-first century. In the 2002 case of *Atkins v Virginia*,[176] a different majority of the Court reversed the *Penry* case and held that executing criminals with intellectual disabilities constituted 'cruel and unusual punishment' prohibited by the Eighth Amendment of the Federal Constitution. Of particular importance was the fact that the *Atkins* Court emphatically returned to the position established in cases predating *Stanford*, namely that 'the Constitution contemplates that in the end our own judgment will be brought to bear on the question of the acceptability of the death penalty under the Eighth Amendment'.[177] Delivering the opinion of the Court, Stevens J stated that 'our own judgement is "brought to bear" by asking whether there is reason to disagree with the judgment reached by the citizenry and its legislators'.[178] Having found that eighteen State legislatures which had recently addressed the matter had concluded that the death penalty was not a suitable punishment for offenders with intellectual disabilities, Stevens J went on to say: 'Our independent evaluation of the issue reveals no reason to disagree with the judgment of [these legislatures]'.[179] However, the dissenting voices have not been muted. For them, the reliance on substantive values inevitably signalled an attempt to conceal personal preferences. Rehnquist CJ and Scalia J both criticized the Court's assessment of the current legislative judgment as resembling a 'post hoc rationalization of the majority's subjectively preferred result rather than any objective effort to ascertain the content of an evolving standard of decency'.[180] Scalia J was typically derisive: 'Seldom has an opinion of this Court rested so obviously upon nothing but the personal views of its members'.[181]

Nevertheless, the substantive approach remained narrowly in the ascendancy in *Roper v Simmons*[182] in 2004, where the Court, by a majority of five–four, reversed

[172] ibid, 833. [173] ibid, 830.

[174] *Stanford v Kentucky* (1989) 492 US 361 (US Supreme Court) 377–78 (Scalia J, joined by Rehnquist CJ, and White and Kennedy JJ).

[175] *Penry v Lynaugh* 492 US 302 (1980) (US Supreme Court). [176] *Atkins v Virginia* (n 8).

[177] *Coker v Georgia* (n 165) 597. [178] *Atkins v Virginia* (n 8) 313. [179] ibid, 321.

[180] ibid, 322. [181] ibid, 338. [182] *Roper v Simmons* (n 7).

Stanford and held that it was constitutionally impermissible to administer the death penalty to juvenile offenders who were over fifteen but under eighteen when they committed the crime.[183] Kennedy J, delivering the judgment of the Court, reiterated the basis in dignity of the Eighth Amendment. 'By protecting even those convicted of heinous crimes, the Eighth Amendment reaffirms the duty of the government to respect the dignity of all persons'.[184] Moreover, in overruling *Stanford*, Kennedy J made it abundantly clear that the Court was also reinstating the principle that the Supreme Court was required to bring its independent judgement to bear on the proportionality of the death penalty for a particular class of crimes or offenders.[185] He therefore followed the *Atkins* Court in relying on both the objective indicia of consensus as expressed by the enactments of legislatures which have addressed the question, and the need to exercise the Court's own independent judgement to determine whether the death penalty is a disproportionate punishment for juveniles.[186] The evidence from State legislatures was mixed, but the Court reassured itself that the key issue was the direction of change, rather than the absolute numbers of legislatures who had moved to remove juveniles from death penalty eligibility since *Stanford*. It therefore moved on to exercise its own judgement, rejecting both deterrence and retribution as good enough bases to justify the death penalty on juveniles as a proportionate punishment.

Notably, in her dissent in *Roper*, O'Connor J did not retract from the Court's right to exert its independent judgement as to the proportionality of the sentence. Indeed, looking back on *Atkins*, she took the view that 'the objective evidence of national consensus, standing alone, was insufficient to dictate the Court's holding in *Atkins*. Rather, the compelling moral proportionality argument against capital punishment of [intellectually disabled] offenders played a *decisive* role in persuading the Court that the practice was inconsistent with the Eighth Amendment'.[187] However, the proportionality argument against the juvenile death penalty was 'so flawed that it can be given little, if any, analytical weight—it proves too weak to resolve the lingering ambiguities in the objective evidence of legislative consensus or to justify the Court's categorical rule'.[188] Scalia J was more forthright.

> Of course, the real force driving today's decision is not the actions of four state legislatures, but the Court's 'own judgment' that murderers younger than 18 can never be as morally culpable as older counterparts ... By what conceivable warrant can nine lawyers presume to be the authoritative conscience of the Nation?[189]

3. *The method of execution*

The wavering majority in the US in favour of a substantive approach in relation to the type of offender has not been sustained when the issue concerns the method of execution. Most recently, this has focused on the administration of the lethal injection. As we saw earlier, the prohibition on the export of drugs for lethal injection

[183] Note that in the meanwhile, the Governor of Kentucky commuted the sentence of Kevin Stanford to life without parole: see ibid, 565.

[184] ibid, 560. [185] ibid, 574. [186] ibid, 564. [187] ibid, 598. [188] ibid, 598.

[189] ibid, 639.

from Europe to the US has been reinforced by the refusal by multinational drug companies to supply the drugs. This led some States to resort to alternative combinations of drugs, which risk subjecting the offender to high levels of pain. The use of such alternative drugs was upheld by a majority of the US Supreme Court in *Glossip v Gross* in 2015,[190] over a strong dissent by Breyer, Ginsburg, Sotomayor, and Kagan JJ. Alito J, giving judgment for the court, did not accept that the drug in use, midazolam, caused unacceptable levels of pain.

> Our decisions in this area have been animated in part by the recognition that because it is settled that capital punishment is constitutional, '[i]t necessarily follows that there must be a [constitutional] means of carrying it out'. ... And because some risk of pain is inherent in any method of execution, we have held that the Constitution does not require the avoidance of all risk of pain. After all, while most humans wish to die a painless death, many do not have that good fortune. Holding that the Eighth Amendment demands the elimination of essentially all risk of pain would effectively outlaw the death penalty altogether.[191]

A similar approach is evident in the decision of the Indian Supreme Court in *Bachan Singh*. The Indian Code of Criminal Procedure prescribes that the sentence of death be carried out by hanging, a provision which has been in place in successive codes for well over 100 years.[192] In *Bachan Singh*, the majority rejected the contention that the death penalty, 'either per se, or because of its execution by hanging, constitutes an unreasonable, cruel or unusual punishment'.[193] In the later case of *Deena v Union of India* in 1983, the provision was challenged directly on the ground that hanging was a cruel and barbarous method of executing the death sentence.[194] The petitioners argued that even if it may be lawful to impose the death sentence in an exceptional class of cases, it was impermissible to execute that sentence unless a humane and dignified mode of executing that sentence could be found. A three-Judge bench of the Indian Supreme Court rejected this argument.

The cases on method of execution, both in the US and India, throw a particularly stark light on the extent to which the death penalty implicates the State in intentional killing. In *Bachan Singh*, Bhagwati J stated that, whether or not hanging was the most humane method of executing, 'one thing is clear, that hanging is undoubtedly accompanied by intense physical torture and pain'.[195] The analysis in *Glossip v Gross* is equally gruesome. As Sotomayor J explained in her dissent, lethal injection required the use of two drugs—rocuronium bromide, and potassium chloride—which cause death in a 'torturous manner, causing burning, searing pain'. It was thus critical that a third drug be used to render and keep the inmate unconscious. But because pharmaceutical companies and European states had refused to supply sodium thiopenthal, the drug of choice for this macabre procedure, Oklahoma had resorted to midazolam. The petitioners produced a range of evidence that midazolam could not be expected to perform that function; and indeed, that it posed constitutionally intolerable risks.

190 *Glossip v Gross* (n 9). 191 ibid. 192 Indian Code of Criminal Procedure, s 354(5).
193 *Bachan Singh v State of Punjab* (n 6) 222–23, per Sarkaria J.
194 *Deena @ Deena Dayal v Union of India* (n 72).
195 *Bachan Singh v State of Punjab* (n 6) 286, per Bhagwati J.

However, the Court upheld what Sotomayor J called 'the scientifically unsupported and implausible testimony of a single expert witness'. Even more worryingly, the majority held that the petitioners bore the burden of showing that there were alternative means causing less pain by which they should be executed. This, Sotomayor J concluded, 'leaves petitioners exposed to what may well be the chemical equivalent of being burned at the stake'.

It is difficult to see how the fundamental values behind human rights could be consistent with a court allowing even the slightest risk of exposing individuals to such pain and suffering. Ultimately, we are left with the spectacle of both the Court and the State as being complicit in acts of extraordinary barbarism. As Sotomayor J put it, it is hard to reconcile this result with the declaration by the Court in *Roper v Simmons* only a decade before, that '[b]y protecting even those convicted of heinous crimes, the Eighth Amendment reaffirms the duty of the government to respect the dignity of all persons'.[196] Avoiding these contortions requires the courts to openly embrace these substantive values. The last word must be with Chaskalson P:

> The rights to life and dignity are the most important of all human rights, and the source of all other personal rights ... By committing ourselves to a society founded on the recognition of human rights we are required to value these two rights above all others. And this must be demonstrated by the State in everything that it does, including the way it punishes criminals.[197]

4. *Equality: substance or procedure?*

The role of equality in striking down death penalty statutes has been similarly contentious. Statistics in many countries show that the poor and racial minorities are disproportionately represented among those sentenced to death and executed. 'Who, by and large, are the men whom the gallows swallow? The white-collar criminals and the corporate criminals whose wilful economic and environmental crimes inflict mass deaths or who hire assassins and murder by remote control?' asked the Indian Supreme Court in *Rajendra Prasad v State of Uttar Pradesh*.[198] The answer was stark:

> Rarely. With a few exceptions, they hardly fear the halter. The feuding villager, ... the striking workers desperate with defeat, the political dissenter and sacrificing liberator ... the waifs and strays whom society has hardened by neglect into street toughs, or the poor householder— husband or wife—driven by dire necessity or burst of tantrums—it is this person who is the morning meal of the macabre executioner.

This is borne out by the data. Surendrenath et al found that nearly 74 per cent of death row convicts in India in the period of study (2012–2015) were from economically vulnerable sections of society, judged by land-holding and occupation.[199] Since over two-thirds of these were sole breadwinners, their families were unlikely to be able to afford the legal expenses critical to ensure fair treatment within the criminal justice

[196] *Roper v Simmons* (n 7) 560. [197] *S v Makwanyane* (n 5) para [144].

[198] *Rajendra Prasad v State of Uttar Pradesh* (1979) 3 SCC 646 (Indian Supreme Court) para [77].

[199] Surendrenath et al (n 83) 101.

system.[200] Moreover, their economic vulnerability could only be worsened over the many years to which they were subject to the process.[201] Surendrenath et al also highlight the extent to which a lack of education can affect an accused's ability to stand up for his or her rights during and after trial. They found that over two-thirds of those on death row had not completed secondary school, and as many as 23 per cent had never attended school.[202] Furthermore, over three-quarters of prisoners sentenced to death in India were found to be from backward classes and religious minorities.[203]

The over-representation of the poor and uneducated among those who are sentenced to death is not a coincidence. Poverty has a direct impact on the quality of the legal advice available and the extent to which the accused is able to protect his or her own rights. Williams shows that in the US, 'whether one ends up in death row is usually determined not by the heinousness of the crime but by the quality of trial counsel'.[204] This reinforces the experience of US Supreme Court Justice Ruth Bader Ginsburg. As she put it in a lecture in 2001: 'I have yet to see a death case, among the dozens coming to the Supreme Court on eve of execution petitions, in which the defendant was well represented at trial'.[205] Although defence counsel is guaranteed to indigent defendants in capital cases in the US, the American Civil Liberties Union in a report in 2010 concluded that appointed attorneys in indigent capital cases are 'overworked, underpaid, lacking critical resources, incompetent, or inexperienced in trying death penalty cases'. Nor was this isolated to a few cases: 'It is a widespread and systematic failure to ensure access to justice for defendants facing capital charges and those convicted of capital crimes'.[206] Despite some important attempts at change, the picture remains bleak for indigent defendants facing the death penalty. The American Bar Association concluded in 2013 that 'jurisdictions have not established the kind of legal services that is necessary to ensure that defendants charged with capital offenses or on death row receive the defence they require'.[207]

A similar picture emerges in India. The Indian Supreme Court has held that the State has a duty to provide a lawyer free of charge to an indigent accused.[208] Legal aid lawyers, however, are very poorly paid.[209] Surendrenath et al found that although there were some examples of positive opinions by defendants of their lawyers, the majority of prisoners reported 'absence during court proceedings, lack of interaction with prisoners and their families, repeated demands for money and dereliction of duties as a defence lawyer'.[210] The result of lack of proper representation is grim. A very large

[200] ibid, 104. [201] ibid, 107. [202] ibid, 108. [203] ibid, 109.

[204] K Williams, *Most Deserving of Death? An Analysis of the Supreme Court's Death Penalty Jurisprudence* (Ashgate 2012) 18.

[205] Ruth Bader Ginsburg, 'In Pursuit of the Public Good: Lawyers who Care' (Joseph L Rauh Lecture, University of the District of Columbia, 9 April 2001) <http://www.supremecourt.gov/publicinfo/speeches/viewspeech/sp_04-09-01a> (accessed 24 February 2018).

[206] American Civil Liberties Union, 'Slamming the Courthouse Doors: Denial of Access to Justice and Remedy in America' (December 2010) 7.

[207] American Bar Association, 'The State of the Modern Death Penalty in America: Key Findings of State Death Penalty Assessments 2006–2013', 7–8. For a detailed discussion of this issue, see Hood and Hoyle (n 29) 272–81.

[208] *Hussainara Khatoon and Others (IV) v Home Secretary, State of Bihar, Patna* (1980) 1 SCC 98 (Indian Supreme Court).

[209] Indian Law Commission 2015 (n 1) para 5.3.12. [210] Surendrenath et al (n 83) 129.

number of death row prisoners interviewed by Surendrenath et al had had no legal representation at the time of pre-trial investigation, yet most alleged that they had been forced to sign 'confessions' provided by the police to match facts already discovered.[211] As seen above, as many as 95.7 per cent of death sentences meted out by trial courts are overturned on appeal.[212] In the meanwhile, prisoners have been subjected to very long periods of detention in appalling conditions.

In the US, there are also clear racial disparities in the imposition of the death penalty. About 41 per cent of death row inmates on 1 July 2017 in the US were African American, and 13 per cent Hispanic, while 42 per cent were white.[213] Yet African Americans only constitute about 13.2 per cent of the population.[214] There is a clear correlation between the race of the victim and the likelihood of a death sentence.[215] Over 75 per cent of murder victims in cases resulting in an execution between 1976 and 2016 were white and only 15 per cent black, even though nationally only 50 per cent of murder victims are white.[216] There is also some evidence for higher rates of conviction and death penalty sentencing for African Americans as against whites. For example, a recent study of juries in Washington State shows that jurors in that State are three times more likely to recommend a death sentence for a black defendant than a white defendant in a similar case.[217] Moreover, there is evidence that juries are selected in a racist manner. In the most recent case, in 2016, the US Supreme Court, with an unusually clear majority (only Thomas J dissented) struck down the conviction of an African American defendant after it became clear that a deliberate policy had been pursued of striking all African American jurors.[218] The Court found a persistent focus on race in the prosecution file: an 'N' appeared next to each of the black prospective jurors' names on the jury venire list, and on the list of qualified prospective jurors. Correspondingly, the names marked with N all appeared on the 'definite NOs list'. The Court concluded that the State's prosecutors were motivated 'in substantial part by race' when they struck at least two jurors. Tellingly, the defendant had been in prison and on death row for thirty years before this determination was made.

These facts have not, however, convinced judicial majorities in India and the US to regard the death penalty as cruel and inhuman. In *Bachan Singh*, the Indian Supreme Court reversed the *Rajendra* decision, which as we have seen had so strongly emphasized the unequal chances of indigent prisoners. Instead, it was Justice Bhagwati's dissent which stressed the discriminatory operation of the death penalty, 'for it strikes

[211] ibid, 132. [212] Indian Law Commission 2015 (n 1) para 5.2.70.

[213] Death Penalty Information Center, 'Facts about the Death Penalty' (updated February 2018) <https://deathpenaltyinfo.org/documents/FactSheet.pdf> (accessed 24 February 2018).

[214] United States Census Bureau, 'Census' (1 July 2017) <https://www.census.gov/quickfacts/table/PST045215/00#headnote-js-a> (accessed 18 February 2018).

[215] Hood and Hoyle (n 29) 372–78. [216] Death Penalty Information Center (n 213).

[217] K Beckett and H Evans, 'The Role of Race in Washington State Capital Sentencing 1981–2012' (University of Washington, January 2014) <https://deathpenaltyinfo.org/documents/WashRaceStudy2014.pdf> (accessed 28 February 2018).

[218] *Foster v Chatman* (2016) 136 S Ct 1737. Previous jurisprudence had established that, on a challenge to striking a jury, the trial court is required to determine whether the defendant has shown purposeful discrimination: *Snyder v Louisiana* 552 US (2008) (US Supreme Court) 472, 477.

mostly against the poor and deprived sections of the community and the rich and the affluent usually escape from its clutches'.[219]

In the US, Douglas J, concurring with the majority in striking down the death penalty in *Furman*, did indeed place this issue at the centre of his concurring judgment: 'These discretionary statutes,' he stated, ' … are pregnant with discrimination and discrimination is an ingredient not compatible with the idea of equal protection of the laws that is implicit in the ban on "cruel and unusual" punishments'.[220] However, as we have seen, the Court in *Gregg* held that revised procedures were sufficient to meet the concerns in *Furman* about arbitrariness. Moreover, the fact that the statistics continued to show racial disparities was not regarded by later judgments as sufficient to prove discrimination. In *McCleskey v Kemp*,[221] McCleskey claimed that, as a black defendant with a white victim, he was subject to unlawful discrimination, rendering the death penalty imposed on him unconstitutional under the Fourteenth and Eighth Amendments. He based his case on a detailed study by Baldus showing that defendants charged with killing white victims were 4.3 times as likely to receive a death sentence as defendants charged with killing black victims. Similarly, black defendants were 1.1 times as likely to receive the death penalty as other defendants. The Court refused to draw an inference of discrimination from the statistical evidence. Instead, it held that the defendant had to prove that the decision-makers in *his* case acted with discriminatory purpose. Indeed, to sustain a challenge to the legislation as a whole, the defendant would need to prove that the State specifically enacted the capital punishment statute to further a discriminatory purpose.[222] He could do neither of these things. By a five–four majority, the Court therefore rejected his claim. As Brennan J put it in his dissent, to insist that the defendant prove intention so strictly ignores the uniquely irrevocable nature of death as a penalty: instead, any capital sentencing system in which race 'more likely than not' plays a role should be held to fall below the uniquely high degree of rationality needed in the context of taking a human life.[223]

It is only the South African Court that has explicitly relied on the inequality inherent in the death penalty as one of the factors in finding the death penalty disproportionate and unconstitutional. As Chaskalson P put it:

> [T]he unpalatable truth is that most capital cases involve poor people who cannot afford and do not receive as good a defence as those who have means. In this process, the poor and the ignorant have proven to be the most vulnerable, and are the persons most likely to be sentenced to death.[224]

These discrepancies were intolerable in the light of the irreversibility of death.[225] Similarly, Mahomed J stated that he had very considerable difficulty in reconciling the death penalty with the right to equality. He recognized that judges seek conscientiously to avoid impermissibly unequal treatment. Unlike the majority in *McCleskey*, however, he did not regard this as sufficient. Instead, he held that there was an

[219] *Bachan Singh v State of Punjab* (n 6) 366 G–H; *Rajendra Prasad v State of Uttar Pradesh* (n 198).
[220] *Furman v Georgia* (n 3) 256–57.
[221] *McCleskey v Kemp* 481 (US) 279 (1987) (US Supreme Court). [222] ibid, 298.
[223] ibid, 335. [224] *S v Makwanyane* (n 5) n 79. [225] ibid, para [54].

inherent risk of arbitrariness: 'The fault is not of the sentencing Court, but in the process itself'.[226]

Ultimately, however, the discrimination argument needs to be allied with a substantive commitment to dignity and equality if it is to hold the weight of the abolition of the death penalty. Otherwise, it would be possible to argue, as in the procedural cases above, that if the discriminatory element were to be removed, the death penalty would be legitimate. Hood and Hoyle refer to a paper written by two US Justice Department officials in 2006, in which it was claimed that

> even if the claim of race of the victim were valid, it would only prove that some crimes against black victims are punished less severely than comparable crimes against white victims ... The solution to such a problem would not be to abolish the death penalty ... but rather ensure that murderers of black victims are more consistently sentenced to death.[227]

V. Conclusion

The chapter began with the contrasting quotations from Cesare Beccaria in 1764 and Scalia J in 2015. For Scalia, the issue of capital punishment was for 'the People' to decide. Becarria saw the absurdity of a system in which the laws 'which are the expression of the public will, and which hate and punish murder, should themselves commit one, and that to deter citizens from murder, they should decree a public murder'. From a human rights perspective, it seems incontestable that attempts to reconcile the death penalty with human rights standards are doomed to failure. There is no doubt that the pace of abolition of the death penalty is quickening, and of course it would be preferable for the momentum to come from democratically elected legislatures. However, if democratically elected legislatures do not prohibit the death penalty, it is precisely the function of human rights instruments, and the judges who enforce them, to ensure that fundamental principles of human rights are adhered to. Leaving the question of capital punishment to 'the People to decide' as Scalia would have it, is an abdication of human rights duties. Two-and-a-half centuries since it was uttered, the wisdom of Becarria seems incontrovertible.

[226] ibid, para [273].

[227] M Griffey and L Rothenberg, 'The Death Penalty in the United States' in *The Death Penalty in the OSCE Area* (2006), Organization for Security and Co-operation in Europe (OSCE) Background Paper 2006, 41; cited in Hood and Hoyle (n 29) 378.

7
Abortion

I. Introduction

Abortion remains one of the most contested issues in the human rights arena. A comparative approach reveals the pivotal role of the characterization of the rights at stake. Is this an issue of the right to life, the right to privacy, or the right to equality and reproductive freedom? The outcome can depend crucially on the answer to this question. If the foetus is accorded personhood, and therefore the right to life in its own right, the result is a head-on collision with the pregnant woman's rights, particularly her right to life, but also her rights to bodily integrity, autonomy, privacy, and equality. The space for negotiating these conflicts is radically reduced. Short of an immediate threat to her life, the foetus may be regarded as trumping all rights of the pregnant woman. Moreover, characterizing the issue in terms of clashes of rights portrays the pregnant woman as an adversary, bringing with it stigma and blame.

In practice, it is unusual for legal systems to accord full personhood to the foetus. The Irish Constitution was, until 2018, the marked exception. Other jurisdictions have instead characterized the issue as concerning potential life. This makes it possible to bring the pregnant woman's rights into greater focus, so that the arena of contestation becomes the extent to which her rights can be limited by the State's interest in protecting potential life. Here again, much depends on the ways in which the pregnant woman's rights are understood. Three main rights have been considered to be central. The first is the woman's own right to life. Both legislative and judicial solutions will generally make some provision for situations of immediate danger to her life. The contentious issue then becomes whether her right to life includes protection for her health, and in particular, her mental and psychological health. The second is the right to privacy. The privacy right, however, is ambiguous. Does it mean an area of intimacy and personal space, into which the State should not intrude,[1] or does it protect autonomy or decision-making from State intervention? In both senses, privacy frames the issue as an individual rather than a social one.

The third relevant right is that of equality. An equality perspective exposes the subliminal assumptions about women and their role as mothers, which shape much of the decision-making in relation to abortion. As Siegel puts it, 'Legislation restricting women's access to abortion forces women to bear children. Today, as in the past, a legislature's decision to save foetal life by compelling pregnancy is one that both reflects and enforces social judgements concerning women's roles'.[2] The right to

[1] *Griswold v Connecticut* 381 US 479 (1965) (US Supreme Court); *McGee v Attorney General* [1974] IR 284 (Irish Supreme Court).

[2] R Siegel, 'Reasoning from the Body: A Historical Perspective on Abortion Regulation and Questions of Equal Protection' (1991–92) 44 Stan L Rev 261 at 266.

substantive equality therefore requires greater attention to be paid to the continuum between the right to abortion and the social consequences of childbearing and childcare on women's opportunities, whether in the workforce, in the family, or in public life more generally. This chapter examines the ways in which these conflicting and contrasting perspectives have shaped both legislative regulation of abortion and judicial responses.

As well as determining what rights of the pregnant woman and those, if any, of the foetus, are at issue, courts in various jurisdictions have been called on to determine third-party rights. Most jurisdictions permit conscientious objection by medical and other staff who believe that abortion is morally wrong. But what if this means that there are no staff available to perform the abortion? Also contentious have been the claims to freedom of speech and the extent to which these are permitted to intrude on pregnant women's rights to abortion.

Running through these substantive issues are the cross-cutting themes identified in this book. Particularly salient has been the interaction between legislatures and the courts. As will be seen in section II, the tension between elected legislatures and courts in relation to abortion pulls in opposing directions. In some jurisdictions, courts have struck down legislative prohibitions on abortion, while in others, courts have invalidated legislative protection for abortion. Other jurisdictions have seen courts and legislatures working together, either to cement prohibitions, or to protect the right to abortion. The second cross-cutting theme is that of interpretation. There are many open-textured terms. Where a human rights instrument states that 'everyone' has the right to life, does 'everyone' include the foetus? What does the right to life for a pregnant woman entail? Does risk to her life include her health, or more broadly her psychological, or even her social health? Even more fundamental is the meaning of liberty. As will be seen, it is from the notion of liberty that the US Court has derived the right to privacy, rather than from an express right in the Constitution.

This highlights the third cross-cutting theme, namely that of comparativism and transnational influence. There has been some active transplantation: as will be seen, the early criminal statutes were exported from the UK to other countries such as India and Ireland, although their trajectories since then have been very different. There has subsequently been much by way of judicial conversation, particularly concerning the meaning of 'everyone' in relation to whether the foetus has a right to life. Particularly important, although often underemphasized, has been the role of international aid in influencing abortion in developing countries. The US refusal to provide aid for abortion-related projects has been a serious impediment to domestic policies in countries which wish to liberalize abortion.

This chapter does not attempt to set out the detailed provisions on abortion in all of the jurisdictions covered. Instead, it considers the ways in which the human rights framework has been used to shape these provisions. Section II considers the ways in which judicial and legislative forces have interacted in the contestation over abortion rights. Sections III, IV, and V look more closely at the three different rights which feature centrally in this debate: the right to life; the right to privacy; and the right to equality. The final part examines the rights of third parties, especially conscientious objection.

II. Courts and Legislatures: Contestation and Compromise

Jeremy Waldron has consistently pointed to the contrast between the highly contentious intervention of the US Court in *Roe v Wade*,[3] and the apparently consensual legislative introduction of the Abortion Act 1967 in the UK. This he regards as demonstrating the importance of leaving such decisions to 'the people' rather than allowing judges to do so through a human rights framework.[4] However, the interaction is less polarized than Waldron suggests. In fact, the earliest UK liberalization of abortion was judge-led, in the case of *R v Bourne*[5] in 1938, which remained the guiding principle for abortion law in the UK until 1967. Although the *Bourne* principle differed from *Roe v Wade* in that it could in principle be overruled by the legislature, the opposite took place, with the legislature finally enacting and broadening the *Bourne* principles.

Moreover, a comparative perspective reveals 'activist' courts operating in both directions: the US Court has struck down prohibitions on abortion, while the German Court has struck down legislation permitting abortion. Here too a closer look demonstrates a much more nuanced position. Although the German Court insists that foetal life should be protected, it permits abortion before twelve weeks after mandatory counselling encouraging women to keep the pregnancy. Abortion within the twelve-week period is now widely available. The US Courts, on the other hand, are permitting increasingly burdensome statutes to erode pregnant women's rights. In other jurisdictions, judiciaries have upheld legislation, whether by endorsing prohibitions on abortion, as in Ireland, or endorsing abortion rights, as in South Africa. It is not therefore possible to draw a bright line between judicial and legislative approaches. This section briefly narrates these complex interactions.

A. Human rights challenges of legislative prohibitions on abortion: the US

As in many of the colonial countries examined here, abortion did not become a criminal offence in the US until the early nineteenth century.[6] From 1821, when the first criminal statute on abortion was enacted, regulation became increasingly more restrictive, so that by the end of the 1950s a large majority of the US states banned abortion whenever performed, unless done to save or preserve the life of the mother.[7]

It was the Texas criminal abortion law, first enacted in 1854, that came before the US Supreme Court in the seminal case of *Roe v Wade* decided in 1973.[8] The statute made it a crime to procure or attempt to procure an abortion, except where the abortion was procured by medical advice to save the life of the mother. Blackmun J, delivering the opinion of the court, struck down the statute as breaching the implied right of privacy in the US Constitution which, he held, was 'broad enough to encompass a woman's

[3] *Roe v Wade* (1973) 410 US 113 (US Supreme Court).

[4] J Waldron, 'The Core of the Case Against Judicial Review' (2006) 115 Yale L J 1346, 1384–85; J Waldron, 'Judges as Moral Reasoners' (2009) 7 Int J of Constitutional Law 2, 19–20.

[5] *R v Bourne* (1938) 1 KB 687 (King's Bench Division).

[6] *Roe v Wade* (n 3) 141–43.

[7] ibid, 139.

[8] ibid.

decision whether or not to terminate her pregnancy'.[9] On the other hand, the privacy right was not absolute and needed to be considered in relation to important state interests, particularly in protecting the potentiality of life. These countervailing interests became stronger as the pregnancy progressed, and the foetus came closer to viability. This led the Court to construct the famous trimester test. In the first trimester, the abortion decision and its effectuation should be left to the medical judgement of the woman's physician. In the second trimester, the State's interest was confined to the health of the mother. It could therefore choose to regulate the abortion procedure in ways that are reasonably related to maternal health. In the final trimester, the State's interest in the potentiality of human life meant that it was legitimate to regulate and even proscribe abortion except where necessary, according to appropriate medical judgement, to preserve the life or health of the mother.[10]

However, the contentiousness of abortion and the accusation that the trimester framework constituted illegitimate judicial activism began to whittle away judicial support for the *Roe v Wade* settlement. This reached a head in 1992 in *Planned Parenthood v Casey*.[11] In the dramatic opening to the joint opinion written by Justices O'Connor, Souter, and Kennedy, the Court stated:

> Liberty finds no refuge in a jurisprudence of doubt. Yet 19 years after our holding that the Constitution protects a woman's right to terminate her pregnancy in its early stages in *Roe v Wade*, that definition of liberty is still questioned . . . the United States, as it has done in five other cases in the last decade, again asks us to overrule *Roe*.[12]

Although the Court proclaimed fidelity to the *Roe* precedent, it abandoned the trimester framework. Instead, it decided that the State's interest in protecting potential life extended to all periods in pregnancy. However, any limitation should not constitute an 'undue burden' on the pregnant women's privacy. Greenhouse and Siegel characterize *Casey*'s undue burden standard as a compromise 'crafted by moderates responding to concerns raised both by those who wanted to overturn *Roe v Wade* and those who wanted to preserve constitutional protection for the abortion right'.[13] The undue burden test is now at the centre of litigation in the US, as individual state legislatures continue to contest the boundaries of judicial legitimation of abortion. This is elaborated further below in section IV.

B. Human rights challenges of legislation permitting abortion: Germany

The contestation between courts and legislatures can also function in the opposite direction: instead of using human rights law to attempt to strike down prohibitions on abortion, human rights are used to challenge statutes permitting abortion. The clearest example of such a situation is that of Germany. Legislation permitting abortion was

[9] ibid, 153. [10] ibid, 164–66.

[11] *Planned Parenthood v Casey* 505 US 833 (1992) (US Supreme Court). [12] ibid, 843.

[13] L Greenhouse and R Seigel, 'Casey and the Clinic Closings: When "Protecting Health" Obstructs Choice' (2016) 125 Yale L J 1428, 1431.

struck down by the German Federal Constitutional Court twice, first in 1973 and again in 1993. Nevertheless, in what might seem to be a paradoxical approach, the Court left open the possibility of abortion which, while not officially sanctioned, was also not punishable. Current legislation indeed makes abortion exempt from punishment in three situations: abortion which takes place after dissuasive counselling within the first twelve weeks of fertilization; abortion on medical grounds; and abortion on grounds relating to a crime. The result is that Germany is generally regarded as a country which permits abortion. Indeed, the number of legal abortions reported per year between 1994 and 2014 ranges from 97,937 to 134,964.[14] The vast majority (around 97 per cent) of abortions take place under the first exemption.

How did this paradoxical situation come about? The complex interaction between the German Federal Constitutional Court and the German legislature began very shortly after *Roe v Wade* had been decided in the US Supreme Court. The political and legal context, however, is strikingly different. The background lies in the shameful practice of forced abortions carried out by the Nazis during the Second World War, which was condemned as a war crime and crime against humanity.[15] Prior to 1974, abortion was a criminal offence under the German Criminal Code, except when carried out by a licensed physician to remove a clear danger to the woman's life or health.[16] After a highly contentious legislative process, the Abortion Reform Act of 1974 was passed with a narrow majority of only fourteen in the German Bundestag. The Act permitted a woman to choose to have an abortion within the first twelve weeks of pregnancy after consulting a medical doctor and a licensed counsellor. After twelve weeks, an abortion could only be secured for a certified medical necessity or, within twenty-two weeks, for serious foetal problems.[17] However, within days, opposition Christian Democratic lawmakers and five States with Christian Democratic majorities invoked the Constitutional Court's abstract power of judicial review, which can determine the validity of a statute without presenting a specific case or controversy.

In February 1975, the Court issued its judgment striking down the statute by a six–two majority.[18] As we see below, it relied primarily on the right to life and the inviolability of human dignity in the German Basic Law. It nevertheless acknowledged that the woman's rights to life and to personal self-determination might in some circumstances be weighed against those of the foetus. In particular, where there was serious danger to the pregnant woman's health or life, or the pregnancy arose from rape or incest, or the foetus was discovered to have serious problems, the pregnant woman should not be compelled by law to carry the pregnancy to term. It also left open the

[14] 'Historical abortion statistics, FR Germany, compiled by Wm. Robert Johnston (last updated 26 February 2018) <http://www.johnstonsarchive.net/policy/abortion/ab-frgermany.html> (accessed 25 February 2018).

[15] See 'Trials of War Criminals before the Nürnberg Military Tribunals, October, 1946–April, 1949' vols IV–V ('The RuSHA Case') (Washington, DC: US Gov't Printing Office 1949) IV: 610, 613; V: 153, 160–61, 166. See J Hunt, 'Out of Respect for Life: Nazi Abortion Policy in the Eastern Occupied Territories' *Life and Learning IX* <http://www.uffl.org/vol%209/hunt9.pdf> (accessed 25 February 2018).

[16] This section draws heavily on D Kommers, 'The Constitutional Law of Abortion in Germany: Should Americans Pay Attention?' (Scholarly Works Paper 733, Notre Dame Law School 1994) <http://scholarship.law.nd.edu/law_faculty_scholarship/733> (accessed 25 February 2018).

[17] Gesetz zur Reform des Strafrechts of 18 June 1974, 218.

[18] 39 BVerfGE 1 (1975).

possibility that the social predicament of a woman might justify an abortion, but only if the hardship to the woman was severe, and only after compulsory counselling and within the first twelve weeks of pregnancy (the social exception). Parliament accepted these requirements in the Abortion Reform Act of 1976, which reinstated the criminal prohibition of abortion except in relation to the circumstances prescribed by the Court. It was under the social exception that most legal abortions occurred in the Federal Republic of Germany for the next two decades, although its definition varied from *Land* to *Land*.[19]

The unification of Germany in 1990 brought with it renewed contestation of the right to abortion. The German Democratic Republic had legislated in 1972 to permit abortion on demand within the first twelve weeks of pregnancy. Unification therefore triggered a reconsideration of the West German legislation. In what Kommers describes as 'long and painful negotiations' in the early part of 1992, a compromise was finally reached which won the support of all the parties and factions.[20] The Pregnancy and Family Assistance Act of June 1992, declared, inter alia, that the interruption of pregnancy in specified circumstances was 'not illegal'. No criminal penalty would be incurred if an abortion was performed within the first twelve weeks of pregnancy, with the woman's consent, by a licensed physician. Counselling stressing the value of unborn life was compulsory and a three-day delay between counselling and abortion was required. After twelve weeks, an abortion was only permitted if there was a serious threat to the pregnant woman's life or physical or mental health.

Despite the difficult and delicate negotiations which had led to the Act, a group of 249 Christian Democratic members of the Bundestag, all from West Germany, again invoked the abstract review jurisdiction of the Constitutional Court.[21] Again, the legislation was struck down. In a decision which took the Court nearly eight months to craft, and which ran to 183 pages in length, the Court reaffirmed the essential core of the 1975 decision, namely that unborn life is a constitutional value that the State has a duty to protect from the moment of implantation.[22] As in the previous decision, the Court held that the duty of protection was not absolute and acknowledged that it conflicted with the rights to life and bodily integrity of the pregnant woman, as well as her human dignity and her right of personality. In drawing this balance, the Court again stated that abortion should be forbidden unless continuation would place unreasonable demands upon the pregnant woman. The result was once more a complex synthesis. The Court held that it was wrong to declare that abortion in the first twelve weeks was 'not illegal'. Nevertheless, it accepted that the State could fulfil its duty to protect unborn life by requiring dissuasive counselling in the first twelve weeks of pregnancy, with the aim of winning over the woman to voluntary continuation of the pregnancy. It also accepted that it was not necessary to provide criminal sanctions during this period.[23] The amended German criminal code now provides

[19] Kommers (n 16) 10. [20] ibid,12. [21] ibid, 15.

[22] G Neuman, 'Casey in the Mirror: Abortion, Abuse and the Right to Protection in the United States and Germany' (1995) 43 The American Journal of Comparative Law 273, 280.

[23] Schwangerschaftsabbruch II (1993) 88 BverfGE 203 (Fed Const Ct) (Germany) [Second Abortion decision]. An official English translation is available on the website of the German Constitutional Court. See BVerfGE, 2 BvF 2/90 (28 May 1993) <http://www.bverfg.de/entscheidungen/fs19930528_2bvf000290en.html> (accessed 25 February 2018).

that abortion during the first twelve weeks should not be punishable as long as there has been dissuasive counselling and a three-day waiting period. Abortion remains lawful in situations falling into one of the four categories: the medical indication (the pregnancy created serious danger to her life or health); the criminological indication (rape or incest); the embryopathic indication (serious foetal problems); and more loosely, the 'general situation of need' indication. All of these, however, need to be verified by medical practitioners.

Kommers argues that the relationship between the courts and legislature in Germany is far more collaborative than in the US. For him, the Abortion decision of 1975 triggered a reaction in the legislature which constituted a conscious attempt to define a policy which was compatible with the Court's approach:

> In many respects, the Bundestag had entered into a conversation with the Constitutional Court, furnishing Americans with an example of creative dialogue across branches of government. *Roe v. Wade*, by contrast, stopped the conversation. It ended the debate over the constitutionality of abortion and on the basis of constitutional language less explicit or commanding than the text of the Basic Law.[24]

Whereas the rigid trimester framework of *Roe* gave little or no discretion to legislatures, Kommers argues that in both 1975 and 1993 the Federal Constitutional Court 'bounced the ball back to parliament, thus continuing the dialogue that had begun there'.[25]

Indeed, although in many ways, the German Court might have been very prescriptive, the ultimate package in practice does not look very different from the original statute, barring the very important removal of the right to statutory health insurance for abortion. On the other hand, it might be argued that since *Casey*, there are signs of an interesting convergence between the approaches of the two courts, albeit from a very different starting point. At the same time, many might find it puzzling and uncomfortable that the German Federal Constitutional Court has insisted that abortion cannot be declared lawful, albeit that the only deterrence required by the State should take the form of dissuasive counselling. Others would see it as a pragmatic approach, underpinned by a recognition that without the woman's co-operation, abortion is unlikely to be deterred, as demonstrated by the reality of back-street abortion, with its disastrous consequences. Ultimately, as the court put it, a woman should be able to choose, after proper reflection, to have a safe and confidential abortion.

C. From contestation to legitimation: the UK

In the UK, by contrast, the initial judicial challenge to criminal abortion was eventually clarified and broadened by statute. Until the nineteenth century, abortion was 'by the common law of England a grave crime',[26] at least after 'quickening',[27] when the soul was believed to enter the body of the foetus. But it was not until the nineteenth century that criminalization was endorsed in statute, with the earliest statute being

[24] Kommers (n 16) 27. [25] ibid, 28. [26] *R v Bourne* (n 5) 690.
[27] Between sixteen and eighteen weeks, when foetal movement can be felt.

Lord Ellenborough's Act in 1803, where abortion after quickening was punishable by the death penalty, and abortion prior to quickening became a punishable felony.[28] Although the death penalty was removed in 1837, the criminalization of abortion was carried forward and consolidated in the Offences Against the Person Act 1861. Section 58 of the Offences against the Person Act 1861, which is still in force today, makes it a criminal offence, carrying a sentence of life imprisonment, for a pregnant woman 'with intent to procure her own miscarriage [to] unlawfully administer to herself any poison or other noxious thing, or [to] unlawfully use any instrument or other means whatsoever'. It is similarly an offence for anyone else to procure the miscarriage of a woman. Section 58 did not explicitly include an exception for abortions necessary to preserve the life of the pregnant woman. The result was that, for over a century, women facing unwanted pregnancies resorted to back-street abortions and dangerous abortifacients, resulting in many deaths and chronic injuries. Statistics show that between 1923 and 1933, 15 per cent of all maternal deaths were due to illegal abortion.[29]

It was, strikingly, a judicial decision in the late 1930s that crafted an exception, and in broad enough terms to cover risk not just to life but also to health, including mental health. Section 58 does not define what it means to 'unlawfully' procure a miscarriage. It was this which allowed McNaughten J in *R v Bourne*[30] in 1938 to carve out an exception for these purposes. In this case, Aleck William Bourne, an obstetrical surgeon at St Mary's Hospital London, was prosecuted under section 58 of the 1861 Act for performing an abortion on a fourteen-year-old girl who had been raped by a soldier. In giving directions to the jury, McNaughten J held that the words 'unlawfully' in section 58 meant that the crime was not committed where it was done in good faith for the purpose only of preserving a pregnant woman's life. He therefore directed the jury that section 58 should be read as including a proviso requiring the Crown to prove beyond reasonable doubt that the defendant did not procure the miscarriage of the girl in good faith for the purpose only of preserving her life.[31] Even more importantly, in a surprisingly generous interpretation, he emphasized that there was no clear distinction between danger to health and danger to life, and that a reasonable view should be taken of the meaning of these words. This meant that the doctor need not wait until the pregnant woman was in immediate danger of death. Instead, 'if the doctor is of the opinion on reasonable grounds that the probable consequence of the pregnancy will be to make the woman a physical or mental wreck, the jury are quite entitled to take the view that the doctor ... is operating for the purpose of preserving the life of the mother'.[32]

[28] Lord Ellenborough's Act, 43 Geo 3, c 58; revised in 1828, 9 Geo 4, c 31, § 13. See generally the historical description in *Roe v Wade* (n 3) 136ff.

[29] Abortion Rights: The National Pro-Choice Campaign, 'A History of Abortion Law in the UK' <http://www.abortionrights.org.uk/history-of-abortion-law-in-the-uk/> (accessed 25 February 2018).

[30] *R v Bourne* (n 5).

[31] ibid, 691. He drew on the proviso in the Infant Life (Preservation) Act 1929 which made it a criminal offence to kill a child wilfully when it was being delivered in the ordinary course of nature, but which included the following proviso to the effect that 'no person shall be found guilty of an offence under this section unless it is proved that the act which caused the death of the child was not done in good faith for the purpose only of preserving the life of the mother'.

[32] ibid, 694.

This meant that abortion could now be lawfully carried out in certain circumstances, both on the NHS and by private practitioners. However, the likelihood of obtaining an abortion varied widely across the country. For example, in Aberdeen in Scotland, lawful abortion was fairly well established, while in other parts of the country it was almost impossible to obtain.[33] In any event, the legal situation remained uncertain, leaving it to individual practitioners to judge whether the abortion was lawful or not. The result was that large numbers of illegal abortions continued to be carried out each year, with estimates ranging between 40,000 and 200,000 each year.[34] The cost to women's lives was unspeakable.

Unlike several US states, which continue to contest judicial intervention by finding ways to enact restrictive legislation, the push in the UK was towards legislative clarification and amplification. For the next three decades, a concerted campaign for the legalization of abortion gradually garnered support. Finally, in 1967, a private member's bill sponsored by David Steel MP became law, in the form of the Abortion Act 1967. It is notable that, although there was still fierce dissent, particularly from the Catholic Church, support for reform came both from the Churches of England and Scotland and from the general population, with two national opinion polls registering that 75 per cent of the population were in favour of reform.[35]

The Abortion Act 1967[36] clarifies the *Bourne* exception but it also goes significantly further. The Act retains criminal liability but provides four wide exceptions. Two exceptions give statutory language to the *Bourne* principle, applying in circumstances in which two registered medical practitioners are of the opinion that the termination is necessary to prevent grave permanent injury to the physical or mental health of the pregnant woman or that the continuance of the pregnancy would involve a greater risk to the life of the pregnant woman than if the pregnancy were terminated.[37] However, the other two exceptions go further. Section 1(1)(d) provides an exemption from criminal liability if two medical practitioners are of the opinion that there is 'a substantial risk that if the child were born it would suffer from such physical or mental abnormalities as to be seriously handicapped'.[38]

But the widest and most innovative is section 1(1)(a) of the Act (the social clause), which applies where a pregnancy is terminated at or before twenty-four weeks (previously twenty-eight weeks). Termination in this period is not a criminal offence where two registered medical practitioners are of the opinion that the continuance of the pregnancy would involve risk of injury to the physical or mental health of the pregnant woman or any existing children of her family greater than if the pregnancy were terminated.[39] Since the risks of continued pregnancy are almost always higher than that of an early abortion carried out by a registered medical practitioner, this makes abortion lawful in most circumstances. Particularly importantly, the statute provides specifically that, 'in determining whether the continuance of a pregnancy would involve such risk of injury to health, account may be taken of the pregnant woman's

[33] See the Hansard debate on the Medical Termination of Pregnancy Bill: HC Deb 22 July 1966, vol 732 cols 1067–1165, col 1070.

[34] ibid. [35] ibid, 1072.

[36] As amended by the Human Fertilisation and Embryology Act 1990.

[37] Abortion Act 1967, s 1(1)(b) and (c). [38] ibid, s 1(1)(d). [39] ibid, s 1(1)(a) as amended.

actual or reasonably foreseeable environment'.[40] Nevertheless, although the result is a relatively permissive regime, it does not provide abortion on demand. All the exceptions are based on the good-faith opinion of two registered medical practitioners, except where termination is immediately necessary to save the woman's life or prevent grave permanent injury, in which case only one medical practitioner will suffice.[41] Moreover, terminations must be carried out by a registered medical practitioner in an NHS hospital or, for terminations taking place at less than twenty-four weeks, at a place approved for these purposes by the Secretary of State.[42]

The UK courts have remained supportive of the Act, taking a broad interpretive approach to allow it to keep pace with medical developments. Thus, in a case in 1981, it held that the Act applied to medically induced abortion, even though this can be carried out in part by nurses.[43] Literally interpreted, the Act only applies to a pregnancy terminated by a registered medical practitioner.[44] Taking an expressly purposive approach, Lord Keith held that interpreting the Act to authorize these procedures was 'fully in accordance with that part of the policy and purpose of the Act which was directed to securing that socially acceptable abortions should be carried out under the safest conditions attainable'.[45] This contrasts with the dissenting opinion of Lord Wilberforce who took the view that, given that abortion was such a controversial subject involving moral and social judgements, a purposive construction was not appropriate, and it should be left to the legislature to include any amendments.[46]

The legislation has had a dramatic effect on morbidity and mortality associated with abortion. In 2014, there were 184,571 lawful abortions in England and Wales, where 98 per cent were funded by the NHS. The vast majority (98 per cent) were undertaken under the social clause, s1(1)(a), almost all of them (92 per cent) at less than thirteen weeks' gestation.[47] Indeed, it is the policy of the Department of Health that women who are legally entitled to an abortion should have access to the procedure as soon as possible.[48]

The Abortion Act 1967 does not, however, apply to Northern Ireland.[49] Instead, abortion remains a criminal offence under the 1861 Offences Against the Person Act, carrying a sentence of life imprisonment, both for the pregnant woman and anyone who assists her.[50] Abortion remains a criminal offence even for fatal foetal abnormality, rape, and incest. The only exception, imported from the *Bourne* case, is for an abortion performed to preserve the life of the mother.[51]

Several important challenges to this position finally materialized in 2018. First, the Convention on the Elimination of all Forms of Discrimination Against Women

[40] ibid, s 1(2). [41] ibid, s 1(4). [42] ibid, s 1(1) and s 1(3).

[43] *Royal College of Nursing v Department of Health and Social Security* [1981] AC 800 (HL).

[44] Abortion Act 1967, s 1(1).

[45] *Royal College of Nursing v Department of Health and Social Security* (n 43) at 835 F.

[46] ibid, 824 C.

[47] Department of Health 'Abortion Statistics, England and Wales 2014' <https://www.gov.uk/government/ uploads/system/uploads/attachment_data/file/433437/2014_Commentary__5_.pdf> (accessed 25 February 2018).

[48] ibid, para 2.25. [49] Abortion Act 1967, s 7(3).

[50] Offences against the Person Act 1861, ss 58 and 59; Criminal Justice Act (NI) 1945, s 25(1).

[51] Criminal Justice Act (NI) 1945, s 25(1).

(CEDAW) Committee found that the UK is responsible for grave and systemic violations of the rights of women in Northern Ireland by unduly restricting their access to abortion.[52] The report concludes that a 'restriction affecting only women from exercising reproductive choice, and resulting in women being forced to carry almost every pregnancy to full term, involves mental and physical suffering constituting violence against women and potentially amounting to torture or cruel, inhuman and degrading treatment'.[53] It recommended the adoption of legislation legalizing abortion at least for rape and incest, severe foetal abnormality, or where there is any threat to the pregnant woman's physical or mental health, regardless of their duration.

Second, the Northern Ireland Human Rights Commission (NIHRC) brought proceedings in the UK Courts, arguing that the lack of any exemptions for rape, incest, or fatal foetal abnormality constituted a breach of women's rights under the European Convention on Human Rights (ECHR). A majority of the UK Supreme Court held that in principle the current law was incompatible with Article 8 (the right to respect for private and family life). In individual cases of rape, incest, or fatal foetal abnormality, this interference might reach the threshold of severity required to constitute inhuman or degrading treatment, contrary to Article 3. Disappointingly, however, a differently constituted majority dismissed the appeal on the ground that the NIHRC did not have standing to bring proceedings without identifying a potential victim of an unlawful Act.[54] At the same time, Lord Mance stated that the law was untenable and in need of radical reconsideration. Unfortunately, the prospects of legislative intervention are small given the absence of a Northern Irish legislative assembly, and the reluctance of the Westminster Parliament to act in its stead. Nevertheless, the Court signalled clearly that if any person affected by an unlawful act were to bring proceedings, the outcome would be almost inevitable. Individual claims by clear victims of the law are imminent.

D. Constitutionalizing foetal rights: Republic of Ireland

Until the dramatic change of heart in a referendum in May 2018, the Irish Constitution contained the clearest example of an express right to life accorded to the foetus. The Irish trajectory has been strikingly different from that of England and Wales, despite their common origins in the 1861 Act, which was exported to Ireland in colonial times. As we have seen, the 1861 Act, criminalized both the pregnant woman and any accomplice to abortion, but did not afford rights to the foetus.[55] This was changed radically by a constitutional amendment introduced after a referendum in 1983, which expressly accorded the right to life to the foetus. Article 40.3.3 of the Irish Constitution (known as the Eighth Amendment) stated: 'The State acknowledges the right to life of the unborn and, with due regard to the equal right to life of the mother,

[52] CEDAW Committee, 'Report of the Inquiry concerning the United Kingdom of Great Britain and Northern Ireland under Article 8 of the Optional Protocol to the Convention on the Elimination of All Forms of Discrimination against Women' (23 February 2018) UN Doc CEDAW/C/OP.8/GBR/1 [72], [83].

[53] ibid, [65].

[54] *In the matter of the application of the Northern Ireland Human Rights Commission for Judicial Review (Northern Ireland)* [2018] UKSC 27 (UK Supreme Court) [73].

[55] Offences Against the Person Act 1861, s 58.

guarantees in its laws to respect, and, as far as practicable, by its laws to defend and vindicate that right'.[56]

Given the implacable resistance to abortion in Ireland, the only space for contestation concerned women's right to travel to the UK for abortions, as well as their rights to information and to assistance in travelling for abortion. As we see in more detail below, spurred by the Society for the Protection of Unborn Children, the Irish courts repeatedly issued injunctions against civil society organizations and student groups to prevent them from disseminating information and helping arrange travel and appointments for women seeking abortion in the UK.[57] Challenges in Europe were partially successful. The Court of Justice of the EU (CJEU) held that in principle, prohibitions on dissemination of information about services abroad could breach EU rules on free movement of services, but this did not apply to the student groups who were the applicants in the cases.[58] The European Court of Human Rights (ECtHR) was somewhat more robust, holding that injunctions on the dissemination of information constituted a breach of the respondents' rights to freedom of speech, which could not be justified in these circumstances.[59]

These cases prompted an amendment in 1992 to specify that Article 40.3.3 did not limit freedom to travel to other countries, or to obtain information relating to services lawfully available in another State.[60] Although this meant that women could travel to obtain an abortion, medical professionals in Ireland were not permitted to refer a pregnant woman to a clinic in a different State or to make an appointment for her in a clinic.[61] On the other hand, so strong were the feelings about abortion that a Protocol was secured to the Maastricht Treaty, which amended the Treaties constituting the European Union in 1992, and again to the Lisbon Treaty in 2008, to make it clear that nothing in the treaties relating to the EU would affect the application in Ireland of Article 40.3.3 of the Constitution of Ireland.[62]

It was only when faced with a similar situation to that in *Bourne*, namely the pregnancy of a fourteen-year-old girl who had been raped by her friend's father, that the Irish Supreme Court carved out a small exception. Even then, it did not go as far as *Bourne*. In the case of *Attorney General v X*[63] in 1992, the Irish Supreme Court held that termination might be permissible only where there was a real and substantial risk to the life of the mother which could only be avoided by the termination of pregnancy. Importantly, this risk included suicide.[64] This small concession, together with the limited permission to travel for safe abortions, had the effect of shutting down any further challenges in the ECtHR. In *A, B and C v Ireland* in 2011, the Court rejected

[56] Constitution of Ireland (1937), Article 40.3.3.

[57] *Society for the Protection of Unborn Children v Grogan* [1990] 1 CMLR 689 (Irish Supreme Court); *Attorney General Ex rel Society for the Protection of Unborn Children (Ireland) Ltd v Open Door Counselling Limited and the Dublin Wellwoman Centre Ltd* [1988] 2 CMLR 442 (Irish Supreme Court).

[58] C-159/90 *Society for the Protection of Unborn Children v Grogan* [1991] 3 CMLR 849 (CJEU).

[59] *Open Door Counselling and Dublin Well Woman v Ireland* (1993) 15 EHRR 244 (ECtHR).

[60] Constitution of Ireland (1937), Article 40.3.3; amended by the 13th and 14th Amendments in December 1992.

[61] Regulation of Information (Availability of Services Outside the State for Termination of Pregnancies) Act 1995, s 8(1).

[62] Protocol 17, Maastricht Treaty on European Union, February 1992; legally binding decision of heads of state or governments of the twenty-seven Member States of the European Union.

[63] *Attorney General v X* [1992] IR 1 (Irish Supreme Court). [64] ibid, 11.

a claim by Irish women that their rights to privacy were infringed by having to travel to have an abortion.[65] A more robust response, however, emanated from the United Nations Human Rights Committee, which in 2016 found that the absence of an exception allowing abortions in Ireland for fatal foetal abnormalities constituted cruel and inhuman treatment under the International Covenant on Civil and Political Rights (ICCPR). The right to travel to have such an abortion was not sufficient to justify such a restriction.[66]

In the meanwhile, the scope of the exception under *X v Ireland* remained unclear, exerting a significant chilling effect on both doctors and pregnant women.[67] So much so that in a tragic case in 2012, Savita Halappanavar died during a protracted miscarriage, after abortion was denied as long as a foetal heartbeat was present.[68] This finally prompted legislation replacing the Offences Against the Person Act 1861, in the form of the Protection of Life During Pregnancy Act 2013. However, the 2013 Act constituted one of the strictest abortion regimes in Europe.[69] There were no exceptions for rape, incest, risk to health short of death, or even fatal foetal abnormalities. The Act made abortion a criminal offence for both the doctor and the pregnant woman except where there was a real and substantial risk to the life of a pregnant woman that emanated from a physical illness and which could only be averted by termination of the pregnancy. This had to be certified by two doctors, except in an emergency situation (in which one doctor sufficed), and the certification had to be carried out in cognizance of the need to preserve foetal life to the extent possible. None of these exceptions applied if the foetus was viable. As de Londras concludes, only a woman who was dying could have a legal abortion in Ireland.[70]

It was not until 2018 that the voices of the countless women who had suffered under this regime were finally heard. In a passionately fought referendum in May 2018, as many as two-thirds of those voting (1.4 million) registered their resounding support for a repeal of the Eighth Amendment, and its replacement with a new article stating: 'Provision may be made by law for the regulation of termination of pregnancy'.[71]

The referendum was not a vote on any legislation following the repeal of the Eighth Amendment, but rather a vote to allow the Oireachtas (the Irish legislature) to pass laws regulating terminations. It remains to be seen what the legal framework regulating abortion will look like, given the differing views on abortion amongst the Irish political parties. Current proposals supported by the Irish Government would allow

[65] *A, B and C v Ireland* (2011) 53 EHRR 13 (European Court of Human Rights).

[66] UN Human Rights Committee, 'Views adopted by the Committee under article 5(4) of the Optional Protocol, concerning communication No 2324/2013' (9 June 2016) CCPR/C/116/D/2324/2013.

[67] *A, B and C v Ireland* (n 65).

[68] K Holland, 'Woman "denied a termination" dies in hospital' *The Irish Times* (14 November 2014) <http://www.irishtimes.com/news/woman-denied-a-termination-dies-in-hospital-1.551412> (accessed 25 February 2018).

[69] F de Londras, 'Constitutionalizing Fetal Rights: A Salutary Tale from Ireland' (2015) 22 Michigan Journal of Gender and Law 243, 251.

[70] ibid, 251.

[71] The Referendum Commission of Ireland, 'The Proposed Change' <https://refcom2018.refcom.ie/about-the-referendum/the-proposed-change/> (accessed 3 July 2018).

terminations where a medical practitioner certifies that the pregnancy concerned has not exceeded twelve weeks. After twelve weeks, if there is a risk to a woman's life or of serious harm to her health, the proposals would allow abortion where two medical practitioners certify that, in their reasonable opinion formed in good faith, an abortion should be permitted, provided the foetus has not reached viability. Only one medical practitioner is needed where there is an immediate risk to the life of, or serious harm to the health of, the pregnant woman. The proposals would also permit abortions in the case of fatal foetal abnormality, without gestational limits.

E. A collaborative approach: South Africa

In yet a further configuration in the relationship between courts and legislatures, permissive legislation might be challenged under constitutional frameworks which are relatively hospitable to abortion and reproductive rights. The South African Constitution, as a result of strong representations by organizations of women during the drafting process, contains a vigorous endorsement of reproductive rights.[72] Section 12 of the Constitution gives everyone the right to bodily and psychological integrity, which includes the rights 'to make decisions concerning reproduction'; to 'security in and control over their body'; and 'not to be subjected to medical or scientific experiments without their informed consent'.[73] Section 27, on the right of access to health care, also expressly includes the right of access to reproductive health-care services.

Soon after the transition to democracy, the Choice on Termination of Pregnancy Act 1996 (CTOPA) was enacted. The Act stands out for its explicit declaration in the preamble that the decision whether to have children is fundamental to women's physical, psychological, and social health and that the State has the responsibility to provide safe conditions under which the right of choice can be exercised without fear of harm. The statute permits abortion on request within the first twelve weeks of pregnancy, thus going further than any of the frameworks described above. Between thirteen and twenty weeks, abortion is permitted if a medical practitioner, in consultation with the pregnant woman, is of the opinion that there is a risk of injury to her physical or mental health, or there is a substantial risk of severe physical or mental abnormality in the foetus, or the pregnancy resulted from rape or incest, or the continued pregnancy would significantly affect the woman's social or economic circumstances. After 20 weeks, abortion is permitted if there is a danger to the woman's life, or continued pregnancy would result in a severe malformation of the foetus or would pose a risk of injury to the foetus, but only if two medical practitioners are of the same opinion.[74] Also salient are the facts that women under eighteen years old do not require parental consent, and that trained midwives can perform abortions.

Despite the positive constitutional language which supported the CTOPA, there have been several legal challenges, dealt with in more detail below. In the first, the

[72] C Albertyn, 'Claiming and Defending Abortion Rights in South Africa' (2015) 11 Rev direito GV 429, 435.

[73] South African Constitution, s 12 (right to life).

[74] Choice on Termination of Pregnancy Act 1996, s 2. The amended Choice on Termination of Pregnancy Act 2008 contains the identical provisions: see s 2.

Christian Lawyers Association challenged the fundamentals of the Act, arguing that it breached the right to life of the foetus. The High Court rejected the claim, not so much on a constitutional basis, but by reiterating the longstanding common law principle that the foetus lacked personhood and therefore could not be the subject of rights.[75] The Christian Lawyers Association, in a similar move to their counterparts in the US, then turned their attention to challenge the breadth of choice permitted to the pregnant woman. In a 2005 case, also before the High Court, they argued that the provisions permitting minors to have abortions without parental consent or notification breached minors' rights to family and parental care. The Court rejected their claim on the ground that it was not age but capacity which determined capacity to consent.[76]

In a third challenge, a different tack was pursued. This time a non-government organization (NGO) challenged a 1996 amendment bill to the Choice on Termination of Pregnancy Act on the grounds that Parliament had failed to comply with its constitutional obligation to facilitate public involvement before passing the Act.[77] The main aim of the amendment bill was to permit registered nurses, other than midwives, to perform abortions, and generally to increase access to safe termination of pregnancy services and achieve better governance. The issue turned not so much on abortion as on the constitutional obligation to facilitate public involvement.[78] However, the abortion context made the need for public involvement particularly pressing.[79] The South African Constitutional Court struck down the amendment bill on the grounds that, with one exception, none of the provinces had conducted public hearings at provincial level.[80] Consultation was duly held, and ultimately all nine provinces supported the Bill, which was passed in 2006.[81]

F. A legislative approach: India

The history of Indian abortion law is most similar to that of the UK. Criminal liability for abortion was entrenched in sections 312–316 of the Indian Penal Code. These provisions were passed during British Rule in 1862 and have remained unchanged. They make it a criminal offence for anyone, including the pregnant woman herself, to voluntarily cause a miscarriage of 'a woman with child'. They differ from their UK counterpart in that there is an explicit exception for saving the life of the woman.

In 1971, four years after the UK Abortion Act, the Indian Parliament passed the Medical Termination of Pregnancy Act 1971. The 1971 Act is similar to the UK Act

[75] *Christian Lawyers Association v Minister of Health* 1998 11 BCLR 1434 (High Court of South Africa (Transvaal division)).

[76] *Christian Lawyers Association v Minister of Health* 2005 1 SA 509 (T) (South African High Court).

[77] Choice on Termination of Pregnancy Amendment Act 38 of 2004.

[78] Constitution of the Republic of South Africa 1996, s 72(1)(a).

[79] *Doctors for Life International v Speaker of the National Assembly (CCT12/05)* [2006] ZACC 11 (South African Constitutional Court).

[80] ibid.

[81] The Choice on Termination of Pregnancy Act 92 of 2006. Most recently (2017), the African Christians Democratic Party introduced a Private Member's Bill to Parliament. The Bill seeks to substantially limit access to abortion in South Africa, in particular by requiring mandatory counselling; prohibiting abortions between the thirteenth and twentieth week of gestation; and requiring extra equipment at abortion facilities, such as ultrasound. The Bill is still in draft form.

in several respects. First, like the UK Act, it provides exemptions from criminal liability for termination of pregnancy in specified circumstances. Outside of these circumstances, abortion remains a criminal offence. Second, while these exemptions are broad, and the woman's consent is required, they are not ultimately based on a principle of choice for women or autonomy over their own bodies, but on the opinion of registered medical practitioners that one of the exemptions applies. For abortions which take place at twelve weeks or less, the opinion of one doctor is required; for abortions between twelve and twenty weeks, two registered medical practitioners are needed,[82] unless there is a medical emergency.[83] Again, abortions must take place at either a government established or maintained hospital or one approved by the government. Abortions must be with the consent of the pregnant woman,[84] but in the case of a minor, the consent of her guardian is required.[85]

The exemptions from criminal liability are also broadly similar to those of the UK Act, although differently phrased. There are two main exemptions. First, abortion is exempt from criminal liability where the continuance of the pregnancy would involve a risk to the life of the pregnant woman or be of grave injury to her physical or mental health.[86] Second, the Act provides for an exemption for terminations where there is a substantial risk that if the child were born, it would suffer from 'such serious physical or mental abnormalities as to be seriously handicapped'.[87] The explanations and further provisions broaden these exemptions substantially. The rape exception comes in the first explanation, which provides that 'where any pregnancy is alleged by the pregnant woman to have been caused by rape, the anguish caused by such pregnancy shall be presumed to constitute a grave injury to the mental health of the pregnant woman'.[88] The social clause comes in two further provisions. One provides that in determining whether there is a risk of injury to health, account may be taken of the pregnant woman's actual or reasonable foreseeable environment.[89] The second comes in Explanation 2, which states that '[w]here any pregnancy occurs as a result of failure of any device or method used by any married woman or her husband for the purpose of limiting the number of children, the anguish caused by such unwanted pregnancy may be presumed to constitute a grave injury to the mental health of the pregnant woman'.[90] The reference to a 'married' woman has, however, proved to be problematic, since it is sometimes understood as excluding single women from the right to abortion altogether.

The context in which the 1971 Act operates is, however, very different from that in the UK. The Act was expressly intended to reduce the incidence of maternal morbidity and mortality due to unsafe abortion. Nevertheless, the majority of women seeking abortion in India seem still to be turning to uncertified providers. It is estimated that of the 6.4 million abortions performed annually in India, as many as 3.6 million are unsafe.[91] The Abortion Assessment Project, a large multi-centre study published in 2004, reported that an estimated 6.7 million unreported abortions were performed

[82] Indian Medical Termination of Pregnancy Act 1971, s 3(1). [83] ibid, s 5.
[84] ibid, s 3(4)(b). [85] ibid, s 3(4)(a). [86] ibid, s 3(2). [87] ibid.
[88] ibid, s 3(2) Explanation 1. [89] ibid, s 3(3). [90] ibid, s 3(2) Explanation 2.
[91] R Duggal and V Ramachandran, 'The Abortion Assessment Project—India: Key Findings and Recommendations' (2004) 12 Reproductive Health Matters 122.

annually in India, by providers who were not registered or recognized, and often using untrained persons working in unhygienic conditions.[92] The risks faced by women using unsafe alternatives are enormous: deaths from unsafe abortions are estimated to constitute 10–13 per cent of total maternal deaths in India,[93] not far from the level in the UK before the 1967 Act was passed. An amendment passed in 2002 attempted to address this problem, by reducing bureaucracy for the registration of abortion facilities. It also recognized medical abortion to complement surgical abortion for very early abortions since the former can reduce risks of infection.[94] However, the insistence that only medically trained practitioners may perform abortions remains a major obstacle. As Hirve points out, the 'physicians only' policy excludes mid-level health providers, and the requirement of a second medical opinion for abortions between twelve and twenty weeks further restricts access, particularly in rural areas.[95] This can be contrasted with the South African legislation, where midwives and other registered nurses can perform abortions, and where no physician consent is required in the first twelve weeks. Krishnan argues that the focus on the medical profession rather than the women is at least in part due to the fact that Indian abortion law grew out of a concern about unsafe abortion and maternal mortality rather than women's autonomy.[96] However, it has in practice functioned as an obstacle to improvements in maternal health.

Other barriers have emerged, even though not in the Act. Hirve notes that although no spousal or any other third-party consent is required except for a minor, abortion providers often insist on such consent, and conversely, many women report that the decision to have an abortion was not taken by themselves but by husbands or other family members. 'Informal' fees charged in the public sector and exorbitant charges in the private sector, as well as other unnecessary requirements, add to the barriers experienced by women.[97]

These problems have led to proposals for amending legislation, in the form of the Medical Termination of Pregnancy (Amendment) Bill, 2014. Most importantly, the Bill provides for first-trimester abortions to be considered a matter of the woman's choice rather than requiring the opinion of a physician.[98] If the Bill becomes law, abortions will be permitted up to twenty-four weeks rather than the twenty weeks currently provided for and only one physician's opinion will be required in the second trimester. Unmarried women are explicitly included. At the same time, the Bill proposes to widen the base of abortion providers to allow mid-level and non-allopathic

[92] ibid.

[93] A L Montgomery, U Ram, R Kumar, P Jha (for Million Death Study Collaborators), 'Maternal Mortality in India: Causes and Healthcare Service Use Based on a Nationally Representative Survey' (15 January 2014) <https://doi.org/10.1371/journal.pone.0083331> (accessed 25 February 2018).

[94] Medical Termination of Pregnancy (Amendment) Act 2003.

[95] S Hirve, 'Abortion Law, Policy and Services in India: A Critical Review' (2004) 12 Reproductive Health Matters 114, at 116.

[96] S Krishnan, 'MTP Amendment Bill, 2014: Towards Re-imagining Abortion Care' (2015) XII Indian Journal of Medical Ethics 43, 44.

[97] Hirve (n 95) 118.

[98] Krishnan (n 96) 43.

health practitioners to perform abortions. This was based on research which found that abortions conducted by trained mid-level healthcare providers were as safe as those conducted by physicians.[99] As Krishnan argues, the fact that women would be able to request an abortion without having to justify it on any grounds, together with the wider access now available, ought to significantly reduce the obstacles women perceive to seeking and obtaining legal and safe abortions.[100] Of course this depends to a large extent on the Indian government taking on the task of training mid-level health practitioners to perform their role properly. The amended bill would strikingly resemble the South African provision. However, at the time of writing, the Bill had still not been passed.

At the same time, better access to safe abortion in India needs to be accompanied by wider policies on access to contraception and proper reproductive rights and freedoms. India's policies on population control have notoriously depended on sterilization rather than access to contraception, with small monetary incentives and widespread ignorance used to entice women to undergo unsafe and undesired sterilizations. In 2014, for example, in a case before the High Court of Punjab, the Human Rights Law Network argued that the Haryana government had disproportionately promoted female sterilization at the expense of access to other forms of modern contraception for years.[101] In the meanwhile, sterilization 'camps' operate in many areas in India, with appallingly low levels of standards of health and safety, high levels of morbidity and mortality, and highly questionable methods of establishing consent.

The issue of abortion in India cannot be discussed without also mentioning the problem of sex-selective abortion. The problem of 'missing girls' was first brought to world attention by Amartya Sen in his seminal work on the subject. Sen demonstrated that, compared to the distribution by gender in other parts of the world, there were millions fewer women in many parts of Asia than there should have been. Comparing the male–female ratio to that of Sub-Saharan Africa, he estimated a total of 37 million 'missing women' in India and 44 million in China at the end of the 1980s.[102] This trend has continued. According to the 2011 census in India, there were only 933 females for every 1,000 males. The ratio for children under six was even worse, with 927 girls for every 1,000 males.[103] This pattern reflects deeply entrenched patriarchal attitudes to women and girls, making girl children unvalued compared to boys. Strong preferences for sons are reinforced by community customs such as dowry, which are perceived as a financial burden on the bride's family during and after marriage. Moreover, as a recent Indian report points out, women are treated with respect in the community if they bear male children, and a son is considered as security for old age.[104]

[99] ibid, 44. [100] ibid, 45.

[101] Centre for Reproductive Rights, 'India: State Must Act on Contraception' (24 January 2014) <http://www.reproductiverights.org/feature/India-state-must-act-on-contraception> (accessed 25 February 2018).

[102] A Sen, *Development as Freedom* (OUP 1999) 106.

[103] S Subramanian and S Selvaraj, 'Social Analysis of Sex Imbalance in India: Before and After the Implementation of the Pre-Natal Diagnostic Techniques (PNDT) Act' (2009) 63 Journal of Epidemiology and Community Health 245.

[104] Public Health Foundation of India 'Implementation of the PCPNDT Act in India: Perspectives and Challenges' (PHFI April 2010) 10.

Sen attributed the distorted male–female ratio in India as primarily due to the comparative neglect of female health and nutrition during childhood.[105] However, since the advent of advanced technologies for detecting the sex of foetuses in utero, this has much more frequently manifested as sex-selective abortion. This can be seen by considering the male to female ratio at birth. This can generally be expected to be about 105 males to 100 females. But this ratio soars to between 110 and 120 males in some areas.[106] The UN Population Division estimates that in the fourteen countries which have a significant incidence of prenatal sex selection or neglect of girls, there is a total gender gap of 117 million missing women, cumulatively over several decades, most of them from China and India.[107] This is allied with dropping fertility rates, so that it becomes particularly important to have a male child within the first two or possibly three births. Jha et al's assessment of sex ratios by birth order in India showed that when the firstborn was a girl, the conditional sex ratio for second births fell sharply between 1990 and 2005, from 906 girls per 1,000 boys in 1990 to 836 girls per 1,000 boys in 2005. By contrast, no significant declines were detected when the firstborn was a boy. They estimated that this implied that there had been between 4.2 million and 12.1 million selective abortions of girls between 1980 and 2010.[108] The sex imbalance is even more pronounced among high socio-economic status groups.[109] As Subramanian and Selvaraj put it: 'High incidence of dowry marriages and prevailing inheritance practices favouring sons, both more common among high [socio-economic status] SES groups, are key motivations for intense preference for sons among high income groups'.[110]

In response to this worrying trend, the Indian Government enacted legislation in 1994 to prohibit sex selection before or after conception and to prevent the misuse of prenatal diagnostic techniques for sex determination leading to female foeticide.[111] However, its effect seems to have been minimal, partly because there is no incentive for either families or physicians to comply and partly because there has been little sustained effort at implementation.[112] A report on the implementation of the Act in 2010 showed that in the more than fifteen years of the law being in place, a mere 600 cases had been lodged, with only about twenty convictions.[113] This suggested that it clearly has not been a 'serious tool to catalyse positive social change'.[114] Nevertheless, as Hirve points out, it would be wrong to regard this issue as a reason for restricting

[105] Sen (n 102) 106.

[106] United Nations Population Fund (UNFPA), 'Sex Imbalances at Birth: Current Trends, Consequences and Policy Implications' (UNFPA 2012) 9.

[107] ibid, 10.

[108] P Jha et al, 'Trends in Selective Abortions of Girls in India: Analysis of Nationally Representative Birth Histories from 1990 to 2005 and Census Data from 1991 to 2011' (2011) 377 The Lancet 1921.

[109] ibid; Subramanian and Selvaraj (n 103).

[110] Subramanian and Selvaraj (n 103) 249.

[111] Prenatal Diagnostic Techniques (Regulation and Prevention of Misuse) Act (No. 57 of 1994); amended and expanded by the Prenatal Diagnostic Techniques (Regulation and Prevention of Misuse) Amendment Act 2002 (No 14 of 2003) now known as the Pre-Conception and Pre-Natal Sex Selection and Determination (Prohibition and Regulation) Act 2002.

[112] Subramanian and Selvaraj (n 103) 251.

[113] Public Health Foundation of India 'Implementation of the PCPNDT Act in India: Perspectives and Challenges (PHFI 2010).

[114] ibid, 11.

access to abortion. Proposals to reduce the gestation period for permissible abortions to twelve weeks are likely to send many more women to backstreet abortions rather than to address this issue.[115] Instead, the key is to address the social norms which regard women as less valuable than men. Proper access to safe contraception and abortion will hasten these changes rather than impede them.

III. Abortion and the Right to Life

Section II assessed the ways in which courts and legislatures have interacted in relation to abortion regulation, against the background of constitutional or international human rights instruments protecting a range of relevant human rights. Parts III, IV, and V examine in more detail how, in adjudicating claims in relation to abortion, courts in different jurisdictions have interpreted the rights to life, privacy, and equality, respectively. This section considers the right to life, both in relation to the foetus and the pregnant woman.

A. Birth as signifying personhood

The vast majority of human rights instruments state that everyone has a right to life. But does 'everyone' include the unborn embryo or foetus? Although the question of when life begins is framed as a scientific one, with many conflicting answers, a closer look reveals that it is in fact a moral or normative question. Many courts have, however, sought to avoid entering into the fraught moral contest by looking to legal precedents. As Baker P put it in the English High Court case of *Paton v British Pregnancy Advisory Service Trustees*:

> In the discussion of human affairs and especially of abortion, controversy can rage over the moral rights, duties, interests, standards and religious views of the parties. Moral values are in issue. I am, in fact, concerned with none of these matters. I am concerned, and concerned only, with the law of England as it applies to this claim. My task is to apply the law free of emotion or predilection.[116]

Echoing this sentiment in the Canadian case of *Tremblay*,[117] the Supreme Court of Canada stated:

> The Court is not required to enter the philosophical and theological debates about whether or not a foetus is a person, but, rather, to answer the legal question of whether the Quebec legislature has accorded the foetus personhood. Metaphysical arguments may be relevant but they are not the primary focus of inquiry. Nor are scientific arguments about the biological status of a foetus determinative in our inquiry.[118]

Notably, in seeking legal precedents, courts have looked to judgments in comparable jurisdictions to support their conclusions on whether a foetus has personhood.

[115] Hirve (n 95) 118.
[116] *Paton v British Pregnancy Advisory Service Trustees* [1979] QB 276 (High Court) 278.
[117] *Tremblay v Daigle* [1989] 2 SCR 530 (Supreme Court of Canada) 552.
[118] ibid.

The consensus has been against characterizing the foetus as a subject of rights. The seminal case remains that of the US Supreme Court in *Roe v Wade*[119] in 1973. The Fourteenth Amendment of the US Constitution provides that the State shall not 'deprive any person of life, liberty, or property, without due process of law'. Although the word 'person' is not defined expressly, the US Supreme Court held in *Roe v Wade* that, as used in the Fourteenth Amendment, 'person' did not include the unborn.[120] This meant that abortion was not inevitably a killing, and the Court could go on to determine the balance between the woman's right to privacy and the State's interest in the protection of unborn life. The balance drawn by the Court has been modified and challenged in subsequent US cases, but the finding that the foetus is not a 'person' for the purposes of the Fourteenth Amendment has remained intact.

Characteristically, the US Court did not cite foreign materials to reach this finding. However, its decision has been part of a transnational sharing of ideas as courts in different jurisdictions grapple with the same question. Thus, when the English High Court was faced with the question of whether the foetus had rights of its own before birth, its first recourse was to the judgment of Blackmun J in *Roe v Wade*. The case in question was *Paton v British Pregnancy Advisory Service Trustees*,[121] in which a husband sought an injunction to prevent his wife having an abortion which had been lawfully certified under the Abortion Act 1967. The Court held that the foetus does not have rights of its own until it is born. Baker P, agreeing with Blackmun J in *Roe v Wade*[122] that abortion 'arouses great emotions, and vigorous opposing views',[123] went on to seek confirmation of his substantive conclusion by reference to the law in other common law countries. Thus, he stated:

> The foetus cannot, in English law, in my view, have a right of its own at least until it is born and has a separate existence from its mother. That permeates the whole of the civil law of this country ... and is, indeed, the basis of the decisions in those countries where law is founded on the common law, that is to say, in America, Canada, Australia and, I have no doubt, in others.[124]

The High Court decision in *Paton* has been cited to support similar conclusions on similar fact situations in both Australia and Canada. Thus, in the Australian High Court, in *Attorney General (Qld) (Ex rel Kerr) v T*,[125] Gibbs CJ refused an application by the father of the foetus for an injunction to restrain an abortion. The applicant argued, inter alia, that the foetus should be regarded as a person whose existence can be protected by the courts. Gibbs CJ stated:

> As at present advised, I would agree with the judgment of Sir George Baker P in *Paton v BPAS Trustees* that a foetus has no right of its own until it is born and has a separate existence from its mother ... There are limits to the extent to which the law should intrude upon personal liberty and personal privacy in the pursuit of moral

119 *Roe v Wade* (n 3).
120 ibid, 157–62. This finding has not been questioned in later decisions.
121 *Paton v British Pregnancy Advisory Service Trustees* (n 116).
122 *Roe v Wade* (n 3) 708–09.
123 *Paton v British Pregnancy Advisory Service Trustees* (n 116) 278.
124 ibid, 279.
125 *Attorney General (Qld) (Ex rel Kerr) v T* (1983) 57 ALJR 285, 46 ALR 275 (High Court of Australia).

and religious aims. Those limits would be overstepped if an injunction were to be granted in the present case.

The Supreme Court of Canada faced a similar challenge in *Tremblay*,[126] where the complainant applied for an injunction to prevent his ex-partner from having an abortion. The trial judge had found that a foetus was a 'human being' under the Quebec Charter of Human Rights and Freedoms and therefore enjoyed a 'right to life' under section 1 of the Quebec Charter, which states: 'Every human being has a right to life, and to personal security, inviolability and freedom'. The Supreme Court of Canada, reversing the judgment, came to the opposite conclusion. The Court concluded that the Quebec Charter did not display any clear intention on the part of its framers to consider the status of a foetus. If the legislature wished to grant foetuses the right to life, it would not have left the protection of the right in such an uncertain state.

In South Africa, too, the constitutional right to life was used by the Christian Lawyers Association to attack the right to abortion contained in the Choice on Termination of Pregnancy Act 1996. The plaintiffs argued that life starts at conception, and therefore, by permitting abortion, the Act violated section 11 of the South African Constitution, which provides that 'everyone has a right to life'. The High Court, like its counterparts in the US, Australia, and Canada, relied on the absence of an explicit definition of 'everyone' to reject the contention that the drafters of the South African Constitution intended to accord the foetus legal personality or protection from conception.[127] This was reinforced both by civil law, which only gave rights to a foetus once born, and other provisions of the Constitution, such as the right to make decisions concerning reproduction and to have control over and security in the person. In a line of reasoning very similar to that of the Commission in *Paton*, the Court also held that the consequences of implying personhood for the foetus would have far-reaching and anomalous consequences for the rights of women.[128]

The claimant in *Paton*,[129] having lost at domestic level, resorted to the European Commission of Human Rights, where, instead of having to rely on the common law, he could rely directly on the right to life in Article 2(1) of the ECHR.[130] Article 2(1) of the ECHR states: 'Everyone's right to life shall be protected by law'. The Commission noted that, as in the US and Canadian cases, the term 'everyone' was not defined in the Convention.[131] However, there were no indications in the Convention that it included the foetus. Moreover, if the Convention were to be construed as recognizing an absolute right to life of the foetus, 'an abortion would have to be considered as prohibited even where the continuance of the pregnancy would involve a serious risk to the life of the pregnant woman. This would mean that the "unborn life" of the foetus would be regarded as being of a higher value than the life of the pregnant woman'. Such an interpretation, the Commission held, 'would be contrary to the object and purpose

[126] *Tremblay v Daigle* [1989] 2 SCR 530 (Supreme Court of Canada) 552–53.

[127] *Christian Lawyers Association v Minister of Health* (n 76).

[128] ibid, citing *Roe v Wade* (n 3); *Borowski v Attorney General for Canada* (1987) 39 DLR (4th) 73 (Saskatchewan Court of Appeal).

[129] *Paton v UK* (1981) 3 EHRR 408 (European Commission of Human Rights).

[130] ibid. [131] ibid, para [7].

of the Convention'.[132] It also noted that at the time of the signature of the Convention on 4 November 1950, all High Contracting Parties, with one possible exception, permitted abortion when necessary to save the life of the mother and that, in the meantime, the national law on termination of pregnancy has shown a tendency towards further liberalization. This would not be consistent with an approach which afforded personhood to the foetus. This approach has been reiterated on several occasions by the ECtHR.[133]

However, the Court has refrained from holding unequivocally that the foetus does not have personhood. This has been particularly pronounced in the Irish cases, in which it was argued that the right to life of the foetus should be included in the 'rights of others' for the purposes of the justification defence.[134] The Court has declined to decide this question. In *A, B and C v Ireland*,[135] the Irish Government argued that it was entitled to restrict the Article 8 right to privacy of the applicants because its aim was to protect the life of the foetus. This the Court rejected. It reiterated that it was neither desirable nor possible to answer the question of whether the unborn was a person for the purposes of Article 2 (right to life) of the Convention, leaving it open to States to choose to consider the unborn to be such a person. Indeed, both Ireland and Germany have taken this view. It is to this we now turn.

B. Life begins at conception

Several major jurisdictions expressly characterize life as beginning at conception and therefore afford the foetus foundational human rights. The inter-American Convention expressly states that life begins at conception. As we have seen, Ireland constitutionalized foetal rights in 1983. The German Federal Constitutional Court has likewise held that 'everyone' includes unborn human beings for the purposes of the right to life in the Basic Law. The implications for the possibility of a right to abortion nevertheless differ across these jurisdictions. This section begins by examining the Irish cases in more detail before moving on to examine the German jurisprudence.

1. *Ireland*

As we have seen, Article 40.3.3 of the Irish Constitution, introduced after a referendum in 1983, expressly accorded the right to life to the foetus. Article 40.3.3 stated: 'The State acknowledges the right to life of the unborn and, with due regard to the equal right to life of the mother, guarantees in its laws to respect, and, as far as practicable, by its laws to defend and vindicate that right'.[136] Notably, as de Londras points out, there is no mention of the woman's rights: instead, the pregnant woman is referred to from the outset as a 'mother'.[137] She argues that, although this was not the

[132] ibid, paras [19]–[20].

[133] *VO v France* (2005) 40 EHRR 12 (ECHR) 85; *A, B and C v Ireland* (n 65).

[134] *Attorney General Ex rel Society for the Protection of Unborn Children (Ireland) Ltd v Open Door Counselling Limited and the Dublin Wellwoman Centre Ltd* (n 57).

[135] *A, B and C v Ireland* (n 65) [212].

[136] Constitution of Ireland (1937), Article 40.3.3.

[137] de Londras (n 69) 263.

inevitable interpretation of the Article, a deeply conservative Irish Supreme Court has endorsed an interpretation of these provisions that 'reduced a woman from being a rights-bearing individual to a foetus-bearing mother'.[138]

Indeed, the response of the Supreme Court of Ireland has almost always been sternly literal. In *Open Door Counselling* case in 1988, it confirmed an injunction restraining Open Door Counselling and the Dublin Well Woman Centre, who provided non-directive counselling in Ireland to pregnant women, from assisting pregnant women to travel abroad to obtain abortions. It also prohibited the respondents from making travel arrangements for pregnant women, or giving them information as to where abortion clinics could be found or how to contact them.[139] The judgment of Finlay CJ was unequivocal: 'I am satisfied beyond reasonable doubt that having regard to the admitted facts the defendants were assisting in the ultimate destruction of the life of the unborn by abortion in that they were helping the pregnant woman who had decided upon that option to get in touch with a clinic in Great Britain which would provide the service of abortion'.[140] A similar injunction was issued in *Grogan* against three Irish student unions which had included information in their student handbooks about the names and locations of abortion clinics in the UK.[141]

It was therefore only the mother's own right to life that could have any countervailing weight in the eyes of the Irish court. *Attorney General v X*[142] concerned a fourteen-year-old girl who became pregnant after being raped by her friend's father, leaving her severely traumatized and suicidal. She and her parents decided to travel to the UK for an abortion, but because they had asked the Irish police whether the foetus could be tested to prove paternity, their plans became known by the Irish Attorney General. He immediately obtained an interim injunction from Costello J in the Irish High Court preventing them from leaving the country for a period of nine months or from procuring or arranging an abortion. Although they had in fact already left the country, they cancelled the arrangements for the abortion and returned to the country, not surprisingly aggravating the distress and suicidal thoughts of the victim. Their appeal against the interim injunction failed, and a permanent injunction was issued by Costello J.

However, the Irish Supreme Court overturned this finding and discharged the injunction. The Court rejected the test propounded by the lower court that an abortion was only permissible if there was an inevitable or immediate risk to the life of the mother. Referring to the *Bourne* case, the Court held that such a high threshold insufficiently vindicated the pregnant woman's right to life. Instead, it held that on the true interpretation of the constitutional provision, a termination was permissible where it was established as a matter of probability that there is a real and substantial risk to the life of the mother which can only be avoided by the termination of the pregnancy. Importantly, suicide was a risk which must be taken into account.[143] On the evidence, the risks to the life of the young defendant in this case satisfied this test. However, the

[138] ibid, 262.

[139] *Attorney General Ex rel Society for the Protection of Unborn Children (Ireland) Ltd v Open Door Counselling Limited and the Dublin Wellwoman Centre Ltd* (n 57).

[140] ibid, para [21].

[141] *Society for the Protection of Unborn Children v Grogan* [1990] (n 57).

[142] *Attorney General v X* (n 63).

[143] ibid, 11.

Court did not go as far as *Bourne*. Finlay CJ made it clear that the proper test referred to the real and substantial risk to the life, as distinct from the health, of the mother.[144] Absent such risk, a pregnant woman could not access abortion even if the pregnancy resulted from rape or incest, and even if there was a fatal foetal abnormality.

Any further moderation of the strength of the right to life accorded to the foetus therefore had to come from other sources, primarily the ECHR, but also the European Union (EU) and the UN Human Rights Committee (HRC). The CJEU was called into action by the student groups who were indicted for distributing information about abortion in the UK in *Grogan*. They argued that the injunction interfered with the right of free movement of services in EU law.[145] To counter this claim, the Society for the Protection of Unborn Children argued that the provision of abortion in jurisdictions in which it is lawful could not be regarded as a service on the grounds that it involves the destruction of the life a human being, namely the unborn child. The Court rejected this proposition: 'Whatever the merits of these arguments on the moral plane', the Court stated, 'they cannot influence the answer to the ... question. It is not for the Court to substitute its assessment for that of the legislature in those member States where the activities in question are practised legally'.[146] However, the link between the students' associations' distribution of information and the clinics in other Member States was too tenuous to be regarded as a restriction on the freedom to provide services in EU law.[147] This also meant that the Court did not have jurisdiction to pronounce on the human rights issues which were raised.

The human rights dimension was therefore pursued to the ECtHR, this time not by the student groups but by Open Door Counselling and Dublin Well Woman Centre.[148] In this case, the rights asserted were the free speech rights of the counsellors employed by these agencies under Article 10 of the ECHR. The ECtHR upheld their claim. There was no doubt that the rights to impart and receive information were interfered with. The question then became whether they were justified under Article 10(2) of the ECHR, which only allows limitations on rights where necessary in a democratic society for the protection of, inter alia, health or morals, or the rights of others. As we have seen, the Court rejected the argument that the foetus was protected by the right to life in Article 2 and therefore fell within the exception for protection for the rights of others.[149] However, it did allow the Irish Government to argue that the restriction could potentially fall within the exception for the protection of morals, finding that the constitutional protection was based on 'profound moral values concerning the nature of life'.[150] Nevertheless, although pursuing a legitimate aim, the restriction could not be said to be necessary. This was due to the heavy-handedness of the injunction, which permanently prevented any dissemination of information; the particular impact of the lack of guidance on vulnerable women with fewer resources; and the added health risks for women whose abortions were delayed because of the difficulty in finding

[144] ibid. [145] *Society for the Protection of Unborn Children v Grogan* [1990] (n 57).
[146] ibid, paras [19]–[20]. [147] ibid, para [24].
[148] *Open Door Counselling and Dublin Well Woman v Ireland* (n 59). [149] ibid, para [66].
[150] ibid, para [63].

information. The Court therefore found a violation of the right to freedom of speech in Article 10.[151]

In the meantime, the constitutional referendum in 1992 established a right to travel and to access information. The Thirteenth Amendment specified that Article 40.3.3 did not limit freedom to travel outside of Ireland, and the Fourteenth Amendment stated that Article 40.3.3 did not limit the freedom to obtain or make available information relating to services lawfully available in another State subject to any conditions laid down by law. These concessions provoked a highly deferent response by the ECtHR. In the subsequent case of *A, B and C v Ireland*, the applicants complained that the lack of an exception for women's health or wellbeing in Irish law infringed their rights to respect for their private life under Article 8 of the ECHR. The Court agreed that the absence of any exception for health or wellbeing meant that the Irish prohibition came within the scope of Article 8.[152] The case therefore turned on whether the prohibition pursued a legitimate aim and was a proportionate means of doing so. Again, the Court rejected the justification based on the right to life of the foetus but held that the aim of the restriction could be legitimately regarded as the protection of morals. But was the restriction proportionate to the protection of morals? Here the majority of the Court, against a powerful dissent by six judges, held that a broad margin of appreciation should be afforded to the Irish State.[153] It was particularly swayed by the fact that women could lawfully travel abroad for an abortion with access to appropriate information and medical care in Ireland.

> From the lengthy, complex and sensitive debate in Ireland as regards the content of its abortion laws, a choice has emerged. Irish law prohibits abortion in Ireland for health and well-being reasons but allows women ... who wish to have an abortion for these reasons, the option of lawfully travelling to another state to do so.[154]

By contrast, the dissenting judgments held that it was not sufficient to regard the right to travel abroad as fulfilling the pregnant woman's rights given the financial, practical, and emotional costs involved.[155] Moreover, they took issue with the way the majority applied the margin of appreciation, which is usually narrowed when there is a consensus among a substantial majority of the Contracting States of Europe. Abortion was available on request in thirty such States, and justified on health and well-being grounds in approximately forty Contracting States.[156] Thus, a far narrower margin for appreciation should have been applied.

On the other hand, the Court did find that the failure to introduce legislation which made it clear whether or not a pregnant woman qualified under the *X v Ireland* exception for an abortion in Ireland constituted a breach of the State's positive obligations under Article 8. The Irish Government has subsequently enacted the Protection of Life During Pregnancy Act 2013. However, as we have seen, the result was highly restrictive. Particularly striking is the absence of any exception for cases where the foetus is highly unlikely to be born alive, or, if born, might suffer from a serious medical condition leading to death soon after birth. Because there is no provision for

[151] ibid, paras [73]–[77]. [152] *A, B and C v Ireland* (n 65) para [212].
[153] ibid, para [233]. [154] ibid, para [239]. [155] ibid, O-III 10. [156] ibid, para [235].

abortion in such a case, the woman is required to bear the foetus until term or until its natural death.[157] The only alternative is to travel to the UK for the abortion, often without the support of family and friends. Moreover, Irish health-care professionals are not allowed to help arrange the abortion and it is unclear what information they are permitted to impart. Because they could be subject to criminal penalties if they give too much information, they tend to give little or no guidance or assistance to pregnant women in this position.

It was this kind of case which came before the HRC.[158] In this case, the complainant discovered at twenty-two weeks that the foetus she was carrying suffered from a serious heart defect and would either die in utero, or shortly after birth. She travelled to the UK for an abortion, but because of shortage of resources had to return within twelve hours of the procedure, despite being weak and very distressed. She argued that her right not to be subjected to cruel or inhuman punishment or torture under the International Covenant on Civil and Political Rights (ICCPR) was violated by having to leave Ireland, without the support of her family and friends, or the Irish medical system, or else remain in Ireland and wait for her foetus to die in utero or shortly after birth. She also argued that her rights to privacy and equality had been breached: the decision she faced was wholly invidious, infringing her right to autonomy and privacy; and the fact that she was treated worse than a man or than women who suffered a stillbirth or miscarriage meant that her rights to equality under the Convention were similarly breached.

The HRC upheld all her claims. The legislative framework, it held, subjected her to 'conditions of intense physical and mental suffering'. This was exacerbated by 'the need to choose between continuing her non-viable pregnancy or traveling to another country while carrying a dying foetus, at personal expense and separated from the support of her family, and to return while not fully recovered; the shame and stigma associated with the criminalization of abortion of a fatally ill foetus; the fact of having to leave the baby's remains behind and later having them unexpectedly delivered to her by courier; and the State's refusal to provide her with necessary and appropriate post-abortion and bereavement care'.[159] Unlike the ECtHR, it did not regard the right to travel to have an abortion in the UK as in any sense a viable alternative. Instead, it held that all of this could have been avoided had she been permitted to have her abortion in Ireland.[160]

2. *Germany*

The German Federal Constitutional Court (FCC) starts from a similar position to that of the Irish Constitution, prior to the 2018 referendum, but lands up with a very different result. When interpreting the provision 'everyone has a right to life' in Article 2.2 of the Basic Law, the Court has held unequivocally that 'life in the sense of the historical

[157] de Londras (n 69) 29.

[158] UN Human Rights Committee, 'Views adopted by the Committee under Article 5(4) of the Optional Protocol, concerning communication No 2324/2013' (9 June 2016) CCPR/C/116/D/2324/2013.

[159] ibid. [160] ibid.

existence of a human individual exists according to established biological and physiological knowledge at least from the 14th day after conception ... "Everyone" in the meaning of Article 2 (2) of the Basic Law ... therefore includes unborn human beings'.[161] As we have seen, the Court relied on this provision in the First Abortion decision in 1975 to strike down the recently reformed Criminal Code, which permitted abortion within the first twelve weeks of pregnancy, with the consent of the pregnant woman and some mandatory counselling procedures. The FCC held that the developing human life is also included in the protection of human dignity in Article 1.1 of the Basic Law:

> Where human life exists, it merits human dignity; it is not decisive whether the holder of this human dignity knows of it and is able to maintain it by himself. The potential capabilities lying in human existence from its inception on are sufficient to justify human dignity.[162]

The judgment of the FCC is, however, complex and nuanced. Two main points should be highlighted. The first is that, unlike the position in Ireland, the FCC recognized that the State also has an interest in protecting women's rights. How then does it resolve the conflict of rights? On the one hand, it is not prepared to regard the embryo as simply a part of the maternal organism, so that termination would fall into the pregnant woman's sphere of private life into which the State could not intrude. 'Because the nasciturus is an independent human being which is protected by the Constitution, the termination of a pregnancy has a social dimension which makes it accessible to and in need of state regulation'.[163] Moreover, while recognizing the pregnant woman's right of self-determination, the FCC stated that this should give way to the protection of foetal life. On the other hand, the pregnant woman's rights are not entirely subordinate. The State's duty to protect the right to life and self-determination of the pregnant woman means that the woman should not be 'forced to sacrifice her own values to an unbearable degree in order to protect the unborn life'.[164] The Court pointed to four relevant circumstances or 'indicators' where the woman would not be expected to sacrifice her right to life and inviolability of the person in the Basic Law Article 2.2. As well as cases in which the termination is necessary to avoid a threat to her life or to avoid serious impairment of her health, the Court specified three other indicators: eugenic (serious foetal problems); ethical (rape or incest); and social or emergency indicators. The last indicator is striking, in the light of the strong background assumption in favour of protecting foetal life. This indicator refers to a situation in which the general social situation of the pregnant woman and her family may produce such conflicts that the State cannot extract sacrifices beyond a certain degree from the pregnant woman.

The second major point to highlight, which might strike readers as surprising, is the approach of the FCC to sanctions, especially criminal sanctions. Although, outside of the indicated situations, the termination of a pregnancy remained a wrong deserving of punishment, the Court held that the legislator was not obliged to use criminal law. The litmus test was effectiveness, and it was acknowledged that the criminal law did

[161] 39 BverfGE (1975) para C.I. 1(b). [162] ibid, para C.I. 2. [163] ibid, para C.II. 2.
[164] ibid, para C.II. 3.

not operate in the same way for protection of unborn life as it did for murder. The priority was prevention as opposed to repression, so that the State should use 'socio-political' means as well as public assistance to safeguard developing life. There was nothing preventing the State from expressing its legal disapproval of abortion by other means than the use of penal sanctions, as long as the sanction indicated the wrongness of the conduct and the disapproval of such conduct. Even in the indicated situations, the State's duty was to express disapproval and aim to deter the pregnant woman. But this could take the form of counselling, encouragement and, especially in cases of social need, support by means of practical assistance.

Applying these principles, the Court struck down the legislation for three main reasons. First, it failed to explicitly articulate legal disapproval for abortion. Second, it did not provide legal sanctions for unconstitutional abortions. Finally, the mandatory counselling procedure insufficiently deterred abortions, because the doctors providing the counselling were not qualified to inform women about available welfare benefits; there was no waiting period between counselling and the procedure, and the same doctors provided the counselling and performed the operation. By contrast, the two dissenting justices argued that the decision went too far in intruding on legislative decision-making. The classic function of the Court was to determine whether the State was *permitted* to control personal freedom through punishment, whereas in this case, the Court was intervening in order to *require* the State to utilize punitive measures, thus encroaching deeply into the sphere of personal freedom. In this case, the legislator was entitled lawfully to drop the threat of a penal sanction, which was, in its view, ineffective, inadequate, and even damaging.

As we have seen, the German legislature accepted the FCC's judgment in the Abortion Reform Act of 1976, which reinstated the criminal prohibition of abortion except in relation to the circumstances prescribed by the Court. However, further litigation was sparked by the Pregnancy and Family Assistance Act of June 1992, passed after the unification of Germany.[165] As we have seen, the crucial change was to remove all requirements, apart from counselling, in the first twelve-week period. The guiding principle of the statute was that the State's duty to protect developing life is best served by improving the social environment for women and families, rather than by the threat of punishment, or the establishment of burdensome procedures to obtain permission for an abortion. Crucially, therefore, the Pregnancy and Family Assistance Act of 1992 included a number of social measures on education, family planning, women's rights in the workplace, and childcare.

There were two particularly controversial issues in the Act which formed the basis of challenge. The first was that non-indicated abortions which fulfilled the counselling requirement were labelled 'not illegal'. Second, the cost of these early abortions was to be covered by general health insurance. It was argued that, while it may be acceptable to remove criminal sanctions, the legislation should not give the message that abortion was actually legal. It was these two issues which led the Court again to

[165] Kommers (n 16) 12.

strike down the legislation.[166] On the first issue, it reiterated that the Basic Law requires the State to protect human life, including that of the unborn, and that even unborn human life is accorded human dignity. The FCC was even more sternly of the view that such protection is only possible if the legislature forbids the mother to terminate her pregnancy and imposes on her the fundamental legal obligation to carry the child to term. The State could not therefore declare non-indicated terminations as 'not illegal' or justified. However, in vivid contrast to the Irish approach, the German Court's approach was again highly nuanced. The obligation to protect unborn human life must be determined with a view to competing legal values, including the right of the pregnant woman to respect for her human dignity, and above all her right to life, physical inviolability, and free development of her personality. As in the earlier decision, the Court drew on the principle that a woman should not be subject to burdens which demand such a degree of sacrifice of her own existential values that she could not be expected to continue with the pregnancy. Importantly, the FCC accepted the principle that the State could protect unborn human life through counselling the pregnant woman to convince her to carry the unborn child to term. In the early phase of pregnancy, the State could thus dispense with the threat of criminal punishment. The Court also accepted the shift away from the indicator approach in this period, and with it the need for third-party verification. The most important aim was to enlist the woman's co-operation: this might be less forthcoming if she were required to gain verification from third parties. Importantly too, the State could not force a woman to consult parents, husband, or family. Thus, in effect, provided the label of 'not illegal' was withdrawn from this type of termination, the appropriate message would be sent.

Its findings were more intrusive in relation to the provision permitting non-indicated abortions to be paid for under the State medical insurance system. This, it held, would give entirely the wrong message and should be struck down. However, this part of the judgment was also nuanced. It did not preclude the granting of social assistance benefits in cases of economic hardship for abortions which were not punishable (but still not lawful) granted under the counselling category: 'No woman will be prevented from going to a licensed physician to procure an abortion merely because she lacks the financial means to do so'.[167] In addition, all 'indicated' or lawful abortions could be State-funded.

The Court, like the statute, situated abortion within the broader context of the effect of childbearing on women's role in the paid workforce. It emphasized the need to ensure that women would not lose their jobs or suffer serious financial hardship as a consequence of pregnancy or childbirth. Respect for a pregnant woman's right to personality required the State to adopt 'legal and actual measures designed to enable both parents simultaneously to raise their children and pursue gainful employment and to return to their jobs without losing the opportunity for professional advancement following periods of child care'.[168] It therefore read the Constitution holistically, having

166 88 BVerfGE, Judgment of the Second Senate of 28 May 1993—2 BvF 2/90—paras [1]–[434] <http://www.bverfg.de/e/fs19930528_2bvf000290en.html> (accessed 25 February 2018).

167 ibid, para [321]. 168 ibid, para [260].

regard also to the declaration in the Basic Law that men and women should have equal rights.

Incorporating the judgment of the Court, the German Criminal Code now makes it an offence punishable with imprisonment to terminate a pregnancy. However, the Code exempts from punishment all non-indicated pregnancies under twelve weeks, provided the woman consents; she has a certificate demonstrating that she had counselling at least three days before; and the termination is performed by a physician. No third-party verification is required, making the German statute in this sense more liberal than its UK counterpart, which requires physicians' authorization. This exemption is not stated as being 'not unlawful'; instead the Code provides that the 'elements of the offence ... have not been fulfilled' in these circumstances.[169] On the other hand, 'indicated' abortions are designated as 'not unlawful'. Indicated abortions include situations in which 'considering the present and future living conditions of the pregnant woman, the termination of the pregnancy is advisable to avert a danger to the life or the danger of a grave impairment of the physical or emotional state of health of the pregnant woman and the danger cannot be averted in another way which is reasonable for her'.[170] Abortions are also 'indicated' or 'not unlawful' within the first twelve weeks where 'according to medical opinion an unlawful act has been committed against the pregnant woman under [the relevant provisions of the Penal Code], [and] strong reasons support the assumption that the pregnancy is based on that act'. There are also detailed provisions as to counselling which should 'serve to protect unborn life' but which should also 'through advice and assistance, contribute to overcoming the conflict situation'.[171]

IV. Abortion and the Right to Privacy

As we have seen, the conversation between courts and legislature in the US is at first sight diametrically opposite to that in Germany. Whereas the German FCC struck down permissive legislation, the US Supreme Court has repeatedly struck down restrictive abortion legislation. Key to this contrast has been the different starting point. As we have seen, the US Supreme Court in *Roe v Wade* held that a foetus was not a person protected by the right to life.[172] Instead, its starting point was the pregnant woman's right to privacy. In this section, we discuss in more detail how the right to privacy has shaped US jurisprudence on abortion.

Notably, unlike the ECHR, which has a right to respect for private life, the right to privacy is not one of the express terms of the US Constitution. Instead, the US Supreme Court has recognized the right to personal privacy in what it calls the 'penumbra' of the Constitution. More specifically, in *Roe*, the Court regarded the right to privacy as founded in the Fourteenth Amendment's concept of personal liberty and its concomitant restriction upon State action.[173] This it was held, was broad enough

[169] German Penal Code 218 and 218a (1). [170] ibid, 218a (2). [171] ibid, 219.

[172] *Roe v Wade* (n 3) 158.

[173] The Due Process clause of the Fourteenth Amendment states that no State shall 'deprive any person of life, liberty or property without due process of law'.

to incorporate a woman's decision as to whether to terminate a pregnancy or not. However, just as the FCC recognized that the foetus' right to life had to be balanced against the woman's right to self-determination, so the US Supreme Court held that the pregnant woman's right to personal privacy was subject to some State regulation in the interest of protecting potential life. As Blackmun J, giving the judgment of the Court, held, '[T]he pregnant woman cannot be isolated in her privacy'.[174] The fact that she carries an embryo, and later a foetus, means that it is reasonable and appropriate for a State to decide that other interests, including the health of the mother and that of potential human life, become significantly involved. The Court in *Roe* envisaged this relationship as temporal: the State's important and legitimate interests in each of these 'grows in substantiality as the woman approaches term and at a point during pregnancy, each becomes "compelling" '.[175]

It is here that Blackmun J developed the trimester approach which was to hold sway for the next nineteen years. The State's interest in the health of the mother only became compelling after the end of the first trimester. This point was chosen because of the well-established medical fact that until this point, mortality in abortion might be less than in normal childbirth. After this point, it was permissible for the State to regulate abortion, but only to the extent that regulation reasonably related to the preservation and protection of maternal health. Such regulation could include requirements as to qualifications of the abortion provider and the facility in which it was performed. The State's interest in potential life, on the other hand, became compelling at the point of viability, or the third trimester, when the foetus was presumed to be capable of meaningful life outside of the womb. After this period, the State would be free to prohibit abortion, provided the health or life of the mother was not at stake.

Notably, although State regulation was not permitted in the first trimester, these provisions were not framed in terms of women's choice. Instead, during the first trimester, Blackmun J stated, '[T]he attending physician, in consultation with his patient, is free to determine, without regulation by the State, that, in his medical judgment, the patient's pregnancy should be terminated'.[176] As in the UK and India, the decision was left in the hands of the physician. This is despite the fact that the right of privacy relied on in *Roe v Wade* was firmly based in a notion of liberty, which was said to underpin the specific rights provided for in the Constitution. As Stewart J put it, '[F]reedom of personal choice in matters of marriage and family life is one of the liberties protected by the Due Process Clause of the Fourteenth Amendment... That right necessarily includes the right of a woman to decide whether or not to terminate her pregnancy'.[177] Yet no justification was given for leaving the decision to a medical physician rather than the pregnant woman herself.

As we have seen, the trimester framework was abandoned in *Planned Parenthood v Casey*.[178] This framework, the Court held, overstated the woman's interest and undervalued the State's interest in the potential life within the woman. Even in the first trimester, the woman's interest should not be seen as free of State regulation. The balance was instead drawn on the basis of whether the interference created an 'undue burden'

[174] *Roe v Wade* (n 3) 158. [175] ibid, 163. [176] ibid, 163. [177] ibid, 169.
[178] *Planned Parenthood v Casey* (n 11).

on the woman's choice. Undue burden was held to be shorthand for the finding that a 'state regulation has the purpose or effect of placing a substantial obstacle in the path of a woman seeking an abortion of a nonviable foetus'.[179] The means chosen by the State to further the interest in potential life must aim to inform the woman's free choice, not hinder it.[180] The undue burden framework was reiterated and reinforced in *Gonzales v Carhart*,[181] where the Court upheld the Partial Birth Abortion Ban Act, a federal statute prohibiting a specific method of performing abortion during the second trimester.

The undue burden test is remarkably similar to the FCC's principle that the pregnant woman should not be 'forced to sacrifice her own values to an unbearable degree in order to protect the unborn life'.[182] This raises the question of how the different starting points of each Court affects the outcome. For the FCC, the primary value is the right to life of the foetus, which can only be limited in cases where the woman's sacrifice is more than she can be expected to bear. In the US jurisprudence, the woman's right to privacy is the primary value, and it is for the State to justify limiting that interest in order to protect the interest in potential life. As we have seen, the FCC balanced the two values in ways which gave significant opportunity for the women's interests to be catered for. How then have US Courts carried out the balancing exercise? In *Roe*, the Court held that, because the pregnant woman's right to personal privacy was a fundamental right, any State regulation limiting her right attracted strict scrutiny. This means that any regulation interfering with the privacy right can only be justified by a 'compelling state interest'. In addition, regulations must be 'narrowly drawn to express only the legitimate state interests at stake'.[183] The extent to which the undue burden test can genuinely protect the pregnant women's privacy rights depends entirely on whether the Court carries over the strict scrutiny test to the many restrictive provisions which have subsequently proliferated.

In *Casey* itself, the Court only struck down one of the requirements in the Pennsylvania statute which had been challenged in the case. This was the requirement that a married woman give notice to her husband. The Court recognized that in some circumstances, this would give an effective veto to the husband and therefore constitute an undue burden. According to the joint opinion: 'We must not blind ourselves to the fact that the significant number of women who fear for their safety and the safety of their children are likely to be deterred from procuring an abortion as surely as if the Commonwealth had outlawed abortion in all cases'.[184] The other requirements were not, however, held to be unduly burdensome. Thus, the Court upheld the requirement that certain information should be supplied to the woman at least twenty-four hours before the procedure, on the basis that it was legitimate to expect a woman to make an informed choice. Such information could include materials designed to persuade a woman to choose childbirth over abortion if reasonably related to the exercise of an informed choice, unless it constituted an undue burden on her choice. Nor was the waiting period of twenty-four hours an undue burden. This was despite the District

[179] ibid, 877. [180] ibid.
[181] *Gonzales v Carhart* 550 US 124 (2007) (US Supreme Court).
[182] 39 BverfGE (1975) para C.II. 3. [183] *Roe v Wade* (n 3) 156.
[184] *Planned Parenthood v Casey* (n 11) 894.

Court's finding that a waiting period was particularly burdensome because of the distances many women might have to travel to reach the clinics and their increased exposure to anti-abortion protestors.

Similarly, the Court upheld the requirement that a pregnant minor should be required to obtain parental consent, with the possibility of applying to court to obtain consent if she did not wish to or could not obtain her parent's consent. A large number of States—as many as forty-four out of fifty in 1994—required pregnant minors to notify their parents, or else persuade judges that they are sufficiently mature and well-informed to make the decision themselves. Sanger, writing in 2004, points to the intrusive and intimidating nature of such judicial hearings and argues that they are a highly legalistic response to the resolution of teenage pregnancy.[185] A key difficulty is the delay it causes, increasing the medical risks of abortion.[186] Girls who do not want to involve their parents in the decision are already in a particularly vulnerable position: yet they are required to speak about intimate matters in court, including their sexual relations; their home life, which might be in disarray; their views on motherhood; and their reasons for wanting an abortion rather than adoption or motherhood.[187]

Both *Roe* and *Casey* identified two kinds of legitimate interests a State might have in interfering with women's choice: the interest in protecting potential life and that of protecting women's health. The interest in protecting potential life was emphasized in *Carhart*.[188] More recently, however, States have imposed restrictive provisions on abortion providers, ostensibly to promote women's health. Known as TRAP laws (targeted regulation of abortion providers), several States have imposed requirements on abortion providers which are not imposed on other potentially greater risk-prone health procedures. This raises the question of whether the reference to women's health is no more than a pretext for restricting abortion. Here the standard of scrutiny used by the Court becomes crucial, and especially the extent to which it demands a strong evidential basis for assertions about women's health. To what extent will the Court insist on evidence to prove that the regulations in question really do protect the health of women?

It was in this context that the judgment in *Whole Woman's Health v Hellerstedt*[189] was eagerly awaited. The case constituted a challenge of Texan legislation, known as HB2 (House Bill 2), which placed onerous requirements on abortion providers in Texas. Physicians performing abortions were required to have admitting privileges at a hospital not more than thirty miles from the abortion facility (the 'admitting privileges' requirement). In addition, the abortion facility was required to meet the minimum standards for ambulatory surgical centres under Texas law (the 'surgical centre' requirement). Abortion is acknowledged to be a safe procedure, with very few complications and almost no deaths. Yet it was subject to a higher level of regulation than many procedures which were less safe. Moreover, the effect of the two requirements would be dramatic, slicing the number of facilities providing abortion in Texas from

[185] C Sanger, 'Regulating Teenage Abortion in the United States: Politics and Policy' (2004) 18 International Journal of Law, Policy and the Family 305.

[186] ibid, 311. [187] ibid, 312. [188] *Gonzales v Carhart* (n 181) 58–59.

[189] *Whole Woman's Health v Hellerstedt* 133 S Ct 2292 (2016) (US Supreme Court).

forty to potentially no more than eight or nine. The District Court therefore found that the provisions created an impermissible obstacle. The Fifth Circuit Court of Appeal, however, reversed. The key difference lay in the standard of scrutiny to which State legislation would be subject. The Fifth Circuit held that all the State needed to show was that the requirements were rationally related to the purpose of protecting women's health, which in this case had been demonstrated.

In a landmark decision, with a majority of five justices, the Court reversed this decision. Crucially, it held that the Fifth Circuit Court of Appeal's articulation of the relevant standard was incorrect. The rational relationship standard wrongly equated the 'judicial review applicable to the regulation of a constitutionally protected personal liberty with the less strict review applicable where for example economic legislation is at issue'.[190] Instead, the Court emphasized, '[U]nnecessary health regulations that have the purpose or effect of presenting a substantial obstacle to a woman seeking an abortion impose an undue burden on the right'.[191]

Equally importantly, the US Supreme Court held that courts should require a proper evidential basis for legislative assertions, even where this included potentially contested medical evidence. The District Court was therefore right to consider the evidence, and then to weigh the asserted benefits against the burdens.

Applying this test, the Court held that the admitting privileges requirement imposed an 'undue burden' on a woman's right to have an abortion. The Court found nothing in the evidence that showed that, 'when compared with the prior law (which required a working arrangement with a doctor with admitting privileges), the new law advanced Texas' legitimate interest in protecting women's health'.[192] At the same time, the evidence showed that this requirement placed a 'substantial obstacle in the path of a woman's choice'. The number of abortion facilities halved, and more clinics might close. This is because admitting privileges are based on criteria not related to clinical competence. For example, hospitals generally require doctors to admit a certain number of cases per year to acquire admitting privileges; and paradoxically, because abortion was so safe, and required so few admissions, this threshold number was not achieved. Closures meant fewer doctors, longer waiting times and increased risk. Although the longer driving distances were not in themselves an undue burden, they were an additional burden, which together with the absence of any health benefit, led the Court to conclude that the evidence supported the conclusion that the requirements constituted an undue burden on the woman's choice. A similar conclusion was drawn in relation to the 'surgical centre' requirement, which obligated abortion facilities to include an operating theatre of a specific size, with many other detailed regulatory standards. The evidence before the Court again showed that these standards do not benefit patients and are not necessary. The careful scrutiny applied by the Court in this case means that a wide range of TRAP laws will now be called into question.[193]

[190] ibid, 2298. [191] *Planned Parenthood v Casey* (n 11) 878.

[192] *Whole Woman's Health v Hellerstedt* (n 189) 2298.

[193] Reva Siegel, 'Whole Women's Health: A Call for Evidence-based Regulation of Abortion' (OxHRH Blog, 19 July 2016) <http://ohrh.law.ox.ac.uk/whole-womens-health-a-call-for-evidence-based-regulation-of-abortion/> (accessed 25 February 2018).

Kommers argues that the contrast between the approaches of the FCC and the US Supreme Court should be understood in terms of the differing underlying ethos in each jurisdiction.

> In the U.S. that ethos is anti-statist individualism. The image of the human person in American constitutional law is that of an autonomous moral agent unconnected to the larger community in any meaningful sense. It is the image of a woman alone, isolated and independent, and bounded by little more than self-interest. German constitutional law, by contrast, has a strong communitarian orientation, and it tells the story of human solidarity, a story that tries to join public virtue to liberty, one that speaks of social integration and the wholeness of life.[194]

This is arguably an unnecessary polarization of the two positions. Communitarianism might also have the consequences we have seen in Ireland, where the responsibility to bear children overwhelms any autonomy of women. The more constructive elements of this position, however, are arguably better captured by the right to equality, which brings in gender relations without subsuming women to a communitarian ideal. It is to this we now turn.

V. Abortion and the Right to Equality

In the contestation between rights to life of the foetus and rights to privacy and autonomy of the pregnant woman, a key missing element is any discussion of the right to gender equality. Legal systems that protect the right to life of the foetus subordinate the pregnant woman's bodily autonomy to the State's regulatory powers. The right to privacy protects important aspects of that autonomy. But the individualism behind the right to privacy can negate the interconnectedness of individuals in society and conceal the gender relations which shape childbearing and childrearing. By overstating women's ability to control their own lives, the privacy approach allows the State to abdicate responsibility for children and parenthood.

It is therefore of great importance to locate abortion within the larger issue of gender inequality. Women's struggle for control over their own reproduction has been central to the possibility of equal opportunities, whether in the family, the paid workforce, or public life. The availability of contraception constituted a revolution for women; but even with such availability, women in situations of gender power imbalances, poverty, lack of information, poor health-care facilities, sexual violence, or conflict might not have full control over pregnancy and childbearing. And of course, nearly all contraceptive methods will sometimes fail. Abortion also needs to be seen in the context of the social forces that place primary responsibility for childbearing and childcare on women, while at the same time patterning the paid workforce on a norm which takes no account of such responsibilities. An equality perspective therefore requires that the question of abortion be determined together with the whole range of reproductive rights, including the right to contraception, as well as social policies which value childcare as a shared social responsibility. Equality also challenges the background

[194] Kommers (n 16) 31.

assumptions about women that pervade much of the abortion discourse. These include the assumptions that abortion should only be permitted for women who are victims (eg of rape); or that women's choice needs to be guided by compulsory counselling, ultrasound images of foetuses, or the like. Instead, equal rights arguments 'generally seek to affirm women's agency, whilst understanding the social and economic context that constrains this'.[195]

An equality perspective brings into focus the shockingly disproportionate impact on women of prohibitions on abortion. Research shows that worldwide 25 million unsafe abortions occurred every year between 2010 and 2014, as many as 97 per cent of which occurred in developing countries in Africa, Asia, and Latin America.[196] Yet, as the Guttmacher Institute shows, highly restrictive abortion laws are not associated with lower abortion rates.[197] The appalling reality of deaths from unsafe abortions should force us to recognize that the institutions which deny women autonomy over their own reproduction are the same institutions which propel women into seeking unsafe abortions.

A breakthrough was achieved in 1994 at the International Conference on Population and Development (ICPD) in Cairo, in which 179 countries recognized reproductive health and rights, as well as women's empowerment and gender equality, as pivotal to population and development programmes.[198] Particularly important was the definition of reproductive rights as:

> the basic right of all couples and individuals to decide freely and responsibly the number, spacing and timing of their children and to have the information and means to do so and the right to attain the highest standard of sexual and reproductive health. It also includes the right of all to make decisions concerning reproduction free of discrimination, coercion and violence as expressed in human rights documents.[199]

The Programme of Action included a provision requiring governments to deal with the health impact of unsafe abortion and to reduce the need for abortion through family-planning services. It also stated that 'in circumstances where abortion is not against the law, such abortion should be safe'.[200] However, the ICPD could not come to an agreement that a safe and legal abortion was a fundamental right,[201] a position which was reflected in the Beijing Platform for Action.[202]

The process towards agreeing the Sustainable Development Goals (SDGs) gave renewed momentum to the recognition of a right to reproductive health.[203] There are several pertinent references in the SDGs Agenda for 2030. Goal Three aims to ensure

[195] Albertyn (n 72) 443.

[196] B Ganatra et al, 'Global, Regional, and Subregional Classification of Abortions by Safety, 2010–14: Estimates from a Bayesian Hierarchical Model' (2017) 390 Lancet 2372–81.

[197] Guttmacher Institute 'Induced Abortion Worldwide' (September 2017 Fact Sheet) <https://www.guttmacher.org/fact-sheet/facts-induced-abortion-worldwide> (accessed 25 February 2018).

[198] International Conference on Population and Development (ICPD) Programme of Action <http://www.unfpa.org/publications/international-conference-population-and-development-programme-action> (accessed 25 February 2018).

[199] ibid, para 7.3. [200] ibid, para 8.25. [201] Albertyn (n 72) 437.

[202] UN Women Beijing Declaration and Platform for Action 1995, para 106 (j) and (k).

[203] United Nations General Assembly, 'Transforming our World: The 2030 Agenda for Sustainable Development' (25 September 2015 A/RES/70/1).

healthy lives and promote well-being for all. One of its targets is to ensure universal access to reproductive health-care services, including for family planning. Similarly, Goal Five, which aims to achieve gender equality and empower all women and girls, includes Target 5.6, which is to ensure universal access to reproductive rights as agreed in the ICPD conference. Again, while there is no express reference to abortion, the concept of a right to reproductive freedom has been widely thought to include a right to abortion. Certainly, there has been a great push to lessen mortality from unsafe abortions and Target 3.1 commits the world to reducing the maternal mortality ratio to less than seventy per 100,000 live births. A report by the UN General Secretary in 2013 highlighted unsafe abortion as a leading cause of maternal deaths and made it clear that the numbers of unsafe abortions would continue to increase unless women's access to safe abortion and contraception were strengthened.[204]

What then would an equality perspective add to a human rights approach to abortion in the jurisdictions studied here? The first step is to provide a range of reproductive rights, including the rights to contraception. The South African Constitution comes closest to this goal: the right to life in section 12 includes the 'right to make decisions concerning reproduction', and to 'security in and control over their body' as explicit parts of the right to bodily and psychological integrity. Section 27, on the right of access to health care, also includes the right of access to reproductive health-care services. The second step is to give women the genuine and effective right to choose abortion. This entails the removal of the need for external authorization, such as that of physicians, parents, or spouses. Notification or authorization of spouses or partners has generally been struck down by courts in various jurisdictions, including the US, the UK, Canada, and Australia, and is not required in others, such as South Africa, and India (although in the latter, it is sometimes assumed to be required). Most recently, the Indian Supreme Court dismissed a petition by a husband seeking damages from his wife on the grounds that she had terminated her pregnancy without his consent.[205] But parental consent for minors is still required in some of the main jurisdictions, endorsed by the US Supreme Court in relation to the US. The South African Court stands out for its affirmation of the South African legislative settlement, which looks to capacity of minors to make decisions rather than age.[206]

Physician authorization has been assumed without question even in some of the more liberal frameworks, such as the UK and India. In India, the difficulties experienced in obtaining such authorization have led to numerous women still resorting to unsafe abortion, leading to a proposed amendment to remove the requirement. Only South Africa leaves the decision fully to the choice of the woman, at least in the first twelve weeks. The extent to which this can operate as an obstruction to women's

[204] United Nations Economic and Social Council, 'Report of the Secretary-General on challenges and achievements in the implementation of the Millennium Development Goals for women and girls' (24 December 2013) UN Doc E/CN.6/2014/3.

[205] *Anil Kumar Malhotra v Ajay Pasricha*, Civil Appeal No 4704/2013 (22 September, 2017) Indian Supreme Court, dismissing the appeal by the husband against the decision of the Punjab and Haryana High Court that the husband had no right to compel his wife not to terminate her pregnancy (CR No 6337 of 2011; 29.11.2011); Aradhana Cherupara Vadekkethil, 'Is Consent of the Husband Needed for an Abortion in India?' (OxHRH Blog, 17 February 2018) <http://ohrh.law.ox.ac.uk/is-consent-of-the-husband-needed-for-an-abortion-in-india/> (accessed 25 February 2018).

[206] *Christian Lawyers Association v Minister of Health* (n 76).

genuine choice has also been recognized in Germany, where the court endorsed the removal of third-party verification even though it upheld the right to life. However, the genuine and effective right to choose abortion also entails removing the stigma attached to it. Thus, although the German framework includes many elements that further equality, its strong message that abortion is illegal remains highly problematic. The experiences of South Africa and India, where stigma persists even though abortion has been legalized, demonstrates how strong the impetus of shame might be. Women will often choose the backstreet, despite its extra risks, rather than facing the stigma, lack of privacy, and disapproval found in abortion facilities.[207]

A further step is to ensure that women can actually access safe abortion. Legalizing abortion does not in itself ensure that it is safe, as the Indian experience shows. Proper investment in healthcare, across the whole spectrum of reproductive health, is a prerequisite. Albertyn shows how in South Africa, the impressive advances achieved by a rights-based framework have been pushed back 'in the face of a declining health-system, pervasive stigma and normative resistance, a less visible non-governmental sector and unclear political will. It is little surprise to learn that poor, black women have borne the brunt of this, once more putting their lives and health at risk in unsafe backstreet abortions'.[208] On the other hand, unnecessarily strict medical requirements can also impede real access. The US Supreme Court's recognition in the *Well Woman* case that regulations which have the effect of reducing access to safe abortion should be judged against a strict standard of scrutiny is of great significance.[209] In addition, as in South Africa, and under suggested reform in India, permitting properly trained midwives and registered nurses to carry out abortions can significantly improve accessibility.

Finally, the right to abortion needs to be embedded in proper provision for protection of the rights of pregnant women at work and parental leave for both parents. This should come together with social provision of childcare and changing working hours to acknowledge the value of childbearing and prevent women from bearing the whole cost. Here again, the German framework stands out for its holistic view of the abortion right. However, the background message of womanhood as motherhood is clearly not one sustained by an equality approach.

VI. Rights of Third Parties: Conscientious Objection

One of the features of abortion regulation has been to seek a compromise between the right to religion or freedom of conscience and the right of reproductive freedom, autonomy, or equality of the pregnant woman. This manifests as an exception for conscientious objection. For example, under the UK Abortion Act 1967, anyone who has a conscientious objection to any treatment authorized by the Act is under no legal duty, whether contractual, statutory, or other, to participate in such treatment. Conscientious objection, however, does not apply in relation to treatment which is necessary to prevent grave permanent injury to the physical or mental health of a pregnant woman or to save her life.[210]

[207] Albertyn (n 72) 446. [208] ibid, 430.
[209] *Whole Woman's Health v Hellerstedt* (n 189). [210] Abortion Act 1967, s 4.

While this might seem to be a sensitive compromise, its operation in practice might be highly problematic. In the context of abortion, a key issue should be the extent to which women's rights to a safe abortion are nevertheless safeguarded. It is clear that too wide a latitude for conscientious objection could materially interfere with the exercise of the right to abortion, especially where there are insufficient alternatives available. The South African experience is therefore salutary. Although conscientious objection was not included in CTOPA, it is widely accepted as applying through the code of medical ethics. Albertyn shows how 'the unregulated nature of conscientious objection, with little guidance offered by policy makers, has seen conscientious objection becoming one of the biggest barriers to abortion service delivery'.[211] This bears out NeJaime and Siegel's argument that it should be recognized that conscientious objection goes further than protecting individual freedom of religion. It also requires third parties whose conduct is considered sinful by religious adherents to bear the burden of the latter's religious beliefs.[212]

In partial recognition of such consequences, the UK Supreme Court has firmly confined the boundaries of the right of conscientious objection under the UK Act. In a case in 1989, it rejected a claim by a secretary and receptionist at a health centre that typing a letter referring a patient to a hospital with a view to a possible termination fell within the right to object to participation in treatment.[213] More contentious was the 2014 case of *Doogan*, where the petitioners, who were co-ordinators on a labour ward in a Scottish hospital, claimed that their right to conscientious objection extended to permitting them to refuse to book in patients for terminations, allocate staff to such patients, and provide guidance, advice, and support to such staff. The Scottish Inner House upheld their claim. 'The right is given because it is recognised that the process of abortion is felt by many people to be morally repugnant ... It is in keeping with the reason for the exemption that the wide interpretation which we favour should be given to it'.[214] However, the UK Supreme Court overturned this decision.[215] Instead, it held that the reference in the Abortion Act to a refusal to 'participate' in treatment referred only to hands-on involvement and not to the ancillary, administrative, and managerial tasks associated with it. The Court left open the possibility that the petitioners could claim under ECHR rights to freedom of religion not to be discriminated against on religious grounds, which might require the employer to make reasonable adjustments to cater for their religious beliefs. However, since these were both limited rights, a balance needed to be drawn in particular cases.

The US Supreme Court has tended instead to favour religious rights over women's reproductive rights. Indeed, in *Burwell v Hobby Lobby Stores*,[216] it went so far as to

[211] Albertyn (n 72) 445, citing K Trueman and M Mawentshu, 'Abortion in a Progressive Legal Environment: The Need for Vigilance in Protecting and Promoting Access to Safe Abortion Services in South Africa' (2013) 103 American Journal of Public Health 397–99.

[212] D NeJaime and R Siegel, 'Conscience Wars: Complicity-Based Conscience Claims in Religion and Politics' (2015) 124 Yale L J 2516.

[213] *R v Salford Health Authority, Ex p Janaway* [1989] AC 537 (HL).

[214] *Doogan v NHS Greater Glasgow and Clyde Health Board* [2013] ScotCS CSIH_36 (Scottish Court of Session) para [38].

[215] *Doogan v Greater Glasgow and Clyde Health Board* [2015] AC 640 (UK Supreme Court).

[216] *Burwell v Hobby Lobby Stores* 134 S Ct 2751 (2014) (US Supreme Court).

accord religious freedom rights not just to individuals but to for-profit corporations for this purpose. In *Burwell*, two companies refused to abide by a federal requirement to provide health insurance coverage for their employees for methods of contraception which they claimed violated the sincerely held religious beliefs of the companies' owners. The requirement had been instituted by the Affordable Care Act, also known as Obamacare, which included as a deliberate policy that the full range of contraceptive methods should be included in health insurance coverage. Notably, during the legislative process, a 'conscience clause' allowing an insurance provider or employer to deny coverage based on its asserted religious beliefs or moral convictions was rejected.[217] Nevertheless, the Court, by a majority of five to four, held that the requirement to provide such health insurance breached the Religious Freedom Restoration Act of 1993 (RFRA), which prohibits the Federal Government from taking any action that substantially burdens the exercise of religion unless such action is the least restrictive means of serving a compelling government interest. According to Justice Alito, giving the opinion of the Court, there was an alternative means which sufficiently protected employees' interests in contraception. However, as Justice Ginsburg stated in her dissent, any proposed alternative placed a very heavy cost on thousands of women employed by the two companies, who did not share the corporation owners' religious faith. Justice Ginsburg reiterated the message in *Casey* that 'the ability of women to participate equally in the economic and social life of the Nation has been facilitated by their ability to control their reproductive lives'.[218] Moreover, she stated, the First Amendment protection of the free exercise of religion did not require accommodations which significantly impinged on third parties. Nor did the RFRA permit such a broad exemption. As a start, she held, it covered 'a person's exercise of religion' which it made no sense to apply to corporations, which have no conscience, beliefs, or feelings, and which employ people with a wide range of beliefs, unlike religious non-profits which might fall within the Act. She also rejected the view that an accommodation was available: 'A "least restrictive means" cannot require employees to relinquish benefits accorded them by federal law in order to ensure that their commercial employers can adhere unreservedly to their religious tenets'.[219]

The US Supreme Court has been similarly solicitous to anti-abortion protesters, who have challenged municipal restrictions aiming to prevent intimidation of women approaching abortion clinics. Thus, in *McCullen v Coakley*,[220] the Court struck down a Massachusetts statute which made it a crime to stand on a public way within 35 feet of an entrance to an abortion facility. The law was designed to address clashes between abortion opponents and advocates outside such clinics. The petitioners claimed that they were therefore unable to reach women going to abortion clinics to dissuade them from going through with the abortion. The Court held that the prohibition breached their First Amendment freedom-of-speech rights.

The endorsement of 'complicity' claims has had even wider effects on foreign aid. Since *Roe v Wade* in 1973, the US has enacted a series of foreign assistance laws placing

[217] ibid, 2789. [218] *Planned Parenthood v Casey* (n 11) 856.

[219] *Burwell v Hobby Lobby Stores* (n 216) 2802: see further Chapter 12 (Freedom of Religion).

[220] *McCullen v Coakley* 134 S Ct 2518 (2014) (US Supreme Court).

restrictions on the federal funding of abortions and family planning activities in other countries. The Helms Amendment to the Foreign Assistance Act 1961 prohibited the use of US funds to perform abortions;[221] the Siljander Amendment prohibited US funds from being used to lobby for or against abortion;[222] and the Tiahrt amendment placed requirements on voluntary family planning projects receiving assistance from the United States Agency for International Development (USAID).[223] As well as legislation, various US Presidents have used their executive powers to place restrictions on abortion and family planning provision overseas. In 1984, President Ronald Reagan required foreign NGOs receiving USAID family planning funding to certify that they would not perform or actively promote abortion as a method of family planning, even if such abortions were themselves not funded by USAID. Known as a global gag order, Reagan's executive order was rescinded by President Bill Clinton, reinstituted by President George W Bush, and rescinded again by President Barack Obama in 2009.[224] In one of the first moves after he took office in January 2017, President Trump revived the Bush restriction and expanded it further to remove funding from health clinics which offer a wide variety of services, including abortion counselling. In May 2017, he expanded it even further to apply to all existing foreign aid provided by the State Department USAID and the Department of Defence. Whereas previously the restriction only applied specifically to US family planning funds (approximately $575m), the newly extended Trump policy extends the restrictions to an estimated $8.8 billion in US global health assistance.[225] The policy removes funding from clinics which receive US funding for other health services if they provide non-US-funded sexual and reproductive health services, unless the latter are restricted or cut.

VII. Conclusion

Abortion remains a topic of deep contestation, arousing strong personal opinions and emotions. In such contexts, the role of human rights law is equally contested. For some, such as Waldron, its resolution should be left entirely to the legislature. However, a comparative insight demonstrates that there is a much more complex relationship between legislatures and courts, with courts being called upon by litigants to enter into the fray regardless. The result has been that in all the jurisdictions considered, there has been an interaction between courts and legislatures, sometimes in tension

[221] Section 104(f)(1) of the Foreign Assistance Act of 1961 (PL 87–195; 22 USC 2151b(f)(1)), as amended by the Foreign Assistance Act of 1973 (PL 93–189), approved 17 December 1973.

[222] Section 525 of the Foreign Assistance and Related Programs Appropriations Act 1982 (PL 97–121; 95 Stat 1657), approved 29 December 1981.

[223] Section 101 of the Omnibus Consolidated and Emergency Supplemental Appropriations Act 1999 (PL 105–277, 112 Stat 2681-154), approved 21 October 1998.

[224] L Blanchfield, 'Abortion and Family Panning-related Provisions in US Foreign Assistance Law and Policy' (Congressional Research Service, 17 May 2016) <https://fas.org/sgp/crs/row/R41360.pdf> (accessed 25 February 2018).

[225] Human Rights Watch, 'Trump's "Mexico City Policy" or "Global Gag Rule"' (updated 8 February 2018) <https://www.hrw.org/news/2017/06/22/trumps-mexico-city-policy-or-global-gag-rule> (accessed 25 February 2018).

and at other times in support. Nor does human rights law provide a straightforward or uncontested response. A comparative approach nevertheless illuminates the different ways in which the central rights to life, privacy, and equality are interpreted and how their interaction shapes the outcomes. These provide a rich deliberative resource for courts to address issues which come before them. We have seen many instances of the comparative conversation which is in fact taking place between courts, as well as drawing out further comparative insights going forward. We have also seen how courts draw on fundamental values such as dignity and autonomy when wrestling with open-textured concepts and balancing conflicting rights and interests. With this in mind, we turn to a broader aspect of the right to life, and one which also straddles the traditional boundary between civil and political rights and socio-economic rights, namely, the right to health. This brings with it complex polycentric issues, testing not just judicial legitimacy but also judicial competence. Here too, the fundamental principles of human rights law provide a broad framework and the insights of comparative law permit us to evaluate and assess different ways to proceed.

and of other states to support. Nor does human rights law [illegible] of an unrelated response. A [illegible] for the way in which [illegible] and their interaction shapes [illegible] the courts to address [illegible]. We [illegible] of the comparative [illegible] as well as developing further [illegible] how courts draw on fundamental [illegible] with [illegible] human rights [illegible] the [illegible] namely the right to health. [illegible] lost [illegible] ciples of human rights law [illegible] law permit us to evaluate and [illegible].

8

The Right to Health

I. Introduction

Is health a human right? Many would maintain that it is not. On this view, health and ill-health are due to natural causes, not to State actions. The function of human rights, by contrast, is to protect individuals against State interference with their liberty. Others claim that any attempted formulation of a right to health is hopelessly vague. As philosopher Onora O'Neill puts it:

> Is this right only a right to the standard of health that a person can attain with locally available and affordable treatment—however meagre that may be? Or is it a right to the highest standard available globally—however expensive that may be? The first is disappointingly minimal, and the latter barely coherent (how can everyone have a right to the best?).[1]

Alternatively, it could be contended that, even if we give the State a role in addressing the effects of ill-health, this should not be in the form of justiciable human rights obligations. This is because health care raises so many complex and inter-related issues, that they are best suited for the political process.

These contestations clearly operate on several levels. One is based on a particular theory of human rights, confining the role of human rights to constraining the State from interfering in individual freedoms. As we saw in Chapter 2, this can be set against a positive view of human rights, requiring the State to facilitate freedom and advance substantive equality. A second level of contestation concerns the difficulty in defining the right to health. Is it a right to health or a right to health care? Is it a right to a particular standard of health, or the highest attainable standard? And how do we define correlative obligations? Is it a duty to deliver health? Or is it to deliver reasonable access to health care? A third level focuses on the institutional division of power as between courts and the legislature or executive. Here the argument is that health and health care are policy decisions, best suited for elected representatives of the people. To this legitimacy-based argument is added one based on judicial competence. Since health care has wide polycentric implications and consumes a significant proportion of State resources, judges are not considered to be competent to adjudicate on health as if it were simply a dispute between the individuals before the court. This can be contrasted with the view that courts and litigation processes can be fashioned in ways that enhance democracy, particularly through holding governments to account for their human rights-impacting decisions, through requiring transparency, and through insisting on non-discrimination.

[1] O O'Neill, 'The Dark Side of Human Rights' (2005) 81 International Affairs 427, 429.

The principle that health is a human rights issue has received growing endorsement. In 2004, Gauri found that of the 165 countries with available written constitutions, seventy-three referred to a right to health care.[2] This comes in parallel with the recognition that ill-health is not simply due to natural causes but can be a direct or indirect result of State action or omission in a variety of fields. States which permit environmental pollution could be said to directly interfere with individuals' health; and the same is true for States which fail to regulate the pricing of medicinal drugs by pharmaceutical companies. Particularly problematic has been the international protection afforded to intellectual property under the Agreement on Trade-Related aspects of Intellectual Property Rights (TRIPS). This allows pharmaceutical companies to patent drugs and therefore to maintain high prices insulated from market competition. TRIPS itself now allows countries to make exceptions for public health, but several countries, under pressure from multinational corporations, are choosing to impose stricter (or TRIPS plus) protections in bilateral trade agreements.[3] Grover and Citro argue that countries which enter into trade agreements interfering with TRIPS exceptions are violating their obligations under the right to health in international law.[4]

Nevertheless, the concern remains that health raises too many polycentric problems to be appropriately dealt with through justiciable human rights. Indeed, scholars and researchers point to jurisdictions in which a justiciable right to health has impeded the State's ability to provide coherent and equitable access to health care by enforcing individual claims to expensive medication at the cost of skewing the public health budget. Ferraz uses the Brazilian experience of a justiciable right to health to suggest that courts adjudicating the right to health might be worsening the country's already pronounced health inequities.[5] Flood and Gross conclude from their study of sixteen countries that individual litigation on the right to health can undermine the ability of governments to run fair and effective health-care systems.[6] Litigation in Canada has challenged the model of publicly provided health care.[7]

In the meantime, as part of the post 2015 Sustainable Development Goals, the global community has made a significant commitment to improving health outcomes, particularly for those living in poverty. This is true for both health itself and the social determinants of health, such as access to food, water, housing, healthy environments, and road safety.[8] What then can a human rights-based approach add to this ambitious agenda? Paul Hunt, previously the UN Special Rapporteur on the right to the highest attainable standard of health, has no doubt of the crucial role of human rights.

[2] V Gauri, 'Social Rights and Economics: Claims to Health Care and Education in Developing Countries' (2004) 32 World Development 465.

[3] A Grover and B Citro, 'India: Access to Affordable Drugs and the Right to Health' (2011) 377 The Lancet 976.

[4] ibid.

[5] O Ferraz, 'The Right to Health in the Courts of Brazil: Worsening Health Inequities' (2009) 11 Health and Human Rights 33.

[6] C Flood and A Gross, 'Litigating the Right to Health: What Can We Learn from a Comparative Law and Health Care Systems Approach' (2014) 16 Health and Human Rights Journal 62.

[7] *Chaoulli v Quebec (Attorney General)* (2005) SCC 35 (Supreme Court of Canada).

[8] UN General Assembly, 'Transforming our world: the 2030 Agenda for Sustainable Development', 21 October 2015 UN Doc A/RES/70/1 <https://sustainabledevelopment.un.org/?menu=1300> (accessed 26 February 2018).

For him, a human rights-based approach to health brings valuable perspectives that otherwise tend to be neglected.[9]

All of these contestations have shaped the way in which the right to health is understood both in the jurisdictions examined here and in the international human rights instruments. This chapter traces these themes by considering the case law that has emerged. In particular, the following sections examine what the textual base of the right is, what substantive content has been given to the right, how this shapes the duties on the State, and the extent to which a justiciable right can address systemic issues rather than simply individual rights to medication. The chapter begins with a brief sketch of the health context in the major jurisdictions examined here: South Africa, India, Canada, and Europe. Section III considers jurisdictions in which there is no express right to health, but such a right has instead been derived from other rights, primarily the right to life and personal integrity, but also the right to privacy. Here the focus is on India, Canada, and the European Convention on Human Rights (ECHR). Section IV contrasts this approach with jurisdictions with an express right to health, examined here in the context of the South African constitution and the International Covenant on Economic, Social and Cultural Rights (ICESCR). Section V examines the role of the right to equality in relation to health, while section VI focuses on reproductive health. The final section returns to the challenges of polycentricity.

II. Social and Political Context

The right to health must be understood within the broader context of the state of health and the system of health care in any particular jurisdiction. Both India and South Africa face enormous challenges in this respect. In South Africa, the legacy of apartheid left serious deficits in health and health care among the majority of the population. After the end of apartheid in 1994, there was a notable attempt to tackle deeply entrenched patterns of inequality in access to health-care services. Policies put in place after apartheid were specifically targeted at reducing inequities, particularly through a focus on primary health care. However, the country was even more sorely challenged by the scourge of HIV/AIDS which became rampant in South Africa over the first decades of the new democracy. AIDS denialism on the part of the Mbeki Government led to a refusal to provide treatment or take preventative action. This considerably worsened the problem, costing millions of lives during Mbeki's period of government from 1999 to 2008. The result was that between 1994 and 2009, life expectancy fell by almost 20 years.[10] As we will see below, it was through litigation under the constitutional right to health brought by the campaigning group Treatment Action Campaign (TAC) that the government was required to change this policy, specifically through the provision of the drug nevirapine to prevent mother–child transmission

[9] P Hunt, 'Report of the Special Rapporteur on the right of everyone to the enjoyment of the highest attainable standard of physical and mental health' UN Doc E/CN.4/2006/48 (United Nations, 2006).

[10] P Jones and N Chingore, 'Health Rights: Politics, Places and the Need for "Sites for Rights"' in M Langford and others (eds), *Socio-Economic Rights in South Africa: Symbols or Substance?* (Cambridge University Press, 2013) 227.

of the HIV virus. The programme to prevent mother–child HIV transmission has seen a drop from a rate of 30 per cent in perinatal transmission to 2.7 per cent.[11] More generally, the reversal of AIDS-denial policies triggered the largest HIV treatment programme in the world, with over three million HIV-positive individuals on anti-retroviral treatment in 2016.[12] While this is a major achievement, it is also very expensive to maintain.

The impacts of both apartheid and AIDS denialism have meant that health inequities in South Africa remain extreme. Despite some positive progress, particularly in the field of primary health,[13] the burden of disease is still primarily carried by poor black people, especially young children and women. Although about 8.5 per cent of gross domestic product (GDP) is now spent on health care, as much as half is spent in the private sector. This leaves 84 per cent of the population, who carry a disproportionate burden of disease, with resort only to the under-resourced public health sector.[14] Health outcomes are poor when compared with other middle-income countries, such as Brazil, with similar spending on health care. Maternal mortality in South Africa stood at 138 deaths per 100,000 live births in 2015, well above that in Brazil, where the corresponding figure was 44.[15] Moreover, enormous health and health-care inequalities remain, whether between the public and private health sectors, between urban and rural, between the nine provinces, or within provinces. Together with a very high rate of infectious diseases, especially tuberculosis, there is a growing problem of non-communicable disease, such as diabetes and stroke, added to disturbing levels of violence, particularly against women, and road accidents.[16]

The question then is whether there is anything a justiciable right might add. Rispel argues that a major reason for the disconnect between progressive policies for health and health care lies in the tolerance of ineptitude, and failures of leadership, management, and governance.[17] Particularly problematic have been clear trends in irregularities in expenditure, used as an indirect measure of corruption. She quotes a recent study which found that between 2009 and 2013, about R24 billion of combined provincial health expenditure was classified as irregular by the Auditor-General.[18] Although it is impossible to tell how much of this is due to corruption and how much to ineptitude, the consequences for those who depend on the public sector are dire. Rispel points to other failures of leadership and governance, including failure to implement

[11] L Rispel, 'Analysing the Progress and Faultlines of Health-sector Transformation in South Africa' [2016] South African Health Review 17, 18.

[12] ibid, 18. [13] ibid. [14] ibid.

[15] The World Health Organization (WHO), the United Nations Childrens' Fund (UNICEF), the United Nations Population Fund (UNFPA), the World Bank Group, and the United Nations Population Division, 'Trends in Maternal Mortality: 1990 to 2015' (WHO, 2015) <http://data.worldbank.org/indicator/SH.STA.MMRT> (accessed 26 February 2018).

[16] R Downie and S Angelo, 'Counting the Cost of South Africa's Health Burden' (CSIS, July 2015) 8–10 <https://www.csis.org/analysis/counting-cost-south-africas-health-burden> (accessed 26 February 2018).

[17] Rispel (n 11) 18.

[18] Auditor-General of South Africa, 'PFMA Consolidated General Report 2012–13' (Pretoria: Auditor-General of South Africa, 2014) <http://www.agsa.co.za/Reporting/PFMAReports/PFMA2011-2012/PFMAdocuments/tabid/220/ArticleID/195/2012-13-PFMA-consolidated-general-report.aspx> (accessed 27 February 2018). Irregular spending is defined as expenditure incurred without complying with applicable laws and regulations.

much-needed reforms in nursing training; a dysfunctional federal system, with inconsistencies between provinces; and lack of functioning systems at district level. This combines with a workforce crisis, with figures showing that significant numbers of nurses are moonlighting or working for an agency at the same time as being employed in the public sector, negatively affecting their ability to perform their jobs in the public sector properly.[19] Arguably, a human rights approach is well suited to tackle these weaknesses. By emphasizing transparency and accountability, as well as substantive values such as equality and accessibility, a human rights approach can be used as one part of a strategy to insist that a government delivers on its promises. This is developed further in section IV below.

The Indian context reveals a similar pattern. A 2012 report points out that India has 25 per cent of the world's maternal deaths every year; and 47 per cent of all children are underweight. Yet total health expenditure is a mere 4.5 per cent of GDP, putting India at 153 out of 193 countries in relation to per capita health-care spending. Even more worrying is the fact that 75 per cent of health expenditure is private: indeed, government expenditure on health is only just over 1 per cent of GDP.[20] Yet on the basis of the Multi-Dimensional Poverty Index, which measures poverty in relation to the three dimensions of education, health, and standard of living, 53.8 per cent of the Indian population are poor.[21]

Parmar and Wahi point to two chief failures in India's health policy which have created a health crisis. The first and most serious is the absence of a political commitment to realize universal health care. A second is the fact that there has been a policy of prioritization of separate specific disease eradication programmes, which were piecemeal, ill-conceived, and cost-ineffective. This in turn meant that no integrated health infrastructure was put in place, and institutional health capacity declined. Unfortunately, this problem was in part caused by the World Bank and the World Health Organization (WHO), who opposed proposals in 1983 to institute universal health care, arguing that poor countries should prioritize limited resources in specific disease eradication programmes. These have now been recognized as ineffective and costly. More recent policies by international and bilateral funding agencies have been no less problematic, favouring commercialization of health care, including user fees, privatization, and promotion of public–private partnerships.[22] A human rights approach would clearly situate health care as a public responsibility, to be delivered without discrimination and with a particular focus on the most disadvantaged. This means that a comprehensive, publicly funded, good-quality service would be optimal.

The context in Canada, on the face of it, contrasts vividly with that of South Africa and India. According to Organization for Economic Cooperation and Development

[19] Rispel (n 11) 19, 20.

[20] N Wahi, 'Litigating the Right to Health in India', CMI Brief (May 2012, Vol 11 No 4); see further S Parmar and N Wahi, 'India: Citizens, Courts and the Right to Health: Between Promise and Progress?' in A Yamin and S Gloppen (eds), *Litigating Health Rights: Can Courts Bring More Justice to Health?* (Harvard University Press, 2011).

[21] Oxford Poverty and Human Development Initiative (2016), 'India Country Briefing', Multidimensional Poverty Index Data Bank (OPHI, University of Oxford' <www.ophi.org.uk/multidimensional-poverty-index/mpi-country-briefings/> (accessed 26 February 2018).

[22] Parmar and Wahi (n 20).

(OECD) figures, the life expectancy in Canada in 2011 stood at 81.5 years, more than a year higher than the OECD average. Health spending in 2012 in Canada accounted for 10.9 per cent of GDP, again noticeably higher than the OECD average of 9.3 per cent. Although this is lower than the 16.9 per cent of GDP spent on health care in the US in 2012, these figures are deceptive because the private sector is the main source of funding in the US, whereas in Canada 70 per cent of health spending was funded by public sources in 2012, a little less than the OECD average of 72 per cent.[23]

On the other hand, these figures mask disturbing disparities in health outcomes and accessibility to health care, particularly in relation to indigenous or aboriginal Canadians.[24] The UN Special Rapporteur on the rights of indigenous peoples, in its 2014 Report, commented that it was difficult to 'reconcile Canada's well-developed legal framework and general prosperity with the human rights problems faced by indigenous peoples in Canada that have reached crisis proportions in some respects'.[25] For him, 'the most jarring manifestation of these human rights problems is the distressing socio-economic conditions of indigenous peoples in a highly developed country'.[26] This is true for the social determinants of both health and access to health-care services. Overcrowded housing is endemic, especially in the north, where the weather can be extreme. This contributes to higher rates of respiratory illness, depression, sleep deprivation, and family violence.[27] Although the overall health situation of indigenous peoples has improved in recent years, there remain significant gaps, including in terms of life expectancy, infant mortality, suicide, injuries, and chronic diseases such as diabetes.[28] The UN Special Rapporteur on the right to food, in his 2012 report on Canada, described food insecurity among aboriginal people as 'deep and severe', reaching as high as 32.6 per cent in Nunaut, a Northern Territory. At the same time, rates of obesity and diabetes were high.

The health-care context in Europe has similar characteristics. Population health has significantly improved over recent decades, but there remain significant disparities in health status, both between countries and within them.[29] Life expectancy at birth in European Union (EU) Member States increased by more than five years on average between 1990 and 2012 to 79.2 years. However, there remains a gap of eight years between countries with the highest life expectancies, namely Spain, Italy, and France, and the lowest, that is to say Lithuania, Latvia, Bulgaria, and Romania. There are also persistent large inequalities within countries between different socio-economic groups. People with higher levels of education and income are likely to live several years longer and be

[23] OECD Health Statistics 2014, 'How Does Canada Compare?' <http://www.oecd.org/els/health-systems/Briefing-Note-CANADA-2014.pdf> (accessed 26 February 2018).

[24] The term 'indigenous' is the preferred terminology; however, the Canadian Constitution uses the word 'aboriginal'. See B Allan and J Smylie, 'First Peoples, Second Class Treatment: The Role of Racism in the Health and Well-being of Indigenous Peoples in Canada' (Wellesley Institute Discussion Paper, 2015) <http://www.wellesleyinstitute.com/publications/first-peoples-second-class-treatment/> (accessed 26 February 2018).

[25] Special Rapporteur on the rights of indigenous peoples, James Anaya, 'The Situation of Indigenous Peoples in Canada' (2014) (hereafter UNSRIP 2014) <http://www.ohchr.org/Documents/Issues/IPeoples/SR/A.HRC.27.52.Add.2-MissionCanada_AUV.pdf> (accessed 26 February 2018) para 14.

[26] ibid, para 15. [27] ibid, para 24. [28] ibid, para 29.

[29] This paragraph is drawn from OECD/EU, 'Executive Summary' in *Health at a Glance: Europe 2014* (OECD Publishing) <http://dx.doi.org/10.1787/health_glance_eur-2014-en> (accessed 26 February 2018).

in better health than those who are more disadvantaged. Such disparities are largely due to differences in access to and quality of care, as well as individual behaviours and lifestyles. The most glaring inequities, however, relate to the Roma population. An estimated 12–15 million Roma live in Europe, particularly in Bulgaria, Slovakia, and Romania. Roma are disproportionately poor, with about 45 per cent living in households that lack at least one of the basic housing amenities, namely an indoor kitchen, indoor toilet, indoor shower or bath, and electricity. About 90 per cent live in households with incomes below national poverty lines. According to the WHO, such living conditions have serious consequences for their health. Indicators suggest that life expectancy among Roma communities can be as much as ten to fifteen years shorter than among non-Roma populations. There are enormous disparities in other indicators, such as childhood nutritional status, low birth weight, diabetes, and coronary artery disease. There is also evidence of significant inequities in access to health care, particularly in relation to antenatal care coverage and vaccination rates.[30]

Most EU countries have universal or near-universal coverage for a core set of health services, with the exception of Cyprus, Greece, and Bulgaria. This is also reflected in the levels of health-care expenditure. In 2012, average health expenditure in EU member states was 8.7 per cent of GDP, a significant increase from 7.3 per cent in 2000. However, after the economic crisis in 2009, health expenditure fell in half of all EU countries and significantly slowed in the remainder.[31] Importantly, too, around three-quarters of health spending comes from public sources. In particular, the Netherlands, UK, and most of the Nordic countries have levels of public financing greater than 80 per cent.[32] Although quality of care improved in most countries, disparities persisted. For Europe, probably the greatest challenge comes from an ageing population, as compared to the challenges facing developing countries such as India and South Africa.

III. Health as a Derivative Right: Rights to Life and Bodily Integrity

The ambivalence as to whether health should be regarded as a human right is reflected in the absence in several major constitutions of an express, justiciable right to health. The Indian Constitution does include health in Article 47 of the 'Directive Principles of Social Policy', which requires the State to regard the improvement of public health as among its primary duties. However, although the Directive Principles are declared to be fundamental in the governance of the country, they are not enforceable in court.[33] The Canada Charter and the ECHR make no reference to health at all.

Nevertheless, courts in India and Canada, as well as the European Court of Human Rights (ECtHR), have derived aspects of the right to health from other rights, primarily the right to life. However, the result has been radically different in each jurisdiction. The Indian Court has been willing to construe the right as giving rise to

[30] WHO, 'Improving the Health of Roma in the WHO European Region' <https://web.ua.es/es/iudesp/documentos/ultima-hora/who-european.pdf> (accessed 26 February 2018).

[31] OECD/EU, 'Health Expenditure in relation to GDP' in *Health at a Glance: Europe 2014* (n 29).

[32] ibid.

[33] Constitution of India, Article 37.

positive duties to provide health care, even if this involves requiring the State to provide resources or to improve the efficiency of its administration. Importantly, this has permitted the Court to consider issues beyond the individual claimant to include systemic deficiencies. The Supreme Court of Canada, by contrast, has construed the right to life as giving rise to a duty not to interfere with individual liberty to seek private health care, rather than to provide a well-funded public service. Both Courts have been activist in the sense of interfering with government policies. But this has had opposite results. While the Indian Supreme Court has required the State to provide better access to public health care, the Canadian Supreme Court has prevented the State from creating a purely public system. This in turn provides an illuminating contrast to South Africa. Here there is an express right to access to health care. Nevertheless, the jurisprudence of the South African Constitutional Court reveals a much greater tendency to deference than its Indian and Canadian counterparts. The ECtHR, for its part, has traditionally focused on breaches of the right so far as it affects the individual. In recent cases, however, it, like the Indian Court, has located the individual breach in wider structural problems, which it has required the State to remedy.

This can be seen by considering the case law more closely. The Indian Supreme Court has implied a right to health from the right to life, in line with its general approach to the right to life as giving rise to a range of positive obligations. In *Consumer Education & Research* in 1995, the Court reiterated that the 'expression "life" in Article 21 ... does not connote mere animal existence or continued drudgery through life. It has a much wider meaning which includes right to livelihood, better standard of life, hygienic conditions in workplace and leisure'.[34] The case was concerned with the serious and long-term adverse effects of exposure to asbestos in mines. At one level, this was a health hazard which could be regarded as the responsibility of the employers and producers, rather than a human rights issue. However, the responsibility of the State was engaged in that regulations in place were not enforced. The Court held that mere adoption of regulations has no meaning without 'professional, industrial and governmental resources and legal and moral determination to implement such regulations'.[35]

The *Consumer Education & Research* case was quickly followed by *Paschim Banga Khet Mazdoor Samity v State of West Bengal* in 1996, a case concerned with the right of access to emergency treatment.[36] The petitioner, an agricultural labourer, suffered serious head injuries and brain haemorrhage when he fell off a train at a station in Bengal. He was taken to no less than seven public hospitals, none of which was able to find him a bed, despite his urgent need. Twelve hours after the accident, he was admitted to a private hospital where he was charged a large sum for his treatment. The Court had no doubt that 'failure on the part of a Government hospital to provide timely medical treatment to a person in need of such treatment results in violation of his right to life guaranteed under Article 21'.[37] The petitioner was awarded compensation, but the Court also went

[34] *Consumer Education & Research v Union of India* AIR 1995 SC 922 (Indian Supreme Court) para [24].

[35] ibid, para [19].

[36] *Paschim Banga Khet Mazdoor Samity v State of West Bengal* AIR 1996 SC 2426, (1996) 4 SCC 37 (Indian Supreme Court).

[37] ibid, para [9].

on to make detailed orders to address the systemic problems with emergency care, not just in West Bengal, but in other Indian States. It endorsed the recommendations that had already been made by a committee established by the State Government in the interim, but also went further. It required the government to make sure, inter alia, that adequate facilities were available at primary health-care centres to stabilize a patient; that hospitals at district level be upgraded to be in a position to treat serious cases; that more beds and facilities for specialist treatment be made available; and that a centralized communication system be set up to direct emergency patients to hospitals where a bed is available.

The Court was not deterred by the argument that this might be a costly exercise. 'It is no doubt true that financial resources are needed for providing these facilities. But at the same time, it cannot be ignored that it is the constitutional obligation of the State to provide adequate medical services to the people. Whatever is necessary for this purpose has to be done'.[38] It did accept that it could not all be done at once, but nevertheless required a 'time-bound plan' to provide the stated services. This can be compared with other formulations of the right to health, which permit progressive realization to the maximum available resources.

Since these cases, the Indian Supreme Court has continued to give specific content to the right to health in a variety of circumstances. Parmar and Wahi analysed a sample of sixty-six Supreme Court cases as part of their examination of the policy impact of litigating the right to health in India.[39] About twenty-eight of these cases (over 40 per cent) involved social justice or public interest claims. They found that the Indian Supreme Court had used a wide range of remedial techniques in adjudicating cases on the right to health. These included: appointing amicus curiae to provide legal assistance; establishing commissions or expert bodies to ascertain facts or to monitor implementation; delivering detailed directions to both public and private respondents to develop policy and regulations; and exercising continuing supervision through mandatory orders, whether interim or final. Where Court guidelines have recommended the adoption of measures to fill existing policy gaps, this appears to have prompted initiatives by the government in several important areas, including the regulation of blood banks, drug regulation, emergency care, mental health care, tobacco control laws, and reproductive rights. While Parmar and Wahi acknowledge that there is no way to be certain that the court decisions were in fact causative, there are clear correlations.[40]

The Canadian approach, while also deriving the right to health from the right to life and personal security has led to diametrically opposite results. As will be recalled, section 7 of the Charter gives everyone the 'right to life, liberty and security of the person and the right not to be deprived thereof except in accordance with the principles of fundamental justice'. The first case on this issue seemed promising. In *Morgentaler*, the Court struck down cumbersome abortion regulations on the grounds that they breached the pregnant woman's section 7 rights.[41] According to the Court, 'The jurisprudence of this Court holds that delays in obtaining medical treatment which affect patients physically and psychologically trigger the protection

[38] ibid, para [16]. [39] Parmar and Wahi (n 20). [40] ibid.

[41] *R v Morgentaler* [1988] 1 SCR 30 (Supreme Court of Canada).

of section 7 of the Charter'.[42] Importantly, the Court framed the issue as concerning the State's duty of restraint. Mandatory procedures imposed by the State led to delays in obtaining therapeutic abortions, increasing the risk of complications. Thus: 'The state has intervened in such a manner as to create an additional risk to health, and consequently this intervention constitutes a violation of the woman's security of the person'.[43]

However, this emphasis on section 7 as creating a duty of restraint opened the way to a conception of the right to health which gave priority to individual freedom of contract to arrange one's own health care, even if this might compromise the State's ability to provide publicly funded health care for all. This can be seen in *Chaouilli v Quebec*.[44] The case was concerned with the balance between public and private provision of health care, an issue which was highly political, and had been the subject of protracted debate across Canada in several provincial and federal elections.[45] Quebec's approach, mandated in a recent election, was to protect its public health-care system and discourage a private or second-tier health sector by prohibiting private health insurance. There were, however, long delays in the public health-care system. The prohibition of private insurance was challenged by a patient who had waited more than a year for a hip operation, and a doctor who wished to establish a private hospital. They argued that the prohibition violated both the Quebec Charter, which guarantees the right to life and personal inviolability, and section 7 of the Canadian Charter, which protects the right to life and security of the person. The Supreme Court of Canada, by a majority of four to three, struck down the prohibition as inconsistent with the Quebec Charter. So far as section 7 of the Canadian Charter was concerned, however, the Court was evenly split: three judges found a breach, three did not, and Deschamps J preferred not to commit herself on this point.

There are several important points to make about the decision. The first is that the breach was framed as one of interference with individual rights to life and personal security, rather than as a positive duty to provide health care. As Deschamps J put it, the State could not validly prevent Quebeckers who were prepared to spend money on health care, from doing so. McLachlan, Major, and Bastarache JJ concluded:

> Prohibiting health insurance that would permit ordinary Canadians to access health care, in circumstances where the government is failing to deliver health care in a reasonable manner, thereby increasing the risk of complications and death, interferes with life and security of the person as protected by section 7 of the Charter.[46]

Rather than requiring the government to repair the serious delays in the public system, they held that patients should have the right to access private health care. Indeed, at the very start of their judgment, McLachlin CJ and Major J emphasized that the appellants were not seeking an order that the government should spend more money on health care, nor that waiting times in the public health care scheme should be reduced. Instead, they were seeking a ruling that, because delays put their health at risk, they should be allowed to take out insurance so that they could access private services.[47]

[42] ibid. [43] ibid, 105–110. [44] *Chaoulli v Quebec (Attorney General)* (n 7).
[45] ibid, para [161]. [46] ibid, para [124]. [47] ibid, para [103].

Thus in effect, the right to health was characterized as a right to freedom of contract. The understanding of human rights as promoting not just individual autonomy, but also solidarity and substantive equality, is missing entirely from this approach.

The second point to note was the use of social fact evidence. The Quebec Government argued that any interference was justified on the basis that private health insurance would undermine the public health system by diverting resources into private health. The trial judge found good reason for the Quebec Government's fear that 'a private health sector fuelled by private insurance would frustrate the achievement of the objectives of the Canada Health Act'.[48] Her findings on the evidence were endorsed in the Quebec Court of Appeal.[49] However, McLachlan CJ and Major J held that '[t]he evidence ... belies that contention'.[50] Rather than accepting the conclusions on the facts reached by the lower courts, they embarked on their own assessment of the evidence. The result, according to Marmor, was to 'violate almost every scholarly standard for competent cross-national policy analysis'.[51] The majority did not specify what methodology they were using for the cross-country analysis, simply considering vignettes of other countries without grounding them in relevant differences and similarities, and relying on a Senate Committee report which itself had reached a different conclusion to that of the Court.[52] The dissent was similarly scathing as to the use of evidence by the majority. This raises serious questions as to how social fact evidence is used in courts and more specifically how comparative cross-national research on policy issues should be used to ground judicial determinations, especially in the highly complex context of health-care systems.

A third issue relates to remedies. The Court initially granted a declaration of invalidity with immediate effect. This would have required fundamental changes in the Quebec system of funding health care. Moreover, although it was strictly binding only in Quebec, its ripple effects were potentially far reaching. Private insurance was not prohibited only in Quebec, but also in five other Canadian provinces.[53] According to Flood, the 'legal impact of *Chaoulli* was dwarfed by its normative impact on policy debates across the country'.[54] However, after the Government of Quebec brought a motion for a rehearing, the Supreme Court suspended the declaration of invalidity for twelve months.[55] This gave the Quebec Government the opportunity to respond constructively to the challenge, by announcing new policies to limit waiting times, at the same time as allowing private insurance in a limited class of cases, namely knee, hip, and cataract surgeries. In particular, it introduced a centralized system to manage waiting lists, and a regulated system of out-of-hospital treatment. Flood regarded this as a 'Goldilocks solution',[56] a measured response to the judgment, which permitted some private insurance, while at the same time creating disincentives for the private sector to flourish.[57] Roach strongly advocates the use of a suspended declaration

[48] ibid, para [166]. [49] ibid, para [168]. [50] ibid, para [152].

[51] T Marmor, 'Canada's Supreme Court and Its National Health Insurance Program: Evaluating the Landmark *Chaoulli* Decision from a Comparative Perspective' (2006) 44 Osgoode Hall L J 311.

[52] ibid, 324. [53] *Chaoulli v Quebec (Attorney General)* (n 7) para [174].

[54] C Flood, '*Chaoulli*'s Legacy for the Future of Canadian Health Care Policy' (2006) 44 Osgoode Hall L J 273, 273.

[55] *Chaoulli v Quebec (Attorney General)* (n 7). [56] Flood (n 54) 305. [57] ibid.

in this way to deal with some of the most difficult problems of polycentric decisions which require resource allocation. In particular, it allows dialogic or participative solutions such as the one reached in *Chaoulli*.[58]

The ECHR is similar to the Canadian Charter in the absence of an express right to health. Instead, the European Social Charter (ESC) includes an express right to the highest attainable standard of health.[59] This reflects the division between civil and political rights, contained in the ECHR, and socio-economic rights, found in the ESC. However, not unexpectedly, the distinction has not been easy to sustain. This is particularly so in light of the recognition by the ECtHR that contracting states have both negative and positive obligations under the Convention. The result has been that, as in India and Canada, aspects of the right to health have been implied from the right to life in Article 2 of the ECHR. The Court has also drawn on the rights not to be subject to cruel or inhuman treatment (Article 3); to respect for home, family, and private life (Article 8); and to non-discrimination in the enjoyment of Convention rights (Article 14).

The ECtHR's strong focus on resolving individual rather than systemic complaints, together with its civil and political orientation, have meant that the decided cases have tended to emphasize procedural aspects of the right to health, such as the right to be informed of risks, free and informed consent, and access to proper investigations in cases of medical negligence.[60] However, in an important new development, the Chamber decision in the 2015 case of *Asiye Genç v Turkey*[61] began to shape the right to life in Article 2 in a way which is better able to address some of the systemic issues. The facts of the case were remarkably similar to those of *Paschim Banga Singh* in the Indian Court.[62] It concerned the tragic death of a new-born baby who had been born prematurely in Gümüshane public hospital in Turkey. As there were no neonatal facilities in the hospital, the doctors decided to transfer the baby to another public hospital, KTÜ Farabi, 110 km away. However, that hospital refused to admit the baby on the ground that there was no space in the neonatal intensive care unit. The baby was transferred to a nearby medical-surgical and obstetrical centre. But the duty doctors there explained that no incubators were available and suggested that the parents take the baby back to KTÜ Farabi public hospital, where doctors again refused to admit the baby due to lack of space in the neonatal unit. The baby died in the ambulance. A subsequent investigation was closed on the ground that no fault had been committed by the staff.

In upholding the parents' complaint of a violation of Article 2, the Court went straight to the systemic problems. It reiterated that Article 2 gave rise not just to negative obligations, to abstain from interfering with life, but also to positive duties on the

[58] K Roach, 'Polycentricity and Queue Jumping in Public Law Remedies: A Two-track Response' (2016) 66 University of Toronto Law Journal 52.

[59] European Social Charter (ESC) Part I Article 11.

[60] For a summary of these cases, see European Convention on Human Rights (ECHR) Factsheet 'Health' (August 2016) <http://www.echr.coe.int/Documents/FS_Health_ENG.pdf> (accessed 26 February 2018).

[61] *Asiye Genç v Turkey* (App No 24109/027) 2015 (European Court of Human Rights).

[62] *Paschim Banga Khet Mazdoor Samity v State of West Bengal* (n 36).

State to take the necessary measures to protect the life of people within its jurisdiction. These positive obligations applied too to the sphere of public health, requiring the State to establish a regulatory framework capable of ensuring a high level of competence among health professionals and to compel hospitals, whether private or public, to adopt measures ensuring the protection of the life of patients. The Court stressed the importance of differentiating between such systemic issues, which could entail a violation of Article 2, and individual errors of judgement of health professionals or poor co-ordination between them in the treatment of a particular patient. Where the State had made adequate provision for securing high professional standards among health professionals and in the protection of the lives of patients, errors of judgement by health professionals or poor co-ordination between them would not, without more, engage the responsibility of the State.[63] Nor was it sufficient if such protective measures existed only in theory: it was especially necessary that they actually worked in practice.[64] This was in addition to the need for prompt independent investigation to establish responsibility for the death of patients.

On the facts of the case, the issue was clearly not one of negligence in relation to an individual patient. Instead, the death of the child occurred because of lack of co-ordination between hospitals; the inadequacy of the current provision for neonatal care; and the total lack of provision for medical emergencies.[65] The Court particularly noted the unsatisfactory quantity and condition of the equipment for neonates in hospitals in the region:[66] the only incubator at Gümüshane was broken, as was one out of only four incubators at the obstetrical centre to which the baby was referred.[67] The child had died because the State had not sufficiently ensured the proper functioning and organization of the public hospital service or its health protection system more generally. This was coupled with the inadequacy of the internal investigation. The Court therefore held that the State had failed to fulfil its obligations under Article 2 of the Convention.[68]

IV. Health as a Socio-economic Right

Rather than implying the right to health from the right to life, several jurisdictions include an express right to health in their human rights instruments. An express right to health can be understood in several different ways. From some perspectives, a human rights approach entails an individually justiciable right to medication or other medical intervention for individual illness. A different perspective would be to focus on a broader framework within which policy initiatives should be structured. Substantively, a right to health could mean a right to access to health care; a right to be healthy; or a right to the highest attainable standard of health. The right could be immediate. Or, in order to acknowledge and accommodate the resource-intensive nature

[63] *Asiye Genç v Turkey* (n 61) para [67], citing *Powell v UK* (App No 45305/99) 2000 (European Court of Human Rights).

[64] ibid, para [70].

[65] ibid, para [77].

[66] ibid, para [80].

[67] ibid, paras [17]–[22].

[68] ibid, paras [87]–[88].

of health care, the right to health could be formulated as one which is not immediately realizable, but can be progressively fulfilled subject to available resources.

This section compares and contrasts two major manifestations of the right to health: at international level, in the form of Article 12 ICESCR, and at domestic level, in the South African Constitution. There are three interconnected themes running through this analysis. The first is the way in which the substance of the right is formulated. Article 12(1) ICESCR provides for the right 'of everyone to the enjoyment of the highest attainable level of physical and mental health'.[69] This contrasts with the formulation in section 27(1) of the South African Constitution, which does not provide for the right to health as such but the right to access health care. The question arises in both cases as to how the substance of the right can be elaborated. As we will see, the South African Constitutional Court has been reluctant to give specific content to the right, preferring to take the role of scrutinizing measures taken by the State. The Committee on Economic, Social and Cultural Rights (CESCR) has been much more forthcoming in this respect.

The second theme concerns the nature of the obligation to which this gives rise, and particularly the temporal framing. As with most of the rights under the ICESCR, Article 12 is not immediately realizable: the general obligation of States Parties under the Covenant is to 'take steps ... to the maximum of its available resources, with a view to achieving progressively the full realization' of the rights in the Covenant.[70] Article 12(2) gives some examples of the steps States should take. These include those necessary for the reduction of the stillbirth rate and of infant mortality; the healthy development of the child; the improvement of environmental and industrial hygiene; and the prevention, treatment, and control of epidemic, endemic, occupational, and other diseases. It also requires States to take the steps necessary for the creation of conditions which would assure medical service and attention to all in the event of sickness.

So far as the South African Constitution is concerned, there are two types of obligations related to the right to health. In relation to emergency medical treatment the right is immediately realizable: 'no-one may be refused emergency medical treatment'.[71] Similarly, the rights of children to 'basic nutrition, shelter, basic health care services and social services'[72] are immediately realizable. On the other hand, the right to access to health-care services does not give rise to an immediate duty. Instead, under section 27(2), the duty on the State is to take 'reasonable ... measures, within its available resources, to achieve progressive realization' of the right.[73] Notably, the ICESCR is more demanding than its South African counterpart: under the Covenant, a State must take steps to the 'maximum of its available resources', whereas the South African provision deliberately refers only to 'reasonable' measures 'within its available resources'. As we will see, the South African Constitutional Court has preferred to adjudicate the cases that have come before it under the progressively realizable right of access to health care, rather than the immediate right to emergency medical treatment or the right to life.

[69] ICESCR Article 12(1). [70] ICESCR Article 2. [71] South African Constitution, s 27(3).
[72] South African Constitution, s 28(1)(c). [73] South African Constitution, s 27(2).

As we saw in Chapter 3, progressively realizable rights are challenging. What is the substantive content of the right at the end of the road and what steps does the State need to take to show that it has fulfilled its duty of progressive realization of the right? Is the goalpost continually moving as technology develops and a country has more resources? For example, it could be argued that the 'highest attainable standard of health' in Article 12 ICESCR is continually rising, so that a country might in fact never achieve the full realization of the right. Moreover, as Chapman shows, it is particularly difficult to evaluate compliance because 'progressive realization' within the context of 'maximum available resources' requires a multiplicity of performance standards for each right in the context of specific countries and their varied social, developmental, and resources contexts.[74] Similar challenges arise in relation to the availability of resources. Which resources are covered under the rubric of maximum availability? And whose word counts—that of the State, the Court, or the international body?

The challenges raised by the progressive realization standard feed back into the difficulty in defining the substance of the right. As we saw in Chapter 3, the South African Constitutional Court sees its role as limited to assessing the reasonableness of measures taken by the State to fulfil the right, rather than giving the right independent normative content. The CESCR has instead formulated what it calls the minimum core content of the right, which must be immediately achieved, regardless of resources. The content of the minimum core, and its relationship to those elements which can be realized progressively, remains contentious.

The third theme is concerned with institutional separation of powers. Some of these differences may be related to the important institutional differences between courts and international supervisory committees. It may be more appropriate for the CESCR to set clear standards for States to achieve, which can then be used in periodic reporting to measure States' progress. Individualized litigation, on the other hand, may throw up ad hoc or non-systemic issues which are not conducive to general standard setting. On the other hand, given the much more authoritative role which can be played by domestic courts, it may be considered an abdication of their role in enforcing the right to health to be too passive or responsive, rather than proactive in defining standards. These themes are elaborated by considering these two jurisdictions in more detail.

The South African Constitutional Court has been acutely conscious of the difficulties which arise if courts intervene inappropriately in polycentric rights such as this one. It has therefore taken very seriously the constitutional framing of the right as one which is progressively realizable rather than immediate. This can give rise to excruciating dilemmas. On the one hand, the individual before the court is in desperate need of treatment. At the same time, it might be equally unfair to allow him or her to jump the queue. The South African Constitutional Court faced precisely this dilemma in *Soobramoney*, one of the first cases under section 27.[75] Mr Soobramoney was a forty-one-year-old man who suffered from heart disease, diabetes, and chronic renal failure.

[74] A Chapman, 'A "Violations Approach" for Monitoring the International Covenant on Economic, Social and Cultural Rights' (1996) 18 Hum Rts Qtr 23, 24.

[75] *Soobramoney v Minister of Health, Kwa-Zulu-Natal* 1998 (1) SA 765 (CC) (South African Constitutional Court).

Without regular renal dialysis, he would certainly die. However, his local hospital, the Addington state hospital in Durban, was woefully under-equipped for renal patients. Its renal unit only had twenty dialysis machines, some of which were in poor condition. This meant that it could only provide dialysis treatment to a limited number of patients. No funds were available in the budget for further expenditure on dialysis. As a result, the hospital authorities had adopted a system of prioritization, which excluded patients who would not be eligible for kidney transplants, for example because of heart disease. The claimant was therefore excluded. He had exhausted his personal resources on private treatment and could no longer afford it. He therefore faced certain death if denied dialysis. He brought an application under the right not to be refused emergency treatment in section 27(3) of the Constitution, and the right to life under section 11.

Chaskalson P was clear that the facts of the case did not invoke the right to emergency treatment in section 27(3). He regarded the right to emergency treatment as applying to a person suffering a sudden catastrophe who should not be denied available emergency services or turned away from a hospital capable of providing the necessary treatment.[76] He therefore took the view that the case therefore differed significantly from the undoubted emergency situation in the Indian Supreme Court case of *Paschim Banga Khet Mazdoor Samity*,[77] which had been cited before him. He also declined to follow the Indian approach of a broad construction of the right to life, since there was an explicit right to health care in section 27. The case therefore fell to be determined according to section 27(1) and (2). Applying these sections, the Court rejected the claim.

Chaskalson P's interpretation of sections 27(1) and (2) laid the foundation for the Court's future approach, not just to the right to health, but to other similarly worded rights in the Constitution. Most importantly, he interpreted the substance of the right in section 27(1) as being integrally shaped by the nature of the obligation in section 27(2).[78] In other words, the right to access to health care could not be determined without considering the available resources.[79] Indeed, he paid no attention to defining the content of the right. Instead, he focused on the State's claim that it could not make additional funds available to provide lifesaving treatment to the appellant. His starting point was that any obligation owed by the State to the individual appellant had to be determined on the basis that the same treatment should be available to everyone in his position. In the context of the overwhelming demand for health care, the State's failure to provide renal dialysis for all persons suffering from chronic renal failure did not constitute a breach of its constitutional obligations. In stark contrast to jurisdictions which see the right to health in individualistic terms, the Court emphasized that the individual might have to give way to the broader public good. The State had to manage its limited resources to address a wide range of claims, and a utilitarian approach might be needed: 'There will be times when this requires it to adopt a holistic approach to the larger needs of society rather than to focus on the specific needs of particular individuals within society'.[80] For support of this position he looked

[76] ibid, para [20]. [77] *Paschim Banga Khet Mazdoor Samity v State of West Bengal* (n 36).
[78] *Soobramoney v Minister of Health, Kwa-Zulu-Natal* (n 75) para [22]. [79] ibid, para [11].
[80] ibid, para [31].

not to other countries with a constitutional right to health, nor to the ICESCR, but to England, where there is no such right and courts adjudicate claims for health care under ordinary administrative law principles. Thus, he cited a 1995 UK case in which it had been held that it was undesirable for a court to determine how scarce medical resources should be applied because of the danger that providing the medication for this particular patient might have the effect of denying those resources to other patients who might benefit more.[81] Chaskalson P recognized that this meant that the ability to access health care for such patients would be dependent on how wealthy they were. 'The hard and unpalatable fact is that if the appellant were a wealthy man, he would be able to procure such treatment from private sources; he is not and has to look to the State to provide him with the treatment'.[82]

A different approach might have been to regard the claim of restricted resources as a limitation of the right and therefore requiring to be justified to a high standard of scrutiny under the limitations clause in the constitution. However, because the decision was taken under section 27(2), there was no question of shifting the burden of proof to the State or requiring a proportionality analysis. Instead, in what appeared to be a light-touch approach, Chaskalson P formulated the standard as simply one of rationality. 'A court will be slow to interfere with rational decisions taken in good faith by the political organs and medical authorities whose responsibility it is to deal with such matters'.[83]

This approach was underlined by Sachs J in his concurring judgment. 'In all the open and democratic societies based on dignity, freedom and equality with which I am familiar', he stated, 'the rationing of access to life-prolonging resources is regarded as integral to, rather than incompatible with, a human rights approach to health care'.[84] His approach, however, did not rest on a simple utilitarian calculus. For him, health-care rights needed to be considered not only in 'a traditional legal context structured around the ideas of human autonomy but in a new analytical framework based on the notion of human interdependence'.[85] A healthy life depended on social interdependence in many complex ways, from the quality of air, to the quality of caring relationships, to the quality of health care and support. Ironically, whereas the individualist approach in *Chaoulli* had granted the individual applicant the right to health, the collective view militated against recognizing that the individual claimant could successfully claim a violation.

> When rights by their very nature are shared and inter-dependent, striking appropriate balances between the equally valid entitlements or expectations of a multitude of claimants should not be seen as imposing limits on those rights (which would then have to be justified in terms of section 36) but as defining the circumstances in which the rights may most fairly and effectively be enjoyed.[86]

It is notable, however, that this was not balanced by an expectation that the State should fulfil the duty progressively. Indeed, the duty of progressive realization seems

[81] ibid, para [30], citing *R v Cambridge Health Authority, ex parte B* [1995] 2 All ER 129 (CA).
[82] *Soobramoney v Minister of Health, Kwa-Zulu-Natal* (n 75) para [31]. [83] ibid, para [29].
[84] ibid, para [52]. [85] ibid, para [54]. [86] ibid.

to have slipped off the Court's radar. This is problematic in that, while it may be acceptable that resources are not available to fulfil the claimant's right at this point in time, the State should still be required to give an account of how and when this might change. Without such a focus, the content of the right to access to health care can become illusory.

The context of the second major right to health case, the *TAC* case, was very different.[87] The case was triggered by the refusal of the government to provide nevirapine to pregnant mothers living with HIV/AIDS. This was despite the fact that it had been clearly established that a single dose of the drug during labour would significantly cut the risk of transmission of the HIV virus from mothers to new-born babies. During the 1990s, the HIV/AIDS epidemic in South Africa had reached catastrophic proportions. One of the most common methods of transmission of HIV in children was from mother to child at birth; indeed, the government estimated that about 70,000 children had been infected in this way each year.[88] Yet the government decided in September 2000 to make nevirapine available only at a very small number of pilot sites, with no possibility of wider roll-out in the foreseeable future. This was despite the fact that the South African Medicines Control Council had approved its use.

The case differed from *Soobramoney* in that the litigation was not brought by an individual claiming care for herself, but as a public-interest litigation on behalf of all pregnant women living with HIV. Moreover, the resource constraints at the centre of the *Soobramoney* case were not at issue in *TAC*, as the manufacturers of nevirapine had offered to make the drug available to the South African Government free for five years. Nevertheless, the judgment of the Court followed the path laid down in *Soobramoney*. Most importantly, the Court held, section 27(1) did not 'give rise to a self-standing and independent positive right enforceable irrespective of the considerations mentioned in s27(2)'.[89] Drawing on both *Soobramoney*[90] and *Grootboom*,[91] the Court held that it was:

> impossible to give everyone access even to a 'core' service immediately. All that is possible, and all that can be expected of the state, is that it act reasonably to provide access to the socio-economic rights identified in sections 26 and 27 on a progressive basis.[92]

The Court defended its rejection of the minimum core by reference both to legitimacy and competence concerns. It was for the State to take measures to eliminate or reduce the severe deprivations of the country: the Court's role under the Constitution was to ensure that those measures were reasonable, bearing in mind that a wide range of possible measures could be adopted by the State which would meet its obligations.[93] In addition, the Court held, courts were not 'institutionally equipped to make the wide-ranging factual and political enquiries necessary for determining what the

[87] *Minister of Health v Treatment Action Campaign (No 2)* (2002) 5 SA 721 (South African Constitutional Court) para [39].
[88] ibid, para [19].
[89] ibid, para [39].
[90] *Soobramoney v Minister of Health, Kwa-Zulu-Natal* (n 75).
[91] *Republic of South Africa v Grootboom* 2001 (1) SA 46 (South African Constitutional Court).
[92] *Minister of Health v Treatment Action Campaign* (n 87) para [35].
[93] ibid, para [41].

minimum-core standards … should be, nor for deciding how revenues should most effectively be spent'.[94] The role contemplated for the courts by the Constitution was to require the State to take measures to meet its constitutional obligations and to subject those measures to evaluation on the grounds of reasonableness.[95] Thus, section 27(1) and (2) must be read together: the rights are to have access to the services that the state is bound to provide.[96]

Nevertheless, the Court took a more robust view of the standard of scrutiny embodied in the reasonableness requirement than it had in *Soobramoney*. It reiterated the principle established in *Grootboom* that 'to be reasonable, measures cannot leave out of account … those whose needs are the most urgent and whose ability to enjoy all rights therefore is most in peril'.[97] For a programme to be reasonable, it must be balanced and flexible and give appropriate attention both to crises and to longer term needs.[98] Unlike *Soobramoney*, and in strong contrast to *Chaoulli*, the Court took seriously the point that, since nevirapine was in fact available in the private sector, it was the poor who would suffer. 'There is a difference in the positions of those who can afford to pay for services and those who cannot. State policy must take account of these differences'.[99] At the same time, the issue was much starker than that of *Soobramoney*. There was no question of lack of resources and the stakes were very high: the Court was clear that in evaluating government policy, regard must be had to the fact that the case was concerned with new-born babies whose lives might be saved by administering nevirapine at birth.[100] Where medically indicated, a single dose of nevirapine was a cheap, simple, and potentially lifesaving medical intervention. The Court therefore held that the government policy constituted a breach of the State's obligations under section 27.

Also of great importance was the Court's development of its remedial powers. The Court rejected the argument that the only appropriate remedy was a declaration, leaving it up to government to determine how to adapt its policies to bring it in line with its constitutional obligations.[101] It was also prepared to accept in principle that a Court could adopt a structural interdict, that is, a remedy which required ongoing supervision by the court: 'Where a breach of any right has taken place, including a socio-economic right, a court is under a duty to ensure that effective relief is granted … Where necessary this may include both the issuing of a mandamus and the exercise of supervisory jurisdiction'.[102] Significantly, it drew support from the results of its comparative survey of similar jurisdictions, including the US, India, Canada, and Germany, where structural interdicts were not considered a breach of the separation of powers doctrine.[103] However, supervisory remedies should only be issued where absolutely necessary, for example in the face of intransigence.[104] The Court did

[94] ibid, para [37]. [95] ibid, para [38]. [96] ibid, para [39].
[97] *Republic of South Africa v Grootboom* (n 91) para [44]. [98] ibid, para [43].
[99] *Minister of Health v Treatment Action Campaign* (n 87) para [70]. [100] ibid, para [72].
[101] ibid, para [99]. [102] ibid, para [106].
[103] *Minister of Health v Treatment Action Campaign* (n 87) paras [107]–[111], citing *Brown v Board of Education* 347 US 483 (1954) (US Supreme Court) and the second German abortion decision as examples, but acknowledging that courts in Canada and England were more cautious.
[104] *Minister of Health v Treatment Action Campaign* (n 87) paras [129] and [135].

not consider it absolutely necessary in the case before it, and therefore refused to confirm the structural interdict issued by the High Court. Instead, the Court issued a mandatory order requiring the government without delay to remove the restrictions preventing nevirapine from being made available at public hospitals and clinics and to permit and facilitate its use. The government was also required to make provision for counsellors to be trained, and to take reasonable measures to extend relevant testing and counselling facilities. In practice, the TAC was able to mobilize a great deal of community support to assist in monitoring implementation. Without ongoing judicial supervision, however, it is difficult to see what the Court makes of the requirement of progressive realization.

V. The Right to Equality

A third basis for protecting the human right to health is through the right to equality. Since almost all countries have some health-care protection for elites in their communities, the key issue could well be inequality in access and underlying distributional distortions. This is clear from the thumbnail sketches of health care in the four major systems above. In relation to health, it is particularly important to move beyond a formal notion of equality, since some individuals' needs for health care might be by their nature greater than others. In addition, particular individuals or groups might be marginalized specifically because of their race, gender, disability, age, religion, sexual orientation, or other protected characteristic. For those who fall at the intersection of all these identities, disadvantage resulting from inequality in health care can be not just additive but synergistic. For example, as we have seen, the ongoing consequences of colonialism and racial discrimination in Canada have had severely detrimental effects on the health of indigenous peoples, and this is exacerbated for women and people with disabilities.

The application of the right to equality to health can be examined by considering two Canadian cases, *Eldridge*[105] and *Auton*,[106] both of which required the Court to confront the extent to which the right to equality required a substantive approach. *Eldridge* raised the question of whether the failure by British Columbia to provide funding for sign language interpreters for deaf persons when they received medical services violated their right to equal benefit of the law under section 15 of the Canadian Charter. Each of the claimants was born deaf and their preferred means of communication was sign language. They argued that without interpreters, their ability to communicate with their doctors was impaired, increasing the risk of misdiagnosis and ineffective treatment. For example, one of the claimants had to give birth to twin babies without the benefit of an interpreter, a process she found frightening and difficult to understand, especially since the babies were born prematurely and she was unable to communicate with her doctor or nurse as to their condition. Her physician similarly testified that communication by written notes was impractical and might result in harm.

[105] *Eldridge v British Columbia* [1997] 3 SCR 624 (Canadian Supreme Court).
[106] *Auton v British Columbia (Attorney General)* [2004] 3 SCR 657 (Canadian Supreme Court).

Section 15(1) of the Charter provides that every individual is 'equal before and under the law and has the right to the equal protection and equal benefit of the law without discrimination'. The central question was whether the appellants had been afforded the equal benefit of the law. It was clearly not appropriate to regard equality as simply entailing that everyone be treated the same. The Medicare system in British Columbia treated everyone alike, with no explicit exclusions for deaf persons. La Forest J, delivering the judgment of the Court, emphasized that legislation equally applicable to everyone could infringe the right to equality if it had a greater impact on certain classes of people due to irrelevant personal characteristics than on the public as a whole.[107] Here, the adverse effects did not stem from the imposition of a burden, but from a failure to ensure that deaf persons benefit equally from a service offered to everyone. For hearing persons, 'an effective means of communication is routinely available, free of charge, as part of every health care service. In order to receive the same quality of care, deaf persons must bear the burden of paying for the means to communicate with their health care providers, despite the fact that the system is intended to make ability to pay irrelevant'.[108] Sign language interpretation was the means by which deaf persons could receive the same quality of medical care as hearing persons. The failure to provide sign language where necessary for effective communication therefore denied deaf people the equal benefit of the law and discriminated against them in comparison with hearing persons. The government would therefore be required to take special measures under section 15(1) to ensure that disadvantaged persons were able to benefit equally from government services.[109]

Three other aspects of this case contribute to making it the high-water mark of the application of the right to equality in relation to health care. The first is that the Court held that it was not necessary for the claimants to prove that their own rights had been infringed, if they had established a violation of the equality rights of the group to which they belong.[110] The second was the role of private entities. Here the Court held that the Charter may apply to non-governmental entities in respect of 'inherently governmental actions', that is, to private bodies implementing a specific government programme or entity. In this case, it was up to hospitals to decide whether to provide sign language. But because the provision of medical services was an expression of government policy, and the discrimination was intimately connected to the medical service delivery system instituted by the legislation, hospitals' decisions must conform with the Charter.

The third striking aspect of the case is the way in which the limitation was dealt with. Having determined a prima facie violation of section 15(1), the respondents would need to justify any limitation under the stringent analysis in section 1 of the Charter. Section 1 provides that Charter rights are 'subject only to such reasonable limits prescribed by law as can be demonstrably justified in a free and democratic society'. La Forest J held that the government had manifestly failed to demonstrate a reasonable basis for the total denial of medical interpretation services for the deaf. Unusually for a court, it was prepared to scrutinize the budgetary implications. Here,

[107] *Eldridge v British Columbia* (n 105) para [64]. [108] ibid, para [72].
[109] ibid, para [77]. [110] ibid, para [83].

the estimated cost of providing sign language interpretation for the whole of British Columbia was only $150,000, or 0.0025 per cent of the provincial health-care budget at the time. The refusal to expend such a 'relatively insignificant sum' could not possibly qualify as a justifiable limitation.[111] This raised the question of whether recognition of this claim would have a ripple effect throughout the health-care system, requiring the government to spend scarce health resources on myriad disadvantaged persons. For La Forest J, the answer was provided in the equality analysis itself. The claim was not for a discrete service, which the government, in the exercise of its discretion to allocate resources, had chosen not to provide. Instead, the claim was only for equal access to services available to all: 'To deny the appellants' claim on such conjectural grounds, in my view, would denude section 15(1) of its egalitarian promise and render the disabled's goal of a barrier-free society distressingly remote'.[112]

The remedy, however, was light-touch. The Court decided that the appropriate remedy was a declaration that the failure to provide services was unconstitutional together with a direction that the government administer the relevant legislation consistently with section 15(1). La Forest J regarded a declaration as more appropriate than an injunction because there were 'myriad options available to the government' to rectify the position and it was not for the Court to determine how it would be accomplished. Moreover, the Court suspended the declaration for six months to allow the government to explore its options and formulate an appropriate response. At the same time, the Court did set a target, namely that after six months had expired, sign language interpreters would be provided wherever necessary for effective communication in the delivery of medical services.[113]

The conclusion was very different in the later case of *Auton*.[114] In this case, parents of children with autism in British Columbia challenged the provincial government's refusal to provide publicly funded applied behaviour analysis/intensive behavioural intervention (ABA/IBI) for children with autism aged between three and five years old. They argued that this breached their rights to equal benefit of the law under section 15 of the Charter. The government justified its refusal on the grounds both of financial constraints and the emergent nature of the therapy. The Court rejected the claim. Its reasoning shows some of the potential risks of an equality analysis which is not underpinned by a substantive right to health. By taking a very narrow approach to the key terms, namely whether a benefit was provided by law, and what the comparator class was, the Court was able in effect to define the claim out of existence.

This can be seen by looking more closely at the Court's reasoning. It reiterated previous equality jurisprudence establishing that for a claim to succeed under section 15(1), the claimants had to show, first, that they had been denied a benefit provided by law, and second, that they were treated less favourably on the ground of their disability than a comparator group. Both were defined very narrowly. On the first question, it was held that section 15(1) requires claimants to establish they failed to receive a benefit that the law provided or were saddled with a burden that the law did not impose on anyone else. The Canadian Medicare scheme did not promise that all

[111] ibid, para [87]. [112] ibid, para [93]. [113] ibid, para [96].
[114] *Auton v British Columbia (Attorney General)* (n 106).

Canadians would receive funding for all medically required treatment. The legislation only conferred core funding for services provided by medical practitioners, leaving it to the Province to provide funding for non-core services in its discretion. ABA/IBI was not provided by medical practitioners and was therefore within the discretionary power of the Province rather than being a 'benefit provided by law'. The Court distinguished *Eldridge* on the grounds that in the latter, the benefit was provided by law, but in a discriminatory fashion. Nor could it be said that it was discriminatory to fund some non-core therapies but not ABA/IBI therapy, since it was inherent in the legislative scheme that only some non-core services could be funded.[115] The Court also interpreted the claimants' position very broadly, as a claim that all medically required treatment should be publicly funded, so that any polycentric implications appeared overwhelming.

The second element to be established in a section 15 claim was that treatment was less favourable than that of the relevant comparator group. Here too the Court took a narrow view of the criteria for choosing the appropriate comparator. In its view, the comparator group should 'mirror' the characteristics of the claimant group except for the personal characteristic related to the section 15 ground. For disability, comparison could be with those suffering a different type of disability or one of greater severity.[116] Applying these criteria, the court concluded that the appropriate comparator was 'a non-disabled person or a person suffering a disability other than a mental disability (here autism), seeking or receiving funding for a non-core therapy important for his or her present and future health, which is emergent and only recently recognized as medically required'.[117] It was not established that any such comparator group was more favourably treated. The claim therefore failed on this basis too.

Auton and *Eldridge* should not, however, be considered in isolation. As a start, the Supreme Court of Canada has subsequently resiled from its strict adherence to a 'mirror' principle in determining a comparator group.[118] Equally importantly, Flood and Chen point out that the impact of these two cases does not map precisely onto the judicial finding. Whereas *Eldridge* can be considered the closest that Canadian plaintiffs have come to establishing a positive right of access to a health service through litigation, in practice its implementation was weak and patchy. On the other hand, the failure of *Auton* in the courts functioned to mobilize public sympathy, which put pressure on the government to take political action.[119]

VI. Reproductive Health

Perhaps one of the most pressing equality issues in relation to the right to health concerns the right to reproductive health. Although there have been advances in maternal health and family planning, maternal mortality remains at shockingly high levels. According to the WHO, about 830 women died every day in 2015 due to complications

[115] ibid, para [43]. [116] ibid, paras [53]–[54]. [117] ibid, para [55].

[118] *Withler v Canada (Attorney General)* [2011] 1 SCR 396 (Supreme Court of Canada).

[119] C Flood and Y Chen, 'Charter Rights and Health Care Funding: A Typology of Canadian Health Rights Litigation' (2010) 19 Annals of Health Law 479, 483.

of pregnancy and childbirth. Almost all occurred in settings with poor resources, and the majority could have been prevented. These figures mask gaping inequalities, between developed and developing countries, between urban and rural areas, and between rich and poor. A woman in a developing country runs a risk of dying from a maternal-related cause which is thirty-three times higher than her counterpart in a developed country. Although numbers decreased globally by 43 per cent between 2000 and 2015, the annual rate of decline was only 2.3 per cent, which was less than half of what was needed to achieve the goal of a reduction of 75 per cent set by the Millennium Development Goals.[120]

The critical breakthrough of the International Conference on Population Control in 1994 was in its recognition of the need for an express right to reproductive health. Indeed, as the UN follow-up report in 2014 put it, the conference represented 'a remarkable consensus among 179 Governments that individual human rights and dignity, including the equal rights of women and girls and universal access to sexual and reproductive health and rights, are a necessary precondition for sustainable development'.[121] However, this has still not gained widespread recognition. Indeed, of the countries in this study, only South Africa has such a right. Thus, as we saw in Chapter 7, the right to have access to health care in section 27 of the Constitution expressly includes the right to have access to reproductive health care. Like the right of access to healthcare services more generally, this is a progressively realizable right, subject to available resources. In South Africa, there has not yet been major litigation on this aspect of section 27, although it is mentioned in the *TAC* case. In other jurisdictions, the right to reproductive health has been litigated under a range of other rights, including the right to life, the right to equality, the right not to be subjected to cruel and inhuman treatment, and the right to respect for private and family life. As in other aspects of the right to health, the choice of right shapes the potential response. In particular, the extent to which the right can address the problem depends on whether a court regards the issue as one of individual negligence or wrongdoing, on the one hand, or as one arising from systemic obstacles rooted in gender and/or race inequality on the other.

These themes can be demonstrated by contrasting the decisions in two tragic cases of death due to pregnancy-related causes, one of which came before the ECtHR and one before the Convention on the Elimination of All Forms of Discrimination Against Women (CEDAW) Committee. In both, the adjudicator was required to navigate the boundary between an individual and systemic approach, and between negligence and a human rights approach. In both, a young woman died after delays in diagnosing and properly treating her after her baby had died in utero. In the ECtHR case of *Mehmet Şentürk and Bekir Şentürk v Turkey*,[122] Mrs Şentürk, who was in her thirty-fourth week of pregnancy, began to experience violent pain. She was taken by her husband, the applicant, to two different public hospitals, both of whom turned her away because

[120] World Health Organization, 'Global Health Observatory Data: Maternal Mortality' <http://www.who.int/gho/maternal_health/mortality/maternal_mortality_text/en/> (accessed 26 February 2018).

[121] UN General Assembly, 'Framework of actions for the follow-up to the Programme of Action of the International Conference on Population and Development beyond 2014' UN Doc A/69/62 (12 February 2014) 1.

[122] *Şentürk v Turkey* (2015) 60 EHRR 4 (European Court of Human Rights).

the ultrasound machine had been turned off and they were short staffed. At the third hospital, after waiting in the emergency department for three to four hours, she was briefly examined and sent home with some painkillers. After a few hours at home, her pain remained so unbearable that the applicant took her to a fourth hospital, the Ege University Medical Faculty Hospital, where she was finally given an ultrasound, which revealed that the baby had died in utero. This necessitated immediate surgery to save the mother's life. However, the applicant was told that the surgery could not go ahead unless the applicant paid 600–700 million Turkish lira immediately. The hospital would not accept an undertaking to pay later, or a deposit in partial payment. Since the applicant did not have the funding immediately available, he was told to call an ambulance to transport her to a nearby maternity hospital. However, she died in the ambulance on the way.

The Court upheld the complaint under the right to life in Article 2 ECHR. As in *Asiye Genç v Turkey*, discussed above, the Court held that to constitute a violation, the problem had to be systemic. Medical negligence must be shown to have occurred in the context of the failure of the State to set up a regulatory system requiring hospitals to take appropriate steps to ensure that patients' lives are protected. At the same time, the Court was careful to emphasize that it was not its task to rule in abstract on the State's public health policy on access to treatment. In navigating the difficult boundary between a general prescription on systemic failures and an individualized negligence decision, it focused on the fact that the provision of treatment at the Ege University Medical Faculty Hospital was subordinated to a prior financial obligation. There was no doubt as to the seriousness of the patient's condition and the need for immediate surgery; and the medical staff were perfectly aware of the risk to her health if she were transferred. Yet there was no provision making it possible to determine what should be done in medical emergencies requiring hospitalization where the fees were not paid. Domestic law therefore did not have provisions capable of preventing the failure to provide medical treatment in her case. Thus, the Court concluded, '[T]he deceased woman, victim of a flagrant malfunctioning of the hospital departments, was deprived of the possibility of access to appropriate emergency care'.[123] The State therefore failed in its obligation to protect her physical integrity under Article 2.

The facts of *Alyne da Silva Pimentel Teixeira v Brazil*,[124] which came before the CEDAW Committee, had strong similarities with the *Şentürk* case. Alyne da Silva Pimentel Teixeira was a young African descendant Brazilian woman, who died of pregnancy-related complications after her condition was severely neglected in a Brazilian health clinic and hospital. Her story, like that of Mrs Şentürk, was a catalogue of mismanagement and neglect. Having presented at her local health centre with severe nausea and abdominal pain, it took a further two days before doctors realized that her twenty-seven-week foetus had died in utero, requiring induced labour. She continued to suffer severe symptoms, including haemorrhaging and low blood pressure for several more days, until the health centre attempted to transfer her to nearby

[123] ibid, paras [94]–[97].

[124] *Alyne da Silva Pimentel Teixeira v Brazil* 2011 (Communication No 17/2008) (Committee on the Elimination of Discrimination against Women).

public and private hospitals with better facilities. Only one municipal hospital had available space but refused to use its only ambulance to transfer her at that hour. Ms da Silva waited in a critical condition for eight hours, having slipped into a coma, before being transported to the hospital by ambulance. Although she arrived in a grave condition and had to be resuscitated, the hospital left her in a makeshift area in the emergency room hallway, where she died less than twenty-four hours later. Since her medical records had not been transferred with her, the hospital was unaware of her recent stillbirth.

In a communication to the CEDAW Committee under the Optional Protocol, her mother argued that her daughter's equality rights, and in particular her rights to life and health had been violated. Crucially, the communication situated the plight of her daughter in the deep structural inequalities in the Brazilian health system. Unlike the *Şentürk* case, which did not deal with the gender equality dimension of the case, the claimant argued that the duty to reduce maternal mortality was a key obligation entailed by the right to health. Yet they pointed to statistics showing that over 4,000 maternal deaths occurred each year in Brazil, representing one-third of maternal deaths in Latin America as a whole. This figure was considerably higher than those of countries with lower levels of economic development. This, they argued, constituted a systematic failure to prioritize and protect women's basic human rights. In response to the State's submission that a national health strategy was in place to eventually achieve improvement, the claimant argued that the requirement that health facilities be available on a non-discriminatory basis was an obligation of immediate effect. Moreover, the mere adoption of a national health strategy was not sufficient to fulfil the progressive elements of the rights. In addition, it had to be implemented and periodically reviewed on the basis of a participatory and transparent process.[125] The position was materially aggravated by inexcusable delays in the Brazilian judicial system, which routinely failed to provide adequate remedies for women in vulnerable groups such as Ms da Silva Pimentel Teixeira and her family. Women from lower socio-economic backgrounds and women of African descent faced widespread difficulties in accessing remedies in relation to acts of violence and discrimination committed against them.[126] The State, on the other hand, attempted to argue that this was an individual case of negligence, not of its own making, but attributable to the private health facilities which had been responsible for her care. Indeed, it went so far as to claim that Ms da Silva's death was not a maternal death but resulted from 'digestive haemorrhage'.

In upholding the complaint, the Committee accepted both the individual breach and the more systemic violations. Its decision resonates strongly with the ECtHR's emphasis on redressing systemic issues. The Committee held that it was not sufficient to have policies in place—policies must be adequately funded, and both action- and result-oriented. Moreover, the policy should ensure that there are strong and focused executive bodies to implement such policies. In addition, the Committee rejected the State's claim that the private health-care institution where she was treated was responsible for the poor level of medical care, rather than the State. Instead, it held, the

[125] ibid, para [5.6]. [126] ibid, para [5.5].

State was directly responsible for the actions of private institutions when it outsourced medical services; and, indeed, always retained the duty to regulate and monitor them. On the basis of Article 2(e) of the Convention, the State Party had an obligation of due diligence to take measures to ensure that private actors' activities in relation to health policies and practices were appropriate.[127]

At the same time, the CEDAW Committee went further and emphasized the crucial gender equality dimensions of the case. As a start, the Committee made it clear that it regarded this as a case of maternal death. This is important in that the government's refusal to classify it as such was symptomatic of widespread misclassification and under-reporting of maternal deaths. Moreover, and particularly importantly, the Committee was able to recognize the role of intersectional discrimination in this case. In its General Recommendation 28, the Committee had recognized that discrimination against women based on gender is 'inextricably linked to other factors that affect women, such as race, ethnicity, religion or belief, health status, age, class, caste and sexual orientation and gender identity'.[128] In accepting the author's argument that Ms da Silva was subjected to multiple discrimination, as a woman of African descent and on the basis of her socio-economic background,[129] the Committee has come to one of the very few decisions in which intersectionality has been concretely applied.

The Committee therefore held that Brazil had violated its obligations under Article 12 in relation to access to health; Article 2(c) in relation to access to justice; and Article 2(e) in relation to its due diligence obligation to regulate the activities of private health service providers. As well as recommending that the State provide reparations to Ms da Silva's surviving daughter, who had been abandoned by her father and lived in conditions of severe poverty with her grandmother, the Committee made some structural recommendations. These included ensuring women's right to safe motherhood; the right to affordable access for all women to adequate emergency obstetric care; and the provision of adequate professional training for health workers, especially for women's reproductive health rights. The State is also required to ensure access to effective remedies for violation of such rights. In addition, the State must ensure that private health-care facilities comply with international and national standards on reproductive health care. Most importantly, the State should reduce preventable maternal deaths through implementing its own policies effectively and throughout all the regions of Brazil.[130]

The right to reproductive health does not only engage positive duties to provide health care. It also performs a crucial role in preventing the State from wrongfully interfering in women's autonomy. This is particularly salient in relation to sterilization without informed consent. We saw in Chapter 7 that India's policies on population control have notoriously depended on sterilization. Small monetary incentives and widespread ignorance are used to entice women to undergo unsafe and undesired sterilizations. In 2014, for example, in a case before the High Court of Punjab, the

[127] ibid, para [7.5].

[128] CEDAW Committee General Recommendation No 28 on the Core Obligations of States Parties under Article 2 of the Convention on the Elimination of All Forms of Discrimination against Women (December 2010) CEDAW/C/2010/47/GC.2.

[129] *Alyne da Silva Pimentel v Brazil* (n 124) para [7.7].

[130] ibid, para [8].

Human Rights Law Network argued that the Haryana Government had disproportionately promoted only female sterilization at the expense of access to other forms of modern contraception for years.[131] In the meanwhile, sterilization 'camps' operate in many areas in India, with appallingly low levels of standards of health and safety, high levels of morbidity and mortality, and highly questionable methods of establishing consent.

There is also a long history of such pernicious abuse in Eastern Europe. Forced sterilization against Roma women was one of the instruments of persecution of Roma people by the Nazi regime in the Second World War. It was continued in communist Czechoslovakia, where government programmes provided monetary incentives and condoned misinformation and coercion, specifically targeting Roma women. It is estimated that as many as 90,000 Romani women were subject to coercive sterilization between 1970 and 1990 in the former Czechoslovakia.[132] Although the Slovak Government claimed that these programmes were ended in 1989 after the fall of communism, a fact-finding report in 2003 found consistent patterns whereby Slovak health-care providers disregarded the need to obtain informed consent to sterilization and failed to provide accurate reproductive health information.[133] Cases continue to be documented in the Czech Republic and Hungary.

Three seminal cases have come before the ECtHR highlighting the extent of these violations: *VC v Slovakia*,[134] *NB v Slovakia*,[135] and *IG v Slovakia*.[136] In all three, the Court made important strides towards recognition of the blatant violation of the rights of the individuals subjected to sterilization without informed consent. The Court found a breach of the right not to be subject to cruel or inhuman treatment in Article 3 of the Convention, as well as the right to respect for home and family life in Article 8. But it stopped short of finding a breach of the right to equality. This was despite sophisticated submissions by the applicants and intervenors highlighting the systematic and intersectional nature of discrimination against Romani women on grounds of sex and race. This meant that the findings, as in many of the right-to-health cases we have seen in this chapter, individualized the problem and faltered at the point of finding systemic shortfalls.

The facts of the cases epitomized the practices of non-consensual sterilization in Slovakia. In all three, the applicants were sterilized immediately after giving birth by caesarean section. The ostensible 'consent' typically took the form of a signature on a typed form, presented to the woman while in the midst of labour or immediately after having been given sedating medication and accompanied by warnings from health-care professionals that she or her child would die if the procedure was not carried

[131] Centre for Reproductive Rights, 'India: State Must Act on Contraception' (24 January 2014) <http://www.reproductiverights.org/feature/India-state-must-act-on-contraception> (accessed 26 February 2018).

[132] S Curran, 'Intersectionality and Human Rights Law: An Examination of the Coercive Sterilisations of Romani Women' (2016) 16 Equal Rights Review 139.

[133] Centre for Reproductive Rights and Poradna pre obcianske a l'udské práva, *Body and Soul Forced Sterilization and Other Assaults on Roma Reproductive Freedom in Slovakia* (2003).

[134] *VC v Slovakia* (2014) 59 EHRR 29 (European Court of Human Rights).

[135] *NB v Slovakia* (2012) App no 29518/10 (European Court of Human Rights).

[136] *IG v Slovakia* (2012) App no 15966/04 (European Court of Human Rights).

out. All the applicants were young, with many reproductive years ahead of them, and all found themselves subject to stigma and ostracism from their own communities due to their subsequent infertility. They suffered permanent psychological and social damage.

In the first case, *VC v Slovakia*,[137] decided in 2012, the Court established several vigorous principles which underpinned the finding that sterilization without informed consent was a violation of the absolute right not to be subject to torture or inhuman or degrading treatment or punishment. The first was its recognition of forced sterilization as a major affront to individual dignity. Sterilization constitutes an extensive interference with a person's reproductive health, bearing on 'manifold aspects of the individual's personal integrity'.[138] Imposition without the consent of a mentally competent adult patient 'is to be regarded as incompatible with the requirement of respect for human freedom and dignity, one of the fundamental principles on which the Convention is based'.[139]

The second principle established by the Court was its insistence that consent should be genuine and informed. The applicant was asked to give her consent in writing two-and-a-half hours after she was brought into hospital, when she was in labour, and immediately before undergoing a caesarean section.[140] She was informed by medical personnel that if she had another child, either she or her baby would die. The Court held that such an approach was not compatible with the principles of respect for human dignity and freedom in the Convention. She was not informed about her health status, the procedure, or the alternatives, and had no opportunity to discuss it with her partner. Nor could this be regarded as an emergency and therefore an exception to the need for informed consent: clearly, sterilization was not a lifesaving procedure. Neither could the Court give any weight to the hospital authorities' assumption that she might act in an irresponsible manner with regard to her health in the future. The way the hospital staff acted was paternalistic, giving her no option but to agree to the doctors' prescription, and therefore violating her essential autonomy.

Third, the Court held that both the procedure itself and the manner in which she was asked to consent were 'degrading' in the sense elaborated in its Article 3 jurisprudence, namely 'treatment which humiliates or debases an individual, showing a lack of respect for, or diminishing his or her human dignity, or arouses feelings of fear, anguish or inferiority'.[141] The combination of these issues meant that her treatment reached the level of severity required to constitute a violation of Article 3. The Court also found a violation of the State's positive obligations under Article 8 (the right to respect for private and family life) to put in place effective legal safeguards to protect the reproductive health of women of Roma origin in particular.[142] However, in the light of its findings under Articles 3 and 8, it held that it was unnecessary to make a decision in relation to Article 14. A similar approach was taken in *NB v Slovakia*, where the applicant was a minor and no attempt had been made to gain either her informed consent or that of her representative.

[137] *VC v Slovakia* (n 134). [138] ibid, para [106]. [139] ibid, para [107].
[140] ibid, para [111]. [141] *IG v Slovakia* (n 136) para [121].
[142] *VC v Slovakia* (n 134) para [145].

The refusal to deal with the equality issue is puzzling. The Court acknowledged at various points of its judgment that the treatment experienced by the claimants was based on prejudicial assumptions about Roma women in general, as well as a long history of similar oppression based on both race and gender. Indeed, its decision under Article 8 was based on the absence of safeguards giving special consideration to the reproductive health of the applicant as a Roma woman. In this part of its judgment, it cited in detail various reports pointing to the widespread negative attitudes among the majority Slovak population towards the relatively high birth rate among the Roma. This had been the conclusion of the Council of Europe Commissioner for Human Rights,[143] echoed in the report of the Emergency Care Research Institute and CEDAW's concluding observations in 2008.[144] The Court itself noted that the section on social and working conditions in the medical records of the applicant's pregnancy simply stated: 'Patient is of Roma origin'.[145] The government's explanation of this statement reflected the deeply prejudicial attitudes towards Roma people, namely that Roma patients frequently neglected social and health care. As the Court put it, this indicates

> a certain mind-set on the part of the medical staff as to the manner in which the medical situation of a Roma woman should be managed. Certainly, it does not suggest that special care was to be, or was in fact, exercised to ensure that the full and informed consent of such a patient was obtained before any sterilization was contemplated.[146]

The later case of *IG v Slovakia* specifically raised the issue of racial prejudice. The applicants in that case, three women who had been subjected to forced sterilization between 2000 and 2002, submitted that racial prejudice had played a significant role in the quality of the treatment they had received. They had been segregated into 'Gypsy rooms', prevented from using the same bathrooms and toilets as non-Roma women, excluded from the communal dining room, and on occasion, subjected to verbal abuse. They also adduced statements by high-level politicians and members of the government calling for the regulation of Roma fertility. As well as race discrimination, they alleged that compulsory sterilization constituted discrimination on grounds of sex: subjecting women in a vulnerable position to sterilization without their full and informed consent was a form of violence against women. Moreover, the ensuing infertility resulted in a particularly heavy burden on women, since in the Roma community, a woman's status was often determined by her fertility.

The reason given in all three cases for avoiding Article 14 was the observation that, although medical staff acted with gross disregard for her right to autonomy as a patient, there was no indication that they had acted with the intention of ill-treating the applicant.[147] In the *IG* case, the Court again held that it could not be established that the doctors involved acted in bad faith, that the sterilization of the applicants was a part of an organized policy, or that the hospital staff were intentionally racially motivated.[148] Yet it juxtaposed this with a reiteration of its finding that 'shortcomings in legislation and practice relating to sterilizations were liable to affect members of the Roma

[143] ibid, para [146]. [144] ibid, para [148]. [145] ibid, para [149]. [146] ibid, para [151].
[147] ibid, paras [106]–[120]. [148] *IG v Slovakia* (n 136) para [165].

community in particular'.[149] This finding, however, established a violation of the positive duties under Article 8 rather than Article 14. This is problematic for two reasons. First, it ignores the Court's own jurisprudence establishing that discrimination means more than intentional differential treatment. Instead it extends to indirect discrimination, or practices which are likely to have a disproportionate effect on individuals with protected characteristics.[150] Second, it short-circuits any potential for addressing systemic violations. As Judge Mijovic put it in his dissenting opinion in *VC*,

> Finding violations of Articles 3 and 8 alone in my opinion reduces this case to the individual level, whereas it is obvious that there was a general State policy of sterilization of Roma women under the communist regime, ... the effects of which continued to be felt up to the time of the facts giving rise to the present case.

Indeed, he continued,

> [T]he fact that there are other cases of this kind pending before the Court reinforces my personal conviction that the sterilisations performed on Roma women were not of an accidental nature, but relics of a long-standing attitude towards the Roma minority in Slovakia. To my mind, the applicant was 'marked out' and observed as a patient who had to be sterilized just because of her origin, since it was obvious there were no medically relevant reasons for sterilizing her. In my view, that represents the strongest form of discrimination and should have led to a finding of a violation of Article 14 in connection with the violation found of Articles 3 and 8 of the Convention.[151]

VII. Health and Polycentricity

The right to health raises acute problems of polycentricity. Granting curative care to one individual might be at the expense not only of another, but of the health system's allocatory principles more generally. Indeed, Flood and Gross conclude from their study of sixteen countries that individual litigation can undermine the ability of governments to run fair and effective health-care systems.[152] They situate the difficulty in the ways in which courts have individualized the right to health, regarding them as immediate rights to a specific benefit. Because of the myopia of courts, which are only able to see the two-way dispute before them, the consequences for equity in access to health care and medications cannot be addressed. Yamin similarly concludes, from her experience in relation to rights to health care in Latin America, that litigation on individual rights poses the greatest challenges to equity. Spurred by low thresholds for standing, countries in this region have experienced high levels of litigation, which exploit the system without transforming it.[153] Similarly, Ferraz is highly critical of the Brazilian approach to a justiciable right to health, which he regards as worsening the

[149] ibid; *VC v Slovakia* (n 134) [177]; *NB v Slovakia* (n 135) [121]–[122].

[150] *DH v Czech Republic* App No 57325/00 (2008) 47 EHRR 3 (European Court of Human Rights).

[151] *VC v Slovakia* (n 134) (Dissenting Opinion of Judge Mijovic).

[152] Flood and Gross (n 6).

[153] A Yamin, 'Promoting Equity in Health: What Role for Courts?' (2014) 16 Health and Human Rights 1.

country's already pronounced health inequities.[154] Notably, some of the litigation for expensive drugs in this region has been instigated by drug companies which can then benefit from the exorbitant drug prices in the unregulated pharmaceutical industry.

However, this does not mean that the right to health cannot be shaped to avoid such inequitable results. As this chapter has shown, it is possible for a court to use a wider lens, to consider not just the individual but also the system. As was argued in Chapter 4, the Court should approach the issue from a deliberative standpoint, focusing on insisting that policy-makers provide reasons for their actions which can be justified as furthering the right and thereby enhancing their accountability. The bounded deliberative approach does not necessarily require courts to make specific allocative decisions themselves. Instead it would require particularly compelling reasons for government action or inaction which deprives the most vulnerable, marginalized, and impoverished of their basic existential needs and dignity. Such an approach resonates with that of Paul Hunt, who stresses that

> a human rights-based approach requires that special attention be given to disadvantaged individuals and communities; it requires the active and informed participation of individuals and communities in policy decisions that affect them; and it requires effective, transparent and accessible monitoring and accountability mechanisms. The combined effect of these is to empower disadvantaged individuals and communities.[155]

Yamin similarly argues for litigation which is able to consider the equity impacts of health-care rights and create opportunities for public learning about health rights. Courts should expect policy-makers to design health-care plans to meet human rights-based criteria, particularly the need to prioritize both socio-economic disadvantage and the specific needs of those with serious illnesses.[156] She also helpfully points to the kind of factors which need to be part of the deliberation sparked by litigation. These should include evidence of the broader impact of decisions in individual cases, an understanding of the complexity of the health-care sector, and in particular, a reckoning with the asymmetries of power and information as between patients on the one hand, and the insurance and pharmaceutical industry on the other. For example, the Colombian Constitutional Court, after a period of intense individual litigation which threatened to skew the health-care budget, issued a ruling in 2008, ordering the government to address the systemic factors behind the health litigation.[157] As part of this, the government was required to draw up a wider restructuring plan which included a participative process. The hope is that such an approach will achieve a greater balance between individual rights and the wider social interest.

Yamin also suggests that adjudication of the right to health should not be singularly focused on health care. It should also deal with the social determinants of health, such as the right to sanitation. Indeed, litigation may be better suited to pursuing such collective goods, where equity considerations are central rather than peripheral

[154] O Ferraz, 'The Right to Health in the Courts of Brazil: Worsening Health Inequities' (2009) 11; ibid, 33.

[155] Hunt (n 9). [156] Yamin (n 153). [157] Ruling T-760 of 2008.

to the claim before the court.[158] Adjudication should also include regulation of both public and private actors, including pharmaceutical companies, which, as we have seen, have often driven individual litigation so that they can benefit from exorbitant prices for drugs where prices are unregulated. Brinks and Gauri argue that litigation which aims at better regulation of aspects of health care, such as pricing of medication, can have greater pro-poor impacts than litigation for direct provision of services to the individual.[159]

In any event, assessing the impact of litigation is considerably more complex than it might first appear. Flood and Chen show that even if there is a successful challenge leading to courts granting a positive right to a particular therapy or care, it is rare for the order to be fully enforced. The under-enforcement of court orders is well illustrated in relation to *Eldridge*, where implementation was weak and patchy. On the other hand, a case might fail in court, but nevertheless galvanize public support and thereby trigger political intervention. *Auton* is a good example of this phenomenon.[160] On the other hand, health rights challenges might fail in court and thereby set back the momentum for achieving political change.[161] Furthermore, as Gauri and Brinks show, it is misleading to focus only on the immediate consequence of the dispute. For example, even if the first generation of cases is dominated by better-resourced claimants, this might have established an entry point for litigation by low-income litigants with the assistance of publicly funded lawyers.[162] In addition, the State might decide to extend the benefits awarded consequent to the initial litigation to all those who are similarly situated. This could be because it is less costly for the State than continuing defensive litigation; or because potential claimants can now articulate their claim through the political process in the form of a 'right' rather than a wish or aspiration; or because equal treatment standards make it politically untenable to continue offering a special service only to those who sue.[163] Gauri and Brinks' empirical work shows that such 'expansive compliance' is more common than the adversarial model of litigation might predict.[164] Indeed, they find that those affected by public policy initiatives triggered by litigation vastly outnumber those who benefit directly from the specific judicial remedy. This is true too for Brazil, which has been one of the jurisdictions most criticized for the ways in which individual litigation might distort the public healthcare provision. A particularly salient example is the AIDS litigation. Although this was spearheaded by the relatively well-off, the innovations introduced by the judiciary were incorporated into the public health system, benefitting large numbers who had never brought a legal claim.[165]

Litigation, in any event, must be used with other strategies to ensure a fully deliberative response. Yamin points to various opportunity structures, such as advocacy, proposing new legislation in the domestic context, and the use of international vehicles such as the individual complaints procedure under the Optional Protocol to the ICESCR, and the Sustainable Development Goals. By embedding litigation within a

[158] Yamin (n 153). [159] V Gauri and D Brinks (eds), *Courting Social Justice* (CUP 2008).
[160] Flood and Chen (n 119) 483. [161] ibid, 482–83.
[162] Gauri and Brinks (eds) (n 159) 23. [163] ibid, 24–25. [164] ibid, 24.
[165] ibid, 339.

wider set of democratic participatory structures, it becomes possible to incorporate the broader perspectives of civil society, to further the expressive function of human rights through education, training, and advocacy, and to mobilize the appropriate actors to monitor compliance.[166] The success in the implementation of the *TAC* case was largely due to the social mobilization of the advocacy group TAC, which was also responsible for bringing the claim.

VIII. Conclusion

This chapter has applied the cross-cutting themes identified in the first part of this book to analyse the many challenges raised by a human right to health. Given the lack of clear consensus as to the place of health in the canon of fundamental rights in the first place, it has been necessary to draw on the values underpinning the concept of a human right. More specifically, where there are no express constitutional rights, judges' theories of interpretation of the text before them have been central to the shaping of the right. The right to health also straddles the boundary between civil and political rights and socio-economic rights, demonstrating the importance of approaching the substance of the right from the perspective of the duties to respect, protect, and fulfil. This in turn challenges the adjudicative frontiers of courts, especially where the right to health takes us into the heartland of positive duties with polycentric implications. Possibly the most salient point which arises from a comparative perspective on the right to health is the importance of a systemic approach by courts to the meaning of the right to health. It is when the right to health is interpreted in terms of individual errors, or individual benefits, that its polycentric implications are obscured. On the other hand, in insisting that governments are accountable for systemic failures in the duty to fulfil the right to health, courts should not lose sight of the substantive nature of human rights. The individual right should not be made to give way to utilitarian concerns. This is the challenge which courts applying the right to health will continue to face.

166 Yamin (n 153).

9

The Right to Housing

I. Introduction

Like health, housing has frequently been regarded as a matter for the political sphere, rather than that of fundamental human rights. This approach is strikingly evident in the judgment of the European Court of Human Rights (ECtHR) in the 2001 case of *Chapman*, where the Court stated:

> While it is clearly desirable that every human being has a place where he or she can live in dignity and which he or she can call home, there are unfortunately in the contracting states many persons who have no home. Whether the state provides funds to enable everyone to have a home is a matter for political not judicial decision.[1]

In those instruments in which housing has been afforded the status of a human right, it is generally regarded as a socio-economic right, and therefore subject to progressive realization, depending on available resources. On the other hand, protection against State intrusion into home, family, or private life is regarded as a paradigm candidate for human rights law. This bifurcation is reflected at international and regional levels. The right to be housed has been assigned to the International Covenant on Economic, Social and Cultural Rights (ICESCR),[2] while the International Covenant on Civil and Political Rights (ICCPR) only includes a right protecting individuals against arbitrary or unlawful interference with their homes, privacy, family, or correspondence.[3] This is replicated at European level. Article 8 of the European Convention on Human Rights (ECHR) gives a right to respect for home, family, and private life; while the right to housing is found in the much less well-known European Social Charter (ESC).[4]

However, on a closer look, the division is deeply problematic. As a start, it is difficult to see how an individual's right to respect for her home can be fulfilled if she has no home. More fundamentally, the division is premised on a background assumption that the role of human rights is to protect individuals against State intrusion on their freedom, where freedom itself is narrowly defined as lack of coercion. On a broader view of the values pursued by human rights, this division becomes unsustainable. As was argued in Chapter 2, freedom should mean more than whether individuals are left alone. It should also be concerned with whether people are able to exercise their autonomy through a range of feasible options. Homelessness and housing insecurity drastically curtail individuals' ability to make any kind of choices beyond mere survival. More than this, they undermine the basic dignity and respect which should be afforded to all human beings.

1 *Chapman v UK* (2001) 33 EHRR 18 (ECtHR) para [99].
2 ICESCR, Article 11(1).
3 ICCPR, Article 17(1).
4 ESC, Article 31.

Homelessness and housing insecurity should also be seen from the perspective of equality.[5] As the UN Housing Rights Programme puts it: 'To live in a place, and to have established one's own personal habitat with peace, security and dignity, should be considered neither a luxury, a privilege nor purely the good fortune of those who can afford a decent home'.[6] In addition, homelessness undermines the value of solidarity which holds communities together. Sachs J articulated this vividly in the South African Constitutional Court:

> It is not only the dignity of the poor that is assailed when homeless people are driven from pillar to post in a desperate quest for a place where they and their families can rest their heads. Our society as a whole is demeaned when State action intensifies, rather than mitigates, their marginalization.[7]

The relegation of housing to the status of a socio-economic right has meant that, like other socio-economic rights, breaches have not been regarded with the same seriousness as violations of civil and political rights. As the UN Special Rapporteur on the Right to Housing has put it: 'The right to adequate housing is too frequently disconnected from the human rights values which form its core, and is treated more as a socioeconomic policy aspiration than as a fundamental right which demands effective, rights-based responses and timely access to justice'.[8] She maintains that the choice to separate the right to adequate housing from the right to life has legitimated a widespread sense that violation of housing rights is not as important or culpable as other violations. Homelessness and grossly inadequate housing, on her view, should be addressed as unacceptable violations of the right to life.

In practice, it has become increasingly difficult to corral the right to housing in the sphere of socio-economic rights. Since the right to life and the right to respect for home and privacy tend to attract stronger censure, whether through justiciable human rights or in human rights advocacy, it is these rights which are increasingly called upon by litigants to address homelessness and grossly inadequate housing. Moreover, most of the very burning issues relate to housing insecurity and evictions. People without homes will inevitably be driven by the need to survive to erect shelters or informal homes for themselves wherever they can. The right to non-interference with one's home then becomes directly allied with the right to have access to fair alternatives if eviction is to be legitimate.

Whatever the source of the right, several central challenges face a human rights conception of housing. Central among these is the question of how to define the substance of the right. Is it an individual right to a home? If so, what is the standard of the home required? The standard set in the ICESCR is one of adequacy, but this too needs further definition. It has been argued that 'the concept of adequate housing is

[5] S Fredman, *Human Rights Transformed: Positive Rights and Positive Duties* (OUP 2008) ch 1, 204ff.

[6] United Nations Human Settlements Programme, 'Housing Rights Legislation: Review of International and National Legal Instruments' United Nations Housing Rights Programme, Report No 1, (2002) 1.

[7] *Port Elizabeth Municipality v Various Occupiers* 2005 (1) SA 217 (South African Constitutional Court) para [18].

[8] Special Rapporteur on adequate housing, 'Adequate housing as a component of the right to an adequate standard of living' (UN General Assembly, UN Doc A/71/30, August 2016) para 5.

no longer constrained to a physical structure of four walls and a roof, but increasingly encompasses the basic structure and the human settlement environment in which that structure finds itself'.[9] This might include sanitation, roads, protection of law and order, electricity, running water, and community facilities, such as schools. This also raises the question of whether the right requires housing which is close to sources of livelihood. It is abundantly clear that, without this essential prerequisite, people leave whatever homes they have and move to places in which they can eke out a means of survival, even if there is an absence of the most fundamental infrastructure.

A different conception might focus on the duty, regarding the right as a right to an act by the State, rather than to a physical object. The role of the court, on such an approach, would be to insist on accountability of the State in achieving its obligations. While there may be several different ways of meeting these duties, the State needs to give a well-reasoned and deliberatively sound account of its choices. Alternatively, the right could primarily consist in procedural protections, for example in relation to evictions. This in turn raises the question of whether procedures are simply a means of legitimating outcomes, or genuinely trigger meaningful engagement with stakeholders and others.

All these challenges raise the further question of whether a justiciable right, elaborated and enforced by a court, is able to deal with the many complex and conflicting demands of housing needs. As in the right to health, affording the right to the individual might have detrimental effects on the State's capacity to afford the same right to everyone else in that position. Does this mean, however, that the individual's right should be postponed, or even emptied of content? It could in any event be argued that the challenges of urbanization, poverty, town planning, and employment opportunities may make it difficult for a court to make a helpful intervention. On the other hand, given that the cases generally come before the court in the form of eviction proceedings, it is not feasible simply to regard housing rights as non-justiciable.

Indeed, most of the major cases considered here concern informal occupation of land or derelict structures, whether public or private. This is largely due to the inability or refusal of public authorities to ensure that the poorest and most disadvantaged of their populations are properly housed close to sources of livelihood. In India, the cases have concerned attempts to evict people from the informal settlements, slums, and pavements which are home to as much as half of the population in cities such as Mumbai. It is estimated that by 2017, India's total slum population was 104 million. Slum dwellers face numerous deprivations, including discrimination, lack of recognition by governments, high exposure to disease and violence, precarious livelihoods, pollution, and the adverse effects of climate change and natural disasters.[10] Most have no electricity, water supply, or cooking gas, and many live in shacks surrounded by open sewers.[11] In Europe, the cases have primarily concerned the Roma and traveller

[9] Statistics South Africa, 'Housing from a Human Settlement Perspective' GHS Series Volume VII (2002–14) <http://www.statssa.gov.za/publications/Report-03-18-06/Report-03-18-062014.pdf> (accessed 27 February 2018).

[10] UN Habitat, 'Slum Almanac: Tracking Improvement in the Lives of Slum Dwellers 2015–2016' 4 <https://unhabitat.org/slum-almanac-2015-2016/> (accessed 27 February 2018).

[11] India Guide, 'Slum Population in India' <http://www.indiaonlinepages.com/population/slum-population-in-india.html> (accessed 27 February 2018).

populations. Even those who have largely abandoned their nomadic cultural history have cultural preferences against high-rise housing and suffer from prejudice and racism. In South Africa, the rapid urbanization consequent on removing the harsh limitations on free movement under the apartheid government, together with decades of refusal to provide urban housing, have led to wide-scale informal settlements. In addition, many people have no option but to squat in derelict and often unsafe inner-city buildings.

More recently, these types of evictions have been joined by housing repossessions by banks and other lenders after the huge crisis caused by sub-prime mortgage lending biased against poor and disadvantaged borrowers. In the US from 2008 until May 2014 there were over 5 million foreclosures. Many of those affected were tenants renting properties foreclosed because of their landlord's default. As many as 40 per cent of families in the US facing eviction due to foreclosure are renters, who are disproportionately of low income and people of colour.[12]

A comparative examination of judicial approaches to these challenges reveals several clear themes. First, courts have recognized that a home is fundamental to both human survival and human dignity. The right to a home therefore functions as a counterweight to courts' traditional concern for the protection of property rights. This is particularly true where the homeless are amongst the poorest and most disadvantaged. Second, courts have frequently reconciled competing interests by focusing on providing procedural protections. The third and most contested theme is the extent to which courts have been willing to link their acknowledgement of a right to a home to a requirement that adequate homes be provided. Whether or not a right to housing is express or derived from another right, and whether it is immediate or subject to progressive realization, it is on this issue that a justiciable right has had the most limited interpretation in the jurisdictions considered here. Each of these themes is elaborated below.

Section II considers the source of rights and how the source shapes the substance of the right. In particular, it contrasts jurisdictions which rely on derivations from the rights to life or respect for home and family life with those with express protections of the right to housing. The following sections consider how these differences manifest in relation to the key challenges raised by the right to housing. Section III looks at the ways in which rights to a home have been balanced against rights of third parties, whether landlords or landowners or other members of the public. Pavement dwellers and other informal occupiers may interfere with others' rights of passage, their safety, or even their health. They may also encroach on public spaces, such as parks or green spaces. This requires a balance between negative and positive duties. This section examines the different ways in which these conflicts have been addressed. It considers, first, procedural protections, and second, substantive protections such as the duty to provide alternative housing or shelter. Section IV looks more closely at the substance of the right. Is it a right to an object or a right to an act? How can we define 'adequacy' in the housing context? This requires us to locate the right

[12] 'Housing and Homelessness in the United States of America: Submission to the UN Universal Periodic Review of the USA', 15 September 2014, para 13 <https://www.nlchp.org/documents/UPR_Housing_Report_2014> (accessed 27 February 2018).

more closely in the social context in which it occurs, and to examine how courts and other adjudicative bodies have dealt with broader polycentric issues, especially in relation to the duty of progressive realization and the need for ongoing implementation. Section V concludes by considering housing as an equality right.

II. Sources and Shape of the Right

The right to housing has been crafted out of a variety of different rights, depending on the nature of the constitution or international instrument. The Indian Court has been at the forefront of deriving the right to housing from the right to life,[13] whereas under the ECtHR, the issue has primarily arisen under the rights to respect for home and private and family life, and to peaceful enjoyment of one's possessions.[14] This can be contrasted with the South African Constitution, which includes an express right to housing. Like the other socio-economic rights in the South African Constitution, this is formulated in two parts: the first part gives a right of access to adequate housing, while the second requires the State to take reasonable measures progressively to realize the right, subject to available resources.[15] This has to be read together with the right to property.[16] The ICESCR similarly gives a right to adequate housing, but formulates the correlative duty as the duty to take steps to the maximum of available resources to realize the right.[17] This section begins by considering civil and political rights as a source of an implied right to be housed, and in particular the use of fundamental values to do so. This is followed by an analysis of express rights to housing. The comparative approach reveals striking similarities, despite the differences in text. Instead, judges' perception of their own role in relation to the executive and legislature has tended to be the primary influence on shaping the outcome.

A. A value-driven right: deriving the right to a home from civil and political rights

Leilani Farha, in her 2016 report as UN Special Rapporteur on the right to housing, argues powerfully that the right to life is not only violated by the deliberate or preventable infliction of death by the State.[18] Violations through State neglect, such as from a failure to take reasonable measures to ensure access to necessities of life such as food, housing, and water, should be given equal importance. Such an approach is exemplified by the Indian Supreme Court. The Indian Constitution has no express mention of a right to a home. Nevertheless, the Court has been able to craft such a right from the right to life. It has largely done so by invoking the fundamental values behind human rights. In *Chamelli Singh*,[19] a three-judge bench vividly affirmed the right to life as encompassing a right to live with dignity and to aspire to self-development:

[13] Indian Constitution, Article 21.

[14] ECHR, Article 8; Protocol 1, Article 1.

[15] South African Constitution, s 26.

[16] South African Constitution, s 25.

[17] ICESCR, Article 11(1) and Article 2(1).

[18] Report of the Special Rapporteur on adequate housing, UN General Assembly, 'Adequate housing as a component of the right to an adequate standard of living' UN Doc A/71/310, 8 August 2016.

[19] *Chameli Singh and Others v State of UP* (1996) 2 SCC 549 (Indian Supreme Court).

> In any organised society, the right to live as a human being is not ensured by meeting only the animal needs of man. It is secured only when he is assured of all facilities to develop himself and is freed from restrictions which inhibit his growth. All human rights are designed to achieve this object.[20]

Shelter is regarded as more than just a protection against danger; it is a 'home where he has opportunities to grow physically, mentally, intellectually and spiritually'. Moreover, rather than seeing the right to a home and shelter as less pressing than civil and political rights, the Court has affirmed their central importance as a precondition to the exercise of such rights: 'The right to life implies the right to food, water, decent environment, education, medical care and shelter, since no civil, political, social or cultural rights either in the Universal Declaration or the Indian constitution could be exercised without them'.[21]

Equally important is the recognition of the close link between the right to housing and the rights to life and livelihood in the famous case of *Olga Tellis*.[22] The petitioners were pavement- and slum-dwellers in Bombay. They faced eviction as a result of a decision by the Bombay Municipal Corporation that all pavement- and slum-dwellers in the city would be forcibly evicted and deported to their respective places of origin or other places outside of the city. This was likely to affect as much as half the population of Bombay, many of whom had come from rural areas with no source of employment to eke out a means of survival in the city. They claimed a breach of the right to life in Article 21. The nature of the challenge was vividly described by Chandrachud CJ:

> Those who have made pavements their homes exist in the midst of filth and squalor, which has to be seen to be believed. Rabid dogs in search of stinking meat and cats in search of hungry rats keep them company. They cook and sleep where they ease for no conveniences are available to them ... It is these men and women who have come to this Court to ask for a judgment that they cannot be evicted from their squalid shelters without being offered alternative accommodation.[23]

The Chief Justice was also mindful of the powerful social forces driving people to live in this way, including the pressures of urbanization triggered by lack of rural development; and poor urban planning, which concentrated employment opportunities in one specific area of Bombay.[24] Most of the pavement-dwellers were employed in the most casual or menial of work. Many were hawkers selling vegetables, flowers, toys, balloons, or buttons. Others were casual labourers, construction workers, domestic servants, and luggage carriers. The Court was acutely aware that it was the availability of opportunities to earn a living, however menial, that was the key driver of squatter settlements in big cities. The connection with the right to livelihood was obvious. People 'choose a pavement or a slum in the vicinity of their place of work, the time otherwise taken in commuting and its cost being forbidden for their slender

[20] ibid.

[21] *Ahmedabad Municipal Corporation v Nawab Khan Bulab Khan* (1997) 11 SCC 121 (Indian Supreme Court).

[22] *Olga Tellis and Others v Bombay Municipal Corporation* AIR 1986 SC 180 (Indian Supreme Court).

[23] ibid, para [1]. [24] ibid.

means. To lose the pavement or the slum is to lose the job'.[25] This was proved by the undisputed fact that people invariably returned to the cities after eviction. Arguably, too, they provided an important and even indispensable service to the community.

For the Court, removing the right to livelihood was a clear breach of the right to life.

> The sweep of the right to life conferred by Article 21 is wide and far reaching. It does not mean merely that life cannot be extinguished or taken away ... An equally important facet of that right is the right to livelihood, because no person can live without the means of living, that is, the means of livelihood.[26]

Notably, the Court drew on the Directive Principles to inform its interpretation of Article 21. It referred both to Article 39(a), which provides that the State shall direct its policy towards securing that citizens have the right to an adequate means of livelihood, and Article 41, which provides that the State should, within the limits of its economic capacity and development, make effective provision for securing the right to work. Although not enforceable by any court, the Directive Principles 'must be regarded as equally fundamental in the understanding and interpretation of the meaning and content of fundamental rights'.[27]

The Indian Court's approach can be contrasted with that of the ECtHR, where the right to a home has been adjudicated under the right to respect for home and family life in Article 8, rather than the right to life. At one level, the ECtHR has preferred to regard the Article 8 right as invoking only rights of non-intervention. As we have seen, the ECtHR in *Chapman* emphatically relegated questions of housing provision to the political sphere in individual countries. However, the division between positive and negative duties has been difficult to sustain in the light of the fact that here, as in other cases, the trigger for invocation of the right is generally an eviction. The rights attendant on eviction are formulated as protection from State intervention; but evictions are highly likely to leave people homeless, raising the question of the State's positive duties to provide adequate housing. This tension has required the ECtHR, like the Indian Court, to look to fundamental values behind human rights in order to develop the Article 8 right appropriately. It has done this, first and foremost, by recognizing the place a person lives in as her home, regardless of its legality. From the mid-1990s, the Court has consistently held that whether an applicant's house should be regarded as their home for the purposes of Article 8 was a matter of fact, independent of whether their occupation was lawful in domestic law.[28] This means that a State cannot rely on the fact that an occupier is unlawful in domestic law to justify evictions. Instead, evictions constitute an interference with an individual's right to respect for her home; and the burden shifts to the State to justify the interference on the grounds of proportionality.

It is in the framing of the test of proportionality that the Court has drawn on background values to affirm the importance of a home. Eschewing the highly deferent standard usually adopted for cases in which social and economic policies are at

[25] ibid, paras [82]–[83]. [26] ibid, paras [79]–[80].

[27] ibid, paras [80]–[81]. See Chapter 3 on Directive Principles.

[28] *Buckley v UK* (1993) 23 EHRR 101 (European Court of Human Rights).

issue, the Court has held that a strict standard should apply to Article 8. This is because the right to respect for one's home 'concerns rights of central importance to the individual's identity, self-determination, physical and moral integrity, maintenance of relationships with others and settled place in the community'.[29] In determining the scope of the margin of appreciation in relation to Article 8, even where general social and economic policy considerations have arisen, particular significance should be attached to the 'extent of the intrusion into the personal sphere of the applicant'.[30] This was reinforced in *Cosic v Croatia*, where the Court reiterated that 'the loss of one's home is a most extreme form of interference with the right to respect for one's home'.[31] This contrasts with its approach to the right to reasonable enjoyment of property in Article 1, Protocol 1 of the Convention. Here the Court would respect the legislature's judgement as to what is in the general interest unless it is 'manifestly without reasonable foundation'.[32]

These themes were vividly affirmed in the case of *Yordanova v Bulgaria* in 2012.[33] Like many ECtHR cases, the issue concerned the abysmal housing conditions of Roma populations, perpetuated by discrimination and racism. In Bulgaria, most Roma no longer pursue an itinerant way of life, and instead live in predominantly Roma neighbourhoods on the fringes of towns. The applicants in the case had settled on vacant State land in a neighbourhood of Sofia in the 1960s and 1970s, creating a small Roma settlement of 200–300 people. They had erected their own houses but there was no sewage or plumbing. They had never sought to regularize their houses, since this was a difficult process for a poor and isolated community, and it was undisputed that in any event their homes fell below basic health and safety construction requirements. Nevertheless, they were permitted to remain in their homes, albeit in an environment which became increasingly hostile to Roma communities. However, in 2005, bowing to pressure from non-Roma residents, the mayor of Sofia ordered the community to be forcibly removed.

The applicants argued that the eviction order interfered with their rights under Article 8. The ECtHR had no difficulty in finding that the makeshift houses of the applicants were their 'homes'. Despite being unlawful in domestic law, there was no doubt that they had lived for many years in the houses they had constructed on State or municipal land. Since the removal order would result in them losing their homes, it was clear that there was an interference with their right to respect for their homes. The question therefore was whether the eviction was proportionate to a legitimate aim. The Court regarded it as legitimate in principle for a State to improve and upgrade the urban environment by removing substandard buildings; or to take measures to cope with health hazards resulting from an unlawful settlement of makeshift houses lacking sewage and sanitary facilities. However, simply evicting them and rendering them homeless without considering other options was not a proportionate means to achieve this aim.

[29] *Connors v UK* (2005) 40 EHRR 9 (European Court of Human Rights) para [82].
[30] ibid, para [82].
[31] *Cosic v Croatia* [2011] 52 EHRR 39 (European Court of Human Rights) para [22].
[32] *Connors v UK* (n 29) para [82].
[33] *Yordanova v Bulgaria* Application No 25446/06 (2012) (European Court of Human Rights).

Notably, the Court refused to accept the applicants' argument that the eviction had been motivated by the desire to satisfy racist demands to free the area of an unwanted Roma settlement. At the same time, it stressed that the government had failed to recognize that socially disadvantaged groups, such as the applicants, may need assistance to be able to effectively enjoy the same rights as the majority population. Although the Court reiterated the principle in *Chapman* that Article 8 does not in terms give a right to be provided with a home, it went on to say that 'an obligation to secure shelter to particularly vulnerable individuals may flow from Article 8 of the Convention in exceptional cases'.[34] Most importantly, the Court held that the underprivileged status of the applicants' group must be a weighty factor in considering approaches to dealing with their unlawful settlement and, if their removal was necessary, in deciding on its timing, modalities and, if possible, arrangements for alternative shelter. This had not been done, and therefore the removal order was found not to be necessary in a democratic society for the achievement of the legitimate aims pursued.

Similarly, the assault on dignity exemplified by enforced homelessness has led the UK Supreme Court to hold that it is a breach of the right not to be subjected to cruel and inhuman or degrading treatment to leave people with no choice but to live rough. 'The exposure to the elements that results from rough-sleeping, the risks to health and safety that it gives rise to, the effects of lack of access to toilet and washing facilities and the humiliation and sense of despair that attaches to those who suffer from deprivations of that kind' are all relevant indicators of a potential breach of this right.[35]

An analogous approach can be seen in relation to the African Charter on Human and Peoples' Rights, which also does not mention the right to housing directly. In *SERAC v Nigeria*,[36] the complainants argued that the military government of Nigeria massively and systematically violated the right to adequate housing of members of the Ogoni community. The case arose from the exploitation by a consortium involving both the State oil company and Shell Petroleum Development Corporation of oil reserves in Ogoniland, causing serious environmental degradation and health problems. In addition, the Nigerian security forces had attacked and destroyed several Ogoni villages and homes in retaliation against a non-violent campaign by Ogoni members against the oil companies. The African Commission on Human and Peoples' Rights held that although the right to housing or shelter was not explicitly provided for under the African Charter, a right to shelter or housing could be read into the Charter as a result of the combined effect of the rights to property,[37] the protection of the family,[38] and the right to health.[39] Moreover, as we saw in Chapter 3, the Commission held that all rights give rise to obligations, not just of restraint, but also to protect, promote, and fulfil. At the very minimum, this meant that the Nigerian Government had

[34] ibid, para [130].

[35] *R (on the application of Limbuela) v Secretary of State for the Home Department* [2005] UKHL 66; [2006] 1 AC 396 (HL) para [71].

[36] *Social and Economic Rights Action Centre (SERAC) and Another v Nigeria* (2001) AHRLR 60 (African Commission on Human and Peoples' Rights).

[37] African Charter of Rights and Freedoms, Article 14.

[38] African Charter of Rights and Freedoms, Article 16.

[39] African Charter of Rights and Freedoms, Article 18(1); *Social and Economic Rights Action Centre (SERAC) and Another v Nigeria* (n 36) para [60].

an obligation not to destroy the housing of its citizens and not to obstruct efforts to rebuild lost homes. It also meant that the State had a duty to protect its citizens, by preventing the violation of any individual's rights by non-state actors. Most importantly, the right to shelter 'even goes further than a roof over one's head. It extends to embody the individual's right to be let alone and to live in peace, whether under a roof or not'.[40]

B. The right to a home as a socio-economic right

Although the South African Constitution contains an express right to access to housing, the interpretation of the right by the South African Constitutional Court converges strikingly with that of the Indian Supreme Court and the ECtHR. Whereas the latter have derived the right to housing from essentially civil and political rights, with limited positive duties attached, the former has seen the positive duties attached to an express right to housing as limiting the substance of the right. The outcomes are remarkably similar.

There are four relevant provisions in the South African Constitution. Section 26(1) gives a right to have access to adequate housing. This is a 'progressively realisable' right: section 26(2) requires the State to 'take reasonable legislative and other measures, within available resources, to achieve the progressive realisation of this right'. Section 26(3) deals with evictions, providing that '[N]o one may be evicted from their home or have their home demolished without an order of the court made after considering all the relevant circumstances'. Section 28(1)(c) gives every child an immediately realizable right to shelter. These should be read together with the right to property in section 25(1), which states: 'No one may be deprived of property except in terms of law of general application, and no law may permit arbitrary deprivation of property'.

The right to housing in South Africa comes in the context of a severe housing shortage owing to the policies of the previous apartheid government, which strictly controlled the numbers of black people allowed to live in the cities. As Sachs J put it, apartheid was institutionalized by 'a cluster of statutes that gave a legal/administrative imprimatur to the usurpation and forced removal of black people from land and compelled them to live in racially designated locations'.[41] The grand scheme of apartheid was to strip all black South Africans of South African citizenship, and create separate 'countries', fragmented and impoverished bits of land, which would be the only parts of South Africa in which they could own land. The law was premised on the principle that Africans should live in rural reserves and come to the cities only as temporary migrant workers.[42] Those who were permitted to live in the cities were subject to the Group Areas Act, which rigidly segregated residential areas. Black people were required to live in 'townships' adjacent to the cities without rights to buy property or conduct businesses. In the Western Cape, there were further restrictions under the so-called 'coloured labour preference policy', which gave coloured people preference over black Africans in access to employment and residence in the Western Cape. This

[40] *Social and Economic Rights Action Centre (SERAC) and Another v Nigeria* (n 36) para [61].

[41] *Port Elizabeth Municipality v Various Occupiers* (n 7) para [9]. [42] ibid.

meant that no family housing for African people was built in the Western Cape over several decades.

When apartheid ended, people flooded to the urban areas in search of jobs, leaving the new government with an enormous inherited housing deficit and a growing flood of people needing housing. The newly elected democratic government was committed to alleviating the housing shortage. However, although the number of formal houses increased by 5 million between 1996 and 2009, there was still a shortage of as many as 2 million, and in 2010 almost a quarter of the population was living in informal housing. There has been some improvement: the urban population living in informal settlements decreased from 17 per cent in 2002 to 11 per cent in 2014. However, the same period saw only a very slight decrease in the percentage of households living in informal dwellings, from 13.6 per cent to 13.1 per cent. This is due to an increase in households living in informal dwellings in the backyards of other dwelling types.[43] Moreover, the improved percentage of households living in formal dwellings does not signal progress for all households. Statistics show that as many as 18.1 per cent of households were living in informal housing in 2013 but had been in formal dwellings five years earlier. This could be due to a deterioration in their socio-economic conditions, migration, or a move from living with parents previously.[44]

It was in this context that the first major housing case, *Grootboom*, was decided.[45] The case concerned a group of 510 children and 390 adults who had previously lived in abysmal conditions in Wallacedene, an informal housing settlement in the eastern suburbs of Cape Town. They were living in desperately overcrowded shacks, constructed on land which was partially waterlogged, dangerously close to a main thoroughfare, and without water, sewage, or refuse removal services. They had been on the waiting list for formal housing for seven years. Attempting to escape from these intolerable conditions, they moved onto nearby private land, but were forcibly evicted by the owner and many of their possessions destroyed. Having nowhere else to go, they took shelter on the Wallacedene sports field. Here conditions were unspeakably bad, particularly since the winter rains had begun. They applied to the Court under the right to housing in section 26 of the Constitution, as well as the right of children to shelter under section 28.

Like his counterparts in India and Europe, Yacoob J, giving the judgment of the Court, stressed that the foundational values of human dignity, freedom, and equality are denied those with no food, clothing, or shelter.[46] Nevertheless, as we saw in Chapter 3, he declined to hold that the right to housing had a 'minimum core', which the State must use all the resources available to it to achieve.[47] The real question was not what the content of the right in section 26(1) was, but whether the duty in section 26(2) had been discharged. In other words, were the measures taken by the State to realize the right reasonable? This standard was not, however, left entirely open-ended. To discharge its duty to take reasonable measures to provide access to housing, the State must have a plan to produce housing. To be reasonable, such a plan

[43] Statistics South Africa (n 9). [44] ibid, para 9.6.

[45] *Republic of South Africa v Grootboom* 2001 (1) SA 46 (South African Constitutional Court).

[46] ibid, para [23]. [47] ibid, paras [32]–[33].

should clearly allocate responsibilities as between different tiers of government and should ensure that the appropriate financial and human resources are available.[48] It should be balanced and flexible and make appropriate provision for crises, as well as for needs which are short-, medium-, and long-term.[49] Nor is it sufficient to formulate a plan: it must also be reasonably implemented.[50] National and provincial government should ensure that duties imposed on the executive by housing legislation are met.[51] Moreover, the right should be progressively realized, so that housing is made available over time to a larger number and wider range of people.[52] It should respond with care and concern to the needs of the most desperate. On the other hand, the State is not required to do more than available resources permit.[53] Nor would the Court reject a plan on the ground that the Court thought that there were better or more desirable means to meet this obligation. The precise content of the plan is for the State to determine so long as it is reasonable.

Having examined the measures taken by the State, the court concluded that the programme being executed was a major achievement. Nevertheless, it was not sufficiently responsive to those in desperate need. This was particularly so in the light of the fact that proper housing would not be available for the immediate future. The Court therefore held that the State had fallen below the standard of reasonableness in failing to provide for those in desperate need. At the same time, responding to those most in need did not mean that Irene Grootboom was herself entitled to a house immediately. Recognition of the immediate needs of desperate people required the government to plan, budget, and fulfil these needs. It also required a significant number of desperate people in need in fact to be afforded relief. However, not all of them received it immediately.[54]

Why then was the Court unwilling to grant individual relief? The case reveals a pervasive theme of the Court's socio-economic rights jurisprudence: the concern that providing relief to the litigant before the Court would be unfair to the hundreds of thousands of others in the same position. Yacoob J stated that he was acutely aware of the 'painful reality' that the circumstances of the respondents were no different from those of thousands of other people at Wallacedene, and that it would be wrong to provide any 'special dispensation' for those who had moved onto private land.[55] Albeit particularly desperate, the situation of the respondents was typical of many people in the Cape area and indeed in South Africa as a whole. The Court noted that the number of shacks in the Cape Metro area had increased by 111 per cent in three years and continued to increase by a further 21 per cent. Although 22,000 houses were built each year, demand was growing by about 20,000 so that the backlog could only be reduced by 2,000 each year.[56] It was this which, as we saw in Chapter 8 in the *Soobramoney* case, tempered the Court's approach. Yacoob J was very keen to give the message that neither queue-jumping nor land invasion should be encouraged by litigation under section 26. As he put it:

48 ibid, para [39].
49 ibid, para [43].
50 ibid, para [42].
51 ibid, para [40].
52 ibid, para [45].
53 ibid, para [46].
54 ibid, para [68].
55 ibid, para [81].
56 ibid, para [58].

> This judgment must not be understood as approving any practice of land invasion for the purpose of coercing a state structure into providing housing on a preferential basis ... Land invasion is inimical to the systematic provision of adequate housing on a planned basis.[57]

Thus, the Court held that neither section 26 nor 28 entitled the respondents to claim shelter or housing immediately on demand.[58] The State's obligation, instead, was to devise, fund, implement, and supervise measures to provide relief for those in desperate need.

The South African provisions can be compared to Article 11 of the ICESCR, which recognizes 'the right of everyone to an adequate standard of living for himself and his family, including adequate food, clothing and housing, and to the continuous improvement of living conditions'.[59] Article 11 requires States Parties to take appropriate steps to ensure the realization of this right. This is in addition to the general provision in Article 2 of the Covenant, which states that each State Party to the present Covenant undertakes to 'take steps, individually and through international assistance and co-operation, especially economic and technical, to the maximum of its available resources, with a view to achieving progressively the full realization of the rights recognized in the present Covenant by all appropriate means, including particularly the adoption of legislative measures'. The South African Constitutional Court in *Grootboom* was keen to point to relevant differences between the South African provision and Article 11 ICESCR. While the Covenant provides a right to adequate housing, the South African Constitution provides a right of *access* to adequate housing. For Yacoob J, the emphasis on access recognized that housing entails more than bricks and mortar, but includes available land, provision of services, and financing. In addition, the focus on access means that it is not only the State which is responsible for providing housing: instead, the State's role is to provide access, whether though facilitating financing, providing subsidies, assisting self-help provision, or actually building houses.[60]

In reality, Article 11 ICESCR has also been understood in a broader sense than bricks and mortar; and indeed, as in the Indian, European and South African jurisdictions, has been rooted in a value-laden approach. In its General Comment on the Right to Housing in 1991, the Committee emphasized that

> the right to housing should not be interpreted in a narrow or restrictive sense which equates it with, for example, the shelter provided by merely having a roof over one's head or views shelter exclusively as a commodity. Rather, it should be seen as the right to live somewhere in security, peace and dignity ... 'The inherent dignity of the human person' from which the rights in the Covenant are said to derive requires that the term 'housing' be interpreted so as to take account of a variety of other considerations, most importantly that the right to housing should be ensured to all persons irrespective of income or access to economic resources.[61]

[57] ibid, para [92]. [58] ibid, para [95].

[59] On the CESCR's rebuttal of the gendered assumptions in this right, see section V below (right to equality) and CESCR General Comment No 4: The Right to Adequate Housing (Art 11 (1) of the Covenant) (1991) UN Doc E/1992/23, para 6.

[60] *Republic of South Africa v Grootboom* (n 45) paras [36]–[37].

[61] CESCR General Comment No 4 (n 59) para 7.

This is fortified by the reference to adequate housing: 'Adequate shelter means ... adequate privacy, adequate space, adequate security, adequate lighting and ventilation, adequate basic infrastructure and adequate location with regard to work and basic facilities—all at a reasonable cost'.[62] Like the South African Constitutional Court, the Committee states that, while there are many appropriate means of realizing the right, this will invariably require the adoption of a national housing strategy, allocating responsibility and budget, and setting a timetable.[63] Such a plan should reflect extensive genuine consultation with all those affected.

The role of the minimum core is more controversial. In its earlier General Comment No 3, the Committee took the view that every State Party has a prima facie duty to ensure the satisfaction of 'at the very least minimum essential levels of each of the rights'.[64] At the same time, the Committee made it clear that resource constraints must be accounted for. 'In order for a State party to be able to attribute its failure to meet at least its minimum core obligations to a lack of available resources it must demonstrate that every effort has been made to use all resources at its disposition to satisfy these minimum obligations as a matter of priority'.[65] While its later General Comment No 4 on the Right to Adequate Housing elaborates the criteria for 'adequacy', it does not mention the minimum core or specify its content. Instead, it refers to steps to be taken immediately, regardless of the state of development of any country. Many measures would only require the government to refrain from interfering with certain practices and to make a commitment to facilitating self-help by affected groups. In addition, steps should immediately be taken to request international co-operation if more resources are needed for this. States should also give due priority to those social groups living in unfavourable conditions 'by giving them particular consideration'.[66] Effective monitoring, such as data collection, is an obligation of immediate effect. Ultimately, then, the approach of the international body is very similar to that of the South African Constitutional Court.

III. Conflicting Pressures: Rights to a Home versus Rights to Property

In practice, litigation about housing almost always arises in the context of eviction. This reflects the fundamental conflict generated by the right to housing with the more traditional right to property. The instinctive priority that the common law accords to property rights is challenged by the recognition of a right not to be arbitrarily deprived of a home. A frankly value-laden approach is required to change that balance. As Sachs J in *Port Elizabeth Municipality* stated, the protection against eviction in the South African Constitution

> evinces special constitutional regard for a person's place of abode. It acknowledges that a home is more than just a shelter from the elements. It is a zone of personal intimacy and family security. Often it will be the only relatively secure space of privacy

[62] ibid, para 7. [63] ibid, para 12.
[64] CESCR General Comment No 3: The Nature of States Parties' Obligations (Art. 2, Para. 1 of the Covenant) (1990) UN Doc E/1991/23, para 10.
[65] ibid. [66] CESCR General Comment No 4 (n 59) para 11.

> and tranquility in what (for poor people in particular) is a turbulent and hostile world.[67]

Moreover, as the CESCR General Comment on Forced Evictions emphasizes, forced evictions may also result in violations of civil and political rights, such as the right to life; the right to security of the person; the right to non-interference with privacy, family, and home; and the right to the peaceful enjoyment of possessions.[68]

However, the resolution of these conflicts is not straightforward. As Sachs J put it, the Constitution

> counterpoises to the normal ownership rights of possession, use and occupation a new and equally relevant right not arbitrarily to be deprived of a home. The expectations that ordinarily go with title could clash head-on with the genuine despair of people in dire need of accommodation. The judicial function in these circumstances is not to establish a hierarchical arrangement between the different interests involved, privileging in an abstract and mechanical way the rights of ownership over the right not to be dispossessed of a home, or vice versa.[69]

These conflicts arise in different constellations, depending on whether the land is public or private, vacant or earmarked for other use, such as urban development or for low-cost housing itself. In India, the cases have concerned pavement-dwellers, whose hutments are said to obstruct the right of way of pedestrians; while in Canada, homeless people have built shelters on public park land, allegedly obstructing the right of the public to leisure.[70] In South Africa, there is now widespread occupation of derelict inner-city buildings, left to decay by their owners due to inner-city blight. Here the conflict is more complex, since the state of the buildings often leads to health-and-safety risks for the occupiers themselves. The conflict can also manifest itself in relation to financial interests in the home, particularly between lenders and mortgage holders, or where property is used as a guarantee against other kinds of debt. These conflicts were exacerbated as a result of the massive collapse of the property market triggered by highly problematic lending practices by banks, in the form of sub-prime mortgages and similar devices. This led to large numbers of people losing their homes through foreclosure by banks and other lending institutions when the former became unable to keep to their repayment schedules. The ways in which courts have attempted to reconcile these tensions is elaborated below.

A. From substance to procedure?

Perhaps the most common way of navigating these deep-seated tensions is to stress procedural protections. Procedural requirements allow courts to appear to afford some semblance of dignity to those whose evictions are being sanctioned at the same

[67] *Port Elizabeth Municipality v Various Occupiers* (n 7) para [17].

[68] CESCR General Comment No 7: The Right to Adequate Housing (Art.11.1): Forced Evictions (1997) UN Doc E/1998/22, para 4.

[69] *Port Elizabeth Municipality v Various Occupiers* (n 7) para [23].

[70] *Olga Tellis and Others v Bombay Municipal Corporation* (n 22); *Ahmedabad Municipal Corporation v Nawab Khan Bulab Khan* (n 21); *Victoria (City) v Adams*, 2009 BCCA 563 (Court of Appeal for British Columbia).

time as protecting property rights. This is strikingly illustrated in the Indian cases. As we have seen, *Olga Tellis* and *Ahmedabad* concerned informal dwellings erected on pavements and public walkways, used both for living and conducting small businesses such as hawking. The Indian Supreme Court in both cases was keen to assert the right of the public to use the pavements unimpeded. The vivid declarations of the right to life and livelihood for the pavement-dwellers were therefore tempered by an assertion of the conflicting needs of other members of the public. The obvious reconciliation is to require the State to provide decent housing for pavement-dwellers, obviating the need to obstruct public rights of way. However, the Indian Supreme Court has tended instead to stress procedural protections. This is based to some extent on the wording of Article 21, which, as will be recalled, states that 'no person shall be deprived of his life or liberty except according to procedure established by law'. Thus, in *Olga Tellis*, the Court declared that the pavement-dwellers should not be removed until they had been properly consulted. In *Ahmedabad*, the Court, while reiterating the right to shelter, also emphasized that it was legitimate for the municipality to keep the pavements clear of hutments:

> The Constitution does not put an absolute embargo on the deprivation of life or personal liberty but such a deprivation must be according to the procedure, in the given circumstances, fair and reasonable. To become fair, just and reasonable, it would not be enough that the procedure prescribed in law is a formality. It must be a pragmatic and realistic one to meet the given fact-situation.[71]

A more formalized procedure requires a proper hearing before a court or tribunal to sanction eviction. This has been central to the protection offered by the ECtHR in cases under the right to respect for home, private, and family life in Article 8 ECHR. Thus, in *Cosic v Croatia*, the ECtHR stressed that the loss of one's home is the most extreme form of interference with the right to respect for the home. It went on to hold, however, that it was the absence of adequate procedural safeguards which constituted the violation. 'Any person at risk of an interference of this magnitude should in principle be able to have the proportionality and reasonableness of the measure determined by an independent tribunal'.[72] Even if the aim is legitimate—owners are not obliged to tolerate unlawful occupation—an eviction without procedural safeguards may not be regarded as necessary to achieve that aim. In *Connors*, the Court held that the eviction of a family of gypsies from a gypsy site by a local authority in the UK was a violation of their rights under Article 8: 'While a legitimate aim was being pursued by the local authority, the eviction of the applicant and his family could not be regarded as necessary in pursuit of that aim as it was not attended by procedural safeguards that would enable the applicant to challenge the factual basis on which the local authority decided to serve the notice'.[73] Similarly, the crucial change introduced in the South African Constitution was to expressly prevent evictions without an order of the Court made after considering all the relevant circumstances.[74]

[71] *Ahmedabad Municipal Corporation v Nawab Khan Bulab Khan* (n 21).
[72] *Cosic v Croatia* (n 31) para [22].
[73] *Connors v UK* (n 29).
[74] South African Constitution, s 26(3).

Can it then be said that procedural protections foster deliberative democracy by enhancing participation? Or are they simply gestures to legitimate evictions? Procedural protections were framed in *Olga Tellis* as having both intrinsic and instrumental value. Their intrinsic value consisted in giving individuals the right to participate in the process by which decisions affecting them are made, 'an opportunity that expresses their dignity as persons'. This value was entirely independent of the right to secure a different outcome. The instrumental value, on the other hand, consisted in giving individuals the means to ensure that the public rules of conduct were in fact accurately and consistently followed.[75] We could go further and insist that its aim is to give those who are affected a voice in the decision-making.[76] Participation in political decision-making is generally illusory for those who are most marginalized by absence of the most basic necessities of life, including housing and access to means of livelihood. Consultation gives them a voice and agency in determining their own lives. It is also likely to produce more durable and effective solutions, partly because the parties involved have closer knowledge of their needs and the parameters for action than judges, and partly because the parties should then feel a sense of ownership of the outcome and willingness to act on it.[77]

Whether it achieves these aims, however, depends on the content of the procedure. It is all too easy to go through the motions of consulting without genuinely involving others in decision-making. Many procedures simply require notice to be given of eviction. But more is required if procedures are to have a real participative value. The amount of information imparted clearly affects how meaningful such consultation can be. Timing is also crucial: should the engagement take place before the eviction decision is made, or is subsequent engagement sufficient? If subsequent, then the actual eviction is not affected, leaving only the details to be discussed and the nature of alternatives. Thus, to be meaningful, consultation should take place in time to have an influence on the outcome, and those involved should have sufficient information to make an appropriate input. In addition, all those affected should be incorporated, as well as all those with the power to make decisions. Importantly, decision-makers should be genuinely open to the views of the participants.[78]

In *Olga Tellis* itself, the Indian Supreme Court declared that the slum-dwellers should not be removed until they had been properly consulted. This went some of the way to recognizing that without the active participation of those affected, no solution would be either legitimate or effective. However, the Court did not put in place any of the elements to ensure that such participation could give an effective voice to the pavement-dwellers. In *Ahmedabad*, the procedural protections were in fact minimal: because of the strength the Court accorded to the right of pedestrians to use pavements, it regarded a notice of ten days to two weeks as sufficient in situations in

[75] *Olga Tellis and Others v Bombay Municipal Corporation* (n 22) paras [90]–[91].

[76] Fredman (n 5).

[77] *Schubart Park v City of Tshwane* [2012] ZACC 26 (South African Constitutional Court) para [44].

[78] 'Basic Principles and Guidelines on Development-based Evictions and Displacement', Annex 1 of the *Report of the Special Rapporteur on Adequate Housing as a Component of the Right to an Adequate Standard of Living* UN Doc A/HRC/4/18, paras 38–40.

which the pavement-dwellers had been left undisturbed for a relatively long time. For more short-term dwellers, notice could be much shorter, or even unnecessary.

This can be compared to the evolution of procedural protections in South Africa. As we have seen, section 26(3) prevents evictions without an order of court, further specified in the Prevention of Illegal Eviction from and Unlawful Occupation of Land Act 19 of 1998 or PIE. Sachs J, in the *Port Elizabeth Municipality*[79] case, strongly endorsed the need for proper discussion and, where appropriate, mediation.[80] In particular, he stressed the need to regard occupiers as agents, whose resourcefulness in finding a place for themselves and their families should be harnessed to work out alternative solutions with the landowner.[81]

This approach was developed in a more sophisticated form in *Occupiers of 51 Olivia Rd* in 2008.[82] In this case, more than 400 occupiers of two dilapidated buildings in central Johannesburg challenged the City's attempts to evict them on the grounds of health and safety. This was only the tip of the iceberg: it was suggested that as many as 67,000 people were living in unsafe and unhealthy buildings in Johannesburg. The occupiers argued that the City had a positive duty to provide appropriate alternative housing. On its own initiative, the Court issued an interim order,[83] which required the parties to 'engage with each other meaningfully … and in the light of the values of the Constitution, the constitutional and statutory duties of the municipality and the duties of citizens concerned' to resolve the dispute. It also required the parties to engage with each other in an effort to alleviate the plight of the applicants in the buildings concerned 'by making the buildings as safe and conducive to health as is reasonably practicable'. The parties were given a period of time to report on the results of the engagement, and the resulting agreement was in due course endorsed by the Court.

In giving its reasons for such an approach, the Court fleshed out the principle of meaningful engagement and its aims. It characterized engagement as a two-way process which had the potential to contribute towards resolving disputes through increased understanding and sympathy.[84] There was no closed list of the objectives of engagement: they might include engagement as to what the consequences of the eviction might be; whether the city could help in alleviating those dire consequences; whether it is possible to render the buildings concerned relatively safe and conducive to health for an interim period; whether the city has any obligations to the occupiers in the prevailing circumstances; and when and how the city could or would fulfil these obligations. The process should take into account the vulnerable situation of people about to be evicted. Importantly, the fact that large numbers of people were affected only enhanced the need for structured, consistent, and careful engagement.[85] On the other hand, as long as the response of the municipality was reasonable, it

[79] *Port Elizabeth Municipality v Various Occupiers* (n 7).

[80] ibid, para [43].

[81] ibid, para [41].

[82] *Occupiers of 51 Olivia Road v City of Johannesburg* Case CCT 24/07 [2008] ZACC 1 (South African Constitutional Court).

[83] *Occupiers of 51 Olivia Road v City of Johannesburg* Case No CCT 24/07 Interim Order dated 30 August 2007.

[84] *Occupiers of 51 Olivia Road v City of Johannesburg* (n 82) para [15].

[85] ibid, para [19].

complied with this duty. This did not necessarily mean that housing had to be provided: according to Yacoob J, it may in some circumstances be reasonable to provide no housing at all.[86]

The principle of meaningful engagement has great potential to empower occupiers facing eviction and to significantly influence State decision-making in eviction proceedings. However, there is always the risk that it becomes a mere gesture, legitimating uncomfortable substantive outcomes. Particularly problematic is the possibility of a 'futility' argument or, in other words, a claim that the absence of proper procedure has not affected the outcome, or that it could be cured by subsequent consultation. This would permit the ends to justify the means, and undermine the intrinsic value, identified in *Olga Tellis*, of affording agency and dignity. In any event, it is problematic to assume that it is ever possible to predict that procedure properly followed would not have changed the outcome.

These issues arose in the subsequent *Joe Slovo* case, which involved the redevelopment of a huge informal settlement close to Cape Town.[87] Developers applied to court for an order for the eviction of almost 20,000 residents of the settlement to make way for low-cost housing development. The plan was to relocate residents to an area known as Delft, 15 km away. As in so many other cases, the residents preferred to endure the 'deplorable' conditions in the informal settlement rather than accept relocation to an area further from their sources of livelihood. The Court ordered the eviction. This was despite the fact that at least three of the judgments held that there had not been meaningful engagement.[88] Instead, the Court required detailed engagement over the process of moving as well as imposing minimum standards on the alternative accommodation to be provided.[89] There was a strong suggestion of the futility argument in O'Regan J's judgment:

> The question we have to ask in this case is whether the failure to have a coherent and meaningful strategy of engagement renders the implementation of the plan unreasonable to the extent that the respondents have failed to establish a right to evict the occupiers. On balance, I think not.[90]

She gave several reasons for this, including that there had been some consultation, although the respondents admitted that it had not been coherent or comprehensive, and at times had even been misleading. She also stressed that it would be against the interests of the many people waiting for the houses to be built to delay the project. In addition, she took the view that the failure of the government to engage meaningfully thus far could at least to some extent be remedied by the court order to engage in relation to

[86] ibid, para [18].

[87] *Residents of Joe Slovo Community v Thubelisha Homes* Case CCT 22/08 [2009] ZACC 16 (South African Constitutional Court).

[88] Moseneke DCJ, O'Regan J, and Sachs J in *Residents of Joe Slovo Community v Thubelisha Homes*, ibid, paras [167], [301], and [384].

[89] It also imposed an obligation on the respondents to set aside at least 70 per cent of the new homes to be built on the sight of the Joe Slovo informal settlement to be allocated to current or very recent residents.

[90] *Residents of Joe Slovo Community v Thubelisha Homes* (n 87) para [302].

implementation of the eviction order.[91] The result was, in Liebenberg's words, to open the way for 'the largest judicially sanctioned eviction in post-apartheid South Africa'.[92]

In the event, it was decided not to go ahead with the relocation because the relevant minister had grave concerns that the massive relocation would cost more than the scheme to upgrade the existing settlement. The Court was therefore asked to suspend the evictions until further notice.[93] This suggests that genuine engagement before the decision has been taken might be essential for orderly and effective decision-making, rather than simply constituting a burden on the State, as O'Regan J's judgment seems to hint. By failing to involve beneficiaries as participants, the huge project ignored issues which were essential to the latter. There was little understanding of the interconnected livelihood strategies by which poor communities survive, which crucially rely on resources available within their settlements. These sources of livelihood would be lost to residents on relocation to Delft. In addition, the social housing units planned for the settlement were aimed at families who earned above the level of income of many of those affected. They were therefore unable to benefit from this project.[94] In any event, Delft was simply too far away, even with the provision of transport.[95]

The role of meaningful engagement has to some extent been shored up in later cases. A series of cases challenged legislation which gave provincial authorities the power to require private landowners to apply to court to evict unlawful occupiers. This was struck down as unconstitutional because it sidestepped the protections in section 26, and particularly the duty to engage.[96] Meaningful engagement has also been helpful to occupiers in their response to threats of evictions, even without resorting to courts. It is therefore important that courts are not tempted to dilute the duty.

Evictions pursuant to mortgage foreclosure are a further area in which protection for the right to housing has manifested in the form of procedural protections. Mortgage financing has traditionally targeted the more affluent segments of society. However, during the 1990s and 2000s, new 'creative' mortgage products were designed specifically for borrowers with low income or a poor credit history. This market ballooned during this period, with credit increasingly awarded to households which would not in normal circumstances be eligible for loans. This generated what have come to be called 'sub-prime' loans. However, as Rolnick and Rabinovich point out, these products introduced subtle but highly discriminatory elements, which worsened the situation of the poor.[97] Since the latter, being lower income, were considered

91 ibid, paras [302]–[303].

92 Sandra Liebenberg, 'Joe Slovo eviction: Vulnerable community feels the law from the top down' <https://docs.escr-net.org/usr_doc/Liebenberg_-_Joe_Slovo_eviction-_Vulnerable_community_feels_the_law_from_the_top_down.pdf> (accessed 1 March 2018).

93 K McLean, 'Meaningful Engagement: One Step Forward or Two Back? Some Thoughts on Joe Slovo' (2010) 3 Constitutional Court Review 223, 232.

94 ibid.

95 Centre on Housing Rights and Evictions, *N2 Gateway Project: Housing Rights Violations as 'Development' in South Africa* (COHRE 2009) 12.

96 *Schubart Park v City of Tshwane* (n 77) para [50]; *Abahlali baseMjondolo v Premier of the Province of KwaZulu-Natal* [2009] ZACC 31 (South African Constitutional Court) paras [69], [114], and [120].

97 R Rolnik and L Rabinovich, 'Late-Neoliberalism: The Financialisation of Home Ownership and the Housing Rights of the Poor' in A Nolan (ed), *Economic and Social Rights after the Global Financial Crisis* (CUP 2014) 69–71.

high-risk borrowers, they were charged higher interest rates than lower-risk borrowers, meaning that mortgages became significantly more expensive for low-income groups. In addition, outright predatory lending policies were used, entailing loans which were even more expensive than the risk profile of a disadvantaged borrower warranted. The increased availability of credit also led to higher house prices: an International Monetary Fund (IMF) analysis from 2011 showed that a 10 per cent increase in household credit is associated on average with about a 6 per cent increase in housing prices.[98] Since much of the credit was financed through global capital markets in increasingly complex ways, national housing markets became overexposed to volatile global finance. This in turn precipitated the US sub-prime mortgage crisis in 2008, and the subsequent spread of the financial crisis globally. The crisis led to spiralling payment default, followed by foreclosures and homelessness, facilitated by legal adjustments simplifying foreclosure.[99] According to Rolnick and Rabinovich, 'the sub-prime and financial crises have disproportionately affected the poorest and most vulnerable, who were the last to join the mortgage markets and the first to suffer the consequences of the crises owing to their low resilience to economic shocks and low repayment abilities'.[100]

It was in this context that a test case was brought under the newly adopted individual communication protocol to the ICESCR. The communication concerned the process of foreclosure in Spain, which had witnessed 350,000 foreclosures between 2007 and 2011, and where 212 foreclosures and 159 evictions were occurring daily in 2011.[101] The author of the communication discovered that her property was being put up for auction after she missed several mortgage repayments (about 11,000 euros), having fallen on difficult times due to the serious economic crisis in Spain and her own personal circumstances.[102] The lending institution used the acceleration clause in the mortgage to call in the full amount of the loan and applied to court under a special mortgage procedure. The relevant court attempted to notify the author of the proceedings on four occasions, but the author was not at home, and no written notification was left at the address. Instead, the court posted the notification on the court notice board, to complete the notification process. It was only once the auction proceedings had been approved unopposed that she received notice of the auction of her home.

The author of the complaint argued that her right to adequate housing under Article 11.1 ICESCR had been violated. She argued that the failure to notify her of the proceedings meant that she had no opportunity to challenge the unfair nature of the terms of the mortgage contract or the way the lending institution calculated the interest. Her case was supported by the International Network for Economic, Social and Cultural Rights, which argued that the Spanish legal framework continued to favour financial institutions over the interest of the persons concerned.

[98] IMF, 'Global Financial Stability Report (2011)', 134 <https://www.imf.org/en/Publications/GFSR/Issues/2016/12/31/Global-Financial-Stability-Report-April-2011-Durable-Financial-Stability-Getting-There-from-24324> (accessed 1 March 2018).

[99] Rolnik and Rabinovich (n 97) 70. [100] ibid. [101] ibid.

[102] *IDG v Spain*, Committee on Economic, Social and Cultural Rights Communication No 2/2014 (adopted June 2015) UN Doc E/C.12/55/D/2/2014.

Where borrowers fail to defend themselves, for whatever reason, there should be strict judicial oversight to ensure that the terms of the foreclosure are fair.

In its decision, the Committee stressed that in the context of procedures that might affect security of tenure, procedures must guarantee, among other things, a real opportunity for consultation with those affected and adequate and reasonable notice prior to the scheduled date of eviction.[103] Insufficient notice of an application for mortgage enforcement, which prevented the person defending their rights in that procedure, therefore violated the right to housing. In the case at hand, the notification was inadequate: although several attempts had been made to serve it in person, no written notice was left in the letterbox or with the caretaker. In an important rebuttal of the futility argument, the Committee also rejected the State's argument that failure to notify was of little consequence in foreclosure proceedings, since the debtor's rights in defence are in any event legally very limited. The State had argued that the debtor had recourse to an ordinary procedure whereby they could mount unlimited defences and even challenge the validity of the mortgage contract. However, the Committee held that this was not a sufficient substitute as the eviction process was not capable of being suspended pending the determination of an ordinary challenge.

While the insistence on proper notification is crucial, the focus on procedure is still an incomplete approach to the right to housing. Even with notification, the debtor might have little success in protecting herself against unfair mortgage terms or excessive interest rates. A more substantive approach would insist on the right to challenge these terms themselves. This has been made possible by a case before the Court of Justice of the European Union (CJEU), which held that the Spanish authorities should give proper protection against unfair contractual terms.[104] The case was brought under EU law provisions requiring Member States to provide that unfair contract terms should not be binding. A term is regarded as unfair if it causes a significant imbalance in the parties' rights and obligations, to the detriment of the consumer, and applies particularly to standard-form contracts.[105] The case was brought by Mr Aziz, whose home was repossessed after he defaulted on his mortgage payments. He argued that the terms of the mortgage were unfair, providing for excessive default interest and giving the lender the right both to call in the mortgage after a relatively short amount of time and to unilaterally quantify the amount due. The CJEU held that Spanish law should permit a challenge to the unfairness of the mortgage before repossession is ordered. It also held that the court's examination should include an assessment of whether the contract places the consumer in a less favourable legal situation, having regard to the means at her disposal to prevent continued use of unfair terms.[106]

Particularly invidious are provisions which permit the sale in execution of people's homes because they have not paid other debts, not specifically secured through their

[103] ibid, para [11.2] referring to CESCR General Comment No 7 (n 68).

[104] Case C-415/11 *Mohamed Aziz v Caixa d'Estalvis de Catalunya, Tarragona i Manresa (Catalunyacaixa)* [2013] 3 CMLR 5 (CJEU).

[105] Council Directive 93/13/EEC of 5 April 1993 on unfair terms in consumer contracts.

[106] *Mohamed Aziz v Caixa d'Estalvis de Catalunya, Tarragona i Manresa (Catalunyacaixa)* (n 104).

property, especially where those debts are small. This was the situation under South African provisions which allowed the sale in execution of property in order to satisfy a debt.[107] These provisions were regularly used to attach houses of extremely poor people in satisfaction of relatively small debts. They were challenged in *Jaftha v Schoeman*[108] as a breach of the right of access to housing in section 26 of the Constitution. Ms Jaftha, a poor woman who suffered from ill health, had borrowed the small sum of R250 in 1998, which she repaid in part, only to find that proceedings had been mounted against her for a rapidly increasing sum, including interest and costs. The creditor subsequently attached her meagre property, which she had bought with the aid of public housing subsidies. She was forced to vacate the house, following its sale in execution of the debt.[109] The consequences were dire, in that a recipient of state-subsidized housing was barred from receiving such assistance in the future if she lost a house pursuant to a sale in execution.

The South African Constitutional Court held that the provision allowing property to be attached in these circumstances constituted a violation of section 26. Mokgoro J drew on CESCR General Comment No 4 to make it clear that security of tenure was an aspect of adequacy.[110] Although it was not necessary to delineate adequacy in full, 'at the very least, any measure which permits a person to be deprived of existing access to adequate housing, limits the rights protected in section 26(1)'.[111] She also stressed that although section 26(1) might not give rise to an independent positive right, it did include a negative obligation on the State. This was immediately realizable as it did not involve State resources and was not subject to progressive realization.

Having found a violation, the Court unusually went on to consider whether the limitation on the right could be justified. Section 36 of the Constitution permits limitations only to the extent that it is 'reasonable and justifiable in an open and democratic society based on human dignity, equality and freedom'. Mokgoro J concluded that 'it is difficult to see how the collection of trifling debts in this case can be sufficiently compelling to allow existing access to adequate housing to be totally eradicated, possibly permanently, especially where other methods exist to enable recovery of the debt'.[112] She therefore held that the provision in question was unconstitutional to the extent that it allows for sales in execution in unjustifiable circumstances and without judicial intervention.[113] The remedy was again to insist on a judicial role, based on substantive criteria. The provision should be read as including a requirement that execution could only be ordered by a court after considering all relevant circumstances, including the size of the debt, the circumstances in which the debt arose, and the availability of alternatives which do not involve attachment of a person's home.[114]

The South African Constitutional Court extended this principle to mortgages in the more recent case of *Gundwana*,[115] where the facts were remarkably similar to the Spanish case before the CESCR. Elsie Gundwana took out a mortgage of R25,000 on a house worth R52,000. When she fell behind in some of her payments, eight years later,

[107] South African Magistrates' Courts Act 32 of 1944, ss 66(1)(a) and 67.
[108] *Jaftha v Schoeman* (2005) 2 SA 140 (South African Constitutional Court).
[109] ibid, para [4]. [110] ibid, para [24]. [111] ibid, para [34]. [112] ibid, para [44].
[113] ibid, paras [48]–[49]. [114] ibid, paras [54]–[60].
[115] *Gundwana v Steko Development CC* (2011) 3 SA 608 (South African Constitutional Court).

the lender invoked the acceleration clause of her loan agreement and demanded the full amount owed immediately. With interest and fees, this was calculated at R33,500, which was well above anything she could afford. She nevertheless borrowed R15,000 to pay off some of her arears. However, without notifying her, the lender had already obtained a court order, granting permission to sell her house in satisfaction of her debt. Meanwhile, the lender continued to accept payments from her, amounting to a further R41,000, before selling the property four years later. She challenged the sale as a breach of her right to housing. Affidavits before the Court indicated that her case was a common one.

The South African Constitutional Court upheld her claim. Froneman J reiterated that '[w]here execution against the homes of indigent debtors who run the risk of losing their security of tenure is sought after judgment on a money debt, further judicial oversight by a court of law of the execution process is a must'.[116] The respondent argued that the case differed from *Jaftha* in that the debtor willingly provided her house as security for the debt. However, Froneman J made it clear that willingness to provide her house as security did not extend to acceptance that the mortgage debt might be enforced without court sanction. Nor did her consent extend to waiving her constitutional rights to have access to adequate housing and to protection against eviction without court sanction; nor that the mortgagee was entitled to enforce in bad faith. A judgment creditor is of course still entitled to execution against the assets of the judgment debtor. However,

> in allowing execution against immovable property, due regard should be taken of the impact that this may have on judgment debtors who are poor and at risk of losing their homes. If the judgment debt can be satisfied in a reasonable manner without involving those drastic consequences, that alternative course should be judicially considered before granting execution orders.[117]

Procedural protections have therefore played a major role in the elaboration by courts of the right to housing. Their value, however, depends heavily on the extent to which they genuinely facilitate participation, democratic engagement, and agency on the part of those in need of homes. Hohmann argues that the Indian experience demonstrates that judicial protection of process can be the focus of political mobilization.[118] For her, 'the availability of fair legal process can make space for the realisation of the right in a way that facilitates freedom, autonomy and participation, unlike a prescriptive interpretation of a substantive right'.[119] She shows that this has indeed provided significant de facto protection for pavement- and slum-dwellers in Mumbai and other Indian urban areas. However, this can only take place if there is an insistence on proper information, proper timing, and a genuine commitment by courts and the State to consider the substantive issues in the course of the procedure.

[116] ibid, para [41]. [117] ibid, para [53].
[118] J Hohmann, *The Right to Housing: Law, Concepts, Possibilities* (Bloomsbury 2013) 131.
[119] ibid.

B. From procedure to substance: the duty to provide

Fair procedures facilitating evictions do not, however, mean that the people evicted from these spaces simply evaporate. This raises the question of what duty falls on the State to provide alternative accommodation, what standards those alternatives should meet, and where they should be located. According to the CESCR General Comment No 7 on Forced Evictions, where people affected by an eviction are unable to provide for themselves, the government must take 'all appropriate measures, to the maximum available resources to ensure that adequate alternative housing, resettlement or access to productive land ... is available'.[120] The crucial linkage between the lawfulness of eviction and the requirement for alternative accommodation has compelled courts to examine the State's responsibility. This is true even in a jurisdiction like the ECHR, where the right to respect for home and family life appears on the surface to be most narrowly delineated. Thus, in the *Yordanova* case mentioned above,[121] the Court made it clear that simply evicting the community and rendering them homeless was not a proportionate means of achieving the aim of upgrading the urban environment. Crucially, the Court held that the authorities should have considered the wide range of available options in relation to eviction, including legalizing buildings where possible, constructing public sewage and water supply facilities, and providing assistance to find alternative housing where eviction is necessary.

The Indian Supreme Court in *Olga Tellis* acknowledged that there was no 'short-term or marginal solution to the question of squatter colonies'. Forcible eviction was no answer. The Court recognized that unless there are sources of livelihood elsewhere, people eventually return. It therefore ordered the government to make good its proposal that pavement-dwellers who had been part of a 1976 census should be given alternative pitches at a site which had been identified nearby. Slums which had been in existence for twenty years or more and had been improved and developed should not be removed unless the land was required for a public purpose, in which case alternative sites should be provided. In addition, the Court required the State government to implement its various programmes for low-income shelter and house-building for the economically weaker sections without delay. This included its programme of making available 85,000 small plots for construction, and upgrading slums with basic civic amenities, for which funding from the World Bank had been obtained. 'The profound rhetoric of socialism must be translated into practice for the problems which confront the State are problems of human destiny'.[122] Hohmann argues that the prescriptive nature of the Indian Supreme Court's order in this case should not be seen as an isolated judicial act of legislation. Instead it should be understood in the context of the political power of India's informal settlers, who represent an important source of votes in the city and see legal cases on the right to housing as only one prong in their wider campaign. The Court's order in effect legalized the results of complex negotiations.[123]

120 CESCR General Comment No 7 (n 68) para 16.

121 *Yordanova v Bulgaria* Application No 25446/06 (2012) (European Court of Human Rights).

122 *Olga Tellis and Others v Bombay Municipal Corporation* (n 22) para [98].

123 Hohmann (n 118) 114.

Similar powerful rhetoric was voiced in the *Ahmedabad* case. The Court referred not just to Article 21, the right to life, but also Article 19(e), which provides all citizens the fundamental right to reside in any part of India. It would be unconstitutional to prevent people from migrating and settling in places in which they find their livelihood. Yet, '[d]ue to want of facilities and opportunities, the right to residence and settlement is an illusion to the rural and urban poor'. The Court also brought into play the Directive Principles, Articles 38, 39, and 46, which mandate the State to minimize inequalities in income, opportunities, and status. 'Though no person has a right to encroach and erect structures or otherwise on footpaths, pavements or public streets or any other place reserved or earmarked for a public purpose, the State has the constitutional duty to provide adequate facilities and opportunities by distributing its wealth and resources for settlement of life and erection of shelter over their heads to make the right to life meaningful'. The Corporation was held to have a constitutional duty to implement these Directive Principles, and therefore to enforce the schemes identified in a planned manner through its annual budgets.

However, in both *Olga Tellis* and *Ahmadebad*, the Court was cautious about prescribing alternate accommodation. In *Olga Tellis*, it refused to insist that the alternative provision was a condition precedent to removals. In *Ahmedabad*, the Indian Supreme Court set aside the direction of the High Court to provide accommodation as a condition of removal of the encroachment. Although it held that each case should be examined on its facts, it stated: 'Normally, the court may not as a rule direct that the encroacher should be provided with an alternative'. It did hold that the financial condition of the corporation should not be a constraint which permitted it to avoid its duty to provide residence to the urban weaker sections. Nevertheless, it held that the Court could not direct the authority to implement a scheme with a particular budget, as this was the executive function of local authorities. In this case, the opportunity should be given to the ten named petitioners to opt for any one of the three named schemes. If they were eligible and satisfied the income criterion, they should be allocated a site or tenement. However, in a refrain familiar from the South African context, the Court emphasized that 'we are not giving any specific direction in this behalf lest it would amount to encouraging the people to abuse the judicial process to avail of such remedy by encroaching public property'.[124]

It is this last theme which has become increasingly powerful. By 1996, when cases were increasingly initiated by environmentalists and middle-class property owners, slum-dwellers were no longer characterized as rights-bearing citizens. In the waste-disposal case of *Almitra,*[125] initiated by a public-interest litigant committed to the improvement of the urban environment, the Court characterized the provision of alternative accommodation as rewarding wrongdoers. According to the Court:

> The promise of free land, at the taxpayers cost, in place of a jhuggi, is a proposal which attracts more land grabbers. Rewarding an encroacher on public land with a free alternate site is like giving a reward to a pickpocket.[126]

[124] *Olga Tellis and Others v Bombay Municipal Corporation* (n 22) para [586]; *Ahmedabad Municipal Corporation v Nawab Khan Bulab Khan* (n 21).

[125] *Almitra Patel v Union of India* (2000) 1 SCALE 568 (Indian Supreme Court).

[126] ibid.

The South African Constitutional Court has been similarly ambivalent. The Court has consistently expressed concern for the fundamental dignity and rights of occupiers. At the same time, a pervasive theme has been its desire to avoid encouraging land invasion as a means of jumping the queue and obtaining housing ahead of others who have waited for an equally long time and in equally miserable conditions. The PIE Act states that, where an unlawful occupier has occupied the land for more than six months, the availability of alternative accommodation is a factor which the court should pay regard to in determining whether to issue an eviction order.[127] However, in the *PE Municipality* case, Sachs J made it clear that this was not a mandatory prerequisite. Nevertheless, a court should be reluctant to allow an eviction of relatively settled occupiers unless a reasonable alternative is available, even as an interim measure.[128]

This raises the question of what might constitute reasonable alternative accommodation. In *Joe Slovo*, the Court sanctioned the proposed eviction of 20,000 people from the Joe Slovo informal settlement to Delft, 15 km away, on condition that the alternative housing provided met specified standards, as agreed by the parties.[129] However, just as in the Indian cases, the main problem with the removal to Delft was not so much the quality of housing, as the distance from sources of livelihood. Occupiers resisted the move because it would double the cost of their commuting, so that travel to work would eat up as much as half their meagre incomes.[130] The Court attempted to meet this concern by requiring the respondents to meaningfully engage with the occupiers about the provision of transport from the temporary accommodation to places of work. But unlike the Indian Supreme Court, which recognized that people will invariably return to areas close to their sources of livelihood, the South African Constitutional Court coupled these requirements with an interdict on the occupiers preventing them from returning to Joe Slovo to erect informal dwellings or taking residence therein.[131] As we have seen, the eviction order was subsequently discharged,[132] when the new provincial government decided instead to examine the possibility of upgrading the settlement *in situ*.[133] In the later case of *Abahlali*, the Court accepted that wherever possible, upgrading should be done *in situ*.[134]

One very difficult issue is how the cost of alternative housing should be spread between private landowners and the public sector. Where the land concerned is private land, one alternative is for the State to be required to purchase the land or compensate the landowner. This was the innovative solution used by the South African Constitutional Court in *Modderklip Boerdery*,[135] where an informal settlement on private land expanded very rapidly, swelling to about 40,000 people. An eviction order

[127] PIE, s 6(3). [128] *Port Elizabeth Municipality v Various Occupiers* (n 7) para [28].

[129] *Residents of Joe Slovo Community v Thubelisha Homes* (n 87) paras [118]–[121].

[130] S Wilson and J Dugard, 'Constitutional Jurisprudence: The First and Second Waves' in M Langford (ed), *Socio-Economic Rights in South Africa: Symbols or Substance?* (CUP 2013) 48.

[131] *Residents of Joe Slovo Community v Thubelisha Homes* (n 87) para [13].

[132] *Residents of Joe Slovo Community, Western Cape v Thebelisha Homes and Others* (2011) (7) BCLR 723 (CC) (South African Constitutional Court).

[133] Wilson and Dugard (n 130) 49.

[134] *Abahlali baseMjondolo v Premier of the Province of KwaZulu-Natal* (n 96) paras [113]–[115].

[135] *President of the Republic of South Africa and Another v Modderklip Boerdery (Pty) Ltd* CCT 20/04 (South African Constitutional Court).

was granted by the High Court. But the cost of evicting the occupiers was far higher than the cost of the land itself. This was before the cost of rehousing the community was even contemplated. In an innovative remedy, the Court required the government to compensate the landowner, while at the same time declaring that the residents were entitled to occupy the land until alternative land was made available to them by the State. Langa CJ emphasized that the State's responsibility stemmed from the major threat of large-scale disruptions to the social fabric:

> Failure by the state to act in an appropriate manner in the circumstances would mean that Modderklip, and others similarly placed, could not look upon the state and its organs to protect them from invasions of their property. That would be a recipe for anarchy'.[136]

At the same time, to 'evict tens of thousands of people with nowhere to go would cause unimaginable social chaos and misery and untold disruption'.[137]

The Court took a very different approach to the division of responsibility in the later case of *Blue Moonlight*.[138] The case concerned the fate of eighty-six people who had been occupying a dilapidated building in Johannesburg. The building had subsequently been bought by Blue Moonlight, a property development company, which wished to evict them in order to develop the property. Blue Moonlight argued that a private owner has no obligation to provide free housing; whereas the City argued that it could not be responsible for providing accommodation to people evicted by private landowners. The question before the Court was whether the eviction order should be linked to an order that the City provide them with accommodation. The Court held that it did. Excluding people in an emergency situation simply because they were evicted by a private landowner was not found to be reasonable. 'Once an emergency of looming homelessness is created, it … matters little to the evicted who the evictor is'.[139] Unusually, the Court rejected the City's argument that it simply did not have the resources to provide emergency accommodation for the occupiers. 'It is not good enough', stated van der Westhuizen J, 'for the City to state that it has not budgeted for something, if it should indeed have planned and budgeted for it in the fulfilment of its obligations'.[140] Since the City had both a constitutional and statutory duty to provide temporary accommodation, it had a correlative duty to plan proactively and to budget for emergency situations in its yearly application for funds.[141]

The Court therefore held that the City's housing policy was unconstitutional to the extent that people who had been evicted by private landlords were excluded from consideration for temporary accommodation.[142] Emergency accommodation should be provided in a location as near as possible to their existing residence. However, the Court was careful to add that the obligation on the City was only to provide emergency housing. Moreover, it refused to retain jurisdiction through a supervisory or structural interdict. The need for longer-term planning for permanent housing is not

[136] ibid, para [45]. [137] ibid, para [47].

[138] *City of Johannesburg v Blue Moonlight Properties* [2011] ZACC 33 (South African Constitutional Court).

[139] ibid, para [92]. [140] ibid, para [74]. [141] ibid, para [66]. [142] ibid, para [95].

directly addressed by the decision, but remains pressing, as will be seen by the sequel to the case, discussed below.

Blue Moonlight is a landmark decision of the South African Constitutional Court. It clearly places responsibility on the State to provide emergency accommodation for those who are evicted, regardless of whether the cause of the eviction was public or private. It does raise the question, however, of what responsibility should be borne by private landlords, who stood to profit from the eviction. As the Court acknowledged, Blue Moonlight was aware of the occupiers when it bought the property,[143] and it might be surmised that the price was considerably reduced as a result. The Court did not absolve Blue Moonlight of all responsibility, as the latter had hoped. 'Although Blue Moonlight cannot be expected to be burdened with providing accommodation to the Occupiers indefinitely, a degree of patience should be reasonably expected of it and the City must be given a reasonable time to comply'.[144] The Court therefore gave the City about four-and-a-half months to find alternative accommodation, and it was only after that that the eviction order would come into play. The question remains whether the private landlord's responsibilities are fulfilled by its duty to pay rates and taxes, which the City could use for its housing programme, or whether there should be specific liabilities to contribute towards affordable housing for developers who have been responsible for evictions.

IV. Quality of Housing and the Underlying Determinants

Even if it is established that the State has a duty to provide housing, the question remains as to whether there is also a right to a minimum quality of housing, and whether this includes underlying determinants, such as sanitation, water, location, transport, and access to communal services such as schools. It is here that litigants have begun to turn back to the values behind the need for shelter, including the rights to dignity, privacy, equality, life, and livelihood. This is highlighted in CESCR General Comment No 4 on the Right to Adequate Housing. In the Committee's view, the right to housing should not simply be seen as having a roof over one's head, but instead as 'the right to live somewhere in security, peace and dignity'. This is captured by the fact that the right is a right to adequate housing. While adequacy is determined in part by local conditions, the Committee enumerates seven key aspects of the right which should be taken into account. As a start, there should be legal security of tenure. Second, there should be availability of services such as safe drinking water, energy for cooking, heating and lighting, sanitation and washing facilities, means of food storage, refuse disposal, site drainage, and emergency service. Third, housing should be affordable; fourth, it should be habitable; fifth, accessible; and sixth, located with access to employment options, health-care services, childcare centres, and other social facilities. Finally, it should be culturally adequate.[145]

The South African Constitutional Court has been more cautious in addressing the issue of the adequacy of housing. This has been particularly so in relation to the

143 ibid, para [39]. 144 ibid, para [100].

145 CESCR General Comment No 4 (n 59) para 8.

underlying determinants of housing, such as infrastructure, sanitation, and electricity. In *Mazibuko*,[146] the Court reinforced its resistance to providing any substantive content to socio-economic rights which might resemble a minimum core. In rejecting the claim that poor residents of Soweto should be entitled to a minimum amount of free water, the Court reiterated its lack of institutional capacity and legitimacy to dictate to government how the complex challenges of poverty and inequality in the young democracy should be dealt with. Instead, the Court reinforced its position that its role was to judge the reasonableness of measures taken to fulfil its duties under the Constitution to provide access to housing, water etc. While this approach can be defended in relation to specifying a minimum core, it is striking that the Court has paid so little attention to the duty of progressive realization. In *Mazibuko* itself, the Court praised the City of Johannesburg for having made important concessions during the course of protracted litigation proceedings. But there was no requirement on the City to show how it would progressively realize the right in the future. Indeed, the fact that the Court rejected the claim and upheld the City's position meant that the City was no longer bargaining in the shadow of the law and, arguably, had no further incentive to improve. Moreover, many of the housing cases reflect poor governance and planning on the part of municipal, provincial, and national authorities. The Court could certainly play a meaningful role in holding authorities to account in these circumstances.

The South African Constitutional Court's extreme caution in prescribing minimum conditions and its substitution of deference for accountability in relation to progressive realization are further reflected in *Nokotyana*.[147] In this case, residents of an informal settlement had been waiting for at least three years for the municipality to decide whether to upgrade it *in situ*. Pending a decision as to the future of the settlement, the municipality refused make transient arrangements for infrastructure, arguing that it was not obliged to do so under the National Housing Code. The residents were therefore caught in limbo: their conditions remained appalling, while the municipality claimed to have no obligations to them, while continuing to drag its feet in coming to a decision about upgrading. In desperation, the residents came to court asking for installation of ventilated pit latrines for each household and of high-mast lighting in key areas to enhance community safety and access for emergency vehicles.

The Court rejected the occupiers' claim. It held that because no decision had yet been made as to whether to upgrade the settlement, it was reasonable for the municipality to refuse to provide these basic services on a temporary basis, in the interests of ensuring that public funds are expended effectively. The Court was not prepared to consider the claim that section 26 of the Constitution should be interpreted to include basic sanitation and electricity. This was on the basis of its longstanding principle that, where legislation has been enacted to give effect to a right, a litigant could not make a direct constitutional challenge. Consistently with its concern that the litigants should not 'jump the queue', Van der Westhuizen J pointed to the fact that the settlement was one of 110 informal settlements in the municipality, comprising 140,000 households.

[146] *Mazibuko v City of Johannesburg* [2009] ZACC 28 (South African Constitutional Court).

[147] *Nokotyana v Ekurhuleni Metropolitan Municipality* [2010] (4) BCLR 312 (CC) (South African Constitutional Court).

Countrywide, about 1.8 million households, representing between 7 and 8 million people, resided in squalid conditions.

> It is tempting to order the Municipality ... to improve the lives of at least the applicants before this Court, by describing their situation as exceptional and unique. Unfortunately, though, it is not so exceptional or unique ... It would not be just and equitable to make an order that benefit only those who approached a court and caused sufficient embarrassment.[148]

Instead, it ordered the Province to come to a decision about upgrading the settlement within the next fourteen months. The occupiers were therefore left to wait yet another extended period before being given even the most basic infrastructure.

Much more nuanced was the Court's approach in the sequel to the *Blue Moonlight* case. As we have seen, the Court required the City to provide temporary housing to the evicted occupiers, but neither prescribed minimum standards for such accommodation nor required the City to give an account of its programme for permanent housing. In practice, the provision of such accommodation has been deeply unsatisfactory. Those occupiers who could not afford to pay rent of R600 a month were housed in a temporary shelter where they were required to vacate the building by day and return no later than 8 pm. Having nowhere to go during the day exposed them both to the elements and to the high levels of crime in inner-city Johannesburg. Those whose work kept them out late were liable to be locked out and remain on the street overnight; and night workers had nowhere to rest and recover during the day. Added to this was the fact that accommodation was in single-sex dormitories, so that families could not be housed together; and those who eked out a living as street vendors had nowhere to store their small stock overnight. The proprietors of the shelter argued that in this way it could accommodate more homeless people on an emergency basis, while keeping the costs down. While this may have been appropriate for very short stays, for which the hostel was intended, in fact no further plans for more permanent accommodation were made for the evicted occupants. As the Socio-Economic Rights Institute (SERI) argues, the problem is that temporary accommodation becomes de facto permanent due to the lack of proper provision for alternative accommodation.[149]

This raises the question of whether the quality of housing should be challenged not under the socio-economic right to housing, but under the rights to privacy and dignity, which may provide more immediate relief. Indeed, the occupants successfully relied on the rights to privacy and dignity to challenge the stringent rules of the shelter in the High Court in Johannesburg. This was reversed by the Supreme Court of Appeal, which held that the rules were not unreasonable in the context of a severe shortage of resources for emergency shelter.[150] The Constitutional Court, for its part, reinstated the decision of the High Court.[151] However, the basis for the decision

[148] ibid, para [54].

[149] Socio-Economic Rights Institute, 'From Saratoga Avenue to MBV 12 and Ekuthuleni' (Community Practice Notes: Johannesburg Inner City Alternative Accommodation Series) <http://www.seri-sa.org/images/Saratoga_Practice_notes_FOR_WEB.pdf> (accessed 1 March 2018).

[150] *City of Johannesburg v Dladla* [2016] ZASCA 66 (South African Supreme Court of Appeal) para [24].

[151] *Dladla v City of Johannesburg* [2017] ZACC 42 (South African Constitutional Court).

differed strikingly as between the three judgments delivered. Mhlantla J, delivering the judgment of the Court, held that the shelter's rules should be struck down because they infringed the occupiers' rights to dignity and privacy.[152] Since the rules could be separated from the provision of accommodation itself, she held, the right of access to housing was not engaged, and therefore the reasonableness criterion in section 26(2) was not the appropriate measure of judicial scrutiny.[153] Instead, any justification had to be determined under section 36 of the Constitution, which states that any limitation of a constitutional right must be by law of general application and legitimate and proportional. Since the rules of the shelter could not be adjudged a 'law of general application', section 36 did not apply.[154]

Cameron J, concurring, took a different view.[155] For him, the provision of temporary accommodation necessarily engaged the right of access to housing in section 26 and was part of the State's obligation to progressively realize the right.[156] Adequate housing comprised not just the shelter itself, but the conditions attached to the accommodation.[157] This meant that the shelter's rules needed to be judged according to the standard of reasonableness in section 26(2).[158] Cameron J's judgment is particularly notable for the way it approaches the meaning of reasonableness. For him, reasonableness in section 26(2) should be read consistently with reasonableness in section 36, the limitations clause.[159] Since the latter expressly incorporates a proportionality analysis, with the burden on the respondent to prove that the measure was proportional, this is potentially an important step beyond the approach to reasonableness in previous cases. At the same time, Cameron J stressed that the strictness of the Court's scrutiny depended on the context, which in turn related to both purpose and circumstances. This meant that some limitations would be scrutinized more intensely than others.[160]

In this case, Cameron J found that the rules were unreasonable, treating the residents in a demeaning manner for no demonstrable purpose. The reliance on the reasonableness principle allowed him to address two difficult arguments posed by the City. First, the City argued, the rules save money, and this money was urgently needed for those even worse off than the occupiers. Cameron J was prepared to look closely at the evidence behind this claim. On the figures provided, very little was saved: the small amount saved monthly per resident was in practice offset by the cost of the day-time drop-in centre provided by the City to ameliorate the lock-out rule. In a crucial acknowledgement of the need to take a more textured view of budgetary claims, Cameron J held that it was simply not established on the evidence that if the residents before the Court were permitted to remain in the shelter during the day, this would be a drain on the budget available for other, worse-off people in Johannesburg.[161]

The second argument went to the heart of the dilemmas faced by courts in adjudicating housing claims in situations of overwhelming need. The City argued that hundreds of thousands of people in Johannesburg were worse off than the residents. Although the rules of the shelter were unpleasant, the occupiers at least had nourishing

[152] ibid, paras [47]–[50]. [153] ibid, para [41]. [154] ibid, paras [52]–[53].
[155] Froneman, Khampepe, and Madlanga JJ concurred with this part of the judgment.
[156] *Dladla v City of Johannesburg* (n 151) para [57]. [157] ibid. [158] ibid, paras [64]–[66].
[159] ibid, para [75]. [160] ibid, paras [76]–[77]. [161] ibid, paras [83]–[86].

meals, shelter from the elements, warmth and protection, and effective ablutions. This might suggest that the limitations imposed by the rules should be judged more leniently. Cameron J acknowledged that this was a difficult dilemma. However, he was clear that the claim to dignified treatment by the litigants before the Court could not be waved away by the fact that others, who are worse off than them, might also have claims:

> The reasonableness of public treatment of the vulnerable cannot depend only on the fact that what they are getting is better than that of others who are worse off. The question is not whether others are worse off, but whether these measures the City is taking here, now, with this vulnerable group, affords them sufficient care, respect and dignity.[162]

The Court should not have to determine who are the worst off, in abstract terms:

> If the comparative welfare of others, or their lack of it, could without more justify deprivation of benefits, this could imply a race to the bottom, where the hierarchy of the worse-off determines who is entitled to dignity. This could lead to infinite regressions of impoverishment and misery.[163]

This sets his approach apart from earlier decisions of the Court. As we saw in Chapter 8, in *Soobramoney*,[164] the Court held that the soundness of the claim could only be determined on the basis that the same treatment should be available to everyone.

This can be contrasted with the novel approach of the Supreme Court of India, which has been recently prepared to take a much more intense supervisory role. The context was the long-running 'Right to Food' case, discussed in Chapter 3. In 2010, the judge in charge of the ongoing case was approached to give directions in relation to a large number of deaths of homeless people in the extreme cold of the Delhi winter. The applicants demonstrated that underlying malnutrition and hunger make people more susceptible to extreme weather conditions. Yet the city of Delhi had only thirty-two shelters, fifteen of them temporary, to cater for at least 15,000 urban homeless families. The Court immediately ordered the City of Delhi to provide night shelters on an urgent basis, with blankets, water, and mobile toilets. In its report to the Court the following month, the City reported that it had doubled the available capacity from 4,165 to 8,575 people, and that electricity, water, toilet, and sanitation facilities, as well as bedding, had been provided. It also set out its plans to provide facilities for a night shelter for every 5 lakh[165] of the population. The Court also required other Indian States and Territories to make a similar provision, and to file affidavits setting out their up-to-date positions.[166] Although the shelters provided are rudimentary, the case nevertheless demonstrates that an ongoing supervisory process is possible so that unforeseen difficulties as well as resistances can be addressed.

[162] ibid, para [88]. [163] ibid, para [89].

[164] *Soobramoney v Minister of Health (Kwazulu-Natal)* 1997 (12) BCLR 1696 (South African Constitutional Court).

[165] One lakh is 100,000.

[166] Compilation of Orders passed by the Supreme Court in *PUCL v UOI* (CWP 196/2001) pertaining to homeless shelters.

V. Housing as an Equality Right

A. Housing and same-sex couples

Discrimination is a major cause of exclusion from access to housing. In jurisdictions with no positive duties to provide housing, the right to equality functions as an important means of securing housing rights to excluded groups. This is clearly evident under the ECHR, where Article 14, the right not to be discriminated against in the enjoyment of Convention rights, can be used in conjunction with the right to respect for home in Article 8. Thus, the ECtHR has held that rules which exclude same-sex partners from the right to succeed to a tenancy constitute a breach of Article 14 in conjunction with Article 8.[167] In applying this principle in the context of UK law, Baroness Hale summed up the role of equality in bridging the gap between the duty of respect for home and the duty to provide housing:

> Everyone has the right to respect for their home. This does not mean that the state—or anyone else—has to supply everyone with a home. Nor does it mean that the state has to grant everyone a secure right to live in their home. But if it does grant that right to some, it must not withhold it from others in the same or an analogous situation. It must grant that right equally, unless the difference in treatment can be objectively justified.[168]

B. Housing and race discrimination

A similar result is found in US cases on race discrimination, albeit by a somewhat different legal route. Although there is no right to housing in the US Constitution, decades of severe racial segregation in housing have brought many litigants to court claiming a breach of their rights to equality in housing. De jure residential segregation by race was declared unconstitutional early in the twentieth century;[169] but vestiges have remained well into the twenty-first century. In the famous case of *Shelley v Kraemer* in 1948, the US Supreme Court was asked to adjudicate on a widespread practice whereby white property owners entered into restrictive covenants, with the aim of excluding people of a particular race or colour from the ownership or occupancy of property in white residential areas. In *Shelley*, thirty property owners in St Louis, self-styled as being of the 'Caucasian race', had entered into a covenant not to sell or rent their houses to 'people of the Negro or Mongolian Race'.[170] When one of the properties was sold to Shelley, an African American, the other property owners brought suit asking the Court to restrain Shelley from taking possession and to divest title from him. The Supreme Court of Michigan granted the order. On appeal to the US Supreme Court, the petitioners claimed a violation of the Fourteenth Amendment's command

[167] *Karner v Austria* (2004) 38 EHRR 24 (European Court of Human Rights); *Kozak v Poland* (2010) 51 EHRR 16 (European Court of Human Rights).

[168] *Ghaidan v Godin-Mendoza* [2004] UKHL 30, [2004] 2 AC 557 (HL) para [135].

[169] *Buchanan v Warley* 245 US 60 (1917) (US Supreme Court); see *Texas Department of Housing and Community Affairs v The Inclusive Communities Project* (2015) 135 S Ct 2507 (US Supreme Court).

[170] *Shelley v Kraemer* 334 US 1 (1948) (US Supreme Court).

that no State shall 'deny to any person within its jurisdiction the equal protection of the laws'. The crucial question was whether judicial enforcement of private covenants could amount to State action. The US Supreme Court held that it did.

> We have noted that freedom from discrimination by the States in the enjoyment of property rights was among the basic objectives sought to be effectuated by the framers of the Fourteenth Amendment. That such discrimination has occurred in these cases is clear. Because of the race or colour of these petitioners they have been denied rights of ownership or occupancy enjoyed as a matter of course by other citizens of different race or colour.[171]

Other practices, however, continued to perpetuate racial segregation in housing, including discriminatory lending practices. By the 1960s, the combination of such policies and prejudices had led to urban patterns whereby inner-city areas were predominantly black, surrounded by more affluent white suburbs.[172] A Commission established by President Lyndon Johnson in 1968 found that nearly two-thirds of all black families living in the central cities 'live in neighbourhoods marked by substandard housing and general urban blight'.[173] Black families were prevented from obtaining better housing and moving to integrated communities by both open and covert racial discrimination.[174] The Commission concluded that '[o]ur Nation is moving toward two societies, one black, one white—separate and unequal'.[175] The assassination of Martin Luther King in 1968 triggered a new sense of urgency to resolve inner-city social tensions. Congress responded by accepting the Commission's report and passing the 1968 Fair Housing Act. The Act makes it unlawful to refuse to sell or rent or otherwise make unavailable or deny a dwelling to any person because of race, colour, religion, sex, familial status, or national origin.[176]

While blatant discrimination on grounds of race may have receded in the ensuing decades, segregation continues to be maintained by apparently neutral practices, such as zoning laws prohibiting multi-family housing, which in practice exclude minorities from certain neighbourhoods. This raises the question of whether the Fair Housing Act precludes practices or policies which, although facially neutral, have a disparate impact on grounds of race which cannot be justified. In the 2015 case of *Texas Department of Housing v Inclusive Communities*,[177] the US Supreme Court held that it did. The case raised the question of where housing for low-income persons should be constructed in Dallas, Texas. The record of the Texas Department of Housing, which was responsible for approving housing subsidies for low-income housing, showed that it rarely subsidized low-cost housing in predominantly white suburban areas. Instead, the vast majority of subsidies were granted to developments in predominantly black, inner-city areas. The result was that low-income families could not easily

[171] ibid, 21.

[172] *Texas Department of Housing and Community Affairs v The Inclusive Communities Project* (n 169).

[173] Report of the National Advisory Commission on Civil Disorders 91 (1968) ('Kerner Commission Report') at 13, cited in *Texas Department of Housing and Community Affairs v The Inclusive Communities Project* (n 169).

[174] ibid. [175] ibid, at 1.

[176] Section 804(a), 42 USC s 3604(a); see also s 805(a), s 3605(a).

[177] *Texas Department of Housing and Community Affairs v The Inclusive Communities Project* (n 169).

find affordable housing in the white suburban neighbourhoods. It was argued that this perpetuated segregated housing patterns.

A divided court upheld the claim. Kennedy J reaffirmed the importance of disparate impact analysis in challenging zoning laws and other housing restrictions that function unfairly to exclude minorities from specific neighbourhoods without sufficient justification. Disparate impact liability could also be used by applicants to counteract unconscious prejudices and illicit stereotyping. At the same time, he reiterated the important role of the justification defence in permitting authorities to properly explain their decisions. This was particularly so in a case such as the present where there could be several reasonable ways for an authority to use its discretion in allocating subsidies for low-income housing. In an approach not far distant in substance from that of Cameron J in *Dladla*, above, Kennedy J stated:

> An important and appropriate means of ensuring that disparate-impact liability is properly limited is to give housing authorities and private developers leeway to state and explain the valid interest served by their policies ... Just as an employer may maintain a workplace requirement that causes a disparate impact if that requirement is a 'reasonable measure[ment] of job performance,' so too must housing authorities and private developers be allowed to maintain a policy if they can prove it is necessary to achieve a valid interest.[178]

Despite reiterating the standard of necessity, however, Kennedy J hedged it with safeguards. Not only was he concerned that valid policies of inner-city development might be blighted by claims of disparate impact, but he also cautioned against the risk that racial quotas would be used to desegregate housing areas. This led him to require applicants to prove clearly that the policy in question caused the racial disparity. Racial imbalance should not, without more, establish a prima facie case of disparate impact. In addition, when courts did find disparate impact, the remedy should strive to eliminate racial disparities through race-neutral means. Nevertheless, Kennedy J did not rule out policies which expressly choose to foster diversity provided they used race-neutral tools: 'Mere awareness of race in attempting to solve the problems facing inner cities does not doom that endeavour at the outset'.

C. Housing and gender equality: engendering housing rights

The feminist perspective has demanded a much more substantive understanding of equality in the right to housing.[179] As Farha argues: 'The gendered nature of social and economic relations within and outside the household means that women experience discrimination and inequality in virtually every aspect of housing'.[180] This manifests in a range of different ways, including unequal access to credit and finance; unequal rights in relation to inheritance and property; customs and traditions denying women

[178] ibid, para [28].

[179] S Fredman, 'Engendering Socio-economic Rights' [2009] 25 South African Journal of Human Rights 1.

[180] L Farha, 'Is There a Woman in the House? Re/conceiving the Human Right to Housing' (2002) 14 Canadian Journal of Women and the Law 118 at 121–22.

rights in relation to their marital homes; and the disproportionate effect on women of forced evictions and poor-quality housing.[181] In some parts of the world, this is a result of blatantly discriminatory laws. As the first Special Rapporteur on the right to housing put it, many women have no rights in relation to their homes, neither the one in which they were born, nor the one they live in once married. This home-without-rights, he called 'essential homelessness'.[182] In thirty-five of the 173 economies covered by the 2016 report 'Women, Business and the Law', female surviving spouses do not have the same inheritance rights as their male counterparts.[183] This could be because in several countries, including India, 'personal laws', or laws broadly related to marriage, inheritance, and property ownership, are regulated by customary or religious laws. Both Hindu and Muslim personal law continue to include discriminatory provisions against women in relation to property ownership, succession, and the right to reside in the residence. In other countries, customary law is expressly excluded from the constitutional right to equality.[184]

In South Africa, by contrast, customary law, while recognized by the Constitution, is expressly subordinated to the right to equality. This allowed Ms Bhe to challenge the customary law of primogeniture, according to which only a male relative of the deceased qualifies as his heir. The facts were stark.[185] Anelisa Bhe lived with the father of her children in a temporary informal shelter in Khayelitsha in Cape Town. Her partner had bought the small patch of land on which they lived with state housing subsidies but died before the house could be built. The rule of primogeniture meant that neither Ms Bhe nor her two minor daughters were entitled to inherit. Instead, the deceased's father was appointed the heir, and he made it clear that he intended to sell the meagre property belonging to the deceased to defray the funeral expenses. Ms Bhe and her children were threatened with homelessness. She challenged the constitutionality of the rule of primogeniture.

The answer was not straightforward. In South Africa, customary law is respected as an equality issue in itself, the rationale being that customary law, having been subordinated by colonial laws, and to some extent distorted by apartheid laws, should be given its proper place in the new constitutional order. As Langa J put it in *Bhe*: 'Quite clearly the Constitution itself envisages a place for customary law in our legal system'.[186] On the other hand, the Constitution establishes a clear hierarchy, allowing the Court to strike down customary laws which infringe equality. This permitted the Court to

[181] M Kothari, 'Women and Adequate Housing' (2003) Study by the Special Rapporteur on adequate housing as a component of the right to an adequate standard of living, and on the right to non-discrimination, UN Doc E/CN.4/2003/55 para 21 (hereafter Kothari 2003).

[182] R Sachar, Special Rapporteur, '*The Right to Adequate Housing: Final Report*' 9 (12 July 1995) UN Doc E/CN.4/Sub.2/1995/12.

[183] World Bank, 'Women, Business and the Law 2016' <http://pubdocs.worldbank.org/en/810421519921949813/Women-Business-and-the-Law-2016.pdf> (accessed 1 March 2018).

[184] CEDAW Committee, 'Concluding observations: Zambia 2011' para 37. See also Lesotho and Zimbabwe: Kothari (2003) (n 181) para 38; Constitution of Botswana, s 15; CEDAW Committee, 'Concluding observations: Botswana 2010' para 13.

[185] *Bhe v Khayelitsha Magistrate (CCT 49/03)* [2004] ZACC 17, 2005 (1) SA 580 (CC), 2005 (1) BCLR 1 (CC) (South African Constitutional Court).

[186] ibid, para [41], referring to ss 39 and 211 of the Constitution.

find the customary law of male primogeniture to be in breach of the Constitution. The Court stated:

> The exclusion of women from inheritance on the grounds of gender is a clear violation of section 9(3) [the right to equality] of the Constitution. It is a form of discrimination that entrenches past patterns of disadvantage among a vulnerable group, exacerbated by old notions of patriarchy and male domination incompatible with the guarantee of equality under this constitutional order. The principle of primogeniture also violates the right of women to human dignity as guaranteed in section 10 of the Constitution as, in one sense, it implies that women are not fit or competent to own and administer property. Its effect is also to subject these women to a status of perpetual minority, placing them automatically under the control of male heirs.[187]

Even apart from expressly discriminatory laws, women's experience of housing insecurity is frequently overlaid by gendered power relations. This is particularly true of violence against women. Violence both results from and causes inadequate and insecure housing. Domestic violence is a major cause of homelessness among women; while at the same time the lack of alternative housing leaves women vulnerable to such violence. Since women have comparatively fewer educational and employment opportunities, they can be disproportionately dependent on family, informal support networks, or a partner or spouse to meet their housing and economic needs. Due to such dependency, fear of homelessness makes many women vulnerable to violence and other forms of exploitation within the family. This is especially problematic for poor women, disabled women, Roma women, and other women who suffer multiple forms of discrimination.[188]

In addition, since women are still ascribed the primary role in domestic work and childcare, poor housing conditions are particularly burdensome for women. Overcrowding, indoor pollution (eg from inadequate cooking facilities), lack of water, sanitation, and electricity disproportionately affect women who spend more time at home.[189] Kothari concludes that 'persistent poverty, where women and others are forced to live in inadequate and insecure housing and living conditions, is itself a form of violence'. He also draws attention to gender-specific types of evictions and insecurity, particularly where a woman faces threats of eviction by family members or other household members.[190] In large parts of South Asia and Africa, widowed, divorced, or separated women are often thrown out of the house in which they had lived with their husbands.[191]

However, women's perspectives, particularly on housing, were not reflected in the 'gender-neutral documents' adopted by the UN on the right to housing. Article

[187] ibid.

[188] M Kothari, 'Women and Adequate Housing' (2006) Report by the Special Rapporteur on Adequate Housing as a Component of the Right to an Adequate Standard of Living, and on the Right to Non-Discrimination, UN Doc E/CN.4/2006/118, para 9 (hereafter Kothari 2006).

[189] Kothari (2003) (n 181) para 30.

[190] Kothari (2003) (n 181); M Kothari, 'Women and Adequate Housing' (2005) Study by the Special Rapporteur on Adequate Housing as a Component of the Right to an Adequate Standard of Living, UN Doc E/CN.4/2005/43; Kothari (2006) (n 188).

[191] Kothari (2003) (n 181), para 28.

11 of the ICESCR refers to 'the right of everyone to an adequate standard of living for himself and his family, including adequate ... housing'. The CESCR has emphasized that the gendered assumptions in this provision have become outdated: 'While the reference to "himself and his family" reflects assumptions as to gender roles and economic activity patterns commonly accepted in 1966 when the Covenant was adopted, the phrase cannot be read today as implying any limitations upon the applicability of the right to individuals or to female-headed households or other such groups'.[192] Nevertheless, Farha argues, the ostensible gender neutrality in the CESCR General Comment on the Right to Adequate Housing has the effect of rendering women's specific experience of housing invisible. For example, although the Comment states that all persons should possess a degree of security of tenure, it fails to capture the particular causes of women's insecure tenure, such as domestic violence and discriminatory inheritance laws, customs, and traditions.[193] Similarly, as Ikdahl points out, the work of the CESCR 'largely focused on threats affecting the household as a unit with shared interests, rather than exploring the potential for conflicts and evictions occurring between members of the household'.[194]

A similar pattern emerges in relation to the Convention on the Elimination of All Forms of Discrimination Against Women (CEDAW). As Ikdahl concludes, 'While the CEDAW Committee has provided detailed analysis of women's unequal property rights within the family, it has not yet engaged systematically with the effects on women's unequal right to [housing]'.[195] Under Article 16 CEDAW, State Parties are required to eliminate discrimination in all matters relating to marriage and family, and ensure in particular the same rights for both spouses in relation to property.[196] In its General Recommendation No 21 on Equality in Marriage and Family Relations, the CEDAW Committee urged recognition of women's unpaid and domestic work as a valued contribution to the property, so that financial and non-financial contributions should be accorded the same weight when marital property was being divided.[197] The Committee also declared that unequal inheritance rights of women contravened the Convention.[198] The right to adequate housing itself, however, is subsumed under the rights of rural women.[199]

The crucial shift towards engendering the right to housing requires a recognition of the interaction between the public and the private, and particularly the ways in which gendered relationships within the family and in the broader society shape the extent to which women can benefit equally from the right to housing.[200] As Ikdahl puts it, 'attention to relations within the household facilitates the articulation of a wider range of women's experiences of housing insecurity as human rights themes'.[201] The Special

[192] CESCR General Comment No 4 (n 59) para 6.

[193] Farha (n 180) 120.

[194] I Ikdahl, 'Property and Security: Articulating Women's Rights to their Homes' in A Hellum and H Sindig-Aasen (eds), *Women's Human Rights* (CUP 2013).

[195] ibid.

[196] CEDAW, Article 16.1.h.

[197] CEDAW Committee General Recommendation No 21 on Equality in Marriage and Family Relations, (4 February 1994) para 32.

[198] ibid, para 35.

[199] CEDAW, Article 14.2.

[200] S Fredman, 'Engendering Socio-economic Rights' in A Hellum and H Sindig-Aasen (eds), *Women's Human Rights* (CUP 2013).

[201] Ikdahl (n 194).

Rapporteur gives valuable guidance in this direction. Notably, he does not necessarily characterize the right to adequate housing as a right to a particular bundle of goods, in this case a house, but as a right to action by the State to protect and expand the range of feasible options available to women, such as the development of gender-sensitive housing policies and legislation; access to affordable utilities such as water, electricity, and heating, as well as to education, employment, and health facilities; and protection against violence.[202]

VI. Conclusion

Traditionally, while the right to respect for home and family has been regarded as a core area for human rights protection, the right to housing has been considered to be primarily a matter for politics, or at most, as the subject of progressively realizable socio-economic rights. However, the fundamental values of dignity and substantive freedom have driven courts in many jurisdictions to bring housing within the settled corpus of human rights. This is fortified by the inevitable interdependence of duties to respect people's homes with duties to provide alternative accommodation. The comparative examination in this chapter reveals a striking convergence in outcomes between jurisdictions with express socio-economic rights regarding housing and those where housing is implied into other rights, such as the right to life and the right to respect for home and family. Particularly important has been the increasing recognition by courts that a right to a home might provide a substantive counterweight to property rights of landlords and landowners.

At the same time, courts have continued to be concerned as to the limits of their own legitimacy and competence in prescribing policy solutions to complex and polycentric problems of housing. As a result, they have tended to prefer procedural interventions, thereby avoiding giving substantive meaning to the right to adequate housing. This places great store on the power of procedure to shape outcomes, but frequently important requirements of equal participation and timely involvement are underplayed. Most striking is the continuing concern of some courts that the decision as to whether a remedy should be provided to the parties before the court should be tempered by the perceived difficulty in providing a similar remedy to others. With rare exceptions, this raises the spectre that courts too easily permit governments to rely on the scale of the problem as a reason to continue in breach of individual rights. In some important exceptional cases, however, courts have paid more attention to the evidence and have recognized their own important role in addressing failures of governance, ineptitude, and recalcitrance in putting into place proper housing. Ultimately, courts should not be deterred by strong utilitarian counter-arguments from giving full endorsement to housing as neither a luxury, a privilege, nor good fortune, but as a fundamental right connected to the foundational values of peace, security, and dignity.

202 Kothari (2006) (n 188) para 65.

10

Freedom of Speech

I. Introduction

Unlike the rights to housing and health, there is universal consensus that speech is a fundamental right. However, there is a surprising lack of agreement as to why this is so. Raz refers to freedom of expression as '[a] liberal puzzle. Liberals are all convinced of its vital importance, yet why it deserves this importance is a mystery'.[1] Alexander acknowledges that he has 'searched for the scope and ground of a human right to freedom of expression and failed', which he finds 'terribly disquieting'.[2] Other theorists are more confident. John Stuart Mill famously focused on the search for truth, while the notion of a 'free market of ideas',[3] coined by Oliver Wendell Holmes, is probably the most widely cited. Some regard the guiding principle as being the right of self-government, while others rely more broadly on the 'moral agency of individuals'.[4] But all are contested.[5]

Paradoxically, then, rights to housing, health, food, and water are still on the margins of human rights protection, even though no one disputes that everyone has a need for shelter, health care, food, and water. On the other hand, freedom of speech is indisputably part of the human rights corpus, while still not being unambiguously matched to an individual interest. For Raz, the source of the problem is simple. Despite the elevated priority given to freedom of expression, most people rightly value other interests, such as employment, much more highly than their freedom of expression.[6]

Since freedom of speech is universally included in human rights instruments, it may be asked why courts should be concerned at the lack of consensus at a theoretical level. For courts, the starting point is the text of the human rights instrument. The question then becomes not so much whether there should be a right to freedom of speech, since that is resolved in the text, but how it should be interpreted. Such challenges are intensified in the modern context, in which the internet has made participation in speech widely available, while also enhancing its power. Have we witnessed an extraordinary democratization of speech, making it truly possible to fight speech with speech and rendering censorship impotent? Or has the internet amplified the potential of speech to cause harm, through vilification, misleading information, pornography, or incitement to violence?

[1] J Raz, 'Free Expression and Personal Identification' (1991) 11 Oxford Journal of Legal Studies 303, 303.

[2] L Alexander, 'Freedom of Expression as a Human Right' in T Campbell, J Goldsworthy, and A Stone (eds), *Protecting Human Rights: Instruments and Institutions* (OUP 2003) 72–73.

[3] *Abrams v US* 250 US 616 (1919) (US Supreme Court) at 630–31.

[4] *Press Media South Africa v Minister for Home Affairs* [2012] ZACC 22 (South African Constitutional Court) para [53].

[5] E Barendt, *Freedom of Speech* (2nd edn, OUP 2005) 13.

[6] Raz (n 1) 303.

This chapter begins with a sketch of the foremost theories justifying freedom of speech, not with a view to developing an overreaching theory, but to provide a framework to evaluate courts' responses to the challenges that come before them. Section II considers the textual differences in freedom-of-speech guarantees in the jurisdictions considered here. Section III considers how courts have dealt with three of the most burning issues confronted in all of these jurisdictions: whether freedom of speech protects subversive speech, pornography, and hate speech. Section IV asks whether the right-bearer extends beyond the speaker to the recipient of speech and assesses the role of freedom of information. This chapter does not attempt to cover all aspects of freedom of speech. It does not deal with, for example, electoral spending; time, manner, and place regulations; prior restraints; or commercial speech. Instead, the chapter gives more detailed attention to the challenges that arise for our cross-cutting themes of comparativism, background values, interaction between civil and political rights and socio-economic rights, the judicial role in relation to the legislature, and judges' theory of interpretation. The aim is to give the reader a framework to analyse these other important topics in freedom of speech.

A comparative approach reveals the importance of the textual basis in shaping judicial decisions on freedom of speech. In particular, the absence of an express limitation clause in the US First Amendment contrasts vividly with other human rights instruments in other jurisdictions, which permit justifiable limitations to freedom of speech. The US Supreme Court's approach to the background values of freedom of speech is also counterpoised to that of other jurisdictions. The need to protect individual autonomy from State intervention looms much larger in US jurisprudence than in other jurisdictions, which tend to balance this imperative with other values, such as dignity and equality. The result has been that, while judges in other jurisdictions refer frequently to US jurisprudence, this is often to explain the divergence in their own approaches with that of their US counterparts. Indeed, in an important application of the deliberative approach to comparative human rights law, the US approach to free speech is often the paradigm which other courts provide sound reasons to diverge from.

So far as the relationship between judges and the legislature is concerned, judges in all jurisdictions, but particularly in the US, are far more confident in their countermajoritarian role than we have seen in previous chapters. Freedom of speech, perceived as falling within the heartland of justiciable human rights, raises few compunctions on the part of courts in striking down legislation. So much so that, as we will see, US Supreme Court Justice Breyer, dissenting in a case in which the majority yet again struck down an attempt by Congress to regulate child pornography, bemoaned the loss of what he called the constructive discourse between legislatures and courts. This greater confidence is partly due to the perceived absence of the kind of polycentric consequences encountered in Chapters 8 and 9. Indeed, when faced with potential positive duties arising from freedom of speech, such as the duty to provide information, courts have generally preferred to abdicate their role in favour of the legislature. So far as the interpretive task is concerned, the main challenge has been to determine justifiable limits on speech. For the US Court, faced with an apparently absolute right, the interpretive challenges are significant. Yet it is striking that in the many ways in which US justices have implied limitations into the right, little if any mention is made of interpretive philosophy, such as original intent. This is largely true too for their counterparts in other jurisdictions. Much more likely is a resort to fundamental values, such as autonomy, dignity, and equality. It is therefore to these that we turn first.

II. The Liberal Puzzle: Why Freedom of Speech?

A. The protection against tyranny

In his work *On Liberty*,[7] Mill took it for granted that freedom of speech and the press was 'one of the securities against corrupt or tyrannical government'.[8] This is reflected in the jurisprudence of apex courts in many jurisdictions. MacIntyre J in the Supreme Court of Canada puts it thus: 'Representative democracy, as we know it today, which is in great part the product of free expression and discussion of varying ideas, depends on its maintenance and protection'.[9]

Protection against tyranny remains the most powerful rationale for freedom of speech. States should not suppress dissenting opinions in order to maintain their own power. Anyone who has lived in a regime with strict censorship has no doubt of the fundamental intrusion on individual thought, social interaction, and political activity that suppression of freedom of speech can entail. Nor is this confined to strictly political speech. Suppression of literature, art, and other cultural expressions, as well as of science and history, can equally be used to prevent the formation of potentially dissenting ideas and movements. In South Africa under apartheid, for example, strict State control extended from the banning of political texts, such as those of Marx and Lenin, to the designation of school textbooks depicting South African history in a particular manner, to the prohibition of films and art which included inter-racial mixing, sexually explicit material, or even bad language.

B. The pursuit of truth

A second familiar rationale for freedom of speech is its role in the pursuit of truth. Mill argued that, even in the absence of tyrannical government, freedom of speech was necessary to the discovery of truth.

> The peculiar evil of silencing an expression of an opinion is that it is robbing the human race, posterity as well as the existing generation ... If the opinion is right, they are deprived of the opportunity of exchanging error for truth: if wrong they lose ... the clearer perception and livelier impression of truth, produced by its collision with error.[10]

[7] JS Mill, *On Liberty* (Longman, Roberts & Green 1869) ch II. [8] ibid, ch II, 1.

[9] *Retail, Wholesale and Department Store Union v Dolphin Delivery* [1986] 2 RCS 573 (Supreme Court of Canada), 583.

[10] Mill (n 7) ch II.

This was echoed by Brandeis J in his famous statement in *Whitney v California* in 1927. 'Freedom to think as you will and to speak as you think are means indispensable to the discovery and spread of political truth' he declared. '[W]ith [free speech and assembly], discussion affords ordinarily adequate protection against the dissemination of noxious doctrine'.[11] This was reiterated with approval as recently as 2015 by the Indian Supreme Court.[12]

The argument from truth on its own has been widely recognized as too limited to sustain a robust right to freedom of speech.[13] A particular risk is that it allows courts to decide that some speech is not worth protecting because, in the court's view, it does not promote truth. This was summed up by US Supreme Court Justice Murphy in *Chaplinsky v New Hampshire*, when he held that there were certain classes of speech which had never been thought to raise any Constitutional problem because they 'are no essential part of any exposition of ideas, and are of such slight social value as a step to truth that any benefit that may be derived from them is clearly outweighed by the social interest in order and morality'.[14] Mill's own view, however, was that falsehoods were equally as important for their role in challenging truth. For the State to decide ahead of time that some sorts of speech are not furthering truth would cut right across this view. This indeed has been reflected in later US cases, where the Supreme Court has made it clear that constitutional protection does not turn upon 'the truth, popularity, or social utility of the ideas and beliefs which are offered'.[15] In *New York v Sullivan*, the Court reiterated that 'erroneous statement is inevitable in free debate and ... must be protected if the freedoms of expression are to have the breathing space that they need ... to survive'.[16] Rather than excluding such expressions by making a threshold decision that they have little value, it is preferable to subject all to scrutiny.[17]

The argument from truth might also yield a principle of freedom of speech which is too broad. Not all speech aspires to truth. Moreover, there may well be situations in which there is a need to suppress speech, whether or not it advances truth, in order to protect other values.[18] Information involving State security or individuals' private lives fall into this category. However, it may be accepted that the function of speech is to further truth, while recognizing that achieving truth is not always the top priority in a social sense. In fact, as we will see, it is usually in the justification for the limitation of speech that the difficult challenges arise. In such situations, it remains helpful to ask how important the truth-seeking aspect of the speech might be.

More problematic is the assumption that freedom of speech necessarily leads to the discovery of truth. Thus, the Nazis came to power in Germany in 1933 although there had been relatively free political debate in the preceding Weimar Republic.[19] This is equally true today. The proliferation of speech on social media and more generally on the internet, including sites with deliberately false news, has led to what could now be called a post-truth society. After the US election in 2016, in which Donald Trump was

[11] *Whitney v California* 274 US 357 (1927) (US Supreme Court) 375.
[12] *Shreya Singhal v UOI* AIR 2015 SC 1523 (Indian Supreme Court). [13] Barendt (n 5) 8ff.
[14] *Chaplinsky v New Hampshire* 315 US 568 (1942) (US Supreme Court) 572.
[15] *NAACP v Burton* 377 US 415 (1963) (US Supreme Court) 445.
[16] *New York Times v Sullivan* 376 (US) 254 (1964) (US Supreme Court) 272. [17] ibid, 269.
[18] Barendt (n 5) 8. [19] ibid, 9.

elected president, there was widespread reporting of fake news, designed to discredit political candidates, not just in the US, but also in Europe.[20]

This might suggest that, turning Mill's theory on its head, it is necessary to protect the pursuit of truth from speech itself. Barendt concludes that some constraints may be required 'to ensure that false propositions do not drive out truths'.[21] Alternatively, it could be argued that instead of constraints, speech should always be countered by more speech. Brandeis J put this view powerfully in *Whitney v California*, when he stated that 'discussion affords ordinarily adequate protection against the dissemination of noxious doctrine ... and that the fitting remedy for evil counsels is good ones'.[22] Yet this assumes that the voice of the powerless is equivalent to that of the powerful. Pornography and hate speech might render its targets speechless, or unable to respond to the volume or power of the speaker. On the other hand, countering speech with speech may be the only practical way forward, given the extreme difficulty of regulation of internet sites. One recently advocated solution might be to require Facebook and Google to crack down on purveyors of fake stories.[23] But is it any safer to require these companies, rather than the State, to vet the truthfulness of news? Facebook itself states that it is difficult to use software or technical means to distinguish between different stories.[24]

C. Free marketplace of ideas

Mill's truth principle has often been conflated with a different justification for freedom of speech, the well-known 'marketplace of ideas' coined by US Justice Oliver Wendell Holmes. In his dissenting judgment in *Abrams v US* in 1919, Holmes J declared that 'the ultimate good desired is better reached by free trade in ideas—that the best test of the power of the thought is to get itself accepted in the competition of the market, and that truth is the only ground upon which [people's] wishes safely can be carried out'.[25]

The marketplace of ideas theory has played a central role in much of the reasoning about freedom of speech, not just in the US but elsewhere.[26] It resonates with a suspicion of State interference in individual decision-making, and with the commitment to the principle that the invisible hand of the market will always lead to optimal outcomes for individuals pursuing their rational self-interest. However, there are many cogent reasons for being cautious about the analogy between speech and the free market. As a start, the imperfections of the market are well known, especially the tendency for

[20] See eg Michael Safi, 'Fake News: an insidious trend that's fast becoming a global problem' *The Guardian* (2 December 2016) <https://www.theguardian.com/media/2016/dec/02/fake-news-facebook-us-election-around-the-world> (accessed 4 March 2018); Elizabeth Dwoskin, Caitlin Dewey, and Craig Timberg, 'Why Facebook and Google are struggling to purge fake news' *The Washington Post* (15 November 2016) <https://www.washingtonpost.com/business/economy/why-facebook-and-google-are-struggling-to-purge-fake-news/2016/11/15/85022897-f765-422e-9f53-c720d1f20071_story.html?tid=a_inl&utm_term=.f3ac4665789d> (accessed 4 March 2018).

[21] Barendt (n 5) 9. [22] *Whitney v California* (n 11) 375.

[23] See eg Alison Little, '"Step Up" Theresa May Takes on Facebook and Twitter with crackdown on abusive content' *Sunday Express* (5 February 2018) <https://www.express.co.uk/news/politics/914849/theresa-may-twitter-facebook-online-abuse-terror-content> (accessed 4 March 2018).

[24] Dwoskin, Dewey, and Timberg (n 20). [25] *Abrams v US* (n 3) 630.

[26] *Shreya Singhal v UOI* (n 12) para [11].

the strongest players to accumulate power, while the weakest become more vulnerable. This tendency is enhanced by the use of speech by large corporations, in the form of advertising. Indeed, the market may encourage distortions of truth, rather than the search for it. In any event, many actors do not engage in speech simply to achieve truth: ideas might be published because they are popular and might increase sales.[27]

The need for regulation of the market to prohibit unfair trading practices and maintain competition is now generally accepted. Does this bring with it a similar need to regulate speech? As we will see, there are few who argue for an absolute, unlimited freedom of speech. The issue, in practice, is what sort of regulation is legitimate. The marketplace of ideas notion is not particularly helpful in determining appropriate limits, particularly if it stands for the principle of unregulated markets, and if it regards the market as furthering truth.

D. Autonomy and self-fulfilment

A closer look at the marketplace of ideas theory reveals that it combines the presumption that unregulated speech will lead to truth with a different principle, namely that the State should not interfere in individual autonomy to make decisions. It is this essentially liberal principle of autonomy that infuses other justifications for freedom of speech. Scanlon rests his justification of freedom of speech on the general principle, 'coming down to us from Kant and others, that a legitimate government is one whose authority citizens can recognize while still regarding themselves as equal, autonomous, rational agents'.[28] On this view, an autonomous person should not accept the judgement of others as to what she should believe or do without her own independent consideration. Autonomy therefore entails that the State should not protect a person against the harm of coming to have false beliefs. Otherwise, the State would be given the authority to decide which views are false and deprive the citizen of grounds for making an independent judgement. Moreover, the State, although permitted to decide that certain conduct is illegal, should not also outlaw the advocacy of such illegal conduct. This would deprive citizens of the right to arrive at an independent judgement as to whether the law should be obeyed.[29]

Scanlon acknowledges that there is a clear parallel between his thesis and Mill's argument that if truth is to prevail, all available arguments should be permitted to be heard. However, his thesis does not depend on an empirical claim that truth is in fact more likely to triumph if free discussion is permitted. Instead, it asks: how could citizens recognize a right of governments to command them while still regarding themselves as equal, autonomous, rational agents?[30] Thus the truth-seeking dimension is at best a by-product of his theory. Scanlon is also quick to point out that his argument rests on a limitation on the authority of the State, rather than a right of individuals to make up their own minds. This means that it does not go so far as to give individuals

[27] Barendt (n 5) 12.
[28] T Scanlon, 'A Theory of Freedom of Expression' (2007) 1 Philosophy & Public Affairs 204, 214.
[29] ibid, 218. [30] ibid, 225.

a right to information necessary for them to make an informed decision. Rights to information, in his view, require different justifications.

Autonomy is also at the core of Meicklejohn's thesis that self-government is the foundational principle of freedom of speech. For Meicklejohn, freedom of speech, at least as expressed in the US Constitution's First Amendment, 'does not protect a "freedom to speak". It protects the freedom of those activities of thought and communication by which we "govern"'.[31] This means that, although the agents of the State 'govern us, we, in a deeper sense, govern them'.[32] He is quick to point out that this does not only protect overtly political speech. It also covers freedom of education, which is necessary to 'cultivate the mind and will of a citizen',[33] philosophy and the sciences, literature and the arts, and public discussion of public issues, together with the spreading of information and opinion relevant to these issues. He expressly includes 'obscenity' in the list of protected speech. Like Scanlon, Meicklejohn does not rest his theory on the expectation that 'in a fair fight between truth and error, truth is sure to win'. Nevertheless, he argues that 'in order to make self-government a reality rather than an illusion, in order that it may become as wise and efficient as its responsibilities require, the judgment-making of the people must be self-educated in the ways of freedom'.[34] At the same time, Meicklejohn argues that there are many forms of communication which are wholly outside the scope of the freedom of speech protection in the First Amendment of the US Constitution. This would largely comprise private speech, such as libel directed against a private individual. He also has no difficulty with regulation of the place and time of speech: freedom of speech is not simply freedom to speak wherever and whenever one pleases.

Emerson adds a further rationale. This is that freedom of speech has intrinsic value, essential to individual self-fulfilment. He argues that the value of speech derives from 'the widely accepted premise of Western thought that the proper end of man is the realization of his character and potentialities as a human being'.[35] Expression, on this view, is an integral part of the development of ideas and the affirmation of self. None of these theories, however, regard it as important to ensure that everyone is equally able to exercise their freedom of speech.

E. State neutrality and liberal tolerance

Behind much of this discussion is the liberal theory that the State should not impose any particular version of the 'good' on its citizens. The right of individuals to make their own decisions as to the good life is seen to be fundamental to liberty. It is here that liberalism makes its decisive break from the Aristotelian view that there is an objective 'good' discernible by the rational faculties. Aristotle saw the polis as not only a political entity but also a community based on a commitment to shared values.[36] Perceiving that such a view would require dissenters to conform to the 'general will',

[31] A Meiklejohn, 'The First Amendment Is an Absolute' [1961] Sup Ct Rev 245, 255.
[32] ibid, 257. [33] ibid, 257. [34] ibid, 263.
[35] T Emerson, 'Toward a General Theory of the First Amendment' (1963) 72 Yale L J 877, 879.
[36] Aristotle, *Politics* (Random House 1943) 1287, 1280–82, 1325, and see T Burns, 'Aristotle' in D Boucher and P Kelly (eds), *Political Thinkers* (OUP 2003) 76–77.

Berlin argued emphatically that the State should be strictly neutral as between different particular values or world views.[37] The problem with this conclusion is that it assumes that the State can remain neutral. In practice, however, the illusion of neutrality disguises particular value commitments. Autonomy is itself a value commitment, as Rawls recognizes.[38] Similarly, the ideal of a 'free market', whether of goods or ideas, embodies a particular understanding of human needs and aspirations, one which downgrades collective goals and interpersonal relationships and ignores the ways in which choice is constrained by individuals' initial endowments, their ability effectively to mobilize resources at their disposal, and their access to social goods such as education and training.[39]

The acknowledgement that the State cannot be value-neutral then requires a different way of determining the line between issues on which the State should not intervene—those areas in which a plurality of values is not only acceptable but essential to maintain equality and freedom in a diverse society—and those areas in which the State is entitled to take positive action to further specific values or prevent the pursuance of what it regards as morally bad goals.[40] The dilemmas are particularly acute in relation to freedom of speech. Does the liberal principle of tolerance for all views require the State to tolerate illiberal views, including views advocating the suppression of freedom of speech, democracy, and liberalism itself? A liberal State cannot be neutral as to the virtues of liberalism itself, which entails guarding against the possibility that advocates of illiberalism might convince others and cause harm to liberalism. However, the suppression of any speech, including illiberal speech, goes against the tenets of liberalism. Alexander argues that 'the great liberal freedoms—freedom of religion, association, and expression—are deeply paradoxical because they rest on the notion of epistemic abstinence—the idea that liberal government cannot impose its view of the Good on dissenters'.[41] The failure to find a cogent and defensible principle defining freedom of speech is therefore 'part and parcel of the failure of liberalism to provide a justification for tolerating illiberal views—which toleration is definitive of liberalism'.[42] As we will see, the paradox of liberalism is one of the chief sources of contestation in the case law.

F. Speech as a public good

Raz approaches the rationale for freedom of speech very differently. He regards people's interest in free speech as rather small. Instead, he defends freedom of speech as a public good, or one in which the interests and rights of others as well as those of the speaker are taken into account.[43] The paradigmatic public good argument for freedom of speech is that it is an integral part of a democratic regime. Even though in any democracy with a sufficiently large electorate, the individual's interest in free public speech, as it is in casting her vote, is in fact very small, freedom of speech is essential

[37] I Berlin, *Four Essays on Liberty* (Clarendon Press 1969) 170. For a fuller discussion, see S Fredman, *Human Rights Transformed: Positive Rights and Positive Duties* (OUP 2008) 18–21.

[38] J Rawls, *Justice as Fairness* (Harvard University Press 2001) 156.

[39] S Deakin and F Wilkinson, *The Law of the Labour Market* (OUP 2005) 285–86.

[40] Fredman (n 37) 21ff. [41] Alexander (n 2) 66–67. [42] ibid, 66. [43] Raz (n 1) 306.

for the survival of democracy. The fundamental principle of democracy, namely governmental responsiveness to the wishes of the governed, is only desirable if those wishes are not entirely a result of manipulation by government. Moreover, the better informed the governed are, and the better they are able to evaluate the information before them, the stronger is the case for taking account of their wishes.[44]

However, there are clearly areas where speech should be protected even though it is unlikely to affect political decisions. Raz proposes that the democratic justification should be complemented by a further public good justification, deriving from the high value placed by contemporary pluralist societies on recognizing the existence of a plurality of valuable ways of life and the possibility of new valuable forms of life.[45] 'Public portrayal and expression of forms of life validate the styles of life portrayed', while 'censoring expression normally expresses authoritative condemnation not merely of the views or opinions censored but of the whole style of life of which they are a part'.[46] The restriction on content-based censorship is particularly crucial. 'Content-based censorship and criminalization are a public and authoritative condemnation. Their repudiation of ways of life which they reject is insulting and hurtful'.[47] This might suggest that positive portrayals of ways of life should be tolerated, while critical or hostile discussion may be prohibited. However, for Raz, bad speech is often part of a good way of life, or at least one which should not be condemned by society through its official organs. His support for pluralism therefore embraces the paradox of liberalism: strong pluralism 'approves as valuable, although imperfect, ways of life which themselves deny the truth of pluralism'.[48] Law should not be used to promote conformism by allowing one group to use the law to promote their views. Instead, pluralism requires the law to promote pluralism in the society. The authoritative voice of society is significantly distinct from criticism or hostility from members of the public.

Notably, failure to provide the means for expression is not an authoritative condemnation of the expression, and therefore does not fall within the protection for freedom of speech advocated by Raz. Thus, his position does not entail positive duties to provide platforms for speech. Like the autonomy arguments, therefore, Raz does not regard it as important to ensure the equal ability of all to exercise their speech.

If political theorists find it difficult to provide a coherent theory of freedom of speech, can these theories be of any value to judges in making decisions in particular disputes? Courts in fact often refer to an amalgam of theories. This was summed up by the South African Constitutional Court when it declared that freedom of expression

> lies at the heart of a democracy. It is valuable for many reasons, including its instrumental function as a guarantor of democracy, its implicit recognition and protection of the moral agency of individuals in our society and its facilitation of the search for truth by individuals and society generally.[49]

Similarly, the European Court of Human Rights (ECtHR) has frequently stated that freedom of expression 'constitutes one of the essential foundations of a democratic

[44] ibid, 308. [45] ibid, 311. [46] ibid, 310. [47] ibid, 314. [48] ibid, 321.

[49] *South African National Defence Union v Minister of Defence* (1999) 4 SA 469 (South African Constitutional Court) para [67].

society and one of the basic conditions for its progress and for each individual's self-fulfilment'.[50] Judges are not, of course, entirely free to adopt whatever political theory they wish. They are constrained by the human rights instrument or text which they are required to interpret. So the first question to be asked is whether and how constitutional texts give a steer to courts as to the meaning and background values of freedom of speech. It is to this that we now turn.

III. Constitutional Texts

The US Constitution is the oldest and most opaque. The First Amendment, famous for its bluntness, simply states: 'Congress shall make no law ... abridging the freedom of speech, or of the press ..'..[51] The First Amendment is particularly conspicuous in that it appears to grant an absolute right. Unlike more recent iterations of the right, it does not include an express limitation clause. This puts pressure on the meaning of 'speech'. If the classification of an act as speech immediately gives it absolute protection, there is a strong temptation to classify an act as non-speech in order to escape protection. The difficulty with this, in turn, is that the usual balancing process of free speech against other interests is short-circuited.

Other constitutional protections are more detailed, leaving less to judicial interpretation. Article 10(1) of the European Convention on Human Rights (ECHR) states as follows: 'Everyone has the right to freedom of expression. This right shall include freedom to hold opinions and to receive and impart information and ideas without interference by public authority and regardless of frontiers ..'..

Article 10 differs from the First Amendment in several important ways. First, while the First Amendment is targeted at preventing laws abridging freedom of speech, Article 10 creates a positive right, to which everyone is entitled. Second, Article 10 refers to both the speaker and the listener, giving a right to receive as well as impart information. Unlike the First Amendment, it does not, however, refer to freedom of the press. Third, and particularly importantly, it creates an express list of potential justifications for restricting freedom of expression. According to Article 10(2):

> The exercise of these freedoms, since it carries with it duties and responsibilities, may be subject to such formalities, conditions, restrictions or penalties as are prescribed by law and are necessary in a democratic society, in the interests of national security, territorial integrity or public safety, for the prevention of disorder or crime, for the protection of health or morals, for the protection of the reputation or rights of others, for preventing the disclosure of information received in confidence, or for maintaining the authority and impartiality of the judiciary.

This is notable in its explicit statement that the right carries with it duties and responsibilities. Even more importantly, it sets out a test to balance such justifications against the core right. Thus, restrictions must be 'prescribed by law and ... necessary

[50] *Animal Defenders International v UK* (2013) 57 EHRR 21 (European Court of Human Rights) para [100].

[51] This applies to States too via the Fourteenth Amendment: *Perry Education Association v Perry Local Educators' Association* 460 US 37 (1983) (US Supreme Court).

in a democratic society'. The right in Article 10 ECHR closely reflects that under Article 19 of the International Covenant on Civil and Political Rights (ICCPR). Article 19, however, importantly includes the right to seek information in addition to the right to receive and impart information.

The right to freedom of speech in the Indian Constitution is contained in Article 19. It states quite simply that 'all citizens shall have the right to freedom of speech and expression', thus including both speech and expression but not expressly mentioning, as Article 10 does, the interests of the recipient as well as the speaker. Nor does it mention freedom of the press, as does the First Amendment. Article 19(2) allows the State to maintain or make any law which 'imposes reasonable restrictions on the exercise of the right [to freedom of speech and expression] in the interests of the sovereignty and integrity of India, the security of the State, friendly relations with foreign States, public order, decency or morality or in relation to contempt of court, defamation or incitement to an offence'. Notably, rather than requiring that any restrictions be 'necessary in a democratic society', the Indian text permits any 'reasonable restrictions'. Although this test seems on the face of it to be markedly more lenient than the ECHR, the Indian Supreme Court in the 2015 case of *Shreya Singhal* stated that to be reasonable, a restriction must be 'narrowly interpreted so as to abridge or restrict only what is absolutely necessary'.[52]

The Canadian provision has a different structure. Section 2(b) of the Charter states that everyone has 'freedom of thought, belief, opinion and expression, including freedom of the press and other media of communication'. Like its US counterpart, it expressly includes freedom of the press. The Charter right differs from the Indian Constitution and the ECHR in that its limitation clause is not specific to the freedom of expression right. Instead, section 1 of the Charter contains a general limitation clause, which states that the rights and freedoms set out in the Charter are guaranteed, 'subject only to such reasonable limits prescribed by law as can be demonstrably justified in a free and democratic society'. The Supreme Court of Canada has developed a detailed proportionality test for the application of section 1.[53]

The South African Constitution adds artistic creativity and academic and scientific freedom to the familiar protections in its counterparts elsewhere. Section 16 states: 'Everyone has the right to freedom of expression, which includes (a) freedom of the press and other media; (b) freedom to receive or impart information or ideas, (c) freedom of artistic creativity and (d) academic freedom and freedom of scientific research'. Although the South African Constitution includes a general limitation clause based on a detailed proportionality test, section 16 also includes some specific limitations. Importantly, section 16(2) states that the right to freedom of expression does not extend to propaganda for war; incitement of imminent violence; or advocacy of hatred that is based on race, ethnicity, gender, or religion, and that constitutes incitement to cause harm.

Although there is a central affirmation of the right to freedom of speech in all these iterations, the principles guiding its application remain challenging. Courts in

[52] *Shreya Singhal v UOI* (n 12) para [17].
[53] *R v Oakes* [1986] 1 SCR 103 (Supreme Court of Canada).

different jurisdictions have dealt with this in different ways. This raises the question of whether there is a universal core of the right to freedom of speech. Or is it at the point of balancing that differences between cultures and value priorities emerges? These questions are explored in more detail in section IV. It should be noted that while some refer to 'speech' and others to 'expression', in practice nothing hangs on the different formulations. This chapter therefore refers to 'speech' throughout, denoting both speech and expression.

IV. Addressing the Liberal Paradox

A. Content and viewpoint-based restrictions

Central to the liberal ideal of freedom of speech is a notion that the State should not prefer one viewpoint over another. This has meant that courts everywhere have held that speech should not be suppressed simply because the State disagrees with its content. In the US in particular, a trenchant opposition to 'viewpoint' discrimination on the part of the State has been a central organizing principle in the Supreme Court's case law. As Brennan J put it, 'In order to secure the First Amendment's guarantee of freedom of speech and to prevent distortions of "the market-place of ideas," governments generally are prohibited from discriminating among viewpoints on issues within the realm of protected speech'.[54] This follows too from other rationales for freedom of speech, whether based on truth, autonomy, or pluralism. As the ECtHR has consistently emphasized, freedom of expression

> is applicable not only to 'information' or 'ideas' that are favourably received or regarded as inoffensive or as a matter of indifference, but also to those that offend, shock or disturb. Such are the demands of pluralism, tolerance and broadmindedness without which there is no 'democratic society'.[55]

However, can the State ever be truly neutral? At the very least, government should be able to advocate its own policies in preference to others. Thus, the US Court has held that government is entitled to advocate particular viewpoints, so long as it does not suppress criticism. According to Breyer J:

> That freedom in part reflects the fact that it is the democratic electoral process that first and foremost provides a check on government speech ... Instead, the Free Speech Clause helps produce informed opinions among members of the public, who are then able to influence the choices of a government that, through words and deeds, will reflect its electoral mandate.[56]

However, the line between advocating a governmental viewpoint and suppressing criticism is easily crossed, especially where the State attaches conditions to government subsidies of private activities. Thus, in *Rust v Sullivan*[57] the Court upheld regulations

[54] *Perry Education Association v Perry Local Educators' Association* (n 51) 71–72.

[55] *Animal Defenders International v UK* (n 50) para [100].

[56] *Walker v Sons of Confederate Veterans, Inc* 135 S Ct 2239 (2015) (US Supreme Court) 2264; *Pleasant Grove City v Summum* 129 S Ct 1125 (2009) (US Supreme Court).

[57] *Rust v Sullivan* 500 US 173 (1991) (US Supreme Court).

prohibiting counselling concerning the use of abortion as a condition of receipt of federal funding for family-planning services. The petitioners argued that by prohibiting all discussion about abortion as a lawful option, while compelling the counsellor to provide information that promotes continuing a pregnancy to term, the regulations amounted to impermissible viewpoint discrimination in breach of their First Amendment rights. Rehnquist CJ, giving the judgment of the Court, simply stated that government was entitled to make a value judgement favouring childbirth over abortion and implement that judgement by the allocation of public funds. Blackmun J penned a powerful dissent:

> Until today, the Court never has upheld viewpoint-based suppression of speech simply because that suppression was a condition upon the acceptance of public funds ... By refusing to fund those family-planning projects that advocate abortion because they advocate abortion, the Government plainly has targeted a particular viewpoint.[58]

Disagreement and offence may not therefore be reasons for trammelling content. But what if the content of the speech is so radical as to discount the values that speech itself is meant to protect, for example by calling for authoritarian government, or calling on others to commit crimes? And what if the speech is not just offensive, but is racist, sexist, anti-Semitic or homophobic? Here too Courts have frequently been called on to determine whether the State has transgressed the boundary between its legitimate functions and censorship of dissenting voices. One approach is to hold that speech is not implicated. A second is to take a broad approach to the meaning of speech and instead determine whether speech has been justifiably limited. The first has primarily been used by US courts. It is dealt with briefly here. The second is dealt with in detail in the remainder of this chapter.

B. When is expression not speech?

One way of regulating the content of speech without appearing to breach the right to freedom of speech is simply to hold that speech is not at issue. This is particularly tempting in the case of 'expressive conduct', or the use of actions rather than words to impart a message. Early US cases resisted this temptation, seeing clearly the dangers of censorship. As early as 1931, the US Supreme Court struck down a State regulation prohibiting the flying of the red flag as a symbol of opposition to organized government.[59] Just over a decade later, it upheld a challenge brought by Jehovah's Witnesses whose children had been disciplined for refusing to salute the US flag, which was compulsory in schools in West Virginia. The Court had no doubt that 'the flag salute is a form of utterance. Symbolism is a primitive but effective way of communicating ideas'.[60] Such symbolic speech attracted full First Amendment protection: 'If there is any fixed star in our constitutional constellation, it is that no official, high or petty, can prescribe what shall be orthodox in politics, nationalism, religion, or other matters of opinion or force citizens to confess by word or act their faith therein'.[61] This was

[58] ibid, 207, 210. [59] *Stromberg v California* 283 US 359 (US Supreme Court).
[60] *West Virginia Board of Education v Barnette* 319 US 624 (1943) (US Supreme Court) 632.
[61] ibid, 643.

initially true too for protests against the war in Vietnam. In *Tinker v DesMoines*, the Court held that disciplinary measures against children for wearing black armbands to school in protest against the war were a clear breach of their freedom of speech.[62]

However, the Court took a very different view of burning the draft card, which became a widespread form of protest against conscription to fight in Vietnam. Responding to these demonstrations, Congress created in 1965 a new federal offence of destroying the draft card. It was under this provision that O'Brien was convicted for publicly burning his draft card. He was sentenced to up to six years in custody. O'Brien argued that the First Amendment protected all modes of communication of ideas by conduct, including burning of the draft card.[63] His challenge was rejected. According to Warren CJ: 'We cannot accept the view that an apparently limitless variety of conduct can be labelled "speech" whenever the person engaging in the conduct intends thereby to express an idea'.[64] The Court held that the defendant was being punished for the 'non-communicative impact of his conduct, and for nothing else',[65] a statement which Alfange trenchantly criticizes as generating an eerie 'never-never land atmosphere'.[66] The Court, he argues, refused to give explicit attention to the context of the draft-burning, which clearly could not obstruct the war itself, but was aimed to make a dramatic gesture expressing opposition to the war.[67] *O'Brien* was nevertheless upheld in 1984 in *Clark v Community*, where sleeping in the Mall in central Washington as part of a protest against homelessness, was not permitted.[68] This can be contrasted with the dissenting opinions, which held that rather than obscuring the expressive content of the conduct, the Court should ask whether limiting such expression was justifiable.[69]

It is this approach that has been favoured by courts in other jurisdictions. Eschewing the speech/conduct distinction, which had previously been used by Canadian courts to weed out certain claims to freedom of speech, the Supreme Court of Canada 'has ensured that all manner of expressive activities qualified for constitutional protection'.[70] In *Dolphin Delivery*, the majority of the Court held that picketing by trade union members in a trade dispute clearly involved some element of expression—namely to persuade customers not to do business with the picketed company.[71] This was reinforced in *Butler*, where the Supreme Court of Canada rejected the Court of Appeal's decision that pornography was a purely physical activity and therefore not a protected form of expression. Unlike the 'purely physical' activity of parking a car, pornography clearly conveyed ideas, opinions, or feelings.[72] The State was required to justify, to a high standard, any regulation of conduct which had an expressive element

[62] *Tinker v Des Moines* 393 US 503 (1969) (US Supreme Court) 513–14. Black J dissented on the question of whether the right to free speech can be used at school.

[63] *US v O'Brien* 391 US 367 (1968) (US Supreme Court) 376. [64] ibid. [65] ibid, 391.

[66] D Alfange, 'Free Speech and Symbolic Conduct: The Draft-Card Burning Case' (1968) The Supreme Court Review 1, 14.

[67] ibid, 15–16: see Universal Military Training and Service Act of 1948, s 12(b)(6).

[68] *Clark v Community for Creative Non-Violence* 468 US 288 (1984) (US Supreme Court).

[69] ibid, 308.

[70] K Roach and D Schneiderman, 'Freedom of Expression in Canada' (2013) 61 SCLR (2d) 429, 433.

[71] *Retail, Wholesale and Department Store Union v Dolphin Delivery* (n 9) 588.

[72] *R v Butler* (1992) 1 SCR 452 (Supreme Court of Canada) 487.

to it. On the other hand, where expressive speech involved conduct which could destroy property or assault individuals, the conduct could be punished.[73]

A similar approach was followed by the SACC in *Case v Minister of Safety and Security*, which concerned the constitutionality of legislation criminalizing 'indecent or obscene' photographic matter.[74] Mokgoro J asked, by way of a preliminary question, whether sexually explicit expression was within the protection of the freedom of expression guarantee. Rejecting the US approach of excluding some expressive conduct from the Free Speech guarantee, she took the view that 'the better approach would seem to be to define the right generously, and to interpose any constitutionally justifiable limitations only at the second stage of the analysis'.[75]

This raises the difficult question of what principles should be used to determine when content-based restrictions are legitimate. Sections V–VII consider how courts have navigated this difficult terrain in three specific substantive areas: subversive speech; obscenity and pornography; and hate speech.

V. Subversive Speech

Perhaps the most difficult dilemma arises when speech is used to advocate suppression of speech or dismantling of democracy. As we have seen, Alexander regards it as paradoxical that liberalism appears to deny the State the right to defend the values of liberal free speech. This is not, however, the whole picture. Censorship is not necessarily the only or even the best way to defend free speech and democracy. The fundamental tenet of freedom of speech is to fight speech with speech. Moreover, there is a real risk that if the State is given the power of censorship, it might be tempted to misuse it against speech it dislikes. As US Supreme Court Justice Douglas declared: 'We have deemed it more costly to liberty to suppress a despised minority than to let them vent their spleen. We have above all else feared the political censor'.[76] The First Amendment makes 'confidence in the common sense of our people and in their maturity of judgment the great postulate of our democracy. Its philosophy is that violence is rarely, if ever, stopped by denying civil liberties to those advocating resort to force'.[77] On the other hand, we are rightly haunted by the spectre of the rise of the Nazi Party, which used democratic means to establish a totalitarian regime with the most egregious human rights violations. The concept of 'militant democracy' has been used to suggest that, paradoxically, the only way to protect fundamental freedoms such as freedom of expression is precisely to deny it when endangered. But does this mean that the very basis of democracy has been sacrificed and those attacking democracy have been victorious after all?

The historical and social context is, as ever, of great importance. Many of the American cases arose when the US was gripped by anxiety about communism. In Europe, both fascism and communism were perceived as serious threats, while in

[73] *Retail, Wholesale and Department Store Union v Dolphin Delivery* (n 9) 588.
[74] *Case v Minister of Safety and Security* (1996) (3) SA 617 (South African Constitutional Court).
[75] ibid, para [21].
[76] *Dennis v United States* 341 US 494 (1951) (US Supreme Court) 584–85.
[77] ibid, 591.

India and Turkey, support for separatist movements attracted highly repressive measures. Most recently, the challenge has come from movements asserting the primacy of religion in political affairs and advocating the substitution of liberalism by religious law. In all these contexts, courts have had to answer similar questions. How resilient is the principle that speech should be countered by speech rather than censorship, criminalization, or banning of political parties? Should the State be entitled to take pre-emptive action to suppress speech before any conduct has taken place, or is it sufficient to criminalize unlawful conduct once it has occurred?

A. 'Clear and present danger' in the US Supreme Court

One way forward, which appears consistent with liberal principles, is to apply the familiar harm principle. The State, on this view, is entitled to limit freedom in order to prevent harm. This requires a difficult determination as to whether the speech can be regarded as harmful in itself, or whether harm is likely to arise as a result of the speech. In *Schenck v US*, Justice Holmes formulated the link between speech and harm through the 'clear and present danger' test: 'The question in every case is whether the words used are used in such circumstances and are of such a nature as to create a clear and present danger that they will bring about the substantive evils that Congress has a right to prevent'.[78] Despite the apparent absolute nature of the First Amendment, he declared: 'The most stringent protection of free speech would not protect a man in falsely shouting fire in a theatre and causing a panic'.[79] The 'clear and present danger' test, however, makes problematic assumptions about the ability of words to cause harm. The person shouting 'fire' in a theatre only causes harm if people believe her, if panic ensues, and if individuals are injured. As we have seen, Scanlon argues that a key tenet of freedom of expression is respect for the autonomy of the listener to make up her own mind as to whether to be persuaded.[80] On this view, it is problematic to claim that the speaker is responsible for the ensuing conduct of the listener.

Third-party agency also makes it difficult to determine when a harmful result is 'clear and present'. The tests formulated by courts are, perhaps inevitably, only as robust as the judges who apply them, and judges are not always immune from the political and social anxieties of their times. Thus, rather than requiring stringent proof of causation as between speech and conduct, the US Court quickly diluted the test to one of 'tendency to cause harm'. These risks can be seen in *Schenck* itself. Schenck had been convicted for distributing leaflets protesting against conscription during World War I. He argued that his First Amendment rights had been breached. The Court accepted that the pamphlets confined themselves to peaceful measures. Nevertheless, the conviction was upheld. Holmes J held that the key issue was whether expression had the tendency to obstruct recruitment and was intended to do so. There was 'no ground for saying that success alone warrants making the act a crime'.[81] The result was

[78] *Schenck v United States* 249 US 47 (1919) (US Supreme Court) 52.
[79] ibid, 52.
[80] Scanlon (n 28) 216.
[81] *Schenck v United States* (n 78) 52.

that 'this insubstantial gesture ... was held to be a clear and present danger of bringing about the evil of military insubordination'.[82]

Having authored three judgments upholding convictions where the link between the expression and the obstruction of the war effort was tenuous at best,[83] Holmes J himself realized the risks of the test and began to join Brandeis J in dissent,[84] pointing out how easily the clear and present danger test can be manipulated to crush free opposition. His dissenting voice became even clearer after the war, when the wrath of the State was turned on supporters of Communism. The majority of the Court was quick to find that such dissent had a 'tendency' to cause harm. Thus, in *Gitlow v New York*,[85] the Court upheld the conviction of the Socialist party for the publication of a manifesto advocating 'revolutionary Socialism' to displace capitalism. There was no evidence of any effect resulting from the distribution of the manifesto. The Court nevertheless held that speech could be punished whenever 'its natural tendency and probable effect' is to bring about some substantive evil which the State was entitled to prevent.[86] Holmes J dissented on the grounds that there was no present danger. Moreover, in a reassertion of the autonomy of individuals to make up their own minds, he stated, '[I]f in the long run the beliefs expressed in proletarian dictatorship are destined to be accepted by the dominant forces of the community, the only meaning of free speech is that they should be given their chance and have their way'.[87]

Nevertheless, judicial support for highly repressive state measures continued with vigour during the Cold War period. This is starkly demonstrated in *Whitney v California*, where the Court upheld the imprisonment of Miss Whitney, on the grounds that she had helped organize the Communist Labour Party, which was formed to advocate the desirability of proletarian revolution by mass action at some date far in the future. The Court held that '[w]ithout more, advocating violent means to effect political and economic change involves such danger to the security of the State that the State may outlaw it'.[88] Only Brandeis J continued to speak out for the power of speech itself to counter speech. Despite concurring in the result, he reiterated that 'the fitting remedy for evil counsels is good ones ... If there be time to expose through discussion the falsehood and fallacies ... the remedy to be applied is more speech.'[89]

This reached its lowest point in *Dennis*, where the 'tendency' test was diluted even further into a test which simply asked whether harm was 'not improbable'. In *Dennis*, the US Supreme Court upheld the conviction of eleven national leaders of the Communist Party on the grounds that they had organized the Party to 'teach and advocate the overthrow and destruction of the government of the US by force and violence', which was a criminal offence under the notorious Smith Act. They were not charged with any actual violence. The defendants argued that their activities presented no clear and present danger of foreseeable overthrow. Vinson J reiterated that success in or probability of achieving the overthrow of the government was not a criterion to

[82] *Dennis v United States* (n 76) 504.

[83] See *Frohwerk v US* 249 US 204 (1919) (US Supreme Court); *Debs v US* 249 US 211 (US Supreme Court).

[84] See eg *Abrams v US* 250 US 616 (US Supreme Court).

[85] *Gitlow v New York* 268 US 652 (1925) (US Supreme Court).

[86] ibid, 671.

[87] ibid, 674.

[88] *Whitney v California* (n 11).

[89] ibid, 275, 377.

determine clear and present danger. The clear and present danger test should not be interpreted in a way that could extend 'unprecedented immunities' to Communists or ensnare the government in a 'judge-made verbal trap' in the face of a well-organized national conspiracy. Instead, the plurality diluted it to a balancing test: 'In each case [courts] must ask whether the gravity of the "evil", discounted by its improbability, justifies such invasion of free speech as is necessary to avoid the danger'.[90] The plurality had no doubt that the defendants' conspiracy created a clear and present danger in accordance with this 'not improbable' test.

This approach was sharply criticized by Black J. As he put it: 'Such a doctrine waters down the First Amendment so that it . . . is not likely to protect any but those "safe" or orthodox views which rarely need its protection'.[91] Indeed, history demonstrated the damaging effect of such a gloss on the First Amendment. Looking back on this period in 1969, Douglas J was moved to say:

> [T]he infamous loyalty-security hearings which, since 1947 when President Truman launched them, have processed 20,000,000 men and women . . . were primarily concerned with one's thoughts, ideas, beliefs, and convictions. They were the most blatant violations of the First Amendment we have ever known.[92]

The dissenting voices eventually did become the majority, as the tide turned back in favour of freedom of speech. In *Brandenburg v Ohio*,[93] members of the Ku Klux Klan, were convicted under the Ohio Criminal Syndicalism statute which punished persons who advocated or taught violence as a means of accomplishing industrial or political reform. Overruling *Whitney v California*, the Court held that mere advocacy of the use of force without more could not be outlawed. It could only be prohibited where three elements were satisfied: intent to incite or produce lawless action; imminence of such action; and likelihood that the speech would produce such imminent lawless action.[94] The imminent lawlessness test in *Brandenburg* remains the standard in US cases and has been applied in a wide range of cases.[95] Ironically, however, the *Brandenburg* case protected the blatantly racist and anti-Semitic speech of the Ku Klux Klan. Arguably, when speech attacks the very dignity and integrity of others, a different sort of test is needed. This is dealt with in section B.

B. Tendency to disorder: The Indian Supreme Court

The harm principle has similarly been used by the Indian Supreme Court to determine the legitimacy of criminal statutes suppressing 'subversive' speech. As in the US, the key issue has been the way the Court has characterized the link between speech and harmful conduct. The test has wavered between a rather lenient requirement of

[90] *Dennis v United States* (n 76) 511.
[91] ibid, 580.
[92] *Brandenburg v Ohio* 395 US 444 (1969) (US Supreme Court) 456.
[93] ibid.
[94] ibid, 447.
[95] *Scales v United States* 367 US 203 (1961); *Noto v United States* 367 US 290 (1961); *Yates v United States* 354 US 298 (1957); *Keyishian v Board of Regents* 385 US 589 (1967); *Elfbrandt v Russell* 384 US 11 (1966); *Cramp v Board of Public Instruction* 368 US 278 (1961); *United States v Robel* 389 US 258 (1967); *Speiser v Randall* 357 US 513 (1958); *Schware v Board of Bar Examiners* 353 US 232 (1957).

intention and tendency to cause harm and a more exacting demand for imminence. Article 19(2)(b) of the Indian Constitution allows the State to pass legislation imposing reasonable restrictions on speech and expression, in the interests of, inter alia, the security of the State, public order, or incitement to an offence. In the early case of *Babulal Parate*, the applicants argued, relying on *Schenck*, that restraints on speech were only permissible if there be a clear and present danger. The Court rejected this approach.

> The American doctrine cannot be imported under our Constitution because the fundamental rights guaranteed under Article 19(1) of the Constitution ... are subject to the restrictions placed in the subsequent clauses of Article 19. There is nothing in the American Constitution corresponding to [these clauses].[96]

A key issue before the Indian Supreme Court has been the constitutionality of sedition laws penalizing words which 'excite or attempt to excite disaffection'.[97] Sedition was widely used by the British during colonial times as a means to suppress the struggle for freedom from the British empire. Mahatma Gandhi famously referred to these laws as 'the prince among the political sections of the Indian Penal Code designed to suppress the liberty of the citizen'.[98] Gandhi was himself found guilty of sedition in 1922 and sentenced to prison. Because of this history, the drafters of the Indian Constitution decided to omit sedition from the list of potentially legitimate reasons to limit freedom of speech. Nevertheless, successive Indian governments have not been averse to making use of precisely the same provisions to prosecute dissidents. The sedition law inherited from the British was maintained in the Indian Penal Code.[99] Section 124A of the Penal Code, as amended in 1950, now reads: 'Whoever by words, either spoken or written, or by signs or by visible representation or otherwise, brings or attempts to bring into hatred or contempt, or excites or attempts to excite disaffection towards the Government established by law in India shall be punished . . '. with a maximum sentence of three years in prison. According to the statutory explanations, 'disaffection' includes disloyalty and all feelings of enmity. Disapprobation of government measures without exciting or attempting to excite hatred, contempt, or disaffection are not included.

The Indian Supreme Court was asked to clarify the constitutionality of this provision in *Kedar Nath Singh* in 1962.[100] The defendant had been sentenced to imprisonment for delivering fiery speeches critical of the current regime, but without calling for revolution. He argued that section 124A was inconsistent with freedom of speech in Article 19. The Court emphasized the need to show a link with incitement to violence to justify limiting the right. 'A citizen has a right to say or write whatever he likes about the Government, or its measures, by way of criticism or comment, so long as he

[96] *Babulal Parate v State of Maharashta* (1961) 3 SCR 423 (Indian Supreme Court) 424–25.

[97] Indian Penal Code, Article 124A. See generally G Bhatia, *Offend, Shock or Disturb: Free Speech under the Indian Constitution* (OUP 2016) ch 4.

[98] Centre for the Study of Social Exclusion and Inclusive Policy, National Law School of India University, Bangalore and Alternative Law Forum, Bangalore: 'Sedition Laws & the Death of Free Speech in India' (February 2011) <https://www.nls.ac.in/resources/csseip/Files/SeditionLaws_cover_Final.pdf> 9 (accessed 4 March 2018).

[99] Indian Penal Code, Article 124A. See generally Bhatia (n 97) ch 4.

[100] *Kedar Nath Singh v State of Bihar* AIR 1962 SC 955 (Indian Supreme Court).

does not incite people to violence against the Government established by law or with the intention of creating public disorder'.[101] It held that section 124A could be construed so that the offence was only committed if the words created a tendency to disorder, or intention to create a disturbance of law and order. Interpreted in this way, it was held to be constitutional. Thus, despite having distanced itself from US case law, the Court nevertheless promulgated a test very similar to the 'tendency' test in the earlier US cases.

A different current of Indian jurisprudence has suggested somewhat more searching scrutiny, based on a test of proximity. In *Lohia,*[102] the General Secretary of the Indian Socialist Party had been arrested under legislation originally introduced by the British in 1932 to offset the Congress Party's defiance campaign of non-payment of taxes. Lohia had addressed audiences urging them not to pay enhanced irrigation rates in protest at the unbearable burden placed on cultivators. The Supreme Court was required to determine whether the legislation constituted a reasonable restriction on freedom of speech in the interests of public order. The Court held that to fulfil this criterion, a restriction 'should be one which has a proximate connection or nexus with public order, but not one far-fetched, hypothetical or problematical or too remote in the chain of its relation with the public order'.[103] In this case, there was no proximate or even foreseeable relationship between the instigation by a single individual and the possibility of a revolutionary movement destroying public order.

Although earlier than *Kedar Nath, Lohia* was not cited therein, so that it is difficult to know how to reconcile the proximity test in *Lohia* with the tendency requirement in *Kedar Nath*. Imminence or proximity have nevertheless reappeared in some forms in more recent cases outside the sedition arena. In *Rangarajan*, the Court established a much higher standard of scrutiny than in *Kedar Nath,* referring to the need to show that expression was intrinsically dangerous to the public interest, or, more graphically, that the 'expression should be inseparably locked up with the action contemplated like the equivalent of a "spark in a powder keg"'.[104] More recently still, in *Arup Bhuyan,*[105] the Court expressly referred to and endorsed the *Brandenburg* test. The case concerned a statute which made mere membership of a banned organization illegal.[106] The Court held that mere membership of a banned party was not sufficient unless it incites to 'imminent lawless action'. It nevertheless remains unclear whether the Indian Court has fully embraced a high level of scrutiny, requiring incitement to imminent lawless action before expression can be curtailed. In the light of continued action in the Indian law courts against dissenters, including university students, the need to maintain such a standard is particularly urgent.[107]

101 ibid. 102 *Superintendent v Ram Monohar Lohia* AIR 1960 SC 633 (Indian Supreme Court).
103 ibid.
104 *Rangarajan v Jagjivan Ram* 1989 SCR (2) 204 (Indian Supreme Court) 226 G–H.
105 *Arup Bhuyan v State of Assam* (2011) 3 SCC 377 (Indian Supreme Court).
106 Terrorist and Disruptive Activities (Prevention) Act 1967, s 3(5).
107 See L Liang, 'Sedition and the Status of Subversive Speech in India' *The Wire* (14 February 2016) <https://thewire.in/21547/sedition-and-the-status-of-subversive-speech-in-india/> (accessed 4 March 2018).

C. Political parties: The European Court of Human Rights

The cases thus far have been predominantly concerned with punitive measures against individuals. What if the State bans a political party? The liberal dilemma is particularly acute if a party, while using the democratic process to gain power, might then utilize its power to dismantle democracy itself. Can the State act pre-emptively to prevent this? The very basis of democracy might appear to be threatened by parties advocating its demise, as so disastrously testified by the Nazi Party in Germany. But at the same time, how far can democracy compromise on its own basic principles to protect itself, without at the same time destroying itself?

The most sustained treatment of this issue has been before the ECtHR, triggered by the banning in Turkey of various political parties over recent decades. In navigating the difficult balance between protection of democratic principles, and protection of democracy itself, the ECtHR has generally taken a robust stand in favour of protecting both freedom of speech and freedom of association. Specifically, political parties are regarded as entitled to seek the protection of Article 10, since they function as part of a collective freedom of expression. At the same time, the Court recognizes that the State should be able to protect its democratic institutions against associations which might jeopardize them. Hence, according to the Court: 'A political party whose officers encourage the use of force or propose a political programme that does not respect the rules of democracy or that aims to destroy democracy and infringe the rights and freedoms that it upholds, cannot rely on the protection of the Convention'.[108]

The more difficult issue is to apply this formula to specific cases. In most cases, the Court has found in favour of freedom of speech. In *United Communist Party v Turkey*,[109] the Court held that by dissolving the United Communist Party of Turkey (TBKP), Turkey was in violation of both Article 10, the right to freedom of speech, and Article 11, freedom of association. Notably, the TBKP had never advocated either violence or the institution of a dictatorship. What really caused the government to move for its dissolution was the TBKP's support for a separate Kurdish state, albeit by peaceful and democratic means. For the Court, free expression of the opinion of the people in the choice of legislature is 'inconceivable without the participation of a plurality of political parties representing the different shades of opinion within a country's population'.[110] Given the essential role of political parties in the proper functioning of democracy, any limitations on their right to freedom of expression should be strictly construed, leaving only a small margin of appreciation to the State.[111] The TBKP was committed to democracy, including political pluralism and universal suffrage. The Court took a similar stance in relation to the Socialist Party, which had likewise been dissolved by the Turkish Constitutional Court, again because of its reference to the right to self-determination of Kurds:[112]

[108] *Yazar v Turkey* (2003) 36 EHRR 6 (European Court of Human Rights) para [49].
[109] *United Communist Party of Turkey* (1998) 26 EHRR 121 (European Court of Human Rights).
[110] ibid, para [35]. [111] ibid, para [46].
[112] *The Socialist Party v Turkey* (1999) 27 EHRR 51 (European Court of Human Rights).

> In the Court's view, the fact that such a political programme is considered incompatible with the current principles and structures of the Turkish State does not make it incompatible with the rules of democracy. It is of the essence of democracy to allow diverse political programmes to be proposed and debated, even those that call into question the way a State is currently organised, provided that they do not harm democracy itself.[113]

However, it took a very different view of the application of these principles in the more recent case of *Refah Partisi v Turkey*.[114] Refah, a large political party, had been dissolved by the Turkish Constitutional Court on the grounds that it was a 'centre' of activities contrary to the principle of secularism in the Turkish Constitution. The party maintained that adherents of each religious movement should obey their own rules rather than that of Turkish law. It also called for the secular political system to be replaced by a theocratic system, if necessary, by force. In its decision to dissolve the party, the Turkish Constitutional Court declared that the principle of secularism was an indispensable condition of democracy in Turkey and that the rules of sharia were incompatible with the democratic regime.

The ECtHR upheld the dissolution. It reiterated the 'primordial role' played by political parties in a democratic regime. Political parties had the right to seek the protection of Article 10 inasmuch as their activities form part of a collective exercise of freedom of expression. Moreover, Article 10 applied not only to inoffensive ideas, but also to those that shock and disturb.[115] At the same time, it emphasized that the freedoms guaranteed by Article 10 could not deprive the State of the right to protect its institutions where an association, through its activities, jeopardizes the State's institutions:

> No-one must be authorised to rely on the Convention's provisions in order to weaken or destroy the ideals and values of a democratic society ... It is not at all improbable that totalitarian movements, organised in the form of political parties, might do away with democracy, after prospering under the democratic regime, there being examples of this in modern European history.[116]

Nor is a State compelled to wait for a political party to seize power before intervening, where the danger for democracy is 'sufficiently established and imminent'.[117] Where such a danger has been established by national courts, after detailed scrutiny and subject to rigorous supervision from Europe, a State may reasonably forestall the execution of a policy before steps are taken to implement a policy which might prejudice the country's democratic regime. Indeed, such a power of preventive intervention might arise under the State's positive duties under Article 1 of the Convention to secure the rights and freedoms of persons within their jurisdiction. Nevertheless, drastic measures such as the dissolution of an entire political party and banning of its leaders should be taken only in the most serious cases.[118] Thus the simple fact that a political

[113] ibid, para [102].
[114] *Refah Partisi (the Welfare Party) v Turkey* (2003) 37 EHRR 1 (European Court of Human Rights).
[115] ibid, paras [193]–[195]. [116] ibid, para [205]. [117] ibid, para [208].
[118] ibid, para [206].

party is animated by religious values cannot be regarded as intrinsically inimical to democracy. In a test resonant of that in *Brandenburg*, the crucial issue for a court to determine was whether there was plausible evidence that the risk to democracy, supposing it had been proved to exist, was sufficiently imminent.[119]

While the court articulated a framework which is sensitive to the difficult balance that needs to be drawn, its application in the *Refah* case itself is problematic. The Grand Chamber agreed with both the Chamber and the Turkish Constitutional Court that 'it is difficult to declare one's respect for democracy and human rights while at the same time supporting a regime based on sharia, which clearly diverges from Convention values, particularly with regard to its criminal law and criminal procedure, its rules on the legal status of women and the way it intervenes in all spheres of public and private life in accordance with religions precepts'.[120] Boyle is highly critical of the Court's assumption that sharia law and democracy are incompatible.[121] While he affirms the background principles used by the Court to determine the question, he regards its application in the case as revealing highly problematic background assumptions on the part of the Court. As Boyle points out, the Refah party was not suppressed for anything it had done in government, but for what it might do in the future, based on its statements and the programme it advocated. Paradoxically, it was the popularity of the party in the polls which the Court regarded as making the threat imminent: at the time of its dissolution, Refah had sixty-two MPs in Parliament. Polls predicted that at the next general election, it might be the majority party, in a position to implement its programme. The Court was mindful that the dissolution of the party only affected five of its MPs, who temporarily forfeited their parliamentary office. The 152 remaining MPs continued to sit in Parliament.[122] Nevertheless, *Refah* is an extraordinary decision, given the fact that when it was taken, Refah was actually part of the governing coalition in Turkey.

The Court's problematic assumptions about the incompatibility of sharia law and democracy are even more conspicuous in the light of its continued support for dissident parties of other creeds, including communist parties and Kurdish separatist parties. Thus, in *Partidul Comunistolor v Romania*, it held that the refusal to register a Communist Party was a breach of freedom of association and freedom of expression. Romania's experience of totalitarian communism prior to 1989 was not itself a justification for violating the rights to freedom of association of the party. The Court reiterated its consistent view that:

> one of the principal characteristics of democracy [is] the possibility it offers of addressing through dialogue, without recourse to violence, issues raised by different strands of political opinion, even when they are irksome or disturbing. Democracy thrives on freedom of expression. From that point of view, there can be no justification for hindering a political group that complies with fundamental democratic

[119] ibid, para [210]. [120] ibid, para [229].

[121] K Boyle, 'Human Rights, Religion and Democracy: The Refah Party Case' (2004) 1 Essex Human Rights Review 1.

[122] *Refah Partisi (the Welfare Party) v Turkey* (n 114) para [240].

principles solely because it has criticised the country's constitutional and legal order and sought a public debate in the political arena.[123]

The emergence of a new communist party should therefore be the subject of democratic debate rather than prohibition. The Court also struck down the dissolution of pro-Kurdish parties in Turkey on two further occasions, on the ground that advocating the right to self-determination for the Kurds could not be equated with supporting acts of terrorism.[124] Only in one case, against Spain, did the Court uphold the dissolution of a Basque party on the grounds that the Spanish courts, after a detailed study of the evidence, had reasonably concluded that there was a link between the applicant parties and terrorist strategies. In view of the situation in regard to terrorist attacks in Spain, which had existed for many years, these links could be objectively regarded as a threat to democracy.[125]

VI. Obscenity and Pornography

The contest between freedom of speech and valid restrictions plays itself out in very different ways in the jurisprudence concerning obscenity and pornography. Courts consistently proclaim that freedom of speech includes speech which is shocking and offensive. Courts in several jurisdictions have nevertheless readily upheld prohibitions on speech which is regarded as 'obscene or depraved'. This is particularly striking in the US, where courts have not been deterred by the apparent absoluteness of the First Amendment when it comes to speech which is regarded as exciting 'prurient interest'. The ECtHR has also been quick to uphold limitations where they can be justified in the interests of 'morality', which is expressly permitted under Article 10(2). Paradoxically, however, the US Supreme Court has distinguished between 'obscenity' and 'pornography', and has systematically struck down attempts by Congress to regulate access to pornographic materials, even for minors.[126] This is in striking contrast with the Canadian jurisprudence, which has rooted its approach to obscenity and pornography firmly in the harm principle.

Behind this lies an acute tension between censorship based on a Victorian morality of sexual repression, and regulation of a highly profitable, highly exploitative commercial market of pornography. Where should the line be drawn between commercial products which are genuinely harmful and speech which represents and experiments with many different life-styles? This dilemma is epitomized by the Canadian experience. Having established a harm-based principle to control pornography, the Canadian Supreme Court found itself faced with a case in which these powers had

[123] *Partidul Comunistilor (Nepeceristi) v Romania* (2007) 44 EHRR 17 (European Court of Human Rights) para [55]; see also *Republican Party of Russia v Russia* (2015) 61 EHRR 20 (European Court of Human Rights).

[124] *HADEP v Turkey* (2013) 56 EHRR 5 (European Court of Human Rights); *Party for a Democratic Society (DTP) v Turkey* (3870/10, 12 January 2016) (European Court of Human Rights).

[125] *Herri Batasuna v Spain* (25803/04, 30 June 2009) (European Court of Human Rights).

[126] Pornography is generally defined as printed or visual material containing the explicit description or display of sexual organs or activity, intended to stimulate sexual excitement, see English Oxford Living Dictionaries <https://en.oxforddictionaries.com/definition/pornography> (accessed 4 March 2018).

been used against a publisher promoting same-sex culture.[127] One way forward might be to ally the harm principle with one based in dignity. In the South African case of *De Reuck v DPP*,[128] Langa J held that child pornography was universally condemned because, as well as causing obvious physical harm, 'there is also harm to the dignity and perception of all children when a society allows sexualised images of children to be available'.[129] The chief purpose of statutory prohibitions against child pornography, he concluded, 'is to protect the dignity, humanity and integrity of children'.[130] On this test, the understanding of what constituted pornography in the context of same-sex culture would be very different from heterosexual culture. Thus, materials promoting same-sex culture would not constitute pornography if they did not create dignity harms.

What is missing from all these formulations is the right to equality. An equality perspective requires us to ask whether everyone has an equal opportunity to speak, or whether speech silences those with less power in society. A key rationale for freedom of speech is to protect individuals against the power of the State. But this evaporates when speech is used to augment power and deprives the powerless of even the ability to counter speech with more speech. It was this perspective which has been articulated so trenchantly by Andrea Dworkin and Catharine Mackinnon. Pornography, on this view, should be recognized as sex discrimination, as a 'practice of civil inequality on the basis of gender, posing the threats to its target population that all socially institutionalized inequalities do'.[131] In the words of Andrea Dworkin, 'the fact is that the speech of the socially worthless, the sexually stigmatised, is hard to hear even when the victims shout'.[132] Or, as MacKinnon puts it: 'The free speech of men silences the free speech of women'.[133]

A. Obscenity: speech as morality

This is not, however, an insight which has convinced the US Supreme Court. Instead, its case law has taken a frankly moralistic approach. Drawing on the long tradition of English law, which punished speech which tended to 'deprave and corrupt',[134] the US court has upheld regulation of obscenity on the grounds of a moralistic notion of 'decency' and 'propriety'. The charge of content-based censorship is avoided by refusing to classify material as speech in the first place. In *Roth v US* in 1958, Brennan J, giving the opinion of the Court, held that obscenity was so 'utterly without redeeming

[127] *Little Sisters Book and Art Emporium v Canada (Minister of Justice)* (2000) 2 SCR 1120 (Supreme Court of Canada).

[128] *De Reuck v Director of Public Prosecutions* [2003] ZACC 19 (South African Constitutional Court).

[129] ibid, para [63]. [130] ibid.

[131] A Dworkin and C MacKinnon, *Pornography and Civil Rights: A New Day for Women's Equality* (1988) 31 <https://www.feministes-radicales.org/wp-content/uploads/2012/05/Catharine-A.-MacKinnon-Andrea-Dworkin-Pornography-and-Civil-Rights-A-New-Day-for-Women%E2%80%99s-Equality-1988.pdf> (accessed 4 March 2018).

[132] C MacKinnon and A Dworkin (eds), *In Harm's Way: The Pornography Civil Rights Hearings* (Harvard University Press 1997) 33.

[133] C MacKinnon, *Feminism Unmodified* (Harvard University Press 1987) 156.

[134] *R v Hicklin* (1868) LR 3 QB 360 (UK Queen's Bench).

social importance' as not to count as expression at all for the purposes of the First Amendment.[135] Even though ideas with the slightest redeeming social importance, including 'unorthodox ideas, controversial ideas, even ideas hateful to the prevailing climate of opinion' had full protection of the First Amendment, obscenity was not within the area of constitutionally protected speech or press.[136] Brennan J rejected the concern that obscenity statutes punished incitement of 'pure sexual thoughts not shown to be related to any overt antisocial conduct'.[137] The short answer to this was that there was no need to prove harm if the material was not classified as speech in the first place. Obscenity can be prohibited simply because a legislature determines that this would protect 'the social interest in order and public morality'.[138]

This puts great weight on the definition of obscenity. Brennan J purported to endorse a stricter standard for the definition of obscenity than the previous *Hicklin* test, which had allowed material to be evaluated from the perspective of particularly sensitive persons.[139] Instead, the standard should be 'whether to the average person, applying contemporary community standards, the dominant theme of the material taken as a whole appeals to prurient interest'.[140] Brennan J was quick to insist that 'sex and obscenity are not synonymous'. It was therefore permissible to punish speech which was 'obscene, lewd, lascivious or filthy, or other publication of an indecent character'. On the other hand, the portrayal of sex in art, literature, and science 'has indisputably been a subject of absorbing interest to mankind through the ages'.[141] This emphasis on morality rather than harm, however, was deeply concerning to Douglas J, dissenting. For him, speech should only be suppressed if it was 'so closely brigaded with illegal action as to be an inseparable part of it'.[142] A test which depended on community standards of morality was wholly unacceptable: 'Literature should not be suppressed merely because it offends the moral code of the censor'.[143]

Despite difficulty in clarifying what Harlan J called the 'intractable obscenity problem',[144] the Court reaffirmed *Roth's* finding that obscene material is unprotected by the First Amendment in *Miller v California* in 1973.[145] For Burger CJ, to equate the robust exchange of ideas and political debate with commercial exploitation of obscene material 'demeans the grand conception of the First Amendment and its high purposes in the historical struggle for freedom'.[146] Keeping it outside of the First Amendment also meant that obscenity regulation could remain expressly moralistic. The *Miller* court's revised test retained the reliance on contemporary community standards, adding a more objective requirement of patent offensiveness, and a more express caveat for material with serious literary, artistic, political, or scientific value. The three-pronged test for obscenity is therefore: '(a) whether the average person, applying contemporary community standards would find that the work, taken as a whole, appeals to the prurient interest; (b) whether the work depicts or describes, in a patently offensive way, sexual conduct specifically defined by the applicable state

[135] *Roth v United States* 354 US 476 (1957) (US Supreme Court) 485. [136] ibid, 484–85.
[137] ibid, 486. [138] ibid, 485. [139] *R v Hicklin* (n 134).
[140] *Roth v United States* (n 135) 489. [141] ibid, 488. [142] ibid, 514. [143] ibid, 513.
[144] Cited in *Miller v California* 413 US 15 (1973) (US Supreme Court) 16; see especially *Memoirs v Massachusetts* 383 US 413 (1966) (US Supreme Court).
[145] *Miller v California*, ibid. [146] ibid, 34.

law; and (c) whether the work, taken as a whole, lacks serious literary, artistic, political, or scientific value'.[147]

The *Miller* standard nevertheless continues to be unpredictable and litigation-prone. In particular, with the growth of the internet, the question arises as to which community's standard is guiding. Given that web publishers cannot control the geographic scope of their communications, the community standards criterion could force all speakers on the Web to abide by the most puritan of community standards. The US Supreme Court nevertheless upheld the community standards test as recently as 2002. According to Thomas J:

> [I]f a publisher chooses to send its material into a particular community, this Court's jurisprudence teaches that it is the publisher's responsibility to abide by that community's standards. The publisher's burden does not change simply because it decides to distribute its material to every community in the Nation.[148]

The ECtHR has reached a similar result to that of the US Supreme Court by a very different route. Unlike its US counterpart, it has not needed to disguise moral judgements behind apparent neutrality, because of an explicit acknowledgement that the State might legitimately limit freedom of speech for the 'protection of morals', provided such a measure is prescribed by law and necessary in the interests of a democratic society.[149] Moreover, it has taken the view that, as a supranational court, it cannot be the arbiter of national public morals. The problematic nature of this uncritical deference to a notion of public morality can be seen in *Handyside v UK*.[150] In this case, an English publisher of *The Little Red Schoolbook* was convicted under the UK Obscene Publications Act, which deemed material to be 'obscene' if its effect was 'such as to tend to deprave and corrupt' persons who are likely to read, see, or hear it.[151] The *Schoolbook*, which included a twenty-six-page chapter on 'sex', had been circulated freely in at least thirteen European countries. Nevertheless, the domestic court held that it tended to deprave and corrupt. Although the information was largely accurate and useful, it was undermined by several subversive suggestions. For example, the treatment of homosexuality was factual and compassionate, but the fact that marriage was not mentioned at all could create incorrect conclusions in children's minds.

The ECtHR held that prosecution and confiscation interfered with the applicant's freedom of expression. However, it was 'prescribed by law' and 'necessary in a democratic society ... for the protection of morals' under Article 10(2). Since it was impossible to find a uniform European conception of morals, State authorities were in a better position than an international court to determine whether restrictions were necessary to protect morals. Moreover, anyone who exercised freedom of expression had not only rights, but also duties and responsibilities, and this was relevant in determining whether restrictions were justified.[152] The Court reminded itself that freedom of speech also applied to ideas that shock, offend, or disturb, and that restrictions must

[147] ibid, 24. [148] *Ashcroft v ACLU* 535 US 564 (2002) (US Supreme Court) 584.
[149] ECHR Article 10(2).
[150] *Handyside v The United Kingdom* (1979–80) 1 EHRR 737 (European Court of Human Rights).
[151] Obscene Publications Act 1959/1964, s 1(1).
[152] *Handyside v The United Kingdom* (n 150) para [49].

be 'necessary' in the interests of protecting morals.[153] Nevertheless, the application of the test was remarkably lenient. Although the book contained information that was generally correct and often useful, it also contained material 'that young people at a critical stage of their development could have interpreted as an encouragement to indulge in precocious activities harmful for them or even to commit certain criminal offences'.[154]

The ECtHR displayed a similar lenience in permitting morality-based restrictions in *Müller v Switzerland* in 1988.[155] Swiss law made it an offence to make or possess 'obscene' items, interpreted by Swiss courts to mean any works which offend the sense of sexual propriety in a manner that it is difficult to accept. Müller had been convicted for publicly exhibiting paintings held to depict sexuality in an offensive form, including one depicting sexual relations between men and animals. The ECtHR held that the interference with freedom of expression could be justified under Article 10(2) as necessary in the interests of a democratic society for the protection of morals. The Court again gestured towards the need to respect pluralism, tolerance, and broadmindedness towards ideas even if they offend, shock, or disturb. It nevertheless reiterated that there was no uniform conception of European morals, and therefore State authorities were in the best position to give an opinion on the necessity of a restriction. However, far from a necessity standard, the Court upheld the Swiss court's approach on the ground that it was not unreasonable.

B. Pornography: harm or inequality

The problem with both the ECtHR and the US Supreme Court's approach is its dislocation from any linkage to harm. For the US Supreme Court, attempts by the State to regulate pornography to protect against harm have been consistently struck down. At the same time, feminist lawyers and writers have increasingly articulated the harms of pornography as rooted in and perpetuating women's subordination in society. This in turn has led to an uneasy alliance between those who wish to control pornography because it is immoral and those who wish to prohibit it because of the harm it causes. As Green puts it:

> To be radical about pornography used to mean that one favored less censorship; now it often means that one favors more ... Until quite recently, most people who believed pornography wrong thought it offended against decency and propriety and was therefore *obscene* ... The new paradigm is importantly different for ... pornography is understood to be harmful to women, and public policy in this area is a special case of fulfilling the duty to prevent harm.[156]

Recognition of the harm caused by pornography has required, as its very first step, the unlocking of the enforced silence of the victims. Hired to draft an amendment to the City of Minneapolis's civil rights law to recognize pornography as a violation of

153 ibid, para [49]. 154 ibid, para [52].

155 *Müller v Switzerland* (1991) 13 EHRR 212 (European Court of Human Rights).

156 L Green, 'Pornographies' (2000) 8 Journal of Political Philosophy 27, 27–28 (italics in the original).

women's rights, Dworkin and MacKinnon began by holding public hearings to provide a legislative record demonstrating the need for such a law. As Dworkin describes it:

> [A] new social truth emerged, one that had been buried in fear, shame, and the silence of the socially powerless ... What the survivors said was speech; the pornography had been through their lives, a means of actively suppressing their speech. They had been turned into pornography in life and made mute; terrorized by and made mute. Now the mute spoke; the socially invisible were seen.'[157]

Their work exposed the unspeakable harm of pornography, for the women involved in the making of it, and the women deeply damaged by the effects of it.

The reliance on the harm principle for prohibiting pornographic speech might be regarded as placing this approach squarely in the liberal tradition. Its radicalism, however, lies in its recognition of the power of words and images themselves to subordinate, discriminate, and silence. Pornography in this sense is not only about the pain it inflicts on the protagonists. It is also harmful in that it legitimizes and normalizes sexual violence and humiliation against women. This approach has been controversial. There is no doubt that serious harm, often reaching the level of torture, is caused to the actors in pornography, whether adult or child.[158] Empirical proof of causative links between pornography and sexual violence and discrimination, on the other hand, is often challenged. The UK Committee on Obscenity and Film Censorship rejected evidence offered to it that pornography increases the crimes of violent assault or sexual abuse.[159] Similarly, in his dissent in *Roth*, Douglas J, although holding that only the harm principle could justify censorship of obscenity, also rejected evidence of harm caused by exposure to obscene literature as too inconclusive to rest restrictions on the harm principle.[160] Such an approach ignores the large amount of literature, both experimental and experiential, showing that explicitly violent and non-violent sexual materials can intensify sexual aggression among men highly predisposed to sexual coercion, as well as triggering copycat sexual violence and objectification.[161] Waltman concludes that

> although 'scientific' evidence of single direct harmful causation is complex and can seldom be absolutely verified ... when considering the preponderance of evidence and convergence of different methodologies and sources on the single conclusion ... not attributing causality from the sexual objectification and violence in pornography is not credible, even though other causes are also present.[162]

The contestation around empirical evidence exposes the limits of the harm principle as the chief reason for permitting regulation of hard pornography. Harm can only be fully understood once infused with an equality perspective, namely that pornography

[157] A Dworkin, *Pornography: Men Possessing Women* (Putnam 1981) ch 3.

[158] See extensive evidence cited in M Waltman, 'Rethinking Democracy: Legal Challenges to Pornography and Sex Inequality in Canada and the United States' (2010) 63 Political Research Quarterly 218, 219–20.

[159] Committee on Obscenity and Film Censorship (Williams Committee) Cmnd 7772 HMSO, London 1979.

[160] *Roth v United States* (n 135).

[161] See evidence cited in Waltman (n 158) 221.

[162] ibid, 221.

is condoned by and perpetuates the sexual subordination of women in broader society. This frankly recognizes that a moral position is inevitable in determining the permissible limits of freedom of speech. Instead of claiming the harm principle as a neutral or scientific means of determining such limits, the relative merits of different moral positions should be openly aired. The existing human rights commitment to equality and dignity makes these values a better contender in the conflict with freedom of speech than Victorian values of sexual repression. This can be seen in the South African Court's use of dignity in the context of child pornography. In *de Reuck*, Langa CJ accepted that it was difficult to find evidence to support the claim that pornography was likely to reinforce beliefs that sex with children was acceptable, or that paedophiles' fantasies were fuelled by child pornography. Nevertheless, he held that common sense indicates that these effects will sometimes occur.[163]

The attempts to infuse US jurisprudence with such an approach have, however, been thwarted. The ordinances drafted by Dworkin and MacKinnon aimed to characterize pornography as a species of sex discrimination. Their ordinance was passed by the Minneapolis City Council in 1983 and 1984 but vetoed by its mayor on both occasions. A similarly drafted ordinance was passed in Indianapolis in 1984 but struck down by a federal court of appeals in *American Booksellers v Hudnut* in 1985.[164] Far from accepting pornography as discriminatory speech, the Court held that the Ordinance discriminated on the basis of the content of the speech:

> Speech treating women in the approved way—in sexual encounters 'premised on equality'—is lawful no matter how sexually explicit. Speech treating women in the disapproved way—as submissive in matters sexual or as enjoying humiliation—is unlawful no matter how significant the literary, artistic, or political qualities of the work taken as a whole. The state may not ordain preferred viewpoints in this way. The Constitution forbids the state to declare one perspective right and silence opponents.[165]

The US Supreme Court's predominant concern with preventing encroachment by the State on free speech has continued to obscure any recognition of State responsibility to protect against the harm of pornography. This has led to a longstanding war of attrition between the US legislature and the Court, which has systematically struck down legislative attempts to protect children from pornography, however carefully the legislature attempted to meet the Court's concerns. The first attempt by Congress to protect children from exposure to pornography took the form of the Communications Decency Act of 1996 (CDA). The CDA prohibited the knowing display on the internet of 'patently offensive' material in a manner available to persons under the age of eighteen. Restricted access to covered material could be provided with proof of age. The Act prohibited material which 'depicts or describes, in terms patently offensive as measured by contemporary community standards, sexual or excretory activities or organs'.[166] Nevertheless, in *Reno v ACLU*, the US Supreme Court struck down the

[163] *De Reuck v Director of Public Prosecutions* (n 128) para [65].
[164] *American Booksellers v Hudnut* 771 F.2d 323 (1985) (US Court of Appeals, Seventh Circuit).
[165] ibid, 325. [166] §223(d)(1).

provision as breaching the First Amendment.[167] In order to deny minors access to potentially harmful speech, it held, the provisions had suppressed a large amount of speech which adults had a constitutional right to receive and to address to each other.[168] The reference to 'patently offensive', while part of the *Miller* test, was not sufficient, largely because it omitted the need to show lack of literary artistic, political or social value.[169]

Congress responded to the *Reno* decision by enacting the Child Online Protection Act of 1998, which restricted 'material that is harmful to minors', produced for commercial purposes. To meet the Court's objection, the legislation's definition of 'harmful materials' replicated the definition of obscenity in *Miller.* Like its predecessor, it included defences where age verification had been put in place. However, in *Ashcroft v ACLU*, by a narrow majority, the Court upheld an injunction preventing the statute from being enforced on the grounds that it was likely to violate the First Amendment.[170] Kennedy J reiterated the view that 'content-based prohibitions, enforced by severe criminal penalties, have the constant potential to be a repressive force in the lives and thoughts of a free people'.[171] The Court held that there were less restrictive alternatives, in the form of blocking and filtering software.

Breyer J disagreed. Filtering software was not, in his view, an equally effective or feasible option.[172] He did not regard the Constitution as requiring 'Government to disprove the existence of magic solutions', which would solve any problem less restrictively with equal effectiveness. Particularly important was his concern as to what had happened to 'the constructive discourse between our courts and our legislatures' that 'is an integral and admirable part of the constitutional design'.[173] Congress, he said, had:

> dedicated itself to the task of drafting a statute that would meet each and every criticism of the predecessor statute that this Court set forth in *Reno.* It incorporated language from the Court's precedents, particularly the *Miller* standard, virtually verbatim. And it created what it believed was a statute that would protect children from exposure to obscene professional pornography without obstructing adult access to material that the First Amendment protects.[174]

The US Supreme Court has endorsed a harm principle only when direct harm is caused to children in producing pornography.[175] However, this has not extended to proscriptions based on indirect harm. In particular, attempts to restrict virtual pornography, depicting harm to children without using live child actors, have been consistently struck down. In *Ashcroft v Free Speech Coalition*, the Free Speech Coalition challenged a federal law prohibiting the possession or distribution of sexually explicit

[167] *Reno v American Civil Liberties Union* 521 US 844 (1997) (US Supreme Court).
[168] ibid, 874. [169] ibid, 873.
[170] *Ashcroft v American Civil Liberties Union* 542 US 656 (2004) (US Supreme Court).
[171] ibid, 660.
[172] Citing *US v American Library Association* 539 US 194 (2003) (US Supreme Court): filters can both over-block and under-block material.
[173] *Ashcroft v American Civil Liberties Union* (n 170) 689, citing *Blakely v Washington* 542 US 296 (2004) (US Supreme Court) at 326.
[174] *Ashcroft v American Civil Liberties Union*, ibid, 690.
[175] *New York v Ferber* 458 US 747 (1982) (US Supreme Court).

images that appear to depict minors but were produced without using real children. The Court held that the legislation violated the First Amendment.[176] Kennedy J, drawing on the principle in *Brandenburg v Ohio* that speech could only be proscribed if it was likely to produce imminent lawless action, found that the connection with possible child abuse was remote and thus insufficient to sustain the prohibition of virtual child pornography.[177]

It was only by reverting to the principle that some material falls outside of the free speech protection that the Court ultimately upheld federal legislation regulating simulated child pornography. Known as PROTECT,[178] this legislation was motivated by the concern that the emergence of new technology made it nearly impossible to prove that actual children were being used, although, given the prohibitive expense of digital technology, it was well known that most child pornography images were made using actual children. The legislation made it an offence, inter alia, knowingly to advertise, promote, distribute, or solicit material that is intended to cause another to believe that the material contains an obscene visual depiction of a minor engaging in sexually explicit conduct. In *US v Williams* in 2008,[179] the legislation was upheld. Scalia J held that offers to provide or requests to obtain child pornography are categorically excluded from the First Amendment. The legislation did not outlaw advocacy of child pornography, and therefore did not prohibit protected speech. Souter J, dissenting, was unconvinced that a strong enough link with actual harm had been established. For him, the decision strayed too far from the imminent lawless action test: '*Brandenburg* unmistakably insists that any limit on speech be grounded in a realistic, factual assessment of harm'.[180] Instead, in his view, the majority decision risked harking back to the *Schenck* tradition of allowing suppression of speech for its tendency and intent rather than its effects.

A very different approach was taken by the South African Constitutional Court in *De Reuck*, where the Court upheld legislation making it an offence to create, produce, import, or possess publications or films containing child pornography. Notably, child pornography was defined to include simulated images. The judgment differs from the US jurisprudence in several key ways. First, Langa CJ rejected the submission that child pornography was not expression in the first place. However, bringing it within the scope of freedom of expression did not give it the extremely high level of protection afforded under US jurisprudence. Instead, the limitation clause could be adjusted to reflect the 'low value' of such expression. Restricted expression was 'expression of little value which is found on the periphery of the right', far from the core values articulated by the Court, namely the protection of democracy, moral agency, and the search for truth.[181] The second difference concerns the approach to the link between words and harm. Langa CJ accepted that child pornography did more than harm the children used in its production. It could also be used to 'groom' children for sexual

[176] *Ashcroft v Free Speech Coalition* 535 US 234 (2002) (US Supreme Court). [177] ibid, 254.

[178] The Prosecutorial Remedies and Other Tools to End the Exploitation of Children Today Act of 2003, 117 Stat 650.

[179] *US v Williams* 128 US 1830 (2008) (US Supreme Court). [180] ibid.

[181] *South African National Defence Union v Minister of Defence and Another* 1999 (4) SA 469 (CC), 1999 (6) BCLR 615 (CC) para [7].

abuse by showing them acts other children have ostensibly performed; to reinforce the belief that sex with children is acceptable; and to fuel paedophiles' fantasies prior to committing sexual abuse. Importantly, empirical evidence was not necessary, since common sense dictated that these effects would occur in at least some cases.[182] Instead, the test was whether there was a reasonable risk that images would be used to harm children. Finally, the fact that there might conceivably be less invasive means was not determinative: the relatively narrow infringement of expression was outweighed by the important legislative purposes of the impugned provision.[183]

Dworkin and MacKinnon have been more influential in the Canadian jurisprudence. In *R v Butler*,[184] the Supreme Court of Canada expressly moved away from the moralistic approach of earlier jurisprudence to a more harm-based principle. The case was brought by Butler, who owned a shop selling and renting 'hard-core' videos and magazines and sexual paraphernalia. He had been charged with selling obscene material contrary to the Criminal Code. Section 163(8) of the Code states that a publication 'a dominant characteristic of which is the undue exploitation of sex, or of sex and any one or more of the following subjects, namely, crime, horror, cruelty and violence, shall be deemed to be obscene'.[185] He challenged the provision as a breach of his right to freedom of expression in section 2(b) of the Charter.

The Court, in rejecting the challenge, incorporated an explicitly harm-based criterion into the definition of obscenity. This it did through the interpretation of 'undue exploitation of sex'. The Court held that this phrase should be determined by community standards. However, in contrast to the US courts, the standard was formulated as the 'community standard of tolerance', not of taste. As Dickson CJ put it: 'What matters is not what Canadians think is right for themselves to see. What matters is what Canadians would not abide other Canadians seeing because it would be beyond the contemporary Canadian standard of tolerance to allow them to see it'.[186] This is where the harm principle comes in. Courts should determine what the community would tolerate others being exposed to on the basis of the degree of harm that may flow from such exposure. Explicit sex with violence will almost always be undue exploitation of sex. Explicit sex without violence but which subjects people to treatment that is degrading or dehumanizing, may be undue if the risk of harm is substantial. Otherwise, explicit sex is generally tolerated unless it employs children in its production. There is a strong presumption that artistic expression when viewed in the context of the work as a whole would be tolerated. Obscenity, when defined in this way, constituted a justifiable limitation on freedom of expression.

The Supreme Court of Canada differed from its US counterpart in two further ways. First, like the South African Constitutional Court, it rejected the argument that obscenity was devoid of meaning and therefore fell outside of the protection of the right to freedom of expression in section 2(b) of the Charter. Instead, it reaffirmed its generous approach to section 2(b) protection, preferring to base its decisions on

182 *De Reuck v Director of Public Prosecutions* (n 128) para [65].
183 ibid, para [70].
184 *R v Butler* (n 72).
185 Criminal Code SC 1953–54, c 51, s 150; now Criminal Code RSC 1985, c C-46, s 163(8).
186 *Towne Cinema Theatres Ltd v The Queen* [1985] 1 SCR 494 (Supreme Court of Canada) 508–09.

the justifiability of limits. This permits a proportionality analysis, rather than the all-or-nothing outcome of the US focus on the meaning of 'speech'. Second, it differed from its US counterpart in relation to the standard of scrutiny to be applied when assessing proportionality. US courts have insisted on a strict standard of scrutiny, leading them to find that even if there is a faintly plausible alternative which is less restrictive, government regulation of pornography should be struck down. The Court in *Butler*, like the South African Constitutional Court, took the view that pornography was not part of the 'core' of freedom of expression values, namely the search for truth, participation in the political process, and individual self-fulfilment. Rather, in the overwhelming majority of cases, it was motivated by profit. Nor did the Court require conclusive evidence of causation. Although social science evidence might be inconclusive, Parliament was 'entitled to have a "reasoned apprehension of harm" resulting from the desensitization of individuals exposed to materials which depict violence, cruelty and dehumanization in sexual relations'. Moreover, in determining possible alternatives, it was not necessary to have a perfect scheme, or to require legislatures to choose the least ambitious means to protect vulnerable groups.

Butler was a major breakthrough in the recognition of the role of pornography in reinforcing and generating women's subordination. Not only did the Court integrate a harm principle into the definition of obscenity, but it characterized harm in a way which is alive to the feminist understanding of pornography. Case law prior to *Butler* had established that material which exploited sex in a 'degrading or dehumanizing manner' would necessarily fail the community standards test even in the absence of cruelty or violence.[187] Sopinka J took this further in *Butler* by emphasizing that, 'among other things, degrading or dehumanizing materials place women (and sometimes men) in positions of subordination, servile submission or humiliation'.[188] He situated his approach squarely within a harm principle: such material would fail the community standards test 'not because it offends against morals but because it is perceived by public opinion to be harmful to society, particularly to women'.[189] It is true that his moral position was not far from the surface: 'This Court has thus recognized that the harm caused by the proliferation of materials which seriously offend the values fundamental to our society is a substantial concern which justifies restricting the otherwise full exercise of the freedom of expression'. Indeed, Green regards *Butler* as an attempt to 'fashion the silk purse of harm-prevention out of the sow's ear of moralism'.[190] Nevertheless, while the harm principle in *Butler* is clearly value-based, the values it endorses are quite different from the Victorian-type moralism of sexual repression.

The problem with any provision for censorship, however, is the power it vests in the censor, particularly where definitions are slippery and open to abuse. This was graphically demonstrated in the *Little Sisters* case,[191] in which a bookstore catering to the gay and lesbian community found that its literature on gay and lesbian erotica was being systematically targeted, labelled obscene, and confiscated at the borders.[192] The

[187] *R v Butler* (n 72) para [478]. [188] ibid, para [479]. [189] ibid.
[190] Green (n 156) 29.
[191] *Little Sisters Book and Art Emporium v Canada (Minister of Justice)* (n 127).
[192] ibid, para [37].

Supreme Court of Canada found that the conduct of customs officials was oppressive and dismissive, and its effect was to isolate and disparage the appellants on the basis of their sexual orientation.[193] It nevertheless held that the customs legislation constituted a reasonable limit on freedom of expression. Only the provision placing the burden of disproving obscenity on the possessors was declared unconstitutional.

Little Sisters raises the complex question of whether the feminist analysis of pornography as reinforcing women's subordination is applicable to gay erotica. The majority insisted that the *Butler* formula did not discriminate against the gay and lesbian community. Minority expression was a key concern behind the adoption of the community standard of tolerance, and, given the centrality of equality under the Canadian Charter, the standard of tolerance could not reasonably be interpreted as suppressing sexual expression in the gay and lesbian community. For Green, however, this simply replicates what he calls the astonishing heterosexual uniformity of our public culture.[194] While heterosexual pornography reinforces women's subordination, this cannot be read across to gay pornography. Here, he argues, the real oppression is not by men over women, but by heterosexuals against Lesbian, Gay, Bisexual, Transgender, and Intersex people, reflected inexorably in suppression of gay pornography.[195] 'Gay pornography contributes to gay life what is everywhere else denied—that gay sexualities exist, that gay men are sexual beings, and that men may be objects of male desire'.[196] For him, the record of the State's attention to pornography after *Butler*, as epitomized by *Little Sisters*, was just as one would have predicted.

VII. Hate Speech

The jurisprudence on hate speech demonstrates a similar polarization between judges who regard any kind of censorship as a slippery slope, and those who regard other values, such as harm, dignity, or equality, as valid justifications for limiting speech rights. The US Supreme Court has generally been highly protective of speech which might be regarded as 'hate speech', regarding any restrictions as content-based discrimination. We have already seen that the high-water mark of protection of 'subversive' speech was *Brandenburg v Ohio*, which, rather than protecting political dissent, gave licence to the Ku Klux Klan to disseminate speech which was deeply anti-Semitic and racist. By contrast, there is widespread consensus in other jurisdictions that hate speech should be regulated. Indeed, international human rights instruments require ratifying states to prohibit hate speech. The ICCPR states that '[a]ny advocacy of national, racial or religious hatred that constitutes incitement to discrimination, hostility or violence shall be prohibited by law'.[197] The International Convention on the Elimination of All Forms of Racial Discrimination (CERD) similarly requires states to make it an offence to disseminate ideas based on racial superiority or hatred and incitement to racial discrimination.[198]

As in other aspects of speech, this controversy entails a conflict of background values. From one perspective, the difficulty in defining 'hate speech' gives too much power to the State to choose between viewpoints it prefers. This is not an unfounded

[193] ibid, para [36]. [194] Green (n 156) 32. [195] ibid, 42. [196] ibid, 48.
[197] ICCPR, Article 20(2). [198] CERD, Article 4(a).

concern: in a reversal of power relations reminiscent of *Little Sisters*, UK prosecutors reserved their first prosecution under the UK's incitement to racial hatred provisions for a black man who made derogatory comments about white people in a public meeting.[199] On this view, if people feel insulted or hurt by others' words, then they should either speak back or put up with it. The opposite perspective recognizes that, as in pornography, hate speech can function to silence its targets, rendering unrealistic any view that speech should be countered with more speech. Waldron argues that hate speech does not only cause significant harm to the dignity of minority groups but also diminishes the public good of inclusiveness that is an essential attribute of our society.[200] This also raises the question of the extent to which definitions of hate speech should be asymmetric, taking into account the difference between speech directed against the powerless and that used by the powerless against the powerful.

The clearest constitutional position is that of the South African Constitution. As we have seen, under section 16(2)(c), freedom of speech does not extend to 'advocacy of hatred that is based on race, ethnicity, gender, or religion, and that constitutes incitement to cause harm'. This is elaborated in section 10(1) of the Equality Act of 2000, which states that 'no person may publish, propagate, advocate or communicate words based on one or more of the prohibited grounds, against any person, that could reasonably be construed to demonstrate a clear intention to (a) be hurtful; (b) be harmful or incite harm; (c) promote or propagate hatred'.[201] This is subject to a proviso for bona fide engagement in artistic creativity, academic and scientific inquiry, and fair and accurate reporting in the public interest.[202] On the face of it, the Act goes beyond the Constitution in including statements intended to be hurtful. This does not appear to include the Constitution's requirement of incitement to cause harm. The constitutionality of this provision was challenged by Jon Qwelane, a popular columnist who wrote an article entitled 'Call me names—but gay is not okay', which was highly derogatory of homosexual people. In proceedings against him under section 10(1) of the Equality Act, he argued that his speech was protected under the constitutional guarantee of freedom of speech and that the Equality Act's provisions in section 10(1) were overbroad.[203] The High Court rejected his defence. The Court emphasized that the requirement in the Constitution for the speech to constitute incitement to cause harm did not require proof of actual harm resulting from the offending statement. Moreover, the fact that section 10 included speech which was merely hurtful did not mean that it was overbroad and therefore went beyond the constitutional protection. Overbreadth only occurred if the statute exceeded its constitutionally legitimate underlying objectives, which was not the case here.

[199] *R v Malik* (1968) 1 WLR 353 (Court of Appeal). He was found guilty of using words, with intent to stir up hatred against a section of the public distinguished by colour and likely to stir up hatred against that section of the public contrary to s 6(1) of the Race Relations Act 1965.

[200] J Waldron, *The Harm in Hate Speech* (Harvard University Press 2014) ch 4.

[201] The Promotion of Equality and Prevention of Unfair Discrimination Act 4 of 2000 (PEPUDA) s 10(1).

[202] PEPUDA s 12.

[203] *South African Human Rights Commission v Qwelane Dubula Jonathan* Case No EQ44/2009 (EQ13/2012) (Equality Court of South Africa). I am indebted to Nomfundo Ramalekana for her analysis of this case.

In all the other jurisdictions, Courts have had to confront the question by interpreting open-textured constitutional provisions. The results have differed widely. Not surprisingly, the US Supreme Court has taken the strongest stand against prohibitions on hate speech. In *RAV v St Paul,* the Court struck down the conviction of a white teenager, who had burned a crudely made cross inside the fenced yard of a neighbouring African American family.[204] The teenager was convicted under an Ordinance making it a criminal misdemeanour to

> place on public or private property, a symbol, object, appellation, characterization or graffiti, including, but not limited to, a burning cross or Nazi swastika, which one knows or has reasonable grounds to know arouses anger, alarm or resentment in others on the basis of race, colour, creed, religion or gender.[205]

Scalia J, delivering the opinion of the Court, accepted that the Ordinance only applied to 'fighting words', which are in principle excluded from First Amendment protection. However, he held, a State cannot selectively prohibit some fighting words and not others. In a curious upending of the 'overbreadth' argument, he held that the exclusion for hate speech was under-inclusive because it focused on race, colour, creed, religion, and gender and not on other possible reasons for hate speech. This preferred some viewpoints, namely the fighting words which were not prohibited.[206] This allowed the city to 'impose special prohibitions on those speakers who express views on disfavoured subjects',[207] constituting unconstitutional content-based discrimination. As White J put it, 'The Court today turns First Amendment law on its head: Communication that was once entirely unprotected (and that still can be wholly proscribed) is now entitled to greater protection than commercial speech—and possibly greater protection than core political speech'.[208]

Even without express mention of race, gender, or religion, legislation banning hate speech has been struck down. Thus, in *Virginia v Black*,[209] the Court struck down a Virginia statute banning cross-burning with 'an intent to intimidate a person or group of persons'. Unlike the Ordinance in *RAV*, the statute did not single out speech directed towards 'one of the particular disfavoured topics'. In an important recognition of the power of expressive conduct, O'Connor J, giving the opinion of the Court, held that cross-burning was a form of expression. Indeed, 'individuals burn crosses as opposed to other means of communication because cross burning carries a message in an effective and dramatic manner'.[210] Nevertheless, the State could regulate this subset of intimidating messages because of their long and pernicious history as a signal of impending violence. But this did not save the statute: it was struck down because of its presumption that burning of a cross was evidence of intent to intimidate, putting the burden on the perpetrator to disprove intent: 'The provision chills constitutionally protected political speech because of the possibility that the Commonwealth will

[204] *RAV v St Paul* 505 US 377 (1992).
[205] St Paul Bias-Motivated Crime Ordinance, St Paul, Minn, Legis Code s 292.02 (1990).
[206] *RAV v St Paul* (n 204) 391. [207] ibid, 391. [208] ibid, 423; White J concurring.
[209] *Virginia v Black* 538 US 343 (2003) (US Supreme Court). [210] ibid, 360.

prosecute—and potentially convict—somebody engaging only in lawful political speech at the core of what the First Amendment is designed to protect'.[211]

This protection extends to what Alito J has called 'vicious verbal assault'.[212] In *Snyder v Phelps*,[213] members of the Westboro Baptist Church gathered near the funeral service of a soldier who had been killed on duty in Iraq with placards stating, 'Thank God for Dead Soldiers', 'You're going to Hell', 'God Hates you', 'God hates fags', and 'Thank God for 9/11'. After being found liable for defamation and intentional infliction of emotional distress, the Church argued that their First Amendment rights had been breached. Upholding the challenge, Roberts CJ, giving the opinion of the Court, held that any distress caused by the picketing turned on the content and viewpoint of the message conveyed. Given that it was at a public place on a matter of public concern, it was entitled to special protection under the First Amendment:

> Speech is powerful. It can stir people to action, move them to tears of both joy and sorrow, and—as it did here—inflict great pain. On the facts before us, we cannot react to that pain by punishing the speaker. As a Nation we have chosen a different course—to protect even hurtful speech on public issues to ensure that we do not stifle public debate.[214]

For Alito J, dissenting, the diametric opposite was true: 'In order to have a society in which public issues can be openly and vigorously debated, it is not necessary to allow the brutalization of innocent victims like the petitioner'.[215] This did not mean he favoured shutting down the respondents' right to voice their opinions. There were countless platforms available to them to do this. However, they chose to picket funerals for the very reason that it attracted publicity.

Similar battles have been fought in the Supreme Court of Canada, with the opposite outcome to its US counterpart. In *R v Keegstra*,[216] the Court upheld the constitutionality of section 319 of the Criminal Code, which made it an offence to 'wilfully promote hatred against any identifiable group'. Like the Ordinance in *RAV*, section 319 defined an 'identifiable group' as one distinguished by colour, race, religion, or ethnic origin. Keegstra, a high-school teacher, was convicted under section 319 for teaching deeply anti-Semitic material to his students. He taught his pupils that Jews were 'treacherous', 'subversive', 'sadistic', 'money-loving', 'power hungry', and 'child killers'; that they 'created the Holocaust to gain sympathy'; that they sought to destroy Christianity and were deceptive, secretive, and inherently evil. He maintained that anyone Jewish must be evil and that anyone evil must be Jewish. He expected his students to repeat these notions in essays and examinations in order to receive good grades.

The Court held that section 319, interpreted narrowly, constituted a prima facie breach of freedom of expression. However, it was justifiable under section 1 of the Charter, which permits 'such reasonable limits prescribed by law as can be demonstrably justified in a free and democratic society'. Dickson CJ recognized the power of speech to undermine individuals' self-image as well as creating the risk that 'prejudiced

[211] ibid, 365. [212] *Snyder v Phelps* 131 S Ct 1207 (2011) (US Supreme Court). [213] ibid.
[214] ibid, 1220. [215] ibid, 1228.
[216] *R v Keegstra* [1990] 3 SCR 697 (Supreme Court of Canada).

messages will gain some credence, with the attendant result of discrimination, and perhaps even violence, against minority groups'. This understanding of harm was reinforced by the Charter's strong commitment to the values of equality and multi-culturalism. Hate speech sends a message

> that members of identifiable groups are not to be given equal standing in society, and are not human beings equally deserving of concern, respect and consideration ... In restricting the promotion of hatred Parliament is therefore seeking to bolster the notion of mutual respect necessary in a nation which venerates the equality of all persons.[217]

This was reinforced by the international human rights obligations taken on by Canada, demonstrating 'the principles of equality and the inherent dignity of all persons that infuse both international human rights and the Charter'. Indeed, the United Nations Human Rights Committee (HRC) has rejected a claim that Canada's prohibition of hate messages by telephone was in breach of freedom of speech in the ICCPR.[218]

Having upheld the legitimacy of the aim of the impugned measure, it was necessary to determine whether it was a proportionate means. Dickson CJ found that hate speech furthered none of the values of freedom of expression, contributing little to the aspirations of Canadians 'in either the quest for truth, the promotion of individual self-development or the protection and fostering of a vibrant democracy where the participation of all individuals is accepted and encouraged'. So far as the search for truth was concerned, 'there is very little chance that statements intended to promote hatred against an identifiable group are true, or that their vision of society will lead to a better world'. Similarly, although it might be true that prohibiting hate speech might hinder the self-fulfilment of its proponents, protection for such speech must be tempered by the fact that it 'advocates with inordinate vitriol an intolerance and prejudice which view as execrable the process of individual self-development and human flourishing among all members of society'. Particularly striking is Dickson CJ's willingness to confront the liberal dilemma whereby the liberal state is required to tolerate illiberal views even if they constitute a danger to liberalism itself. For him, the answer was clear.

> The suppression of hate propaganda undeniably muzzles the participation of a few individuals in the democratic process.... Nonetheless, expression can work to undermine our commitment to democracy where employed to propagate ideas anathemic to democratic values. Hate propaganda works in just such a way.... This brand of expressive activity is thus wholly inimical to the democratic aspirations of the free expression guarantee.[219]

McLachlan J dissented. She agreed that hate speech could lead to harm and this could be a sufficient objective for limiting speech. However, criminal prohibitions were a

[217] Canadian Charter, ss 15, 27.

[218] *Taylor and Western Guard Party v Canada*, Communication No 104/1981, Report of the Human Rights Committee, 38 UN GAOR, Supp No 40 (A/38/40) 231 (1983) para 8(b) (decision reported in part at (1983), 5 CHRR D/2397).

[219] *R v Keegstra* (n 216) 764.

disproportionate means to this end. Rather than curbing hate-mongers, criminal prosecutions had given wide publicity to precisely such speech. Moreover, the offence was formulated in such a broad and subjective manner, particularly the definition of hatred, as to give the State a wide margin of dangerous discretion, creating a chilling effect.[220]

Keegstra was reaffirmed in a unanimous decision in *Whatcott*.[221] Whatcott had been prosecuted for distributing flyers entitled 'Keep Homosexuality out of Saskatoon's Public Schools!' and 'Sodomites in our Public Schools'. The flyers were found to contravene section 14(1)(b) of the Saskatchewan Human Rights Code, which prohibited the publication or display of any representation that 'exposes or tends to expose to hatred, ridicules, belittles or otherwise affronts the dignity of any person or class of persons on the basis of a prohibited ground'. Prohibited grounds included sexual orientation. The penalties for infringement were not criminal, as in *Keegstra*, but Whatcott was ordered to cease publishing and distributing them and to pay damages to the complainants. The Supreme Court of Canada held that section 14(1)(b) was constitutional.

The case is important for its foregrounding of the definition of 'hatred', widely criticized as being too subjective, giving too much power to the censor, and being too vague, creating a chilling effect on debate and discussion. Rothstein J held that 'hatred' referred only to extreme and egregious expression which exposed a group to 'detestation' and vilification.[222] The question was not whether the ideas expressed were offensive, but whether they exposed vulnerable groups to hatred. Intention was irrelevant. Less convincing is the test proposed by Rothstein J, namely whether 'a reasonable person, aware of the context and circumstances surrounding the expression, [would] view it as exposing the protected group to hatred'.[223] The effectiveness of this test depends largely on whether the courts can construct a reasonable person with sufficient empathy for experiences which the majority, by definition, might never have been exposed to.[224]

Like Dickson CJ in *Keegstra*, Rothstein J was sensitive to the particular type of harm generated by hate speech, namely seeking 'to delegitimize group members in the eyes of the majority, reducing their social standing and acceptance within society'.[225] Moreover, it operates by silencing those whom it targets:

> Indeed, a particularly insidious aspect of hate speech is that it acts to cut off any path of reply by the group under attack. It does this not only by attempting to marginalize the group so that their reply will be ignored: it also forces the group to argue for their basic humanity or social standing, as a precondition to participating in the deliberative aspects of our democracy.[226]

[220] *R v Keegstra* (n 216); see further *R v Zundel* [1992] 2 SCR 731 (Canadian Supreme Court).

[221] *Saskatchewan (Human Rights Commission) v Whatcott* 2013 SCC 11 (Supreme Court of Canada).

[222] ibid, para [41]. [223] ibid, para [56].

[224] L Curran, 'Freedom of Speech or Enabling a Right to Insult? The Australian Debate over section 18C of the Racial Discrimination Act 1975' (OxHRH Blog, 16 May 2017) <http://ohrh.law.ox.ac.uk/freedom-of-speech-or-enabling-a-right-to-insult-the-australian-debate-over-section-18c-of-the-racial-discrimination-act-1975> (accessed 22 June 2018).

[225] *Saskatchewan (Human Rights Commission) v Whatcott* (n 221) para [71].

[226] ibid, para [75].

Rejecting the arguments against effectiveness endorsed by McLachlan J, he held that it is not fatal that the prohibition does not render hate speech extinct: even the process of hearing a complaint reminds Canadians of their fundamental commitment to the eradication of intolerance. Nor was he persuaded by the proposed alternative of leaving the regulation of hate speech to the 'marketplace of ideas'. The marketplace is unlikely to function effectively if the targets of hate speech are silenced and discredited in that very marketplace. Notably, the *Whatcott* approach to hate speech was quoted verbatim and adopted in the Indian case of *Pravasi Bhalai Sangathan*.[227]

Like the Canadian Supreme Court, the ECtHR has upheld prohibitions on hate speech. However, it has taken a different route in some key cases. This is to confront the liberal dilemma squarely by finding that hate speech breaches the separate provision on abuse of rights in Article 17. This states: 'Nothing in [the] Convention may be interpreted as implying for any State, group or person any right to engage in any activity or perform any act aimed at the destruction of any of the rights and freedoms set forth herein or at their limitation to a greater extent than is provided for in the Convention'. Thus in *Seurot v France*, the Court declared: '[T]here is no doubt that any remark directed against the Convention's underlying values would be removed from the protection of Article 10 by Article 17'.[228]

The ECtHR has declared several applications inadmissible on these grounds. In *Pavel Ivanov v Russia*, the applicant claimed a breach of his Article 10 rights after having been convicted of public incitement to ethnic, racial, and religious hatred through the use of mass media.[229] Ivanov had published a series of articles portraying the Jews as the source of evil in Russia and called for their exclusion from social life. The Court held that his claim was inadmissible:

> Such a general and vehement attack on one ethnic group is in contradiction with the Convention's underlying values, notably tolerance, social peace and non-discrimination. Consequently, the Court finds that, by reason of Article 17 of the Convention, the applicant may not benefit from the protection afforded by Article 10 of the Convention.[230]

Similarly, in *Norwood v UK*, the applicant was convicted of aggravated hostility towards a religious group after he displayed a British National Party poster, representing the Twin Towers in flames, with the caption 'Islam out of Britain—Protect the British People'. Reiterating the principles in *Ivanov* that such an attack was incompatible with the fundamental values guaranteed by the Convention, the Court found that the poster constituted an abuse of rights contrary to Article 17, precluding the protection of Article 10.[231]

Even where Article 17 does not apply, the ECtHR has held that it is justifiable to prohibit hate speech. In *Vejdeland v Sweden*, the applicants were convicted of agitation

[227] *Pravasi Bhalai Sangathan v UOI* Writ Petition (C) No 157 of 2013 (12 March 2014) (Indian Supreme Court) paras [7]–[8].
[228] *Seurot v France* (57383/00) 2004 (European Court of Human Rights).
[229] *Pavel Ivanov v Russia* (3522/04) 2007 (European Court of Human Rights).
[230] ibid, para 1. See also *Garaudy v France* (6583/101) 2003 (European Court of Human Rights).
[231] *Norwood v UK* (23131/03) 2004 (European Court of Human Rights).

against a national or ethnic group after distributing highly offensive homophobic pamphlets at an upper secondary school.[232] The Court rejected their claim of a breach of Article 10. Although there had been a prima facie interference, this was justified under Article 10(2). Like the Canadian Court, the ECtHR did not confine the harm to express calls for violence or other criminal acts. 'Insulting, holding up to ridicule or slandering specific groups of the population can be sufficient for the authorities to favour combating racist speech'.[233] The severity of penalties was also a factor to be taken into account in assessing proportionality. In this case, the penalties—suspended sentences with fines—were not excessive in the circumstances.

The recognition that hate speech should be a justifiable limitation on freedom of speech should not, however, obscure the risk of giving too much power to the State to determine what constitutes hate speech. It is this risk which has been at the forefront of Indian jurisprudence. Indian legislation contains numerous statutory provisions against various forms of speech considered as hate speech. This has given rise to a pattern of selective enforcement, so that powerful figures remain immune from prosecution, while private individuals might find themselves arbitrarily arrested. The 2015 case of *Shreya Singhal*[234] was prompted by the arrest of a young woman, who had posted a comment on her Facebook page questioning the shutdown in Mumbai following the death of a controversial Hindu nationalist politician. Her friend, who had 'liked' the post, was arrested with her. They were initially charged under provisions of the Indian Penal Code criminalizing statements creating or promoting enmity, hatred, or ill-will between classes, and later under the Information Technology Act 2000. Although these charges were ultimately withdrawn, their case prompted a public interest litigation challenging the constitutionality of the provisions.

The focus of *Shreya Singhal* was section 66A of the Information Technology Act of 2000. This made it a criminal offence to send by computer or other device any information that is 'grossly offensive or has menacing character' or which the sender knows to be false but sends with the aim of causing annoyance or inconvenience; or any email message for the purpose of causing annoyance or inconvenience. The Court struck down the provision. Freedom of speech should prevail unless it constituted incitement with an imminent causal connection to public disorder: 'Mere discussion or even advocacy of a particular cause, howsoever unpopular, is at the heart of Article 19(1)(a). It is only when such discussion or advocacy reaches the level of incitement that Article 19(2) kicks in'.[235] Section 66A clearly infringed Article 19(1), since it prohibited discussion or advocacy of annoying material regardless of whether this constituted incitement. Nor could the restriction be justified under Article 19(2), which permits 'reasonable restrictions' in the interests of a list of enumerated objectives.[236] Reiterating that speech could only be curtailed in the interests of the enumerated objectives, and not to protect the general public interest, the Court held that the provision could not be justified under any of those objectives. Crucially, the Court endorsed the higher standard of scrutiny set out in *Lohia*,[237] requiring an intimate

[232] *Vejdeland v Sweden* (2014) 58 EHRR 15 (European Court of Human Rights).
[233] ibid, para [55]. [234] *Shreya Singhal v UOI* (n 12). [235] ibid, para [13].
[236] See above at text relating to n 52.
[237] *Superintendent v Ram Monohar Lohia* (n 102) 834–36.

connection between the speech in question and the aim to be achieved. It was not sufficient for the connection to be far-fetched, hypothetical, or problematic.[238] By proscribing speech simply because it created annoyance or inconvenience, the statute fell far short of both the US Supreme Court test of 'clear and present danger' or the Court's own 'tendency' test. Moreover, the width of the provision created a serious chilling effect: it 'was cast so widely that any serious opinion dissenting with the mores of the day would be caught in its net'.[239]

This raises the further question of whether hate speech should be dealt with differently depending on whether it is used by those in power to vilify the powerless or by those who are less powerful to attack those in power. This issue arose in South Africa, when a prominent politician, Julius Malema, was sued for breach of the Equality Act's hate speech provisions for singing a song known as 'Dubul'ibhunu', translated as meaning 'Shoot the Boer [Afrikaans farmer]'.[240] Malema argued that the words were part of a liberation song referring to representatives of the apartheid regime. The complainants argued that it undermined the human dignity of Afrikaners and could reasonably be construed to demonstrate a clear intention to be hurtful to a particular ethnic group. The judge accepted that as originally sung the words were used to denote 'Destroy the Regime'. However, the context and widely conveyed meaning had been changed. 'The Equality Act allows no justification on the basis of fairness for historic practices which are hurtful to the target group but loved by the other group'.[241]

A similar question has arisen in the US. In *Matal v Tam*,[242] a rock group called itself 'The Slants' in a deliberate attempt to drain its denigrating force as a derogatory term for Asian persons. Their application for federal registration of this name as a trademark was denied under legislation prohibiting the registration of trademarks that may 'disparage ... or bring ... into contempt or disrepute' any person.[243] The US Supreme Court held that the disparagement clause constituted impermissible viewpoint discrimination. The applicant could register a positive or benign mark but not a derogatory one, reflecting the Government's disapproval of a subset of messages it finds offensive. The Court's reasoning reaffirms its consistent position that prohibiting hate speech breaches the First Amendment. For present purposes, its interest lies in the way in which the case dealt with the argument that the speech aimed to correct prejudice rather than to create or reinforce hatred. For Kennedy J, the only response was a strictly symmetric prohibition on all limitations of speech.

> A law that can be directed against speech found offensive to some portion of the public can be turned against minority and dissenting views to the detriment of all. The First Amendment does not entrust that power to the government's benevolence. Instead, our reliance must be on the substantial safeguards of free and open discussion in a democratic society.[244]

[238] *Shreya Singhal v UOI* (n 12) para [22]. [239] ibid, para [83].
[240] *Afri-Forum v Malema* (2011) 4 All SA 293 (EqC) (Equality Court SA).
[241] ibid, para [108]. [242] *Matal v Tam* 137 S Ct 1744 (2017) (US Supreme Court).
[243] 15 USC § 1052(a). [244] *Matal v Tam* (n 242) 1769.

This leaves open the question of whether it is possible or desirable to design provisions which protect against hate speech directed against the less powerful while permitting the latter to use speech, including hate speech, to redress inequalities of power.

Perhaps the most present modern question concerns the extent to which internet providers and online platforms can be held responsible for hate speech posted on their sites. The power and reach of the internet, together with the blanket of anonymity it casts over speakers, has led to calls for platform-providers to be made legally responsible for removing the material. But is this simply turning private parties into censors? This was the question confronted by the ECtHR in the 2015 case of *Delfi v Estonia*.[245] Delfi was one of the largest internet news portals in Estonia. Its comments section, which was not moderated by the company, received about 10,000 readers' comments daily, the majority posted under pseudonyms. There were certain safeguards: any reader could mark a comment as insulting, in which case it was taken down, and an automatic filter deleted comments with specified obscene words. Nevertheless, Delfi had a notorious history of publishing degrading and defamatory comments. After an article published on the Delfi website attracted virulent comments against the applicant in person, he successfully sued Delfi for defamation. Delfi claimed this to be a violation of their right to freedom of speech.

The Court held that Delfi's freedom of speech had indisputably been interfered with by the tort of defamation. The main question therefore became whether the interference was justified under Article 10(2). The aim of defamation is clearly to protect the reputation and rights of others. But was the measure necessary in a democratic society to achieve that aim? For the Court, the key was how much control Delfi exercised over comments on its portal. In this case, Delfi had exercised a substantial degree of control: only the company could remove or modify comments once posted. Given this degree of control, the Court concluded that the imposition of an obligation to remove hate speech and incitements to violence without delay after publication was not a disproportionate interference with the portal owner's freedom of expression. Nor could this be regarded as 'private censorship', given the fact that there are ample possibilities to make one's voice heard on the internet.[246] Moreover, the responsibility was not sufficiently discharged by notice-and-take-down systems. Significantly, the Court attached weight to the difference in power between an individual victim of hate speech and a large, commercial internet provider, whose ability to prevent or rapidly remove such comments from the internet was much greater. The Court was also influenced by the fact that Delfi had only been required to pay a tiny sum in damages.

The Indian Supreme Court in *Shreya Singhal* similarly upheld a provision placing liability on an intermediary. But it read down the contested provision to avoid any possibility that the intermediary would have to exercise its own judgement in determining whether material should be removed. Instead, it only permitted intermediaries to be held liable if they failed expeditiously to remove material having actual knowledge of a court order to the effect that the material was being used to commit an unlawful act.[247]

[245] *Delfi AS v Estonia* (2016) 62 EHRR 6 (European Court of Human Rights).
[246] ibid, para [157]. [247] *Shreya Singhal v UOI* (n 12) para [119].

VIII. Whose Right Is It? Freedom of Information

Thus far, the discussion has assumed that freedom of speech creates rights for the speaker. However, speech is essentially a communicative act. Does this mean that the listener also has rights? Some human rights texts expressly refer to recipients' rights. Article 10 ECHR includes the right to impart and receive information and ideas, while Article 19(2) ICCPR additionally contains the right to seek information.[248] The South African Constitution is less explicit, referring to the 'freedom to impart information or ideas'.[249] Others do not refer to recipients' rights, but do include the press. The First Amendment prohibits laws abridging freedom of the press, while the Canadian Charter includes freedom of the press and 'other media of communication',[250] and the South African Constitution includes 'freedom of speech and other media'.[251]

Courts have had little difficulty in accepting that the basic rationales of freedom of speech support rights for recipients of speech. This is true whether or not there is an express mention of such rights in the constitutional text. In *Lamont v Postmaster General*, Brennan J acknowledged that the First Amendment contained no specific guarantee of access to publications. However, freedom of speech would mean nothing without the right to receive publications. Brennan J linked this closely to the 'free market of ideas' rationale for freedom of speech: 'The dissemination of ideas can accomplish nothing if otherwise willing addressees are not free to receive and consider them. It would be a barren marketplace of ideas that had only sellers and no buyers'.[252] Similarly, the Court has stressed that '[t]he State may not, consistently with the spirit of the First Amendment, contract the spectrum of available knowledge'.[253] Thus in *Griswold v Connecticut*, it was held that individuals had a right to receive information on contraception. This is true even if the State wishes to protect its citizens against harmful advertising. In *Virginia Pharmacy Board*, the Court held that a ban on advertising pharmaceuticals was unnecessarily paternalistic. In a dictum strongly reminiscent of Meicklejohn's autonomy principle, the Court stated: 'People will perceive their own best interest if only they are well enough informed and ... the best means to that end is to open the channels of communication rather than to close them'.[254] Brennan J has also regarded the right to receive information as a precondition for the meaningful exercise of speech. [255]

Where there is a willing speaker, the position is relatively straightforward. But what if the speaker chooses not to speak? Can the recipient compel the speaker to release information? This is particularly apt for the State: does the individual right to receive information impose a correlative obligation on the State to provide that information? On one view, rights to information are best dealt with through legislation rather than human rights, and there is now a vigorous movement towards statutory provision for

248 ICCPR, Article 19(2).

249 South African Constitution, s 16(1)(b).

250 Canadian Charter of Rights and Freedoms, s 2(b).

251 South African Constitution, s 16(1)(a).

252 *Lamont v Postmaster General* 381 US 301 (1965) (US Supreme Court) 308.

253 *Griswold v Connecticut* 381 US 479 (1965) (US Supreme Court) 482.

254 *Virginia Pharmacy Board v Virginia Consumer Council* 425 US 748 (US Supreme Court) 770.

255 *Board of Education v Pico* 457 US 853 (1982) (US Supreme Court) 867.

freedom of information, which generally includes criteria for access and permits the State to withhold information for specified reasons.[256] Should courts therefore regard this issue as entirely one of political choice, or can freedom-of-information legislation be challenged as insufficiently protecting freedom of speech?

The response of courts can be placed along a spectrum. Most reluctant to intervene has been the US Supreme Court. In *Houchins v KQED*,[257] a local TV station was refused permission to inspect prison conditions and interview prisoners in a San Francisco jail after a report suggesting that poor conditions had contributed to the suicide of an inmate. The Court held that there was no right of access to information and no special privilege for the press above that of the ordinary public. A demand for access to information of this sort would invite the Court to involve itself in a legislative task: standards governing disclosure and access to information should not be devised by courts but by legislatures. Stevens J dissented. In his view, an informed public is essential to hold governments to account, and information-gathering is entitled to constitutional protection. While some governmental activity was entitled to secrecy, a 'special importance attached to allowing a democratic community access to knowledge about how its servants were treating some of its members who have been committed to their custody'. Nevertheless, the Court has maintained its view that access to government records is a policy question for the legislature, rather than a constitutional question for courts.[258]

The Supreme Court of Canada, while not as firmly resisting the notion of a constitutional right of access to government documents, has nevertheless closely circumscribed any such principle. In the *Criminal Lawyers' Association* case in 2010, the Court held that section 2(b) of the Charter guarantees freedom of expression, not access to information.[259] Freedom of information is a derivative right, which can only be implied into the section 2(b) guarantee of freedom of expression if it is consistent with the background value of freedom of speech, namely to facilitate public discussion. Thus, a prima facie right to access documents in government's hands only arises where access is necessary to permit meaningful discussion on a matter of public importance. Even then, it will only be protected if it does not encroach on protected privileges and is compatible with the function of the institution concerned.[260] Importantly, the Court has insisted that this is essentially a question about the scope of freedom of expression, not about justifiable limits.[261]

At the other end of the spectrum is the approach of the HRC, aided by the reference in the ICCPR to the right to seek information. The HRC published a General Comment on Freedom of Opinion and Expression in 2011 which made it clear that Article 19 ICCPR on freedom of expression embraces a right of

[256] Report of the United Nations Special Rapporteur on the promotion and protection of the right to freedom of opinion and expression to the General Assembly on the right to access information, published on 4 September 2013 (A/68/362).

[257] *Houchins v KQED* 438 US 1 (US Supreme Court).

[258] *McBurney v Young* 133 S Ct 1709, 1718 (2013).

[259] *Ministry of Public Safety and Security v Criminal Lawyers' Association* [2010] 1 SCR 815 (Supreme Court of Canada).

[260] ibid, para [5]. [261] ibid, para [34].

access to information held by public bodies.[262] Notably, the HRC linked this right, not just to the text of Article 19, but also to the separate right in Article 25 ICCPR to take part in the conduct of public affairs.[263] Crucially, the right of the individual to receive State-held information triggers a duty on the State to provide such information, or at least to give a legitimate justification for refusing.[264]

The ECtHR has moved gradually along the spectrum from the more restrictive position in the US and Canada, to one which resembles aspects of the HRC approach. Until 2016, the Court, like its US counterpart, confined the right to information to information received from a willing speaker. This was set out in what came to be known as the *Leander* principle, namely:

> [T]he right to freedom to receive information basically prohibits a Government from restricting a person from receiving information that others wish or may be willing to impart to him. Article 10 does not ... embody an obligation on the Government to impart such information to the individual.[265]

Similarly, in *Guerra*, the applicants argued that their right to receive information under Article 10 had been infringed because of the State's failure to provide them with information about the risks associated with severe environmental pollution from a neighbouring chemical factory. Here the Court held that freedom to receive information could not, in the circumstances of the case, be construed as imposing a positive obligation on the State to collect and disseminate information of its own motion.[266] Notably, the Court, while rejecting the Article 10 claim, nevertheless found a violation of the State's positive duty under Article 8 (respect for home, family, and private life).[267] This was because the failure to make the information available made it impossible for the applicants to assess the risks of continuing to live in their town.[268]

The opportunity to revisit the *Leander* principle came in the 2016 case of *Magyar v Hungary*.[269] The case is of particular interest because of the respondents' attempt to rely on the original intention of the drafters. The Hungarian Government argued that the drafters of the Convention had omitted a reference to the right of access to information in the text of Article 10 'precisely because they did not intend that Contracting Parties should assume any such obligation'.[270] The argument from original intent was pursued even more forcefully by the UK government, which maintained that the clear objective of Article 10 was only to impose negative duties on the State to refrain from interfering with the right of communication. It argued that the absence of any positive duty to provide access to information was confirmed by the *travaux préparatoires*, which showed that the right to 'seek' information had been deliberately omitted, thus

262 HRC General Comment No 34 on Article 19 of the ICCPR (freedoms of opinion and expression) (2011) UN Doc CCPR/C/GC/34.

263 ibid; see also *Robert W Gauthier v Canada*, Communication No 633/1995, UN Doc CCPR/C/65/D/633/1995 (5 May 1999).

264 *Toktakunov v Kyrgyzstan*, Communication No 1470/2006, UN Doc CCPR/C/101/D/1470/2006 (28 March 2011) para 7.4.

265 *Leander v Sweden* (1987) 9 EHRR 433 (European Court of Human Rights) para [74].

266 *Guerra v Italy* (1998) 26 EHRR 357 (European Court of Human Rights) para [53].

267 ibid, para [58].

268 ibid, para [60].

269 *Magyar v Hungary* ECtHR App No 18030/11 (8 November 2016).

270 ibid, para [126].

defining the scope of the right more narrowly than that under Article 19 ICCPR, which, as we have seen, includes such a right.

The Grand Chamber reaffirmed its 'living tree' approach.[271] The *travaux préparatoires* could be a relevant consideration; but they were not determinative where the existence of a right was supported by a growing consensus.[272] The broad consensus on the need to recognize an individual right of access to State-held information both within the Council of Europe and at the international level demonstrated that the textual differences between the ECHR and the ICCPR were not decisive. Instead, the consensus reflected the fundamental principle that the right of access to public interest data and documents was inherent in freedom of expression.[273] This in turn derived from the background value of enabling the public 'to scrutinise and form an opinion on any matters of public interest, including on the manner of functioning of public authorities in a democratic society'.[274]

The case is also important for the Court's willingness to give flesh to the right. Unlike the US Supreme Court, which regarded legislation as performing the functions of delineating the right, the Court went on to establish a set of principles to determine when documents should be disclosed. First, the purpose must be to receive and impart information and ideas to others. Second, the information must fulfil a public interest test, closely determined by the function of information in vitalizing democracy. Thus, the need for disclosure might exist 'where disclosure provides transparency on the manner or conduct of public affairs and on matters of interest for society as a whole and thereby allows participation in public governance by the public at large'.[275] Importantly, the public interest was limited to matters which affected the public to such an extent that the public could legitimately take an interest in them. It could not be reduced to 'the public's thirst for information about the private life of others, or to an audience's wish for sensationalism or even voyeurism'.[276]

The Court also played close attention to the role of the seeker of information. Although Article 10 differs from the Canadian and US texts in that it makes no reference to the press, the ECtHR has always been particularly protective of the role of the press. Prior to *Magyar*, the Court had already begun to develop a limited right of access to information in relation to the 'social watchdog' role, paradigmatically by the press, but also by other civil society bodies. This applied where access to information was part of the legitimate gathering of information of public interest to contribute to public debate.[277] In *Magyar*, the Court emphasized the special importance of the seeker of information in 'receiving and imparting' information to the public. This reinforces the position of the Human Rights Committee in *Toktakunov v Kyrgyzstan*, where it held that the function of circulating information of public concern to individuals was not limited to the press. It could equally be provided by individuals performing a 'watchdog' function. In the case in question, the government of Kyrgyzstan had refused to release figures to the Youth Human Rights Group on the number of people who had been sentenced to death. The State maintained that the figures remained

[271] See Chapter 5. [272] *Magyar v Hungary* (n 269) para [125]. [273] ibid, para [143].
[274] ibid, para [139]. [275] ibid, para [161]. [276] ibid, para [162].
[277] ibid, para 130ff and cases cited therein.

'confidential to the press'. This was not sufficient, in the view of the HRC. Nor was there a legitimate national security justification for refusing to disclose.[278]

The more difficult question of how far the State needs to go to collect the information remained unanswered in *Magyar*. In earlier cases, the Court had had regard to whether the information was 'ready and available' and did not require the collection of any new information. On the other hand, the Court has held that the State cannot rely on the anticipated difficulty in gathering information as an excuse for not providing it, where the difficulty in generating information is due to the authority's own practice. In *Magyar*, the Grand Chamber held that the fact that the information is ready and available should constitute an important criterion in assessing whether a refusal to provide the information is an interference with this right.[279] Nevertheless, any claim by the State to withhold such information must be justified according to Article 10's strict standards of scrutiny.

IX. Conclusion

Freedom of speech, although in the heartland of justiciable human rights, continues to raise highly contested questions. As this chapter has shown, the resolution of these issues benefits richly from a comparative approach. In this area, divergences are shown to be as important as similarities: the absence of a limitations clause in the US First Amendment has driven much of its jurisprudence, including in relation to the meaning of speech itself, as compared to other jurisdictions which can apply an express limitations clause. At the other end of the spectrum, the inclusion of morality as a justifiable aim under the ECHR would seem anathema to other jurisdictions, especially the US, which regard the possibility of the State using morality to censor speech as a serious breach of State neutrality. The dilemma of where the limits of liberal tolerance should lie nevertheless remains a persistent challenge for courts in all jurisdictions. While the harm principle provides a starting point to address these challenges, much depends on how harm is interpreted and what the causal relationship between harm and speech is perceived to be. All these challenges are heightened in the age of the internet, which has both democratized speech and magnified the voices of the powerful. Ultimately, the rationale behind freedom of speech, which is to curb the power of the State to censor expression it dislikes, needs to be recalibrated so that the right to free speech can be exercised in conditions of genuine equality. This requires not total abstention of the State, but appropriate intervention. The challenge for courts is to continue to strive towards determining when intervention is appropriate to achieve equal freedom of speech.

[278] *Toktakunov v Kyrgyzstan* (n 264).

[279] *Magyar v Hungary* (n 269) paras [169]–[170].

11

The Right to Education

I. Introduction

> Education is both a human right in itself and an indispensable means of realizing other human rights. As an empowerment right, education is the primary vehicle by which economically and socially marginalized adults and children can lift themselves out of poverty and obtain the means to participate fully in their communities ... Increasingly, education is recognized as one of the best financial investments States can make. But the importance of education is not just practical: a well-educated, enlightened and active mind, able to wander freely and widely, is one of the joys and rewards of human existence.[1]

Education is a multiplier right. Without education, other rights and freedoms cannot be fully enjoyed. Freedom of speech, rights to democratic participation, and rights to employment are enhanced by the right to education. Education is also an accelerator right: it equips people to enter the labour force, to participate in public life, and to be productive members of society. Indeed, education has been placed at the heart of the struggle to alleviate poverty and disadvantage in the world. The Sustainable Development Goals (SDGs), agreed in 2015, committed the world to ensure inclusive and equitable quality education and to promote lifelong learning opportunities for all by 2030.[2]

However, education is more than an instrumental right. It is popular nowadays to talk of education in terms of developing 'human capital', or as an investment in human resources to promote economic prosperity.[3] However, to see education only in instrumental terms risks depriving individuals of the right to education if they are not able to achieve these ends. Children with profound learning difficulties may be deprived of an education. Or education, seen instrumentally, may be deliberately formulated to prevent individuals from 'rising above their station', as in colonial India, or apartheid South Africa. The notorious Bantu Education Act of 1953 in South Africa prescribed separate and deliberately inferior education for black South Africans. The apartheid government explicitly designed the curriculum to limit their progress, training black children to be 'hewers of wood and drawers of water' rather than imparting skills and

[1] Committee on Economic, Social and Cultural Rights (CESCR) General Comment No 13 on the Right to Education (1999) UN Doc E/C.12/1999/10, para 1.

[2] UN General Assembly, 'Transforming Our World: The 2030 Agenda for Sustainable Development' 21 October 2015, A/RES/70/1, Goal 4 <https://sustainabledevelopment.un.org/post2015/transformingourworld> (accessed 5 March 2018).

[3] Y Rabin, 'The Many Faces of the Right to Education' in D Barak-Erez and A Gross (eds), *Exploring Social Rights* (Hart 2007) 269.

learning that might allow them to compete with white workers.[4] Regarding education as simply an investment in human capital might also drive out subjects in the arts and humanities, which cannot be mapped straightforwardly onto greater productivity. Thus, education should primarily be regarded as an intrinsic right, valuable in its own terms. As Rawls put it:

> The value of education should not be assessed solely in terms of economic efficiency and social welfare. Equally if not more important is the role of education in enabling a person to enjoy the culture of his [or her] society and to take part in its affairs, and in this way to provide for each individual a secure sense of his [or her] own worth.[5]

Education is a multifaceted right, bridging the boundaries between socio-economic rights and civil and political rights. It is a social right, a freedom right, and an equality right. As a social right, it entitles individuals to free and compulsory primary education provided by the State.[6] As a freedom right, it protects individuals against the risk that the State might use education to promote State propaganda or to impose the dominant culture, language, or religion. The freedom dimension of the right also involves parental choice as to schooling for their children, especially respect for parents' rights to educate their children in accordance with their religious beliefs.[7] Education is also an equality right, as demonstrated by the famous US Supreme Court desegregation case, *Brown v Board of Education*.[8] All these components should be considered simultaneously. Education as a social right is also a freedom and equality-enhancing right. As expressed by the capabilities theory of Sen and Nussbaum, education aims to expand positive freedoms for individuals to be and do as they would like to be and do.[9] There is also the possibility that these aspects of the right might conflict with each other. The right to equal education might conflict with the right to choose education, especially where minority schools exclude non-minority learners. The social right might conflict with the freedom right where distribution of resources is at issue.

The chapter begins by exploring the ways in which the freedom, social, and equality components of the right are reflected in different human rights instruments. It also compares and contrasts these to the characterization of education as a development goal in the SDGs. Section III considers the meaning of 'free and compulsory' education and particularly the paradoxical nature of a compulsory right. Section IV examines the complex contestations between the freedom and equality dimensions of the right, especially in the context of parental choice as to the religious, moral, or political nature of the education. Section V is concerned with the extent to which a human rights approach to education can be used to achieve quality education, and particularly again the complex ways in which education as an equality right interacts with education as a social right.

[4] 'Bantu Education' (South Africa: Overcoming apartheid, building democracy <http://overcomingapartheid.msu.edu/sidebar.php?id=65-258-2&page=1> (accessed 5 March 2018).

[5] J Rawls, *A Theory of Justice* (rev edn) (Harvard University Press 1999) 87.

[6] ICESCR, Article 13.

[7] ICCPR, Article 18(4).

[8] *Brown v Board of Education* 347 US 483 (1954) (US Supreme Court).

[9] M Nussbaum, *Creating Capabilities* (Harvard University Press 2011).

II. A Freedom Right, a Social Right, or an Equality Right: The Textual Basis

This section examines the ways in which the freedom, social, and equality components of the right are reflected in different human rights instruments. The right was originally expressed in a holistic form in the Universal Declaration of Human Rights (UDHR), which declared that everyone has the right to free and compulsory education. Importantly, education must be 'directed to the full development of the human personality' and 'promote understanding, tolerance and friendship among all nations, racial or religious groups'.[10] However, subsequent international and regional human rights documents separated the different components along the boundary between civil and political as against socio-economic rights. Reflecting the familiar hierarchy, human rights documents have given priority to the freedom aspect of the right, with the primary focus on the right of parents to educate their children according to their own beliefs. The only reference to education in the International Covenant on Civil and Political Rights (ICCPR) falls within the right to freedom of thought, conscience, and religion. Under Article 18(4) ICCPR, parties undertake to have respect for the liberty of parents and legal guardians to 'ensure the religious and moral education of their children in conformity with their own convictions'.[11] The European Convention on Human Rights (ECHR) has a specific provision for education, but framed in negative terms. Thus Protocol 1 Article 2 states: 'No person shall be denied the right to education'. As in the ICCPR, the main substance of the provision is to require the State to respect the right of parents 'to ensure such education and teaching in conformity with their own religious and philosophical convictions'.[12]

The social aspect of the right has been given lesser status in the international and regional human rights instruments. In the *Belgian Linguistic* case, the European Court of Human Rights (ECtHR) stated unequivocally that the negative formulation of the right to education meant that it did not require Contracting Parties to establish at their own expense or to subsidize education of any particular type or at any particular level.[13] It was left to the European Social Charter (ESC), adopted nearly a decade after the ECHR, to establish the social substance of the right. However, the ESC frames the right as progressively realizable rather than immediate. Under Article 17 of the Revised ESC, the Parties to the Covenant undertake to 'take all appropriate and necessary measures designed ... to provide to children and young persons a free primary and secondary education as well as to encourage regular attendance at schools'.[14] Similarly, the International Covenant on Economic, Social and Cultural Rights (ICESCR) provides a right to free and compulsory primary education.[15] But, like the ESC, this right is only progressively realizable. Thus, the right to education is subject to Article 2 ICESCR, which states that each State Party undertakes to 'take steps ... to the maximum of its available resources, to achieving progressively the full realization of

[10] UDHR, Article 26(2). [11] ICCPR, Article 18(4). [12] ECHR, Protocol 1, Article 2.
[13] *Belgian Linguistic Case (No 2)* (1979–80) 1 EHRR 252 (European Court of Human Rights) para [3].
[14] ESC 1996, Article 17(2). [15] ICESCR, Article 13.

the rights recognized in the present Covenant'.[16] Secondary education should be made generally available and accessible to all, primarily through the progressive introduction of free education. This is echoed in the Convention on the Rights of the Child (CRC), according to which States Parties recognize the right of the child to education. Under Article 28(1)(a) CRC, States Parties undertake to 'make primary education compulsory and available free to all'. Although the CRC specifies that the right should be made available on the basis of equal opportunity, it too includes a caveat stating that the right need only be achieved progressively.[17]

Education as an equality right has filled some of the gaps created by the relative weakness of the social facet of the right in international human rights law. The Convention on the Elimination of All Forms of Discrimination Against Women (CEDAW) includes a duty on States Parties to ensure that women enjoy equal rights with men in the field of education.[18] All treaties specify that the rights therein should be enjoyed without discrimination, and the obligation of non-discrimination is immediate. Article 3 ICESCR states that there is an immediate obligation to ensure that all rights enunciated in the Covenant, including education, can be exercised without discrimination on grounds of race, colour, sex, language, religion, political or other opinion, national or social origin, property, birth, or other status. Non-discrimination can also be used to give greater power to the right to education in the civil and political rights treaties, as has been the case with the non-discrimination provision in Article 14 ECHR.

At national level, human rights instruments give varying emphasis to the freedom, social, and equality facets of the right, often reflecting national history and priorities. The Indian Constitution from its inception protected the freedom aspect of education, particularly in relation to freedom of religion and language within education. Article 28 states that no-one attending an educational institution recognized by the State or receiving State funds should be required to take part in religious instruction or religious worship without their consent or that of their guardians.[19] The Constitution also specifically protects the rights of both religious and linguistic minorities to establish and administer educational institutions, and it is unlawful for the State to discriminate in the granting of aid to an educational institution on the grounds that it is under the management of a religious or linguistic minority.[20] The equality facet of the right to education has primarily been protected through special provision or reservations in educational institutions for 'the advancement of any socially and educationally backward classes of citizens or for the Scheduled Castes or the Scheduled Tribes'.[21]

The social facet of the right to education has been more contested in India. In the Indian Constitution as originally drafted in 1948, education was referred to as a 'directive principle of state policy', rather than a fundamental right. Article 45 of the Indian Constitution states that 'the State *shall endeavour to provide* free and compulsory education for all children under 14 within 10 years', while Article 41 states that the

[16] ICESCR, Article 2(1).
[17] CRC, Article 28(1)(a).
[18] CEDAW, Article 10. See also CRC, Article 28.
[19] Indian Constitution, Article 28(3).
[20] Indian Constitution, Article 30.
[21] Indian Constitution, Article 15(5).

State shall, '*within the limits of its economic capacity and development*, make effective provision for securing the right ... to education'.[22] Directive principles are expressly declared to be 'unenforceable in any court of law'.[23] Nevertheless, the Constitution provides, they are 'fundamental in the governance of the country and it shall be the duty of the State to apply these principles in making laws'.[24]

Although Article 45 committed the State to endeavour to provide free and compulsory education within ten years of the Constitution's ratification in 1949, the faith in the political process to ensure this commitment was realized proved to be too optimistic. By 1992, the promise of education for all was far from being fulfilled. This led the Court, in the case of *Mohini Jain* in 1992, to find that education can be implied as a fundamental right from the right to life in Article 21 of the Constitution.[25] In doing so, it endorsed education as both intrinsic to the dignity of the individual and a multiplier right. As the Court put it, 'It is primarily the education which brings forth the dignity of a man ... An individual cannot be assured of human dignity unless his personality is developed and the only way to do that is to educate him'.[26] The right to life, in the Court's view, is 'the compendious expression for those rights which the Court must enforce because they are basic to the dignified enjoyment of life ... The right to life under Article 21 and the dignity of an individual cannot be assured unless it is accompanied by the right to education'.[27] Unless the promise of education in the Directive Principles was fulfilled, fundamental rights 'shall remain beyond the reach of the large majority which is illiterate'.[28] This meant that the State was under a duty to establish educational institutions, which could be State owned or State recognized.

The journey from directive principles through implied right to an express right was completed in 2002 with a constitutional amendment giving education the status of a fundamental right. This is found in Article 21A, which provides: 'The State shall provide free and compulsory education to all children of the age of six to fourteen years'.[29] It took another seven years for legislation to be passed, in the form of the Right of Children to Free and Compulsory Education Act, 2009 (RTE Act). The RTE Act sets minimum norms and standards for all schools, whether public or private. It also harnesses the private sector to the goal of addressing disadvantaged learners, by requiring private schools to set aside 25 per cent of the places in their incoming class for children from socially and economically deprived backgrounds. As we shall see, these aspects of the RTE Act have come into conflict with the freedom aspects of the right to education in fiercely contested litigation from minority schools claiming exemptions from the RTE Act. Meanwhile, the right to life continues to play a central role, primarily through the 'Right to Food' litigation, which requires all schools to provide a cooked meal at school.[30]

In the US Constitution, by contrast, there is no express protection for the right to education in either its freedom or its social form. This has meant that all efforts to

[22] Italics added. [23] Indian Constitution, Article 37. [24] ibid.

[25] *Mohini Jain v State of Karnataka* 1992 SCR (3) 658 (Indian Supreme Court).

[26] ibid, 667F. [27] ibid, 669F–G. [28] ibid, 668E.

[29] Constitution (86th Amendment) Act 2002, Article 21A.

[30] Right to Food Campaign <http://www.righttofoodcampaign.in/> (accessed 5 March 2018). See Chapter 4.

protect a right to education at federal level have had to focus on its equality component under the Fourteenth Amendment. As will be recalled, this states simply that 'no state shall ... deny to any person within its jurisdiction the equal protection of the laws'. Under settled US Supreme Court jurisprudence, any legislation impinging on the exercise of a 'fundamental right', or which operates to the detriment of a 'suspect class', is subject to strict judicial scrutiny in order to comply with the Fourteenth Amendment.[31] Otherwise, the State simply has to demonstrate a rational basis for a classification. This raises the question of whether education is a fundamental right attracting strict scrutiny. The unanimous court in *Brown v Board of Education* in 1954 proclaimed: 'In these days, it is doubtful that any child may reasonably be expected to succeed in life if he is denied the opportunity of an education. Such an opportunity, where the state has undertaken to provide it, is a right which must be made available to all on equal terms'.[32] However, nearly two decades later in *San Antonio v Rodriguez*, the Court, by a narrow majority of five to four, refused to hold that the right to education was a fundamental right either explicitly or implicitly protected by the Constitution.[33] Although the Court reiterated the 'grave significance of education to the individual and society', it insisted that 'the importance of a service performed by the State does not determine whether it must be regarded as fundamental for purposes of examination under the Equal Protection Clause'.[34] Nor was the Court prepared to accept the argument that education was a fundamental right because it was essential to the exercise of the rights to freedom of speech or to vote. 'The Court has long afforded zealous protection against unjustifiable governmental interference with the individual's rights to speak and to vote', declared Powell J. 'Yet we have never presumed to possess either the ability or the authority to guarantee to the citizenry the most *effective* speech or the most *informed* electoral choice'.[35]

A more nuanced position was taken in *Plyler v Doe*, where a majority of the Court struck down a Texas statute denying children of unlawful immigrants the right to be educated in State public schools.[36] The Court distinguished *Rodriguez* on the grounds that in *Plyler* children were being denied education altogether, rather than being given some, albeit inferior, schooling, as in *Rodriguez*. While Brennan J acknowledged that education is not a 'right' granted to individuals under the Constitution, he also held that it is not merely a governmental benefit.

> Education has a fundamental role in maintaining the fabric of our society. We cannot ignore the significant social costs borne by our Nation when select groups are denied the means to absorb the values and skills upon which our social order rests.[37]

Children who are deprived of an education are subjected to an 'enduring disability' which takes an 'inestimable toll' on the 'social, economic, intellectual and psychological well-being of the individual' and also on the community.[38] He accepted, following *Rodriguez*, that education was not a fundamental right, and therefore the State

[31] See eg *Plyler v Doe* 457 US 202 (1982) (US Supreme Court) 217.

[32] *Brown v Board of Education* (n 8) 493; for earlier decisions, see *Meyer v Nebraska* 262 US 390 (1923) (US Supreme Court).

[33] *San Antonio Independent School District v Rodriguez* 411 US 1 (1973) (US Supreme Court).

[34] ibid, 31. [35] ibid, 36. [36] *Plyler v Doe* (n 31). [37] ibid, 221. [38] ibid, 222.

was not required to justify the way it provides education to a standard of compelling necessity. Nevertheless, the Court was entitled to review the legislation against the standard of rationality, and in determining the legislation's rationality, the Court was entitled to take into account 'its costs to the Nation and to the innocent children who are its victims'.[39] Applying this test, the Court found that the exclusion of children of unlawful immigrants was irrational.

By contrast to the federal level, the vast majority of State constitutions in the US include provision for education, usually in the form of a duty to provide free public education.[40] For example, the first Texas State Constitution, promulgated in 1845, provided for the establishment of a system of free schools.[41] Similarly, Article XI of the Constitution of the State of New York, which dates back to 1938, states: 'The legislature shall provide for the maintenance and support of a system of free common schools, wherein all the children of this state may be educated'.[42] The real issue has therefore been about quality and equity. The refusal in *Rodriguez* to recognize the right to education at federal level has led litigators to focus their energies litigating under State constitutions, emphasizing inadequate school financing.[43] As we will see below, there has been a fierce debate between education rights advocates about the respective merits of an equality as against an adequacy approach. Wieshart, however, sensibly argues that the two principles should be regarded as complementary.[44]

The South African Constitution fully embraces education as a social right. Section 29 provides: 'Everyone has the right to a basic education, including adult basic education',[45] while section 29(1)(b) provides for a right to further education 'which the state, through reasonable measures, must make progressively available and accessible'. Education stands out from the other socio-economic rights in the Constitution in that it is immediately realizable. This contrasts with the right to further education, which, like the rights to housing and health, should be achieved progressively.[46] The immediate nature of the right was endorsed in the important case of *Juma Musjid*.[47] On the other hand, the South African Constitution contrasts strikingly with human rights instruments at international and national level in that it does not provide for free education.

So far as the freedom aspect of the right is concerned, the South African Constitution gives everyone the right to receive education in the official language of their choice.[48]

[39] ibid, 224.

[40] Education Commission of the States, '50 State Review: Constitutional Obligations for Public Education' (March 2016) <http://www.ecs.org/ec-content/uploads/2016-Constitutional-obligations-for-public-education-1.pdf> (accessed 5 March 2018).

[41] Texas Constitution, Article X, s 1 (1845): 'A general diffusion of knowledge being essential to the preservation of the rights and liberties of the people, it shall be the duty of the Legislature of this State to make suitable provision for the support and maintenance of public schools'.

[42] The Constitution of the State of New York, Article XI: Education <https://www.dos.ny.gov/info/constitution/article_11_education.html> (accessed 5 March 2018).

[43] J Wieshart, 'Transcending Equality Versus Adequacy' (2014) 66 Stanford Law Review 478, 501; M Rebell, 'Ensuring Adequate Funding: The Role of Courts' in W Mathis and T Trujilo (eds), *Learning from the Federal Test-based Reforms: Lessons for ESSA* (Information Age Publishing 2016) 510.

[44] Wieshart, ibid.

[45] South African Constitution, s 29(1)(a).

[46] South African Constitution, s 29(1)(b).

[47] *Juma Musjid v Essay* [2011] ZACC 13 (South African Constitutional Court).

[48] South African Constitution, s 29(2).

Notably, there is no express right to receive an education in accordance with one's religion, although there is a general right to freedom of religion. The South African Schools Act permits religious observances to be conducted at public schools provided they are conducted on 'an equitable basis and attendance at them by learners and members of staff is free and voluntary'.[49] In a recent judgment, the South Gauteng High Court held that it was a violation of this provision for a public school to promote or allow its staff to promote that it, as a public school, adheres to only one or predominantly only one religion to the exclusion of others, and to hold out that it promotes the interests of any one religion in favour of others.[50] However, there is as yet no Constitutional Court judgment on this point. The range of provisions in the Indian and South African Constitutions contrasts with the Canadian Charter, where the right to education is expressed almost exclusively in relation to minority language rights.[51] This has meant that major educational cases have been litigated under other provisions, such as freedom of religion[52] and equality.[53]

Closely allied to the freedom of parents to educate their children in the religion or language of their choice is the right to establish private schools. The CRC, for example, includes a liberty to establish and run educational institutions, subject to the minimum standards laid down by the State and the provisions of the Convention.[54] The right to establish private educational establishments is also protected in domestic constitutions. Thus, under the Indian Constitution, both religious and linguistic minorities have the right to establish and administer educational institutions of their choice.[55] Similarly, the South African Constitution provides for the right to establish independent private educational institutions.[56] This is also the position of the ECtHR, which has held that the State cannot prevent individuals from forming private schools.[57]

But does this mean that the State should be under an obligation to fund such institutions? The answer has generally been in the negative. In the *Belgian Linguistic* case, the ECtHR firmly set its face against requiring the State to establish at its own expense or to subsidize schools of any particular type or at any particular level.[58] In South Africa, in a case in 2013, private schools contested the withdrawal of State subsidy of private schools as a breach of contract and the right to education. The South African Constitutional Court held, by a majority, that there could be no binding contractual right to such subsidies. Provided the State provided reasonable notice, and fulfilled existing obligations, it was entitled to withdraw such funding.[59]

[49] South African Schools Act 84 of 1996, s 7.

[50] *Organisasie vir Godsdienste-Onderrig en Demokrasie v Laerskool Randhart and Others* (29847/2014) [2017] ZAGPJHC 160 (South African South Gauteng High Court).

[51] Canadian Charter, ss 16(1) and 23.

[52] *Loyola High School v Quebec* (2015) SCC 12 (Supreme Court of Canada); see further below.

[53] *Auton v British Columbia (Attorney General)* [2004] 3 SCR 657 (Supreme Court of Canada).

[54] CRC, Article 29(2); see further below.

[55] Indian Constitution, Article 30.

[56] South African Constitution, s 29(3).

[57] *Belgian Linguistic Case (No 2)* (n 13).

[58] ibid, para [3].

[59] *KwaZulu-Natal Joint Liaison Committee v MEC Department of Education* [2013] ZACC 10 (South African Constitutional Court).

On the other hand, the role of the State in regulating private institutions has become a central issue for human rights law. This is because of the exponential growth in commercial firms operating low fee schools for profit in disadvantaged areas. In a crucial General Comment published in 2017, the Committee on Economic, Social and Cultural Rights (CESCR) sets out its authoritative interpretation of the regulatory framework that States should put in place in relation to business.[60] In particular, it deals with the role and impact of private actors in traditionally public sectors, including education.[61] The Comment emphasizes that the 'States retain at all times the obligation to regulate private actors' and should put in place 'strict regulations' to do so. Particularly important is the requirement that States should prevent 'new forms of socio-economic segregation' and ensure that the enjoyment of Covenant rights should not be made 'conditional on the ability to pay'.[62] Currently, a group of stakeholders is working on developing a set of Human Rights Guiding Principles on States' Obligations Regarding Private Schools, which it hopes will be endorsed by States and UN bodies, and will form the basis for shaping policy.[63]

The binding human rights commitments outlined above are now being complemented by a strong emphasis on education as a development goal. The Millennium Development Goals (MDGs) agreed in 2000, set out eight goals to eradicate poverty by 2015. The second goal was the achievement of universal primary education. Its target was to ensure that, by 2015, 'children everywhere, boys and girls alike, will be able to complete a full course of primary schooling'. During the fifteen-year period, there were some notable successes. Enrolment in primary education in developing regions increased from 83 per cent in 2000 to 91 per cent in 2015.[64] In addition, the global literacy rate among youth aged fifteen to twenty-four reached 91 per cent, up from 83 per cent in 1990. However, there were still as many as 57 million children of primary school age out of school in 2015, and many of them will never go to school. Moreover, statistics refer to enrolment rather than completion. In fact, the MDGs 2015 report states that almost 100 million adolescents are still not completing primary school. Equally disturbingly, the proportion of out-of-school children in countries affected by conflict rose from 30 per cent in 1999 to 36 per cent in 2012.[65]

An equality component was also part of the MDGs. The third goal of the MDGs was to promote gender equality and empower women. Its specific target was to eliminate gender disparity in primary and secondary education. In 2015, the United Nations Development Programme proudly proclaimed: 'The world has achieved

[60] UN Committee on Economic, Social and Cultural Rights General Comment No 24 on State Obligations under the ICESCR in the Context of Business Activities (23 June 2017) UN Doc E/C.12/GC/24.

[61] ibid, paras 21 and 22, and see generally Sylvain Aubry, 'The New UN General Comment on Business and Human Rights, Part 1: What Regulations Must States Put in Place When Private Actors Are Involved in the Delivery of Essential Services?' (OxHRH Blog, 13 July 2017) <http://ohrh.law.ox.ac.uk/the-new-un-general-comment-on-business-and-human-rights-part-1-what-regulations-must-states-put-in-place-when-private-actors-are-involved-in-the-delivery-of-essential-services> (accessed 5 March 2018).

[62] CESCR General Comment No 24 (n 60) para 22.

[63] The Global Initiative for Economic, Social and Cultural Rights, 'Human Rights Guiding Principles on States' Obligations Regarding Private Schools FAQS' <http://globalinitiative-escr.org/human-rights-guiding-principles-on-states-obligations-regarding-private-schools-faqs/#3> (accessed 5 March 2018).

[64] <http://www.un.org/millenniumgoals/education.shtml> (accessed 2 June 2017).

[65] ibid.

equality in primary education between girls and boys'. However, a closer look at the statistics shows that in fact only 64 per cent of countries in the developing regions had achieved gender parity by 2012. More worrying still, of the 57 million out-of-school children of primary school age in 2015, 55 per cent were girls. Moreover, nearly half (48 per cent) of out-of-school girls are unlikely to ever go to school, compared to about 37 per cent of out-of-school boys.[66]

A new set of development goals, the SDGs, were agreed in 2015, to be achieved by 2030.[67] The education commitment is considerably more ambitious. SDG4 commits the world to ensuring inclusive and equitable quality education and to promote lifelong learning opportunities for all. Its specific targets include ensuring that all girls and boys complete free, equitable, and quality primary and secondary education leading to relevant and effective learning outcomes. It also commits to building and upgrading education facilities that are child-, disability-, and gender-sensitive and to increasing the supply of qualified teachers. Importantly, it aims to provide access to quality early childhood development, care, and pre-primary education, as well as affordable quality technical, vocational, and tertiary education, including university. Gender disparities in education should be eliminated, and equal access provided for persons with disabilities, indigenous peoples, and children in vulnerable situations. Finally, and particularly significantly, it aims to increase the supply of qualified teachers.

This raises the question of the relationship between development goals and human rights. First, development goals are political commitments, vulnerable to changing priorities. Certainly, wavering political priorities are one reason for the fact that some of the MDGs were not fully achieved. Human rights, by contrast, are legally binding commitments, both internationally and by individual States. Second, development goals are seen as transfers of aid, or even charity. A human rights approach characterizes individuals as rights bearers, capable of insisting on their rights, rather than as beneficiaries of charity or aid. Third, human rights are universal. The focus of the MDGs was on developing regions, although a major step forward for the SDGs is that they now also apply to developed countries. This is important because in developed countries there are vast inequalities and pockets of real poverty. Fourth, the success of development goals is measured in aggregate quantitative terms—hence the claim that the goal of equality in primary education between girls and boys has been achieved. Human rights insist that each individual matters. The fact that there are 57 million out-of-school children means that there are 57 million children whose rights are being breached.

At the same time, there are many ways in which development goals and binding human rights should be regarded as working in tandem. The SDGs for the first time expressly refer to human rights in their preamble, committing 'to protect human rights and promote gender equality and the empowerment of women and girls'.[68] This

[66] UN, 'The Millennium Development Goals Report 2015' <http://mdgs.un.org/unsd/mdg/Resources/Static/Products/Progress2015/English2015.pdf> (accessed 5 March 2018).
[67] 'Transforming Our World: The 2030 Agenda for Sustainable Development' (n 2) Goal 4.
[68] ibid, para 3.

is of great importance. Existing human rights standards can be used to give binding force to SDGs, and SDGs can in turn provide detailed content to broad-brush human rights guarantees. At the same time, both largely depend on the commitment by State institutions to provide resources to fulfil their aims. Moreover, although in principle human rights are binding, enforcement remains difficult to achieve, particularly at international level. Indeed, the effectiveness of the international reporting mechanisms, such as the CESCR, largely depends on their power to galvanize political support at domestic level. This is true both in the preparation of shadow reports to submit to the Committee in the periodic reporting process, and in the use that can be made of the Committee's recommendations and conclusions in the domestic political arena.

III. Free and Compulsory Education: A Paradoxical Right

A. Education as a compulsory right

Education is unusual in being a 'compulsory' right. As we have seen, almost all human rights instruments provide that education should be 'free and compulsory'. On the surface, there is something deeply paradoxical about the notion of a compulsory right. Does it mean, as Rousseau maintained, that individuals can be 'forced to be free',[69] a conclusion which was anathema to liberal thinkers such as Isaiah Berlin?[70] Or is the notion of a compulsory right simply self-contradictory? Some regard it as an essential element of the definition of a right that the right-holder can choose not to exercise the right.[71] Thus Hart maintains that a right makes the right holder 'a small-scale sovereign'[72] in the sense that she can control whether or not the correlative duty-bearer exercises her duty. This means that there can be no such thing as a non-waivable right. This is true too for the more substantive capabilities theories of Sen and Nussbaum. As Nussbaum puts it, 'Capability means opportunity to select. The notion of *freedom to choose* is thus built into the notion of capability'.[73]

How then can we justify the compulsory nature of education? As MacCormick demonstrates, some of the most important rights that we have are non-waivable. A key example is the right not to be enslaved.[74] This is based on the premise that freedom itself cannot be waived. Building on this, it could be argued that compulsory education is necessary to develop children's capabilities for the future, thus enabling them to achieve substantive freedoms. Nussbaum goes on to state: 'Children, of course, are different; requiring certain sorts of functioning of them (as in compulsory education) is

[69] Jean-Jacques Rousseau, *The Social Contract and Discourses by Jean-Jacques Rousseau* (translated with an Introduction by G D H Cole) (London and Toronto: J M Dent and Sons 1923) ch VII <http://oll.libertyfund.org/titles/638> (accessed 16 July 2018).

[70] I Berlin, *Four Essays on Liberty* (Clarendon Press 1969); see further S Fredman, *Human Rights Transformed: Positive Rights and Positive Duties* (OUP 2008) ch 1.

[71] See S Besson, 'Human Rights Waivers and the Right to Do Wrong under the ECHR' in J Casadevall et al (eds), *Mélanges for Dean Spielmann* (Wolf Legal Publishers 2015) 23–35.

[72] H Hart, *Essays on Bentham: Studies in Jurisprudence and Political Theory* (Clarendon Press 1982) 182.

[73] Nussbaum (n 9) 25.

[74] N MacCormick, 'Rights in Legislation' in P Hacker and J Raz (eds), *Law, Morality and Society: Essays in Honour of HLA Hart* (OUP 1977) 197; and see generally L Wenar, 'Rights' in E Zalta (ed), *The Stanford Encyclopedia of Philosophy* (Fall 2015 edition) (2015).

defensible as a necessary prelude to adult capability'.[75] This should not, however, stifle all choice on the part of children. There may be no choice as to whether to be educated; but without giving children a growing degree of choice within education, it is hard to see how education could develop the more general capacity to make choices.

A second justification for compulsory education is to recognize that the compulsion is not directed only or even primarily at the child as rights-bearer. Its main targets are the various duty-bearers in relation to the child's right to education, primarily the parents and the State. 'The element of compulsion highlights the fact that none of the "duty bearers", neither parents, nor guardians, communities or the state are entitled to treat as optional the decision as to whether the child should have access to primary education'.[76] Indeed, statutes making education compulsory generally provide punitive measures against the parents, rather than the child. This is also the way in which John Stuart Mill justified his staunch advocacy of compulsory education, despite its apparent conflict with his liberal theories of individual choice and non-intervention by the State. For Mill, the State was entitled to intervene to prevent harm, including the harm of failing to perform the parent's duty to provide for the proper education of the child.[77] Mill argued that the power of the parent over the child was delegated by the State, and therefore the State could intervene when parents were abusing this power by causing harm to the child, including neglecting to develop the child's mental facilities. This in turn implied that the child had the right to a minimum of education.

If education is compulsory, however, does it leave the way open for the State to use the education system to advance its own views?[78] Mill was acutely aware of the potential for compulsory education to become the engine of State propaganda. As he put it:

> A general State education is a mere contrivance for moulding people to be exactly like one another; and as the mould in which it casts them is that which pleases the predominant power in the government ... [i]t establishes a despotism over the mind.[79]

There are two possible responses to this concern. The first is to protect the right of parents to educate their children according to their beliefs, be they religious, moral, or political. The choice is not whether to educate children, but how. We have seen that this is strongly reflected in human rights instruments. The second, complementary response, is to regard the right to education as including not just access to education but access to quality education which is in fact freedom-enhancing, in that it develops individuals' abilities to make their own choices. This aspect is still under-developed in the human rights canon.

A further strong impetus for making education a compulsory right is its close relationship to prohibitions on child labour. Compulsory education can form a powerful antidote to child labour: children who are at school are simply not available for work

[75] Nussbaum (n 9) 26.

[76] A Fyfe, 'Compulsory Education and Child Labour: Historical Lessons, Contemporary Challenges and Future Directions', Working Draft (2005) 14 <http://www.ilo.org/ipecinfo/product/download.do?type=document&id=1099> (accessed 5 March 2018).

[77] JS Mill, 'On Liberty' in John Stuart Mill, *On Liberty* (OUP 1998) 117.

[78] E West, 'Liberty and Education: John Stuart Mill's Dilemma' [1965] 40 The Journal of the Royal Institute of Philosophy 129.

[79] Mill (n 77) 117–18.

during school hours. It has also been argued that school attendance is easier to enforce than laws preventing children from working for below a minimum wage.[80] At the same time, child labour is one of the chief obstacles to the achievement of education for all. For example, the demand for child labour in England in the first half of the nineteenth century was one reason why attempts to introduce compulsory schooling were unsuccessful until 1880.[81] On the other hand, once the political will to introduce compulsory schooling is ignited, the drop in child labour can be exponential. In England in the nineteenth century, as Fyfe shows:

> Successive governments took the view that mass public education was beyond the financial means of the state. When the foundations of a national school system were finally laid [in 1870], the results were extraordinary. Within the space of ten years, the number of children in state schools increased from fewer than 10,000 to over 1 million. Over the next ten years, numbers doubled. Child labour declined dramatically.[82]

Nevertheless, part-time education still meant that child labour was common until 1910, when legislation required all children to attend school full-time until fourteen years old. This was consolidated in the Education Act of 1918, which prohibited the employment of school-age children.

In India, by contrast, compulsory education was not introduced until the Constitutional Amendment in 2001, followed by the RTE Act in 2009. India continues to have a significant number of child labourers, whether as paid workers or as unpaid family workers. The 2001 census recorded 12.67 million child workers, a figure which, disturbingly, had increased from 11.28 million in the previous census ten years before.[83] One estimate, dating from 2006, puts the number of children out of school at as much as 38.5 million, a staggering 20 per cent of the number of children aged between seven and fourteen in India.[84] Indeed, India has only just signified its intention to ratify the International Labour Organization (ILO) Convention No 182 on the Worst Forms of Child Labour (1999)[85] and issued regulations putting this prohibition into effect.[86]

Compulsory education also enhances children's labour market prospects once they reach adulthood. The World Report on Child Labour, issued in 2015, found consistent evidence from all twelve countries from which data was available that involvement in

[80] Fyfe (n 76) 4–5. [81] ibid, 8. [82] ibid, 37–38.

[83] Government of India Ministry of Labour and Employment, *Indian Labour Year Book 2011 and 2012*, 37 <http://www.labourbureau.nic.in/ILYB_2011_2012.pdf> (accessed 7 March 2018).

[84] India Demographic and Health Survey DHS 2006 <https://www.epdc.org/sites/default/files/documents/India_OOSC_Profile.pdf> (accessed 5 March 2018) and see J Kothari and G Mukherjee, 'The Out of School Children Case: A Model for Court-facilitated Dialogue?' (OxHRH Blog, 18 September 2015) <http://ohrh.law.ox.ac.uk/the-out-of-school-children-case-a-model-for-court-facilitated-dialogue/> (accessed 5 March 2018).

[85] According to the International Labour Organization (ILO), India has, on 13 June 2017, 'deposited with the International Labour Office the instruments of ratification of the two fundamental ILO Conventions concerning the elimination of child labour, the Minimum Age Convention, 1973 (No 138) and the Worst Forms of Child Labour Convention, 1999 (No 182)', see <http://www.ilo.org/global/about-the-ilo/newsroom/news/WCMS_557295/lang--en/index.htm> (accessed 5 March 2018).

[86] See the Child Labour (Prohibition and Regulation) Amendment Act No 35 of 2016.

child labour is associated with lower educational attainment.[87] Moreover, young persons who were required to work as children are consistently more likely to be in low-paying jobs or unpaid family jobs. This is true too for those leaving school prior to the age of fifteen.

The Indian experience shows the importance of parental commitment to education, again pointing to the need for a compulsory element. On the other hand, the extent of compliance is very closely linked to quality of education. Parents will not believe that investment in the child's education is worthwhile if schooling standards are poor or irrelevant. Moreover, employment prospects are crucial: where there are few opportunities for decent work which requires skills learnt at school, parents have little incentive to delay children's entry into work, while at the same time incurring the costs associated with schooling.[88] This is particularly true for girl children. Early marriage and domestic responsibilities in the home mean that girl children face specific difficulties in entering and remaining in school. Because they have fewer opportunities in the labour market and are confined to a narrower range of occupations, there may be less incentive on families to send their girl children to school.

It is also important to ensure that poor families have alternative sources of income, so that child labour is not an essential plank of family survival. Accumulated evidence and experience therefore points to two essential policy pillars for combating child labour: education and social protection.

> Ensuring free, compulsory and quality education through to the minimum age of employment, provides families with the opportunity to invest in their children's education as an alternative to child labour and makes it worthwhile for them to do so. Expanding social protection helps prevent child labour from being used as a household survival strategy in the face of economic shocks and social vulnerability.[89]

B. The right to free education

The correlative of compulsory education is that it should be available for free to all. This is required by the ICESCR and the CRC, both of which provide for free, compulsory primary education. However, South Africa stands out for the absence of a constitutional requirement that education should be free. The end of apartheid brought with it the enormous challenge of achieving equity in a school system which had been racially stratified, with dramatically inferior resources allocated to education for the black majority as compared with their white counterparts. In abolishing racially divided schooling, and making education compulsory for the first time for black South Africans, the newly elected government nevertheless made the decision to depart from the principle that education should be free. This was despite the fact that free compulsory education is enshrined in international human rights law and had been the declared policy of the African National Congress (ANC) since its inception.

[87] ILO, *World Report on Child Labour 2015: Paving the Way to Decent Work for Young People*, 2015, xiv <http://www.ilo.org/ipec/Informationresources/WCMS_358969/lang--en/index.htm> (accessed 5 March 2018).

[88] ibid, xviii. [89] ibid, xxiv.

The famous 1955 Freedom Charter adopted at the Congress of the People in Kliptown on 26 June 1955 provided that 'Education shall be free, compulsory, universal and equal for all children'.[90] This was echoed during the first democratic elections in 1994, when the ANC in its manifesto committed to 'Introduce one education system that provides ten years of free and compulsory education for all children'.[91]

Nevertheless, once it came to power, the ANC decided that school fees should be charged by public schools to supplement minimum State subsidies,[92] with fee waivers for those who could not afford to pay. This was partly due to the limited availability of funds. But the primary reason was to deter white flight to private schools by maintaining the standards of previously white schools. The South African Schools Act requires the School Governing Body (SGB) to 'take all reasonable measures within its means to supplement the resources supplied by the State in order to improve the quality of education provided by the school to all learners at the school'.[93] This is largely done by setting school fees. Once the SGB has approved a fee, all parents must pay. Parents may, however, apply for a full or partial exemption based on income and verified through means testing.[94] Automatic exemptions apply to orphans and abandoned children as well as to parents receiving a poverty-linked State social grant.[95] A school may not deny a learner admission because of their parents' failure to pay fees.[96] However, parents can be sued by the SGB for non-payment.[97]

This inevitably builds in inequalities in schools. Schools with higher numbers of non-fee-paying learners will fare worse than schools whose parents are able to supplement the school's budget. Moreover, there are substantial variations in fee levels as between schools, with schools serving more affluent communities able to set higher fees and thereby protect and enhance their position. This is borne out by Fiske and Ladd's research. Although fees have not deterred learners from attending school, poorer learners will choose schools with lower fees. Class has begun to replace race in determining access to the formerly white schools. Even more seriously, they conclude: 'Fees have reinforced the advantages enjoyed by the formerly white schools without at the same time increasing the resources available to schools serving historically disadvantaged students'.[98] Similarly, Motala and Sayed describe the South

[90] African National Congress, *The Freedom Charter* <http://www.anc.org.za/content/freedom-charter> (accessed 5 March 2018).

[91] African National Congress, *1994 National Election Manifesto* <http://www.anc.org.za/content/1994-national-elections-manifesto> (accessed 5 March 2018).

[92] E Fiske and H Ladd, 'Balancing Public and Private Resources for Basic Education: School Fees in Post-apartheid South Africa' in L Chisholm (ed), *Changing Class: Education and Social Change in Post-apartheid South Africa* (HSRC Press 2004) 57; and see S Lewis and S Motala, 'Educational De/centralisation and the Quest for Equity, Democracy and Quality' in Chisholm, ibid, 118.

[93] South African Schools Act No 84 of 1996, s 36(1).

[94] See South African Schools Act, s 39(2)(b) and the Regulations for the Exemption of Parents from the Payment of School Fees, 2005, 1025 GG No 29311 3.

[95] Regulation 4(3) of the Regulations for the Exemption of Parents from the Payment of School Fees, 2005, 1025 GG No 29311 3.

[96] South African Schools Act, s 5(3)(a).

[97] South African Schools Act, s 41.

[98] Fiske and Ladd (n 92) 57–58.

African public schooling system as 'characterised by a vast number of distinctly disadvantaged schools and a small pocket of highly privileged schools'.[99]

This difficulty is exacerbated by the fact that fee exemptions for poor learners in non-poor schools are not compensated by extra resources for the school, creating an incentive for SGBs to find ways to exclude poor learners. Fiske and Ladd show that although schools have to be careful not to discriminate unlawfully against students eligible for fee exemptions, 'there is little doubt that many schools consider a family's likely ability to pay their fees when making admissions policies'.[100] In an attempt to prevent discrimination based on the family's ability to pay fees, regulations were promulgated by one of the provinces—Gauteng— prohibiting schools from accessing confidential reports on applicant students during the admissions process. A 'confidential report' is defined in the regulations as 'a report containing information about the financial status of a parent, whether the parent can afford school fees and employment details of a parent or any other information that may be used to unfairly discriminate against a learner'. The Federation of School Governing Bodies challenged the regulation as infringing on the powers of SGBs to determine who to admit.[101] The South African Constitutional Court rejected the challenge, holding that the regulation served a legitimate purpose, namely to protect learners against the real prospect of unfair discrimination during the admissions process. Justice Moseneke stated:

> It is so that when a school fashions its admission policy it will be actuated by the internal interests of its learners. It is also quite in order that a school seeks to be a centre of excellence and to produce glittering examination and other good outcomes. But public schools are not rarefied spaces only for the bright, well-mannered and financially well-heeled learners. They are public assets which must advance not only the parochial interest of its immediate learners but may, by law, also be required to help achieve universal and non-discriminatory access to education.[102]

Partly because of the recognition that a two-tier education system had developed in South Africa, with disadvantaged schools remaining almost entirely black, government policy was changed to designate the most disadvantaged schools as 'no-fee' schools.[103] Since 2007, the schools in the lowest two quintiles, and more recently also in the third quintile, were given the opportunity to apply to the Provincial Education Department to be declared 'no-fee' schools.[104] No-fee schools receive larger State allocations per learner, and a higher allocation for non-personnel, non-capital expenditure

[99] S Motala and Y Sayed, '"No Fee" Schools in South Africa' (Consortium for Research on Education, Access, Transitions and Equity (Create) Policy Brief No 7, August 2009) 2.

[100] Fiske and Ladd (n 92) 72.

[101] *Federation of Governing Bodies of South African Schools (FEDSAS) v Member of the Executive Council for Education, Gauteng (CCT 209/15)* [2016] ZACC 14 (South African Constitutional Court).

[102] ibid, para [44].

[103] Education Laws Amendment Act 2005; Amended National Norms and Standards for School Funding (Government Notice 869 in Government Gazette 261789 of 31 August 2006).

[104] R Mestry and R Ndhlovu, 'The Implications of the National Norms and Standards for School Funding Policy on Equity in South African Public Schools' (2014) 34 South African Journal of Education 1, 3.

to compensate for lack of fee revenue. In other schools, parents may continue to apply for exemptions from fees.

While the no-fee policy has been welcomed as a pro-poor intervention, it remains the case that public schools which can bring in high levels of private income through fees attract better qualified teachers, have smaller class sizes, and can offer better infrastructural resources.[105] In their 2014 quantitative study, Mestry and Ndhlovu found that although the State was making concerted efforts to achieve equity in public schooling, the policy of increasing funds for no-fee schools in quintiles 1, 2, and 3 and reducing funding for quintile 4 and 5 schools has not led to the improvement of educational outcomes and learner achievement, especially for rural, poor, and illiterate children.[106] They argue that the reduction of State funding in affluent schools has been more than compensated for through school fees and other fundraising initiatives. Similarly, Transparency International found that, despite the laudable aims behind the no-fee schools policies, 40 per cent of educator respondents in their study believed that learners in no-fee schools received a lower quality of education than students in other types of school.[107] Mestry and Ndhlovu conclude that despite the emphasis on redress and equity, the school funding provisions 'appear to have worked thus far to the advantage of public schools patronized by middle-class and wealthy parents of all racial groups'.[108]

This also raises the question of the age range for which the right to free, compulsory education is provided. While the international human rights documents are silent on the age to which the right applies, the Indian Constitution has a fixed age of six to fourteen years. The South African Constitution, by contrast, specifically includes a right to adult basic education. This is particularly important in countries where free compulsory education is relatively recent, leaving older generations without basic skills. On the other hand, there is a recent surge of interest in pre-school education. In a series of cases in New Jersey in the US, the courts have held that pre-school education for three- and four-year-olds is essential to overcome educational disadvantage in the poorest districts of the State. The New Jersey Constitution requires the legislature to 'provide for the maintenance and support of a thorough and efficient system of free public schools for the instruction of all the children in the State between the ages of five and eighteen years'.[109] Despite the express reference to a minimum age, the standard of 'thorough and efficient' has nevertheless been used to give constitutional underpinning to the provision of pre-school education. The court emphasized that strong empirical evidence demonstrates that early learning is:

> a critical condition for the attainment of a thorough and efficient education once a child enters regular public school. Stated conversely, because the absence of such early educational intervention deleteriously undermines educational performance once the child enters public school, the provision of pre-school education also has strong constitutional underpinning.[110]

[105] Motala and Sayed (n 99). [106] Mestry and Ndhlovu (n 104).

[107] H Døssing, L Mokeki, and M Weideman, 'Mapping Transparency, Accountability and Integrity in Primary Education in South Africa' (Transparency International 2011) 41.

[108] Mestry and Ndhlovu (n 104) 2. [109] New Jersey Constitution, Article VIII, § 4, para 1.

[110] *Abbott v Burke* 710 A 2d 450 (1998) (New Jersey Supreme Court).

Few other courts, however, have cast such a wide lens over the provision of the right to education.

IV. Integration or Assimilation: Conflicting Equalities

As we have seen, one of the risks of compulsory education is that it might be used to impose the dominant culture, religion, or State ideology. Indeed, compulsory education was introduced in the US in the nineteenth century precisely to assimilate the many different immigrant communities into a common culture. While some degree of integration may be essential for a cohesive society, this should not amount to subordination or extinction of different religions, cultures, and beliefs. It is for this reason that the right of parents to educate their children according to their beliefs has been an important complement to the compulsory nature of education. Chapter 12 considers the extent to which the State can promote religion in schools without breaching the right to freedom of religion of parents or learners. This section concentrates on the conflicting demands of integration and identity within the confines of education as a compulsory right. In this respect, the right to education continues to be the site of acute conflict, challenging the shifting meanings of choice and equality. On the one hand, minority groups have claimed the right to separate schools to protect their cultural, religious, or linguistic identities. For them, integrated schooling can stand for assimilation and cultural domination. On the other hand, enforced segregation has been a key weapon of dominant groups in the maintenance of supremacy and oppression. These opposing forces are overlaid with the challenges of competing inequalities. One such conflict is between the rights of parents and those of children. Should parental choice be protected even if it constrains future choices of their children? Equally complex are the conflicting inequalities entailed when minority groups claim a right to retain privileges against a socio-economically disadvantaged majority. In all these ways, the simple meaning of equality as treating likes alike is seriously deficient. Instead, a more searching conception of substantive equality is required.

The conundrum of assimilation or segregation can be partially resolved by focusing on choice: a group that chooses separation is very different from one on which segregation is forced. But choice too is complex. On the one hand, parental choice might be a function of overriding constraints. For example, Roma parents might choose to send their children to segregated and even inferior schools because of stigma and bullying in majority schools. In such situations, the conditions under which choice is exercised need to be scrutinized. On the other hand, protecting the choice of a relatively privileged minority might in effect curtail the choices of disadvantaged groups in the same society. This has been seen in both South Africa and India, where privileged minorities have attempted to maintain their privileges through recourse to minority rights at the expense of poor and disadvantaged majorities. Even more complex is the situation of linguistic minorities. Since language is essentially communicative and cannot be exercised alone, and since education is frequently the main means of survival and flourishing of minority languages, to what extent can minority linguistic groups compel their own members to send their children to a minority language school? These issues are explored below.

A. Assimilation as inequality

The danger that free and compulsory education can mask attempts to assimilate minority groups was clearly recognized by the International Court of Justice (ICJ) as long ago as 1933 in the *Minority Schools in Albania* case.[111] In that year, the Albanian National Assembly modified its constitution to provide free and compulsory primary education for all Albanian subjects while at the same time requiring all private schools to be closed. The Greek minority in Albania claimed that this breached its rights under the Albanian Declaration of 1921, which stated that Albanian racial, linguistic, or religious minorities will enjoy 'the same treatment and security in law and in fact as other Albanian nationals'. The Albanian Government argued that everyone was treated equally. No private schools were allowed and all Albanians were offered free and compulsory education. However, the applicants contended that 'same treatment' of this sort was simply a means to extinguish their separate national identity and that real equality required different treatment in this context. In a remarkably prescient advisory opinion,[112] the ICJ distinguished between equality before the law and equality in fact. Drawing on the reference to equality both in law and in fact in the 1921 Declaration, the Court stated: 'Equality in law precludes discrimination of any kind; whereas equality in fact may involve the necessity of different treatment in order to attain a result which establishes an equilibrium between different situations'.[113] The rights to establish and maintain religious and social institutions, including schools and other educational establishments, are

> indispensable to enable the minority to enjoy the same treatment as the majority, not only in law but in fact ... Far from creating a privilege in favour of the minority, as the Albanian Government avers, the stipulation ensures that the majority shall not be given a privileged situation as compared with the minority.[114]

Otherwise, the majority would have its needs catered for by institutions created by the State, whereas the minority would be deprived of institutions appropriate to its needs.

A similar result was achieved by the US Supreme Court in *Wisconsin v Yoder*,[115] this time applying the right to freedom of religion, rather than building on the meaning of equality. In this case, the Court upheld the right of members of the Old Order Amish to withdraw their children from mainstream schools after the eighth grade (ages fourteen to fifteen), in breach of Wisconsin's compulsory school attendance law, which required them to send their children to school until the age of sixteen. The parents argued that this law violated their rights under the protection for freedom of religion in the First Amendment.[116] Secondary school education, they argued, would expose their children to 'worldly' influences in conflict with their beliefs, which required them to live aloof from the world and make their living through farming and activities close to nature. While high school emphasizes competitiveness, self-distinction, worldly

[111] *Minority Schools in Albania, Advisory Opinion* 1935 PCIJ (ser A/B) No 64 (April) (Permanent Court of International Justice).

[112] ibid. [113] ibid, para [64]. [114] ibid, paras [67]–[68].

[115] *Wisconsin v Yoder* 406 US 205 (1972) (US Supreme Court).

[116] This is applied to States under the Fourteenth Amendment. See further Chapter 12.

success, and social life with other pupils, Amish society is based on informal learning through doing; community welfare rather than competition; goodness rather than intellect; and separation from contemporary worldly society. They accepted the need for elementary education through the first eight grades, above all to learn literacy so that their children could read the Bible. But adolescent years should be spent within the community, acquiring Amish attitudes favouring manual work and self-reliance.

The Court accepted that a degree of education is necessary to prepare citizens to participate effectively and intelligently in the political system, and to be self-reliant and self-sufficient participants in society. However, compulsory high-school education would wrongly require the Amish to assimilate into society at large.[117] The Amish system of 'informal education', or learning-by-doing, was sufficient to equip their children for life in their communities—and even if they chose to leave the community, to life outside. The fact that they had functioned effectively as a self-sufficient community for more than 200 years was 'strong evidence that they are capable of fulfilling the social and political responsibilities of citizenship without compelled attendance beyond the eighth grade at the price of jeopardizing their free exercise of religious belief'.[118]

The case, however, also exposes some of the risks of permitting minority groups to determine the content of education according to their own beliefs. By taking their children out of mainstream education, are parents risking closing off opportunities created by education viewed as an accelerator right? For Burger CJ, this was unequivocally within the scope of parental rights. As he put it, 'This case involves the fundamental interest of parents, as contrasted with that of the State, to guide the religious future and education of their children'.[119] Since it was the parents who were subject to prosecution, it was their right of free exercise of religion, not that of their children, which was at issue.[120] At the same time, he regarded the right as quintessentially a religious one: Burger CJ made it clear that such protection would not be accorded to parental dissent on secular grounds.[121] Burger CJ was also prepared to defer to parents as to the content of the alternative learning provided by the Amish. In particular, he was unperturbed by the risk that Amish 'learning-by-doing' might undermine prohibitions on child labour. He recognized that compulsory school attendance to age sixteen should be viewed both as providing educational opportunities for children and as an alternative to 'the equally undesirable consequence of unhealthful child labour displacing adult workers'.[122] However, he did not consider that the agricultural work performed by Amish children was problematic. 'For, while agricultural employment is not totally outside the legitimate concerns of the child labour laws, employment of children under parental guidance and on the family farm from age fourteen to age sixteen is an ancient tradition that lies at the periphery of the objectives of such laws. There is no intimation that the Amish employment of their children on family farms is in any way deleterious to their health or that Amish parents exploit children at tender years'.[123] At the same time, he left open the possibility of some State regulation of the content of the informal vocational education provided by the Amish.[124]

[117] *Wisconsin v Yoder* (n 115) 218. [118] ibid, 225. [119] ibid, 232. [120] ibid, 231.
[121] ibid, 216. [122] ibid, 228. [123] ibid, 229. [124] ibid, 236.

It was only the lone dissenting voice of Douglas J who was concerned with the wishes of the Amish children themselves. Douglas J refused to see the case as concerned only with a conflict between the interests of Amish parents and those of the State. The inevitable effect of permitting a religious exemption for the parents, was to impose the parents' notions of religious duty on their children. 'Where the child is mature enough to express potentially conflicting desires, it would be an invasion of the child's rights to permit such an imposition without canvassing his views'.[125] Although one of the children testified that her own religious views were opposed to high-school education, the children of the other two respondents had not expressed their views.

> It is the future of the student, not the future of the parents, that is imperilled by today's decision. If a parent keeps his child out of school beyond the grade school, then the child will be forever barred from entry into the new and amazing world of diversity that we have today. The child may decide that that is the preferred course, or he may rebel. It is the student's judgment, not his parents', that is essential if we are to give full meaning to what we have said about the Bill of Rights and of the right of students to be masters of their own destiny.[126]

B. Segregation as inequality

The equality dimension of the right to education has a very different meaning in the context of enforced segregation. Here the response is not to require the State to permit separate schools, but to insist on integration. At the same time, the risks that integration simply signals assimilation do not disappear. Equality is not achieved by confining the right to access to education; attention must also be paid to equality in education. Genuine equality requires schools to ensure an inclusive set of values, which incorporates and respects those who have previously been excluded. These complex interactions can be seen both in the US in the famous *Brown v Board of Education* case and in the Roma segregation cases in Europe. Until the *Brown* case in 1954, widespread segregation of African-American children throughout the Southern States of America was consistently defended on the basis that there was no contradiction between segregation and equality, as captured by the slogan 'separate but equal'. Indeed, in the notorious case of *Plessy v Ferguson* in 1896, the US Supreme Court upheld a law mandating racial segregation on trains. The object, the Court declared, 'was undoubtedly to enforce the absolute equality of the two races before the law, but in the nature of things it could not have been intended to abolish distinctions based upon colour, or to enforce social, as distinguished from political equality, or a commingling of the two races upon terms unsatisfactory to either'.[127] At the same time, the Court specifically endorsed 'the establishment of separate schools for white and coloured children'.[128]

It was not until 1954 that the Court registered a seismic change. In *Brown v Board of Education*,[129] a unanimous Court held that 'in the field of public education, separate but equal has no place. Separate educational facilities are inherently unequal'.[130] Even

[125] ibid, 242. [126] ibid, 245.
[127] *Plessy v Ferguson* 163 US 537 (1896) (US Supreme Court) 544.
[128] ibid, 544 and see cases cited therein. [129] *Brown v Board of Education* (n 8).
[130] ibid, 495.

if 'tangible factors' such as building, curricula, and teachers were asserted to be equal, the effect of segregation itself meant that the result could never be equal. 'To separate [African-American] children from others of similar age and qualifications solely because of their race generates a feeling of inferiority in their status in the community that may affect their hearts and minds in a way unlikely ever to be undone'.[131] In the subsequent case of *Brown II*, the Court required States to desegregate schools 'with all deliberate speed'.[132]

The case was of far-reaching symbolic effect. However, the Court's ability to counter the deep-seated racism which lay behind segregated schools soon came under pressure. In a notorious incident, three years after *Brown*, the Governor of Arkansas ordered the National Guard to block the doors of a white schoolhouse so that black children could not enter. For three weeks, units of the Arkansas National Guard 'acting pursuant to the Governor's order, stood shoulder to shoulder at the school grounds and thereby forcibly prevented' nine African-American students from entering. It was only when the President of the US dispatched federal troops to the school to supervise the admission of the students that the Court order was respected.[133] It took another decade for the legislature to endorse the Court's position. In 1965, Congress enacted the Elementary and Secondary Education Act to facilitate the dismantling of segregated schooling. Officially mandated segregation on grounds of race in schools thereby became unlawful.

However, this has not led to genuine freedom of choice of education for African-American and Latino children. As Minow puts it: 'Because of *Brown*, schools stopped explicitly assigning students to schools that separate them by race, but parents and communities can produce similar results indirectly through housing patterns, district lines, and even some forms of school choice'.[134] Courts, moreover, have withdrawn from school desegregation suits on the grounds that there is a significant difference between officially mandated segregation and socially produced patterns.[135] This culminated in the 2007 decision in *Parents Involved v Seattle*.[136] In this case, the Court struck down the policy of a Seattle school district to promote racial integration by allocating students to oversubscribed high schools according to their race. Although Seattle had no history of de jure segregation, it used a 'racial tiebreaker' in an attempt to address the effects of racially identifiable housing patterns on access to good-quality schools. Parents of students who had been denied assignment to particular schools solely on the basis of their race claimed that the policy violated the Equal Protection Clause. By a five to four majority, the Court held that, unless mandated by courts as a remedy for proven race discrimination, policies by school boards to promote racial integration by classifying students by race were themselves racially discriminatory.

The respondent argued that it was legitimate to assign students by race to ensure that, despite residential segregation, African-American children from disadvantaged

131 ibid, 494.

132 *Brown v Board of Education (Brown II)* 349 US 294 (1955) (US Supreme Court) 301.

133 *Cooper v Aaron* 358 US 1 (1958) (US Supreme Court) 12.

134 M Minow, *In Brown's Wake* (OUP 2010) 8.

135 Rebell (n 43) 509.

136 *Parents Involved in Community Schools v Seattle School District* 127 S Ct 2738 (2007) (US Supreme Court).

areas could access better schools. Rejecting this argument, Roberts CJ took a strictly symmetric view of *Brown*, regarding assignment on the basis of race as invidious even if its aim was to correct past disadvantage. 'Before *Brown*', he declared, 'schoolchildren were told where they could and could not go to school based on the colour of their skin … The way to stop discrimination on the basis of race is to stop discriminating on the basis of race'.[137] Breyer J, dissenting, saw the legacy of *Brown* from the opposite direction. 'All of those plans represent local efforts to bring about the kind of racially integrated education that *Brown v. Board of Education*, long ago promised'.[138] For him, the principle that *Brown* stood for was decidedly asymmetric: the basic objective of those who wrote the Equal Protection clause, he argued, was to forbid practices leading to racial exclusion. 'There is reason to believe that those who drafted an Amendment with this basic purpose in mind would have understood the legal and practical difference between the use of race-conscious criteria in defiance of that purpose, namely to keep the races apart, and the use of race-conscious criteria to further that purpose, namely to bring the races together'.[139]

The result has been increasing racial 'resegregation' in public schools in the US. In fact, schools are now more racially segregated than they were when the effort to achieve racial desegregation was at its height.[140] More worrying still is the finding of the Harvard Civil Rights Project that

> the vast majority of intensely segregated minority schools face conditions of concentrated poverty, which are powerfully related to unequal educational opportunity. Students in segregated minority schools can expect to face conditions which students in the very large number of segregated white schools seldom experience.[141]

The strategy of litigators has therefore turned away from using the right to equality to tackle segregation and instead has focused on educational adequacy and decreasing disadvantage more directly. This is dealt with further in Section V Part A below.

Enforced segregation on grounds of race has similarly been imposed indirectly but effectively in Europe, this time against Roma children. The European Monitoring Centre on Racism and Xenophobia has concluded that 'in many EU Member States, the Roma/Sinti/Gypsies/Travellers group constitutes the most vulnerable group in education'.[142] One particularly insidious practice in the Czech Republic was to use educational psychology tests to segregate Roma children in 'special' schools. Such schools were ostensibly designed for children with learning disabilities but were markedly inferior to mainstream schools. Although the tests were apparently applied equally to all children, an overwhelming majority of those who were placed in special schools were Roma. Data from the Czech Republic as a whole showed that more than half of all Roma children attended special schools.[143] Data from Ostrava, which was the subject of litigation before the ECtHR, revealed that as many as 50.3 per cent of Roma pupils

[137] ibid, 2768. [138] ibid, 2800. [139] ibid, 2815. [140] Minow (n 134) 5.

[141] Cited in Minow, ibid, 7.

[142] European Monitoring Centre on Racism and Xenophobia, Annual Report 2005, Part II (EUMC I) 67.

[143] *DH v Czech Republic* App No 57325/00 (2006) 43 EHRR 41 (European Court of Human Rights) para [18].

were assigned to special schools, whereas a miniscule 1.8 per cent of non-Roma pupils were so assigned.

In the ground-breaking case of *DH v Czech Republic* in 2008, the Grand Chamber of the ECtHR held that this practice contravened the right to non-discrimination in Article 14 together with the right to education in Protocol 1 Article 2 ECHR. The Court rejected two major contentions made by the Government of the Czech Republic, one based on equality and the second on choice. The first was that the applicants had in fact been treated equally: the psychological tests carried out to determine their intelligence was applied to all children, both Roma and non-Roma. Here the Court accepted, for the first time, that the right to equality comprised more than like treatment. Where the same treatment disproportionately disadvantages a group, there is no need to prove discriminatory intent on the part of the relevant authorities. Instead, a presumption of indirect discrimination arises. The burden then shifts to the government to show that the difference in impact is a result of objective factors unrelated to ethnic origin. Nor could the results of the tests constitute such a justification. It was clear in this context that the tests were not adapted to Roma needs, and there was a clear danger that they were biased.[144]

The second contention rejected by the Court was based on choice. The government argued that the parents had consented to the placement of their children in special schools and in some cases even requested this. In dismissing this argument, the Court was sensitive to the constraints on the choice of Roma parents. Consent was given by signature on a pre-completed form with no information on available alternatives or on the differences between the curriculum of the special school and that in other schools. Nor did the Czech Government make any attempt to ensure that ordinary schools were accommodating and welcoming to Roma children. The Court had no doubt that 'Roma parents were faced with a dilemma: a choice between ordinary schools that were ill-equipped to cater for their children's social and cultural differences and in which their children risked isolation and ostracism, and special schools where the majority of the pupils were Roma'.[145] In any event, the right not to be subjected to racial discrimination was so important that it could not be waived.

This conclusion was reinforced in the later case of *Oršuš v Croatia*[146] in which, instead of placing Roma children in separate schools, they were assigned to segregated classrooms, with a curriculum diminished by up to 30 per cent. This policy was challenged before the Court on the grounds that it was discriminatory and violated their rights to education. In its response, the Croatian Government argued that Roma children were placed in such classes because of their inadequate command of the Croatian language, and this position was accepted by the ECtHR at first instance. The Grand Chamber reversed this decision. This case differed from *DH* in that the statistics alone did not demonstrate that a disproportionate number of Roma children were in segregated classes.[147] However, the Court held that statistics were not the only means of establishing indirect discrimination.[148] In this case, the policy of placing children in

144 ibid, paras [198]–[203]. 145 ibid, para [203].

146 *Oršuš v Croatia* (2011) 52 EHRR 7 (European Court of Human Rights).

147 ibid, para [152]. 148 ibid, para [153].

separate classes because of insufficient command of the Croatian language was only applied to Roma children. Moreover, there was clear evidence of hostility on the part of non-Roma parents to integrated schooling, with some schools having witnessed angry protests by such parents.[149] These two factors, in the Court's view, meant that a prima facie case had been established and the burden of justification shifted to the government. The Court made it clear that the history of disadvantage of Roma people in Europe meant that they required special protection, particularly in the field of education. In addition, special consideration should be given to their needs and their different lifestyle.[150] In this case, although insufficient command of Croatian could be a legitimate purpose in principle, segregating such pupils was only applied to Roma children, and the tests used to make the decision were not targeted at language proficiency. Moreover, once in the classes, they were not given any specific language teaching to improve their Croatian.[151] Instead, a diminished syllabus in Croatian was provided. Nor was any attempt made to move them to mixed classes once their proficiency improved. In the result, the Court found a violation of Article 14 of the Convention (the right to equality) taken together with Article 2 of Protocol 1 (the right to education).

As in *Brown*, however, the judicial findings of discrimination have had little impact on patterns of segregation of Roma children in schools in Europe. In December 2013, the European Council adopted a Recommendation on effective Roma integration measures in the Member States, in which it noted that the situation of Roma children in the European Union (EU) is particularly worrying. In particular, segregation remains a serious barrier to preventing access to quality education. The Recommendation provides inter alia that Member States should eliminate school segregation, end inappropriate placement of Roma pupils in special needs schools, and use inclusive and tailor-made teaching and learning methods, including encouraging greater parental involvement.[152] Nevertheless, a survey conducted by the EU Fundamental Rights Agency in 2016 found that over 60 per cent of Romani children in Slovakia, Hungary, and Bulgaria attend schools where all or most of their schoolmates are Roma.[153] In its July 2016 review of Slovakia, the UN Committee on the Rights of the Child expressed concern that Romani children continue to be subjected to de facto segregation in the school system, with over 50 per cent being taught in Roma-only classes or attending classes in separate school facilities, often providing inferior education.[154] In an effort to ratchet up the legal approach, the European Commission is bringing proceedings in the Court of Justice of the EU to achieve compliance.[155]

[149] ibid, paras [153]–[155]. [150] ibid, para [148]. [151] ibid, para [173].

[152] Council of the European Union Recommendation on Effective Roma Integration Measures in the Member States (2013/C 378/01) (Brussels, 9 and 10 December 2013).

[153] European Union Agency for Fundamental Rights, 'Second European Union Minorities and Discrimination Survey (EU-MIDIS II) Roma', 27 <http://fra.europa.eu/en/publication/2016/eumidis-ii-roma-selected-findings> (accessed 5 March 2018).

[154] UN Committee on the Rights of the Child Concluding Observations on the Combined Third to Fifth Periodic Reports of Slovakia (20 July 2016) 13.

[155] See Equinet: European Network of Equality Bodies, 'European Commission Targets School Segregation of Roma Children in Hungary with Launch of Infringement Procedure' (27 May 2016) <http://www.equineteurope.org/European-Commission-targets-school-segregation-of-Roma-children-in-Hungary-with> (accessed 5 March 2018).

The Indian approach to segregation along caste and class lines has been different. The RTE Act is radical in its redistributive aims, requiring unaided private schools to set aside 25 per cent of the places in their incoming class for children from socially and economically deprived backgrounds, free of charge.[156] The State is required to recompense schools with the subsidy it would have paid for those children to go to State schools. The key purpose of this provision is to eliminate segregation and discrimination and foster diversity in schools.[157] The quota covers 'disadvantaged' groups defined as children 'belonging to a Scheduled Caste, Scheduled Tribe, a socially and educationally backward class or such other group having disadvantages owing to social, cultural, economical, geographical, linguistic, gender or such other fact, as may be specified by the appropriate Government, by notification'.[158] The 25 per cent quota also covers children belonging to the 'weaker section', which refers to children whose parents' annual income is lower than a minimum limit specified by the State government.[159]

This provision was challenged by private proprietors on the basis that it interfered with their freedom of occupation.[160] The Indian Supreme Court rejected the challenge.[161] The Court recognized that freedom of occupation was an important right. However, it reiterated the fundamental principle that

> a child who is denied the right to access education is not only deprived of his right to live with dignity, he is also deprived of his right to freedom of speech and expression ... The 2009 Act seeks to remove all those barriers including financial and psychological barriers which a child belonging to the weaker section and disadvantaged group has to face while seeking admission.[162]

The requirement was therefore a reasonable restriction on the right of occupation.

This raises the question of whether attempts to use the law to integrate social groups in India will follow the same trajectory as that experienced after *Brown* and *DH*. It is too soon to give any conclusive answer on this. Implementation has clearly been patchy. Figures show that in 2012–13 only two States in India filled more than half of the available seats for the economically weaker section/disadvantaged groups (EWS/DG). While there has been an impressive increase in some States, others have decreased, and some were only filling a meagre 2–4 per cent of seats.[163] A more detailed study conducted in Delhi in 2017[164] found that compliance had been improving, with only 6 per cent of places at schools assigned to the EWS/DG category in 2010–11,

[156] Right of Children to Free and Compulsory Education Act, 2009 (hereafter RTE Act) s 12(1)(c).

[157] RTE Act, Statement of Objects and Reasons; see further J Kothari, 'Calling the Farce on Minority Schools' in M Campbell, S Fredman, and H Taylor (eds), *The Value of a Human Rights-based Approach for Achieving Equality in Education: Comparative Perspectives on the Right to Education for Minorities and Disadvantaged Groups* (Policy Press 2018).

[158] RTE Act, s 2(d). [159] ibid. [160] Indian Constitution, Article 19(1)(g).

[161] *Society for Unaided Private Schools of Rajasthan v Union of India* (2012) 6 SCC 1 (Indian Supreme Court).

[162] ibid, para [10].

[163] KPMG/CII, 'Assessing the Impact of the Right to Education Act' (March 2016) 11–13.

[164] National Commission for Protection of Child Rights, 'A Study on Implementation of Section 12(1)(c) RTE Act 2009 in Delhi Pertaining to Admission of Children from Disadvantaged Sections in Private Schools' (2017).

reaching 18 per cent in 2016–17. However, this figure had flattened out, sticking at 18 per cent in 2015–16 and 2016–17. Notably, there has been a steady drop-out rate of 10 per cent since 2014. The study also investigated the extent of social discrimination experienced by beneficiaries of the quota. Crucially, it did not find any kind of discriminating behaviour between pupils from the general category and those admitted under the EWS/DG category in over 94 per cent of the schools surveyed. Rather, any negative attitudes seem to come from principals and teachers, a proportion of whom were opposed to the quota, and about one-third of whom regarded the EWS category as unable to cope academically. A major reason cited for this achievement gap was the lack of English language skills among this group, as well as lack of support by families and social environment. The report attributes these perceptions to stereotypes rather than reality, demonstrating that since all the children who come into the pre-primary year speak their mother-tongue rather than English, they should all be in a similar position. In the view of the authors of the report, the responsibility for achievement gaps therefore lies with the school and cannot be attributed to families or parents. A real obstacle for such families, however, is the cost of books. Although the State should provide sufficient funding to cover the cost of uniforms and books to the level that would have been provided in government schools, the fact that private schools choose to use more expensive textbooks means that there is inevitably a deficit for individual students. The report's main recommendation therefore concerns training of principals and teachers, and sensible pricing for books.

C. Identity and privilege: language of education as a clash of equalities

The question of whether and to what extent there is a right to choice of language in education casts a particularly complex light on the issue of choice, since it pits collective autonomy against individual choice. Language can only be sustained and developed through collective communication. But does this mean that minority language instruction can be made compulsory for individuals in the minority linguistic community to preserve the language for the group as a whole? Language rights in education also raise a different sort of conflict: that between privileged minorities, who use language to maintain privilege, and poor and disadvantaged learners who do not share their language. These conflicts are elaborated below.

Not all human rights instruments give parents' choice of language of instruction for their children the same priority as religious beliefs. As we have seen, the US Supreme Court in *Yoder* confined parental rights in relation to their children's education to those motivated by religion. The ECtHR has come to a similar conclusion. In *Belgian Linguistic*,[165] the Court held that the State's obligation to respect parents' right to ensure education in conformity with their own religious and philosophical convictions did not require the State also to ensure parents' linguistic preferences. The right to education under the Convention guaranteed a right of access to an educational

[165] *Belgian Linguistic Case (No 2)* (n 13).

establishment, but did not import any linguistic requirements. Nor could the requirement that a child study a national language which is not her own in depth be regarded as 'depersonalizing' pupils in breach of the right to private and family life in Article 8.[166]

This contrasts with the South African Constitution, which expressly includes a right to receive education in the official language of one's choice in a public educational institution where it is reasonably practicable.[167] This augments the collective right to enjoy and use one's language and culture,[168] together with the prohibition in section 9(3) against unfair discrimination on grounds, inter alia, of language. The Canadian Charter's provisions on language of education, for their part, reflect the fraught politics of the relationship between Quebec and the national government. Indeed, Quebec nationalism has frequently revolved around the preservation of the French language. This has raised in stark terms the conflict between the rights of one linguistic group to preserve their language through requiring it to be taught in schools, and the rights of individual parents to determine the language of instruction for their children. This is particularly problematic since the French-speaking population is a minority in Canada as a whole, but a majority in Quebec.

The dispute over language rights in Canadian schools pre-dates the Canadian Charter. Until the 1960s, parents in Quebec had a free choice as to whether to send their children to French or English schools, with both systems being relatively well developed.[169] However, with the rise of nationalism in Quebec came pressures to curtail the freedom of choice of language of instruction, because of anxieties about the possible decline of the French language. This was heightened by the concern that the large numbers of immigrants to Quebec, who almost invariably choose to send their children to English-speaking schools, would alter the demography of Quebec in a way which permanently marginalized the French language. At the same time, French education was side-lined and at times deliberately neglected in the other Canadian provinces, so that the French minority in those provinces had little genuine opportunity for French education.

These concerns led Quebec to adopt legislation, known as Bill 101, which required all Francophones as well as immigrants to send their children to French schools. Only Anglophones living in Quebec retained the choice as to whether to send their children to English schools.[170] Nor could individuals choose whether to identify as Anglophone. The Quebec government rejected the use of mother tongue as a criterion, concerned at its vagueness and openness to abuse. Instead, it used the criterion of whether the father or the mother of the child had received English language elementary education in Quebec. The result was radically to reduce parental choice as to the language of instruction of their children in Quebec. Neither Francophones nor immigrants could choose English language instruction, even if, in the case of immigrants, the mother

[166] ibid, 305.

[167] South African Constitution, s 29(2); see also the Framework Convention for the Protection of National Minorities, Article 14.

[168] South African Constitution, s 31(1).

[169] S Grammond, *Identity Captured by Law* (McGill-Queen's University Press 2009) 154–55.

[170] ibid, 150.

tongue was English. This was true too for English-speaking residents of Quebec who had been educated in a different province.

Negotiations over protection for minority language education in the Canadian Charter were predictably fraught, and the ultimate provision reflects the resulting compromises. The Charter aims to give minority French-speaking parents residing in provinces outside of Quebec the right to have their children educated in French; with the same rights for English-speaking parents residing in Quebec. Thus, under Section 23(1)(a) of the Charter, citizens of Canada whose first language is that of the English or French linguistic minority population of the province in which they reside have the right to have their children educated, both at primary and secondary level, in the minority language in question in that province. This 'mother tongue' definition, however, has always been rejected by Quebec, and the Quebec Government secured a compromise whereby section 23(1)(a) would not apply in Quebec. Therefore, while children of parents whose first language is French can be educated in French in all provinces in Canada, the same is not true for their English-speaking counterparts in Quebec. Instead, English-speaking parents in Quebec need to prove that their own schooling was in English in order to be entitled to have their children educated in English in Quebec. In addition, once one child is being educated in English, their siblings have the same rights. These rights are provided for in section 23(1)(b) and 23(2) of the Charter.

These provisions have led to fierce contestation, both in court and outside of it, on behalf of parents asserting their rights to freedom of choice of language of instruction. Parents began to argue that even a very short spell in English elementary education, whether in a public or a non-subsidized private school, would give them the rights guaranteed in section 23(1)(b). In an attempt to forestall such loopholes, the Quebec National Assembly amended the law to provide that French language instruction is compulsory for everyone except those who are certified as having received the 'major part' of their elementary instruction in English.[171] Education in private schools is not counted. Not surprisingly, these provisions have been a major source of contention, not just by Anglophones, but also by immigrants and some Francophones seeking an effective bilingual education for their children.

A trilogy of cases beginning in 2005 tested the legitimacy of the Quebec policy. In *Solski v Quebec*, the Court stated that the strict arithmetic calculation used by the Quebec Government to determine whether the 'major part' of elementary education was in English did not conform to the spirit of the Charter.[172] Instead, a qualitative approach was required, depending on whether there was 'a genuine commitment to a minority language educational experience'.[173] Four years later, in *Nguyen*,[174] parents challenged the provision which disregarded periods of attendance at an unsubsidized private school. They had enrolled their children for short periods at such schools and then requested that their children be declared eligible for English instruction in public or subsidized private schools. The Supreme Court of Canada struck down the

[171] Charter of the French Language, RSQ c C-11, s 72.
[172] *Solski v Quebec* (2005) SCC 14 (Supreme Court of Canada).
[173] *Solski (Tutor of) v Quebec (Attorney General)* [2005] 1 SCR 201 (Supreme Court of Canada) para [47].
[174] *Nguyen v Quebec* 2009 SCC 47 (Supreme Court of Canada).

provision. Building on the *Solski* judgment, the Court held that disregarding time spent in English education, albeit at an unsubsidized primary school, would mean that a misleading picture is gained, contrary to the principle that a global qualitative study of the child's educational pathway is required. These two judgments gave some degree of choice to parents. By educating a child in an unsubsidized English school, a family could show a 'genuine commitment' to the language as required by *Solski* and therefore gain access to the publicly funded English system. Importantly, this right would itself become hereditary in the sense that these children would be able to send their own children to publicly funded, English-speaking schools.[175]

The Supreme Court of Canada was less welcoming of claims by members of the French language majority in Quebec who wished to have their children educated in English. As French speakers, they did not qualify as rights-holders under section 73 of the Charter of the French Language, which provides access to English-language schools in Quebec only to children who have received or are receiving English-language instruction in Canada or whose parents studied in English in Canada at primary level. They argued that their right to equality had been violated because the language provisions discriminated between children who qualify for English-language education and those who do not. Equality, the parents argued, requires that all children in Quebec be given access to publicly funded English-language education. In *Gosselin v Quebec*,[176] the Court dismissed the claim. Since the parents were members of the French-language majority in Quebec, their purpose in having their children educated in English did not fall within the purpose of section 23 of the Charter. Indeed,

> if adopted, the practical effect of the appellants' equality argument would be to read out of the Constitution the carefully crafted compromise contained in s. 23 of the Canadian Charter of Rights and Freedoms. This is impermissible. As the Court has stated on numerous occasions, there is no hierarchy amongst constitutional provisions, and equality guarantees cannot therefore be used to invalidate other rights expressly conferred by the Constitution. All parts of the Constitution must be read together. It cannot be said, therefore, that in implementing s. 23, the Quebec legislature has violated either [the right to equality in] s. 15(1) of the Canadian Charter or ss. 10 and 12 of the Quebec Charter.[177]

This emboldened the Quebec Government to enact further legislation, known as Bill 115, which aimed to reinforce the previous strictures on the availability of English-language instruction in the public sector. Birks argues that the new measure is 'so opaque and complex that it can be used to keep transfers into the publicly funded English school system [from the private sector] to minuscule levels'.[178] Indeed,

> in preventing access to publicly funded English-language schools by everyone but a narrowly defined group of hereditary language rights-holders, the Quebec

[175] S Birks, 'Impact Study: Evaluating *Nguyen v Quebec* [2009] 3 SCR 208 and Bill 115: Section 23 of the Canadian Charter' (December 2011) 8 <https://padl-lrsp.uottawa.ca/sites/default/files/images/stories/Publications_and_Media/6_EI_-_Birks_Nguyen_LRSP_Impact_Study_12_11__Final.pdf> (accessed 5 March 2018).

[176] *Gosselin (Tutor of) v Quebec* [2005] SCC 15, [2005] 1 SCR 238 (Supreme Court of Canada).

[177] ibid, para [2].

[178] Birks (n 175) 9–10.

> Government had ... set the existing publicly funded English education system on a path to extinction or virtual extinction, as the group of hereditary rights holders could not grow, except through in-migration of people from other parts of Canada, natural increase of the English-educated Quebec Anglophone population or through intermarriage between rights-holding Anglophones and Francophones or naturalised newcomers.[179]

The result, as intended, is to privatize English-language education in Quebec.[180]

A different sort of conflict around language rights in education has been fought out in courts in South Africa and India, namely the use of language rights to protect minority privileges in relation to schooling. In South Africa, language has always been inextricably bound up with race and power. The Nationalist Party which established and enforced apartheid in South Africa was an Afrikaner party, and Afrikaans became the language of dominance and oppression. Indeed, it was the imposition of Afrikaans which triggered the student uprising in Soweto in 1976, where Afrikaans was rejected as an instrument of domination. Once South Africa transitioned into democracy, Afrikaners and the Afrikaans language became a minority, but one which retained much of the privilege and power of the apartheid regime. This is especially true of Afrikaans medium schools.

The protection of Afrikaans as a minority language has therefore come to represent a clash of equalities. This is because the vast majority of black South Africans prefer their children to be taught in English, even if that is not their mother tongue. As a result, Afrikaans medium schools are heavily undersubscribed, despite an acute shortage of space for English medium learners. On the other hand, many Afrikaners fear that the Anglicization of Afrikaans schools will lead to the demise of the language and cultural and linguistic assimilation.[181] Such was the position of Ermelo High School, which had an average of about twenty-one learners per classroom, as against the surrounding schools, where class sizes ranged from thirty-three to a staggering sixty-two learners per classroom. Despite many requests by the provincial government to create an English medium stream and thereby make more places available at Ermelo High School for the very disadvantaged local population, the SGB refused. This meant that 118 learners in their area would be unable to go to school at all for the year in question. The provincial head of the department of education purported to suspend the SGB and appoint an interim SGB to put an alternative language policy in place. In the case of *Mpumalanga Department of Education v Hoërskool Ermelo*[182] the SGB challenged the legality of this order.

[179] ibid, 7. [180] ibid, 4.

[181] M Smit, '"Collateral Irony" and "Insular Construction"—Justifying Single-medium Schools, Equal Access and Quality Education' (2011) 27 SAJHR 398 at 421; and see M Bishop, 'The Challenge of Afrikaans Language Rights in South African Education' in M Campbell, S Fredman, and H Taylor (eds), *The Value of a Human Rights-based Approach for Achieving Equality in Education: Comparative Perspectives on the Right to Education for Minorities and Disadvantaged Groups* (Policy Press 2017).

[182] *Mpumalanga Department of Education v Hoërskool Ermelo and Another (CCT 40/09)* [2009] ZACC 32 (South African Constitutional Court).

How then should Afrikaans speakers' rights to language and culture be weighed against the rights of Black people to quality education?[183] The South African Constitutional Court has expressly recognized that

> the Afrikaans language is one of the cultural treasures of South African national life.... In approaching the question of the future of the Afrikaans language, then, the issue should not be regarded as simply one of satisfying the self-centred wishes, legitimate or otherwise, of a particular group, but as a question of promoting the rich development of an integral part of the variegated South African national character contemplated by the Constitution.[184]

On the other hand, the Court is acutely aware of the risk that this would maintain white privilege in the educational system. The potential for a compromise solution is to some extent found in the Constitutional provision itself. Section 27(2) gives the right to receive education in the official language of their choice in state schools where 'reasonably practicable'. To ensure effective access to the right, the State should consider all reasonable educational alternatives, taking into account, as well as equity and practicability, the need to 'redress the results of past racially discriminatory laws and practices'.[185] In the *Ermelo* case, Moseneke DCJ highlighted the crucial fact that this is not an all-or-nothing solution. A school need not adopt a single medium policy, but could put in place a parallel system, or even a dual-medium approach.[186]

The South African situation is complicated by the fact that many of the powers to run a school are devolved to the SGB, which is made up of parents and local residents. The SGB has the duty to promote the best interests of the school and all learners at the school. This is seen as a vital part of the democratic governance of schools. However, it also means the SGB is inevitably inward-looking. On the other hand, the provincial education authority has the duty to ensure that all learners in the province are provided with an education. There is therefore enormous potential for conflict between an SGB wishing to preserve the language of its school, and the provincial authority. Indeed, many of the cases which have come before the South African Constitutional Court are formulated as a conflict between the SGB and the provincial authority, rather than dealing directly with the substantive issues.

In *Ermelo*, the Court held that the provincial authority had no power to remove the SGB and put another in its place to promulgate a new language policy. To that extent, the Head of Department acted unlawfully and the new language policy adopted by the interim SGB was void. On the other hand, the SGB did not have unlimited discretion as to the language policy it adopted. Instead, it was 'entrusted with a public resource which should be managed not just in the interests of those who happen to be learners and parents at the time but also in the interests of the broader community in which the school is located and in the light of the values of our Constitution'.[187] This led the Court to 'place

[183] Bishop (n 181).

[184] *In Re Dispute Concerning the Constitutionality of Certain Provisions of the Gauteng School Education Bill of 1995* (1996) 3 SA 165 (South African Constitutional Court) para [49].

[185] South African Constitution, s 29(2).

[186] *Mpumalanga Department of Education v Hoërskool Ermelo and Another (CCT40/09)* (n 182) paras [52]–[53].

[187] ibid, para [80].

substance above form' in devising a remedy even though it had found in favour of the SGB. It held that the SGB should reconsider its language policy in the light of dwindling enrolment numbers and in recognition of the great demand for admission of learners who prefer English as a medium of instruction. At the same time, the provincial authority should plan better to ensure sufficient places for learners who preferred English as their medium of instruction.

As in South Africa, the pressing question in India is how human rights law responds to attempts by those privileged in the education sector to use minority rights to retain that privilege. This has arisen out of contestation over the reach of the RTE Act. The RTE Act sets minimum norms and standards for all schools, whether public or private. These include minimum standards for toilets, playgrounds, drinking water, midday meals, and the ratio of teachers to students.[188] As we have seen, it requires unaided private schools to set aside 25 per cent of the places in their incoming class for children from socially and economically deprived backgrounds.[189]

This provision has been vociferously challenged, both by minority religious and linguistic schools. The Indian Constitution specifically provides for the rights of minorities, whether based on religion or language, to establish and administer educational institutions of their choice.[190] In *Society for Unaided Private Schools*, the Supreme Court of India found that the 25 per cent requirement interfered with this fundamental right because it risked undermining the minority character of these institutions. Although the Court upheld the RTE Act as a whole, it provided an exemption for private, unaided minority schools, on the basis that they were entitled to preserve their minority character.[191] In the subsequent *Pramati* decision, the Court extended this exemption to minority schools even if they received state funding, relying again on the principle that there was a risk that the provision might undermine the minority character of the school.[192] Surprisingly, the Court went beyond exempting minority schools from the requirement to admit 25 per cent disadvantaged students. It also exempted minority schools from all the provisions of the Act, including minimum norms and standards.

A direct consequence of the decision in *Pramati* has been that 'more and more private schools are clamouring for minority status, and proposing to be religious and linguistic minority schools so that they can be exempt from the Act's coverage'.[193] As in Canada, the question has therefore become who counts as a 'minority' for the purposes of the Act. Although Article 30 refers to the right of 'linguistic and religious minorities' to establish and administer educational institutions, it does not provide any principles by which minority status can be identified. The Court has held that the institution must be established and managed by a minority community, and a significant proportion of the school's student body should be from that minority community.[194] However, it has also held that the question of the minority status of schools

[188] RTE Act, s 28. [189] RTE Act, s 12(1)(c). [190] Indian Constitution, Article 30(1).

[191] *Society for Unaided Private Schools of Rajasthan v Union of India* (n 161).

[192] *Pramati Educational and Cultural Trust v Union of India* [2014] 8 SCC 1 (Indian Supreme Court).

[193] J Kothari and A Ravi, 'A Battle of Rights: The Right of Education of Children versus Rights of Minority Schools' (2016) 16 Oxford University Commonwealth Law Journal 195, 200.

[194] *PA Inamdar v State of Maharashtra* (2005) 6 SCC 537 (Indian Supreme Court).

should be determined locally rather than nationally. This has led to vastly different criteria in different States, with some States, such as Andhra Pradesh requiring at least 70 per cent of students in the school to be from the minority community, while others, such as Karnataka, require only 25 per cent. Other States have no requirement as to the proportion of minority students, or have a very vague definition. Private schools have therefore put pressure on authorities to reduce the minimum proportion. Within months of the *Pramati* decision, as many as 80 per cent of private schools in the State of Maharashtra had acquired minority status.[195] Kothari and Ravi demonstrate how far this has moved from the basic principle established by the Court, namely that there should be no more than a 'sprinkling of students from non-minority communities'.[196]

Whatever the definition of minorities, it is difficult to see why such establishments should be exempted from the RTE Act. As a report from the Vidhi institute argues, there is no good reason to suggest that admitting 25 per cent of students from minorities would necessarily be inimical to the school's minority character. Children from EWS/DG, to whom the 25 per cent reservation applies, would themselves be from a variety of religious and linguistic communities.[197] Indeed, the more the definition of a minority is expanded, the less cogent is the concern that the minority character of the school will be diluted. It is paradoxical for a school to argue that a minimal degree of minority input is sufficient for an exemption which is ostensibly aimed at preserving the minority character of the school. Still less is there any justification for exempting minority schools from all the norms and standards in the RTE Act, which include basic necessities such as separate toilets, drinking water, and adequate teaching and non-teaching staff, as well as the prohibition on corporal punishment.[198] On the other hand, as Kothari and Ravi argue, exempting such schools from these basic requirements 'seriously compromises the RTE Act's vision of providing equal access to quality education for all children'.[199]

V. Quality Education: Equal or Adequate?

The above discussion has shown that education as a freedom right is inextricably bound up with education as a social right and an equality right. Freedoms guaranteed to minorities and other groups may conflict with or complement social rights. Those with power, whether in the majority or the minority, have been able to ensure good quality education for their children, facilitating the latters' pathways in life, while others have been left behind. Human rights should therefore play a central role in ensuring that quality education is available to all. But education as a social right brings with it many challenges. Education can be provided according to a range of different models, with differing emphases on syllabus, teacher–learner ratio, distance of school from home, teacher training, urban–rural balance, mother tongue instruction, and many other factors. How then should the right to quality education be assessed? In

[195] Kothari and Ravi (n 193) 200.
[196] *Re the Kerala Education Bill* (1959) 1 SCR 995 (Indian Supreme Court).
[197] A Sangai et al, 'Right to Education and Minority Rights' (Vidhi Centre for Legal Policy 2016) 22.
[198] ibid, 19. [199] Kothari and Ravi (n 193) 196.

addition, the level of resources allocated to education is an intensely political decision. These issues put in question the role of the court. There is no reason to believe that a court is better at problem-solving than the other participants in the decision-making process. On the other hand, a court is well placed to insist on accountability through proper deliberate justification. As argued in Chapter 4, the State should be required to justify, on the basis of reasons which are plausible and based on demonstrable evidence, why it has made its decisions as to quality standards and resource allocation and how this has advanced the right to education. This enhances the accountability of the State and it facilitates full deliberative debate, both within the court and in the broader political process.[200] Moreover, although it is not feasible to enunciate detailed standards, the basic scaffolding can be provided. Probably the most helpful is the 'four A framework', identified by the former UN Special Rapporteur for Education, Katarina Tomaševski: *availability* of infrastructure and teachers; *accessibility* for all in a non-discriminatory manner; *acceptability* in terms of culture, language, and religion; and *adaptability* to changing circumstances.[201] These provide a framework for the Court to evaluate policies set out by governments.

Education as a social right also raises the familiar challenges of positive duties, which require State implementation. Breaches of education rights might well be due to incapacity, incompetence, or intransigence, as discussed in Chapter 4. The role of the court in determining appropriate remedies and devising accountability structures is then under the spotlight. All these issues can be seen in the two case studies below: the New York City education cases, and the South African school cases.

A. Adequately equal and equally adequate: the New York cases

The preliminary hurdle in determining the substance of the right to quality education in the US has concerned the framing of the right itself.[202] As we have seen, the initial impetus was to use the equality principle, found in the Equal Protection clause of the Fourteenth Amendment. In *Brown v Board of Education*,[203] Warren CJ proclaimed in ringing terms:

> It is doubtful that any child may reasonably be expected to succeed in life if he is denied the opportunity of an education. Such an opportunity, where the state has undertaken to provide it, is a right that must be made available to all on equal terms.

The Court in *Brown* assumed that integration was sufficient to achieve quality education. This meant that no attention was paid to the poor quality of black and Hispanic schools. The result has been that not only has the desegregation project failed in its aspirations to integration, it has also failed to improve the conditions of disadvantaged schools, largely populated by American Hispanics and African-Americans. It was therefore necessary to take a further step and establish that the inferior quality of

[200] See Fredman (n 70) 103–09.

[201] K Tomaševski, *Human Rights Obligations: Making Education Available, Accessible, Acceptable and Adaptable* (Right to education Primers No 3, Swedish International Development Agency 2001).

[202] Wieshart (n 43) 483.

[203] *Brown v Board of Education* (n 8).

education and in particular the lower budgetary allocations for inner-city disadvantaged schools were a breach of the equality guarantee.

At federal level, such arguments fell on stony ground. This was epitomized by *Rodriguez v San Antonio*.[204] This case arose out of the extreme inequities in the State system of funding schools, due to the fact that public education was funded by local taxes. Schools in poor districts, with low property values, would inevitably be vastly worse off than schools in well-off districts. San Antonio was a school district in Texas, in which 90 per cent of students were Mexican-American, and 6 per cent African-American. Property values were so low that even though local rates were substantially higher than the neighbouring largely white district, the per capita spending on education was only just over half that of the neighbouring school district. The claimants, Mexican-American parents of children attending school in San Antonio, argued that this breached their rights under the Equal Protection clause. To sustain their claim, they had to establish either that education was a fundamental right, or that poverty was a 'suspect class' attracting strict scrutiny by the Court when treated less favourably than others. The US Supreme Court, by a narrow majority of five to four, rejected both claims. As we saw above, it refused to regard education as a fundamental right. It also rejected the claim that poverty could itself be a ground for discrimination. The disadvantaged class was not a 'discrete and insular minority' similar to racial or ethnic minority groups: 'The system of alleged discrimination and the class it defines have none of the traditional indicia of suspectness: the class is not saddled with such disabilities, or subjected to such a history of purposeful unequal treatment, or relegated to such a position of political powerlessness as to command extraordinary protection from the majoritarian political process'.[205]

Marshall J's dissent was astute:

> The majority's holding can only be seen as a retreat from our historic commitment to equality of educational opportunity and as unsupportable acquiescence in a system which deprives children in their earliest years of the chance to reach their full potential as citizens. The Court does this despite the absence of any substantial justification for a scheme which arbitrarily channels educational resources in accordance with the fortuity of the amount of taxable wealth within each district. In my judgment, the right of every American to an equal start in life, so far as the provision of a state service as important as education is concerned, is far too vital to permit state discrimination on grounds as tenuous as those presented by this record.[206]

The political process had 'proved singularly unsuited to the task of providing a remedy for this discrimination'.[207] As we have seen, the refusal to recognize poverty as a ground for discrimination in education came together with a retreat from the pursuit of racial integration as the main way to provide equal opportunity in education.[208]

The quest for equal opportunity in schools therefore turned to State constitutions, which, as we have seen, include express rights to education. Initially, litigators pursued

204 *San Antonio Independent School District v Rodriguez* (n 33). 205 ibid, 28.
206 ibid, 71. 207 ibid, 71.
208 *Parents Involved in Community Schools v Seattle School District* (n 136).

the equity route, aiming to reduce disparities in educational expenditure by claiming that school financing systems were discriminatory. However, applying a concept of 'equality' as merely the same treatment, courts sanctioned solutions to inequalities which reduced the budgetary allocations of privileged groups rather than levelling up the allocation of the disadvantaged group. For example, Californian courts' finding that wealth-related disparities among school districts must be reduced to insignificant difference led to a dramatic levelling down of educational expenditures. California's ranking fell from fifth in the nation's per pupil spending to forty-second in the three decades from 1964 to 1994.[209]

Taking this lesson to heart, litigators, rather than focusing on equity claims, turned to 'adequacy' claims based on the substantive right to education. This in effect makes it mandatory for budgetary allocations to be based on human rights, rather than human rights being conditional on budgets.[210] Adequacy claims were launched in forty-five out of fifty States, aimed at giving substance to the right to education in State constitutions. These are variously worded as the requirement to provide all students with an 'adequate public education', 'a thorough and efficient education', a 'high quality system of free public schools', or a 'sound basic education'.[211] These claims have had substantial success, with plaintiffs prevailing in over 60 per cent of the final liability decisions on this issue.[212] Such success was in part facilitated by the fact that the vast majority of States had already made a commitment to develop standards for quality education, identifying academic content, specifying requirements for teacher training, and providing curricula, books facilities, and other resources necessary for proper instruction in accordance with the standards. Courts could then test educational provision against these criteria.

These developments are clearly reflected in a series of ground-breaking cases brought by the Campaign for Fiscal Equity (CFE) beginning in 1995, in which New York courts upheld applicants' claims of a violation by New York of its obligations under the New York State Constitution.[213] This required the Court to navigate the relationship between the judicial and policy-making processes in determining the standard of adequacy and the resource required to achieve it. Rather than specifying the detail of the adequacy standard, the New York Court derived the content of the duty directly from the underlying value which it attached to education, namely the ability to undertake civil responsibilities meaningfully. This allowed the Court of Appeals to set the standards for a 'sound basic education' as consisting of 'the basic literacy, calculating, and verbal skills necessary to enable children to eventually function productively as civic participants capable of voting and serving on a jury'. The duty on the State therefore required 'minimally adequate' physical facilities, and teaching by adequately trained teachers. New York City public schools had breached this duty.[214] In the second *CFE* case (*CFE II*), it added that students should have the opportunity for 'a meaningful high school education, one which prepares them to

[209] Rebell (n 43) 511. [210] Fredman (n 70) 219. [211] Cited in Rebell (n 43) nn 9–12.

[212] ibid, 507. [213] New York State Constitution, Article XI, s 1.

[214] *Campaign for Fiscal Equity v State of New York (CFE I)* 86 NY2d 307 (1995) (New York State Court of Appeals); 100 NY2d at 908.

function productively as civic participants' and 'compete for jobs that enable them to support themselves'.[215] Importantly, too, the Court acknowledged the key judicial role in supervising this standard, holding that there is a 'constitutional floor in respect of educational adequacy' and the courts are 'responsible for adjudicating the nature of [the State's] duty'.[216] In *CFE II*, the Court concluded that the State had deprived schoolchildren of a sound basic education.[217] It upheld the trial court's finding that the 'inputs' into these children's education, in the form of teaching, facilities, and instrumentalities of learning, were insufficient, as reflected by the deficiencies in the 'outputs', namely test results, graduation rates, and dropout rates.[218] A causal link between the funding system and the failure to provide a sound basic education had therefore been established.

On the second challenge, that of resources, the Court has been surprisingly robust in scrutinizing the budgetary allocation, while at the same time drawing a careful line around the judicial role. This was directly facilitated by its deliberative approach. During the first round of appeals, the New York State Court of Appeal stressed that the courts 'have neither the authority, nor the ability, nor the will, to micromanage education financing'.[219] Instead, the Court set targets to be achieved: reforms to the current system of financing school funding should ensure that 'every school in New York City would have the resources necessary for providing the opportunity for a sound basic education'.[220] This included a crucial accountability component: the State was required to 'ensure a system of accountability to measure whether the reforms actually provide the opportunity for a sound basic education'.[221] Applying these principles, the Court of Appeals, the highest State court, upheld the trial court's finding that the State had failed to fund New York City schools adequately to provide a sound basic education. It directed the State to ascertain the actual cost of providing a sound basic education, to reform the current system of school funding and management, and to furnish every school in the City with the resources necessary for providing the opportunity for a sound basic education.[222] The State was given approximately twelve months to comply and develop the required reforms, a process which the lower court was given jurisdiction to supervise.[223]

When the deadline passed without the order being implemented, the Court was faced with a greater challenge. The trial judge appointed a panel of referees to recommend a model for determining how much was needed per learner to ensure an adequate education, which concluded that the State had understated the cost of providing a sound basic education in New York City by as much as $3.7 billion. This, however, was regarded by New York State Court of Appeals as stepping beyond the mandate of the Court. The obligation to determine the amount and allocation of funds was a peculiarly legislative function. The Court's role was to decide whether the State's estimate was reasonable, and whether the State had produced a plan which incorporated

[215] *Campaign for Fiscal Equity v State of New York (CFE II)* 100 NY2d 893 (2003) (Court of Appeals of the State of New York), 903, 906.

[216] *Campaign for Fiscal Equity v State of New York (CFE I)* (n 214) 315, 316.

[217] *Campaign for Fiscal Equity v State of New York (CFE II)* (n 215) 918–19.

[218] ibid, 908.

[219] ibid, 925.

[220] ibid, 930.

[221] ibid.

[222] ibid.

[223] ibid, 932.

that sound basic education expenditure and ensured a system of accountability.[224] Using this standard, it found that the State had proffered sufficient evidence to justify its estimate as rational and declared that the constitutionally required funding for the New York City School District included additional operating funds of $1.93 billion.[225] In March 2006, the Appellate Division of New York State held that 'the State, in enacting a budget for the fiscal year commencing April 1, 2006, must appropriate the constitutionally required funding for the New York City schools'.[226] Nevertheless, the highest New York court rejected the trial court's retention of an ongoing supervisory role to ensure accountability. The 'minimally adequate accountability mechanisms' for the evaluation of New York schools were seen as sufficient. The decision in *CFE III* therefore terminated that litigation; and no ongoing injunctive relief was given.

Unfortunately, this turned out to be the Achilles' heel of the process. Plaintiffs have had to commence renewed litigation, claiming that the State has failed to carry out its commitment to provide the resources it itself had determined necessary to provide all its students with a sound basic education.[227] The New York State Court of Appeals in June 2017 struck out many of the claims, holding that the lack of compliance with the orders in the *CFE* cases could not be the basis of litigation between different parties. It also held that any claims based on the State as a whole could not be sustained, requiring the plaintiffs to provide detailed evidence district by district. Nevertheless, the Court allowed the claim that the State had not provided adequate funding for sound basic education in New York City and Syracuse to go forward to trial. Further stages of the process are awaited.

B. Establishing minimum standards: the South African experience

In South Africa, the dire conditions in which countless children go to school, coupled with the lack of responsiveness of the State, have propelled the right to education into the forefront of achieving change. Litigation has led to some significant advances, while also demonstrating the limits of the law in bringing about social change. As in the New York cases, two main issues have been central: the definition of the substance of the right itself; and how to achieve compliance by a State apparatus which is frequently incompetent and often recalcitrant.

1. *Substantive content*

As we have seen, the right to basic education stands out from the other socio-economic rights in the Constitution in that it is immediately realizable. Does this mean that courts will be more open to defining the substance of the right than it has for other rights, where it has firmly rejected the possibility of defining a minimum substantive core? In a series of cases relating to abysmal schooling environments, litigants

[224] *Campaign for Fiscal Equity, Inc v State of New York (CFE III)* 8 NY3d 14 (2006) (New York State Court of Appeals) 30.

[225] ibid, 31. [226] ibid.

[227] *New Yorkers for Students' Educational Rights (NYSER) v State of New York* 29 NY3d 501 (2017) (Court of Appeals of the State of New York).

have pressed the courts to establish that the right to education includes the conditions in which a child is educated. These cases have not reached the South African Constitutional Court, but in a development of potentially great importance, high courts and the Supreme Court of Appeal (SCA) have been willing to find that that the right includes basic conditions for learning, including proper buildings, textbooks, desks and chairs, and teachers.[228] Thus in *Madzozo*, Goosen J stated:

> The state's obligation to provide basic education as guaranteed by the Constitution is not confined to making places available at schools. It necessarily requires the provision of a range of educational resources:—schools, classrooms, teachers, teaching materials and appropriate facilities for learners.[229]

In particular, the right to basic education includes the provision of adequate and age-appropriate furniture so that each child has a desk of her own with sufficient space.

> Learners ... are entitled to have immediate access to basic education. They are also entitled as of right to be treated equally and with dignity. The lack of adequate age and grade appropriate furniture in public schools, particularly public schools located in deep rural and impoverished areas, undermines the right to basic education.[230]

This has been endorsed by several other decisions of the High Court and SCA. Thus, Kollapen J has held that the provision of textbooks is an essential component of the right to basic education: 'In fact, it is difficult to conceive, even with the best of intentions, how the right to basic education can be given effect to in the absence of textbooks'.[231] In a case concerning scholar transport, Plasket J was similarly unequivocal: 'The right to education is meaningless without teachers to teach, administrators to keep schools running, desks and other furniture to allow scholars to do their work, text books from which to learn and transport to and from school at State expense in appropriate cases'.[232] Moreover, the State is under a duty to fulfil these substantive components. 'Where scholars' access to schools is hindered by distance and an inability to afford the costs of transport, the State is obliged to provide transport to them in order to meet its obligations, in terms of s 7(2) of the Constitution, to promote and fulfil the right to basic education'.[233]

As in the *CFE* cases, South African courts are more comfortable holding the executive to their own standards than creating them. In the SCA in the *Limpopo textbook* case, the Court refused to accept the government's contention that its own target of providing a textbook to each learner was simply a 'lofty' ideal or the 'standard of perfection'. Navsa JA held that the government should be held to the standard it set for itself:

[228] *Madzodzo v Minister of Basic Education* [2014] 2 All SA 339 (ECM) (South African Eastern Cape High Court).

[229] ibid, para [20].

[230] ibid, para [36].

[231] *Section 27 v Minister of Education (Textbooks I)* (2013) 2 SA 40 (GNP) (South African High Court) para [25].

[232] *Tripartite Steering Committee v Minister of Basic Education* (2015) 3 All SA 718 (ECG) (South African Eastern Cape High Court) para [18].

[233] ibid, para [19].

> The Minister, acting in terms of the Constitution and legislation, took a decision that textbooks were essential to promote and protect the right to a basic education and devised a plan towards providing a textbook for every learner ... The law is clear ... The [Department of Basic Education] is obliged to provide a textbook to every learner to ensure compliance with s 29(1)(a) of the Constitution.[234]

The government argued that requiring each child to have her own textbook was equivalent to imposing a minimum core obligation, contrary to the consistent stance of the South African Constitutional Court culminating in *Mazibuko*.[235] Instead, the standard should merely be whether reasonable steps had been taken to fulfil the right. This argument was rejected by the SCA, in a move which Veriava argues 'bucks a trend in South Africa's socio-economic rights jurisprudence which has been towards "normative emptiness"'.[236] Similarly, in *Madzodzo*, the Court had no difficulty in rejecting the State's claim that it should be given an open-ended time period within which to carry out its duty to provide desks and chairs for learners in the Eastern Cape: 'Learners in this province are entitled as of right to have immediate access to basic education'.[237] In addition, the SCA has refused to accept an argument that, provided textbooks were supplied to the majority of schools, it was not a violation to have failed to supply textbooks to the remaining 22,000 learners. Navsa JA was clear that each learner was a rights-holder in herself, and if she did not receive a textbook, her right was breached.[238]

Nevertheless, courts remain reluctant to set their own standards when no standards have been set, or when the standards which have been set are deficient. In the scholar transport case, Plasket J was prepared to issue a mandamus to enforce a decision which had in fact been taken to provide transport, but had not been implemented. Similarly, where a decision was arbitrary, and taken without consideration of the merits of each applicant's application, it could be set aside. But Plasket J was also quick to reject what he regarded as the applicants' attempt to seek orders that 'have the effect of dictating the content of the policy that is currently being formulated'. The development and formulation of policy was the province of the executive branch of government, not the judiciary. If a policy, once adopted and implemented, has an impact on rights, it may be scrutinized by courts for constitutional compliance.[239] A less cautious approach was taken by Tuchten J in the High Court in the *Limpopo textbook* case: 'I wish to guard myself against the proposition that the content of a right may be determined without more by reference to the policies of the executive'.[240] In the SCA, however, Navsa JA, was reluctant to do more than hold the executive to the standard it had set for itself.

[234] *Minister of Basic Education v Basic Education for All* [2015] ZASCA 198 (South African Supreme Court of Appeal) para [50].

[235] *Mazibuko v City of Johannesburg* [2009] ZACC 28 (South African Constitutional Court).

[236] F Veriava, 'The Limpopo Textbook Litigation: A Case Study into the Possibilities of a Transformative Constitutionalism' (2016) SAJHR 321, 333.

[237] *Madzodzo v Minister of Basic Education* (n 228) para [36].

[238] *Minister of Basic Education v Basic Education for All* (n 234).

[239] *Tripartite Steering Committee v Minister of Basic Education* (n 232) para [63].

[240] *Basic Education for All and Others v Minister of Basic Education and Others 23949/2014* [2014] ZAGPPHC 251 para 46 (South African North Gauteng High Court).

While in this case, it might not have been necessary to go further, Veriava rightly argues that the absence of an objective test could undermine the role of the fundamental right in future education provision, especially given that education is an immediate right and not subject to progressive realization. In particular, the reluctance to set objective standards may act as a disincentive to government to set itself high standards.[241] This is not to say that the courts should make detailed prescriptions on complex issues above the minimum. Instead, they should follow the deliberative approach above, scaffolded by the principles underpinning the right to basic education. The ICESCR standards of availability, accessibility, acceptability, and adaptability, together with the standards of participation in public life established in the *CFE* case, could fulfil this role.

One salient example of using litigation to facilitate or endorse a substantive content to the right is in relation to the process of determining minimum norms and standards for all schools. Litigation aimed at compelling government to enact minimum standards elicited an agreement by the Minister to publish Norms and Standards Regulations immediately before proceedings were due to begin in the High Court. Public interest litigators and social movements played a vigorous role in the consultation process leading up to the adoption of regulations brought into force in November 2013.[242] The resulting norms and standards have constituted an important foundation for ongoing litigation. Most recently, in July 2018, the High Court ruled that the Norms and Standards Regulations were unconstitutional in permitting the government to indefinitely delay repairing unsafe and inadequate infrastructure in South African schools.

As well as developing the substance of the right to basic education, High Courts and the SCA have been relatively forceful in rejecting government claims of lack of sufficient budget to realize individuals' right to basic education. In the *Limpopo textbook* case, the government argued that it was unable to provide a textbook for each learner because of budgetary constraints. Navsa JA held that there was no statement anywhere in the affidavits filed by the respondent to the effect that it would be unable to procure the funds necessary to meet the shortfall. Indeed, it regarded its reliance on budgetary constraints as 'fallacious' and 'contrived'.[243] Similarly, in *Madzozo*, Goosen J gave short shrift to the respondent's argument that inadequate funds had been budgeted to meet the needs for school furniture. The respondent had had sufficient information for the past two years for it to make reasonable estimates of the funding required and to plan for such expenditure. Indeed, it is not primarily lack of resources that has impeded the realization of the right. The budgetary allocation in South Africa is relatively healthy, as compared to other lower- and middle-income countries.[244]

[241] Veriava (n 236) 17.

[242] Regulations Relating to Minimum Uniform Norms and Standards for Public School Infrastructure Promulgated under Section 5A(1)(a) South African Schools Act 1996, Government Notice R920 in Government Gazette 37081 (29 November 2013).

[243] *Minister of Basic Education v Basic Education for All* (n 234) para [43].

[244] World Bank Data, 'South Africa: Education' <https://data.worldbank.org/topic/education?locations=ZA> (accessed 5 March 2018).

2. Compliance

Achieving compliance has been much more challenging. While the New York litigation focused directly on adequate resources, the South African litigation has been concerned with lack of capacity, intransigence, and corruption.[245] In the face of flagrant disregard of court orders, an increasingly creative range of remedies and compliance mechanisms is being devised in an attempt to achieve a substantive implementation of minimum standards.

This is demonstrated by the series of 'mud school' cases, brought by public interest litigators in the Eastern Cape, to compel the State to provide proper buildings, sanitation, furniture, and teachers to schools in the area. During the apartheid era, when spending on black education was appallingly low, many communities in the former Transkei built their own community schools using whatever materials were available, including mud, corrugated iron, asbestos, and wooden planks. Well into the democratic era, these schools remained, in a state of increasing neglect and decay. Conditions for children at school were abysmal. Structures were unsafe and were easily blown down in the Cape winds. They were damp, airless, and hot in the summer, cold in the winter. Corrugated iron roofs flapped in the wind, drowning out teachers' voices. There was no furniture: learners were required to sit on the floor. And there were frequently no toilets or other sanitation, with both learners and teachers having to relieve themselves in the surrounding bushveld, sometimes perilously close to streams which also supplied drinking water. This was not only an assault to their dignity and privacy, but created severe health risks. The problem was even further exacerbated by the fact that teachers were not being deployed to these schools, with publicly funded posts remaining unfilled. The result was that these very poor communities were having to raise their own funds to pay community-employed teachers.

In 2010, when political routes failed to produce a remedy, litigation was launched by the Legal Resources Centre (LRC) on behalf of a representative group of seven of the most disadvantaged schools, alleging a violation of the right to basic education because of a failure to provide adequate and safe infrastructure, sufficient desks and chairs, or potable water.[246] The applicants sought orders declaring that the failure to provide the schools with proper facilities, access to water, and desks and chairs was unconstitutional, and directing the respondents to provide a plan, in consultation with the seven schools, to provide infrastructure and water. The applicants also sought orders directing the respondents to provide the seven schools with sufficient numbers of desks and chairs. The government initially opposed the application. However, rather than facing litigation, it suddenly changed its mind and offered a generous settlement. This included the immediate provision of temporary classrooms and furniture at the seven schools, and the construction of permanent classrooms within a year.

[245] C Abdoll and C Barberton, *Mud to Bricks: A Review of School Infrastructure Spending and Delivery* (Pretoria University Law Press 2014).

[246] This description is taken from Legal Resources Centre, *Ready to Learn: A Legal Resource for Realising the Right to Education* (Legal Resources Centre 2013); see also A Skelton, 'Leveraging Funds for School Infrastructure: The South African "Mud Schools" Case Study' (2014) 39 International Journal of Educational Development 59, 59, 61.

Even more importantly, it agreed to provide funding of R8.2 billion to replace inadequate school structure country-wide, with R6.36 billion allocated to replace approximately 500 inappropriate school structures in the Eastern Cape over a three-year period. This programme is called the Accelerated School Infrastructure Development Initiative (ASIDI).

Construction of some new schools was undertaken, often providing high-quality facilities.[247] However, compliance became more and more erratic. By January 2014, the programme was far behind schedule. As many as 200 schools listed in the ASIDI plan still needed assistance; many schools where learners' conditions remained appalling were not on the list at all; and there was a general lack of transparency, leading to confusion among schools as to whether and when they might receive new school buildings. Most problematically, only one-quarter of the budget allocated to the three-year period had been spent. This led the LRC to launch a second round of litigation ordering the government to develop and publish plans and to put in place a system to ensure that all mud schools were included. This too led to a significant settlement, in August 2014. There was also widespread lack of compliance with the order requiring a desk and chair to be delivered to every schoolchild in every public school in the Eastern Cape. In *Madzodzo*, Goosen J ordered the respondents within ninety days to provide adequate age-appropriate furniture so that each child had sufficient space. This too has yielded only patchy compliance.[248]

Similarly problematic has been the failure of the State to comply with orders requiring teachers to be deployed and paid. In some communities, parents, themselves with few resources, scraped together sufficient money to pay temporary teachers; others went without teachers, and in a few schools, teachers simply worked for little or no pay.[249] Flagrant disregard of court orders triggered a search for more effective remedies and led to new solutions. Three strategies were used. The first was to bring a class action on behalf of thirty-two schools, asking the court to permanently fill all vacant teacher posts and to reimburse the schools for the teachers' salaries they had paid out of school funds. Importantly, the litigants asked the court to certify an 'opt-in' class action, so that all schools in a similar situation could join as parties. This was the first certified class action of its kind in South African jurisprudence, and was accepted by the Court in *Linkside v Minister of Basic Education*.[250] A further fifty-eight schools opted in to the litigation. Even this was not sufficient to propel the government to redeploy excess teachers to vacant posts, so that in 2014, schools were in the same position as they had been in 2011. Two further innovative tactics were then attempted. The first relied on a Court order that teachers would be deemed to be employed and remunerated by the State from the date set out. This meant that the failure to pay became an enforceable debt under the State Liability Act.[251] On 4 September 2014, the LRC

[247] Legal Resources Centre, ibid, 20.

[248] *Madzodzo v Minister of Basic Education* (n 228).

[249] Legal Resources Centre, *Fighting to Learn: A Legal Resource for Realising the Right to Education* (Legal Resources Centre 2015) 53.

[250] See Shona Gazidis, 'Victory in First Certified Class Action Sees Teachers Appointed and Paid' (OxHRH Blog, 18 April 2014) <http://ohrh.law.ox.ac.uk/victory-in-first-certified-class-action-sees-teachers-appointed-and-paid/> (accessed 5 March 2018).

[251] Legal Resources Centre (n 249) 53.

moved to enforce the debt. In a highly unusual move, it informed the Department of Education that if it did not pay the R28m debt owed to the original thirty-two schools, it would issue a writ to seize State assets to justify the debt. The debt was cleared within a few days.[252] The third tactic was to request the Court to appoint a claims administrator to oversee the payment of the outstanding salaries. The Court took the novel step of appointing a claims administrator to supervise the payment of R81m in outstanding salaries owed to schools in the Eastern Cape.[253]

VI. Conclusion

There are many challenges for the further development of the right to education. Perhaps the most salient is the extent to which human rights obligations in relation to education can be harnessed to achieve the ambitious promises of the SDGs. The SDGs address some of the weaknesses of the binding human right. They supply content to the right, and set down a clear timetable of fifteen years from 2015 for its achievement. But they lack the binding force of human rights law, and tend to ignore individual rights through aggregate measurements. The comparative insights in this chapter demonstrate ways in which courts and human rights bodies have approached the content and enforcement of a justiciable right to education. The hope would be that, going forward, the SDGs and binding human rights can work together.

[252] ibid, 54.

[253] *Linkside v Minister of Basic Education* [2014] ZAECHC 111 (High Court of South Africa).

moved to enforce the debt. In a b[illegible] [illegible] of [illegible] [illegible] may be [illegible] [illegible] it would [illegible] [illegible] [illegible] the debt. [illegible] [illegible] The third [illegible] [illegible] Court [illegible] [illegible] to oversee the payment [illegible] [illegible] [illegible] [illegible] step [illegible] [illegible] [illegible] [illegible] [illegible] [illegible] [illegible] [illegible]

[illegible] Conclusion

There are [illegible] challenges for the [illegible] [illegible] conclusion. Perhaps the most [illegible] is that [illegible] [illegible] [illegible] [illegible] [illegible] [illegible] address some of the weaknesses of [illegible] [illegible] the [illegible] and set down a clear [illegible] [illegible] [illegible] binding [illegible] [illegible] [illegible] through [illegible] [illegible] [illegible] and [illegible] way [illegible] [illegible] and enforcement [illegible] [illegible] [illegible] [illegible]

12

Freedom of Religion

I. Introduction

In determining the contours of freedom of religion in comparative human rights law, it is crucial to locate religion in the political and social contexts in which it operates. Although the rationale of the right is to protect an individual's innermost beliefs from State intervention, in practice, religion has been deeply enmeshed with politics, power, community identities, custom, and tradition. As Sieghart puts it, 'For a substantial proportion of the worst atrocities perpetrated in recorded history, the ostensible justification has been the alleged need for the dominance or maintenance of one belief system rather than another'.[1]

This is further complicated by the fact that many religions entail belief in a source of authority which is higher than law. Such normative ordering is challenging for those who regard the liberal state as gaining its legitimacy, not from religion or Divine rule, but from democracy and the possibility of public justification, even where there is disagreement. To emerge from the religious wars of early modern times required a constitutional state which separated religion from the State, while at the same time, preserving the freedom of believers to follow their religion. As Habermas argues:

> [C]onstitutional freedom of religion is the appropriate political answer to the challenges of political pluralism. In this way, the potential for conflict at the level of citizens' social interaction can be restrained, while at the cognitive level, deep-reaching conflicts may well continue to exist between the existentially relevant convictions of believers, believers of other denominations and non-believers.[2]

However, he also recognizes that the secular State, while a necessary condition for guaranteeing equal religious freedom, is not sufficient.

> It is not enough to rely on the condescending benevolence of a secularized authority that comes to tolerate minorities hitherto discriminated against. The parties themselves must reach agreement on the always contested delimitations between a positive liberty to practice a religion of one's own and the negative liberty to remain spared from the religious practices of the others.[3]

This requires the parties involved to learn to take the perspective of others, a process for which the deliberative mode of democratic decision-making is best suited. It is precisely here that courts, using the deliberative mode of decision-making, should be in a position to navigate the difficult territory between respecting religion's claim

[1] P Sieghart, *The International Law of Human Rights* (Clarendon Press 1983) 324.
[2] J Habermas, 'Religion in the Public Sphere' (2006) 14 European Journal of Philosophy 1, 4.
[3] ibid, 4.

on individual loyalty and the human rights commitment to accept and tolerate each other's beliefs.

This chapter considers freedom of religion in relation to three main interwoven themes. The first concerns the extent to which freedom of religion requires separation of State and religion. Although a strict separation is seen as fundamental in some jurisdictions, such as the US, others see religion as central to society and therefore a legitimate area of State involvement. The second concerns the extent to which the State should respect individual beliefs and accommodate their manifestation. The third principle is that of equality and non-discrimination. Where freedom of religion clashes with equality, which should take precedence? Or can they be reconciled?

Section II of the chapter shows how the different themes are expressed in constitutional texts. Section III deals with the relationship between the State and religion, particularly the established Church or its equivalent. In section IV, we ask which beliefs count as religious beliefs for the purpose of the special protection for individual freedom of religion, and how the Courts position themselves in relation to this question. Section V moves from the definition of religion to the legitimacy of State limitations on it, together with the responsibility of the State to accommodate individual freedoms. Section VI turns to situations in which freedom of religion conflicts with other rights, particularly the right to equality. Freedom of religion expects tolerance of religious adherents, but can religious adherents be expected to be tolerant of others?

It should be stressed that the chapter does not attempt a comprehensive survey of all the issues relating to freedom of religion. It concentrates on issues which have most saliently been dealt with in a comparative context, and which highlight the main cross-cutting themes in this book, namely, the role of comparativism, the relationships of courts to other institutions of the State, and the broader question of how human rights interact with social and political forces in the realm of religion.

II. Textual Provisions

The three inter-related facets to freedom of religion are configured in different ways in human rights instruments. The First Amendment of the US Constitution, in characteristically unadorned language, states: 'Congress shall make no law respecting an establishment of religion, or prohibiting the free exercise thereof'. This has been interpreted as creating two separate pillars, one dealing with separation of State and religion ('Free Establishment'), and the second with individual freedom of religion ('Free Exercise'). No more detail is provided to guide courts on key issues such as whether and how free exercise of religion can be limited, or the meaning of religion. Equality, which is implicit in the first two facets, is also reflected in the Equal Protection clause of the Fourteenth Amendment. But this too is lacking in detail: it does not expressly mention any grounds, let alone religion, nor how conflicts between religion and other grounds, such as gender and sexual orientation, should be determined. At the same time, the Civil Rights Act of 1964, expressly prohibits workplace discrimination on grounds of religion (together with race, colour, sex, and national origin).[4]

[4] Title VII of the Civil Rights Act of 1964, 42 USC 2000E-2.

The European Convention on Human Rights (ECHR) is more elaborate than its US counterpart. Article 9 establishes a right to freedom of religion, thought, and conscience. This expressly includes the rights to change one's religion or belief, and to manifest religion or belief, either alone or in community with others, in worship, teaching practice, and observance. Unlike the First Amendment, the ECHR contains an express set of justifiable limitations of the right, although only in respect of freedom to manifest religion or belief (*forum externum*). This is distinguished from the freedom to hold such beliefs (*forum internum*), which remains absolute and inviolable. Thus, under Article 9(2), freedom to manifest religion or beliefs may only be limited where prescribed by law and necessary in a democratic society in the interests of public safety, for the protection of public order, health, or morals, or for the protection of the rights and freedoms of others. Notably, the powerful emphasis on separation between State and religion in the US is not mirrored in Europe, where the ECHR's understatement of this principle reflects a long history of enmeshment of State and religion. The principle of State neutrality, to the extent that it exists, is found in Article 14, which states that Convention rights should be secured without discrimination on grounds, inter alia, of religion. This is complemented by Article 2 Protocol 2, which requires the State, in exercising any of the functions it assumes in relation to education and teaching, to respect the right of parents to ensure that such education and teaching is in conformity with their own religious and philosophical convictions.

The three facets of freedom of religion have been woven into the Indian Constitution in complex ways, reflecting the fact that religious and sectarian strife have been a central feature of Indian history. Free exercise of religion is found in Article 25(1), which states: 'All persons are equally entitled to freedom of conscience and the right freely to profess, practise and propagate religion'. Like the ECHR, this can be limited: Article 25(1) is stated to be 'subject to public order, morality, and health' and the other fundamental rights in the Constitution. The Indian provision differs from Article 9 ECHR in two ways, however. The first is that no distinction is made between *forum internum* and *forum externum*: both freedom of conscience and the right to profess, practise, and propagate religion are subject to these limits. Second, there is no requirement that the limitation be 'necessary in a democratic society' comparable to the high level of scrutiny provided for in the ECHR.

Particularly salient in the Indian Constitution is the tension between strong protection for religious autonomy on the one hand and a relatively strong role for the State in regulating religion on the other. Thus Article 26 gives religious denominations the right to establish institutions for religious and charitable purposes, to manage their own affairs in matters of religion, and to own, acquire, and administer immovable property, subject to public order, morality, and health. At the same time, Article 25(2) specifically states that the right to freedom of religion does not prevent the State from making any law regulating or restricting activities which may be associated with religious practice. The State is also expressly permitted to provide for social welfare and reform and 'the throwing open of Hindu religious institutions of a public character to all classes and sections of Hindus'.[5] (Sikhs, Jains, and Buddhists are included in the

[5] Indian Constitution, Article 25(2)(b).

reference to Hindu.[6]) This does not, however, mean that State neutrality is not provided for in any way. Article 27 provides that 'no person should be compelled to pay taxes, the proceeds of which are specifically appropriated in payment of expenses for the promotion or maintenance of any particular religion or religious denomination'.

The co-existence of protection for religious autonomy and legitimation of State regulation is further reflected in relation to education. Article 28 takes an initially strong position on State neutrality in relation to education, stating that no religious instruction should be provided in any educational institution wholly maintained out of State funds. However, there is an exception for educational institutions administered by the State established under an endowment or trust requiring religious instruction. In such cases, freedom of religion is protected by the requirement that no individual should be required to attend either religious instruction or religious worship unless she or her guardian consents.[7] Moreover, Article 30 gives religious minorities the right to establish and administer educational institutions of their choice and prevents the State from discriminating on grounds of religion in granting aid to minority educational institutions.

The chief thrust of the protection for individuals against State partiality for one religion over others is found in the non-discrimination provisions. Untouchability and its practice in any form is forbidden by Article 17, and Article 15(1) prohibits discrimination on grounds of caste or religion. Article 16(2) prohibits the State from discriminating on grounds, inter alia, of religion in respect of any State employment or office. At the same time, it permits laws providing that officers in religious institutions belong to a particular religion or denomination.[8] Finally, and importantly, is the protection against religious discrimination in relation to the right to vote. Article 325 states that no one should be ineligible for inclusion on the electoral roll on grounds only of religion, race, caste, sex, or any combination of them.

The Canadian Charter has a much sparser textual structure, leaving correspondingly more to judicial interpretation. Section 2(a) of the Charter simply states that everyone has 'freedom of conscience and religion'. This is subject to the general limitation clause in section 1, which states that the rights and freedoms in the Charter are 'subject only to such reasonable limits prescribed by law as can be demonstrably justified in a free and democratic society'. Protection against State partiality is subsumed into the non-discrimination provision, section 15(1), which prevents discrimination based, inter alia, on religion. Notably too, section 15(2) permits measures to be taken with the object of ameliorating the conditions of those who are disadvantaged because, inter alia, of religion.

South Africa has had a more troubled relationship between politics and religion. During the constitutional negotiations, the role of religion in the democratic State was hotly contested. On the one hand, it was imperative to reverse the legacy of apartheid, with its pernicious use of religious precepts from the Dutch Reformed Church to legitimate the subordination of black South Africans.[9] On the other hand, an approach of

[6] Indian Constitution, Article 25(2), Explanation II.

[7] Indian Constitution, Article 28(2) and (3).

[8] Indian Constitution, Article 15(5).

[9] *S v Lawrence* [1997] ZACC 11 (South African Constitutional Court) para [149].

strict secularism or neutrality of the State was seen as paying insufficient respect to the value accorded to religion by the majority of South Africans.[10] The balance between these imperatives is reflected in the constellation of rights in the final Constitution. Section 15(1) gives everyone the right to freedom of conscience, religion, thought, belief, and opinion. The collective aspect is found in section 31, which states that persons belonging to a cultural, religious, or linguistic community may not be denied the right to enjoy their culture, practise their religion, and use their language. Similar to the Indian provision, they are also entitled to form, join, and maintain cultural, religious, and linguistic associations and other organs of civil society. All of these rights are subject to the general limitation clause, but section 31 also expressly provides that the rights in this section 'may not be exercised in a manner inconsistent with any provision of the Bill of Rights'.

However, as in India and the ECHR, the South African Constitution eschews a strict divide between State and religion. Thus section 15(2) expressly permits religious observances to be conducted at state or state-aided institutions, provided those observances follow rules made by the appropriate public authorities; they are conducted on an equitable basis; and attendance at them is free and voluntary. Moreover, section 15(3) permits legislation recognizing marriages concluded under any system of religious, personal, or family law, provided they are consistent with other provisions of the Constitution. Again, as in India and the ECHR, State partiality is restricted by the non-discrimination provisions. Thus section 9(3) provides that the State may not unfairly discriminate against anyone on grounds inter alia of religion, conscience, belief, or culture.

III. State and Religion: A Contested Boundary

The extent to which freedom of religion requires the State to remain aloof from religion has been a point of key contention in many jurisdictions. Judges in the US are fond of talking of a 'wall between Church and State', whereas courts in other jurisdictions take a softer view of the division between Church and State. It is helpful to begin with Cliteur's typology of the relationship between the State and religion.[11] At the two extremes are theocracies and political atheism. Political atheism aims to eradicate religion altogether and instead foster atheism in its citizenship. The opposite is true of the theocratic State, where one religion permeates the state apparatus, while others are suppressed, often by force and through law. Political atheism was epitomized by the Soviet Union and has largely disappeared with the fall of the Berlin Wall. Theocracy, however, is clearly on the rise in many parts of the world; prompting a reinvigorated emphasis on freedom of religion. Cliteur describes three other models: the State–Church model; multiculturalism; and the religiously neutral or secular State. The 'State–Church' model refers to States which have a close connection with the Church. While other religions are not suppressed, they are also not given the same priority as the established Church. The UK is one example of such a

[10] ibid, para [122].
[11] P Cliteur, 'State and Religion against the Backdrop of Religious Radicalism' (2012) 10 I CON 127.

relationship. The 'multicultural' model requires the State to treat all religions equally by helping them equally, for example through giving State subsidies to maintain places of worship. However, there is no requirement that non-religious activities or beliefs should be treated in the same way as religious beliefs. Finally, the 'religiously neutral or secular' State, does not permit the State to finance religious institutions of any sort or to advocate for religion in any way. While a key tenet is religious freedom and non-discrimination as between religions, it is central to this approach that the State's functions should not include upholding religion per se. Freedom of religion therefore protects freedom not to believe, to manifest one's non-belief, and to refuse to participate in religious observance.[12]

The US comes closest to the aspirations of the religiously neutral or secular State. It is generally agreed that the words 'Congress shall make no law respecting an establishment of religion' in the First Amendment go further than simply prohibiting the State from establishing a State-sponsored church.[13] In the 1946 case of *Everson v Board of Education*, the Court held that these words meant that neither a State nor the Federal Government could pass laws which aid one religion, or aid all religions, or prefer one religion over another. No tax could be levied to support any religious activities or institutions; nor could the government participate in the affairs of religious organizations or groups or vice versa: 'In the words of Jefferson, the clause against establishment of religion was intended to erect "a wall of separation between church and State." '[14] For Black J, giving judgment of the Court, this wall 'must be kept high and impregnable'.[15]

O'Connor J in *Lynch v Donnelly* provided the clearest articulation of the rationale for such a separation. The first concerns the importance of preventing undue influence of religious institutions over politics, and of politics over religious institutions: 'Excessive entanglement with religious institutions ... may interfere with the independence of the institutions, give the institutions access to government or governmental powers not fully shared by non-adherents of the religions and foster the creations of political constituencies defined along religious lines'. The second is the failure to pay all individuals equal concern and respect in matters of religion. Government endorsement of religion

> sends a message to non-adherents that they are outsiders, not full members of the political community, and an accompanying message to adherents that they are insiders, favoured members of the political community. Disapproval sends the opposite message.[16]

The 'wall-of-separation' metaphor has, however, been highly contested among US Supreme Court justices. In *Lemon v Kurtzman*, the Court held that 'total separation is not possible in an absolute sense. Some relationship between government and religious organizations is inevitable'.[17] In *Lynch v Donnelly*, Burger CJ was not convinced

[12] *R v Big M Drug Mart Ltd* [1985] 1 SCR 295 (Supreme Court of Canada) para [70].
[13] *Lemon v Krutzman* 403 US 602 (1971) (US Supreme Court) 612.
[14] *Everson v Board of Education* 330 US 1 (1947) (US Supreme Court) 15–16. [15] ibid.
[16] *Lynch v Donnelly* 465 US 668 (1984) (US Supreme Court) 688.
[17] *Lemon v Krutzman* (n 13) 614.

by the metaphor of a wall of separation. Instead, he held, the Constitution 'affirmatively mandates accommodation, not merely tolerance, of all religions ... Anything less would require the "callous indifference" we have said was never intended by the Establishment clause'.[18]

Various tests have been propounded in an attempt to tie down the meaning of the Free Establishment Clause. The most frequently cited is the *Lemon* test, which requires a statute to fulfil three criteria to avoid violating the Establishment Clause. First, the statute must have a secular legislative purpose. Second, its principal or primary effect must neither advance nor inhibit religion. Third, the statute must not foster 'an excessive government entanglement with religion'.[19] This test, however, has permitted two quite different judicial approaches. In *Zorach v Clauson*, Douglas J stated frankly:

> We are a religious people whose institutions presuppose a Supreme Being ... When the state encourages religious instruction or cooperates with religious authorities by adjusting the schedule of public events to sectarian needs, it follows the best of our traditions ...To hold that it may not would be ... preferring those who believe in no religion over those who do believe.[20]

However, Black J, dissenting, reminded his fellow judges that it was because

> Americans are a religious people divided into many fighting sects that they gave the Court a constitutional mandate to keep church and state completely separate ... Now as then, it is only by wholly isolating the state from the religious sphere and compelling it to be completely neutral, that the freedom of each and every denomination and of all nonbelievers can be maintained.[21]

This ongoing contestation led Rehnquist CJ to declare:

> Our cases, Janus like, point in two directions in applying the Establishment Clause. One face looks toward the strong role played by religion and religious traditions throughout our nation's history ... The other face looks toward the principle that governmental intervention in religious matters can itself endanger religious freedom.[22]

Reconciling these opposing forces, he held, 'requires that we neither abdicate our responsibility to maintain a division between church and state nor evince a hostility to religion by disabling the government from in some ways recognizing our religious heritage'.[23]

Particularly contested has been the question of whether the State can privilege religion over non-religion. In *Zorach v Clauson*, what concerned Black J was the 'Court's legal exaltation of the orthodox and its derogation of unbelievers'.[24] This is vividly reflected in the dissent by Scalia J in *McCreary*, where he rejected the view that the First Amendment mandates government neutrality between religion and non-religion. 'Who says so? Surely not the words of the Constitution. Surely not the history and

[18] *Lynch v Donnelly* (n 16) 673; citing Douglas J in *Zorach v Clauson* 343 US 306 (1952) (US Supreme Court) 313–14.

[19] *Lemon v Krutzman* (n 13) 612–13.

[20] *Zorach v Clauson* (n 18) 313–14.

[21] ibid, 319.

[22] *Van Orden v Perry* 545 US 677 (2005) (US Supreme Court) 683.

[23] ibid, 683–84.

[24] *Zorach v Clauson* (n 18) 319.

traditions that reflect our society's constant understanding of these words'.[25] Indeed, the State could express a preference, not just for religion per se, but for monotheistic religions.[26] By contrast, Souter J, giving the judgment of the court, held that this was 'a remarkable view … a view that should trouble anyone who prizes religious liberty',[27] and indeed, was fundamentally at odds with the notion of a right to freedom of religion. O'Connor J added:

> Allowing government to be a potential mouthpiece for competing religious ideas risks the sort of division that might easily spill over into suppression of rival beliefs. Tying secular and religious authority together poses risks to both.[28]

In Canada, by contrast, the absence of an express non-establishment clause has required courts to determine the State–religion relationship through its interpretation of the simple statement in section 2(a) of the Charter that everyone has freedom of conscience and religion. In the seminal case of *R v Big M Drug Mart*, the State relied on the absence of a non-establishment clause in the Charter to contend that the only challenge of State action could be on the basis of intrusion into the 'free exercise' of religion. Dickson J held that 'recourse to categories from the American jurisprudence is not particularly helpful in defining the meaning of freedom of conscience and religion under the Charter'.[29] Nevertheless, the principles set out by the Canadian Court bear some similarities to those of the US Supreme Court. Dickson J identified the background principle as being the prohibition of preferential treatment of, or state financial support to, particular religions or religious institutions.[30] Whereas the US Supreme Court's three-pronged test in *Lemon* includes both purpose and effects, Dickson J preferred to focus on the State's purpose, which gives readier and more vigorous protection for individual rights than a focus on effects, which were more difficult to prove.[31]

A more detailed elaboration of the State–religion relationship was given in 2015 in *Mouvement laïque québécois v Saguenay*, where the recital of Christian prayers at public meetings of a municipal council was challenged by a local citizen as a breach of his freedom of religion under the Quebec Charter.[32] (Because of the similarity between the relevant provisions in the Quebec Charter and the Canadian Charter, the Court held that the same principles applied to both.[33]) Gascon J held that the State should neither favour nor hinder any particular belief or non-belief, thereby preserving a 'neutral public space that is free of discrimination in which true freedom to believe or not to believe is enjoyed by everyone equally, given that everyone is valued equally'.[34] Such a neutral public space promotes the multicultural nature of Canadian society, encouraging everyone to participate freely in public life regardless of their beliefs. 'It follows that the state may not, by expressing its own religious preference, promote the participation of believers to the exclusion of non-believers or vice versa'.[35]

[25] *McCreary County v American Civil Liberties Union of Kentucky* 545 US 844 (2005) (US Supreme Court) 890.
[26] ibid, 893. [27] ibid, 879–80. [28] ibid, 893.
[29] *R v Big M Drug Mart Ltd* (n 12) para [105]. [30] ibid, para [107]. [31] ibid, para [120].
[32] *Mouvement laïque québécois v Saguenay* [2015] 2 SCR 3 (Supreme Court of Canada).
[33] ibid, para [68]. [34] ibid, para [74]. [35] ibid, para [75].

On the other hand, neutrality did not mean complete secularity or require the State to abstain from celebrating and preserving its religious heritage, bearing in mind that the State should recognize it as religious expression and not disguise it as cultural or historical reality or heritage.[36] Nor was the Court swayed by the declaration in the preamble to the Charter that Canada 'is founded upon principles that recognize the supremacy of God and the rule of law'. This did not limit the scope of freedom of religion and conscience or grant privileged status to theistic religious practices.[37]

The South African Constitution strikes a different type of balance between religion and the State, closer to Cliteur's multicultural model. As in Canada, there is no express establishment clause, and the Constitutional Court has been keen to distance itself from the US attempt at a strict demarcation between Church and State. In the early case of *S v Lawrence*,[38] the Court considered whether the jurisprudence on the US Establishment Clause was appropriate and relevant in South Africa. Chaskalson P was emphatic that the right to freedom of religion in the South African Constitution[39] could not 'be elevated into a constitutional principle ... that the State abstain from action that might advance or inhibit religion'.[40] The recognition that religion was a valued aspect of the lives of many South Africans was reflected in the permission in the Constitution to conduct religious observances at state institutions. At the same time, the Constitution requires the State to conduct such observances on an equitable basis. The result is that instead of a demand for strict secularism or neutrality, the South African Constitution requires the State to act even-handedly and not favour one religion to the exclusion of others.[41]

The Indian Constitution has faced similar challenges in determining the boundary between State and religion, but the trajectory of the jurisprudence has been markedly different. Freedom of religion has been crucial in enabling co-existence within a single nation of a great diversity of religions and cultures. As the Indian Supreme Court put it in 1994:

> The British policy of divide and rule, aggravated by separate electorates based on religion, had added a new dimension of mixing religion with politics ... which could only be countered if the people realised the need for national unity and integrity. It was with the weapons of secularism and non-violence that Mahatma Gandhi fought the battle for independence.[42]

The Court quoted Gandhi himself, when he wrote in 1946:

> I swear by my religion. I will die for it. But it is my personal affair. The State has nothing to do with it. The State will look after your secular welfare, health, communication, foreign relations, currency and so on, but not my religion. That is everybody's personal concern.[43]

[36] ibid, para [78]. [37] ibid, para [148]. [38] *S v Lawrence* (n 9).

[39] Interim Constitution, s 14. The almost identically worded provision in the 1996 Constitution is found in s 15.

[40] *S v Lawrence* (n 9) para [103]. [41] ibid, para [122].

[42] *Bommai v Union of India* AIR 1994 SC 1918 (Indian Supreme Court) para [25].

[43] ibid, para [25].

The preamble to the Constitution was amended in 1976 to include a reference to secularism. It now declares: 'We the people of India, having solemnly resolved to constitute India into a sovereign, socialist, secular, democratic republic . . '.. However, secularity has a complex meaning. Kapur takes the view that 'the separation of religion from the state, and state neutrality in the sphere of religion have not informed the dominant understanding of secularism in India'.[44] Instead, resonating with Cliteur's multicultural model, the Indian understanding of secularism expects the State to intervene to promote equal treatment of religions.[45] This vision of secularism was set out in *Bommai*,[46] a decision of the full constitutional bench. Sawant J stated:

> The ideal of a secular State in the sense of a State which treats all religions alike and displays benevolence towards them is in a way more suited to the Indian environment and climate than that of a truly secular State by which [is] meant a state which creates complete separation between religion and the State.[47]

Tolerance of religion did not, however, make India a theocratic state.

> Secularism under our Constitution is that whatever the attitude of the State towards the religions, religious sects and denominations, religion cannot be mixed with any secular activity of the State. In fact, the encroachment of religion into secular activities is strictly prohibited.[48]

This meant, in the context of the case before it, that it would be unconstitutional for a political party to fight an election on the basis of an agenda which would erode this secular philosophy: 'Under our Constitution, no party or organization can simultaneously be a political and a religious party'.[49]

However, the Indian Supreme Court has subsequently subtly reconfigured the notion of secularism set out in *Bommai* to equate it with tolerance and therefore with the Hindu faith more generally. Thus, only a year later, Justice Verma took the view that because Hinduism is a tolerant faith that enables all the other religions to thrive in India, tolerance has its roots in Hinduism. He therefore saw Indian secularism as encapsulated by Hinduism.[50] This shift was reinforced in the *Hindutva* cases in 1995, where the election of several members of right-wing parties was challenged on the grounds that they had appealed to religion in the course of their election campaigns and incited religious hatred, in breach of the Representation of Peoples Act 1951.[51] In particular, candidates had argued that protection of minority rights for Muslim religious minorities constituted special treatment and therefore a breach of the requirement that the State treat all individuals equally in relation to religion. In a highly contentious finding, the Court held that Hinduism, being founded on tolerance, was the 'way of life of people of the subcontinent' and therefore epitomized secularism. Moreover, the Court regarded Indian secularism as requiring a narrow notion of equality, which

[44] R Kapur, 'The "Ayodhya" Case: Hindu Majoritarianism and the Right to Religious Liberty' (2014) 29 Maryland Journal of International Law 305, 312.

[45] ibid, 314. [46] *Bommai v Union of India* (n 42). [47] ibid, para [146].

[48] ibid, paras [146]–[148]. [49] ibid, per Jeevan Reddy J at 236.

[50] *M Ismail Faruqui v Union of India* AIR 1995 SC 605 (Indian Supreme Court).

[51] *Ramesh Yeshwant Prabhoo v Prabhakar Kashinath Kunte* AIR 1996 SC 1113 (Indian Supreme Court).

required everyone to be treated the same. On this view, minority rights appeared as special treatment. This in turn meant that the campaigning promise to remove minority rights could be regarded as rectifying discrimination against the Hindu majority and thus consistent with secularism.

Kapur argues that by conflating 'Hinduism' with 'Indian-ness', the Court shut off any possibility of a non-Hindu form of being Indian, erasing Muslim religion and culture. Ultimately, this permitted a 'profoundly anti-secular vision' of secularism.[52] Sen takes this further and argues that the Court preferred a particular version of Hinduism or Hindutva, subtly moving from the inclusive understanding of Hinduism to one which was exclusivist and homogenizing of Hinduism. Moreover, the equation of Hindutva with 'Indianization' gave the Court's 'seal of approval—in a sense—to the Hindu nationalists' conception of the nation'.[53] This notion of Indian secularism is particularly contested in the light of the rise of the Hindu Right, culminating in the victory in 2014 of the BJP (the Bharatiya Janata Party), which explicitly defines itself in terms of Hindutva or Hindu nationalism, replacing the traditionally secular Congress Party.

The European Court of Human Rights (ECtHR) has taken a much more permissive view of the notion of neutrality and the extent to which the State should be separate from religion. This is a reflection of the great diversity between Member States, with some, like France, Belgium, and Turkey, having a strong constitutional commitment to secularism, while others, like the UK, Greece, and Denmark, have an established Church. The Convention itself does not include an establishment clause equivalent to that in the US. The boundary between religion and the State therefore needs to be derived from the three articles which address religion: Article 9 (freedom of religion); Article 14 (non-discrimination); and Protocol 1 Article 2 (parental rights to educate their children in the religion of their choice). In his concurring opinion in the Grand Chamber case of *Lautsi v Italy*, Judge Bonello vividly described the position under the ECHR thus:

> The Convention has given this Court the remit to enforce freedom of religion and of conscience, but has not empowered it to bully States into secularism or to coerce countries into schemes of religious neutrality. It is for each individual State to choose whether to be secular or not, and whether, and to what extent, to separate Church and governance. What is not for the State to do is to deny freedom of religion and of conscience to anyone.[54]

Nevertheless, to ensure the State does not deny freedom of religion, it is necessary to have some view of the extent to which the State can privilege one religious group or can allow religion to influence State policy. The settled way in which the ECtHR has navigated these diverse claims is through the prism of 'pluralism'. Freedom of religion, the Court stated in *Kokkinakis v Greece*,

[52] Kapur (n 44) 330.

[53] R Sen, *Articles of Faith: Religion, Secularism and the Indian Supreme Court* (OUP 2010) 60.

[54] *Lautsi v Italy* (2012) 54 EHRR 3 (European Court of Human Rights (Grand Chamber)) paras [2.2]–[2.3].

> is one of the most vital elements that go to make up the identity of believers and their conception of life, but it is also a precious asset for atheists, agnostics, sceptics and the unconcerned. The pluralism indissociable from a democratic society, which has been dearly won over the centuries, depends on it.[55]

But what does pluralism say about whether the State is permitted to interfere in the autonomy of religious organizations and, conversely, whether religion can interfere in the running of the State?[56]

Preventing interference in the autonomy of religious organizations is the more straightforward side of the equation. In *Hasan v Bulgaria*, the Court made it clear that the collective aspect of the right to freedom of religion in Article 9 includes the right to participate in the life of a religious community.[57] Together with freedom of association, freedom of religion encompasses the expectation that the community is permitted to function free from arbitrary State intervention. As the Court stressed:

> The autonomous existence of religious communities is indispensable for pluralism in a democratic society and is thus an issue at the very heart of the protection which Article 9 affords ... Were the organisational life of the community not protected by Article 9 of the Convention, all other aspects of the individual's freedom of religion would become vulnerable.[58]

More contentious is the converse, namely that religion should not interfere in the running of the State. This principle was powerfully tested in *Refah Partisi v Turkey*, which we have already seen in Chapter 10 on Freedom of Speech. It will be recalled that the Refah Partisi Party was banned by the Turkish authorities on the grounds that it was advocating for a theocratic regime in Turkey, based on Sharia law, in contravention of the constitutional principle of secularism in the Turkish constitution. Upholding the ban on the party, the Court emphasized the State's role as the 'neutral and impartial organizer of the exercise of various religions, faiths and beliefs', a role which is 'conducive to public order, religious harmony and tolerance in a democratic society'.[59] Refah's advocacy of divine rules as the basis for the political regime was, in the Court's view, a return to a theistic regime in Turkey which was incompatible with democracy. Sharia in particular, was difficult to reconcile with Convention values, especially with regard to its criminal law and criminal procedure, its rules on the legal status of women, and its intervention in all spheres of public and private life in accordance with religious precepts.[60] The proposal to set up a plurality of legal systems, where each individual was subject to the law of their own religion,

[55] *Kokkinakis v Greece* (1994) 17 EHRR 397 (European Court of Human Rights) para [31].

[56] J Ringelheim, 'Rights, Religion and the Public Sphere: The European Court of Human Rights in Search of a Theory?' in L Zucca and C Ungureanu (eds), *Law, State and Religion in the New Europe: Debates and Dilemmas* (Cambridge University Press 2012).

[57] *Hasan v Bulgaria* (2002) 34 EHRR 55 (European Court of Human Rights).

[58] ibid, para [62].

[59] *Refah Partisi (the Welfare Party) v Turkey* (2003) 37 EHRR 1 (European Court of Human Rights) para [91].

[60] ibid, para [123].

> would do away with the State's role as the guarantor of individual rights and freedoms and the impartial organizer of the practice of the various beliefs and religions in a democratic society, since it would oblige individuals to obey, not rules laid down by the State in the exercise of its above-mentioned functions, but static rules of law imposed by the religion concerned.[61]

Likewise, it would infringe on the principle of non-discrimination between individuals, since it would require different treatment of individuals according to their religion.[62] Since there was no dispute that everyone in Turkey could observe the requirements of their religion in their private life, it was legitimate for Turkey to prevent the application within its jurisdiction of private laws of religious inspiration prejudicial to public order and the values of democracy for Convention purposes (such as rules permitting discrimination based on the gender of the parties concerned, as in polygamy and privileges for the male sex in matters of divorce and succession).[63]

The broad principles set out in different jurisdictions on the boundary between State and religion often take on a different hue when applied to particular issues. Three main arenas of contestation will be dealt with below: religious expression by the State, through public symbols in public spaces or schools; State endorsement of rest days and holy days of the dominant religion; and religious observance or teaching in schools.

A. Religious expression by the State: symbols and schools

The contestation over State neutrality frequently focuses on the degree to which religious expression by the State is permitted. Can public symbols or monuments express support for a particular religion, or even religion in general? Although Courts' responses have differed over the different jurisdictions, several common attempts to justify public expressions of religion emerge. One is the claim by the State that religious symbols have secular meanings and therefore do not breach State neutrality. This, however, reveals a fundamental inability to perceive the extent to which the dominant religion has permeated the culture. A Christian might regard a nativity scene or a crucifix as a cultural rather than a religious symbol. But for adherents of minority religion or non-believers, the very lack of appreciation of the religious nature of the symbol could constitute a negation of their religion or secular position. A second common approach is to distinguish between passive and active religious expression, with the former constituting less encroachment on the State–religion divide. A third, particularly in the schools' cases, is to emphasize the importance of the right to withdraw from official religious expression. These approaches can be contrasted with the few cases in which State neutrality is said to require a robust rejection of any support for religious expression whatsoever.

The first approach, namely to ascribe secular, cultural significance to religious symbols, was taken in the US case of *Lynch v Donnelly*.[64] *Lynch* constituted a claim by residents of Pawtucket that the Free Establishment Clause had been violated when their

[61] ibid, para [119], citing the Chamber decision at para [70].
[62] ibid, para [119].
[63] ibid, para [128].
[64] *Lynch v Donnelly* (n 16).

municipality exhibited a life-size crèche depicting the infant Jesus, Mary, and Joseph as part of their Christmas decorations. By a narrow majority, the US Supreme Court held there had been no violation. Although the Mayor had openly campaigned to 'keep Christ in Christmas', the Court found the city's purpose to be secular, to celebrate the Christmas holiday and to show its origins. However, as Blackmun J, dissenting, so pertinently put it:

> Ironically, the majority does an injustice to the crèche and the message it manifests ... The crèche has been relegated to the role of a neutral harbinger of the holiday season, useful for commercial purposes, but devoid of any inherent meaning and incapable of enhancing the religious tenor of a display of which it is an integral part. The city has its victory—but it is a Pyrrhic one indeed.[65]

The opposite approach was taken in the 2005 case of *McCreary County*,[66] which concerned the legitimacy of a display of the Ten Commandments on a courthouse in Kentucky. Here, the question was whether the Ten Commandments had come to constitute a cultural, and arguably secular, symbol. Upholding the complaint by non-religious citizens of McCreary county, the Court held that the county had displayed the Ten Commandments with a clearly religious purpose. In O'Connor J's words, 'The purpose behind the count[y's] display is relevant because it conveys an unmistakable message of endorsement to the reasonable observer'.[67] As Souter J re-emphasized: 'The Framers and the citizens of their time intended not only to protect the integrity of individual conscience in religious matters, but to guard against the civic divisiveness that follows when the government weighs in on one side of religious debate'.[68] Scalia J, however, took a radically different approach. He acknowledged the religious purpose but did not see anything amiss with State endorsement of religion per se, as long as it did not favour a particular religious viewpoint.

> Publicly honouring the Ten Commandments is ... indistinguishable, insofar as discriminating against other religions is concerned, from publicly honouring God. Both practices are recognized across such a broad and diverse range of the population—from Christians to Muslims—that they cannot be reasonably understood as a government endorsement of a particular religious viewpoint.[69]

The second position, which would permit 'passive' expression of religion by the State, was taken by the majority in the case of *Van Orden*.[70] This time the case concerned whether the Establishment Clause permitted the display of a monument inscribed with the Ten Commandments on the Texas State Capitol ground. The Court held that it did. Giving judgment of the court, Rehnquist CJ regarded the *Lemon* test, with its focus on governmental purpose, as not useful in dealing with the sort of 'passive monument' in question. Notably, like Scalia J, he did not deny that the Ten Commandments are religious or claim them as a purely cultural symbol: 'Simply having religious content or promoting a message consistent with a religious doctrine does not run afoul of the Establishment Clause'.[71]

[65] ibid, 727. [66] *McCreary County v American Civil Liberties Union of Kentucky* (n 25).
[67] ibid, 883. [68] ibid, 875. [69] ibid, 894. [70] *Van Orden v Perry* (n 22).
[71] ibid, 690.

On the other hand, US courts have taken a strong stand against the display of religious symbols in public schoolrooms. In *Stone v Graham*, the Court struck down a Kentucky statute requiring the Ten Commandments to be displayed on the wall of every public classroom in the State.[72] The State trial court had upheld the statute on the basis that its avowed purpose was secular, not religious. The Supreme Court disagreed. The pre-eminent purpose for posting the Ten Commandments was plainly religious. This differed from a case in which the Ten Commandments were integrated into the school curriculum, where it could be used as part of an appropriate study of religion. The fact that it was left to pupils to read for themselves did not make it a 'passive' symbol. In the later case of *Van Orden*, Rehnquist J was clear that a monument was a far more passive symbol than the display of the Ten Commandments in a classroom, where the children were exposed to it daily.[73]

This sets the US jurisprudence clearly apart from that of the ECtHR, where the opposite position has been taken. In *Lautsi v Italy*, the Grand Chamber of the ECtHR held that the display of the crucifix in public school classrooms in Italy did not offend against the right to freedom of religion in Article 9 ECHR. The obligation to hang crucifixes in primary school classrooms has a long history in Italy, dating back to the period in which Catholicism was the State religion. After the Republican Constitution of 1948, which provides for freedom of religion, and the explicit severance of the State from the Catholic Church, the Italian Constitutional Court held that the principle of secularism was derived from the Constitution.[74] Nevertheless, a Ministerial instruction as recently as 2002 reiterated the obligation of school governors to ensure the presence of crucifixes in classrooms. The Minister took the view that this could not be considered to be a limitation of freedom of conscience because the presence of crucifixes 'constitutes only an expression of Christian civilization and culture, and that it therefore forms part of the universal heritage of mankind'.[75]

The applicants claimed that this infringed their rights under both Article 9 and Article 2 Protocol 1. They argued that the display of crucifixes in the classroom was the expression of the State's preference for a particular religion, disregarding the State's obligation to give special protection to minors against indoctrination. It also infringed the parent's right to have her children educated in conformity with her own secular beliefs. The government strenuously argued that the sign of the cross was open to different interpretations, not just as a religious symbol, but also as one of cultural identity. It also argued that the crucifix was a passive symbol: indeed, it had not been claimed that the content of teaching provided in Italy was influenced by the presence of crucifixes in the classroom.

Faced with both the argument that the crucifix was a cultural symbol and that it was a passive one, the Court's response was the converse to that of US courts: it rejected the cultural argument, but accepted the passive one. Finding no evidence that the display of a religious symbol on a classroom wall might influence pupils, the Court held that the crucifix was essentially a passive symbol, and could not be deemed to have an influence on pupils comparable to didactic speech or participation in religious

[72] *Stone v Graham* 449 US 39 (1980) (US Supreme Court).
[73] *Van Orden v Perry* (n 22) 691.
[74] *Lautsi v Italy* (n 54) paras [17]–[23].
[75] Cited in ibid, para [24].

activities.[76] The Court did recognize that the crucifix is 'above all, a religious symbol'.[77] It also acknowledged that the presence of a crucifix in State school classrooms confers preponderant visibility on the country's majority religion in the school environment. However, reflecting the much more porous nature of the boundary between religion and State in Europe as compared to the US, it held that this in itself was not sufficient to establish a breach of Article 2 Protocol 1. Given the great diversity of practices among Contracting States, the Court had a duty to respect the latter's decision as to the organization of the school environment and the setting and planning of the curriculum. Thus, the decision as to whether crucifixes should be present in State-school classrooms was a matter falling within the margin of appreciation of the respondent State.

B. Religious rest days and holy days

An issue which has put pressure on the demarcation between cultural affirmation and religious partiality on the part of the State concerns State endorsement of Sunday as a national rest day. Criminal prohibitions on Sunday trading have a long history, dating back to fourteenth-century England, and exported to its colonies, including the US, Canada, and South Africa. For several centuries, such prohibitions were unashamedly religious in purpose; indeed, they generally referred to Sunday as the Lord's Day, and often specifically stated that no 'worldly labour' could be done so that people could go to church.[78] However, beginning in the eighteenth century, Sunday closing laws began to take on a different, more secular purpose, namely to guarantee a day of rest to workers and to protect them against exploitative employers. The fact that Sunday was chosen as this day was perhaps one of convenience and custom, rather than religion per se. However, this choice inevitably burdens those whose religion prescribes a different day of rest, and privileges those for whom religion and State ordained rest days coincide. It was in the context of this history that courts in the US, Canada, and South Africa have been asked to determine whether Sunday closing laws are an illegitimate breach of the right to freedom of religion or of the State–religion divide. There is a striking similarity between the themes addressed in the different judgments, although the conclusions vary.

For the US Supreme Court, the key issue has been whether Sunday closing laws have retained their religious character or could now be characterized as serving a secular purpose. In *McGowan v Maryland*,[79] the Court held that Maryland's criminal prohibition of Sunday trading did not infringe the Free Establishment Clause. After a detailed examination of the way in which Sunday closing laws had transmuted from their religious origins, the Court held that the statute's present purpose and effect was 'not to aid religion but to set aside a day of rest and recreation'.[80] The difficulty was to justify why this day should be Sunday. Warren CJ, giving judgment for the Court, recognized that if the State's interest were simply to provide a day of rest, it could legislate

[76] ibid, para [72]. [77] ibid, para [66].
[78] *McGowan v Maryland* 366 US 420 (1961) (US Supreme Court) 432. [79] ibid.
[80] ibid, 449.

that everyone should rest one day in seven, and leave the choice of the day to the individual. However, the Court stressed the value of a common day of rest, where all members of a family and a community could spend the day together. It also went further and held that Sunday had come to be regarded as that special day of rest.

Douglas J, dissenting, saw things very differently. For him, the question was not whether one day a week could be imposed by the State as a day of rest. Nor was it whether Sunday by force of custom could be retained as that day of rest.[81] 'It seems to me plain that by these laws the States compel one, under sanction of law, to refrain from work or recreation on Sunday because of the majority's religious views about that day'.[82] Freedom of religion, he stressed, centrally included freedom from religion. Moreover, there was a real cost to individuals whose religion prescribed a different day of rest. Orthodox Jews and Sabbatarians, who observe the rest day on Saturdays, are compelled to observe a second Sabbath, reducing their trade to a five-day week. For him, this was a clear preference for one religion over others.

It was precisely these facts which were presented to the Court in the 1961 case of *Braunfield v Brown*, but here too the majority of the Court were unable to see that prohibiting Sunday trading could constitute a State preference for the Christian religion over others. The case was brought by Orthodox Jewish retail merchants who were prosecuted under a Pennsylvania criminal statute, enacted two years previously, proscribing retail sales on Sundays. Because the Jewish religion requires that no work be done between nightfall on a Friday and nightfall on a Saturday, these merchants had always compensated by doing a substantial amount of their business on Sundays.[83] The appellants claimed that the criminalization of Sunday trading impaired their ability to earn a livelihood, putting them in a position of having to make an invidious choice between giving up a basic tenet of their faith, or being put at a serious economic disadvantage. Warren CJ held that the Sunday law did not make any religious practice of the appellants unlawful; it simply operated to make the practice of their religious beliefs more expensive. The Court placed particular emphasis on the diversity of religions in the US, but instead of leaning against giving preference to the dominant religion, it concluded that since any chosen day of rest would offend some religion, it was acceptable to choose the Christian day. The Court also rejected the appellants' submission that an exemption should be provided for those whose religion requires them to have a different rest day. Even though such an exemption had been provided by a number of States, the Court held that an exemption might undermine the objective of a total day of rest or even give those with the exemption a competitive advantage on a Sunday.

The dissenting judge, Stewart J, summed up the opposite view:

> Pennsylvania has passed a law which compels an Orthodox Jew to choose between his religious faith and his economic survival. That is a cruel choice. It is a choice which I think no State can constitutionally demand. For me this is not something that can be swept under the rug and forgotten in the interest of enforced Sunday

[81] ibid, 561. [82] ibid, 573.

[83] *Braunfeld v Brown* 366 US 599 (1961) (US Supreme Court).

> togetherness. I think the impact of this law upon these appellants grossly violates their constitutional right to the free exercise of their religion.[84]

It is this latter position which has been taken by the Supreme Court of Canada. In *R v Big M Drug Mart*,[85] the applicants were charged with selling goods on a Sunday, in contravention of the Lord's Day Act. They challenged the constitutionality of the statute. The Canadian Court explicitly distanced itself from the US Court's characterization of Sunday observance laws as having a secular purpose, providing a uniform day of rest and recreation for all citizens.[86] Dickson J had no doubt that the purpose of the Lord's Day Act was religious. Moreover, he refused to follow what he called the 'shifting purpose' doctrine in US jurisprudence, whereby legislation initiated with an avowedly religious purpose could come to have a secular meaning. Like Douglas J in *McGowan*, the Canadian Court regarded freedom from compulsory religious observance as a key principle of freedom of religion.[87] The Lord's Day Act, to the extent that it binds all to a sectarian Christian ideal, constitutes 'a form of coercion inimical to the spirit of the Charter and the dignity of all non-Christians … The arm of the state requires all to remember the Lord's Day of the Christians and to keep it holy'.[88]

However, by focusing on a purpose test, the Canadian Court left open the possibility that the prohibition on Sunday trading could be upheld if its purpose was characterized as secular. This was the conclusion in *R v Edwards Books and Art Ltd*,[89] where four Ontario retailers were charged with offering goods for sale by retail on a Sunday contrary to the Retail Business Holidays Act. Dickson CJ, applying the purpose test set out in *R v Big M Drug Mart*, held that on the evidence the Retail Business Holidays Act 'was enacted with the intent of providing uniform holidays to retail workers. I am unable to conclude that the Act was a surreptitious attempt to encourage religious worship'.[90] Legislation with a secular inspiration does not violate freedom of religion simply because the outcome coincides with the tenets of one religion.[91]

At the same time, the Canadian Court was explicit in distancing itself from the views of the majority of the US Supreme Court that no legislative effort needs to be made to accommodate the interests of Saturday observing retailers.[92] Dickson CJ recognized that the Sunday closing laws created substantial pressure on observant Jewish or Seventh Day Adventist retailers to abandon the observance of a Saturday Sabbath. He thus held that there was a prima facie breach of their freedom of religion.[93] On the other hand, he agreed with the majority of the US Supreme Court in *Braunfeld* that it was legitimate for the legislature to be concerned to minimize the effect of exemptions on workers, and in particular, on the right not to do involuntary work on a Sunday. The real purpose of the statute was to benefit retail employees by ensuring they had a weekly holiday which coincided with the rest of the community. Such workers, according to the statistics, were low-paid, female, non-unionized, and therefore very unlikely to have the power to refuse Sunday working if asked. The statute exempted employers with no more than seven employees and this was held to be satisfactory:

[84] ibid, 616. [85] *R v Big M Drug Mart Ltd* (n 12). [86] ibid, para [77].
[87] ibid, para [96]. [88] ibid, paras [97]–[98].
[89] *R v Edwards Books and Art Ltd* [1986] 2 SCR 713 (Supreme Court of Canada).
[90] ibid, para [62]. [91] ibid, para [99]. [92] ibid, para [148]. [93] ibid, para [115].

> In interpreting and applying the Charter I believe that the courts must be cautious to ensure that it does not simply become an instrument of better situated individuals to roll back legislation which has as its object the improvement of the condition of less advantaged persons. When the interests of more than seven vulnerable employees in securing a Sunday holiday are weighed against the interests of their employer in transacting business on a Sunday, I cannot fault the Legislature for determining that the protection of the employees ought to prevail.[94]

As Wilson J held in her dissent, it was not clear why it should be justifiable to distinguish between Saturday observing retailers on the ground of how many workers they employed. Nor was there sufficient evidence to show that permitting all Saturday observers to open on Sundays would in fact have a detrimental effect on workers' right to a common day of rest. She would therefore have retained the exemption for Saturday observers, but removed the limit of seven employees.

A similar challenge was addressed by the South African Constitutional Court in *S v Lawrence*,[95] where the Court rejected a claim that a statutory provision prohibiting the sale of alcohol on Sundays constituted a breach of the right to freedom of religion.[96] Again, one of the issues in *Lawrence* was the extent to which religious symbols or holidays had come to have secular or cultural significance. Chaskalson P held that in South Africa, Sundays had acquired a secular as well as a religious character, as evidenced by the fact that most people spent Sundays in sport and recreation, rather than worship. Sachs J, however, disagreed with Chaskalson P:

> By endorsing a particular faith as a direct and sectarian source of values for legislation binding on the whole nation, it exceeds the competence granted to it by the Constitution. Even if there is no compulsory requirement to observe or not to observe a particular religious practice, the effect is to divide the nation into insiders who belong, and outsiders who are tolerated. This is impermissible in the multi-faith, heterodox society contemplated by our Constitution.[97]

Notably, the case was not brought on the basis of a competing religious belief as in the Canadian and US jurisprudence, but rather on the basis of trading interests.

C. Religious education in public schools

Schools are inevitably an arena for deep contestation over religion, where normative commitments of parents jostle with those of the school and the State. A comparative perspective reveals the various ways in which State neutrality, free exercise of religion, and non-discrimination are called upon to configure the State–religion relationship in this context. The US Supreme Court, reflecting the strong adherence to State neutrality, has generally held fast to the concept of a 'wall of separation' when it comes to religion in public schools. The dominant principle has been that public schools should not be partial towards any religion, and should not endorse either a specific religion, or religion as against non-religion.[98] Thus in *McCollum v Board of Education* in

[94] ibid, para [141]. [95] *S v Lawrence* (n 9). [96] ibid. [97] ibid, para [179].
[98] See *Everson v Board of Education* (n 14).

1948, the Court struck down a programme allowing religious teachers, employed by private religious groups, to run voluntary religious classes on school premises weekly during school time in public schools in the district. Black J, delivering the opinion of the court, found that the programme was 'beyond all question a utilization of the tax-established and tax-supported public school system to aid religious groups to spread their faith. And it falls squarely under the ban of the First Amendment'.[99] He made it clear that this did not constitute hostility to religion. Nevertheless, reiterating his longstanding view that the First Amendment has erected a wall between Church and State 'which must be kept high and impregnable', he declared that both religion and government can work best if each is left free from each other.[100] In the words of Frankfurter J, 'good fences make good neighbours'.[101]

Similarly, in *Abington School District v Schemp*, the Court held that state legislation requiring schools to begin each day with readings from the Bible was unconstitutional under the Establishment Clause.[102] It was not sufficient that parents could withdraw their children if they wished, nor that this was a relatively minor infringement. 'The breach of neutrality that is today a trickling stream may all too soon become a raging torrent'.[103] As we have seen, the Court took a similar view in invalidating a Kentucky statute which required the posting of a copy of the Ten Commandments on the wall of each public classroom in the State.[104] Similarly, in *Lee v Weismann*, the Court held that to invite clergy, albeit from a range of different religions, to give the address at a graduation ceremony at a high school was an unconstitutional violation of the Free Establishment Clause.[105] As Kennedy J put it: 'One timeless lesson is that if citizens are subjected to state sponsored religious exercises, the State disavows its own duty to guard and respect that sphere of inviolable conscience and belief which is the mark of a free people'.[106]

The South African Constitution takes a very different view of the role of religion in public education, closer to Cliteur's multicultural approach. As we have seen, section 15(2) states that 'religious observances may be conducted at state or state-aided institutions'. This is subject to three constitutional provisos: any religious observances should follow rules made by the appropriate public authorities; they should be conducted on an equitable basis; and attendance at them should be free and voluntary. This constitutional settlement was arrived at as a result of much contestation, given the apartheid history in South Africa of perpetuating the system of white racial supremacy explicitly set out in the Christian National Education Policy of 1948. During the negotiations over a national education policy, the option of eliminating religion entirely from the school curriculum was rejected as being inappropriate for South Africa's deeply religious society. The Constitutional provisions are mirrored in the South African Schools Act, which permits religious observances to be conducted at public schools under rules issued by School Governing Bodies, provided they are conducted equitably and attendance is free and voluntary.

99 *Illinois ex rel McCollum v Board of Education* 333 US 203 (1948) (US Supreme Court) 210.
100 ibid, 212.
101 ibid, 232.
102 *Abington School District v Kemp* 374 US 203 (1963) (US Supreme Court).
103 ibid, 226.
104 *Stone v Graham* (n 72).
105 *Lee v Weisman* 505 US 557 (1992) (US Supreme Court).
106 ibid, 592.

However, whether this meant that schools can expressly adopt a specific religion is not settled. Some general principles were canvassed in *Lawrence*, although this was not in issue in that case. Chaskalson P stated that it was acceptable to offer prayers that were appropriate for the particular school, even if this meant that provision was not made for as many denominations as might exist within the pupil body. For Chaskalson P, there were sufficient safeguards in the Constitutional provisos. Sachs J was more concerned at the ways in which public endorsement of a particular religion could result in indirect coercion:

> Compulsory attendance at school prayers would infringe freedom of religion. In the context of a school community and the pervasive peer pressure that is often present in such communities, voluntary school prayer could also amount to the coercion of pupils to participate in the prayers of the favoured religion.[107]

In a 2017 High Court case, it was held that it was not compatible with the Constitution for a public school to hold out that it has adopted one religion to the exclusion of others.[108] Where a learner had no choice but to attend a school which held itself out to be of a different religion, there was clearly a possibility that this might inculcate a sense of inferior differentness.

The ECtHR has been even more accepting of religion within schools than South Africa, reflecting the fact that Member States range from the State–Church model to strict secularity. Indeed, all over Europe, religious education remains closely tied in with secular education. As many as forty-three Council of Europe Member States provide religious education classes in State schools. In twenty-five of these, religious education is a compulsory subject.[109] The Court has attempted to navigate this difficult terrain by accepting that religious and philosophical doctrine is too pervasive to exclude entirely from school syllabuses. Instead it has emphasized the need to convey information in an objective, critical, and pluralistic manner. 'The State is forbidden to pursue an aim of indoctrination that might be considered as not respecting parents' religious and philosophical convictions. That is the limit that must not be exceeded'.[110] The foundational principles were set out in *Kjeldsen v Denmark*.[111] In this case, parents objected to the Danish law making sex education compulsory and an integral part of the curriculum in State primary schools, on the grounds that this was contrary to the beliefs they held as Christian parents. The Court rejected the view that religion should be excluded entirely from schools. The breadth of the concept of religious and philosophical convictions meant that it would be impractical to expect a school curriculum not to impart knowledge of a directly or indirectly religious or philosophical kind.[112] Article 2 of the Protocol did not therefore permit parents to object to the teaching of such material in the school curriculum. On the other hand, the State must take care

[107] *S v Lawrence* (n 9) para [103].

[108] *Organisasie vir Godsdienste-Onderrig en Demokrasie v Laerskool Randhart* [2017] 3 All SA 943 (GJ) (High Court of South Africa).

[109] *Zengin v Turkey* (2008) 46 EHRR 44 (European Court of Human Rights) para [30].

[110] *Kjeldson, Busk Madsen and Pederson v Denmark* (1979-80) 1 EHRR 711 (European Court of Human Rights) para [53].

[111] ibid. [112] ibid.

to convey the information in an objective, critical, and pluralistic manner. In the case of the sex education offered in Danish public schools, the Court held that the curriculum did not overstep these bounds. Although the content inevitably included considerations of a 'moral order', they were very general in character and did not amount to indoctrination. Parents remained free to educate their children in their own way and to send them to private schools if they objected. Therefore, no violation was found.

As in the case of Sunday trading laws, one way of navigating this tension is through exemptions, giving parents the right to withdraw their children from religious education. This re-characterizes the issue as one of free exercise of religion, rather than separation of State and religion. It also enables the Court to preserve the right to freedom of religion while desisting from any attempt to uncouple the State–Church relationship which is foundational to some of the Member States. This can be clearly seen in *Folgerø v Norway*, where parents challenged the compulsory religious education in State schools in Norway. The Grand Chamber took particular note of the fact that the Evangelical Lutheran Religion was declared to be the State's official religion by the Norwegian Constitution. In view of the place occupied by Christianity in the history and tradition of Norway, it held that the fact that the school syllabus gave a larger share to knowledge of the Christian religion than other religions did not depart from the principle of pluralism or amount to indoctrination.[113] On the other hand, the parents' rights under Article 2 Protocol 1 had been infringed as the relevant legislation only granted a partial exemption for religious education, as well as infringing on their privacy by requiring reasons for withdrawing their children.

This was reinforced in *Zengin v Turkey*, where the applicants were followers of Alevism, a branch of Islam which is widespread in Turkey, and whose religious practices differ from Sunni Islam in many significant ways. They complained that compulsory religious education in State schools breached their rights under the Convention. The Court upheld their complaint. Although Turkey was constitutionally a secular State, it was acceptable for the school syllabus to give prominence to knowledge of Islam given that Islam was the majority religion practised in the country. However, the lack of acknowledgement of the religious diversity of Turkey and the total absence of any teaching on the Alevi faith meant that the curriculum did not meet the Court's criteria of objectivity and pluralism, or respect the religious and philosophical convictions of the applicants.[114] Moreover, the provision for exemption was too limited to provide sufficient protection, especially because parents had to inform the school authorities of their religious or philosophical convictions to be eligible.

Canadian courts have confronted the question from the opposite direction, namely challenges by religious parents opposed to the introduction of school curricula recognizing a diversity of religions. The Supreme Court of Canada has had to address the question in several recent cases arising out of the introduction by Quebec of curricula which recognize a diversity of religions. In a clear break with the tradition of denominational public schools in Quebec, a compulsory ethics and religious culture (ERC) programme was introduced in 1997 in all public schools aimed at fostering

[113] *Folgerø v Norway* (2008) 46 EHRR 47 (European Court of Human Rights).
[114] *Zengin v Turkey* (n 109) para [70].

an understanding of several religious traditions but giving particular prominence to the historical and cultural importance of Catholicism and Protestantism. In *SL v Commission scolaire des Chênes*, Catholic parents at a State school challenged the programme after their claim for an exemption had been rejected. They argued that their right to choose an education consistent with their own religious principles would be lost because their children would be forced to take a course that did not reflect their parents' religious beliefs. The Court rejected their claim. Deschamps J accepted that absolute State neutrality is not possible, but nor is it required. Instead, neutrality is assured when the State shows respect for all postures towards religion, including that of having no religious beliefs whatsoever, while taking into account the competing constitutional rights of the individuals affected.[115] These principles were not breached by the course. Simply exposing children to different religions without forcing them to join could not constitute indoctrination which would infringe the parents' freedom of religion. In fact, such exposure might be necessary to teach children what tolerance involves.

The Court took a very different position in relation to private faith schools. In *Loyola v Quebec*,[116] the challenge came from Loyola, a private Catholic high school for boys, administered by the Jesuit Order. The law permitted private schools to apply for an exemption from the ERC programme if they offered an alternative programme deemed equivalent by the Minister. Loyola applied for an exemption. It proposed an alternative course which would teach the doctrines and practices of other world religions from a neutral perspective. On the other hand, the ethics of other religions would be taught from a Catholic perspective. It also proposed to teach Catholic doctrine and ethics from a Catholic perspective. The Minister rejected the request, stating that no part of the programme could be taught from a Catholic perspective. The Court unanimously held that the Minister's decision limited freedom of religion more than necessary.

For Abella J, state regulation of religious schools posed the difficult question of how to balance robust protection of religious freedom with the values of a secular State. Secularism, in her view, did not entail the absence of religion. 'A secular state respects religious differences, it does not seek to extinguish them'.[117] A secular State could not interfere with the beliefs or practices of a religious group, unless they conflict with or harm overriding public interests. At the same time, the State was entitled to promote the core values of its society through education and had a legitimate interest in ensuring that all students would be capable in adulthood of openness and respect towards religious and cultural differences.[118] She agreed with the decision in *SL* that the ERC programme in a public school did not impose limits on individual parents and students' freedom of religion. The State was entitled to devise curricula which aimed to transmit its core values of pluralism and mutual respect, and parents were free to practise and transmit their religious beliefs to their children. However, a private school was in a different position from a public school. A private faith school should

[115] *SL v Commission scolaire des Chênes* [2012] SCC 7 (Supreme Court of Canada) para [32].
[116] *Loyola High School v Quebec* (2015) SCC 12 (Supreme Court of Canada).
[117] ibid, para [43]. [118] ibid, para [48].

be considered as a communal institution which was entitled to convey the faith of its members to their children: 'To tell a Catholic school how to explain its faith undermines the liberty of the members of its community who have chosen to give effect to the collective dimension of their religious beliefs by participating in a denominational school'.[119] As well as interfering with the freedom of Loyola's teachers, by telling them to teach Catholicism in terms defined by the State, this interfered with the rights of parents to transmit the Catholic faith to their children. On the other hand, Abella J differed from the concurring judgments in finding no significant impairment in requiring Loyola to explain other religions, including their beliefs, ethics, and practices, in as objective and neutral a way as possible, rather than from a Catholic perspective. She agreed with Deschamps J that it is not a breach of anyone's freedom of religion to be required to learn or teach about the doctrines and ethics of other world religions in a neutral and respectful way, even in a private denominational school.

One way forward was to regard a private school as having its own right to religious freedom. This was the path taken by the concurring justices. McLachlin CJ held that freedom of religion of individuals could not flourish without freedom of religion for the organizations through which these individuals express their religious practices and transmit their faith.[120] Abella J, however, did not believe it was necessary to decide whether corporations enjoy religious freedom in their own right under section 2(a) of the Charter. Loyola had standing to require the minister to exercise her discretion lawfully and in a way that respects Charter-protected religious freedom for members of the Loyola community, without having to demand the right to religious freedom itself.[121] Her caution was arguably very sensible, given the recent decision of the US Supreme Court in *Hobby Lobby*,[122] where, as we will see, a corporation was accorded freedom of religion with problematic consequences for the right of its employees to receive contraception on their medical insurance.

IV. Elusive and Intangible: The Meaning of Religion

Thus far, we have proceeded as if the meaning of religion were either clear or unnecessary to determine. Yet, as US Justice Burger put it:

> Only beliefs rooted in religion are protected by the Free Exercise Clause, which . . . gives special protection to the exercise of religion. Yet the determination of what is a 'religious' belief or practice is a difficult and delicate task.[123]

This is a crucial question when individuals are claiming a breach of their freedom of religion, especially when this entails the duty to accommodate religious practice. Should courts take it on themselves to determine whether a practice is objectively required by a religion? Or should they accept the applicant's word and instead focus on whether the prima facie breach of the right is justifiable?

[119] ibid, para [62]. [120] ibid, para [95]. [121] ibid, para [34].
[122] *Burwell v Hobby Lobby Stores* 134 S Ct 2751 (2014) (US Supreme Court).
[123] *Thomas v Review Board of Indiana Employment Security Div* 450 US 707 (1981) (US Supreme Court) 714.

Courts in most of the jurisdictions studied here have preferred the second approach. This was the unequivocal position taken by the US Supreme Court in the 1944 case of *US v Ballard*, where the respondents were accused of fraudulent procurement of money by false statements as to their religious experience. The question before the Supreme Court was whether it was for the jury to determine the truth of their asserted religious experience, or whether only the sincerity of their beliefs should be at issue. Douglas J had no doubt that it was the latter.

> Men may believe what they cannot prove. They may not be put to the proof of their religious doctrines or beliefs. Religious experiences which are as real as life to some may be incomprehensible to others. Yet the fact that they may be beyond the ken of mortals does not mean that they can be made suspect before the law.[124]

Similarly, the ECtHR has frequently reiterated that in a pluralist democratic society, the State's duty of impartiality and neutrality is incompatible with any assessment by the State of the legitimacy of religious beliefs or the ways they are expressed.[125]

This approach becomes challenging when the applicant is asking for a special dispensation to accommodate religious beliefs. Should the applicant have to prove that the belief or practice is a mandatory tenet of her religion before such an exemption is granted? Here too courts in several jurisdictions have held that an individual's subjective decision is sufficient, as long as she is sincere. In the US case of *Thomas v Review Board*,[126] a Jehovah's Witness terminated his job because his religious beliefs forbade participation in the production of armaments. He was denied unemployment benefits on the ground that he had not left for 'good cause', the condition for eligibility. The Review Board brought evidence that his belief was not a mandatory tenet of the Jehovah's Witness religion and other members of the faith might have accepted this job. The Court refused to enter into this question. As Burger CJ put it:

> The guarantee of free exercise is not limited to beliefs which are shared by all of the members of a religious sect. Particularly in this sensitive area, it is not within the judicial function and judicial competence to inquire whether the petitioner or his fellow worker more correctly perceived the commands of their common faith ... The narrow function of a reviewing court in this context is to determine whether there was an appropriate finding that [the] petitioner terminated his work because of an honest conviction that such work was forbidden by his religion.[127]

The Court took a similar position in *Frazee v Illinois*.[128] Here the applicant claimed that his refusal to work on a Sunday stemmed from his Christian beliefs, even though he did not assert that this resulted from a tenet, belief, or teaching of an established religious body. The Court held that as long as he had a sincere belief that his religion required him to refrain from work, there was no requirement to prove that the belief should represent a tenet of a religious organization.[129]

[124] *US v Ballard* 322 US 78 (1944) (US Supreme Court) 86–87.
[125] *Zengin v Turkey* (n 109) para [54].
[126] *Thomas v Review Board of Indiana Employment Security Div* (n 123). [127] ibid, 715–16.
[128] *Frazee v Illinois Department of Employment Security* 428 US 829 (1989) (US Supreme Court).
[129] ibid.

The Supreme Court of Canada has similarly held that it is not for the Court to determine whether a claimed custom or practice is a requirement of the applicant's religion. This was tested in *Syndicat Northcrest v Amselem*,[130] which concerned an attempt by the co-owners of apartments in Quebec to prohibit their neighbours, Orthodox Jews, from erecting sukkot, or temporary shelters, on the balconies of their apartments during the nine-day festival of Sukkot. During Sukkot, Jews commemorate the temporary shacks in which the biblical Jews lived during the forty years wandering in the desert after being freed from slavery in Egypt. The co-owners claimed that the sukkot violated the by-laws of the apartment complex, which prohibited decorations, alterations, and constructions on the balconies. The trial judge granted an injunction, holding that it was not obligatory but only customary for Orthodox Jews to build a sukkah on their own premises, and therefore there was no infringement of freedom of religion.

The Supreme Court of Canada allowed the appeal. Citing the US cases of *Thomas* and *Frazee*, the Court held that all that was required was sincerity of belief, irrespective of whether a particular practice or belief is required by official religious dogma: 'To require a person to prove that his or her religious practices are supported by a mandatory doctrine of faith, leaving it for judges to determine what those mandatory doctrines of faith are, would require courts to interfere with profoundly personal beliefs'.[131] At the same time, Iaccobucci J regarded it as necessary to set the outer boundaries of the meaning of religion to differentiate such beliefs, convictions, and practices from those which are secular, socially based, or conscientiously held.

> Religion typically involves a particular and comprehensive system of faith and worship. Religion also tends to involve the belief in a divine, superhuman or controlling power. In essence, religion is about freely and deeply held personal convictions or beliefs connected to an individual's spiritual faith and integrally linked to one's self-definition and spiritual fulfilment, the practices of which allow individuals to foster a connection with the divine or with the subject or object of that spiritual faith.[132]

This was reinforced in *Multani*,[133] where a Sikh pupil was barred from a school in Quebec for wearing a kirpan to school. A kirpan, which is a metal dagger or sword, is one of five religious symbols which orthodox Sikhs are required to wear. Despite its form, the religious symbolism of the kirpan is not one of aggression or threat, but the opposite, deriving from the word 'kirpa' which means mercy and kindness. The school nevertheless took the view that it was a dangerous weapon and offered to allow him to wear a wooden or plastic version. The pupil and his father refused, on the grounds that this would not fulfil their religious obligations. The Supreme Court of Canada reiterated that all that the pupil needed to prove was that he sincerely believed he should adhere to this practice in order to comply with the requirements of his religion. The fact that other Sikhs might have accepted a compromise was not relevant, since people

[130] *Syndicat Northcrest v Amselem* (2004) 2 SCR 551 (Supreme Court of Canada).
[131] ibid, para [49]. [132] ibid, para [39].
[133] *Multani v Commission scolaire Marguerite-Bourgeoys* (2006) SCC 6 (Supreme Court of Canada).

who profess the same religion might adhere to its dogma and practices to varying degrees of rigour.

The South African Constitutional Court has taken a similar stand. In *Prince v President of the Law Society*, the applicant, convicted of smoking cannabis, claimed that cannabis was a central practice of the Rastafari religion. The respondents challenged this assertion. Ngcobo J had no doubt that the Court should not be concerned with the question of whether a particular practice was central to the religion:

> Human beings may freely believe in what they cannot prove. Yet, that their beliefs are bizarre, illogical or irrational to others or are incapable of scientific proof, does not detract from the fact that these are religious beliefs for the purposes of enjoying the protection guaranteed by the right to freedom of religion. The believers should not be put to the proof of their beliefs or faith.[134]

This raises the further question whether practices, which the religion itself regards as voluntary, should be protected and accommodated as part of freedom of religion. The traditional basis for invalidating laws which prohibit the exercise of obligatory religious practices is that it puts adherents in the painful position of having to choose between observance of their faith and a breach of the law. A wider principle is necessary to include voluntary practices, particularly since such practices are often on the boundary between religion and culture. This question arose before the South African Constitutional Court in *Pillay*,[135] where a schoolgirl was disciplined for wearing a nose stud to school. Her mother claimed that the school rule banning the wearing of jewellery constituted unfair discrimination on grounds of religion and culture. Expert witnesses on Hinduism informed the court that the practice of wearing a nose-stud was an expression of South Indian Tamil Hindu culture, but that it was not obligatory, nor a religious rite. Langa CJ, citing the stream of cases described above, agreed that in order to determine if a practice or belief qualifies as religious, the only question to be answered by the court is whether the claimant's belief is sincere. The same was true for culture.[136] But what principle can be used to extend protection to voluntary practices? For Langa CJ, the answer lies in the centrality of religious and cultural practices to human dignity and identity. Human dignity is rooted in freedom to choose the ends which we value. 'That we choose voluntarily rather than through a feeling of obligation only enhances the significance of a practice to our autonomy, our identity and our dignity'.[137]

The ECtHR, while broadly endorsing the sincerity of belief test, has also required such beliefs to reach a threshold of cogency, seriousness, cohesion, and importance. This has been partly necessary because Article 2 of Protocol 1 refers not just to religion, but 'religious and philosophical convictions'. Thus, in *Campbell and Cosans*, parents objected to the use of corporal punishment as a disciplinary measure in the schools attended by their children.[138] The UK Government argued that the applicants'

[134] *Prince v President of the Law Society of the Cape of Good Hope (CCT 36/00)* [2002] ZACC 1; 2002 (2) SA 794 (South African Constitutional Court) para [42].

[135] *MEC for Education: Kwazulu-Natal and Others v Pillay (CCT 51/06)* [2007] ZACC 21; 2008 (1) SA 474 (CC); 2008 (2) BCLR 99 (South African Constitutional Court).

[136] ibid, para [54].

[137] ibid, para [64].

[138] *Campbell and Cosans v UK* (1982) 4 EHRR 293 (European Court of Human Rights).

views on the use of corporal punishment did not amount to 'philosophical convictions', but were merely opinions on the issue of discipline. The Court held that the word 'convictions' required more than opinions and ideas. Instead, it was similar to the concept of 'beliefs' in Article 9, which 'denotes views that attain a certain level of cogency, seriousness, cohesion and importance'. The expression 'philosophical convictions', in turn, denoted 'such convictions as are worthy of respect in a "democratic society" and are not incompatible with human dignity; in addition, they must not conflict with the fundamental right of the child to education'. In this case, the parents' views satisfied these criteria; they

> relate[d] to a weighty and substantial aspect of human life and behaviour, namely the integrity of the person, the propriety or otherwise of the infliction of corporal punishment and the exclusion of the distress which the risk of such punishment entails ... [I]t is this that distinguishes them from opinions that might be held on other methods of discipline or on discipline in general.[139]

The Court's approach was, however, more intrusive in *Valsamis v Greece*,[140] where Jehovah's Witnesses complained that a penalty of one day's suspension had been imposed by the school on their children for refusing to take part in a parade commemorating the outbreak of war between Greece and Fascist Italy in 1940. The applicants argued that pacifism is a fundamental tenet of their religion and forbids any conduct associated with war or violence. The Court rejected their claim. Reiterating the principle that 'religious and philosophical convictions' does not simply refer to any opinions or ideas but denotes views that attain a certain level of cogency, seriousness, cohesion, and importance, the Court did not accept the parents' assertion that the parade violated their pacifist convictions. Instead, it held that such commemorations of national events serve both pacifist objectives and the public interest. It also refused to enter into the question of whether other ways could be found of achieving these objectives.[141] This contrasts with the dissenters, who held that the parents' perception of the symbolism of the school parade and its religious and philosophical connotations should be accepted by the Court unless it was obviously unfounded and unreasonable.

The Indian approach goes much further than that of the ECtHR. Whereas courts in other jurisdictions are loath to look behind 'sincerely held' beliefs, the Indian Court has stridden confidently into this marshy terrain. This is partly a result of the constitutional framework, which, as we saw above, combines strong protection for religious autonomy with a mandate for the State to become involved in religious affairs, including regulating economic, political, or other secular activity associated with religious practice. It also permits the State to provide for 'the throwing open of Hindu religious institutions of a public character to all classes and sections of Hindus'.[142] There are two main factors fuelling the Court's scrutiny of claims of the religious source of contested practices. The first is to prevent religious sects from claiming not to be Hindu in order to evade the requirement to open their temples to Dalits (castes

139 ibid, para [36].

140 *Valsamis v Greece* (1997) 24 EHRR 294 (European Court of Human Rights).

141 ibid, paras [31]–[32].

142 Article 25(2)(b).

which have been subjected to untouchability). The second is to increase accountability and diminish opportunities for corruption by those in charge of the rich resources of India's many religious denominations. By narrowing the definition of exclusively religious practices, State regulation over the affairs of religious institutions is increased.[143]

One way of achieving this is to apply the 'broad and inclusive' understanding of Hinduism seen above. Thus, in its quest for a broad application of the prohibition on the exclusion of Dalits from temples, the Indian Supreme Court has sought a correspondingly broad and flexible definition of Hinduism. This was the approach in the *Satsangi* case,[144] in which the Swaminarayan sect claimed that they were distinct and separate from the Hindu religion, and therefore were entitled to exclude Dalits from their temples. In rejecting their claim, the Court stressed the breadth and inclusiveness of the Hindu religion. Acknowledging that the Hindu religion is difficult, if not impossible to define, because it does not claim any one god, subscribe to any one dogma, or follow any one set of religious practices, the Court preferred to describe it as 'a way of life and nothing more'. Above all, it characterized the Hindu religion as tolerant and inclusive, so that all sects which grew out of it feature a 'kind of subtle indescribable unity which keeps them within the sweep of the broad and progressive Hindu religion'.[145] The result was that, despite describing itself as a separate sect, the Swaminarayan sect remained part of Hinduism and therefore had to permit Dalits to worship in its temples.

The breadth of the conception of religion, however, opened the way to argue that the duty to allow temples to be accessible violated the right of a religious denomination to manage its own affairs 'in matters of religion'.[146] This was the challenge mounted by the Gowda Saraswath Brahmins against the Madras Temple Entry Act, which required that all public Hindu temples be accessible to Dalits.[147] The Court acknowledged that there was a clash between the duty to open public Hindu temples to all castes (Article 25(2)(b)) and religious autonomy (Article 26(b)). However, by classing itself as a denomination, the Gowda Saraswath Brahmins could not exclude itself from the broad sweep of the provision, which applied to all 'Hindu religious institutions' without qualification. In the interests of a harmonious reading of potentially conflicting provisions in the Constitution, the Court held that Article 25(2) took priority over the provision for religious autonomy.

The Court's broad approach to the meaning of Hinduism has extended to the benefits as well as the responsibilities attached to being Hindu. Reservations (or affirmative action) in India are based on membership of a scheduled caste, making it very important for candidates to prove that they are indeed Hindus and members of scheduled castes. In *Gampat v Returning Officer*,[148] an unsuccessful candidate in an election challenged the election results by claiming that one of the successful candidates should not have been regarded as eligible for a seat reserved for scheduled castes, given that,

[143] Sen (n 53) 65.
[144] *Sastri Yagnapurushadji v Muldas Brudardas Vaishya* AIR 1966 SC 1119 (Indian Supreme Court).
[145] ibid, 18. [146] Article 26(b).
[147] *Sri Venkataramana Devaruand v State of Mysore* AIR 1958 SC 255 (Indian Supreme Court).
[148] *Gampat v Returning Officer* AIR 1975 SC 420 (Indian Supreme Court).

although born and married as a Hindu, he had allegedly converted to Buddhism. The Court held that

> Hinduism is so tolerant and Hindu religious practices so varied and eclectic that one would find it difficult to say whether one is practising or professing Hindu religion or not. Especially when one is born a Hindu the fact that he goes to a Buddhist temple or a church or a durgah cannot be said to show that they are no more Hindus unless it is clearly proved that they have changed their religion from Hinduism to some other religion.

All the practices submitted to evince Buddhism could easily have fallen under Hinduism, and therefore it could not be said that there had been a conversion.

Similarly, the Court has suggested that communities such as Jains should be regarded as part of the wider Hindu community and that 'Hinduism can be called a general religion and common faith of India whereas "Jainism" is a special religion formed on the basis of quintessence of Hindu religion'.[149] This militated against their claim for minority status in their own right, and the special protection which comes with such status. Behind this is the Court's concern that to recognize too many religious minorities for the purposes of special rights and reservations would be divisive and a threat to the secular structure of the State.[150]

A different way of keeping judicial control over religious autonomy has been the controversial 'essential practices' doctrine. The doctrine was first articulated in *Shirur Mutt* in 1954,[151] in which a religious denomination argued that legislation regulating the affairs of Hindu religious endowments violated their right under Article 26 to manage their own affairs 'in matters of religion'. This required the Court to articulate what constituted a religious matter. Expressly distancing itself from US theistic approaches to religion, the Court emphasized that freedom of religion protected both religious belief and religious practices. According to Mukherjea J:

> Religion is ... not necessarily theistic. There are well known religions in India like Buddhism and Jainism which do not believe in God or in any Intelligent First Cause. A religion undoubtedly has its basis in a system of beliefs or doctrines ... but it would not be correct to say that religion is nothing else, but a doctrine or belief. A religion may not only lay down a code of ethical rules for its followers to accept, it might prescribe rituals and observances, ceremonies and modes of worship which are regarded as integral parts of religion.[152]

The Court went on to hold that the State could only regulate activities which were economic, commercial, or political in their character, although associated with a religious practice. Where practices were an 'essential part of the religion', the fact that they involved the expenditure of money, or the employment of priests or other employees,

[149] *Bal Patil and Another v Union of India and Others* 8 August, 2005 (Indian Supreme Court), 7 <https://indiankanoon.org/doc/502741/> (accessed 7 March 2018).

[150] ibid, 9.

[151] *The Commissioner, Hindu Religious Endowments, Madras v Sri Lakshmindra Thirtha Swamiar of Sri Shirur Mutt* AIR 1954 SC 282, (1954) SCR 1005 (Indian Supreme Court).

[152] ibid, para [17].

or the use of marketable commodities, did not mean that they became commercial. Equally importantly, 'what constitutes the essential part of a religion is primarily to be ascertained with reference to the doctrines of that religion itself'.[153]

Although *Shirur Mutt* is usually credited with the development of the essential practices doctrine, it can be seen from this dictum that Mukherjea J regarded it as a deferential principle, referring to the doctrines of the religion itself to determine what was essential. In fact, as Surendrenath points out, the Court in that case was only concerned at drawing a line between the religious and the secular, rather than determining which parts of the religion were essential and which were not.[154] Later cases, however, used this notion in a far more intrusive way, with the Court taking responsibility not only for determining the distinction between secular and religious practices, but also of sifting out superstitious beliefs from genuinely religious practice.[155] Thus, in a dispute over the management of a sacred tomb, Chishti Sufis claimed that they should be regarded as a separate sect from the broader group of Hanafi Muslims. The Court found it necessary to enquire into 'the nature of the tenets and beliefs to which Soofism subscribes', to determine whether the sect could be regarded as a religious denomination for the purposes of Article 26. Its main concern was that secular practices or superstitious beliefs would be 'clothed in religious form' in order to found a claim to be a religious denomination for the purposes of claiming religious autonomy. Thus, Gajendragadkar J stated:

> Even practices though religious may have sprung from merely superstitious beliefs and may in that sense be extraneous and unessential accretions to religion itself. Unless such practices are found to constitute an essential and integral part of a religion their claim for the protection under Art. 26 may have to be carefully scrutinised; in other words, the protection must be confined to such religious practices as are an essential and an integral part of it and no other.[156]

As Sen comments,

> This extraordinary statement by the Court pushed the essential practices doctrine in a new direction. The Court was not only going to play the role of the gatekeeper as to what qualified as religion; but now it was also taking up the role of sifting superstition from 'real' religion.[157]

This was reinforced in *Govindlalji*,[158] where Gajendragadkar J made it clear, in stark contrast to the US Supreme Court, that it was up to the Court to resolve rival contentions within a religious group in relation to religious practices. Since the community may 'speak with more than one voice', the question should always be decided by the Court, not just as to whether a practice was religious or secular, but also if it was an

[153] ibid, para [20].

[154] A Surendranath, 'Essential Practices Doctrine: Towards an Inevitable Constitutional Burial' (2016) 15 Journal of the National Human Rights Commission 159.

[155] *The Durgah Committee, Ajmer v Syed Hussain Ali* AIR 1961 SC 1402, [1962] SCR (1) 383 (Indian Supreme Court).

[156] ibid. [157] Sen (n 53) 55.

[158] *Govindlalji v Rajasthan* AIR 1963 SC 1638, [1964] SCR (1) 561 (Indian Supreme Court).

integral or essential part of the religion. Later cases elaborated on what constituted an essential practice. In the 2004 case of *Commissioner of Police v Acharya*, the Court stated:

> Essential part of a religion means the core beliefs upon which a religion is founded ... Test to determine whether a part or practice is essential to a religion is to find out whether the nature of the religion be changed without that part or practice ... It is such permanent essential parts which are protected by the Constitution.[159]

The result of the Court's narrowing down of the concept of religion to include only essential practices has been to correspondingly narrow the applicability of the right to religious autonomy in Article 26.

As Surendranath persuasively argues, it would be preferable for Indian courts, like courts in other jurisdictions, to take a broad view of religion and instead place the primary emphasis on whether State intervention can be justified in the ways provided for in the Constitution.[160] This would mean, as in other jurisdictions, that rather than ruling out the applicability of the right at the threshold, leaving State intervention unregulated, the Court could weigh up the proportionality of the interference against the public interest or the rights of others.

V. Free Exercise and Neutral Laws

The discussion in section IV concerned whether an individual is entitled to claim that her beliefs or practices are religious and therefore within the protection of freedom of religion. But this is not the end of the matter. This section asks how courts have decided whether a State is justified in limiting that right, or, alternatively, required to accommodate religious manifestation. This issue has arisen in numerous contexts, too many to cover here. Instead it focuses on one key issue, which has attracted much comparative jurisprudence. This concerns rules which are apparently neutral on their face, but which in fact burden religious adherents more than others. To what extent is the State entitled to require believers to conform to the general law of the land; and when should exceptions be created to accommodate believers? This issue is complicated by the conflicts of normative authority created by religion: at its starkest, it puts believers in the predicament of risking 'divine punishment' by conforming to secular rules, or secular punishment by conforming to the dictates of their religion. For courts, the difficulty is often dealt with through calibrating the standard of review, so that many cases are fought on the question of the strictness of judicial scrutiny.

These themes are captured well in Brennan J's strong statement in favour of accommodation in the US Court case of *Sherbert v Verner*.[161] In this case, a member of the Seventh-day Adventists Church was dismissed by her employer for refusing to work on Saturdays, the Sabbath day of her faith. She was disqualified from claiming unemployment benefits on the ground that she had failed 'without good cause' to accept 'suitable work' as required by relevant legislation. The Supreme Court held that

[159] *Commissioner of Police v Acharya* 2004 (12) SCC 770 (Indian Supreme Court) 782–83.

[160] Surendranath (n 154).

[161] *Sherbert v Verner* 374 US 398 (1963) (US Supreme Court).

her First Amendment freedom of religion rights had been violated. According to Brennan J, giving judgment for the Court:

> The ruling forces her to choose between following the precepts of her religion and forfeiting benefits, on the one hand, and abandoning one of the precepts of her religion in order to accept work, on the other hand. Governmental imposition of such a choice puts the same kind of burden upon the free exercise of religion as would a fine imposed against [the] appellant for her Saturday worship.[162]

The Court went on to consider whether some compelling State interest justified this infringement. Importantly, the Court set the standard of justification high. A mere rational relationship to a colourable State interest would not be sufficient; only a grave abuse or danger could constitute justification. Here no such danger had been advanced: the State's argument that this would invite fraudulent claims feigning religious objections was not sustained on the evidence. This, as Stewart J pointed out in his concurrence, conflicts strikingly with *Braunfield v Brown* where the burden of Sunday closing rules was far more onerous. In his view, *Braunfeld* was wrongly decided and should be overruled.

Much more difficult are cases in which the challenged law clearly promotes individual safety or well-being, such as the prohibition of child labour, the prevention of drug abuse, or health and safety requirements on the road or on construction sites. Courts in different jurisdictions have struggled to find an appropriate accommodation, generally leaning in favour of requiring individuals to conform to the laws of the land. Thus, in the US case *Prince v Massachusetts*,[163] a Jehovah's Witness was convicted of breaching the child labour laws when she positioned her nine-year-old niece on a city pavement to offer copies of religious pamphlets for sale to passers-by. Both the accused and her niece stated that proselytism was a religious duty, breach of which would condemn them to 'everlasting destruction at Armageddon'.[164] In rejecting her claim, the Court simply held that child labour laws were within the authority of the State. It did not apply a compelling interest test. This can be contrasted with *Yoder*, where, as we saw in Chapter 11, the Court was willing to accept that Amish children over the age of fourteen could be required to work on the Amish lands when this was regarded as part of their religious education.[165]

What if the law is aimed at protecting the individual believer's health and safety, but the latter considers that her beliefs require her to take the risk? These dilemmas have specifically focused on health and safety laws requiring builders on construction sites to wear a hard hat, or motorcyclists to wear helmets. Should an exemption be provided for turban-wearing Sikhs? The United Nations Human Rights Committee (HRC) in *Bhinder v Canada* held that although such a provision was prima facie indirectly discriminatory, it could nevertheless be reasonably justified on the ground that it aimed at protecting workers from injury and was reasonable under the International Covenant on Civil and Political Rights (ICCPR). The Supreme Court of Canada, by contrast, has taken a more accommodating approach, holding that since the applicant's failure to wear a

[162] ibid, 404.
[163] *Prince v Massachusetts* 321 US 158 (1944) (US Supreme Court).
[164] ibid 163.
[165] *Wisconsin v Yoder* 406 US 205 (1972) (US Supreme Court).

hard hat would only increase the risk to himself marginally, the hard hat rule could not be regarded as a reasonably necessary limitation on the right. For a case where a neutral rule has particular adverse effects on an individual for religious reasons, the test is not whether the rule is valid in its entirety, but whether the individual can be accommodated by way of exception to the general rule without undue hardship on the part of the employer.[166] In the UK, Sikhs have been exempted from wearing crash helmets on motor cycles since 1976[167] and hard hats on construction sites since 1989,[168] and this was extended to all other sectors where hard hats are required for safety reasons in 2015. This is accompanied by protection for employers from liability for injuries incurred by individuals through not wearing a hard hat. On the other hand, such exemptions are not cost free for society. Individuals injured in such circumstances are still eligible for National Health Service care.

The extent to which society should be able to override individual beliefs raises particularly acute challenges in relation to the criminal prohibition of drug abuse. The apex courts in both the US and South Africa have confronted claims that prohibitions on religiously inspired use of prohibited drugs constitute a breach of the free exercise of religion. *Oregon v Smith* concerned the sacramental use of peyote, a hallucinogen which was prohibited for possession and use. The respondents were fired from their jobs at a drug rehabilitation centre because they ingested peyote for sacramental purposes at a ceremony of the Native American Church. They were denied unemployment benefit on the grounds that they were discharged for work-related misconduct. The US Supreme Court rejected their claim under the Free Exercise Clause. Giving the judgment of the Court, Scalia J held that the right of free exercise did not relieve an individual of the obligation to comply with a valid and neutral law of general applicability on the ground that the law proscribes conduct that their religion requires, or requires conduct that their religion prohibits.[169] Scalia J went further and held that the 'compelling interest' test in *Sherbert v Verner* should not be applied generally to Free Exercise cases, and especially not to across-the-board criminal prohibitions on a particular form of conduct:

> To make an individual's obligation to obey such a law contingent upon the law's coincidence with his religious beliefs, except where the State's interest is 'compelling'—permitting him, by virtue of his beliefs, 'to become a law unto himself,' contradicts both constitutional tradition and common sense.[170]

The 'compelling state interest' test, in his view, was appropriate for race discrimination or freedom of speech, but not, as he put it, to a 'private right to ignore generally applicable rules'.[171] Instead, he concluded, 'if prohibiting the exercise of religion is merely the incidental effect of a generally applicable and otherwise valid provision,

[166] *Central Alberta Dairy Pool v Alberta (Human Rights Commission)* [1990] 2 SCR 489 (Canadian Supreme Court) 517.

[167] Motor-Cycle Crash Helmets (Religious Exemption) Act 1976, s 2A.

[168] Employment Act 1989, s 11.

[169] *Employment Division, Department of Human Resources of Oregon v Smith* 494 US 872 (1990) (US Supreme Court) 879.

[170] ibid, 885, citing *Reynolds v United States* 98 US 145 (1879) (US Supreme Court) 167.

[171] *Employment Division, Department of Human Resources of Oregon v Smith* (n 169) 885.

the First Amendment has not been offended'.[172] O'Connor J, while concurring in the result, gave a robust defence of the compelling interest test. For her,

> the essence of a free exercise claim is relief from a burden imposed by government on religious practices or beliefs, whether the burden is imposed directly through laws that prohibit or compel specific religious practices, or indirectly through laws that, in effect, make abandonment of one's own religion or conformity to the religious beliefs of others the price of an equal place in the civil community.[173]

Free exercise of religion could only be limited if the State had a compelling interest in doing so and there were no less intrusive means.

Scalia and O'Connor JJ also disagreed over the extent to which individual belief can be accommodated through exceptions. Scalia J acknowledged that a number of States had made an exception to their drug laws for sacramental peyote use. But this was a matter for the political process and could not be imposed by courts. He recognized that 'leaving accommodation to the political process will place at a relative disadvantage those religious practices that are not widely engaged in'. Nevertheless, in his view, 'that unavoidable consequence of democratic government must be preferred to a system in which each conscience is a law unto itself or in which judges weigh the social importance of all laws against the centrality of all religious beliefs'.[174] O'Connor J took issue with the view that the disfavouring of minority religions was an unavoidable consequence of the US system of government and that accommodation should be left to the political process: 'In my view ... the First Amendment was enacted precisely to protect the rights of those whose religious practices are not shared by the majority and may be viewed with hostility'.[175] In the case before the Court, however, she found that the State had discharged its burden of proof of compelling interest, namely the protection of the health and safety of its citizens. This was notwithstanding the fact that several States do in fact provide an exemption.

These crucially different perspectives set in motion a battle of wills between legislators and shifting judicial majorities. Three years after *Oregon v Smith*, Congress passed the Religious Freedom Restoration Act of 1993 (RFRA), which aimed to restore the 'compelling interest' test in *Sherbert v Verner*. The legislation prohibited the government from substantially burdening a person's exercise of religion even if the burden followed from a rule of general applicability, unless the government demonstrated that the burden as applied to an individual furthers a compelling government interest and is the least restrictive means of furthering that interest. At the same time, a regulatory exemption for the religious use of peyote was extended to all members of every recognized Native American or Indian Tribe.[176]

However, this was not the end of the matter. In *City of Boerne v Flores*,[177] the Court held that the RFRA was unconstitutional as applied to States, because it was not a proper exercise of the enforcement power of Congress. In response, a number of States

[172] ibid, 878. [173] ibid, 897. [174] ibid, 890. [175] ibid, 902.

[176] *Gonzales v O Centro Espirita Beneficente União do Vegetal* 546 US 418 (2006) (US Supreme Court) 433.

[177] *City of Boerne v Flores* 521 US 507 (1997) (US Supreme Court).

passed their own versions of the statute, which allowed them to restore the compelling interest test to their own State laws. In 2006 in *Gonzales*, on the other hand, the Supreme Court upheld the RFRA at federal level. The case concerned a small Christian spiritist sect União do Vegetal (UDV) with origins in the Amazon Rainforest, which receives Communion by drinking a sacramental tea, brewed from plants unique to the region which contain a prohibited hallucinogen. The Court applied the compelling interest test set out in the RFRA and found that the government had not discharged its burden. Roberts CJ put particular weight on the fact that an exemption had been granted for sacramental use of peyote for hundreds of thousands of Native Americans; whereas no consideration had been given to doing the same for approximately 130 American members of UDV. This also undermined the government's claim that the effectiveness of the Controlled Substances Act would be undercut if it were not uniformly applied.

This approach can be contrasted with the South African case of *Prince v President of the Law Society*,[178] where the South African Constitutional Court held that it was too difficult to craft an exemption to the prohibition on cannabis to accommodate Rastafarian religious use of the substance. The Court found a prima facie breach of the applicant's freedom of religion: followers of the Rastafari religion were forced to choose between following their religion or complying with the law. As in the US cases, the outcome therefore depended on whether the limitation on the right was legitimate. Referring to *Smith v Oregon*, Chaskalson P and Ackermann and Kriegler JJ preferred the compelling interest test in principle, although they reiterated that the South African approach is not expressly based on different levels of scrutiny, but 'a nuanced and context-sensitive form of balancing' in the section 36 proportionality analysis. On this view, the test was 'whether the failure to accommodate the appellant's religious belief and practice by means of the exemption … can be accepted as reasonable and justifiable in an open and democratic society based on human dignity, freedom and equality'.[179]

The Court recognized that failure to accommodate Rastafari religious use of cannabis 'strikes at the very core of their human dignity. It says that their religion is not worthy of protection. The impact of the limitation is profound indeed'.[180] On the other hand, the government objective in prohibiting the use of cannabis, namely to protect the public from psychological and physical harm, was undoubted. The question therefore was whether an appropriate exception could be carved out without undermining the objective of the prohibition. By a narrow majority of five to four, the Court concluded that it could not. The majority held that the use of cannabis by Rastafarians differed in important ways from that of peyote in *Smith v Oregon*. Whereas the latter was confined to church ceremonies, there was a flourishing illicit trade in cannabis and Rastafari use was not confined to the particular context of a religious ceremony.[181] There was no objective way a law enforcement official could distinguish between the

[178] *Prince v President of the Law Society of the Cape of Good Hope (CCT 36/00)* (n 134).

[179] ibid, para 46, citing *Christian Education South Africa v Minister of Education* 2000 (4) SA 757 (CC), 2000 (10) BCLR 1051 (CC) (South African Constitutional court) para [32].

[180] *Prince v President of the Law Society of the Cape of Good Hope (CCT 36/00)* (n 134) para [51].

[181] ibid, para [129].

use of cannabis for religious purposes and for recreation.[182] This was even more so for its possession and acquisition. The Court therefore concluded that if an exemption were to be permitted for the possession and use of harmful drugs by persons for religious purposes, the State's ability to enforce its drug legislation would be substantially impaired. The court was also concerned with the potential for harm of the Rastafarian user himself, subject only to his own self-control. This conclusion was upheld by both the HRC[183] and the African Commission.[184]

VI. Conflicting Rights: Religious Freedom and Equalities

Freedom of religion demands tolerance and accommodation of religious belief and manifestation, particularly by those who do not believe or believe differently. But does it demand that religious adherents tolerate other value systems and identities, even when this might conflict with their religious belief? The major theistic religions give women secondary status, and many regard homosexuality as contrary to their fundamental beliefs. Some religions have been openly racist, an example being the Dutch Reformed Church in South Africa during apartheid. How then does human rights law reconcile conflicts between two fundamental rights, the right to freedom of religion and the right to equality? A different way forward could be to avoid characterizing this as a conflict of rights. Instead, it could be argued that nothing in the right to freedom of religion includes the right to harm others, where harm includes treating them with less than equal concern and respect. While religious adherents are not compelled to change their beliefs, manifestation of belief should not be permitted to trump the overriding right of each person to equal respect and concern. Increasingly, however, religious adherents are claiming that they should not be required to be 'complicit' in what they regard as sinful behaviour, such as same-sex marriage or abortion and contraception.[185] The first part of this section addresses such claims, and the second turns to the foundational conflicts based on religious personal laws and their implications for sexual orientation and gender equality.

A. Complicity claims

'Complicity-based conscience claims' are distinctive in that accommodating them may inflict material and dignitary harms on others. As NeJaime and Siegel point out, 'accommodating the claim has the distinctive power to stigmatize and demean third parties'.[186] This is particularly so where such objections, although couched in religious terms, feed into and reinforce existing social prejudices.

[182] ibid, para [130].
[183] *Prince v South Africa* (2007) AHRLR 40 (HRC 2007) (Human Rights Committee).
[184] *Prince v South Africa* (2004) AHRLR 105 (ACHPR 2004) (African Commission on People's and Human Rights).
[185] D NeJaime and R Siegel, 'Conscience Wars: Complicity Based Conscience Claims in Religion and Politics' (2015) 124 Yale L J 2516, 2516.
[186] ibid, 2566.

Thus far, courts in the UK and the ECtHR have resisted complicity claims, rightly rejecting assertions by religious adherents that the right to religion permits them to infringe on the equality, privacy, and dignity rights of others. This was clearly asserted in *Eweida v UK*,[187] which involved two complicity claims. The first was by Ladele, a marriage registrar who refused to conduct same-sex civil partnerships because she believed they were contrary to God's law. The second was by McFarlane, a counsellor for a private charity, who refused to provide psycho-sexual counselling to same-sex couples because of his belief that homosexual activity is sinful. Both were dismissed by their employers in pursuance of their equal opportunities policies. They claimed that this breached their freedom of religion and constituted religious discrimination. The ECtHR held that it was legitimate for the employers to give priority to pursuing equality and non-discrimination on grounds of sexual orientation. Although the Court recognized the serious consequences for the applicants, it held that the State had a wide margin of appreciation when it came to balancing rights, which had not been exceeded in this case.[188] At the same time, the Court rejected the argument that the applicants had waived their rights by accepting employment which included responsibilities impacting on their freedom of religion. In a significant reversal of its previous position, the Court held that this did not preclude them from claiming an interference with Article 9 rights. Any awareness of the demands of the job should instead be a factor in determining the proportionality of the measure.

A similar stand against complicity claims can be seen in the UK and Northern Ireland courts. The UK Supreme Court case of *Bull v Hall* was an express complicity claim by religious proprietors of a small hotel, Mr and Mrs Bull. They believed that sexual relations should only take place within heterosexual marriage, and that if they permitted unmarried couples to share a double bed, they would be involved in promoting sinful behaviour. They therefore restricted the rental of their double-bedded rooms to heterosexual married couples. Preddy and Hall, a same-sex couple in a civil partnership, were refused a room in the hotel. When they successfully argued that they had been discriminated against on grounds of sexual orientation, Mr and Mrs Bull, complained that their freedom of religion under Article 9 ECHR had been violated. The Supreme Court held that freedom of religion in this case could not justify the discrimination. The restriction on freedom of religion was a proportionate means of protecting the claimants' rights not to be discriminated against on grounds of sexual orientation. Given the continuing legacy of centuries of discrimination and persecution on grounds of sexual orientation, 'we should be slow to accept that prohibiting hotel keepers from discriminating against homosexuals is a disproportionate limitation on their right to manifest their religion'.[189]

This approach was closely followed by the Northern Ireland Court of Appeal in the vividly named 'cake wars' litigation. In the *Ashers* case, a bakery refused to go ahead with an order placed by Lee for a cake decorated with the headline caption 'Support Gay Marriage'.[190] The proprietors regarded gay marriage as sinful and against God's

[187] *Eweida v UK* [2013] 57 EHRR 8 (European Court of Human Rights).
[188] ibid, para [106]. [189] *Bull v Hall* [2013] UKSC 73 (Supreme Court (UK)) para [53].
[190] *Lee v McArthur and Others* [2016] NICA 39 (24 October 2016) (Northern Ireland Court of Appeal).

law. The bakery was found to have discriminated against Lee on the grounds of sexual orientation under the relevant Northern Ireland legislation.[191] The bakery challenged this decision under Article 9 ECHR. The Northern Ireland Court of Appeal rejected this argument. Given that there was clearly a legitimate aim, namely the protection of the rights and interests of others, the key question was whether there was a reasonable relationship of proportionality between the aim of the legislation and the means used to achieve it. The Court held that there was. In a robust articulation of the arguments against a 'complicity' exemption, Sir Declan Morgan LCJ stated: 'If businesses were free to choose what services to provide to the gay community on the basis of religious belief the potential for arbitrary abuse would be substantial'.[192] The case has been appealed to the UK Supreme Court but judgment had not yet been handed down at the time of writing.[193]

The US Supreme Court took a different view of similar facts in *Masterpiece Cake Shop v Colorado Civil Rights Commission*,[194] decided in 2018. In this case, Phillips, the proprietor of Masterpiece Cake Shop, refused to create a wedding cake for a same sex-couple because of his religious opposition to same-sex marriage. The couple alleged that this constituted discrimination on grounds of sexual orientation in violation of Colorado's Anti-Discrimination Act. The claim was upheld by an administrative court judge, the Colorado Civil Rights Commission, and the Colorado Court of Appeals.

The Supreme Court held by a 7–2 majority that Phillips' freedom of religion had been breached. However, it did so on narrow grounds relating to the particular facts of the case, namely that the Colorado Commission acted with hostility to the baker's religious beliefs and was therefore not 'neutral' towards religion. The Court reaffirmed that it was legitimate for Colorado to enact legislation to protect gay persons in acquiring products and services on the same terms as offered to other members of the public. According to Kennedy J, 'Our society has come to the recognition that gay persons and gay couples cannot be treated as social outcasts or as inferior in dignity and worth'. While it was acceptable to create an exception for clergy who refuse to perform gay weddings, such an exception should be narrowly confined. Otherwise 'a long list of persons who provide goods and services for weddings and marriage might refuse to do so for gay persons, thus resulting in a community-wide stigma inconsistent with the history and dynamics of civil rights laws that ensure equal access to goods, services and public accommodations'.

On the other hand, the principle that the law had to be applied in a manner neutral to religion had not been fulfilled in this case. First, the Court found evidence of hostility to religion in statements by individual Commissioners. Second, it found that the Commission had not acted consistently, indicating a bias against religion. Thus, the Commission had pursued a claim against Phillips for refusing to create a cake for a same-sex wedding. But it had previously refused to take the same steps against three

[191] Equality Act (Sexual Orientation) Regulations (Northern Ireland) 2006.
[192] *Lee v McArthur and Others* (n 190) para [64].
[193] *Lee v Ashers Baking Company Ltd and Others* (Northern Ireland) Case ID: UKSC 2017/0020.
[194] 584 US ______(2018) (US Supreme Court).

bakers who refused to create a cake requested by a customer with slogans hostile to gay rights, including a quote from Leviticus stating that 'homosexuality is a detestable sin'.

In her dissenting opinion, however, Ginsburg rejected both these findings. First, she held that the statements of one or two individual Commissioners should not vitiate a multi-layer set of independent decision-making, starting with an administrative law judge, and ending with a de novo hearing by the Colorado Court of Appeals. Second, and particularly importantly, she held that there is a legitimate distinction between the refusal to bake a wedding cake for a same-sex couple, and a refusal to place a demeaning message on a cake. The bakers in the earlier decisions had regularly refused to place any demeaning message on a cake, regardless of the customer's religious beliefs. The wedding cake requested by the same-sex couple in the *Masterpiece* case, by contrast, was identical to any other wedding cake. Thus, she concluded, Philips' refusal to provide the requested cake was not based on a refusal to convey a demeaning message, but directly on the identity of the same-sex couple.

A much more robust position was taken by the Supreme Court of Canada in *Trinity Western University*.[195] In this case, Trinity Western University (TWU), an evangelical Christian post-secondary institution, sought to open a law school that required its students and faculty to adhere to a religiously based code of conduct prohibiting 'sexual intimacy that violates the sacredness of marriage between a man and a woman'. The Covenant applied even when students were off-campus in their own homes. This led the Law Society of British Columbia and the Law Society of Ontario, which are responsible for determining the entry requirements to the legal profession in their provinces, to declare that the proposed law school was not an approved faculty of law. TWU and a prospective student challenged the decision as a violation of freedom of religion.

The Supreme Court of Canada rejected the claim. It accepted that the Law Societies' decisions constituted a limitation on the claimants' sincere belief that studying in an environment in which members follow particular rules of conduct furthered their spiritual development. However, it held that the Law Societies had acted proportionately in balancing the limitation on religious protections with its statutory objective of upholding and protecting the public interest. The Law Societies were entitled to conclude that ensuring equal access to the legal profession, supporting diversity within the bar, and preventing harm to LGBTQ law students were valid means to pursue the public interest.

Importantly, the Court emphasized that, at the balancing stage, the impact of religious practices on others can be taken into account. The Covenant enforced a religiously based code of conduct not just on the believer but also on others. 'Being required by someone else's religious beliefs to behave contrary to one's sexual identity is degrading and disrespectful. Being required to do so offends the public perception that freedom of religion includes freedom from religion'.[196] In the end, the Court held that the Law Societies' decisions did not deny any evangelical Christian the right to

[195] *Law Society of British Columbia v Trinity Western University* (2018) SCC 32 (Supreme Court of Canada); *Trinity Western University v Law Society of Upper Canada* (2018) SCC 33.

[196] *Law Society of British Columbia*, ibid [101].

practise their religion as and where they choose. At the same time, members of the TWU religious community were not free to impose those religious beliefs on fellow law students. As the majority put it: 'The [Law Society]'s decision ensures that equal access to the legal profession is not undermined and prevents the risk of significant harm to LGBTQ people who feel they have no choice but to attend TWU's proposed law school. It also maintains public confidence in the legal profession, which could be undermined by the [Law Society]'s decision to approve a law school that forces LGBTQ people to deny who they are for three years to receive a legal education'.[197]

The resistance to complicity claims in relation to sexual orientation has not, however, been replicated in relation to gender equality, at least on the part of the US Supreme Court. The most serious of such claims have taken the form of objections by religious employers to legislation requiring them to provide health insurance which includes contraception. They argue that this would make them complicit in employees purchasing forms of contraception (abortifacients) which they regarded as sinful. As we saw in Chapter 7, this was the basis on which Hobby Lobby claimed an exemption from the requirement to provide such insurance to their employees. In *Burley v Hobby Lobby Stores*, the Court upheld the claim.[198] Justice Alito, giving the opinion of the Court, accepted that Congress has a compelling interest in ensuring women's free access to contraception. However, because he took the view that there was an alternative means which sufficiently protected employees' interests in contraception, he held that the requirement to provide health insurance including contraception was not narrowly tailored to achieve that compelling interest. Although, in principle, the majority treated as weighty both the claimants' claim to religious freedom and Congress's interest in promoting women's health, NeJaime and Siegel argue that *Hobby Lobby* is now widely cited to support accommodation of complicity-based conscience claims in a wide range of contexts.[199] Far preferable is Justice Ginsburg's dissent, where she argued powerfully that First Amendment accommodation should not cover cases in which the free exercise of religion significantly impinges on third parties, here the heavy cost borne by thousands of female employees who did not share the corporation owners' religious faith. 'A "least restrictive means" cannot require employees to relinquish benefits accorded them by federal law in order to ensure that their commercial employers can adhere unreservedly to their religious tenets'.[200]

B. Marriage, divorce, and religious personal law

The reconciliation of religion and gender equality becomes particularly acute in relation to marriage and divorce. At one level, this appears as a conflict between the right of religious groups to have autonomy over their own affairs and a secular principle of gender equality.[201] However, this assumes a uniform reading of religious law and practice, ignoring contestation within the religion about the role of gender equality.

[197] ibid, [103]. [198] *Burwell v Hobby Lobby Stores* (n 122).
[199] NeJaime and Siegel (n 185) 2532. [200] *Burwell v Hobby Lobby Stores* (n 122) 2802.
[201] B Parekh, *Rethinking Multiculturalism* (Palgrave 2000); S Mulally, 'Feminism and Multicultural Dilemmas in India: Revisiting the Shah Bano Case' (2004) 24 Oxford Journal of Legal Studies 671, 687.

Recognition of internal contestation could nevertheless be reconciled with religious autonomy by regarding such contestation as an internal matter, for the religious group to determine according to its own culture of resolution. On another view, the principle of internal democracy or contestation becomes vacuous when women are routinely afforded secondary status. It is for this reason that Susan Moller Orkin has argued vehemently that multiculturalism is bad for women.[202] Others have argued that this too quickly dismisses the possibility of 'arriving at just multicultural arrangements'.[203] A further complexity is introduced once it is recognized that there is a need to incorporate pluralism among women's voices themselves. Women are entitled to articulate their own understanding of religion. But are some women entitled to renounce equality for themselves without derailing the right to gender equality itself?

These dilemmas play out in particularly acute form in relation to marriage. Many religions regard marriage as governed by religious laws, some of which conflict with the commitment to gender equality in human rights instruments. How then should these conflicting human rights be mediated? The Convention on the Elimination of All Forms of Discrimination Against Women (CEDAW) has no doubt that gender equality has priority. Article 16(1) requires States Parties to eliminate discrimination against women in all matters relating to marriage and family relations. Article 5(a) requires States Parties to take all appropriate measures to

> modify the social and cultural patterns of conduct of men and women, with a view to achieving the elimination of prejudices and customary and other practices which are based on the idea of the inferiority or the superiority of either of the sexes or on stereotyped roles for men and women.

Similarly, the HRC requires State Parties to ensure that 'traditional, historical, religious or cultural attitudes' do not serve as the basis of justifying 'violations of women's right to equality before the law and to equal enjoyment of all Covenant rights'.[204]

However, not all jurisdictions give such unequivocal primacy to gender equality. In India, the right of religions to govern personal law, including marriage, divorce, and succession, has been protected as part of a commitment to pluralism and the autonomy of religious communities, validated by the constitutional protection for minority and religious cultures. At the time of the drafting of the Constitution, the aspiration for a uniform civil code was not turned into an immediate binding commitment. Instead, it became one of the Directive Principles. Thus Article 44 of the Constitution directs the State to 'endeavour to secure a uniform civil code'. However, despite many calls by the Indian Supreme Court to fulfil this mandate, it has proved impossible to achieve, and personal law in India is still governed by the laws of the different religious communities. India has therefore entered a declaration to CEDAW stating that it will only comply with Articles 5(a) and Article 16(1) of CEDAW 'in conformity with its policy

[202] S Okin, 'Is Multiculturalism Bad for Women?' in J Cohen, J Howard, and N Nussbaum (eds), *Is Multiculturalism Bad for Women?* (Princeton University Press 1999).

[203] Mulally (n 201) 675.

[204] Human Rights Committee, General Comment No 28: Article 3 (The Equality of Rights Between Men and Women) (2000) UN Doc CCPR/C/21/Rev.1/Add.10.

of non-interference in the personal affairs of any Community without its initiative and consent'. The result is that, in Agnes's words: 'Group rights are awarded equal legitimacy and recognition as individual rights'.[205] Since there is no clear hierarchy between these norms,

> the interface between provisions of equality and non-discrimination enshrined in the Constitution and the prevalence of gender-discriminatory personal laws has led to a contestation between individual claims to equality, and the right of religious communities as collective units of a democracy.[206]

Law reform attempts primarily focused on granting rights to Hindu women, whose position was well behind those of other religious groups. This culminated in the Hindu Marriage Act 1955, which gave Hindu marriages contractual status, introduced divorce and other matrimonial remedies, and granted Hindu women equal inheritance rights.[207] The Act also applies to Buddhists, Sikhs, and Jains. Resistance to this process meant that many compromises were made: 'While projecting the reforms as pro-women, male privileges had to be protected. The Acts were neither Hindu in character nor based on modern principles of equality, but reflected the worst tendencies of both'.[208] Christian law reforms took even longer, and it was not until 2001 that the law was amended to introduce egalitarian grounds of divorce.[209]

Even more contested has been the relationship of gender equality and Muslim Personal Law. The Muslim Personal Law (Shariat) Application Act 1937, a colonial statute, provides that, 'notwithstanding any custom or usage to the contrary', in all questions regarding intestate succession, special property of females, marriage, dissolution of marriage, and other related issues, 'the rule of decision where the parties are Muslims shall be the Muslim Personal Law (Shariat)'.[210] Because the Hanafi Code of Muslim Law had no proviso allowing a married Muslim woman to dissolve her marriage, the Dissolution of Muslim Marriages Act 1939 provided the grounds on which a Muslim woman could divorce her husband. However, Muslim Personal Law remains the rule of decision in relation to the husband's right to divorce his wife.

The difficulty in reconciling gender equality and Muslim Personal Law is compounded by a strong line of authority to the effect that personal laws are insulated from judicial review so that they may not be scrutinized for fundamental rights violations. This is because of the wording of Article 13 of the Constitution, the key provision allowing judicial review for fundamental rights violations. Article 13(1) states that all laws in force in India immediately before the commencement of the Constitution would be void to the extent that they are inconsistent with the fundamental rights in the Constitution, while Article 13(2) declares that 'the State shall not make any law which takes away or abridges the rights conferred by this Part and any law made in contravention of this clause shall ... be void'. This raises the question of whether personal laws constitute 'law' within the purview of the Constitution.[211] In a much-cited

[205] F Agnes, 'Personal Laws' in S Choudhry, M Khosla, and P Mehta (eds), *The Oxford Handbook of the Indian Constitution* (OUP 2015) 909.

[206] ibid, 909. [207] ibid, 907. [208] ibid, 908. [209] ibid, 916. [210] Section 2.

[211] 'Law' includes custom or usage having the 'force of law' (Article 13(3)(a)) but force of law only refers to law made by a competent authority (Explanation 1).

case dating back to 1952,[212] *Narasu Appa Mali*, the Bombay High Court interpreted the phrases 'law' and 'law in force' in Article 13 to exclude personal law, thus putting personal law outside of the pale of judicial scrutiny for fundamental rights breaches. According to the two eminent judges in the case, the drafters of the Constitution intended to exclude personal law from Article 13, because they regarded reform of personal law as the responsibility of the legislature, rather than the courts.[213] This decision has been supported on several occasions by the Supreme Court.[214] In the 2017 *Triple Talaq* case,[215] two judges held that *Narasu Appa Mali* should be considered as the 'presently declared position of law';[216] two held that it was unnecessary to decide in this case; and the fifth judge did not deal directly with this point. It was argued in that case that the 1937 Act gives statutory force to Muslim Personal Law and therefore has the 'force of law' under Article 13. This would open it up to judicial scrutiny for compliance with the fundamental rights in the Constitution.[217] However, three judges held that the aim of the 1937 statute was merely to override oppressive customs and usages adopted by Muslims towards women, and instead to ensure that only codified Muslim law, or the Shariat, applied to them.[218] This reading keeps Muslim Personal Law outside of the reach of judicial scrutiny for rights violations.[219]

Pluralism is also a feature of South African law, especially in the field of family law.[220] However, as Albertyn shows, whereas

> customary marital reform saw the state able to resolve disputes of custom and gender largely in favour of legally entrenched equality rights ... religious marital reform has been far more contested, not only in the manner in which women are accorded rights, but also in the role of state law in regulating relationships whose rules are derived (directly or indirectly) from religious texts.[221]

As in India, the South African Constitution aims to protect and encourage its cultural and religious diversity. Thus section 15 (freedom of belief) permits legislation recognizing marriages concluded under any tradition or system of religious, personal, or family law and systems of personal and family law under any tradition or adhered to by persons professing a particular religion.[222] On the other hand, unlike the Indian Constitution, the South African Constitution creates a clear hierarchy. Section 15

[212] *State of Bombay v Narasu Appa Mali* AIR 1952 Bom 82 (Bombay High Court).

[213] ibid, paras [13] and [23].

[214] *Krishna Singh v Mathura Ahir* (1981) 3 SCC 689 (Indian Supreme Court); *Maharshi Avdhesh v Union of India* (1994) Supp (1) SCC 713 (Indian Supreme Court).

[215] *Shayara Bano v Union of India* (2017) 9 SCC 1 (Indian Supreme Court).

[216] ibid, per Jagdish Singh Khehar CJI, para [160] of his judgment.

[217] ibid. See submissions of petitioners.

[218] See the statement of objects and reasons of the 1937 Act, reproduced, at para [22] of Jagdish Singh Khehar CJI in *Shayara Bano v Union of India* (n 215); see also Kurian J at para [3] of his judgment in ibid.

[219] See ibid, Kurian J at para [4].

[220] E Bonthuys, 'A Patchwork of Marriages: The Legal Relevance of Marriage in a Plural Legal System' (2016) 6 Oñati Socio-legal Series [online] 1303, 1308 <http://opo.iisj.net/index.php/osls/article/viewFile/707/962> (accessed 7 March 2018).

[221] C Albertyn, 'Religion, Custom and Gender: Marital Law Reform in South Africa' (2013) 9 International Journal of Law in Context 386, 387.

[222] South African Constitution, s 15(3)(a).

expressly requires that legislative recognition of customary and religious law must be consistent with the provisions of the Constitution.[223]

Customary marriages have now been recognized through legislation in South Africa. But Muslim marriages remain in legal limbo. In the pre-Constitutional era, Muslim Personal Law operated entirely outside of State regulation. The result was that unless Muslim marriages were given civil law sanction, women in such marriages were not able to secure common law benefits of maintenance and inheritance and were dependent on the Muslim authorities for enforcement of proprietary benefits recognized under Muslim law.[224] This had not changed by 2017, despite many calls for recognition of Muslim marriages. This has meant that, whereas in India, Muslim women have turned to the courts to counter the discriminatory effects of recognition of Muslim Personal Law, South African Muslim women are turning to the courts to achieve recognition of Muslim marriages. Their aim has been to obtain the statutory rights available to women in civil law marriages. But do calls for recognition of Muslim marriages in South Africa mean that, as in India, the gender discriminatory aspects of Muslim Personal Law will also be imported? South African courts have thus far attempted to draw a bright line between the recognition of Muslim marriages and the importation of Muslim Personal Law. Indian courts, for their part, have looked for a means to achieve gender equality which has resonance within the religion, although their attempt to achieve a synthesis has generated some controversy. In the following sections, we consider how these complex issues have played out in key areas of contestation: polygamy; maintenance and succession; and divorce.

C. Polygamy

In its 2000 General Comment on equality between men and women, the HRC made it clear that polygamy violates the dignity of women and should be abolished.[225] This has been the position of the US Supreme Court since the 1879 case of *Reynolds v US*,[226] where the applicant, a Mormon, was charged with polygamy. He argued that it was an accepted doctrine of his church that male members had a religious duty to practise polygamy, and that refusing to do so would be punished by damnation in the life to come. The question before the Court was whether an act made criminal by the law of the land could be justified on the basis of a religious belief that the law is wrong. The Court had no doubt that it could not: 'Laws are made for the government of actions, and while they cannot interfere with mere religious belief and opinions, they may with practices'.[227] Any other approach would lead to unacceptable anomalies; for example, a non-believer who practised polygamy might be convicted, while a believer might not be.

The *Reynolds* case did not consider the question from the point of view of a woman in a polygamous marriage, who might be left vulnerable by lack of recognition of her

[223] South African Constitution, s 15(3)(b). [224] Albertyn (n 221) 399.
[225] Human Rights Committee, General Comment No 28 (n 204) para 24.
[226] *Reynolds v United States* (n 170). [227] ibid, 166.

marriage, especially on the death of the husband. Should a State assume that such marriages may continue to occur and recognize them for the purpose of protecting the women in the marriage, rather than prohibiting them and leaving the wives in legal limbo? Or does this perpetuate inequality? South Africa has taken the first route. Polygynous marriages[228] have long been practised and recognized in customary law in South Africa,[229] and despite international human rights law norms to the contrary, polygyny in customary law is recognized by the Recognition of Customary Marriages Act 120 of 1998. Feminist lawyers and rural women defended its inclusion on the basis that it would provide rights to women and children in polygynous marriages.[230] The statute does not require the consent of existing wives to the second or subsequent marriages,[231] although the Court may enforce the requirement of consent if that is required by applicable customary law.[232]

However, Muslim marriages have been treated differently. Unlike customary marriages, the potential for polygyny in Muslim marriages has constituted an obstacle for the recognition of the legal validity of such marriages.[233] The differential treatment of Muslim and customary law women in polygynous marriages was challenged in *Hassam v Jacobs*.[234] In this case, the first wife of the deceased argued that legislation on intestate succession was discriminatory because it excluded widows in polygynous Muslim marriages from its protection. The South African Constitutional Court upheld the claim. The refusal to recognize such a marriage in this legislation meant that wives in such marriages had no rights on intestate succession, causing significant material disadvantage. This constituted a breach of equality on both religious and gender grounds: wives in customary polygynous marriages and widows in Muslim marriages were given rights on intestacy. The Court attempted to draw a line between the constitutionality of polygynous Muslim marriages per se, and their implications for the women involved. Nkabinde J stressed that the issue was decided on the basis of discrimination, without determining whether polygynous marriages were themselves consistent with the Constitution:

> Whatever the answer to that question may be, one we leave strictly open now, it could not result in refusing appropriate protection to those women who are parties to such marriages. Such a result would be to lose sight of a key message of our Constitution: each person is of equal worth and must be treated accordingly.[235]

However, it is difficult to see how recognition for the purposes of intestate succession does not entail affirmation of polygyny in the first place.

The Indian position remains fluid. Christian, Hindu, Buddhist, Jain, and Sikh polygamy is prohibited by statute[236] and Jewish law in any event requires monogamy. For Muslims, marriage is governed by Muslim Personal Law, which, on the traditional

[228] Under polygyny, a husband can have more than wife, but a wife cannot have more than one husband.

[229] Bonthuys (n 220) 1303.

[230] Albertyn (n 221) 397.

[231] *Mayelane v Ngwenyama* [2013] ZACC 14 (South African Constitutional Court) para [41].

[232] ibid.

[233] Bonthuys (n 220) 1308.

[234] J Griffin, *On Human Rights* (OUP 2009).

[235] ibid, para [34].

[236] Christian Marriage Act 1872; Hindu Marriage Act of 1955; Parsi Marriage and Divorce Act 1936.

reading, permits marriage with four women.[237] Paradoxically, rather than Muslim women claiming that they are treated less favourably than Hindu women, some Hindu men have complained that that they are worse off than Muslim men, regarding this as an '"appeasement" of Muslims by privileging them with the option of bigamy/polygamy' as contrasted with the imposition of monogamy on Hindus.[238] It was on this basis that the Bombay Prevention of Hindu Bigamous Marriages Act 1946 was challenged as a violation of the rights to freedom of religion (Article 25) and equality (Articles 14 and 15) in *State of Bombay v Narasu Appa Mali*.[239] A two-judge Division Bench of the Court rejected their claim. According to Chagla CJ and Gajendragadkar J:

> If the State of Bombay compels Hindus to become monogamists, it is a measure of social reform, and if it is a measure of social reform then the State is empowered to legislate with regard to social reform under Article 25(2)(b) notwithstanding the fact that it may interfere with the right of a citizen freely to profess, practise and propagate religion.[240]

This statement was endorsed by the Supreme Court in *Javed*.[241]

However, the statutory prohibition of polygyny among Hindus has not ended the social practice. Agnes notes that official reports show that bigamy is in fact more common among Hindus than Muslims.[242] As in South Africa, it is the women that are left vulnerable by the non-recognition of their marriages, since the husband can avoid responsibility for maintenance by pleading that the woman is his second wife. By contrast, a Muslim woman in a polygynous marriage would be entitled to rights of maintenance, shelter, dignity, and equal status.[243] This social reality was recognized by the Indian Supreme Court in the 2014 case of *Badsha*,[244] where the respondent concealed his first marriage from his second wife. On the break-up of the relationship, he claimed that he had no legal responsibility to pay maintenance. Earlier decisions of the Indian Supreme Court had been sympathetic to that claim, holding that the statutory duty to pay maintenance in section 125 of the Criminal Procedure Code[245] only referred to a 'legally wedded wife', and not to a woman married in contravention of the Hindu Marriage Act.[246] The Supreme Court in *Badshah*, by contrast, held that the provision of maintenance should fall into the category of 'social justice' adjudication, 'which aims at empowering the destitute and achieving social justice or equality and dignity of the individual'.[247] This entailed taking a purposive view of the statute, rather than interpreting it in such a way as to give 'a premium to the husband for defrauding the wife'.[248] In a conclusion remarkably similar to that of the South

[237] *Javed v State of Haryana* (2003) 8 SCC 369 (Indian Supreme Court) para [24].

[238] Agnes (n 205) 919.

[239] *State of Bombay v Narasu Appa Mali* (n 212).

[240] ibid, para [7].

[241] *Javed v State of Haryana* (n 237).

[242] Agnes (n 205) 909.

[243] *Danial Latifi v Union of India* 2001 AIR SC 3958 (Indian Supreme Court). Note that this might be more limited under Muslim Personal Law than under secular law: see further below.

[244] *Badshah v Urmila Badshah Godse* (2014) 1 SCC 188 (Indian Supreme Court).

[245] Section 125 provides that any person who has sufficient means and refuses to maintain his wife (including a divorced woman who has not remarried) can be ordered to provide maintenance to her is she is unable to maintain herself. See further below.

[246] *Yamunabai Anantrao Adhav A v Ranantrao Shivram Adhav* 1988 AIR SC 644, [1988] SCR (2) 809 (Indian Supreme Court).

[247] *Badshah v Urmila Badshah Godse* (n 244) para [19].

[248] ibid, para [25].

African Constitutional Court, the Indian Court held that, 'at least for the purpose of claiming maintenance under Section 125 ..., such a woman is to be treated as the legally wedded wife'.[249]

Polygamy in Muslim Personal Law was directly challenged as violating the rights to equality, life, and religion in a recent petition to the Indian Supreme Court. In the matter of *Ashwini Kumar Upadhyay v Union of India*,[250] filed in March 2018, the petitioner argued that the practice of polygamy is injurious to basic rights guaranteed under the rights to equality in Articles 14 and 15 of the Indian Constitution, and to the right to life in Article 21. The petition submits that the fact that bigamy has been made unlawful by statute for Christians, Parsis, Hindus, Buddhists, Sikhs, and Jains demonstrates that family law is not a part of religious law. Instead, the failure to secure the same equal rights and dignity for Muslim women violates their fundamental right to equality. The case has still to be decided at the time of writing (July 2018).

D. Divorce, maintenance, and succession

Gender inequality in marriage is not confined to polygamous situations. Provision for divorce, maintenance, and succession to property have triggered conflicts between religious freedom and gender equality. Paradoxically, in South African law this is a consequence of the failure to recognize Muslim marriages, while in India it is a consequence of the primacy afforded to Muslim Personal Law. In both jurisdictions, the apex court has attempted to mitigate the consequences for women without heading into the more wide-ranging consequences of their decisions.

In the South African case of *Daniels v Campbell*,[251] a woman married according to Muslim law, argued that legislation providing for maintenance and succession was unconstitutional on the grounds that it failed to include persons married according to Muslim rites. Both the Intestate Succession Act and the Maintenance of Surviving Spouses Act made provision for surviving spouses, but neither provided a definition of 'spouse'. The executors argued that 'spouse' meant a lawfully married wife; and that nothing had precluded her from formalizing her marriage under civil law. This interpretation would leave her with no recourse to statutory protection, and nor could she secure benefits under Muslim Personal Law, since the latter was not recognized or enforceable in the courts. Like the Indian court in *Badshah*, Sachs J, with the support of seven of the other judges, took the view that a purposive interpretation should be used to interpret the word 'spouse' to include parties to a Muslim marriage: 'The constitutional values of equality, tolerance and respect for diversity point strongly in favour of giving the word "spouse" a broad and inclusive construction'.[252] This was particularly so since an important purpose of the statute was to provide relief to a particularly vulnerable section of the population, namely widows. Thus 'the central question is not whether the applicant was lawfully married to the deceased, but whether the

[249] ibid.

[250] The petition can be found at <http://www.livelaw.in/triple-talaq-petition-sc-declaring-polygamy-nikah-halala-unconstitutional/> (accessed 12 July 2018).

[251] *Daniels v Campbell* 2004 7 BCLR 735 (CC) (South African Constitutional Court).

[252] ibid, para [21].

protection which the Acts intended widows to enjoy should be withheld from relationships such as hers'.[253] However, Sachs J was also quick to 'underline the limited effect of such an inclusive interpretation ... [namely that it] eliminates a discriminatory application of particular statutes without implying a general recognition of the consequences of Muslim marriages for other purposes'.[254]

The caution as to the recognition of Muslim marriages for other purposes is borne out in the Indian jurisprudence, which has had to deal with the consequences of giving primacy to Muslim Personal Law in cases where ex-wives or widows are not given equivalent protection to that available under statutory law. These deeply divisive issues have played out in the sequence of events triggered by the *Shah Bano* case in 1985.[255] Shah Bano, a Muslim woman, was divorced by her husband in her old age and after forty-five years of marriage. Elderly and ill, she was left destitute and without any means of survival. As the Court noted, she had managed the matrimonial home for more than forty years, had borne and brought up five children, and was unable to remarry or take up a career at this stage of her life. She applied for an order of maintenance against her ex-husband, a lawyer earning a good income. Under section 125 of the Code of Criminal Procedure 1973 (CrPC), a magistrate may order a husband or ex-husband who has sufficient means to provide a monthly allowance to his wife, ex-wife, or minor children if the latter are unable to maintain themselves. However, section 127 of the Code provides that such an order should be cancelled if the woman has received 'the whole of the sum which, under any customary or personal law applicable to the parties, is payable on such divorce'.[256] Relying on this provision, the husband, supported by the Muslim Personal Law Board, argued that Muslim law absolved a husband from any responsibility for his divorced wife beyond an amount to cover maintenance during the 'iddat' period (about three months), and her mahr or dowry. Other Muslim organizations, intervening on the part of the wife, contested this interpretation of Muslim law. They pointed to other principles in Muslim Personal Law, known as 'mata', to suggest that a divorced Muslim woman could claim provision for maintenance after the iddat period.[257] Thus, as Veena Das puts it, the Court was required to find a way of resolving conflicts between the desire of an ethnic or religious minority to preserve culture, and an overlapping community of women, who wish to reinterpret that culture according to a different set of principles.[258]

The Court upheld the woman's claim. A five-judge bench of the Indian Supreme Court held that if there was a conflict between the CrPC and the personal law of the parties, the former would prevail. At the same time, in an attempt to reconcile the two sources of law, the Court held that, on a close reading of the Quran, the maintenance obligation under Muslim Personal Law was not meant to apply to situations in which the divorced wife was unable to maintain herself. Instead, it came to the view that the

[253] ibid, para [25]. [254] ibid, para [26].

[255] *Mohd Ahmed Khan v Shah Bano Begum* (1985) 2 SCC 556 (Indian Supreme Court).

[256] Code of Criminal Procedure 1973, s 127(3)(b).

[257] See the very helpful summary of the case in the later case of *Danial Latifi v Union of India* ((n 243) para [1]).

[258] V Das, 'Cultural Rights and the Definition of Community' in O Mendelsohn and U Baxi (eds), *The Rights of Subordinated Peoples* (OUP 1994) 137.

Holy Quran imposes an obligation on the Muslim husband to provide for a divorced wife if she is destitute. The result was that there need not be a conflict between the two provisions.

The judgment provoked a fierce backlash among Muslim leaders and followers, who accused the bench, consisting entirely of Hindu judges, of meddling in their religious affairs. Responding to calls by the Muslim Personal Law Board to reverse the results of *Shah Bano*, the legislature passed the Muslim Women (Protection of Rights on Divorce) Act 1986. In what Mulally calls an attempt to silence feminist and other emancipatory interpretations of the Shariah,[259] the Act provides for a 'reasonable and fair provision and maintenance' by the former husband, but only within the period of iddat, as well as the mahr or dowry and any gifts given to her. If she is unable to provide for herself after the period of iddat, she is required to resort to her own relatives for further maintenance, and, failing that, to the State Wakf Board (a Muslim charity), rather than section 125 CrPC, as other women could.

It took a further decade-and-a-half for the constitutionality of the 1986 Act to reach the Indian Supreme Court. The petitioner, Danial Latifi, the lawyer in the *Shah Bano* case, submitted that the Act was discriminatory against Muslim women by depriving them of the benefit of compulsory maintenance under section 125 CrPC, violating the rights to life and equality.[260] Like the *Shah Bano* Court before it, the five-judge bench in *Danial Latifi* attempted to reconcile the two sources of law:

> [Compensation] in terms of money towards her livelihood and such a relief which partakes basic human rights to secure gender and social justice is universally recognized by persons belonging to all religions and it is difficult to perceive that Muslim law intends to provide a different kind of responsibility by passing on the same to those unconnected with the matrimonial life such as the heirs who were likely to inherit the property from her or the wakf boards.

This led the Court to hold that the provisions of the 1986 Act could be interpreted to provide for the equivalent protection to that found in section 125. It did this by focusing on the requirement in the 1986 Act that a reasonable and fair provision was required. This was distinct from the obligation to pay maintenance, which lasted only for the iddat period. Reasonable and fair provision meant that the liability of a Muslim husband to his divorced wife was not confined to the iddat period. Calculated with reference to the needs of the divorced woman, her standard of living, and the means of the husband, reasonable and fair provision might be paid as a lump sum during the iddat period, but, the Court held, there is no reason why such provision should not also take the form of a regular payment of alimony to the divorced woman. On this construction, it concluded, the 1986 Act could not be held to infringe the right to equality or the right to life in the Constitution. Thus, while upholding the constitutionality of the 1986 Act, the Court held that a Muslim husband was liable to make reasonable and fair provision for the future of the divorced wife extending beyond the iddat period. As the Court acknowledged, 'It may look ironical that the enactment

[259] Mulally (n 201) 681. [260] *Danial Latifi v Union of India* (n 243).

intended to reverse the decision in *Shah Bano*'s case, actually codifies the rationale contained therein'.[261]

Perhaps the closest a Court has come to addressing inequality directly, rather than reading in gender-sensitive interpretations to religious personal laws, has concerned the practice of the 'triple talaq'. This practice permits a Muslim husband to unilaterally and irrevocably divorce his wife with immediate effect by simply pronouncing the word 'talaq' three times in the presence of witnesses. In the 2017 *Shayara Bano* case, a woman contested triple talaq as being an unconstitutional violation of gender equality. It was argued on behalf of the respondent husband that the triple talaq fulfilled all the requirements of a valid divorce according to the Hanafi sect of Sunni Muslims and was in consonance with the Shariat, or Muslim Personal Law. In India, about 90 per cent of Sunni Muslims belong to the Hanafi school and it was not in dispute that they had been adopting the triple talaq as a valid form of divorce for hundreds of years.[262] The practice had been upheld by the Privy Council in 1932.[263]

By a narrow majority of three to two, the Court held that the practice was unconstitutional. Before determining whether the triple talaq breached the right to equality, the Court had to decide whether the triple talaq was insulated from further challenge because it fell within the protection of freedom of religion in Article 25. As will be recalled, the Court has taken an objective view of religious claims, giving itself the authority to determine whether a practice is an 'essential practice' of the religion to warrant protection under Article 25. To be an essential practice, it was necessary to prove that triple talaq was at the core of the religion, in the sense that the fundamental nature of Islam, seen through an Indian Sunni Muslim's eyes, would change without the practice. Applying this test, the three majority judges held that the triple talaq was not an essential practice.[264] Kurian J made it particularly clear that 'triple talaq is against the basic tenets of the Holy Quran' because it does not permit the possibility of reconciliation which is required by the Quran.[265] His answer was therefore simple: 'What is held to be bad in the Holy Quran cannot be good in Shariat and, in that sense, what is bad in theology is bad in law as well'.[266] This contrasts with the minority judges, who decided not to 'enter into the thicket of determining ... whether or not ... triple talaq constituted a valid practice under the Muslim personal law'.[267] Instead, they accepted that it was to be considered integral to the Hanafi school and part of their 'personal law'.[268] This meant that the practice could only be altered by legislation, which they urged the legislature to enact as soon as possible.

The majority decision that triple talaq was not protected by Article 25 opened the way for scrutiny under Article 14, the right to equality. The two judgments that held that Article 14 had been breached, however, specifically declined to deal with the many careful arguments about gender equality submitted to them. Instead, they held that the right to equality in Article 14 was primarily aimed at preventing ad hoc and arbitrary treatment. Since equality before the law was the diametric opposite of

[261] ibid. [262] *Shayara Bano* (n 215) para [144]ff, Nariman J, para [7].
[263] *Rashid Ahmad v Anisa Khatun* AIR 1932 PC 25 (Privy Council).
[264] *Shayara Bano* (n 215) per Nariman J, para [25]. [265] ibid, per Kurian J, para [10].
[266] ibid, per Kurian J, para [26]. [267] ibid, para [137]. [268] ibid, para [145].

arbitrariness, any arbitrary law was unequal and in violation of Article 14.[269] Manifest arbitrariness, which included legislation which was excessive and disproportionate, would violate Article 14.[270] Under this test,

> it is clear that this form of Talaq is manifestly arbitrary in the sense that the marital tie can be broken capriciously and whimsically by a Muslim man without any attempt at reconciliation so as to save it. This form of Talaq must therefore be held to be violative of the fundamental right contained under Article 14 of the Constitution.[271]

The majority decided that insofar as the 1937 Muslim Personal Law (Shariat) Application Act recognizes and enforces the triple talaq, it should be struck down as void.[272] Although the outcome was victory in practice for the women, it is unfortunate that the opportunity was lost to make a decision on the basis of the submissions on gender equality put before the Court.

E. Dress codes and freedom of religion

In Europe, the tension between equality and freedom of religion, has focused on dress requirements, and particularly religious dress based on expectations of women's modesty. Several of the principles we have already seen in other contexts of religious freedom are at play here. One concerns respect for autonomy. Where women are coerced to adhere to these modesty codes, as they are in many parts of the world, there is a clear breach of their right both to religious freedom and to equality. However, where women choose to cover themselves, is this an issue entirely for their own autonomy? This is further complicated by the fact that individuals' choices might be influenced by a range of issues, including whether they have viable exit options; stigma and pressure within their community; or even internalization of women's separate or subordinate roles in communities and society. This raises a second issue, namely, what principles justify State intervention to restrict religious freedom? The familiar harm principle would need to be elaborated. Can the State intervene when a woman chooses to wear religious dress which might cause harm to herself, for example by impeding her mobility? The analogy with Sikh turbans and motorbikes or construction site safety rules might be appropriate. Alternatively, can the State intervene when such dress is considered as creating a harm to society more generally. This in turn requires an understanding of religious modesty codes in relation to dress as being more than an individual choice, but an act of communication or expression reflecting underlying values in relation to the proper role of women. Even so, are criminal prohibitions the appropriate way for society to promote these values?

This complex confluence of issues has brought several acutely challenging cases before the ECtHR. Where the issue is simply the wearing of a headscarf, there seems little to justify State intervention. However, does this change in relation to the burqa, a full-body covering including a mesh over the face, or the niqab, a full-face veil leaving an opening only for the eyes? *SAS v France* concerned a French law which prohibited anyone from concealing their face in public places.[273] The applicant, a devout

[269] ibid, per Nariman J, para [45].
[270] ibid, per Nariman J, para [55].
[271] ibid, per Nariman J, para [57].
[272] ibid.
[273] *SAS v France* (2015) 60 EHRR 11 (European Court of Human Rights (Grand Chamber)).

Muslim, wore the burqa and niqab both in public and privately. She maintained that no member of her family had put any pressure on her to wear these garments; her decision was in accordance with her religious faith, culture, and personal convictions. She added that she did not always wear the niqab: she might not wear it when she wanted to socialize in public, and she did not demand to wear it for security or identity checks. She did, however, claim the right to choose to wear it, depending on her spiritual feelings. She claimed a breach of her rights to privacy, freedom of religion, and non-discrimination, under Articles 8, 9, and 14 ECHR. The ECtHR rejected her challenge. Although the French legislation interfered with both her right to respect for private life and her freedom to manifest her beliefs, this interference was justified under Articles 8(2) and 9(2).

The Court's reasoning has been much criticized. The judges were not persuaded by the government's argument that the legislation's objective was respect for gender equality. While this might be applicable to coerced veiling, the Court held that a State Party could not invoke gender equality in order to ban a practice that is defended by women.[274] Nor could a blanket ban be justified on the grounds of respect for human dignity.

> The Court is aware that the clothing in question is perceived as strange by many of those who observe it. It would point out, however, that it is the expression of a cultural identity which contributes to the pluralism that is inherent in democracy. It notes in this connection the variability of the notions of virtuousness and decency that are applied to the uncovering of the human body.[275]

Nor did the Court find that there was any evidence that wearers of a full-face veil expressed a form of contempt against others they encounter.

Instead, the Court upheld the government's argument that its aim was to respect the minimum requirements of 'living together' in a society. Under certain conditions, such an aim could be regarded as a legitimate 'protection of the rights and freedoms of others'.[276] The Court took into account the State's view that the face plays an important part in social interaction, and that individuals who are present in public places would not want to see practices which fundamentally called into question the possibility of open interpersonal relationships. It therefore accepted that the barrier raised against others by a veil concealing the face could be perceived to be breaching the right of others to 'live in a space of socialisation which makes living together easier'. Indeed, it regarded the principle of interaction between individuals as essential, not just to pluralism but also to tolerance and broadmindedness. The sense that this was a legitimate choice for society led the Court to hold that France should have a wide margin of appreciation, a finding which was backed up by the lack of overall consensus in Europe. It acknowledged that because of the flexibility of the notion of living together, and the risk of abuse, the Court should examine the necessity of the limitation very carefully. Nevertheless, it held that the blanket ban could be regarded as necessary to protect the French value of social interaction and living together.[277] It took into account the possibility that the ban might give women no choice but to remain at home if they wished

[274] ibid, para [119]. [275] ibid, para [120]. [276] ibid, para [121]. [277] ibid, para [141].

to manifest their religious beliefs. On the other hand, the ban only referred to face-coverings. All other kinds of religious dress were permitted in public places. Moreover, the criminal sanction, albeit stigmatizing, was very light, being a maximum of €150.

The concept of 'living together' as a legitimate expression of the 'rights and interests of others' has been widely criticized. The dissenting judges in the case expressed strong reservations about this conception as being farfetched and vague. They reiterated that there is no right not to be shocked by different models of cultural or religious identity. Nor could it be argued that an individual has a right to enter into contact with other people against their will. The dissenters also questioned the proportionality of the measure, in particular the paradoxical claim that an intolerant ban would promote greater tolerance. Raday agrees that '"unease" when encountering the "other" can scarcely be considered a good stand-alone ground for restricting a minority's cultural practices'. However, she argues that the equality ground was too quickly dismissed: 'The community has a valid interest in negating the message to all women that they are required to be self-effacing in order not to be immodest, and in preventing … the shadow effect of gendered modesty'.[278] It is notable too, that the religious basis for modesty rules has been challenged from within Islam itself,[279] although the Court's strong principle of deference to the sincerity of religious belief precludes airing of these contestations in determining whether freedom of religion has been breached in the first place.

So, is a society permitted to stipulate minimum levels of dress requirements, regardless of religion? This can be tested by considering the opposite scenario: whether society should be permitted to criminalize nudity in public. In *Gough v UK*,[280] the applicant had a strong belief in social nudity, which he expressed by being naked in public. He had been repeatedly arrested, prosecuted, and convicted for breach of the peace and public indecency. The ECtHR rejected his claim of breach of his right to freedom of expression and respect for private life. The Court held that the applicant was entitled to initiate a debate about public nudity, but the right to freedom of speech

> does not go so far as to enable individuals, even those sincerely convinced of the virtue of their own beliefs, to repeatedly impose their antisocial conduct on other, unwilling members of society and then to claim a disproportionate interference with the exercise of their freedom of expression when the state, in the performance of its duty to protect the public from public nuisances, enforces the law in respect of such deliberately repetitive antisocial conduct.[281]

Moreover, the police were entitled to arrest him on the basis that he had caused alarm to members of the public. Particularly since he was asking for tolerance of his own conduct, he was under a duty to demonstrate tolerance to others.

[278] F Raday, 'Professor Frances Raday Comments on SAS v France' (OxHRH Blog, 19 July 2014) <http://ohrh.law.ox.ac.uk/professor-frances-raday-comments-on-sas-v-france/> (accessed 7 March 2018).

[279] J Alibhai-Brown, *Refusing the Veil (Provocations)* (Biteback Publishing 2014); Z Sardar and Z Malik, *Introducing Islam* (Icon Books Ltd 2000) 160.

[280] *Gough v UK* (2015) 61 EHRR 8 (European Court of Human Rights).

[281] ibid, para [176].

The Court is arguably wholly consistent in its approach in *SAS v France* and *Gough v UK*, in both cases allowing societies to decree their own minimum irreducible standards of dress. However, it would be interesting to speculate whether those who defend their right to wear full face-veils in public would also defend Gough's right to appear nude in public, in pursuance of his sincerely held beliefs in the inoffensive nature of the human body. Posing the question in this way makes us realize that there are several quite different principles at play in this debate. Those who support both Gough's nudity and women's right to cover assume the principle at stake is one of autonomy. Those who require Gough to cover but that women display at least their faces accept that the communicative quality of dress and its relationship to interpersonal relationships can be determined, at least so far as minimum demands are concerned, by prevailing social norms. But there is a different possible principle behind the position that opposes Gough's nudity but supports the total covering of women's faces. Such a position suggests that the issue is not about autonomy or minimum social standards of interaction, but of the meaning of sexuality, modesty, and attitudes towards the human body. Alarm at Gough's nudity is premised on the assumption that displays of male nudity are sexually dangerous or predatory. Equivalently, the assumption behind gendered modesty rules is that women's bodies are sexually tempting to men and should be covered.

The above discussion has focused on full face-veiling because of its specific interference with both personal mobility and interpersonal communication. Arguably, very different considerations apply to religious dress which does not have these implications: the wearing of a cross, a headscarf, a kippah, or a Sikh turban. The application of the principle of proportionality should therefore be very differently weighted, with little weight being given to an employer's desire for uniformity in its corporate image, and a stronger requirement of evidence of harm, going beyond risk of loss of profits. This was recognized by the ECtHR in *Eweida*, where the Court upheld a claim by a British Airways employee to the right to wear a cross, in breach of company rules against jewellery of any sort. While it considered that the wish to project a corporate image on the part of the employer was undoubtedly legitimate, the prohibition was not proportionate, since the cross was discrete and there was no evidence of any real encroachment on the interests of others.[282] On the other hand, it rejected a similar claim by a nurse, on the grounds that her employer had a valid claim that a hanging pendant might cause harm to a patient or permit a patient to cause harm to the nurse.[283]

Much less convincing was the judgment of the Court of Justice of the European Union in *Achbita v G4S*, dismissing a claim of discrimination by a Muslim employee who was dismissed from her work as a receptionist for wearing a headscarf to work.[284] It was held that since all visible signs of political, philosophical, or religious beliefs in the workplace were banned, there was no direct discrimination against her as a Muslim. The Court left open the possibility that this was a case of indirect discrimination, in that an apparently neutral rule impacted disproportionately on Muslim women. However, it held that an employer's wish to project an image of neutrality towards customers was

[282] *Eweida v UK* (n 187). [283] ibid.
[284] *Achbita v G4S Secure Solutions* (2017) 3 CMLR 21 (CJEU (Grand Chamber)).

in principle legitimate, given that the freedom to conduct a business is recognized as a right under the EU Charter, but only where this aim involves workers who come into contact with the employers' customers. Instead, the employer should attempt to accommodate this employee in a non-customer-facing job. This ignores the familiar principle that a rule requiring 'neutrality' in display simply favours the majority way of dressing, which carries with it no cost to their beliefs.

VII. Conclusion

The enmeshment of religion, politics, and identity has undergone a resurgence in recent decades, challenging the secular settlement established by constitutional freedom of religion. Habermas's aspiration that all parties involved should learn to take the perspectives of others remains elusive, as the claim for the positive liberty to practice one's own religion increasingly encroaches on the negative liberty to be spared from the religious practices of others. In these circumstances, it is more important than ever that deep disagreement can be resolved through deliberative processes rather than resorting to violent conflict. As this chapter has shown, the comparative approach illuminates the ways in which courts in different jurisdictions, within the framework of differing textual mandates and diverse histories and cultures, have navigated these issues. Comparativism is especially helpful in casting new light on assumptions made about religion itself, with the Christian paradigm found in much human rights law put into perspective by its comparison with other religions which operate from very different premises. Courts in all jurisdictions, faced with this comparative perspective, need to be wary of regarding the majority religion as simply a matter of national culture. On the other hand, acceptance of sincerity of belief as compared to an objective view of religion should not signify a retreat into relativism. When it comes to manifestation of belief, or the customs associated with belief, the rights of others need to be given appropriate weight. It is in drawing this balance that, as we have seen, judges face the most challenges.

13
Conclusion

We have now reached the end of this phase of the journey through comparative human rights. Struck by the fact that judges in different jurisdictions face the same demanding questions about the meaning and application of human rights, we have sought to find the commonalities and understand the divergences. The deliberative method has triggered countless new insights and perspectives. We have unsettled assumptions that had previously gone unquestioned, and required renewed justification based on the possibility of a range of different substantive answers. The aim has not been to provide a comprehensive textbook of human rights law, but to trigger a vibrant conversation based on asking a range of questions and being open to considering different ways of answering them. It is hoped that the reader, having joined the incipient conversation about the possibilities of cross-fertilization of principles in human rights law, will now take this conversation further.

This chapter briefly draws together the threads of the issues canvassed in this book. The first five chapters set out the main cross-cutting themes which form the analytic framework for the subsequent substantive chapters: the role of comparative materials; the meaning of human rights; the relationship between civil and political rights and socio-economic rights; the role of adjudication; and different approaches to judicial interpretation. The following chapters apply these themes to some of the most challenging issues in comparative human rights law. By considering the same topics over five different jurisdictions, and drawing on international human rights law where relevant, many of the themes in the first part are illuminated, and in turn cast light on these difficult issues. The coverage is not intended to be complete, but challenging and thought-provoking.

Chapter 1 throws down the gauntlet with Scalia's J's trenchant criticism of comparative human rights law as 'dangerous dicta' attempting to impose 'foreign moods, fads or fashions' on Americans. Where there is no express constitutional mandate to refer to foreign norms, is it illegitimate and undemocratic for Courts to do so? The chapter argues that while these difficulties arise in comparative law more generally, human rights law is distinctive. On the one hand, there is a broadly similar common core of human rights both internationally and domestically, and human rights guarantees in different jurisdictions have important affinities, often through conscious adoption or adaptation. On the other hand, human rights are inevitably formulated in open-textured terms, requiring interpretation and application in specific contexts. The differences in text, culture, history, and institutions might be more important than the similarities. Thus, posing the same questions does not necessarily entail that different jurisdictions should give the same answers.

It is argued in this book that the main function of comparative law is deliberative. Judges making decisions on complex issues of human rights law need to adopt a reasoning process which is thorough and persuasive. Judicial accountability depends centrally on the quality of the reasons adduced. In contested human rights cases there will be no single right answer; but the suspicion that judges are imposing their own subjective beliefs can only be dispelled by reasoning which is capable of being persuasive and openly canvasses a range of alternative solutions. Comparative materials constitute an important contribution to the rigour of this process, particularly with respect to canvassing alternative solutions. A deliberative approach does not regard the function of comparativism as tending towards convergence in human rights decision-making worldwide. Even apart from the difficulty in establishing a universal meaning of human rights, there are important and relevant differences in constitutional texts, legal institutions, and social, cultural, historical, and political contexts. But whether the outcomes converge or diverge, there need to be good reasons, articulated in the decision, to explain why the textual, institutional, legal, social, or cultural context demands convergence or divergence.

Chapters 2 to 5 elaborate on the kinds of issues that need to be considered as part of a deliberative approach to comparative human rights law. The first is the question of whether there is a universal understanding of human rights. If there is no such universal understanding, is the only alternative to accept pure relativity, where comparison is futile since no common meanings exist? These issues are examined in Chapter 2. The chapter demonstrates the difficulty in finding fundamental values which underpin human rights in ways that all can accept. At the same time, it is possible to draw on the strengths of different theories of rationality, liberty, dignity, and autonomy to fashion principles of substantive freedom and equality, which recognize the embeddedness of the individual in society and the need to provide a range of options if choice and autonomy are to be real. The chapter also shows the important contribution of relativists in unmasking the risk of hegemony by powerful forces in shaping the meaning of human rights. On the other hand, the relativists' refusal to countenance the possibility of cross-cultural interchange on the meaning of human rights can mask a different sort of hegemony, that of the powerful voices within particular communities seeking to prevent human rights from unsettling their power. Yet this is precisely the function of human rights, in all States, both in the West and the East. The chapter concludes by demonstrating that there is in fact a widespread consensus on what are human rights. But this occurs at a high level of abstraction. It is in their interpretation and application that divergences arise. The very contestation about the meaning and application of human rights, and above all the justification for their limits, contribute to the dynamism of human rights law. And it is here that the comparative, deliberative approach has a key role to play. By insisting on public reasoning, accountability on the basis of evidence and cogency, and wide participation, as well as the importance of comparative insights, the interpretation and application of human rights law will continue to evolve and respond to complex social and political issues.

It would not have gone unnoticed that much of the traditional discourse about what counts as a human right takes civil and political rights as the paradigm case. Many are sceptical as to whether socio-economic rights, such as rights to housing and health, can be credited with the status of justiciable fundamental human rights. Some are sceptical because they regard judicial intervention into this area as overstepping the bounds of judicial legitimacy, regarding socio-economic rights as concerned with policy issues, which should rightfully remain within the political arena. Others emphasize the limits of courts' competence in addressing issues with wide polycentric ramifications. Chapter 3 examines these objections, and the responses within comparative human rights law. It considers different ways of demarcating the boundary between civil and political rights and socio-economic rights, including competing ideologies, content, and the duties attributed to each. Finding that none of these create a clear bright line between socio-economic rights and civil and political rights, the chapter endorses the notion that all rights are indivisible and interconnected.

Instead, the focus is on the duties to respect, protect, and provide, to which all rights give rise. The challenge for justiciable rights often comes with adjudicating positive duties to protect and provide. Several human rights instruments attempt to deal with this by framing socio-economic rights as subject to available resources and therefore only realizable progressively. This in turn raises the difficult questions of how to frame the substantive right at the end of the road; how to measure progressive realization; and what is the standard of scrutiny in relation to available resources. Without some idea of the answers to these questions, it is difficult to determine when a State is in breach. In response to this, the Committee on Economic, Social and Cultural Rights (CESCR) has developed the notion of a minimum core of the right, to which priority must be given. This has raised more questions than it has answered. The debate about the meaning and function of the minimum core is dealt with in the chapter and various options canvassed. At the same time, the concepts of progressive realization and maximum available resources, which are often given little attention, are considered in more detail.

A key part of the debate about the status of socio-economic rights concerns the role of the court. But this is only part of the broader question of the role of adjudication in human rights and, more specifically, how the role of the court differs as between jurisdictions. It is this that is the subject of Chapter 4. This chapter considers the tension between the democratic commitment to participation by the people in all decision-making, and the need for human rights to counter the risk that the majority might invade the human rights of individuals and minorities. It poses the question of whether we can create a role for justiciable human rights which reinforces democracy. This requires more consideration of the limitations of courts both from a legitimacy and a competence perspective.

The first half of the chapter examines comparative perspectives on legitimacy. In particular, it considers different ways of configuring the relationship between the judiciary, the legislature, and the executive: representation-reinforcing, dialogic, and deliberative theories. It draws on the strengths of each of these to develop a role for the court which is one of bounded deliberative democracy. Drawing on Habermas's distinction between 'value-oriented' and 'interest-based' co-ordination, it is argued that human rights resolution should never be the subject of interest bargaining. Instead, they should be addressed through 'value-oriented' decision-making, where the outcome is determined according to the persuasiveness of the argument rather than the power of the parties. Courts are in a position to augment deliberative democracy in human rights adjudication in two complementary ways. First, the court functions as a deliberative forum in its own right. Second, courts can steer legislative and executive decision-making away from interest bargaining and towards deliberation. They do this by insisting that decision-makers justify their decisions on the interpretation or limitation of human rights in a deliberative manner, substantiating their reasons, with evidence where appropriate. At the same time, courts are not entitled to impose their views on open-ended moral grounds. The deliberative approach is bounded in that it operates within the constraints of human rights, which are themselves a product of prior deliberative consensus. Decision-makers must be in a position to persuade the court that they have fulfilled their human rights obligations, account being taken both of the pre-existing deliberative consensus and of the fact that there is room for reasonable disagreement. The use of comparative law is central to this deliberative process.

Gauri and Brinks' rich empirical research also bears out the insights gained from the discussion above. They found that courts can help overcome political blockages, challenge lack of implementation of existing policies, and hold governments to account for 'incomplete commitments', that is, announced projects of social transformation which have imparted great legitimacy to a government but which have not been implemented. Courts can also create spaces of deliberation and compromise between competing interests and channel important information to political and bureaucratic actors; and they can reprioritize claims so that protection of human rights, and in particular access to social and economic goods, is extended. On the other hand, the very structure of litigation may militate against these achievements.

The second part of Chapter 4 is concerned with the limits of the court's competence to deal with complex issues with polycentric implications. Using the example of India's public interest litigation, it examines ways in which the court structure might be adapted to address these concerns. In the final section, the chapter considers the remedies and ongoing implications of justiciable human rights. It suggests that more attention should be paid to organizational structures of the State, and to discovering where the blockages to implementation lie, so that remedies and implementation can be properly targeted.

The chapter concludes by reiterating that courts cannot be a substitute for either political activity or recalcitrant governments. Instead, they can act as a catalyst for the democratic pressures which ultimately make recalcitrant governments act. Courts, in adjudicating human rights, should enable ordinary people to require governments to explain and justify their actions or inactivity. Beyond that, human rights adjudication should facilitate deliberative reasoning rather than pure interest bargaining, which in turn requires governments to listen and interact with civil society, and groups within civil society to listen and interact with each other. Most importantly, human rights adjudication should require deliberation to take place on equal terms. To maintain this, courts should take care to avoid capture by those who already have political power in society.

Debates about the legitimate role of courts crystallize when judges are faced with the need to interpret open-textured human rights instruments in order to resolve the dispute before them. In order to give substance to human rights guarantees, what values can judges legitimately draw on? Some judges regard judicial interpretation as gaining legitimacy only from the intentions of the drafters, or the natural meaning of words. Other see Bills of Rights as necessarily responsive to changing times, preferring a 'living tree' or purposive approach. A third approach is that of transformative constitutionalism, which suggests that Bills of Rights could be interpreted expressly to bring about social change. Chapter 5 explores the ramifications of these different approaches, and what implications they have had in the case law of the different jurisdictions examined here. On closer inspection, the contrast between these approaches proves to be less vivid than judicial dicta might suggest. The intent of the original drafter might be impossible to discover, especially in relation to issues that they could not have envisaged. In any event, it is not clear why the original drafters retain their legitimacy over generations. At the same time, even under the 'living tree' approach, text and history are factors which need to be considered to avoid free-floating, unaccountable value judgements. Under any approach, judges are required to make value judgements: even the choice of an 'original intent' theory requires a value judgement. As Dworkin puts it: 'The issue is rather what reasons are, in [a court's] hands, good reasons'.[1] Rather than following Dworkin's own distinction, however, between principle and policy, the chapter argues that a deliberative model requires all judicial interpretations of human rights, whether on principle or policy, to be convincingly defended in the context of the overall commitment to furthering human rights.

Part I of the book having set out the main cross-cutting themes in comparative law, the chapters in Part II apply these themes to some of the most challenging issues in comparative human rights law. Each chapter examines the crucial role of the human rights texts which judges in each jurisdiction are concerned with. The text often determines the constellation of rights which are put to use. But this is only the beginning of the decision-making process. The substantive chapters chart the ways in which judges interpret the rights in the text, comparing and contrasting interpretive theories, together with the values which judges draw on. As well as using comparative law to cast light on the ways in which judges in different jurisdictions make decisions on similar issues, the chapters consider the extent to which judges draw on comparative materials and for which purposes. Framing these questions is the judicial consciousness of the limits of their own role, both from a legitimacy and a competence perspective. Since the substance of the chapters spans both civil and political rights and socio-economic rights, it is possible to highlight their interaction, particularly when it comes to positive duties. In addition, each chapter provides a critical focus on equality and considers how different jurisdictions include the equality dimension in their resolution of complex human rights issues.

Chapter 6 on capital punishment again uses one of Scalia J's pithy dicta to frame the issue. Drawing on both his theory of original intent and that of judicial deference to the legislature, he maintains that capital punishment presents such deeply contested moral questions that the framers of the Constitution left the people to decide whether it is acceptable. This contrasts strikingly with the view of the South African Constitutional Court, which held that precisely because the drafters of the South African Constitution could not come to a conclusion about the legitimacy of the death penalty, it should be for the Court to decide. Judges' interpretive theories are further put to the test in

[1] R Dworkin, *A Matter of Principle* (OUP 1985) 34 (hereafter Dworkin, *A Matter of Principle*) 69.

interpreting the text of human rights instruments which seem to sanction the death penalty as long as it is carried out with due process of law, but at the same time prohibit cruel and inhuman punishment. Original intent, natural meaning, and living tree approaches have all been relied on to achieve a mosaic of different and vehemently contested approaches.

The chapter explores divergent judicial approaches on three main issues: whether there can be a fair procedure for imposing the death penalty; whether it can be justified by penological goals; and whether there are clear value-based reasons for determining compliance with human rights. It shows how judges' choice of answers to these issues further depends on their background positions on the cross-cutting issues identified earlier, particularly their constitutional interpretation, their view of the proper role of the court, their approach to comparativism, and their background values. Some judges have clearly articulated a value-based view, derived from human rights or constitutional values such as dignity and equality. For others, the issue is firmly one for the legislature, regardless of the judges' own personal opinion. Alternatively, procedural safeguards might be perceived to be an approach more compatible with the judicial role than a substantive position. Judges increasingly refer to decisions in other jurisdictions, but the way they do so depends on their background theory of comparativism. At the same time, the chapter demonstrates the inter-connectedness of different jurisdictions, not just through the jurisprudence on extradition, but also due to restrictions imposed by some countries on the export of drugs which might be used for the death penalty.

Chapter 7 turns to the highly contested issue of abortion. Given the emotive nature of abortion, there are many trenchant voices that argue that, like capital punishment, this should be an issue left entirely to the legislature. However, a comparative insight demonstrates that in all jurisdictions there has been a complex relationship between legislatures and courts, both complementary and conflictual. The comparative approach also reveals the pivotal role of the characterization of the rights at stake. Is this an issue of the right to life, the right to privacy, or the right to equality and reproductive freedom? From the rich deliberative resource which comparison of different jurisdictions provides, it can be seen not only that these rights interact in complex and decisive ways, but also that the rights themselves are reshaped as a result. The chapter also shows how courts draw on fundamental values such as dignity, equality, and autonomy to enrich the ongoing comparative conversation between courts across jurisdictions.

From the chapters on capital punishment and abortion, we turn to two different sorts of challenges, namely health and housing, whose very status as fundamental rights remains a source of controversy. Chapter 8 on the right to health shows that these contestations operate on several levels, reflecting the cross-cutting themes of the book. One concerns differing theories of human rights. An approach confining the role of human rights to restraining State interference generates a very limited view, which would exclude health from the human rights canon. This can be set against a positive view of human rights, requiring the State to facilitate freedom and advance substantive equality. A different approach focuses on the limits of judicial legitimacy and competence in relation to complex, polycentric issues such as the provision of health. This can be contrasted with the view that courts and litigation processes can be fashioned in ways that enhance democracy, particularly through holding governments to account for their human rights impacting decisions, through requiring transparency, and through insisting on non-discrimination. A comparative approach reveals too that much depends on the characterization of the right, such as a right to life, a right to freedom of contract, a right to access to health care, or a right to the highest attainable standard of health. Concerns at the legitimacy of courts have also led to a formulation of the right as progressively realizable and subject to the availability of resources.

Possibly the most salient point which arises from a comparative perspective on the right to health is the importance of a systemic approach by courts to the meaning of the right to health. It is when the right to health is interpreted in terms of individual responsibility, or individual benefits, that its polycentric implications are obscured. On the other hand, in insisting that governments are accountable for systemic failures in the duty to fulfil the right to health, courts should not lose sight of the substantive nature of human rights. The individual right must not be made to give way to utilitarian concerns. This is the challenge which courts applying the right to health will continue to face.

Like health, housing, the subject of Chapter 9, has frequently been regarded as a matter for the political sphere, rather than that of fundamental human rights. Where it is regarded as a right, it is generally only progressively realizable subject to available resources. On the other hand, protection against State intrusion into home, family, or private life is regarded as a paradigm candidate for human rights law. A comparative approach reveals that in practice this distinction has been impossible to sustain, as litigants seek to rely on the right to life and the right to respect for home and family to protect them against housing insecurity and homelessness. Indeed, given that the cases generally come before the court in the form of eviction proceedings, it is not feasible simply to regard housing rights as non-justiciable.

A comparative examination of judicial approaches reveals several clear themes. First, courts have drawn on the fundamental values of dignity and autonomy to fuel their recognition that a home is fundamental to both human survival and human dignity. The right to a home therefore functions as a counterweight to courts' traditional concern for the protection of property rights. This is particularly true where the homeless are amongst the poorest and most disadvantaged. This has been reinforced by the inevitable interdependence of duties to respect people's homes with duties on the State to provide alternative housing. The result has been a striking convergence in outcomes between jurisdictions where housing is implied into civil and political rights and those with express socio-economic rights regarding housing. Second, courts, cognizant of separation of powers and their own limitations in relation to legitimacy and competence, have preferred procedural interventions, such as the right to be heard or to participate in decision-making, avoiding giving substantive meaning to the right to adequate housing. This places great store on the power of procedure to shape outcomes. However, important requirements of equal participation and timely involvement are frequently underplayed. Third, and relatedly, courts have been reluctant to link their acknowledgement of a right to a home to a requirement that adequate homes be provided. Whether or not a right to housing is express or derived from another right, and whether it is immediate or subject to progressive realization, it is on this issue that a justiciable right has had the most limited interpretation in the jurisdictions considered here. This has been largely due to a deference to the State on issues which are perceived to have significant polycentric and resource implications. As a result, courts have tended to dilute their own role in requiring strong evidence for resource claims by governments, assuming that any reassignment of resources to claimants before the court would inevitably divert such resources from other equally meritorious government priorities. This has meant that breaches due to failures of governance, ineptitude, incapacity, and corruption have not been brought into focus, and courts have not followed through on their role in insisting on good, well-substantiated reasons for breaching fundamental human rights. In this sense, an insistence on bounded deliberative democracy as a framework for judicial intervention would yield a greater commitment to achieving fundamental rights, including housing, while not overstepping the separation of powers.

Chapter 10 on freedom of speech moves back into the heartland of justiciable human rights. Despite judicial confidence in courts' counter-majoritarian role in this context, the values behind freedom of speech remain highly contested. Particularly challenging has been the need to resolve the paradox of pure tolerance. The risk of giving too much power to the censor suggests that the role of the court should be to prevent States from interfering with speech, relying on the power of speech to be countered by speech. However, this might overestimate the genuine ability of the less powerful to speak out. At what point then should some people's speech be restrained to preserve others' right to genuinely exercise their freedom of speech? Whereas the harm principle provides a starting point, the meaning of harm itself requires further elaboration, in particular to include the imperatives of equality and dignity. These challenges are highlighted by the transnational power of the internet, which has both democratized speech and magnified the voices of the powerful.

A comparative perspective reveals the ways in which these difficult balances are drawn by judges through interpreting the text of the human rights instrument in the light of the background values, their perception of their role in relation to the legislature, and their interpretive philosophy. The starting point is the vivid difference between the apparently unlimited or absolute nature of the US freedom of speech guarantee, and the more nuanced provisions in other jurisdictions, especially the possibility of justifying limitations. The US approach to free speech is often the paradigm which other courts provide reasons to diverge from, an important application of the deliberative approach to comparative human rights law. At the other end of the spectrum, the inclusion of morality as a justifiable aim under the European Convention on Human Rights (ECHR) would seem anathema to the US, where the Court would regard the possibility of the State using morality to censor speech as a serious breach of State neutrality. The chapter traces these themes by looking more closely at three challenging issues, namely subversive speech, hate speech, and pornography. It also asks whether the right extends to the recipient of speech, thereby raising the question of whether freedom of speech carries with it positive duties on the part of the State to provide information. Perhaps not unexpectedly, courts which have been robust in protecting speech against State interference have been cautious in expecting positive duties from the State to facilitate freedom of speech through the provision of information, preferring to leave this issue to the legislature.

From freedom of speech, we turn in Chapter 11 to the right to education, which can be characterized as a many-dimensional right, including a freedom right, a social right, and an equality right. Here too the cross-cutting themes in comparative law illuminate many of the key challenges and point to different potential ways forward. The starting point, as ever, is the textual basis. Both at international and domestic level, different human rights instruments give varying emphasis to the freedom, social, and equality facets of the right. Jurisprudence in the various jurisdictions begins from different starting points, depending on whether education is primarily litigated as an express right to education, or as part of the right to equality, or in the context of freedom of religion, conscience, and thought. The development of the jurisprudence is also heavily influenced by the social, historical, and economic factors which are most prominent in each jurisdiction. Nevertheless, as in other contexts, the questions faced by courts are strikingly similar, and a comparative approach provides a rich opportunity to highlight the ways in which courts use the legal starting points to address these issues.

As in freedom of speech, courts are most confident when adjudicating the freedom aspects of the right, and in particular, protection of parents' rights to direct the religious, linguistic, or cultural development of their children. However, this rapidly spills over into the question of whether the State has positive duties to provide quality education. Here the familiar concern of courts not to step beyond their sphere of legitimacy and competence reasserts itself. This is particularly salient in the light of the paradoxical nature of education as being a compulsory right. For the right to be properly realized, it is not sufficient to prevent the State from using education as a propaganda tool. It is also essential to provide an adequate education. Here courts have had to confront the question of what the substance is of the right to quality education, and what role judges can play in achieving this. An important way of addressing this is the deliberative approach of holding governments sternly to account for how their decisions on provision of education ensure the right of everyone to quality education. Courts have also had to hold the balance between different sorts of equality demands, such as the potential conflict between minorities requiring accommodation of their religious, cultural, or linguistic imperatives and poor and disadvantaged learners requiring good-quality education in sound structures.

The chapter ends with the challenge of harnessing human rights to achieve the ambitious goals of the 2030 Sustainable Development Goals (SDGs) Agenda. The SDGs address some of the weaknesses of the binding human rights. They supply content to the right and set down a clear timetable of fifteen years from 2015 for its achievement. But they lack the binding force of human rights law and tend to ignore individual rights through aggregate measurements. The comparative insights in this chapter demonstrate ways in which courts and human rights bodies have approached the content and enforcement of a justiciable right to education. The hope would be that, going forward, the SDGs and binding human rights can work together.

Freedom of religion, the subject of our final chapter, brings with it the added complexity created by belief in an authority which is higher than the law of the land. Chapter 2 rejected the possibility of grounding human rights in divine or natural law;

but the human right to freedom of religion and belief is uncontested. What is more difficult is to reach a secular agreement on the limits of freedom of religion, particularly in relation to manifestation, custom, and practice. The comparative approach reveals a wider divergence than might have been expected. In particular, the relationship between the State and religion is calibrated in very different ways across jurisdictions. The strong focus on non-establishment of religion in the US First Amendment, epitomized by the metaphor of a wall between Church and State, is not replicated in other jurisdictions. Indeed, courts in several jurisdictions have expressly rejected the US doctrine of non-establishment, instead accepting a positive role for the State in promoting diverse religions. This in turn contrasts with the acceptance of a State Church in some European countries. The Indian Constitution, for its part, stands out for its endorsement of both strong protection for the autonomy of religious institutions and a robust commitment to the role of the State in regulating religion. In addition, religious pluralism so far as personal law is concerned contrasts vividly with the commitment to secularism in the preamble of the Indian Constitution. The Indian Supreme Court also contrasts with its counterparts in other jurisdictions in its approach to the definition of what counts as a religious belief or practice for the purpose of human rights protection. Whereas most courts defer to the believer on this question, provided she is sincere, and instead adjudicate the issue on the acceptability of limitations, the Indian courts have been willing to set an objective test, based on a doctrine of essential practices. A closer look at the context of this approach, however, reveals that by confining protection for religious autonomy to essential practices of the religion, the Court has set limits on the freedom of religious institutions to cut across other constitutional imperatives, such as the abolition of untouchability, rather than inevitably impinging on individual freedom of belief. This demonstrates again the importance in comparative human rights law of sensitivity to legal and political context.

The aim of this book has been to bring comparative human rights to life. It has asked similar questions across several jurisdictions, and a range of human rights topics. I have not sought only for abstract legal principles; I have looked for the stories which are brought before courts, the urgent issues which real people in many countries pursue all the way to apex courts and beyond. For the prisoner on death row and the victim of their crime; the pregnant woman seeking an abortion and her opponents; the homeless person among many millions of other homeless people; the women seeking religion and the women oppressed by religion, what can a comparative approach to human rights law add? Judges faced with acutely difficult questions need to refer to their textual mandate, the fundamental values informing the text, their own interpretive philosophy, and their perception of their role relative to the legislature. But more and more, their decision-making can be enriched by considering how judges in other jurisdictions have faced these questions, not to be bound by them, but in a deliberative sense. I have been enormously enriched in my own perceptions of these issues by discussions and debates with generations of human rights law students from many different jurisdictions, and with colleagues and friends across national and disciplinary boundaries. I hope the reader will continue this project by asking these questions, and others, in relation to human rights topics not covered in this book. This is a journey which requires much thoughtfulness and an openness to new perspectives, but also the commitment to the ultimate destination of human rights for all. It is a journey best taken together.

Index